D0987273

Jim Mason

An American Melodrama

Melodrama . . . Now, a dramatic piece characterized by sensational incident and violent appeals to the emotions, but with a happy ending.

—The Shorter Oxford English Dictionary

An
American
Melodrama

NEW YORK

THE PRESIDENTIAL

CAMPAIGN OF 1968

Lewis Chester

Godfrey Hodgson

Bruce Page

THE VIKING PRESS

Copyright © 1969 by Times Newspapers Ltd.
All rights reserved

First published in 1969 by The Viking Press, Inc.
625 Madison Avenue, New York, N.Y. 10022

Library of Congress catalog card number: 69–13666

Printed in U.S.A.

Acknowledgments

Bedminster Press, Inc.: From *Economy and Society* by Max Weber. Copyright © 1968 by Bedminster Press, Inc. Reprinted by permission of Bedminster Press, Inc.

Farrar, Straus & Giroux: From *Near the Ocean* by Robert Lowell, "Waking Early Sunday Morning." Copyright © 1965, 1967 by Robert Lowell. First published in the *New York Review of Books*. Reprinted by permission of Farrar, Straus & Giroux.

Jules Feiffer: Text from the cartoon "The Big Texan." Copyright © 1966 by Jules Feiffer; text from the cartoon "Bobby Twins." Copyright © 1968 by Jules Feiffer.

Senator Eugene J. McCarthy: "Lament of an Aging Politician."

Harold Ober Associates, Incorporated: "Hoppity (or A. A. Milne revised)" by Marya Mannes. Copyright © 1968 by New York Magazine Company. "Sales Campaign" from *Subverse* by Marya Mannes. Copyright © 1959 by Marya Mannes. Both reprinted by permission of Harold Ober Associates Incorporated.

RESEARCH AND REPORTING

John Barry, Tony Clifton, Anne Darnborough, Hilary Lamb, Cal McCrystal, and Emma Rothschild—all of the *Sunday Times* of London. Also Stephen Jessel of the *Times*.

Contents

Preface   xi

ACT I *A Firebell in the Night*

    Seven Days in April   3

ACT II *Two Symptoms in Search of a Sickness*

    1. Some Loss of Blood   21
    2. Indications of Malignancy   33
    3. A Slight Case of Hubris?   37

ACT III *What Is to Be Done?*

    1. The Search for a Champion   51
    2. The Conservative as Insurgent   68
    3. Dove Bites Hawk   78

ACT IV *The Tide of Fearful Faction*

    1. The Restless Tiger   105
    2. The Charisma Machine   127
    3. The Double Incumbent   142
    4. Venture into the Interior   156

ACT V *The Republican Phoenix*

    1. The Field, Ten to One, Bar One   183
    2. Hamlet on Fifth Avenue   209
    3. The New Tenant   224

ACT VI *George Wallace, the Man Who Talked in Code*

    1. The Professional Southerner   *261*
    2. Where Is That Mason-Dixon Line?   *276*

ACT VII *California: Right Back Where We Started From*

    1. Oregon: The Twenty-eighth Election   *297*
    2. The King Must Die   *311*
    3. The Grief Machine   *356*

ACT VIII *New Politics and Old Pols*

    1. Two Case Studies in Insurgency   *375*
    2. The Price of Loyalty   *402*

ACT IX *Miami: An Illusion of Unity*

    1. If Only They'd Grown More Nuts   *427*
    2. Suspicion of Arson   *433*
    3. Trompe l'Oeil   *451*
    4. One Strom   *476*
    5. The Strange Death of the Liberal Republicans   *482*

ACT X *Chicago: The Reign of Piety and Iron*

    1. You Wonderful Town   *503*
    2. The Phantom Armies of the Night   *513*
    3. Wheeling and Dealing for Peace   *524*
    4. No Way to Break It   *538*
    5. The Ted Offensive   *564*
    6. A Throne of Bayonets   *577*
    7. The Big Lie   *592*

ACT XI *See How They Run*

    1. The Ghost of 1960   607
    2. You Taught Me How to Love You, Now
       Teach Me to Forget   632
    3. The Rednecks Are Coming   651

ACT XII *Some of the People, Part of the Time*

    1. The Old Quarterback   673
    2. Bombs Away with Curt LeMay   690
    3. "A Damned Close-Run Thing"   711
    4. The End of an Affair   736
    5. And Then There Was the One   746
    6. A Great Day for Key Biscayne   765

CODA

    And He Shall Judge among the Nations   775

    Index   791

Preface

There is a historian's joke that we know too much about the nineteenth century to write its history, and sometimes it seems that we know too much about our own times to understand them. The pressure of events, and the pressure of information about them, can become overwhelming. The Presidential campaign of 1968, with its entries, withdrawals, startling victories, startling defeats, sudden compromises, violence, apathy, and enterprise, was something of a case in point.

This book is an attempt to retrieve, report, and interpret the events of that contest: very largely, it is an attempt to distinguish between the apparent and the real. It is a report, and not a history—the history of the time will require a considerable perspective. But we have tried to go below the immediate surface of events, to peel away as many layers as possible from the onion. We have tried to record in some detail what people said, and also why they said it; what people did, and also why they did it. The reasons, as usual, were not always the ones they gave in public.

There is, of course, a question: What are three British reporters doing writing a book about this American election? The simplest answer is that we are interested and involved: our society is intimately entangled with America's. In the conditions of the late sixties, it might well be argued that the prosperous middle class of Britain is more a part of American culture than some millions of Americans: the blacks of the Mississippi Delta; the poorest whites of the Appalachian highlands; the *chicanos* of the Great Valley of California. And if we find sins and failings in America, it is usually the case that our own society shares the guilt for them. It is a general truth of the nuclear age that everybody's future is bound up with America's—but it is a particular truth in Britain's case. Nearly all questions in Britain turn, in the end, upon the American relationship.

Whether this is good or bad, should or should not be so, is an issue someone else must debate elsewhere. Here, we mention only as justification: if we should sometimes seem too rough or caustic about the institutions of American politics, that is because of our concern. We cannot afford to be overrespectful of American affairs, any more than we can afford to be of our own.

This book grew out of work we did while covering the election for the *Sunday Times* of London. *"Out* of" is the operative word. The book has relatively little to do with the stories we wrote during the campaign. Some of them were right, some of them were wrong, but all of them needed to be thought through again. (Neither does the book represent any editorial attitude of the *Sunday Times.*)

We have done a good deal of "team journalism," as it is sometimes called, and it seems to us that the concept is often misunderstood. In our view, at least, this sort of journalism, whether for a newspaper or a book, does not consist in large armies of legmen submitting voluminous memoranda which are then written up by desk-bound wordsmiths. Apart from anything else, the work involved would be too boring to be tolerable.

Although there are differences of function within the teams we assemble for particular assignments, these differences should derive more from the extent of each person's involvement than from anything else. Some members do more footwork than others, but everybody does some, and differences in perception and interpretation are resolved by extended —sometimes, it must be admitted, violent—argument. It can be an emotionally exhausting way to write a book, but the process, if carried through, is likely to heighten everybody's performance. Sometimes the charge is made that it is an assault on individual imagination—frequently, though, by people who are trying to eke out rather meager personal supplies of that quality. The ideal book is usually produced by an entirely personal obsession, but that does not mean that useful books cannot be produced by the collective method. Those who doubt the validity of this might ask themselves how often books of this sort which bear a single name do so only because credit has not been fairly apportioned.

One reason for writing about American politics is that it matters. But another reason is that it is so often entertaining. At least, we find it so and, quite obviously, so do many of the practitioners. There are naturally large areas of boredom: interludes as chilly and flaccid as a shrimp cocktail at a fundraising dinner. But taken as a whole, the politicians of the United States, despite the alleged blandness of the age, continue to project a feeling of humor, uproarious diversity, and plain enjoyment of the political life. We have perhaps spent more time trying to convey this flavor than celebrating the grandeur of the democratic process. Dashes of grandeur may be added to taste.

Another noticeable characteristic of American politicians is their patience with journalistic interrogators. The active pleasure which many of them take in the retailing of anecdote and observation is a working asset for reporters that is hard to match elsewhere. We therefore find ourselves indebted, for time and information, to so many of these interesting men and women that it is hardly possible to list them all. In addition, we should not name many of them for reasons of confidence. It seems best, therefore, to make do with an expression of thanks which is no less sincere because it must be generalized.

There is another group of people who, through books or conversations or both, gave us ideas. (Naturally, the groups overlap somewhat.) We may well have gotten the ideas wrong or hopelessly misinterpreted them—certainly, we have tried to rethink them for ourselves. But our feeling of guilt at the possibility that we have mangled the ideas does not lessen our indebtedness toward their authors. People to whom we feel particularly grateful for such reasons include:

Herbert M. Alexander, Citizens' Research Foundation, Princeton; Gar Alperovitz, codirector of the Cambridge Institute, Cambridge, Massachusetts, and author of *Atomic Diplomacy;* Harry S. Ashmore, Center for the Study of Democratic Institutions, Santa Barbara, California; Richard J. Barnet, codirector of the Institute for Policy Studies, Washington, D.C., and author of *Intervention and Revolution;* Professor Alexander M. Bickel, Yale Law School; Marvin Brody, United Auto Workers' union, Los Angeles; David Butler, Fellow of Nuffield College, Oxford, England; Eldridge Cleaver, author of *Soul on Ice;* Reese Cleghorn of the *Atlanta Constitution,* Atlanta, Georgia; Frederick P. Currier, of Market Opinion Research, Detroit; Frederick G. Dutton, of Dutton, Gwirtzman, Zumas, Wise and Boasberg, Washington, D.C.; Marshall Frady, Atlanta, Georgia, author of *Wallace;* John Kenneth Galbraith, Paul M. Warburg Professor of Economics at Harvard and author of too many ideas to list; Edwin O. Guthman, National Editor of the *Los Angeles Times;* Roy V. Harris, attorney, Augusta, Georgia; Stephen Hess, co-author of *Nixon: A Political Portrait;* Richard Hofstadter, DeWitt Clinton Professor of History at Columbia and author of among other works *The Paranoid Style in American Politics;* Emmett John Hughes, *Newsweek;* William Bradford Huie, author of *Three Lives for Mississippi* and many other classic investigations of brutality in the South; the Institute for Social Research at the University of Michigan, especially for *The American Voter;* Christopher Jencks, Institute for Policy Study; John F. Kain, Associate Professor of Economics, Harvard; Seymour Martin Lipset,

Professor of Government and Social Relations, Harvard; Stuart Loory, Washington correspondent, the *Los Angeles Times;* Harry C. McPherson, attorney, Washington, D.C., formerly Special Assistant to President Johnson; Earl Mazo, associate editor, *Reader's Digest;* Thomas B. Mechling, formerly of the Xerox Corporation; David Mermelstein, editor (with Marvin Gettleman) of *The Great Society Reader;* Charles Morgan, Jr., American Civil Liberties Union, Atlanta, Georgia; Raymond Moley, *Newsweek;* Daniel P. Moynihan, Special Assistant to President Nixon for Urban Affairs; Donald S. Muchmore, Opinion Research of California, Los Angeles; Jack Newfield, *Village Voice,* New York; Robert D. Novak, Evans and Novak, Washington, D.C.; Marcus Raskin, codirector of the Institute for Policy Studies; David Riesman, Henry Ford II Professor of Social Science, Harvard; Michael Rogin, University of California at Berkeley; Professor Richard Rose, Strathclyde University, Scotland; Walt W. Rostow, formerly Special Assistant to President Johnson; Bayard Rustin, A. Philip Randolph Institute, New York; Kermit J. Scott, CORE, New York; Robert Sherrill, Washington correspondent of the *Nation* and author of *Gothic Politics in the Deep South;* Irwin Shulman, Anti-Defamation League of B'nai B'rith; Laurence M. Stern, assistant managing editor of the *Washington Post;* I. F. Stone, who is indispensable; Humphrey Taylor, Opinion Research Centre, London; Walter D. De Vries, Fellow of the Institute of Politics at the Kennedy School of Government, Harvard; Franklin Wallick, managing editor of the UAW *Washington Report;* and C. Vann Woodward, Sterling Professor of History at Yale, without whose books it would be impossible to begin to understand the relationship between reunion and reaction in any generation.

We owe an immense debt to Aaron Asher, Elisabeth Sifton, and their colleagues at The Viking Press for all their care, judgment, and tolerance.

There are also immediate, professional colleagues to whom our thanks are due: most of all, to Harold Evans, editor of the *Sunday Times,* whose support, forbearance, generosity, and strong nerves made this project possible and who deserves a better book, in return, than we could possibly write. Also, Frank Giles, Deputy Editor and Foreign Editor, and—very particularly—Ron Hall, Managing Editor (Features), who did the work we should have been doing when we weren't there. Our debt to Henry Brandon, the legendary Washington correspondent of the *Sunday Times,* is immeasurable.

Many other colleagues in London aided and comforted, but we must mention in particular our secretary, Anne Dark, who rescued us from innumerable organizational confusions. We should like also to thank people not on our staff, who made particular inquiries for us: John Shirley, Alex Finer, Derek Barton, and Margaret McGaughey.

We must also thank our colleagues on the *Times* of London. (Although the *Times* and the *Sunday Times* have a combined existence as Times Newspapers Ltd., they are editorially and reportorially independent of each other.) Chief among these is Louis Heren, Washington correspondent of the *Times,* unfailingly generous, and unfailingly professional. We are also grateful to Ian MacDonald, Louis's No. 2 man, for his help, and Innis MacBeath, New York correspondent of the *Times,* for his patience.

Mrs. Margaret Horton, who organizes the *Times'* office in Washington with flawless precision, incorporated us effortlessly into her ministrations. In the New York office of Times Newspapers, we owe much to Robert Ducas, whose existence demonstrates that the supposed gulf between the editorial and commercial staffs of newspapers need be no gulf at all. Also in the New York office were Mrs. Lois Bidel, Mrs. Mildred Temple, Miss Marlise Simons, and Miss Sheila Rumpf—and if they had not been there we would have had to invent them, especially Lois, who is very good at getting people aboard airplanes. There is a question whether Joe Petta, of the New York office, is the best teleprinter operator in the world, or whether it is Mrs. Alma Dever, in Washington. They have, in any case, no competition. And there was also Fred Crawford, who keeps a lot of things going in New York.

We have tried to make this book as comprehensive as seems reasonable in a work aimed at the general reader. However, we have not been able to include references to all the contestants in the Presidential race, and we therefore apologize to the supporters of such forgotten battlers as E. Harold Munn, Sr., who ran on the Prohibition ticket for President. He got only .02 per cent of the vote. But, then, it was a year when people probably felt the need of a drink.

—LEWIS CHESTER
GODFREY HODGSON
BRUCE PAGE

New York City, February 1969

ACT I

A Firebell in the Night

Seven Days in April

"... This momentous question, like a firebell in the night, awakened me and filled me with terror. I considered it at once as the knell of the Union. It is hushed, indeed, for the moment. But this is a reprieve only. ... We have the wolf by the ears, and we can neither hold him, nor safely let him go. Justice is in one scale, and self-preservation in the other."

> —Thomas Jefferson, letter written in April 1820,
> at the time of the Missouri crisis

"Thou seest the world, Volumnius, how it goes;
Our enemies have beat us to the pit:
It is more worthy to leap in ourselves,
Than tarry till they push us."

> —William Shakespeare, *Julius Caesar*

When great waves break, there is a moment when it seems as if everything in their way must be destroyed. Even those who have watched the water rising and guessed the force of the wind and the tides driving it are shocked by the vehemence of the impact. But in that same moment the destructive force of the wave is temporarily spent. Whatever has been unable to withstand it is safe in the slack waters of the trough—until the next wave breaks.

For nearly five years, since the assassination of President Kennedy, two long waves of danger had been racing toward the safe and settled shore where most Americans live—the danger of war from Southeast Asia and the danger of black rebellion in the heart of American cities. The first week of April 1968 was the week the waves broke.

3

By the end of the week, with the capital of the United States under military occupation by its own troops, it looked as if it was a matter of preserving the nation. But for the President, just as that week began, it was a matter of preserving the Constitution. The President of the United States swears that he will, "to the best of my ability, preserve, protect, and defend the Constitution of the United States" and its stated purposes of insuring domestic tranquillity, providing for the common defense, and promoting the general welfare. It was the President's most sober judgment that he stood in danger of losing the power to perform those duties, and he did what he had to do.

Lyndon Johnson stared toward the television camera. He was not looking straight into the lens, but at a teleprompter screen just below it. This useful device, flashing the words of his script to him at a suitable rate for his slow and impressive rate of reading, had enabled him to get through a speech nine thousand words long without once dropping his eyes to the desk in front of him. Eighty-five million of his fellow citizens had thus been able to watch the powerful emotions registered on his familiar face.

It was nine-thirty-five p.m. in Washington, on March 31, 1968. The President had just read, "I would ask all Americans, whatever their personal interest or concern, to guard against divisiveness and all its ugly consequences." He glanced across at his wife, and raised his right arm. It was a prearranged signal that he would, after all, read some additional words which had been prepared for the machine later than the rest. Mrs. Johnson, and very few other people, knew what those words would be.

"Fifty-two months and ten days ago," the President read, "in a moment of tragedy and trauma, the duties of this office fell upon me." Many of his watchers divined now that he was off on another tack, away from the discussion of Vietnam which had been the main burden of his speech. Where on earth was he headed now? "I have concluded," Johnson said, "that I should not permit the Presidency to become involved in the partisan divisions that are developing in this political year." It was a startling proposition—to take out of politics the most important elective office in the Western world. But it prepared the way for his next statement, which —for theatrical effect if nothing else—must compare with anything that any President has ever said: "Accordingly, I shall not seek, and I will not accept, the nomination of my party for another term as your President."

The President had been tired. Bill Moyers, who worked for him and whom the President loved almost as a son until the war destroyed their relationship, as it destroyed so many other things, has said, "The Presidency is a long-distance race, and Lyndon Johnson had been running it like a hundred-yard sprint."

A few days before his announcement, the President had received a British visitor and told him, "God, I'm tired. I wonder what it was like to be as alone as Churchill was in nineteen-forty." He was asked how he would like to be remembered—as what sort of a President? "Four years ago," he said, "I could have given you an answer to that. Today, I can't even think about it. I don't think four years ahead today. I don't even think four weeks ahead. I just think four days ahead."

The fact of the President's exhaustion was well known in Washington in the spring of 1968. When he made his telecast on March 31, it showed in the movements of his hands. Once or twice, tears stood in his eyes. But until the telecast, there remained an almost superstitious belief in his demonic energy. Surely he would refresh his energy from some inner well and gird himself again to scatter his enemies. And one enemy, of course, in particular.

There were some in Washington who, without actual knowledge, had long suspected that the President would decide not to run again. One of these people, a close personal friend of Johnson's, was asked in late March whether he still thought the President would not run. The friend laughed and said, "With Robert Kennedy in the race, he won't be able to resist running against him!"

It was characteristic of the tempo of American politics that of the four men then openly competing for the Presidency two were in the air when Lyndon Johnson made his move. Richard Nixon was in his own campaign plane, a Boeing 727 jet, about twenty minutes out of New York on a trip from Milwaukee. Robert Kennedy was in an American Airlines Astrojet making its approach to John F. Kennedy Airport, New York, incoming from Phoenix, Arizona.

Eugene McCarthy was finishing a speech in Waukesha, Wisconsin.

And the fourth candidate, George Wallace, was immobilized for the moment. He was in Montgomery, Alabama, with his wife Lurleen, then shortly to undergo her last operation for cancer.

Senator McCarthy first realized that something had happened when a group of reporters burst through the doors of the Carroll College auditorium where he was speaking. As the crowd applauded McCarthy's peroration, several of them dashed excitedly on to the stage and shouted, "The President says he isn't running!"

McCarthy observed laconically that the news "came as a surprise" to him. But that night, back at the Sheraton-Schroeder Hotel in Milwaukee, he let his excitement show. He sat up late with his old friend Herman Schauinger, whose office he had shared when he was a raw young college professor. His wife sent his daughter Mary down to fetch him up to bed. Ten minutes later, he was down again. They sat up until past three o'clock talking and drinking a little whisky. Almost wistfully, McCarthy said, "If I do get to the White House, we'll have a lot of fun."

As Robert Kennedy's plane taxied to a halt, Dall Forsythe, a young man who worked in his New York office, pushed through the usual waiting crowd of two or three hundred teen-agers, closely followed by John Burns, State Democratic Chairman. They forced their way past the disembarking passengers until they got to Kennedy, sitting quietly next to his wife, Ethel. It was Forsythe who got the words out first.

Kennedy, as usual, was under control. Fred Dutton, later one of his campaign managers, swore sharply. "What do you think?" Kennedy asked. "Say nothing now," Dutton advised urgently. Without a word to the reporters who had been traveling with him, Kennedy drove to his apartment, 14F United Nations Plaza. Only there, at the entrance, did he make a brief nonstatement. "I've thought of what I could say tonight, but I've decided there was nothing I could say. I'll say something tomorrow."

Inside the apartment, there was something like a carnival atmosphere. Kennedy alone was self-contained, almost grim. "We were all euphoric," says his old friend William vanden Heuvel. "He was the one who understood the dangers ahead. He said, with that tight smile of his, 'The joy is premature.'"

In his own plane, equipped with radio, Richard Nixon had heard the President's words as they were spoken. So he had had time to sort out his thoughts before he landed, and being a professional of twenty-three-years' standing, he knew exactly what to say. He met the reporters at LaGuardia (the other side of Queens from Kennedy), and said, "We must assume that someone within the Democratic Party who represents the Johnson viewpoint will be the candidate." He had seen the point clearly. The bulk of Johnson's figure was so massive that it obscured the real effect of his departure. The way was now clear for the succession of his Vice-President.

Shortly after ten o'clock on the morning of the broadcast, Lyndon Johnson and his daughter arrived at Hubert Humphrey's apartment in

South-West Washington. Ostensibly the purpose of the surprise visit was to say good-by; the Vice-President was due to leave that afternoon on an official visit to Mexico. The President handed him a copy of his much-revised speech on Vietnam to be delivered that night, and asked Humphrey to read it. "Mr. President," Humphrey said as he finished reading, "that's a beautiful speech—just beautiful. Especially that last part about national unity and your untiring efforts for peace. I think it will be the best speech you've ever made."

"Yes, Hubert," said the President starkly, "but they won't believe me."

"Yes, they will, Mr. President."

"No, they won't, Hubert." And he fished in his breast pocket for a single sheet of paper which he had been carrying about with him for two months. "Just read it aloud." Humphrey began to read rapidly. He read until he reached the withdrawal statement: "Accordingly, I shall not seek, and I will not accept, the nomination of my party for another term as your President."

"No, Mr. President," said Humphrey, "you don't mean it!" And he burst into tears.

The President took Humphrey aside and warned him that he had still not finally decided to read the alternative ending that night. As he left, Johnson placed a finger to his lips. Mrs. Humphrey sensed that something was wrong and asked whether the President was ill. Again, on the way to the airport, she asked, "Hubert, what did the President say?" "Nothing, Muriel, nothing."

That night, while he was listening to the President's speech crackling over short-wave radio in the library of the American Embassy in Mexico City, Humphrey was called to the telephone. It was Johnson's special assistant, Marvin Watson. "The President says to tell you it will be the number-two ending," he said.

"I'm sorry," Humphrey said, "terribly sorry."

For all the other candidates, it was as though Christian, in *Pilgrim's Progress,* had braced himself to fight the giant Apollyon, who bestrode the way—and Apollyon, at the challenge, had turned aside with a courteous smile. For Humphrey, it was as if Christian had been called on to substitute for Apollyon.

It was a measure of President Johnson's unpopularity at that moment that to ascribe honorable motives for this supreme gesture of his was in most political circles to invite a reputation for naïveté. Richard Goodwin, for example, who had once worked for Johnson, had long been telling Robert Kennedy that Johnson was a coward. That Johnson should not attempt to defend his record now seemed to Goodwin the final corroboration of this thesis.

In reality, Johnson's decision sprang from the understanding his predicament had taught him of a fundamental contradiction in the nature of his august and dangerous office. Like a Prime Minister—though in crucial respects with fewer resources—the President must be the master of the political process. Like a monarch, he must at the same time be above it. In the raging waters of national division, this contradiction had been mercilessly exposed.

Two days after Johnson announced his decision, on April 2, the primary election in Wisconsin would fall due. When he spoke, Johnson already knew he was going to be badly beaten, and perhaps humiliated, in that election by Eugene McCarthy.

Before the New Hampshire primary on March 12, the President and James H. Rowe, a Washington lawyer whom he had chosen to run his campaign, had expected no trouble in Wisconsin. Ten days before the vote, Rowe began to worry. He sent out half a dozen tried political operators to make the state safe. One of them was Neil Staebler, a veteran politician from Michigan. Every night, they called the White House and told the President's aides what they had found. There was no organization and too little money, and McCarthy was riding on a wave of enthusiasm. In the end, Staebler flew to Washington and gave it to Jim Rowe without varnish. "I told him," he says, "that it was quite evident that the President would be beaten." A few days later, Staebler's report was gloomily corroborated by no less an authority than Lawrence F. O'Brien, who had managed John F. Kennedy's campaign in 1960, had been the President's campaign manager in 1964, and was expected to be the President's campaign manager in 1968 too. O'Brien spent two nights in Wisconsin, talked to the men who were managing Johnson's campaign, took a good look around, and, in two phone calls, concealed nothing of their diagnosis from his boss. "I had to express to him candidly," O'Brien says with careful understatement, "that it didn't look good."

These reports came at a moment when the President already knew that the Gallup poll was going to publish, on March 31, figures showing that the percentage of voters who supported his actions as President had dwindled to thirty-five. After New Hampshire and Wisconsin, there were other important primaries to come, in most of which the President—or his representative—would be compelled by law or by practice to compete. There was scarcely one of them in which he could hope to avoid comprehensive and humiliating defeat by Eugene McCarthy or, what was worse, by Robert Kennedy.

Primary elections are not everything, of course. As the leader of his party, the President could still hope to command the allegiance of a majority of the delegates to the convention. But even here, the little-noticed fact that Lyndon Johnson, the great legislator, was a poor party manager, made his grasp uncertain. It was entirely possible by late March that the incumbent President might fail to win the Presidential nomination of his own party.

No doubt for such a proud man the prospect and even the danger of such a humiliation was anguish. But there was an even greater risk. Short of death or impeachment, Johnson still had nine months to serve as President. The shadow of domestic revolt had already compromised his authority. The disastrous turning of an intensely unpopular foreign war now threatened to destroy it completely.

Only a few days before his announcement, he had been debating with his generals such alarming "options" as the invasion of Laos and the invasion of North Vietnam. Confronted by their estimate that such drastic policies to end the war would demand the sending of two hundred thousand more American troops to Vietnam, he had chosen to keep the war "limited." But that meant a daily struggle against the intrinsic momentum of the war. And he had chosen to negotiate. Apart from his strong feeling that it was improper to divert time and energies to campaigning from the supervision of the war and the peace talks, there was the realization that the two roles might well prove irreconcilable. His White House adviser, Walt Rostow, might argue with jesuitical ingenuity that the Tet offensive had been "the greatest blunder of Ho Chi Minh's career." The President might even believe, as he told the Australian Cabinet in December, that after a cold winter the war would be won. But he knew how hard it would be to sell those arguments on the hustings. Least of all could they be sold there by Lyndon Johnson, whose mere appearances seemed only too likely to provoke civil disorder.

If Johnson were to fight and lose in the primaries, he could hope to keep the nomination only by the most ruthless demands on the loyalty of the party machine. And that effort was likely to be self-defeating. It might make him so disastrous an electoral liability that the politicians would turn to Kennedy in sheer self-defense. To put it at its simplest, Johnson was losing control of his party.

In most democracies, there is an easy escape for a leader who loses his party. He falls from office. But an American President does not fall. That was Johnson's predicament. The office he occupied had been designed by the Founding Fathers before the rise of party. Grounded on the separation of powers and endowed with a fixed term, its construction did not recognize the reality that a modern President's legitimacy in large measure derives from acceptance by his party. The processes of primary election and nomination had evolved outside the Constitution to test that legitimacy. In Johnson's case, a clash was possible between the theory and the reality of power which threatened to strip him of authority without freeing him from responsibility, and that at a critical point in the history of the country.

For all the boundless cynicism which he has attracted—and perhaps invited—Johnson has never taken the responsibility of his office lightly. He took his oath of office in literal earnest. "It all goes back to the oath I took," he said a few days later, explaining his decision to one of his White House advisers. He quoted the sonorous catalogue of his duties from the preamble to the Constitution: "to form a more perfect Union, establish justice, insure domestic tranquillity, provide for the common defense, promote the general welfare, and secure the blessings of liberty." And then he listed the simultaneous crises which, in his judgment, directly threatened the purposes he had sworn to uphold. He mentioned the pursuit of peace in Vietnam and the danger of war in the Middle East. He foresaw the likelihood of even more trouble in the cities and showed that he was aware of a particular dilemma if he were running for re-election: if he reacted toughly to civil disorder, he would be accused of currying favor on the right; if not, he would be vulnerable to the opposite charge. And last, he mentioned the international monetary crisis and the danger that the dollar might have to be devalued if the tax bill were not passed. The deepest fears of his generation were riding again: "We are literally facing nineteen-twenty-nine again," he said.

Of all these apocalyptic preoccupations, it was the duty of defense, and the deep division that his conception of it had produced in the country, that were in the forefront of the President's mind. There was no way out of the dilemma. If he did what he would have to do to be elected to a second term, then he risked losing control of these great external threats. If he ran and failed, he risked reducing the Presidency to its lowest ebb in a hundred years: since his namesake, Abraham Lincoln's successor, had come within a single vote of successful impeachment. His wife's anxiety for his health helped him to accept the inevitable.

And the advance intelligence from Wisconsin meant there was no time to lose.

Since he was pent about by such large dangers, it was not surprising that the President and his staff failed to notice the small advance warning of the danger they had dreaded most of all. On the Thursday before the withdrawal speech, the President's experienced press secretary, George Christian, was holding his routine afternoon briefing in his office in the west wing of the White House.

As he finished, and the reporters began to leave, one correspondent called out, "George, do you have any comment on the thing in Memphis?" "What thing in Memphis?" asked Christian. The reporter told him that, according to the wire services, sixty people had been injured and one person killed as a result of a demonstration in Memphis led by the Reverend Dr. Martin Luther King. "Oh, that," said Christian. "No comment on that."

Almost exactly seven days later, at suppertime on Thursday, April 4, Martin Luther King stepped out of his room on the second floor of the Lorraine Motel in Memphis. He had spent most of the day in the room with his disciples, Jesse Jackson, Andrew Young, Ralph Abernathy. They were all young black clergymen whose toughness and militancy had been hardened by years of nonviolent campaigning in the streets, the black churches, and the white jails of the South. They had seen how, in Birmingham in 1963 and in Selma in 1965, King had been able to use the technique of nonviolent confrontation to keep the Negro's demands at the top of the agenda for white America. But now they were wavering about nonviolence. King himself knew as well as any of them how hard it was going to be to restrain the anger of their people and to compete with those who sneered at his creed and wanted to brush it aside. Only the Sunday before, in the National Cathedral in Washington, a few hours before the President's announcement, he had said, "I don't like to predict violence, but if nothing is done between now and June to raise ghetto hope, I feel that this summer will not only be as bad, but worse than last year."

Now, in the close motel room, he preached his philosophy to his friends as he had done so often before. He spoke of Jesus and of Gandhi, and he told them in his slow, quiet voice, "I have conquered the fear of death." In substance, he repeated to them the sermon he had given the night before in a Memphis church, ending with these words: "Like anybody, I would like to live a long life. Longevity has its grace. But I'm not concerned about that now. I just want to do God's will. And he's allowed me to go up to the mountain. And I've looked over, and I've seen the promised land."

He stepped out of room 306 to the balcony. Jesse Jackson pointed out to him the organist who was going to play at the church where he was to speak that night. "Oh, yeah," said King. "He's my man." And he leaned over the railing. "Tell him to play 'Precious Lord,' and play it real pretty!"

Two hundred and five feet away, across the motel courtyard, across the unmended back-street roadway and the scrubby, untended gardens of a row of sleazy brick houses, a man was watching. He was white. He had been watching for two hours, his feet in a dingy bathtub, his left hand braced against the window, and his right eye to the telescopic sight of a rifle. It was a .30-'06 pump-action Remington, but at that range, with a scope, there was no question of missing with any weapon. As Dr. King straightened up to go, the man fired.

There was no particular reason why George Christian should have blamed himself for not noticing the significance of the news item from Memphis the week before. It was an episode, after all, in a garbage strike. Larger and more deadly events crowded through his office, demanding his attention more urgently. Yet the train of events that led to King's death was not really either trivial or accidental. In retrospect, it is a case history in which most of the poisoned elements of racial conflict in America can be isolated and examined as if they were on slides in a laboratory.

There was the caste system of the South, now spreading more and more to the North, with its hierarchy of "white jobs" and "Negro jobs."

There was desperate poverty and urban decay.

There was Southern political conservatism, and a tradition of the local establishment's using the race issue—almost without realizing what it was doing—to weaken the labor unions.

There was sheer ignorance on the part of even the well-disposed sections of the white community about what was happening in the ghetto south of W. C. Handy's Beale Street, less than a mile from the offices of the mayor, the police chief, and the solid citizens of Memphis.

And there was a new, deadly competition within the black world, between the nonviolent protest Dr. King believed in and the new militancy of the children of the slums.

To be a garbage collector in Memphis is a Negro job. The city of Memphis did not recognize the garbage-collectors' union, the American Federation of State, County and Municipal Employees. On February 12, more than a thousand garbage men, virtually all Negro, went on strike. They had two main demands: recognition of their union and the city's agreement to deduct union dues from their pay packets. The mayor, a shopkeeper called Henry Loeb, flatly refused both requests and began to hire white strikebreakers. By February 22, the strikers were angry enough to march on the auditorium where the city council was meeting to discuss a compromise. The council turned the plan down, and the police dispersed the demonstrating strikers with truncheons and tear gas.

The most influential Negro leader in Memphis was the Reverend James Lawson, pastor of a prosperous Negro church in south Memphis. He was one of the founders of the Student Nonviolent Coordinating Committee, from which many of the Black Power leaders have emerged. But Lawson is a minister and has remained a believer in nonviolence.

From the last week of February, Lawson organized daily demonstrations in sympathy with the garbage strikers. There were sit-ins, and silent single-file marches down Main Street by black sandwich men whose boards proclaimed simply I AM A MAN. The Negroes in Memphis had long been leaderless and divided into middle class, working class, and the unemployed at the bottom of the heap. Lawson began to get them to unite behind the strike.

Memphis is a hard town. Culturally it is an extension of the Delta cotton country of Mississippi to the south, where many citizens, white and black, have their roots. White Memphians say their race relations have been good. In a sense, it is true. But it is also true that, while a substantial Negro middle class has made real economic progress, white men have ruled Memphis with an iron hand since the days of Boss Crump, whose office building still towers over the police headquarters next door, as he towered over politics in Tennessee for most of the first forty years of this century. And Mr. Crump, as W. C. Handy wrote, "don't allow no easy ridin' here."

The days when Crump gave Memphis Negroes the vote and then bought it back from them for a few dollars and a little whisky at election time are long over. Mayor Loeb is an honest and a decent man. But the Memphis Negroes say that he has so little knowledge of life in the black slums south of Beale Street that if the river broke its banks and drowned them all it would be three weeks before the Mayor noticed.

And so, faced with the new situation of Lawson's united front, but without an inkling of the new mood in Negro Memphis, Loeb did what all Southern instinct and tradition taught: he cracked down.

Lawson looked around for allies. On March 14, nine thousand Memphis Negroes listened to speeches of encouragement from two of the most powerful—and moderate—of the national Negro leaders: Bayard Rustin, and Roy Wilkins, of the National Association for the Advancement of Colored People. And on March 16, Martin Luther King came to Memphis.

It was not, in a sense, a deliberate journey. As at the outset of his career in Montgomery in 1955, and again in its first great crisis, in Birmingham in 1963, King did not thrust himself into the situation. He waited until he was asked. He had been in Mississippi recruiting enthusiasm for the Poor People's Crusade he was planning to take to Washington in the summer. He stopped in Memphis, and agreed to come back on March 28.

Technically and politically, as an exercise in nonviolent protest, the March 28 march can only be called a disaster. Lawson had too few experienced organizers, and King did not bring his men with him in time to prepare so big a demonstration.

The marchers met at Clayborne Temple, a large gray-brick Negro church. They were surrounded from the start by burly, unsympathetic police in full riot kit. King arrived late, and Lawson was never quite able to channel the milling mass into an orderly column. The demonstrators had been given I AM A MAN banners, mounted on stout wooden poles. From the outset, twenty or thirty young militants tore off the banners and used the poles to smash in shop windows.

For a while, the police did nothing. Then, as the head of the column was wheeling out of Beale Street into Main Street and toward the white part of town, some of the young men began to javelin their poles clear over the marchers' heads into the windows on the other side of the street. The police waded into them, and a riot became inevitable.

The black leaders began to be afraid for King's life. They had already had threats, both from white racists and from Black Power militants. Lawson took a bullhorn and turned the column around. When they got back to the church, the older people dispersed as they were asked to do, but the young wouldn't go. They grabbed sticks and bottles and began to throw them at the police. Stupidly, the police used tear gas to herd them into the church, where firebrand Black Power orators were lashing them back into the fight. All hell broke loose. Young Negroes started to throw Molotov cocktails, and the police opened fire.

Before the night was over, King had suffered the worst defeat of his career. He called a press conference and said he would not come back to Memphis. Some newspapers openly reported that he fled. But it was not his courage that had failed. What had happened was a terrible setback to his faith in that self-discipline under provocation which, he had always argued, could alone give nonviolent protest its power to persuade.

Lawson went on with his daily demonstrations, and King was persuaded to change his mind. His lieutenants began to work with Lawson on careful preparations for a second march. On Wednesday, April 3, King came back to lead it. He had been criticized for living in luxurious white motels, so this time he checked into the Lorraine Motel, room 306.

His death was not, therefore, in any sense an accident. It was the logical and the foreseen culmination of a story whose roots go back deep into American history—at least as deep as the failure, after the Civil War, to give the freed slaves equality to match their legal freedom. And there is another sense in which it may not have been an accident. A man has been indicted for King's murder. His name is James Earl Ray, and his case is at the time of writing *sub judice*. But while in prison he has told his story to the writer William Bradford Huie.

Most people would assume that the motive for King's murder was racism: the racial hatred either of a solitary assassin or of a conspiracy of which one man was the agent. Huie's investigations have led him to a different conclusion. He believes that "Dr. King was murdered for effect. His murder was planned, not by impulsive men who hated him personally, though they probably did hate him, but by calculating men who wanted to use his murder to trigger violent conflict between white and Negro citizens." That, Huie believes, is why he was murdered in an election year; and not when he was at home in Atlanta, but at some dramatic time and place. There was a plot, Huie maintains, but Dr. King was its secondary—not its primary—target. "The primary target," he asserts, "was the United States of America."

However that may be, the explosion was instantaneous. King was shot a few seconds after six o'clock, Memphis time, which is seven o'clock on the East Coast. Within a quarter of an hour, blacks in Harlem and the south side of Chicago and on upper Fourteenth Street in Washington had heard the news on their transistor radios. The wire-service copy was handed to the President in his oval office as he was talking about the Vietnam peace negotiations with his ambassador to Moscow, Llewellyn Thompson. A few minutes later Johnson's secretary, Juanita Roberts, typed a second message on a slip of paper and handed it to him. "Mr. President," it read, "Martin Luther King is dead."

The President was scheduled to leave that night for Hawaii to talk about the war and his new initiative for peace with his generals. That afternoon, he had held a surprise meeting with U Thant at the United Nations. All that must now be laid aside. He sat down and wrote out a short statement and read it into the television cameras.

"America is shocked and saddened by the brutal slaying tonight of Dr. Martin Luther King," he began, in a voice heavy with sorrow and concern. "I ask every citizen to reject the blind violence that has struck Dr. King. . . . We can achieve nothing by lawlessness and divisiveness among the American people. . . ."

At Fourteenth and U Streets, less than a mile to the north, his voice was coming over the radio in the People's Drugstore. Black staff and customers gathered round to listen to their President. "Honky!" shouted one man. "He's a murderer himself," said another. "This will mean a thousand Detroits," said a third.

Within two hours, the prophecy was well on the way to fulfillment. In Washington, an angry black river poured into the streets. At Fourteenth and U, at the heart of the crowded, dingy black city of slums which mocks the pompous monuments and cool green spaces of the white capital, a middle-aged man began to shout. There were tears in his eyes. He picked up a trash can and hurled it through a drugstore window.

"This is it, baby," said another man. "The shit is going to hit the fan now. We ought to burn the place down right now." And to the best of their ability, that is just what they did. "Man!" said a militant leader— one who had helped to set the fires with Molotov cocktails and dynamite—"when that window broke, that was like—the shot that was heard round the world when the honkies were fighting their own people!"

In Chicago, with more than eight hundred thousand Negroes, violence was slower to start. But before it was over, twenty blocks of West Madison Street had been burned and Federal troops had been called in. Mayor Daley was so shaken and so angry that he ordered his policemen, if it ever happened again, to "shoot to kill arsonists, and shoot to maim looters."

There were rioting and arson, shooting by snipers and by police—

in New York, Detroit, Newark, Cincinnati. In Baltimore, the Republican governor took the outbreak of rioting almost as a personal affront. His name was Spiro T. Agnew.

By the end of the week, thirty-seven people had been killed and there had been riots in more than a hundred cities. For the first time in history, the situation room in the basement of the west wing of the White House was plotting the course of a domestic crisis. Into that nerve center of America as a great power there flowed reports of fighting—not in Khe Sanh or on the Jordan, but on Sixty-third Street in Chicago, One hundred twenty-fifth Street in New York, Fourteenth Street in Washington: the White House is on Sixteenth Street.

At last it could be said that in one sense Johnson had been lucky. Had his withdrawal speech not come four days earlier, it is not certain that he could have contained the crisis as he did. As he had himself foreseen, whatever he did must have been suspected of being politically motivated if he were at one and the same time the President striving to bind up the nation's wounds and a candidate striving to fight his way back into office. As it was, he withstood the shock of the waves. But for the future, it would no longer be up to him. When the next wave came, the duty of being ready for it would devolve upon one of a small group of men.

There was George Corley Wallace, Jr., ex-Governor of Alabama, who had nothing to say.

There was Ronald Reagan, Governor of California, who said that this was the sort of "great tragedy that began when we began compromising with law and order, and people started choosing which laws they'd break." Neither Wallace nor Reagan went to the funeral.

Senator Eugene J. McCarthy did. The night King was shot, McCarthy sat in a hotel suite and watched Washington burn on TV. To himself as much as to anyone, he said, "If I were a Negro, I don't know what I'd do!"

And Governor Nelson A. Rockefeller of New York went too; his brother Winthrop, Governor of Arkansas, had predicted only a matter of hours before King's death that Rockefeller would be a candidate in spite of his denials.

There was Hubert Humphrey. He called on all Americans to resolve that "we will never, never, never let this happen again!" Yet, even at this moment, he found cause for optimism: He predicted that equality for all would be King's memorial.

And there was Robert Kennedy. When he heard that King was dead, he went out onto a street corner in Indianapolis and told the small crowd of Negroes who gathered what had happened. Standing under a street lamp, he waited until the shouts of the men and the wails of the women had died away. Then he quoted Aeschylus: "Even in our sleep, pain which cannot forget falls drop by drop upon the heart, until in our despair, against our own will, comes wisdom through the awful grace of God."

Finally, there was Richard Nixon. Before the President's withdrawal, he had been planning to make a speech on Vietnam. There is reason to believe that in it he intended to moderate his stance on Vietnam. He had felt the strength of the desire for peace that swept the country after the Tet offensive. The reason he gave for canceling his speech was a foretaste of the cautious technique he was to use all year long. He did not wish, he said, to embarrass "our negotiators" in Paris. Now he again moved with sure-footed caution. He went to the funeral. He expressed his condolences. And that same day, a man named Brad Hayes, his Southern regional campaign director, made a number of phone calls to Southern Republican leaders. "I called up every single one of them, before they could call me," he recalled later. "And I said, 'Yes, I'm as concerned as you are about this, but it was something the candidate felt he had to do.'" One should not judge the small treasons of politics too harshly. But as it turned out, Hayes' instinctive professionalism was all too prophetic of the price that Nixon would pay for the Presidency.

Upon one of those seven men the next waves would break. One of them, seven months later, would be chosen to do his best to steer the country through what was universally conceded at the time to be what Nelson Rockefeller called it: "a time of crisis and confusion probably without parallel in our history." Which of them would be chosen would depend not so much, in the last analysis, on the preferences of the American people as on the working of the American political system. But before we see how that system made its choice, we must take a closer look at the nature of the crisis which every prophet and pundit in the land discerned, and try to see if we can distinguish the surface waves and the spray from the deep tides and current underneath.

ACT II

Two Symptoms in Search of a Sickness

1

Some Loss of Blood

"Is this a case of magnanimity, forbearance, love, gentleness, mercy, protection of the weak—this strange and overshowy onslaught of an elephant upon a nest of field mice, on the pretext that the mice had squeaked an insolence at him—conduct which 'no self respecting government could allow to pass unavenged'?"

—Mark Twain on the Boer War

Nothing is clearer than the imperative that an account of the politics of 1968 must start with Vietnam, the progress of which dominated the struggle for the Presidency from first to last. Of course, the nature of its effect was not always agreed upon; it was often more oblique than was supposed; the war was perhaps not the simple and overriding moral issue that many honest crusaders perceived it to be. Perhaps the electoral statistician Richard Scammon was correct to argue —as he did in a conversation with the authors—that foreign policy and marginal war are not the kind of matter upon which, at the end of the day, great blocs of votes turn.

It remains true that the narrative without Vietnam would be like *Hamlet* without the murdered king. Yet no subject is harder to deal with briefly. Once it is touched upon, narrative almost irresistibly disappears in complex and important arguments about first causes, special justifications, and even cosmic debate about the rise and fall of civilizations. Other books, and specially equipped writers, must explore such areas. Our concern is with the effect of particular forces upon a particular political apparatus.

What matters here is that, at the beginning of 1968, we find a President and an Administration engaged in an armed conflict which is not supported by a sufficient consensus of American opinion. The policy does have ardent supporters, but its opponents—some of them former supporters—are now winning the argument. And these opponents make up a large proportion of those active classes without whose consent American affairs can scarcely be managed. The opposition of these people to the war forms a focus of dissent to which many other grievances become attached and around which a series of challenges to the President is organized. The President is caught in a position in which the military logic of the war demands a further commitment of resources—but in which the domestic political climate precludes it. Although the causes of this situation are many and complex, there are certain identifiable ones related to the nature of the Presidency and to the political outlook of the people who have controlled and guided it in recent years.

Few wars are fought with clear purposes and well-defined objectives. But one of the most important political points about America's war in Vietnam was that, to an unusual degree, involvement preceded rationale: the war was well advanced before there was any structured national debate about its purpose. Virtually all protagonists concede that early decisions about the war were made within a limited circle— and frequently mistakenly. Therefore, one must ask what sort of people made the early policy and on what sort of premises they based it.

To begin with, there is evidence that they were largely the wrong people. James C. Thomson, Jr., who left the government in 1966 over Vietnam, having served in the White House and in the State Department, wrote afterward that the Department's Bureau of Far Eastern Affairs "had been purged of its best China expertise . . . as a result of McCarthyism." (Thus one obsession prepares the ground for the next. When the State Department deals with the complexities of the future, how much will it suffer for the lack of the Thomsons it lost over Vietnam?) The members of the Bureau, according to Thomson, "were generally committed to one policy line: the close containment and isolation of Communist China . . . and the maintenance of a network of alliances with anti-Communist client states on China's periphery."

The facile transference of containment policy from Europe to Asia was made by men who assumed that the Chinese controlled most or all revolutionaries in Asia. These men appear to have been insufficiently aware of such details of nationalism as the tension between Vietnamese and Chinese which dates back at least to the ejection of the Chinese

from the peninsula in A.D. 939. Out of such fatal oversimplification grew
the Domino Theory.

The much-described Vietnam war eventually became so horrible
that it was difficult for many to believe that those who began and directed
it were not monsters. But demonology clouds understanding: indeed,
there is a special demonology which actually misrepresents the nature of
the crisis. This is the notion which is given force, perhaps unintentionally,
by the work of some liberal dissidents such as Roger C. Hilsman, in
which the war in Vietnam is blamed on the stupidity and ferocity of
American military officers. The role of the military establishment has
been more complex than that, as is shown by what happened in 1954
when the question arose of going to the aid of the French in Dienbienphu.

Admiral Radford, chairman of the Joint Chiefs of Staff, favored an
air strike in support of the fortress—if necessary, one involving tactical
nuclear weapons. The Air Chief of Staff, General Twining, and the Chief
of Naval Operations, Admiral Carney, were also in favor. Secretary of
State Dulles favored intervention, and the idea was vividly promoted
to the public by another civilian, Vice-President Nixon, who told a
group of newspaper editors that America, "as a leader of the Free
World," could not afford further retreat in Asia. If necessary, he said,
"the Administration must face up to the situation and dispatch forces."
It is ironic that a man brought to the Presidency in 1968 largely because
of the consequences of land war in Asia should have been so ready to
begin one in 1954.

But the idea of intervention, even by air strike, was strongly opposed
by the Army Chief of Staff, General Matthew B. Ridgway. According to
his Chief of Plans, General James M. Gavin:

> Though under tremendous pressure to conform, Ridgway refused
> to endorse the majority view. Instead, he carried his disagreement over
> the air strike . . . up to the President. I am convinced that Ridgway's
> determined opposition plus that of our allies was crucial in aborting this
> early effort to involve us in Vietnam.

Obviously, this does not mean that military advice was not sometimes mistaken and simplistic—indeed, General Gavin admits that it
frequently was, and he includes his own. But it does mean that it was
not monolithically so. (And it is important that Ridgway carried his
objections firmly to the President: something that later dissenters have
not always dared or been encouraged to do.)

The machinery which was to grind so many people to death was essentially set in motion not by any ordinary military ideas, but by the consciously heterodox doctrines of "limited war" and "counterinsurgency." It was under these auspices, early in 1962, that President Kennedy sent to Vietnam the two air-support companies which began the process of escalation. Looking back through a curtain of blood and disillusionment, one cannot easily recapture the mood of almost boyish enthusiasm with which the idea of counterinsurgency was embraced by the official Washington of New Frontier days. One useful memory is of the same Roger Hilsman who was then at the State Department. He was, at that time, famous for his enthusiasm for guerrilla derring-do and the knife-between-the-teeth brand of personal combat. Some part of that mood was apparently connected with an eager desire to demonstrate to the world the vitality and toughness of the individual American spirit in confrontation with the Communists. Perhaps it was an understandable desire—but the world had not chosen to doubt the personal toughness of individual Americans. What was more open to question was another intellectual bastion of the counterinsurgency theory—at least in the version proposed by such influential fellows as Walt Rostow—which was that America was itself a revolutionary society. This proposition insisted on the corollary pretense that the revolutionaries of the Third World were really reactionaries deserving of suppression. Use of such arguments suggests in their advocates errors in the observation of their own society so greatly as to induce self-delusion. Professor Rostow, for one, made much use of mirror-Marxism of the crudest sort. "Communism is best understood as a disease of the transition to modernization," he said when speeding Special Forces trainees on their way from Fort Bragg to the jungles of Vietnam.

Why was it that, in 1962, President Kennedy, uneasily, felt he must send those three hundred soldiers to Vietnam? One reason, says James Thomson, was that the Administration "inherited and somewhat shared" (largely through the flawed bureaucracy of the State Department) "a general perception of China-on-the-march." (In an article in the *Atlantic Monthly,* April 1968, Thomson wrote that this was "fed by Chinese intervention in the Korean War, an intervention actually based on appallingly bad communications and mutual miscalculation on the part of Washington and Peking. But the careful unraveling of that tragedy, which scholars have accomplished, had not yet become part of the conventional wisdom.") Officials tended to see the insurrections in Vietnam, which followed the final collapse of the Geneva Accords that had settled the Indochina war in 1954 by dividing the country, as directed by

Chinese malevolence—or at least, if they were not so already, they soon would be. Another argument was provided by the pressure of liberal lobby groups, such as the American Friends of Vietnam, which believed that it was important to demonstrate that a liberal democracy, or some passable facsimile of one, could be erected in an underdeveloped country.

Kennedy had made a powerful speech against intervention in 1954: "For the United States to intervene unilaterally and to send troops to the most difficult terrain in the world, with the Chinese able to pour in unlimited manpower, would mean that we would face a situation which would be far more difficult than even that we encountered in Korea." But he was still dealing in terms of a Sino-Vietnamese monolith. In office, Kennedy was susceptible to a more subtle and oblique version of intervention. Unfortunately, he had been an early backer of Ngo Dinh Diem, the pig-headed mystic in whom the Friends of Vietnam were able to discern a stout-hearted democrat not visible to many other people.

Counterinsurgency and limited war were two separate items in the calibration of United States power as it was then being developed. Counterinsurgency was the more obviously dangerous, at least if the view that we have implied of it is acceptable—that is, revolutionary guerrilla warfare without its essential mainspring of revolutionary ideology. Men spent weeks in South Carolina learning to live off snakes but emerged with no political ideas to present to an Asian peasant except some generalities about Freedom. This is a classic example of obsession with style and technique to the exclusion of content: military McLuhanism in which the medium is the message.

Limited war was a less obviously flawed idea, being no more than the idea that finely calculated increments of conventional power should be progressively applied until the enemy gave up. It appeared to be the sensible alternative to massive retaliation; nevertheless, when Rostow proposed a policy of "graduated retaliation" against North Vietnam— bluntly, bombing them to make them cease aiding the Vietcong—the cautious Kennedy was not happy. He declined the bombing plan, but sent some troops. "It's like taking a drink," he complained. "The effect wears off and you have to take another." But as a former State Department officer, Richard J. Barnet, put it in *Intervention and Revolution,* "The President had rejected major military intervention as a conscious policy, but he had set in force the bureaucratic momentum that would make it a certainty."

The contradictions of the limited-war theory did not become apparent for some time, and it is possible, as apologists like Arthur

Schlesinger claim, that Kennedy might have been able to reverse the trend toward disaster. He had an inestimable advantage over Johnson in having passed through the Bay of Pigs crisis, in which it had been revealed to him how dangerously misleading might be the expert advice tendered to a President. The man who succeeded Kennedy was not naturally a skeptic, especially in affairs involving patriotic emotion, and he had not passed through the same disillusioning experience. Kennedy mixed the advice he took with conscious knowledge of the weaknesses of those who gave it: but Johnson, aware of his own limitations in foreign affairs, seemed to be more easily impressed. After some movements and maneuvers, he settled on three Kennedy men as his primary advisers on Vietnam: Dean Rusk, his fellow-Southerner, whom he liked and trusted; Walt Rostow, his industrious Special Assistant; and Robert McNamara, whose mind he deeply admired ("McNamara is the ablest man I ever met," he said). Unfortunately, Rusk was an inflexible bureaucrat, Rostow was an ideologue, and McNamara was a brilliant but naïve administrator. The trio was not a fortunate one: as the crisis progressed, McNamara's special limitations, because of his otherwise impressive stature, were to emerge as the most damaging.

Lyndon Johnson, very shortly after his assumption of office, expressed to his advisers a determination that he was not going to "lose Vietnam." (Indeed, he restated the Chinese obsession and the Domino Theory; he would not let "Southeast Asia go the way China went.") If the Vietcong and North Vietnamese were committed to the limits of their endurance—as was the case—there were implicit in this policy a number of developments for which the public certainly was not prepared and which Johnson had probably not thought through himself. In the mock-industrial jargon which McNamara's Pentagon revealingly used, there were a number of "inputs" which could contribute toward the end of not "losing" Vietnam. Certain of these had already been taken up: the United States had assumed such military functions in Vietnam like airlifting and reconnaissance. And the troop commitment had rapidly escalated: by summer 1964, there were twenty-five thousand Americans in Vietnam. Other "inputs," such as the bombing of the North, which Kennedy had rejected, remained unused for the moment.

This process was being conducted with relatively little concern on the part of the public at large, who were given by the media no inkling that the assumptions had been made, and the machinery set in motion, which would shortly plunge them into a major political crisis. During most of 1964, opinion polls reflected generally low interest in the Vietnam issue.

That is not to say some legislators did not feel a certain unease. For instance, Representative Charles Halleck of Indiana—incidentally, a most aggressive hawk—recalls that, in 1962, he attended a bipartisan meeting at the White House when President Kennedy announced the dispatch of more troops to Vietnam. Halleck said to Kennedy that "it looks as though we're going to get a lot of American boys killed"—and he asked the President to "tell the American people just how serious the involvement [is]." Kennedy replied that he would tell the people "if and when the war [gets] that bad." By the logic of limited war, such a time would be too late.

One further development, the Tonkin Gulf incident of August 1964, removed the last inhibitions from the process of escalation. The alleged North Vietnamese attack upon the American destroyers *Turner Joy* and *Maddox* was so dubious, and the retaliation by air raid against North Vietnam so swift, that suspicions were aroused among close observers. It seemed likely that the American command wanted to make a show of force and was only looking for a pretext. But opinion polls showed that eighty-five per cent of voters approved of what the President had done. He described it as a "limited response," yet used this spasm of public enthusiasm to extract from Congress that famous resolution empowering him to "take all measures . . . to repulse aggression and prevent further aggression." This was an *unlimited* brief.

Once the egregious Goldwater had been defeated in the 1964 election, American commitment in Vietnam took what Richard Barnet calls "a series of quantum jumps." The determination to somehow defeat the National Liberation Front had been made when relatively few U.S. troops were involved, either in counterinsurgency or limited conventional action. But the NLF guerrillas were effective and well-entrenched: by early 1965, it was apparent that the degree of force required to oppose them had been grossly underestimated. In October 1963, Secretary McNamara had predicted that 1965 should see the end of the "major part of the U.S. military task." Instead, it was just beginning, with systematic bombing of North Vietnam starting in February 1965 and the dispatch of a hundred thousand troops in the summer.

Such an effort required more justification than the support of a morally dubious government in a small country. Therefore, Vietnam was described as the test case, chosen by international Communism to prove that American power could be brought down by "wars of national liberation." The war which, as recently as the 1964 election, had been labeled as a Vietnamese concern was now described by the embattled

President Johnson as "part of a wider pattern of aggressive purposes."
The American public was now informed that it was engaged in an
international confrontation with North Vietnam and China. The original
low estimates of the "limited strength" required to deal with the NLF
guerrillas were retrospectively justified by claims that the enemy was
getting outside support. The year 1965 saw the launching of the State
Department claim that the war was "aggression from the North"—although even in 1967, the Defense Department could still find only 50,000
North Vietnamese troops among the 286,000 of the enemy. By such
posterior rationalizations, earlier political and military misjudgments
were protected from criticism.

The crucial misjudgment was about the nature of limited war. There
were enough theorists of the subject, both governmental and academic,
but too few of them asked the question: *for whom is the war limited?*
In a symposium in 1968, Theodore Draper said,

> Great powers tend to think of "limited wars" in terms of them-
> selves. . . . A great power may use only a very limited portion of its
> power, but it will be enough to make a small power feel that it must
> fight an unlimited war or not fight at all.

Failure to take this point was well exemplified by Professor Robert
Scalapino of the University of California, who claimed that American
restraint was demonstrated by the decision to risk American lives in
battle rather then "eradicate North Vietnam from the map." Draper
comments dryly: "Presumably this act of self-denial on the part of the
United States should have persuaded North Vietnam to place certain
limitations upon its power."

Once the war had entered a stage where automatic expansion was
all too likely, it was clearly important that the President base his decisions on the most realistic knowledge available. Yet it seems clear that
he did not do so. It may be that no man at the center of so many problems as the President can be expected to make sensible decisions upon
all, or even most, of them. If so, the trend to centralized power in the
White House is not reassuring. In any case, Johnson compounded the
problems by his own hot temperament. According to his former White
House aide and close confidant, Bill Moyers, Johnson was at first more
dubious than many people believe about dispatching troops to Vietnam.
"But once they had gone, he never had any doubt they should be backed
up, and he assumed that every red-blooded American would feel the
same." Such loyalty to men he had sent to risk their lives was no doubt

a virtue: but nothing could have been better calculated to reinforce the limited-war syndrome.

Then there is the question of the quality of the advice he was getting, and here Robert McNamara's way of gathering information was important. During 1963 and 1964, McNamara made journeys to Vietnam with the Director of the CIA, John A. McCone. McCone, by early 1965 at least, had come to the conclusion that the military and political situation in Vietnam was little short of disastrous. According to some of his immediate advisers, his disagreements with McNamara on this question were the essential cause of his departure from the agency in 1965. These two servants of the Presidency make an interesting contrast: McNamara, a kind, emotional organization man of conscious rectitude; McCone, flinty and somewhat ruthless—nearer to the old buccaneering tradition of individualistic capitalism. Their working methods in Vietnam also made a sharp contrast. McNamara relied heavily on the "group briefing," a characteristic tool of rationalistic modern bureaucracy. Experts are gathered around a table, and in crisp rotation they project their expertise at the visiting chieftain. In the case of Vietnam, this was usually quantified as far as possible: that is, numerical ideas like "kill ratios" received more prominence than such intangibles as political mood. McCone attended group briefings, but, according to his executive director, Lyman B. Kirkpatrick, he was skeptical of their usefulness. His reason was that the "official line" prevails in such a situation and few officials are willing to voice doubts which conflict with it. McCone relied on getting people alone and asking them for their views. He therefore acquired a very different picture of Vietnam, for the ordinary Americans who served there had not suffered any gross failure of perception. They saw what was happening: the trouble was that the official information machine filtered out their views. As a result, one of the last men to know what was going on was the President, sitting at the apex of the machine.

Not surprisingly, McNamara and McCone returned with diametrically opposed views. When they reported to the President, McNamara's view prevailed, although his optimism was as erroneous as it had been before. It appears that McCone did not feel able to press his objections with the President in the way that Ridgway had felt able to in 1954— obviously at least partly because of the characters of Lyndon Johnson and John McCone. But a contributory factor, probably, was the fact that, since Eisenhower's time, the "institutional" structure of the Presidency had been weakened. First Kennedy, and then Johnson, had personalized the office intensely: the weight advisers carried with them was measured less by their rank in the formal hierarchy and more by their personal standing with the President. McCone's standing with the President was not high, because of his previous lack of enthusiasm about the war. (He was, by this time, not being invited to the Tuesday lunch meetings at which Johnson talked matters over informally with his advisers.) McCone's skepticism merely hastened his departure from office.

The heavy build-up of ground forces which began in summer 1965 was still presented as a series of increments. No clear understanding was given to the public of where the "limits" of the war were to be found. At this stage, there might have been a case for the Administration's attempting a forthright commitment of U. S. power in one clear-cut decision. At least, the inevitable public debate could have established the degree of commitment the country would find tolerable. But that was precisely what the Administration wished to avoid: this was to be war without hard decisions. And in the Tonkin resolution, the President and his advisers had what amounted to a blank check—even if it had been obtained, as many people thought, by false pretenses. Now that the mechanism of escalating military commitment, escalating rationale, and hopelessly misleading information was complete, it seemed that the war might continue to grow forever. In fact, there was an upper limit—but it did not become evident until three years after the major escalations of 1965. In the wake of the Tet offensive, it was to become clear that the American people, uncertain and reluctant in pursuit of the thundering moralisms with which Lyndon Johnson justified the war, would draw the line somewhere. In the end, faced with mounting casualties, a troop commitment of just over half a million, and a financial cost sufficient to imperil America's gold reserves and, in turn, the dollar itself, the American people decided that too much was too much.

Finally, there is a question that will echo later in the narrative. After all the criticism—justified as it is—can one be sure that any *one man,* even one subtler and better-equipped than Johnson, could have done significantly better at the center of the crisis than he did? In Omaha in July 1966, he said, "Now there are many, many, many who can recommend and advise and sometimes a few of them consent. But there is only one that has been chosen by the American people to decide." The system had placed an extraordinary responsibility on one man: to detect a misconception of the nature of Asian Communism to which he himself originally subscribed; to detect a misapprehension of the nature of his own society by a number of plausible intellectuals; to detect the logical difficulties in the theory of limited war, and resist the temptations it offered to commit the nation to intervention by sleight of legislative hand; and to discount the mechanistic fallacies of the rambling bureaucracy which was his eyes and ears.

And it was not as though Johnson did not have other troubles on his mind.

Indications of Malignancy

"It is a reproach to religion and government to suffer too much poverty and excess."

—William Penn, *Reflections and Maxims*

In the summer of 1964, the sociologist Lee Rainwater, one of the not overlarge body of writers who have taken an interest in the white working class, conducted a set of interviews as part of a privately sponsored research program. He talked to working-class and some middle-class families, trying, among other things, to get a fairly comprehensive account of their social and political emotions. Rainwater found his respondents sympathetic to the rhetoric of social reform which then dominated Democratic politics, and which led up to the Great Society program and the War on Poverty. These industrious, respectable white Americans felt that the poor and the black poor were going to be given a chance to work their way out of poverty, and they approved of the intention.

It was perhaps the last opportunity for some time to record so generous and optimistic a mood: only four years later, it appeared to have collapsed into bitterness and frustration. White factory workers thronged to hear George Wallace. Practical politicians found that white middle-class audiences had never been so delighted to listen to diatribes against relief payments. And intellectuals of the left and right announced the end of the liberal-reformist tradition which had engaged the energies of America's most effective politicians for nearly thirty years.

This swift despair among whites was remarkable enough. But there was an even more startling condition to be observed among black Americans, whose alienation had been at first exaggerated and then excessively discounted. Plainly, the claims that some militants made about the revolutionary temper of the blacks were as absurd as their threats to "destroy America" from their disorganized minority position. In all the pain and passion, it was difficult to see what was really happening.

But at least 1968 produced some serious and comprehensive evidence on the matter, most notably in the brilliant report published that June, *Racial Attitudes in Fifteen American Cities*—Baltimore, Boston, Chicago, Cincinnati, Cleveland, Detroit, Gary, Milwaukee, Newark, New York (Brooklyn), Philadelphia, Pittsburgh, San Francisco, St. Louis, and Washington, D.C. The report, by Angus Campbell and Howard Schuman, grew out of work undertaken for the Riot Commission by the University of Michigan's Institute for Social Research, one of the pioneering centers in quantifying social response, particularly voting behavior. Based on a sample—five thousand blacks and whites— designed as a cross section of the population from sixteen to nineteen years old, the study explored the urban relationship between black and white with a precision not previously attempted. Interviewing began on January 6 and was virtually finished on March 30, the day before the President withdrew and four days before the death of Martin Luther King. The survey is thus a photograph of the racial situation on the brink of a major crisis.

The evidence it produces on the nature of social change may be relevant at later points in this account of Presidential politics. What is interesting here is the degree of separatism and rejection it revealed. The great majority of Negroes were found, as one would expect, to be cautious in social outlook and committed to the ideal of integration. Just before his death, King overshadowed all other black leaders in the respect of his people. Of those interviewed, seventy-two per cent approved, without qualification, of what he stood for. Though some black people had mixed feelings, only one in twenty disliked what he stood for. By contrast, Stokely Carmichael and H. Rap Brown had low scores for approval and high scores for disapproval.

But six per cent of the people interviewed said they favored the formation of a separate black nation. This may seem low at first glance, but it represents a considerable number of people: in the words of the Report, "we are implying that some 200,000 Negroes in these fifteen cities feel so little a part of American society that they favor withdrawing allegiance." The report continues:

> In a formal election six per cent of the vote means little, but in a campaign to change minds and influence policies, six per cent of the

population can represent a considerable force. . . . It is likely that many of those who hold to the majority position do so with little thought or commitment. To deviate from a very widely-held norm probably requires more conviction than to hold it. . . . We might find the force behind black nationalism to be considerably greater than its numbers suggest.

Had not sensibilities been dulled by so much inchoate alarmism, this sober measurement might have caused more disturbance. Nobody knows precisely how long such alienation has existed, nor how rapidly it is increasing, but clearly this finding demonstrates a serious discontinuity in the social fabric. And the extent is probably much greater, as it is likely that the hard core would be surrounded by a penumbra of somewhat less intense alienation: a phenomenon of the sort that was discovered in black reactions to riot and violence. Only a small proportion of Negroes accepted violence as a means of protest—the highest proportion, as one would expect, occurring among young men, where it reached twenty per cent in response to an abstract question and declined sharply when specific propositions were discussed. "The most important fact about those inclined toward violence," wrote Campbell and Schuman, "is that they are not an isolated band of deviants condemned by almost all other Negroes, but are linked to a much larger group by a common definition of the problems that beset the Negro in America."

Only a few days after Campbell and Schuman completed their survey, this point was acted out in one of the cities where their interviewers worked—Washington, D.C. One of the more ominous scenes after the assassination took place when black high-school students left their classes and milled about in the street, while Assistant Superintendent of Schools George Rhodes tried to enlist the help of student leaders to keep the others in school. But, he said, "they found it quite reasonable that the students would react in a violent manner to what had happened." The student leaders felt that "people in the community had to say in no uncertain terms that looting was wrong" if violence was to be avoided. No such unequivocal declaration was forthcoming: by the end of the day, two young blacks had been burned to death, white motorists had been harassed and beaten, firemen had been stoned, and shops and tenements throughout the area lay in smoking ruins.

Without doubt, the explosions of April 1968, and those previous explosions in Detroit, Newark, and Watts, came as a shock and disappointment to most whites—and perhaps as a surprise to many blacks. The relationship of forces at work here is subtle and dangerous, and not all of it can yet be exposed in definitive detail. But, remembering some history and the measurements of the ISR survey, the outline of the mechanism becomes visible.

The crucial point is that black and white perceptions of the progress of the last few years' reform differ radically—*and there is a further radical divergence of perceptions within the black community itself.* In the decade between the 1954 Supreme Court decision and the Civil Rights Act of 1964, a series of great national dramas was enacted: the Court's "all deliberate speed" order (1955); the Montgomery bus boycotts (1955–56); the Birmingham confrontation (1963); and the March on Washington (August 1963). The burden of this dramatic progress was that goods were being conferred upon the Negro, some real, some symbolic. Sometimes the symbolic content was dangerously larger than the real. For instance, before the Birmingham confrontation, Attorney General Robert Kennedy and his staff had been quietly concentrating on legal battles to enable Southern Negroes to register as voters and win other rights for themselves. This policy, which might have hastened the black experience of electoral power and weakened the hold of many white supremacists on local and national power structures, was largely abandoned after Birmingham. In its place came the policy of confrontation with maximum publicity which produced the Civil Rights Act of 1964. But as the main thrust of this Act dealt with public accommodations—the *casus belli* in Birmingham—its effect, in many cases, was to give Negroes access to middle-class hotels and golf courses which they could not afford anyway, rather than gains in real power or prosperity commensurate with the political excitement deployed.

Thus, in every way, circumstances, even down to such emotional details as Lyndon Johnson's use of "We Shall Overcome," conspired to implant in the white community a feeling that real progress had been made. Only one-fifth of the white people in the fifteen cities believed that many Negroes suffered from job discrimination, for instance. And although another third thought that it might affect some Negroes, "perhaps more impressive is the fact that nearly four out of ten white people apparently believe that few if any Negroes are subject to discrimination in hiring or promotions." At the beginning of 1967, the white perception appeared to be that *a great deal had been done* but that *the results were disappointing* (i.e., racial tension was even worse).

What was the blacks' perception? At first glance, optimistic, in that the majority (sixty-two per cent of the fifteen-city sample) believed that a lot of progress had been made. But more than one-third saw little or no change—"the basic assumption of major improvement," wrote Campbell and Schuman, "so seemingly obvious to many white Americans, is not accepted by many black Americans." And, crucially, younger Negroes were much less likely to see improvement than older ones.

There is, of course, an argument over whether or not there have been substantive gains, and this devolves into details about special cases in particular social and geographic situations. But what matters in national politics is the broad movement and the perceptions that result from it. The likeliest proposition here is that some substantive progress *has* been made and has been perceived as progress by older people with memories of harsher discrimination. But it is not perceived by the young, who see only their own predicament, poised agonizingly between full and half citizenship. In the ISR sample nearly half the male teen-agers rejected the idea that progress had been made. What progress there is makes their aspirations possible; its incompleteness enforces the tension from which alienation and violence derive. At the same time, these violent manifestations, by offending the white majority, make less likely the concessions which alone can give relief. It is a syndrome which could easily produce a disaster, failing political intervention—for which the system does not yet seem prepared. And here, in a chapter which has deliberately been kept free of value judgments, it might be worth qualifying the word "disaster."

To some people, the proposition of racial confrontation, conflict, and separation, in various combinations, is not disastrous. They have systematic ideas of superior arrangements that would ensue. Perhaps they are right—their argument is an interesting one. But what cannot be doubted is that the immediate result of such racial conflict will be the destruction or misery of many black people and a violent distortion of the lives of many whites. In a world where so many predictions have been misleading, the word "disaster" still seems applicable.

One further finding by the ISR team—this time about white attitudes—needs to be kept in mind while one examines the politics of 1968:

> The superficially simple solution to the problem of urban riots—more rigid police control of the Negro areas—is not generally seen by white urban residents as an adequate answer. *The large majority of people accept the proposition that there must be an improvement in the conditions of Negro life.* [Our italics.]

How much was the belief in that proposition, which existed so clearly at the beginning of the year, eroded by the events of the 1968 campaign?

3

A Slight Case of Hubris?

"America's leadership must be guided by the lights of learning and reason—or else those who confuse rhetoric with reality and the plausible with the possible will gain the popular ascendancy with their seemingly swift and simple solutions."

> —President John F. Kennedy, in a speech intended for delivery in Dallas on November 22, 1963

"It is an easy thing for one whose foot
Is outside of calamity
To give advice and to rebuke the sufferer."

> —Aeschylus, *Prometheus Bound*

To apply to Lyndon Johnson as an individual the word *hubris* in its modern, dictionary-defined sense of "wanton arrogance" would be both abusive and unfair. But the word has an older and richer meaning. It was the term for the second stage in a progression which is perhaps the fundamental idea in the ancient Greek tragedy, a moral system as deep and as universal as the Christian cycle of sin, grace, and redemption, though a far less comfortable one. The Greeks believed that the danger of success was that it bred hubris; that hubris might lead to *nemesis*— divine retribution—and that nemesis led in the end to *ate*, total black destruction and annihilation.

It is worth pointing out that hubris, in their system, was not necessarily evilly motivated. On the contrary, the classic instance of hubris was the presumption of Prometheus, who stole the divine fire from heaven out of a wish to start mankind on the way to the Great

Society. "In helping man I brought my troubles on me," he said as he lay chained to the rock and at the mercy of his enemies, and the titan from Texas was heard to make similar complaints in the privacy of the White House. No: the sin of hubris lies not in any evil motives, but in a systematic conception of one's powers and one's place in the universe so proud, so presumptuous, and so erroneous that it can only end in disaster.

At a preliminary diagnosis, hubris might seem a strange name for the American malady at the beginning of 1968: a hysterical form of social hypochondria was more in evidence. From television and from the press, from every kind of expert and leader, Americans were inundated with an almost unprecedented torrent of gloom. Every kind of authority produced new reasons for believing that America had become what she was called by Nelson Rockefeller, scarcely the most radical of social critics: "the Afflicted Society." The New Left earnestly predicted the imminent establishment of Fascism; the Right foresaw decadence and mob rule. No prophecy and no denunciation was too wild for the new generation of black leaders; and yet even their antithesis, Senator William Fulbright, most urbane of conservatives, soberly warned that "unmistakably America is showing signs of that arrogance of power which has afflicted, weakened, and in some cases destroyed great nations in the past."

The politicians said that rarely had the country respected its President so little—and the polls bore them out.

The economists feared that the cost of the war and the persistent deficit in foreign payments would lead to devaluation of the dollar (technically, to an increase in the price of gold, which would amount to much the same thing) and to an eventual recession.

The sociologists described the failure of the War on Poverty and pointed out the appalling spread of pauperization in the midst of wealth.

Ordinary people worried over the alarming rise in the crime statistics and the actual alarming, though not quite so steep, rise in crime itself.

And moralists of every school threw up their hands at the vogue for marijuana, LSD, and other new fashions in escapism, and puzzled over the younger generation's lack of respect for their elders.

But two great problems above all were singled out as in some measure the cause of all the Republic's other troubles: the two downward spirals, described in the two previous chapters, which became labeled for convenience, and sometimes, it seemed, with an almost affectionate familiarity, The War and The Cities.

There was good reason, in all conscience, for alarm on both counts. The war was killing more and more Americans. It was costing an astronomical amount of money. And it was beginning to do economic damage: from early 1968 it was noticed that, for the first time anyone could remember, peace was bullish on the Stock Exchange. Most important of all, as it turned out, the war was causing a massive rebellion among young people. The draft was so unpopular that a considerable number of young people were leaving the country and going to Canada or Europe—not a significant number in themselves but apparently, from the attention they attracted, enough to be psychologically wounding to a country that had always thought of itself as the last hope of troubled people from other parts of the world.

There was even more reason to be disturbed by the crisis in the relations between black and white Americans. At the beginning of 1968, the optimism of 1963—when Dr. King had a dream, everyone sang, "Black and white together, We shall overcome," and all that seemed needed for a second emancipation was an act of Congress—had been replaced by a mood of despair which could not be said entirely to lack foundation. In more than a hundred cities, black ghettos had exploded—from Watts in 1965 to Detroit in 1967—and it was generally assumed that each summer would be hotter than the last. What was more, it was getting harder and harder to dismiss these explosions as trivial incidents on the road to a solution of the country's oldest political problem, still less as the work of a handful of agitators. As the Kerner Commission was to say with shocking frankness at the end of February, there was a growing body of evidence that white racism was the cause of the new black militancy; and there was little reason to believe that the white majority was ready in practice to abandon the half-conscious assumption of white supremacy.

The majority of Americans, in short, approached the Presidential politics of 1968 with a strong, and simple, and unhappy picture of what was happening to their country. It was, in a catchphrase of the time, "being torn apart by the war and the cities." No one, it seems to us, can hope to understand what 1968 was about unless he accepts that with infinite variations, that, was the theme of the year for most Americans. But it also seems to us that the picture was not an altogether true one. It was at once too gloomy and too sanguine.

Both the War and the Cities were real enough, and bad enough. But the particular form in which these problems troubled so many Americans was not likely to last forever. There was every possibility that the situation would improve in Vietnam and that the cities would exhaust their anger and their energies in a futile eruption and then relapse into torpor; that people would then return with a sigh of relief to the mild complacency which is a far more natural state of mind for the most "successful" country in the world.

And that is exactly what happened. The escalation of the war did stop, and the peace talks began. The ghettos went up in one incandescent flare in April, and were then quieter than they had been for a long time. The United States triumphed in the Olympic Games. The gross national product went up seven per cent. Detroit had its best year ever, and so did the New York Stock Exchange. To crown it all, three American astronauts beat the Russians around the moon. Already, by the fall of the year, the jeremiads in the news magazines began to be replaced by self-congratulation, cautious at first and then gradually more confident.

Yet nothing that was achieved by the political process in 1968, it seems to us, did anything to heal what was actually wrong with American society. Vietnam and The Cities were not the disease. They were symptoms—real inflammations, but still effects, not causes. The disease was the whole complex of attitudes, traditions, interests, values, past choices, and hopes for the future which made it possible for the strongest country in the world to embroil itself in a cruel and futile war under the illusion that it was safeguarding the freedom of the world; and, at the same time, made it impossible for Americans to cut through the surface with realism and determination to get at the problems underneath at home.

The disease, in a word, was hubris.

We do not need to be reminded of the rebuke that Prometheus most deservedly hurled at the self-satisfied busybodies of the chorus. We know how much easier it is "for one whose foot is outside of calamity to give advice and to rebuke the sufferer." And, when we suggest that America's problem in 1968 stems from hubris, we are not striving to say something vulgarly abusive. We are using not the modern, but the old, tragic sense of the word. Hubris can spring from honorable pride in great powers and great achievements, and its motives may be as high as the improvement of mankind. We still think that when a society's perception of its mission rises too high above reality, there is the danger of nemesis.

It is certainly not hard to trace the failure both of the Great Society program at home and of the Vietnam adventure abroad to typically hubristic conceptions of America's unique power and mission.

The Great Society was not the most daring, but it was perhaps the most bellicose program of social reform in history. It was to be a *war* on poverty. Federal funds were to be "fired in" to pockets of poverty in what was known in Washington as "the rifle-shot approach." "This nation," Johnson had said at a dinner to raise funds for his 1964 election campaign, "this people, this generation, has man's first chance to create a Great Society. . . . No one will stop America," he warned grimly, "from wiping out racial injustice." On another occasion, he actually spoke of "throttling want." It was as if the President and the comfortable middle-class Americans who supported and helped to frame his program were intolerably affronted by the impudent persistence of poverty, rather than concerned at the condition of the poor.

The same initial burst of aggressive confidence characterized the 1963 and 1964 efforts of the Administration and, for example, the great foundations to destroy segregation and "achieve integration." The Congress did pass a long schedule of reform legislation, pieces of which —particularly those concerned with civil rights—are probably of historic importance. But it is fair to say that this program was sold more energetically than it was carried out and that it was, from the start, more aggressive than radical. The Administration's approach seemed curiously industrial. A problem was identified: in this case, that there were too many poor people in the United States. Right. Let the problem be bulldozed out of existence. Experts were consulted and suggested "solutions." These suggestions were priced, and a carefully graduated "mix" of "programs" applied. Elaborate public-relations antics were directed where persuasion was thought necessary—to Congress; to the press, of course; even in certain instances to the proposed recipients, if they proved recalcitrant. Finally, quantitative estimates of the success of the program were proudly produced. Johnson's aide Joseph Califano was a great one for producing lists showing how many fewer poor people there were this year than at some earlier time.

But the point of social reform, of course, ought not to be to push *x* million people above some notional "poverty line." As poverty is relative, so there can be no useful "attack" on it that does not involve the effective redistribution of goods, services, and wealth. But redistribution hurts. It demands hard decisions. And these the Johnson Administration did not seem willing to make. Indeed, it is very doubtful whether the classes that exercise political power in the United States really want to abolish poverty or any other major social problem if it is going to mean paying a price that will hurt. And it is hubristic to think that you can conquer problems that have never been conquered before, however rich you are, if you are not prepared to pay a price to do so.

There are striking parallels between the failure of the Great Society —for, whatever particular successes it did achieve, it *was* a failure in terms of the original rhetorical claims made for it—and the failure in Vietnam. Each involved a refusal to make difficult decisions. This, we have suggested was the inherent, though concealed, weakness of the attractive doctrine of "limited war." And each was based on a premise that the United States was now so rich, so powerful, so omnipotent that it could do *without giving up any other desired goal,* whatever its President wanted to do. "The Johnson-Rusk policy in Asia," wrote Walter Lippmann, "is based on the assumption that two hundred million Americans, because they have a superior technology, can lead and direct the two-thirds of the human race who inhabit the continent of Asia. It cannot be done." He was perfectly right. But the very words, "It cannot be done," applied to a proposed policy of the United States, are regarded by too many of its citizens as tantamount to defeatism. "The impossible takes a little longer." The Johnson Administration thought nothing of proposing, *as a mere incident* in the military defense of South Vietnam, to impose an entirely exotic and imported social revolution. The Kennedy Administration proposed to export a social revolution to the whole of Latin America. And President Johnson not infrequently spoke as if his ambition was to make the whole world part of his Great, unhappy, Society.

One day in the spring of 1968, Senator Eugene McCarthy was asked whether he thought American foreign policy was imperialist. "Well, yes," he answered, "it is a kind of imperialism, but a new kind. It is almost a kind of ideological imperialism. It is an idea we seem to have of the world as our *imperium.*"

It is almost certainly hard for Americans to appreciate the sense, not of arrogance, but of sheer unreality and fantasy, which their own view of themselves and of their place in the universe produces on the foreigner. A foreigner opens *Look* magazine, and he reads Eric Sevareid's opinion that "intelligent foreigners know that much of the world will be transformed in the American image. . . . They know that the struggle is really over—it is the Western way of living and doing, our way and the way of Europe combined, that the world wants." He turns in bewilderment to *Life* magazine, and—hoping, perhaps, for a respite from this messianism—turns to a pleasant little essay on jogging. But what is this? The author is describing the happy camaraderie "in heartland America," when one jogger meets another. "Charlie—corporate officer, community leader, man of substance and affairs, philanthropist, father of a Princeton man and another son on the way there—responds with a cheery wave and jogs on his way, caught up in the task of self-improvement and, *by tacit premise, the betterment of the world*" (our italics).

Such examples might seem too slight to found a thesis on. But they can be multiplied almost infinitely. Here, for example, is the peroration of a book by a professor of history at Harvard, Frederick Merk, *Manifest Destiny and Mission*. Professor Merk's thesis is that while manifest destiny was bad, "a truer expression of the national spirit" was a purer, more godly form of imperialism called mission:

> Manifest destiny, in the twentieth century, vanished. . . . Mission, on the contrary, remained alive, and is as much alive at present as it ever was. It is still the beacon lighting the way to political and individual freedoms. . . . It is still, as always in the past, the torch held aloft by the nation at its gate—to the world and to itself.

Or here is the chairman of the political science department at M.I.T., Dr. Ithiel de Sola Pool:

> The world has become a smaller place. In various ways we will all become more alike, and more like America. People everywhere want some aspects of American culture, such as automobiles, TV sets, refrigerators, and Coca-Cola . . . participant politics, civil liberties, social mobility, pragmatism, and a pacific orientation. . . . We can live safely only in a world in which the political systems of all states are democratic. . . . I predict there will be a number of effective interventions in foreign crises in America's future.

(We have extracted three passages from Dr. Pool's contributions to a colloquy printed in the *Atlantic Monthly* in November 1968 and we have reversed their order. We do not think we have distorted the impression he gave that he considered the world an American *imperium*. That an educated man, let alone a professor of political science, can be under the impression that participant politics, civil liberties—or indeed the automobile—are either American inventions or American monopolies, passes belief.)

Last, here is the thought which Richard Nixon chose to leave before the American people in his last speech before the election of 1960:

> My friends, it is because we are on the side of right: it is because we are on God's side: [*cheers and applause*] that America will meet this challenge and that we will build a better America at home and that that better America will lead the forces of freedom in building a new world.

All nations live by myths, and there is nothing new about the myth of a God-given mission to "build a new world" in one's own image. The history of Europe in modern times can be written around the successive aspirations of its nation-states—Spain, France, Britain, Germany, Russia—to a universal "civilizing mission," to "make the world a better place" by making it more like themselves. Nor is the delusion specifically a heritage of European blood. Such pathetically weak states as Indonesia, Ghana, and India have all aspired to world leadership in the last few years.

But America is not pathetically weak. She is enormously, though not infinitely, strong. The real economic and military power the United States has acquired in the last twenty-five years makes the delusions both of an inherently better society at home and of a God-given universal mission abroad more plausible and therefore more dangerous. Nor is the temptation a new one for Americans. The historian Richard Hofstadter has pointed out that

> the American frame of mind was created by a long history that encouraged our belief that we have an almost magical capacity to have our way in the world, that the national will can be made entirely effective, as against other peoples, at a relatively small price. . . . Free security, easy expansion, inexpensive victories, decisive triumphs—such was almost our whole experience with the rest of the world down to the twentieth century.

All nations have their myths, and there is some merit in them as the bond of unity and the spur to effort. The danger, for a nation as for an individual, comes when the gap betwen rhetoric and reality becomes too wide. In an individual, such a gap between self-perception and reality is known as psychosis. A nation that indulges in too much self-glorifying rhetoric while unable to win a small war or to prevent deterioration in its social fabric is unlikely to be able to heal its real distempers.

ITEM: Americans cherished the myth that theirs is an anti-colonial, revolutionary tradition. Yet they found themselves with a quasi-colonial position in every continent, often with the advantages of possessing colonies without the responsibility of administering them. And they had become committed, almost without realizing it, to a global campaign to frustrate revolution.

ITEM: Americans "hold this truth to be inalienable," that the rights of Americans include the pursuit of happiness. Yet, by the beginning of 1968, an increasing number of them wondered whether they and their forebears had been intoning this sonorous promise with a muttered reservation: "except for black Americans."

ITEM: Americans believe with passionate and creditable intensity that their country offers a unique degree of social and economic equality of opportunity. Even one of the most radical social critics of America, Michael Harrington, has called America "the most radical country in the world," because "the worker on the assembly line has always known . . . that he is just as good as Henry Ford." Yet one of the few sociologists who has bothered to go and ask the worker on the assembly line, Ely Chinoy, found that "among the workers interviewed none spoke of any ambitions in the plant higher than foremanship. . . . 'For a fellow starting as an hourly worker,' " one twenty-four-year-old said, " 'there isn't much chance of going up there in the company. That's in the past now.' " Most Americans believe that the distribution of income in the United States "is the greatest social revolution in history," as President Eisenhower once said. The fact is that, though average incomes in America are very high by international standards (and have been since the eighteenth century), the distribution of wealth in America is noticeably top-heavy and has changed less than in most other countries. The lower half of the population received twenty-two per cent of the national personal income in 1964—which was just one per cent more than thirty years earlier. Some revolution . . .

ITEM: Americans believe that they are set apart from the rest of the world by far greater personal freedom and individualism. Yet more and more, in practice, their freedom and their individualism have been circumscribed by bureaucracy of many kinds—not just by George Wallace's Federal bureaucrats with beards and briefcases. Most of all, perhaps, the traditional American values are threatened by the bureaucrats of private business, with their building passes and their security checks, their credit ratings and their all-knowing computers, their consuming passion for judging a man as employee, customer, or debtor by his wife, his opinions, and his haircut. A man may cleave to his constitutional freedoms. But if he is to get the job, the house, the loan, or the credit he wants, if he is to register at a college or marry the boss's daughter, he learns that cautious conformity is safer than individualism. Far more than his cousin in Western Europe, he must learn to get his mind right.

There is another point. It is not only that the *content* of the American political creed, with its optimism, its faith in progress, its universality, tends to clothe the realities of politics with the cloak of rhetoric more than is acceptable in other cultures. There is also something in the *modus* whereby Americans receive their political ideas and information which encourages exceptionally shameless flights of rhetoric.

In the District of Columbia, in the summer of 1968, there had been so many robberies on the buses that the bus company decided to stop issuing change. Instead it announced that passengers who did not give the exact fare would be issued with "scrip" which would be useless for anything except bus rides and therefore not worth stealing. It was a sensible solution to a real problem. But the bus company didn't stop there. It posted on the sides of all its buses the following notice:

NO CHANGE GIVEN

TO SPEED YOUR RIDE

ONLY SCRIP ISSUED

"To speed your ride"! Whom did they think they were kidding? Americans have grown used to, and cynical about, and even perversely fond of the world's most preposterously audacious advertising. "The Springtime of a Woman's Life Should Begin at 55," says the ad for Information Incorporated. Who believes it? Yet who would pay for it if it had no effect? But—and this is the crucial point—Americans have come to get their information and their ideas about politics, especially in election year, from media that are deeply penetrated by the ethos and the techniques of advertising.

It is not just that Presidential candidates are "packaged" and "sold" —their words, not ours—by advertising professionals. It is not only that, whether citizens watch a serious documentary on urban problems or a candidate's speech on television, the political information is sandwiched between ads, so that it is psychologically all but impossible to switch the cynicism on and off in the right places. It is not just that the most serious political journalism, in the *New York Times Magazine* or *The New Yorker,* stretches like a lonely ribbon of gray between bright temptations to shop at Bergdorf Goodman or Van Cleef & Arpels. Advertising itself has become permeated with politics, until the confusion is complete.

"If you're concerned about the times we live in," says the Equitable Life Assurance Company, under a display of slum pictures deliberately laid out to look like photo reportage, "so are we at Equitable." Thus the agony of the ghettos is made to sell insurance policies to the middle class. "Independence Day," proclaims the ad for Lewis & Thomas Saltz, gentlemen's outfitters, over a picture of the American flag, and then comes a little poem:

> This day of ours is full of sacred joy;
> > The proud glad moments weaving golden hours
> Which patriot souls, of purpose great, employ
> > To pledge ourselves anew with wakened powers.

Thus patriotism is twisted to sell English tweeds and Italian silks. The Army even pays for a full page in the trendiest copywriters' camp to sell war itself:

> Vietnam.
> Hot. Wet. Muddy. Perilous. To prove
> yourself here is to prove yourself
> to the world. No test is harder. No trial
> more demanding.
> But when a man serves here,
> he proves himself a man.
> To his Country. To himself.

Who believes advertising? Yes, but who is uninfluenced by it?

It can be argued, again, that this is not unique to America; that the difference in the audacity of advertising, is only a matter of degree or of time. But the difference of degree, at this point in time, seems to us to amount to a difference in kind. Certainly American advertising men themselves would be the last to deny that they have pushed the technique and the ambitions of their craft further than anywhere else in the world.

And so the great Bullshine Machine rolls forward, extending the field of fire for its shiny product from the advertising pages to the news columns, from skinless sausages ("oxygen intercepted") and mass-produced cakes ("like Grandma used to bake") to the personality of candidates and the great issues that divide society. The constant exposure to this shower of matter—half-true, untrue, or even true, but always simplified, always loud, always self-serving—induces a peculiar mixture of gullibility and cynicism that is close to neurosis. It is not an attitude that is well adapted for distinguishing between bullshine and brass tacks, rhetoric and reality.

ACT III

What Is to Be Done?

1

The Search for a Champion

"For Al, who knew the lesson of Emerson and taught it to the rest of us: . . . 'that if a single man plant himself on his convictions and there abide, the huge world will come round to him.' "

—Note scribbled by Robert Kennedy to Allard K. Lowenstein on a bus in late March 1968

One day in the spring of 1966, three men met for lunch at a restaurant on the East Side of midtown Manhattan called the Quo Vadis. In spite of its name, and an entrance ornamented with pseudo-Pompeian mosaics, it is a rather quiet place. Its red plush banquettes are normally occupied by dealers from the neighboring art galleries with their clients, or by wealthy ladies taking a break from their shopping to discuss hats and husbands. It is perhaps the last place in New York where you would expect to find anybody talking about the end of the world. And yet, that lunchtime, that is exactly what three of the best-known intellectuals in America were talking about.

One of the three men was enormously tall, in his late fifties, with a gaunt, hollow-cheeked face, jutting nose, and forelock, which give him a faint air of Abraham Lincoln. The second was in his middle thirties, dark and saturnine, with a remarkably deep and full bass voice. And the third, who was between the other two in age, was a jaunty man, the sort of man who looks well in a bow tie—which he often wears—an intellectual in fact more in the genre of Paris than of New York, which is to say more worldly than professorial. The tall man's name was John Kenneth Galbraith, economist, satirist, ambassador, and authority on Indian painting. The dark man was Richard Goodwin, political *condottiere*. And the man with them was the historian and political moralist Arthur M.

51

Schlesinger, Jr. That is to list and label them alphabetically, rather than to attempt to place them in proper order in the hierarchy of the American liberal and intellectual Establishment. But by any test all three would have to be accorded membership in the nonexistent steering committee of that mythical body, and their lunch that day at the Quo Vadis was in effect a subcommittee, convened by themselves, to discuss the state of the nation, the war, and what could be done about either of them.

None of the three could fairly be called unsophisticated about politics. They had all long been active in Americans for Democratic Action, the liberal pressure group which thinks of itself as the conscience of the Democratic Party. All three had been brought into government by President Kennedy: Schlesinger and for a while Goodwin as White House staff assistants, Galbraith as Ambassador to India. All three were close to Senator Robert Kennedy and were charter members of a Kennedy "connection" that was already being called the "government in exile." They were liberals, certainly—even, in American terms, men of the Left—but tough-minded, pragmatic, realistic. And yet that day, as they talked about the war which seemed so distant from East Sixty-third Street, they found themselves thinking in almost catastrophic terms. The war seemed to have become a juggernaut, to have taken over, so that while each successive step of escalation might be explained with some ostensibly rational excuse, actually the war seemed to have become its own justification. "We suddenly found ourselves," one of these hard-headed men remembers, "seriously discussing the possibility that the world might come to an end. We decided that at least we didn't want to feel we had done nothing to stop it."

Before they left the restaurant each of the three friends promised to do what he could to end the war. Galbraith set the weight of his vast prestige in Cambridge and throughout the academic community against the war. Goodwin sat down to write a long article which appeared in *The New Yorker* and was then published as a book with the title *Triumph or Tragedy: Reflections on Vietnam*. "I do not doubt Lyndon Johnson's desire to end the war . . . ," he wrote. "It is killing Americans. . . . It has already reduced resources for . . . the war against poverty. It is endangering our prosperity. It is, far more than is yet clear, seriously weakening support for the Democratic Party and the President himself." And he ended in the Quo Vadis mood: "If large-scale war comes . . . it will be no one's fault, but it will be the fault of many. . . . There will be no act of madness, no single villain on whom to discharge guilt; just the flow of history." And Schlesinger wrote an article for the *New York Times Magazine,* which was also republished as an impassioned little book with the title *The Bitter Heritage: Vietnam and American Democracy.* He listed the "ugly side-effects of war: inflation; frustration; indignation; protest; panic; angry divisions within the national community; premonitions of McCarthyism." And he asked a somber question: "The war began as a struggle for the soul of Vietnam: will it end as a struggle for the soul of America?"

It would be foolish to underestimate the personal influence of these three men—each of them, in a different way, was to play an important part in the earlier acts of the 1968 drama—but the larger significance of their lunch at the Quo Vadis was symbolic. It may be said to mark the moment at which Lyndon Johnson had lost not just the support but the tolerance of the American intellectual elite.

"Is there an American upper class?" asked a writer not so long ago in the *New York Review of Books;* then he answered his own question: "Of course there is, though the admission may go against the American grain." There is still a similar reluctance to admit the existence of an intellectual Establishment in America. Yet of course there is one. It is often argued that because its membership is hard to define, or because its members do not always agree, it does not exist. Yet the intellectual elites in Britain and France, for example, are neither united nor easy to define. How many Americans would say that therefore they do not exist?

Once, perhaps—even, it might be argued, not so long ago—there was no such intellectual Establishment in America, but only separate cliques and worlds of intellectuals living and working in isolation. Now, as Lyndon Johnson has learned to his cost, there is one. It has no rigidly defined, perhaps even no indisputable membership—though Galbraith and Schlesinger, McGeorge Bundy of the Ford Foundation, Richard Neustadt of the Kennedy Institute, Henry Kissinger, and Daniel Patrick Moynihan would certainly be among the dozen whom it would be hardest to blackball. Theodore H. White coined his own name for the American intellectual establishment in an admiring series of articles in *Life,* in 1967. He called them the "priesthood" of the "action intellectuals," and praised them for having "subtly transformed our old tree-shaded campuses into brokerage houses of ideas." Besides Bundy, Neustadt, Moynihan, Schlesinger, and Galbraith, he named Henry Rowen of the Rand Corporation; Carl Kaysen of the Institute for Advanced Study at Princeton; Kermit Gordon of the Brookings Institution in Washington; Charles Hitch, late of Rand and now of the University

of California at Berkeley; Francis Keppel, Adam Yarmolinsky, and
Edwin O. Reischauer from Harvard; Jerome Wiesner and Walt W.
Rostow from M.I.T.; and many others. White laid some stress on the
experience of World War II as an influence on this generation of
American academics and quoted one remark of Kaysen's which irresistibly caught the flavor of the Establishment: "We were kids, captains
and majors, telling the whole world what to do!"

There are, of course, whole groups within the Establishment who
have little contact with other subsections except through intermediaries,
but it is nevertheless a real and an immensely powerful factor in American life. It is based, as its enemies suspect, in the Northeast. Its three
main chapters are in Manhattan, in Washington, and in Cambridge,
Massachusetts; a typical member spends an extraordinary amount of
time on the Eastern Airlines shuttles between those three points. But
there are smaller chapters in New Haven, in Princeton, at Ann Arbor,
Michigan, in California, and in Chicago.

There is a certain overlap between this intellectual Establishment
and two quite different worlds: the frivolous world which used to be
called "café society" and the earnest world of the board rooms and
executive offices of the great corporations. But money is not the card of
membership. Nor is membership entirely controlled by the great elite
graduate schools—Harvard and Yale and Columbia, and their law
schools, and M.I.T. Their dominance is great and growing, though it has
not yet perhaps quite reached that of Oxford and Cambridge in Britain,
or of the *grandes écoles* in France. The members of the Establishment
include men who teach or have taught law, government, economics, and
even the physical sciences at these schools; people who work for the
Federal government in Washington and for law firms, newspapers, magazines, publishing houses, television networks, research institutes, and the
great foundations in New York. But not everybody in that long list of
jobs qualifies. The real test of membership is the ability to move and
impress people and to uphold a reputation for being both "bright" and
"effective"—two key words in the Establishment, as "sound" once was
in Britain—simultaneously in three overlapping worlds: the communications world in New York; the academic community, centered in Boston;
and the government in Washington.

Lyndon Johnson was never popular with the intellectual Establishment, and the feeling was reciprocated. Out of a characteristic mixture of
insecurity and aggressive pride he is said to have pointed out at his
first Cabinet meeting that there were so many there from Harvard, so

many from Yale—and only one from the South-West Texas Teachers College at San Marcos! The President was not altogether paranoid in suspecting that some of the hostility which the Establishment showed toward him had its roots in something hardly more creditable than plain, old-fashioned snobbery. In both Washington and Cambridge, we heard President Johnson criticized for the curious reason that he did not, in the critics' judgment, pronounce the word "America" properly. But it was more than that. There were political differences. There was a sincere, though not altogether justified, belief that Senator Johnson had been little better than a reactionary Southern baron of the all too familiar pattern. Then there was the resentment, again perfectly natural but often felt with more than rational intensity, of the fact that Johnson had succeeded the Establishment's own beloved President, John Kennedy. The unseemly furor over William Manchester's book *Death of a President* showed that for many otherwise rational members of the Establishment, Lyndon Johnson could never be anything but a usurper in the White House. Yet this point should not be exaggerated. Many Establishment men— Bundy, Schlesinger, Goodwin among them—worked for Johnson.

Then came the war. Johnson and his friends have been quick to taunt the liberal Establishment with being "neo-isolationist." Dean Rusk, no Establishment member for all that his career was divided between Washington and the Rockefeller Foundation, has even proclaimed his vocation to spend his years of retirement fighting this heresy. The charge is unfounded to an ironic degree. Far from being isolationist, the members of the American intellectual Establishment consistently upheld the extension of American power and influence in the world. Like their heroes and patrons the Kennedy brothers, they are proud of America and ambitious for her. The vision they brought to Washington with them when John Kennedy became President was of an America rich and harmonious at home, powerful and respected abroad, exporting her material graces and her political philosophy to a world in which she would soon have no rival. They believed that Communism was obsolete and that Europe—which, in a somewhat patronizing way, they claimed to appreciate—must inevitably continue what seemed to them a predestined decline. They stood for more and more foreign aid, used more and more consciously to make the world over in the American image; for higher defense budgets more "cost-effectively" used to build an unrivaled military power; for "counterinsurgency," the gunboat diplomacy of the post-imperialist empire.

Specifically, with the honorable exception of a small minority

(John Kenneth Galbraith, for example, visited Vietnam in 1961 and opposed Walt Rostow's recommendation that American commitment should be increased), the Establishment intellectuals were originally in favor of the American commitment to Southeast Asia. McGeorge Bundy and Arthur Schlesinger argued for it in the White House, and Walt Rostow in the State Department. The supreme irony is that Lyndon Johnson may actually have committed himself to the Vietnam policy which destroyed him out of respect for the expertise of the Establishment that did so much to destroy him. This, at least, seems to be the view of Tom Wicker, the able *New York Times* bureau chief at the time. "Because he respected [Rusk and McNamara]," Wicker wrote in his book *JFK and LBJ,* "and men like McGeorge Bundy, and because he needed desperately to win the confidence and keep the services of these links to the Kennedy Administration, Johnson was unusually deferential to these men and to their views in the first months of his Presidency."

The Establishment intellectuals, in fact, with the optimism that comes easily to men with the world at their feet, were liberal imperialists, very much like those in Britain in the 1890s. (The word "imperialist" is not used to imply that any of these gentlemen advocated setting up American colonies. It is used, rather, as a writer like Ronald Steel has used the phrase "the American empire," as shorthand to describe Americans' desire to extend their power and influence in the world by any means—from sending Peace Corps volunteers abroad in order to advertise the American way of life, by way of capital export and diplomatic pressure, to actual military intervention.) Vietnam was their Boer War. It did not immediately turn the Establishment intellectuals against the President. It did not even split them down the middle. It exposed a latent division that had been there all along, between those who were so to speak more imperialist than liberal and those who were more liberal than imperialist. As the horror of the war escalated and its futility became more apparent, majority opinion within the Establishment gradually shifted, so that a man like Walt Rostow, who felt that freedom was the primary value and that one should have the courage to fight for it whatever the cost, found himself in a dwindling minority, while a man like Galbraith, who had felt deep reservations about military intervention from the start, found himself at the head of an overwhelming majority.

Most members of the New York–Washington–Cambridge Establishment had supported the original decision to commit America to the support of the Diem regime in 1961. By February 1965, when President

Johnson took the crucial escalatory step of bombing North Vietnam, Arthur Schlesinger and Richard Goodwin had left the White House, and both soon began to criticize the war publicly. By the spring of 1967, open disenchantment with the war and with the President had become orthodox within the Establishment. Bundy had resigned from the government a few months before, though his sense of propriety prevented him from criticizing the policy he had done so much to form until its failure was even more widely accepted. Rostow, reinforced by the recruitment into the State Department of his brother Eugene, Dean of the Yale Law School, was left as the lonely survivor of the intellectual hawks in Washington. More important still, the man who could be expected to give political weight and effectiveness to the intellectuals' new opposition to the war began to come out into the open against it: Robert Kennedy.

There had been a movement of sorts against the war from the start, of course. Soon after the nuclear-test-ban treaty of 1963 many of those active in the "peace groups"—SANE, for example, and Women Strike for Peace—turned their attention to Vietnam as a more immediate danger. They were joined by many in the Society of Friends and in Protestant churches, especially the upper-middle-class ones such as the Episcopalians; by splinter groups on the Left; and by most of the militant Negroes.

But the politicians had learned from their past experience on other issues that they could well afford to ignore this coalition. The dismal showing of the independent "peace" candidate Professor H. Stuart Hughes, of the Harvard history department, in the 1962 senatorial campaign in Massachusetts was the standard by which orthodox politicians judged the strength of the "peace vote."

In June 1966 Robert Scheer, running as a peace candidate, got forty-five per cent of the vote in a Democratic primary in the Seventh Congressional District in California. The White House was worried enough to spend three hours on the phone to the courthouse on election night.

It would be naïve to base too much on a direct comparison between the Hughes and Scheer campaigns. Hughes was rash enough to run against a Kennedy, for one thing, and Scheer got support from the Oakland ghetto as well as white antiwar votes. Just the same, the two campaigns made a rough yardstick of how much more formidable the peace vote had become.

The students were far ahead of their elders. As early as April 1965, only two months after the crucial escalation steps, fifteen thousand students picketed the White House, and less than a month later more than a hundred thousand students on a hundred campuses heard Arthur Schlesinger *defend* the war at a teach-in relayed from Washington. Professor Galbraith has made the point to us that those who, like himself, were outside Washington and in touch with young people in the universities were helped to see more clearly about the war than those in Washington. "The most important thing about the earlier phases of the campaign," he believes, "is how much the Washington people were out of touch with the country." Above all, they were out of touch with the young.

By the middle of 1967, in any case, the students, particularly the abler and more articulate students in universities in New York, California, New England, and the Middle West, were in a state of almost open rebellion against the war. Idealism was reinforced by self-interest. The threat that the government might remove deferment for graduate studies meant that even those who did oppose the war and the draft on moral grounds opposed them because they didn't want to be sent overseas to be killed. Here was a great political army standing waiting to be recruited. But the students by themselves, like the "peace groups," were politically impotent. It was significant that one of the first major rallies against the war, in the summer of 1966, was organized by a group who called themselves the Assembly of Unrepresented People. If the students were to go beyond disruption and achieve anything positive within the political system, they must be led. That was why it was so important that Lyndon Johnson lost the support of the intellectual Establishment, of the Galbraiths and Schlesingers and Goodwins who could get their ideas published in the *New York Times* and in books and could lobby their friends in the Senate. But the Establishment was not about to take the students seriously as a political force. And the students were not overdisposed to trust the Establishment.

There was one person who in the summer of 1967 was in a position to bridge this abyss between the troubled mandarins and the infuriated, despairing young people in the universities. His name was Allard K. Lowenstein, and at the time he was virtually unknown. Yet it was he, almost single-handed, who set off the political fission process in 1968. He planted himself on his conviction that "when a President is both wrong and unpopular, to refuse to oppose him is both a moral abdica-

tion and a political stupidity," and he there abided. By so doing he
drove Johnson from the White House.

Al Lowenstein is in every respect a surprising and exotic figure in
American politics. Very superficially, he resembles the stereotype of the
Jewish intellectual. He does have thinning hair; he wears thick glasses.
But he is a man of action rather than introspection. His physical energy
and stamina are legendary among his friends. His hobby is wrestling, and
he is said to grab opportunities for a bout even between planes on a cross-
country trip. He will make an appointment with you at half past midnight
and talk until three, interrupted by long-distance calls from friends who
want his help to organize a political campaign here, a fact-finding trip
there, a life-saving mission to Biafra. At three he will excuse himself
because he has another appointment. He is not so much an intellectual as
a fierce, though not a self-righteous, moralist. His two great heroes are
Eleanor Roosevelt and Norman Thomas: he keeps a bronze of the former
and a set of photographs of the latter in his unbelievably chaotic New
York apartment. He is an activist, but an activist liberal, not an activist
radical. He believes to an unusual degree in acting on his beliefs, but the
beliefs themselves are not extreme. Unlike the radicals of the New Left,
he has faith in the essential goodness of the American society in which
his immigrant family has prospered. (His father owns a restaurant near
Grand Central Station, which is the sort of place where the middle-aged
waitress, who has been there for twenty years, will reminisce with tears
in her eyes about the high debates she overheard there when Judge Thurgood Marshall used to drop in for coffee.) Because he believes that
Americans are at bottom to be trusted, he believes in working within the
system.

Lowenstein was President of the National Student Association in
1951—the last president of that unhappy organization before it was
taken over as a front by the CIA. (His enemies in the New Left have
tried to smear him as a "spook," which is nonsense.) He taught law at
Stanford and later at North Carolina State, where he got into trouble for
joining Negro demonstrations. Later he worked as a civil-rights leader
in the South. But his two most extraordinary adventures were abroad.
Every liberal in the universities of the world is outraged by fascism in
Spain and racism in South Africa. Lowenstein is one of the few who
have actually tried to do something about them. In 1959 he smuggled
a "colored" student out of South-West Africa in order to draw attention
at the United Nations to the way South Africa was abusing her UN

mandate over that territory. And he also helped political refugees to leave Spain. In each case, very real physical risk was involved.

In the summer of 1967 Lowenstein was thirty-eight, and it was not unreasonable to say, as many of his friends did say, that he was frittering away great talents by spreading himself across too many good causes. But now he had found the one great task for which he was uniquely equipped. In touch with the Establishment, though not of it (he was a vice-chairman of ADA and was becoming a friend of Robert Kennedy's; not a student, but known and trusted for the battles he had fought on every campus in America) he was the one man who could move between the two worlds with the insistent message for each: "You are not alone!" He saw with absolute clarity not just that the war must be stopped but that the only way to stop it was to challenge and if possible to prevent Johnson's renomination. "It may seem difficult at first," he told a wavering conference of liberals a few months later, "to wage a battle against the power of the Presidency, but that is how the battle must be waged."

To call taking on an incumbent President, let alone so morose and vindictive a titan as Johnson, "difficult" was a breathtaking understatement. To many liberals that summer it sounded like suicide. And liberals as a group have not been given to political *kamikaze*.

There were two main centers where Lowenstein might hope to urge his case with some faint chance of success. The first was in California, where the California Democratic Council, with thirty-three thousand members, voted in March 1967 to wait six months and then, if no action had been taken to end the war, to run a slate of delegates against the President in the California primary.

The other was ADA. Many of the paladins of the intellectual Establishment were among its leading lights. So too were most of the "doves" in Congress—men like Senator Joseph S. Clark of Pennsylvania, Senator George McGovern of South Dakota, and Senator Frank Church of Idaho. So, too, for that matter, was Vice-President Humphrey, as stanch an apologist for the war as could be found. But the moving spirit from a practical point of view has been for many years a Washington lawyer called Joseph Rauh. Rauh is a pleasant, youthful man in his fifties, with a gruff, husky voice. He is every bit as much technician in the ways of getting things done in Washington as a Clark Clifford or a James Rowe, but the clients he gets things done for are more likely to be labor unions.

The dilemma Joe Rauh found himself in, like so many of those in Washington who had supposed they were as liberal as a man could be without being positively dangerous, is suggested by a photograph which had pride of place on his office wall. It showed Mr. and Mrs. Rauh with Humphrey, and was dedicated to them as "two of the dearest people I know—Hubert."

(The war in Vietnam was not in fact the first dilemma that Rauh's friendship with Humphrey had led him into. In 1964, at the Democratic convention in Atlantic City, he was the attorney for the Mississippi Freedom Democratic Party, a hastily organized, mainly Negro organization which was challenging the credentials of the segregationist regular delegation. Humphrey was the favorite for the Vice-Presidency. Rauh has indignantly denied that he was under any pressure from Humphrey to ease up in his efforts lest it cost his friend the Vice-Presidential nomination. But he concedes that "half Humphrey's crowd" did lean on him. And the Mississippi Negroes and their white allies—including specifically Al Lowenstein—believe that Rauh's loyalties were divided.)

At the end of July 1967, Rauh wrote a paper which he called "a proposal to maximize political support for an end to the war in Vietnam." A more suitable description might have been "an argument against the disturbing talk on the part of Allard Lowenstein and others about organizing opposition to Lyndon Johnson's re-election." The paper argued that any conceivable candidate who might run would be weaker than the peace movement and would "hurt rather than help the cause of peace." Instead, Rauh suggested, liberals ought to forget about challenging the President and organize to fight for a "peace plank" in the Democratic platform.

What persuaded Rauh and his ADA friends that no serious candidate would oppose Johnson? Rauh himself cites two reasons. The first was that on June 3, at a fund-raising dinner in New York, Robert Kennedy hailed Johnson as one who had "borne the burdens of the world as few other men have ever borne them": a clear enough indication, it seemed, that Kennedy did not mean to run, and Kennedy was the man with by far the best chance of winning. And second, on July 25 Rauh had a long talk with his friend George McGovern, who told him that he had no intention of being a candidate and that, what was more, neither had any of the other prominent "doves" in the Senate.

Lowenstein dismissed, and still dismisses, Rauh's characteristic calculation of alternatives as little better than sabotage. "The mood of that period," as he remembered it later, "was that everybody agreed that Johnson was a disaster, so let's get rid of Johnson first, and then let's see. You had to keep pumping the bellows, because you knew there was a spark." Nevertheless it has to be said that there were both method and foresight to his pumping. By the middle of 1967, in fact, Lowenstein was not merely determined to overthrow Johnson; he had a plan. It had two mutually necessary wings; he had to fan a "Dump Johnson" fire in the grassroots, and he had to get a candidate.

His most important ally in those early days was a young man on the staff of ADA named Curtis Gans, a viper, so to speak, in Rauh's bosom. Gans, a slim, dark New Yorker who helped to found Students for a Democratic Society in 1961, can lay claim to have been the first to argue within influential left-wing circles that Johnson could be opposed within the Democratic Party. In March 1967, during the first discussions of liberal strategy for 1968, Lowenstein and his hero, Norman Thomas, inclined toward the idea of putting up Martin Luther King as a third-party peace candidate. Gans argued that, while it might be possible to get a broad national consensus against the war, "the snag was that you couldn't get such a consensus against any particular remedial program." And he suggested that Johnson was so unpopular that you could get a consensus against him too.

It is hard to convey the furious pace of Lowenstein's travels once he had decided that this could be done. In August, for example, he packed his battered hold-all and flew to Saigon to observe the elections there. When asked by a friend what on earth he was doing there, he answered that he intended to be criticizing Vietnamese politics in the year to come, and he didn't intend to be one-upped by people asking him whether he'd been there.

On August 4, Jesse Unruh had arranged a big fund-raising dinner in California at which Robert Kennedy was to speak. Lowenstein flew out on the same plane. "He was traveling first class," Lowenstein says, "I was tourist. That's the story of my life." After a while Kennedy's press secretary, Frank Mankiewicz, offered to swap seats so Lowenstein and Kennedy could have several hours of uninterrupted talk. Lowenstein told Kennedy frankly what he was doing and said they wanted a candidate. Kidding, he said, "If you want to run, we'll let you." Kennedy was sympathetic, but uninterested in the idea of running. They discussed other possible candidates, and Lowenstein said he was going out to talk to some of the CDC people. Kennedy warned him against them, saying that they were dangerous left-wingers and that Lowenstein had too good a future in politics to get mixed up with people like that. Lowenstein said this was ridiculous, and then he set Kennedy a little private test. He said, "If you really think the CDC people are so bad, why don't you say so to the reporters who meet us when the plane gets in?"

When the plane arrived, the reporters duly asked Kennedy what he thought of the peace movement in California, and he said, "That's a matter for the people of California to decide for themselves." Gerald Hill, a San Francisco lawyer and chairman of the CDC, was disgusted, but Lowenstein understood. Kennedy might not be ready to commit himself, but he was not ready to denounce the peace movement either.

The next day, Lowenstein and Hill met. They decided they needed money and staff. They agreed to raise three thousand dollars, half in California, half elsewhere, and called Curtis Gans in Washington in the middle of the night, Washington time, and asked him, "Are you willing to put your body where your mouth is?" It turned out that the Marine Corps had a prior option on Gans's body for two weeks, but he agreed to set up an office in Washington on September 1, after he had finished his reserve training. (One cannot help wondering what his fellow Marines would have done if they had known what Gans was a party to; he is a surprising enough Marine at the best of times.)

On August 15, at the convention of the National Student Association at the University of Maryland, just outside Washington, Lowenstein formally launched "Dump Johnson." From then on, he and Gans were working on two, or, strictly speaking, three parallel lines: with the politicians, the peace groups, and the students. "We wanted to be politically effective," says Gans of their strategy. "We didn't want to be just the peace movement playing at politics. But we didn't want to turn off the energy, fervor, paranoia, and other virtues of the peace movement either." In the end they worked through three separate organizations. Dissenting Democrats was for the peace movement. Concerned Democrats—a subtly less alarming adjective—was for the politicians. And then there were student groups forming, under the energetic hands of Sam Brown, a twenty-four-year-old Harvard divinity student from Omaha, Nebraska. "We had to start with the students," Lowenstein explained later, "because we had no money and therefore no hope of getting anybody else to work for us." At the same time they set about finding "concerned Democrats" in as many states as possible.

There was still no candidate. Those early groups went to work to persuade people simply to vote no. In the last two weeks of August and the first three weeks of September, they lit fires in eight states—Michigan, Minnesota, Wisconsin, New York, New Jersey, Pennsylvania, and California—as well as the District of Columbia. After he came back from his reserve training, Gans went ahead as the organizer; on one occasion he spent all but ninety minutes out of a total of forty-eight hours in a hotel bedroom, and ran up a phone bill for $296. Then Lowenstein would appear, deliver an impassioned speech in a church or small hall, and depart for the airport leaving the faithful with the sense that they were not alone, but part of a mighty army of holy warriors.

The movement caught on satisfactorily in New York and California. But if it was not to be dismissed as a peripheral, un-American aberration bred in the superheated air of the New York and San Francisco salons, it had to show strength in the heartland too. That was why it was a feather in Lowenstein's cap when he recruited his first state legislator, Alpha Smaby from Minnesota. Wisconsin was another example. The obvious leader there was an ADA board member, Donald O. Peterson, a pizzeria proprietor from Eau Claire. Lowenstein found him nervous about joining a movement that in Wisconsin might bring reflections on his patriotism. Yet, after hours of talk, he suddenly looked up and said, "That sounds like what we should be doing. I think I'm with you." To make him feel that he was indeed a soldier in a mighty army, Al Lowenstein's friends, the charming hostesses of the West Side reform movement, arranged little dinners for him in New York, and the ladies even rallied round and paid for a suite at the Waldorf out of their pin money, so he would feel that he was in touch with a powerful and well-financed organization. But Lowenstein knew—it was the essence of his disagreement with Rauh—that none of all this would amount to anything until he had a candidate.

Obviously Robert Kennedy had to be the first choice. Lowenstein was never a close friend of his, but he liked what Kennedy was trying to say about the Negro and the cities, and, while he found Kennedy's public statements on the war infuriatingly Delphic, he sensed that Kennedy was deeply troubled in private. He understood him well enough, in fact, to know that "what was going on in his head was always more complicated than what was going on in the heads of the people who were trying to analyze him."

The ADA board meeting in Washington on Saturday, September 23, was a great gathering of the liberal clans. Lowenstein came down from New York, and on both Friday night and Saturday night Lowenstein went out to dinner with the Kennedys at Hickory Hill. On the Friday night, Richard Goodwin was there, and Arthur Schlesinger, and a large and cheerful party of "Kennedy people." Kennedy talked about the possibility that Johnson might not run at all in 1968 but instead would withdraw dramatically on the eve of the convention. (In July 1967, a bizarre encounter had taken place in, of all places, Leningrad. The ubiquitous Schlesinger ran into Senator Vance Hartke, Democrat of Indiana, a dove but no friend of Kennedy's. Schlesinger ventured the prediction that "a few more years of LBJ would kill us all." Hartke said there was no need for such gloom: Johnson would never run in 1968, because he couldn't bear to face even the risk of defeat. On April 1, 1968, Schlesinger sent Hartke a telegram congratulating him on his prescience.)

Schlesinger had come to agree with Goodwin's thesis that Johnson was a coward and so feared defeat at Kennedy's hands that he would do anything, even end the war, even lose the Presidency, rather than risk taking him on. That night, too, they talked about another of Goodwin's speculations: that the President was clinically, certifiably mad. But the atmosphere was loose dinner-party talk, black humor, not serious political discussion.

The next night the atmosphere was very different. The evening turned into a debate. The motion before the house: that Robert Kennedy should challenge Lyndon Johnson for the Democratic nomination. For the motion: Allard Lowenstein and Jack Newfield, a writer for the *Village Voice* and Kennedy's biographer. Against the motion: Arthur Schlesinger and James Loeb, a newspaper publisher from New York who had been John Kennedy's ambassador in Peru and Guinea. Moderator, with the right of final decision: Robert Kennedy. The moderator was wearing hippy beads and lounging on a sofa, but his mood was not frivolous. He said very little. Once, when Schlesinger made Rauh's case for a peace plank, Kennedy said, "You're a historian, Arthur. When was the last time millions of people rallied behind a *plank*?" Lowenstein sensed Kennedy was sympathetic, even tempted, but that he himself had failed.

We shall see that Lowenstein did not accept this "No" as a final answer, that he was in fact to make another earnest attempt to change Kennedy's mind later. But for the moment, from a practical point of view, he knew he would have to look elsewhere for his candidate.

He talked to Congressman Don Edwards of California, whom he admired. He approached Senator Frank Church of Idaho, one of the more distinguished opponents of the war in the Senate. Both said no. He tried to persuade Galbraith to run, in spite of the fact that he was born in Canada, and Galbraith went to the length of consulting more than one lawyer on his qualification. In the end he decided that if he were a candidate the question of his birth would distract attention from the war, and so he said no too. Lowenstein went up to Boston to talk to General James M. Gavin, who had published powerful denunciations of the war. (Gavin's book *Crisis Now* was published in 1968. He had already made his views known in articles and in testimony before the Senate Committee on Foreign Relations.) He found the general most pleasant and sympathetic, and even willing to be a candidate, but not a Democratic candidiate. "Do you see yourself getting the *Republican* nomination?" said Lowenstein in horror.

The next most attractive choice after Robert Kennedy, Lowenstein had to agree with Joe Rauh, was George McGovern. Only J. William Fulbright, of the Senators who had spoken out against the war, had more stature. But Fulbright, as a Southerner who had signed the notorious Southern Manifesto against desegregation in 1956, was simply unacceptable to the liberals.

McGovern is an updated version of those old prairie radicals who have fought the smug Babbitry of farm-belt conservatism since the days of William Jennings Bryan. In manner and appearance he is the antithesis of those shaggy tub-thumpers. He is a tall, quiet man in his middle forties who looks like a professor at a small denominational college, which is what he was. His politics were formed by the Great Depression. He can remember seeing a grown man weep when the check he was paid for a whole truckload of hogs exactly covered the cost of hauling them to market. His father was not a farmer but a coal miner turned professional baseball player, who settled down as a fundamentalist Methodist preacher in a Great Plains village with less than six hundred souls to save. McGovern dropped his original intention of following his father's vocation after the war, but his politics are still grounded in his religion. Unlike the old Farm Belt radicals, he is no isolationist. He ran the Food for Peace program in the Kennedy administration, perhaps the most disinterested and successful of all American aid programs. He was also one of the first men in Congress to come out against the war in Vietnam. He is, in short, in a different tradition, every bit as much a moralist as Al Lowenstein, and therefore a man who might just be persuaded that he had a duty to run for the Presidency.

Lowenstein made the overtures through Marcus Raskin, the young and very radical director of the Institute for Policy Planning in Washington, who knew McGovern better than he did. "Lowenstein said he felt I could successfully challenge Johnson," McGovern recalls, "or at least get enough votes in the primaries to make a real impact on the war."

But after thinking about it for a couple of weeks, McGovern turned the idea down. He felt the challenge was hopeless and that it ought therefore to be made by a Senator who was not up for re-election in 1968. He himself faced a very hard race. He had been elected in 1962 by only 597 votes—his opponent incidentally rejoiced in the richly agrarian name of Joe Bottum—and he had every reason to think the race would be as close this time. "I then got the Congressional Directory to remind myself," he told us, "and was rather surprised to see how many of the Senate 'doves' were up for election in 1968: Fulbright, Frank Church, Wayne Morse, Joe Clark." There were only two "doves" worth Lowenstein's consideration, as McGovern saw it, running his finger down the alphabetical list. "My eye fell on Metcalf and McCarthy," he remembers. "I didn't honestly think either of them would run."

Lee Metcalf, the junior Senator from Montana, is a pleasant, competent liberal, but he is undeniably the kind of man you are apt to forget in an inventory of Presidential timber. And yet McGovern, and his friend Rauh, talking it over, found they both judged Metcalf more likely to take the plunge than McCarthy. They were wrong. At the end of October, McGovern ran into McCarthy on the floor of the Senate and apologized casually for sending Lowenstein to see him. He got the shock of his life. "Not at all," said Gene McCarthy. "I think I may do it."

Lowenstein was not quite so surprised when McCarthy showed interest. In mid-August Gerry Hill in San Francisco had written to Kennedy, McGovern, Church, and McCarthy asking them all about their interest in running and inviting them out to California. All but McCarthy merely acknowledged the letter. McCarthy wrote that he would be in California in October. In the meantime Lowenstein got Senators McGovern, Church, and McCarthy to allow him to use their names as "the sort of people" who might be the candidate. It was not reassuring to those of a practical political bent, but it was better than nothing.

On October 20, McCarthy went to Los Angeles, and so did Lowenstein. They met for breakfast in McCarthy's suite: Hill, Lowenstein, a friend of Hill's, and McCarthy's faithful legislative aide Jerome Eller. During breakfast McCarthy was kidding, but the others noticed that he also asked some very practical questions: "Where's labor in this thing? Do you have any money? Can you get enough volunteers?" About ten-fifteen, after they had been there an hour and a quarter, McCarthy turned to Lowenstein and Hill and said, "You fellows have been talking about three or four names." And he gave them a big smile. "I guess you can cut it down to one."

2

The Conservative
as Insurgent

"Some forty years ago G. K. Chesterton wrote that every time the world was in trouble the demand went up for a practical man. Unfortunately, he said, each time the demand went up there was a practical man available. As he pointed out then, usually what was needed to deal with an impractical muddle was a theorist or philosopher."

—Senator Eugene J. McCarthy, May 9, 1965

Americans like to call the United States Senate "the greatest deliberative body on earth." But in the autumn of 1967, with nearly nine years' experience of its powers, pleasures, and privileges, that was not what Senator Eugene McCarthy thought of it. He called it "the last primitive society left on earth," and traced in scathing detail a comparison between the savages of New Guinea and the society of old men on Capitol Hill—obsessed with seniority, with taboo, and with precedent. On another occasion he called it "the leper colony."

But a Senator's life is indeed both pleasant and privileged. It is true that by contemporary American standards the salary—thirty thousand dollars a year—is less than princely. For many Senators, no doubt, this is scarcely relevant. The Associated Press, in a survey published on March 5, 1968, found that at least twenty Senators were millionaires. But even for those, like Senator McCarthy, who have no private means and a large family's education to pay for, the Senate has its compensations. It is lavish with those little luxuries and dignities which cost so much in America, when they can be bought at all. A Senator, for example, is always spoken to politely. Unlike a Congressman, a Senator is recognized. He can count on a table in a restaurant, a smile from the waitress, even on getting a taxi on a wet night outside a busy hotel.

His quarters are splendid, and he is generously provided with a staff, paid for out of public funds. Each of the one hundred Senators has a suite of four or five comfortable rooms, with pompous seals of office, deep leather armchairs, and attentive secretaries. He has a large budget with which to hire bright young men to write his speeches—or, if he is not too scrupulous, his books. He has political assistants to make on his behalf those phone calls that keep the Senatorial toga unspotted by the sordid necessities of fund-raising and patronage, and to keep at bay the ceaseless importunity of the lobbyists. He has opportunities for free travel anywhere in the world. He has special privileges in one of the two or three finest libraries in the world, and even a private underground railway a couple of hundred yards long, specially built so that when he does feel like going over to the Senate floor for a little actual deliberating he will not be obliged to go out in the rain to do it.

The Senate can offer, in fact, to a contented man that ultimate aspiration of the gentleman in every society, *otium cum dignitate,* ease with dignity. And it offers security of tenure. A Congressman, up for re-election every two years, is never done with his campaigning. The Senator, in office for six years, can afford to act the statesman. In 1964, Eugene McCarthy, the Junior Senator from Minnesota, had been triumphantly re-elected by the largest majority ever achieved by a Democrat in Minnesota. He had begun to accumulate a little of that precious seniority which means so much in the gerontocracy of the Senate's committee system. He had been lucky in his committee assignments: he was a member of the two most important committees from the point of view of national policy, Finance and Foreign Relations. But he was not contented. He was bored. And he was angry.

To his friends he spoke, perhaps idly, of leaving the Senate and going back to be a college professor in Minnesota, as he had been twenty years before. He stood aloof from "The Club," the inner circle of Senators, mostly elderly, mostly conservative, and mostly Southerners, whose delight it is to operate the painstaking processes of bargaining and compromise by which a majority is put together—or frustrated—on every single clause and amendment. And this was a matter of choice. McCarthy's colleague from Minnesota, Hubert Humphrey, had not found being a Northerner, and a relatively young man, and a liberal, a bar to membership in the inner circle. Yet at the same time McCarthy stood aloof from the liberals also.

His ability was admitted: "the most intelligent man in Congress," a colleague conceded with no special warmth. Yet he seemed not to be using it, or rather, to be using it for its own sake. Nobody was his equal as a legislative craftsman in unraveling the intricacies of tax bills, and yet, the liberals felt, he seemed more interested in details, and sometimes even in some rather dubious special-interest amendments, than in the broad lines of liberal policy. Sometimes, too, he seemed oddly in tune with the late Senator Robert Kerr, that arch-manipulator and prince of log-rollers. No one suggested that there was anything financially corrupt about an interest in special amendments for the drug industry, or whatever it might be, but rather that McCarthy found in them the opportunity to show off his sardonic intelligence and his contempt for the banalities of liberal rhetoric.

At fifty-one, Gene McCarthy looked like a Senator. He had the height—a little over six feet—the silver hair neatly brushed back, the dignified smile that starts at the corners of the eyes. But the prevailing opinion among his fellow politicians was that he didn't act like a Senator. They regarded him as aloof, indolent, arrogant, and annoying. They resented it, for example, when he proposed a measure to extend Social Security coverage to Mexican migrant workers and then was nowhere to be found when it came to drumming up the votes to pass it. They didn't like the way he spent so much of his time telling wicked little stories about his distinguished colleagues to reporters like Mary McGrory of the *Washington Star;* and the fact that the stories were always pointed enough to draw blood made it all the worse. They thought him "a truly deeply cynical man, a scoffer," as Geri Joseph, the handsome, hard-eyed Democratic committeewoman from Minnesota put it. But in fact he was an unhappy man, deeply, philosophically troubled by the futility and impotence of the Senate which they professed to respect more than he did.

McCarthy did have one distinctly un-Senatorial habit. He had read poetry all his life, his favorites the more cerebral moderns: Wallace Stevens, William Carlos Williams, Vernon Watkins, Dylan Thomas, Yeats, and Robert Lowell. Recently he had met and rapidly become a close friend of Lowell, who is often called the greatest living American poet. And he had begun to write poetry himself, scribbling it on scraps of paper on plane journeys and neatly typing out the fair copies in his Senate office. "I've never had time to develop my own style," McCarthy says himself, admitting that he imitates Lowell, among others. But the content of his poetry is intensely personal: complex, always intelligent, wry, and sometimes almost desperate, as in a poem he wrote in the spring of 1967 and called "The Lament of an Aging Politician":

> The dream of Gerontion is my dream
> And Lowell's self-salted
> night sweat wet flannel my morning's
> shoulder shroud.
>
> Now far-sighted I see the distant danger
> beyond the coffin confines of telephone booths,
> my arms stretched to read in vain.
>
> Stubbornness and penicillin hold
> the aged above me.
> My metaphors grow cold and old,
> my enemies, both young and bold.
>
> I have left Act I, for involution
> And Act II. There mired in complexity
> I cannot write Act III.

Luckily, McCarthy himself has offered a key: "You know the old rules," he has explained. "Act I states the problem. Act II deals with the complications. And Act III resolves them. I'm an Act II man. That's where I live—involution and complexity."

McCarthy was not writing only poetry that spring. He was also writing a book about American foreign policy, which he called *The Limits of Power*. It is neither involuted nor complex. It is a clear, cold, nail-driving critique of the shoddy thinking in which American policy was developed, of the muddy language in which it is justified, and of the bloody consequences to which it has led. It covers the whole field of foreign policy, but it leads up to a quiet but unqualified rejection of policy in Vietnam in particular:

"If this book has a principal theme," McCarthy wrote in a preface, "it is that our foreign policy should be more restrained . . . more in keeping with the movement of history." That is a voice that his Senatorial colleagues would expect from him: the scholar-intellectual's voice, doubting the political imperative. But he said something else. He listed three practical conclusions of his book which he particularly wanted to underline. The third was that the Senate should more effectively exercise its constitutional responsibility for foreign policy.

So there he sat, in the summer of 1967, in a suite on the top floor of the Old Senate Office Building, a bored, proud man, contemptuously

aloof from the masonic bonhomie and the routines of the life of the
Senate around him, yet seeing as clearly as anyone the futility and the
consequences of the war, and taking moreover a loftier view of the
Senate's duties and prerogatives than the men who felt he did not belong
in it. Mired in complexity, he was confronting the onset of old age and
the probability that private ambitions might never be fulfilled. Yet still
he could not begin Act III.

"He's beautiful," a lady admirer gushed to one of us. "He's like
an El Greco!" He is not. The former first baseman in the Great Soo
baseball league is too robust for that; nor can one easily imagine an El
Greco playing ice hockey. But there is something about McCarthy,
some mark of an enviable inner self-confidence, that recalls the tranquil
faces of saints painted in a tougher age by Giotto or by Cimabue. You
would start with a sense of security if you grew up in Watkins, Minnesota.

Seen from the outside, at least, there is still something idyllic about
the tiny settlements in the rich, lake-studded farmland west of Minneapolis. They are places where people have managed to work out a
modest but real fulfillment of the Jeffersonian dream, of a community
of free and equal farmers responsible for their own destiny and free from
the corruptions and temptations of the city. The road sign says:

WELCOME TO
WATKINS
POPULATION 760 FRIENDLY PEOPLE
PLUS A FEW GROUCHES
A TOWN OF FREE ENTERPRISE

Like virtually everybody else for miles around, the McCarthys were
farmers. (The Senator's father has just retired from running the family
farm: he is ninety-two years old.) Gene McCarthy was never particularly interested in farming, but he has done it—for a brief period after
the war—and he can still demolish a political opponent with a rustic
allusion. In one of his campaigns his opponent was a wealthy Republican,
a tax-loss farmer who was foolish enough to mention that he had sold
a bull for ten cents a pound and lost six hundred dollars. McCarthy had
the whole state chortling by saying, "The way I figure it, that's six thousand pounds. He should have sold it to a circus and made a fortune!"

McCarthy's background was authentically rustic, but it was not
underprivileged, and there were opportunities to get a good education in
spite of the Depression—if you wanted to enough. As a child, Gene
McCarthy's brother, who is now the doctor in Watkins, can remember

his brother forever nipping across to a neighbor's to borrow another volume of the Harvard Classics. And in due course he went to college. Both sides of the family were Catholic: Irish on the father's side, of course, but German on his mother's, which is a very different tradition in the American church, far more intellectual and far more liberal. So Gene went to St. John's, a small Catholic college twenty-five miles away, and loved it. He was an excellent student, and he was a baseball and ice-hockey star. But it was more than that. His religion mattered enough to him that he later very seriously considered taking monastic vows.

After he left St. John's, he taught in high schools for four years, and then returned there to teach economics and education. Then came the war, and in 1942 McCarthy went to Washington for the first time as a coding clerk in Army intelligence. After the war, he went back to high-school teaching again, this time in North Dakota, and there he met Abigail Quigley. He was teaching English now, and so was she. And it was at this point he went to St. John's as a novice. "Oh, I don't know," McCarthy has said about this experiment, "it was a mixed sort of case. I was inclined to give it a test. On the other hand, if it didn't really prove out, it doesn't really hurt to spend eight or ten months away from it all."

He and Abigail were married, and he got a job teaching at St. Thomas, another Roman Catholic college in St. Paul, which is the sleepier and also the more academic half of the Twin Cities of Minneapolis and St. Paul. It was there that he took his first step into politics, and within a year he was chairman of the nearly moribund county Democratic party. A year later, he narrowly squeaked through in a primary and then handsomely beat the incumbent Republican for a seat in Congress. There are two points to be made here, without going into the byzantine and sometimes very bitter feuds of Minnesota politics at the time. One is that his first constituency was a largely academic one. The other is that his rise in politics had very little to do with that of Hubert Humphrey, who in 1948 was winning a national reputation as the fire-brand mayor of Minneapolis, which as far as people in St. Paul are concerned might be in a different world instead of on the other side of the Mississippi River.

In Congress, McCarthy was both happy and active. He became one of the ringleaders of a group of young liberals, mostly from the Middle West, who were known as McCarthy's Marauders before they called themselves the Democratic Study Group—which has now become the quasi-official caucus of liberal Democrats in the House. Then, in 1958, came his election to the Senate and a gradual but growing sense of frustration, interrupted by two brief but startling episodes on the stage of national politics, each in its way still shrouded by puzzling questions of motivation.

In 1960, John Kennedy came to the convention in Los Angeles virtually certain of the nomination. There were only two outside possibilities of denying it to him: if a combination could be put together for Lyndon Johnson or if the sentimental fervor of the liberals for Adlai Stevenson could be whipped into a stampede. Eugene McCarthy nominated Stevenson in a speech of unforgettable eloquence. "Do not turn your back upon this man," he cried, and the Stevenson galleries unleased one of the most famous of those spontaneous demonstrations which are unlikely to be allowed at future conventions. McCarthy's admiration for Stevenson was unquestionably sincere. Yet he went out of his way to tell a press conference that Johnson was his first choice and Kennedy "nowhere." What was his motive? Admiration for Stevenson? A Machiavellian move for Johnson? Or hatred of Kennedy? Or some subtle McCarthyesque mixture of all three?

The origins of the feud between McCarthy and the Kennedys have been traced to specific causes. It is alleged by some that there was a falling-out over a Senate committee assignment, and by others that McCarthy was shocked by rumors of John Kennedy's sexual indiscretions. It is far more likely that the cause was more general, and that McCarthy came close to disclosing it in an ill-natured half joke he made in 1960, when he said he almost thought of running for the Presidency himself because "I'm twice as liberal as Hubert Humphrey, and twice as intelligent as Stuart Symington, and twice as Catholic as Jack Kennedy." Perhaps the origin of the quarrel lay in the bitterness that McCarthy must have felt as he watched Kennedy rise by successively laying claim to the very attributes that McCarthy was most proud of in himself—his religion, his liberal political faith, his academic constituency—and to which, with some reason, McCarthy felt he had the better claim. If so, it should be said that once McCarthy had dared to oppose them in 1960, the bitterness was fully reciprocated by the Kennedys.

For the three years of the Kennedy Administration, McCarthy languished in obscurity. Then, abruptly, in 1964, he was taken up into the mountain and shown the kingdoms of the world. Once again, his opportunity was an episode in the great feud between Lyndon Johnson and the Kennedy brothers which dominated American politics for eight years like the quarrel of Guelph against Ghibelline or Lancaster and York.

As the hour of his coronation at the Democratic convention of 1964 approached, Lyndon Johnson began to fire into the ears of any journalist he could find to listen to him—and he could find many—the names of possible Vice-Presidential candidates who were not Robert Kennedy. As the game of elimination went on, only two names stood out: those of the two Senators from Minnesota, Hubert Humphrey and Eugene McCarthy.

In the end, McCarthy took his own name out of the contest. But a sour taste remained in his mouth. He knew that he had used the episode to help himself to a smashing victory in Minnesota: the talk about him as a possible Vice-President gave him publicity of the kind that money cannot buy. He told his friend and campaign manager Herman Schauinger, a historian who had shared a cluttered office with him at St. Thomas after the war, that he was going to "run hard for the Senate and soft for the Vice-Presidency." But he also knew that he was being used by Johnson.

For almost ten years, Gene McCarthy had been sitting there in the Senate, growing older, and never moving except for those two fitful moments out of the shadow of his own obscurity into the circle of light in which there performed men whom he privately felt to be his moral and intellectual inferiors: John Kennedy, Lyndon Johnson, Hubert Humphrey, and now Robert Kennedy. They were able to start Act III, while he remained mired in complexity, his great gifts curdling into bitterness.

Something like this, perhaps, were his private thoughts, only half-acknowledged. Certainly there were enough publicly admissible thoughts to push a man in the same direction. There was the logic which showed up the catastrophic consequences of the war, the intellectual fastidiousness that despised the constantly shifting justifications put forward for it. In August, he broke out angrily after listening to a particularly sophistical performance by Rusk's deputy, Nicholas deB. Katzenbach, at a Foreign Relations Committee hearing. Things moved too fast these days, Katzenbach argued, for a President to be able to consult the Senate before starting a war. "In that case," McCarthy fumed, "there's nothing left but to take it to the people."

Religious conviction reinforced logic. Had not the Pope earnestly enjoined Catholics to work for peace in his encyclical, *Pacem in terris*? Didn't McCarthy's favorite writer of all, Sir Thomas More, seem to be

saying the same in a passage in the *Utopia* which the Senator was reading in the spring?

> Once upon a time they had gone to war to win for their king
> another kingdom. . . . They realized they would have to fight con-
> stantly for them or against them and to keep an army in constant readi-
> ness. In the meantime, they were being plundered, their money was
> being taken out of the country, they were shedding their blood for the
> little glory of someone else. Peace was no more secure than before, their
> morals at home were being corrupted by war, the lust for robbery was
> becoming second nature, criminal recklessness was emboldened by kill-
> ings in war—all because the king, being distracted with the charge of
> two kingdoms, could not properly attend to either.

"That's it flat out, isn't it?" said Senator McCarthy to a visitor,
closing the book one day at the beginning of December 1967. A few
days earlier, he had announced that he was a candidate for President of
the United States. "There comes a time," he said, with *Utopia* still in
his hand, "when an honorable man simply has to raise the flag."

And yet, even so, all these converging pressures, arguments, and
influences might not have brought him to the point of decision if it had
not been for one more. As early as May, McCarthy told a friend, James
Wechsler, of the *New York Post,* that he was not sure he could live with
his children unless he did something about the war. It was Mary, the
second of his four children, whom he was particularly thinking about.
She had just finished her first year at Radcliffe and had plunged into
the peace movement that was blazing fiercely there and at Harvard next
door. She pleaded with her father not to go down in history as one of
those who had supported Lyndon Johnson and the war. All summer
she and the other McCarthy children and their friends urged their feelings on him. By October, Mary was able to report to Curtis Gans that
her father was "edging along." And it was after a thrilling reception
from her generation at Berkeley that he finally made up his mind to go.
The aging politician raised the flag for a children's crusade.

Four days after his formal announcement, on December 2, he
arrived to make the first major speech of his campaign at Al Lowenstein's National Conference of Concerned Democrats in Chicago. He
was to be the only speaker, but he was late. Lowenstein went on as the
warm-up man, to keep the crowd happy. There were four thousand
people in the ballroom at the Hilton, and another two thousand outside.
Lowenstein said, "I'm going to give you a little pep talk," and pulled
out a wad of notes. What he then proceeded to give them was a hell-

raising, bawl-and-jump speech. Lowenstein maintains that he was only keeping going until McCarthy arrived, and that when he heard McCarthy was ready he stopped "in mid-idea." But the consensus of horrified witnesses is against him. The second half of his idea lasted an agonizing ten minutes.

By then, McCarthy, in his suite, was raging like a caged lion. Eventually he said to Jerry Eller, "Let's go!" and stormed over to the ballroom. Lowenstein was boiling up to a peak, and every time he mentioned Lyndon Johnson the crowd howled for blood. "Get this straight," he was bellowing. "If a man cheats you once, shame on him. But if he cheats you twice, shame on you!"

McCarthy was at the back of the hall, almost going out of his mind. He found a Dixie cup and was kicking it up against the wall, muttering and fuming. Curtis Gans ran to the front of the hall and shouted, "Stop it!" to Lowenstein. "Someone get him to stop it, for Christ's sake!" Lowenstein turned around, waved his notes, and said, "There's only a little bit left."

In the end, Lowenstein did stop, and McCarthy went up to the platform and read his speech, quickly. He talked about the Dreyfus affair in France and the Punic Wars of Rome. He never mentioned Lyndon Johnson, and left the crowd floundering in anticlimax, wondering what sort of leader this was under whose banners they had enrolled. Lowenstein was so grateful to have a candidate at last that he didn't care—indeed, hardly even noticed. But for the more prescient crusaders it was the first hint that their new leader was a strange kind of hero.

3

Dove Bites Hawk

"College students . . . have suddenly discovered a use for people over thirty—voting for McCarthy."

—Mary McGrory, news column, March 11, 1968

"How's the Senator this morning?"
—New Hampshire campaign worker

"Oh! Alienated as usual."
—Eugene McCarthy's daughter Mary

There were a few who had realized that the emperor had no clothes. Long before the election year began, Richard Goodwin had been telling anyone who would listen—and some, like Bobby Kennedy, who wouldn't —that Lyndon Johnson was the easiest President to beat since Herbert Hoover, inviting those who would not take his word for it to ask ten friends at random what they thought of the President. From a radically dissimilar vantage point, Art Buchwald, the country's most widely syndicated humorous columnist, had come to roughly the same conclusion. Buchwald had long been used to finding his jibes at the great resented by shoals of furious letter-writers. But Buchwald found that he could write virtually anything about the President, and hardly anyone would lift a pen on Johnson's behalf. "Whatever LBJ has going for him," Buchwald told his friends, "it's very thin."

Such sentiments, however, swam vainly against the tide of "expert" opinion. The conventional wisdom could point to Johnson in 1964 as the biggest Presidential vote-getter in American history (more accurately, of course, Goldwater was the biggest vote-loser), and to the fact that throughout the twentieth century every incumbent who had sought his party's renomination had achieved it. The peace groups might be up in arms, but the prevailing assumptions about the American electorate were that its instincts were profoundly conservative and that it was in no sense "issue-oriented." That flourishing offshoot of media politics, the campaign-consultancy business, had little time for candidates who tried to make a case through issues. In the jargon of the profession, such methods simply produced "cross-pressuring of the electorate"—that is, they made the bewildered voters react against the man who had caused them discomfort. The wise men in Washington could see no reason to doubt that Johnson's position at the head of the Democratic Party was unassailable. In their view Eugene McCarthy's challenge in the New Hampshire primary was at best quixotic and at worst absurd.

Besides, New Hampshire had been traditionally hawkish. Recently, too, its new industry in the electronics field had waxed fat on Defense Department contracts. Its registered Democrats were thought to be of the loyalist, rather than the cerebral, variety, the majority of them being working men of Irish and French-Canadian descent. On the surface, nothing seemed less likely than an upset—an impression confirmed by the published polls. In the last week of February, *Time* unveiled a poll of New Hampshire Democrats taken by the sophisticated New York firm Elmo Roper Associates. It showed McCarthy trailing the President hopelessly, with only 11 per cent of the vote. *Time* made the seemingly obvious deduction: Senator McCarthy's campaign "has so far drummed up scant support." Then, on the night of March 12, came the result. And the man so often described as a "lackluster candidate" had come within an ace of defeating the highly organized write-in campaign on behalf of President Johnson. McCarthy's share of the Democratic vote was 42 per cent; Johnson's 49 (the final figures were 27,243 votes for the President, 23,380 for McCarthy). With Republican write-in votes—5511 for McCarthy and 1778 for Johnson—taken into account, the gap between the obscure Minnesotan and the President of the United States narrowed to less than one percentage point. But the implications went deeper than mere figures.

The central feature of the later stages of the McCarthy campaign had been its lavish use of "student power." More than ten thousand students had come into New Hampshire to lick envelopes, draw up voter lists, and engage in a massive house-to-house canvassing drive. As a political operation, it was unprecedented—and productive. Nor was there any reason why it should stop. In fact, the next major primary, in Wisconsin, was likely to be even more susceptible to this technique.

Wisconsin had a student population of over a hundred thousand, and a survey of student attitudes in the summer of 1967 revealed that as many as half of them were inclined to engage in some form of political activity. It was unlikely to be on behalf of Johnson.

The White House did what it could to belittle the New Hampshire primary. Lyndon Johnson, speaking at a Veterans of Foreign Wars meeting on the night of the polling, remarked, "I think New Hampshire is the only place where a candidate can claim that twenty per cent of the vote is a landslide and forty per cent is a mandate and sixty per cent is unanimous." George Christian told the White House press corps, "There's not going to be a great deal of attention here at present to primaries, polls, and politics." Coming from the press secretary of a President who had acquired a reputation as history's most obsessive poll-watcher, this was rather laughable. For New Hampshire could not be dimissed as a freak result. A little more confirmation would be required, but March 12 was effectively the date when Johnson was "dumped."

In every election year the primaries have some importance, but in 1968 they were uniquely significant. It was through them that a new corps of political activists, not only students, but a small army of the educated middle class, attacked the political system at the grass roots. And the level of debate, in these Democratic primaries at least, exceeded anything that came later in the year.

The original idea of primary elections was to put an end to choosing candidates in those notorious smoke-filled rooms. About half a century ago, a principle was introduced which attempted to put the nominating power into the hands of the common voters of each party. That, at least, was the idea. In practice, the original purpose has been largely defeated. There has never been any unanimity among the states on how, or even whether, to implement the principle. The South for instance, which has its reasons for preserving party solidarity, has never favored the Presidential primary.

The result is a system so intricate—and so constantly changing—that it is quite beyond the comprehension of most voters and, for that matter, most politicians too. The present status of the primary has not eliminated backroom deals. Rather, dramatized and influenced by the national news media, the primaries have become costly battles between the candidates for cards to play when the backroom dealing starts. There are two things that can be acquired in primaries: delegates at the convention and, less tangibly, a reputation as a big vote-getter. The second

acquisition is much the more crucial. It is useful to pick up solid convention votes in the primaries, but there are not nearly enough available to
assure nomination. In the Democratic Party, for instance, the number of
delegate votes required for nomination is 1312, and it is impractical to
hope for even half of these through the primary mechanism.

Ultimately, of the fourteen primaries scheduled between March and
July, only seven—New Hampshire, Wisconsin, Indiana, Nebraska, Oregon, South Dakota, and California—proved to be of real significance, and
all for different reasons. In a formal sense, the most important were Wisconsin, Oregon, and California, where delegates were bound as a result
of the popular vote. California was supremely important, not only because of its whopping 174 delegates, but because of its timing. As the last
major primary (June 4), its impact on delegate thinking in other states
was, in theory at least, of great psychological importance.

A system of such random complexity has produced many demands
for reform. The more passionate rationalists advocate a supercolossal
national primary with one common procedure throughout the fifty states.
Although it would certainly ease the task of the political commentator, it
has one basic, perhaps fatal, flaw: by making the primary constituency a
national one, it would automatically favor those candidates capable of
mobilizing the largest publicity machines. Image politics would become
paramount. The present primary system, for all its absurdities, does offer
an opportunity for an insurgent candidate, with comparatively little
money, to get into contention. The primary route is not cheap in the long
run, but it starts comparatively inexpensively. A candidate who starts
well can, with luck, pick up backers before he moves on to the next campaign. Such was the nature of Senator McCarthy's campaign.

The New Hampshire primary has virtually no importance in terms
of ultimate voting power at the convention. Only twenty-four delegate
seats were at stake. But as the first shot in the 1968 Presidential election campaign, attracting an army of media men from their billets in
Washington and New York, it had enormous psychological implications—
the more so in 1968, because the state Democratic organization had made
it patent in advance that they were looking to the primary for a massive
display of enthusiasm for their President. Johnson's name would not be
on the ballot, but the local Democrats were zealously bent on organizing
a write-in campaign on his behalf.

Since it was assumed that this drive would be overwhelmingly successful, most reporters directed their attention to the Republican pri-

mary struggle between Governor George Romney of Michigan, the nearest approximation to a Republican peace candidate, and Richard Milhous Nixon, who, as the saying goes, needs no introduction. (Much of the press punditry revolved around the question whether or not there was a New Nixon. A local editor, Ed DeCourcy of Newport's *Argus-Champion*, delivered one of the more acute judgments: "There is no New Nixon. What we have here is the old Nixon, a little older.") The Democratic primary campaign was, until its final weeks, little more than a side show. At one point, an embittered McCarthy supporter sent a letter to the *New York Times* complaining of the leanness of the reporting on her champion. She received in reply a lofty missive to the effect that, as McCarthy was a "one-issue" candidate, he could not seriously be regarded as a major contender; under these circumstances he merited no more coverage than he was already receiving.

At the turn of the year, before McCarthy decided to enter the New Hampshire primary, there were many in the peace movement itself who were equally dismissive. To say that McCarthy did not live up to the initial expectations of his newly found acolytes is to put it mildly. Even among that small cabal of people who had persuaded him to run, the candidate suddenly seemed not merely less than heart's desire, but potentially counterproductive. "We spent most of the time," said one of them, "lying like rugs for him." They had hoped for a roaring peace-proselytizer with a passion for knocking spots off the hated LBJ. They found themselves saddled with a man who seemed to find it difficult to be animated, let alone passionate. Among the insiders, McCarthy's reluctance to muddy his hands with "nuts-and-bolts" organization work and the subtle sycophancies of fundraising was causing a condition verging on despair. At a fashionable New York fundraising party attended by over a hundred people, McCarthy came in, shook three hands, and then, apparently overcome by boredom, retired to the bar. Later, when candidate and constituency became more attuned to each other's foibles, his staff began to realize that McCarthy is unpolitical enough to have off days and let it show. It was a minus—and it became a minus among a lot of plusses. There was no doubt that a lot of money and sentiment could be mobilized. But was McCarthy the man to do it?

Letters of support and offers of money came into the Senator's office at a colossal rate. It was some weeks—and almost a hundred thousand letters—before Al Lowenstein discovered that virtually none of them had been answered. The induction of student scribes solved this problem. But there was no way to stem cries of disenchantment from the left. The more paranoid among the disappointed maintained that McCarthy must be a stalking horse for Johnson—meaning that the fragility of his candidacy was designed to suggest how little support the dove position on Vietnam had. *Ramparts,* the radical magazine published in San Francisco, which had become a bible for disbelievers in the "system," proclaimed that McCarthy was out to destroy the peace movement. At a more exalted level of dissent, Joseph Rauh, who with John Kenneth Galbraith was now maneuvering to secure McCarthy's endorsement by the Americans for Democratic Action, was advised by a friend to lay off. "Gene's entry into the race," he said, "is the greatest thing that could happen to Johnson; he's so weak he makes even Johnson look good."

By December, it was apparent that if McCarthy did not show results soon even his peace constituency would begin to fragment: either into impassioned public appeals for Bobby Kennedy, or into to-hell-with-the-system rhetoric. The only possible course was to persuade McCarthy to run in New Hampshire. This was difficult. At the Chicago CDA meeting, the Senator had been inclined to confine his primary efforts to Wisconsin, Massachusetts, Oregon, and California. Bobby Kennedy had advised him that New Hampshire might be a better bet than Massachusetts—on the reasonable grounds that in New Hampshire, a predominantly Republican state, the Democratic machine was much weaker. It would be easier for an anti-establishment candidate to outflank the state organization. McCarthy, however, had no particular relish for advice from the Kennedys; he suspected—accurately, as it turned out—that Bobby wanted him to put his toe into the electoral waters as early as possible in order to gauge whether it was the right temperature for himself. Fortunately, there were less suspect streams of advice to the same effect.

At the Chicago meeting there had been a small contingent of New Hampshire activists, the most conspicuous of whom, Gerry Studds and David Hoeh, both aged thirty, went on to become McCarthy's campaign coordinators in the state. Neither fell into the wild-eyed-radical mold. Studds had spent a few years in Washington working in the Kennedy Administration and had since settled down to schoolmastering at St. Paul's School—an elaborate derivative of the English public-school which in many respects outdoes the original article—on the outskirts of New Hampshire's capital, Concord. Hoeh taught at Dartmouth College and had been active in state politics for almost ten years. His diminutive but hyperactive wife, Sandy, was the number-four Democrat on the state committee. Both Studds and Hoeh, through their contact with bright young pupils, were fully aware of the extent of disenchantment about the war. (Even the rarefied atmosphere of St. Paul's was infested with anti-Administration sentiment. On parents' day that winter, Robert McNamara, then still Secretary of Defense, went to see his son play football for the school team. Furious attempts were made to conceal the fact that a trenchantly antiwar pamphlet was then going the rounds of the faculty and the upper forms.) More important, both men felt that McCarthy's wry, witty style was perfectly adapted to their state. They urged him at least to come and have a look.

The occasion for such an introduction was rapidly fixed: the Sidor Lecture in Manchester, New Hampshire's largest industrial town, on December 14. McCarthy agreed to deliver an address on the theme "The New Civil Rights," and the New Hampshire group, naturally wanting to make an event of the visit, pulled out all the stops in assembling a big crowd.

The implicit drawing card was some energetic Administration-baiting and a possible declaration of McCarthy's intention to come into New Hampshire's primary. Not so. McCarthy came, as promised, and delivered, as promised, a lecture. It was an urbane, logical piece of work, but not the kind of thing fourteen hundred people had braved a cold winter's night for. "There was no getting away from it," said Hoeh, recalling his first effort in stage management on the Minnesotan's behalf. "He killed them."

After this performance, McCarthy was wheeled around to the house of one of Hoeh's friends to meet some of the key figures in the state who had expressed interest in his candidacy. There were about sixty people there, not the very top-echelon Democrats, but influential nonetheless: two county chairmen, a few state representatives, and the Mayor of Nashua. McCarthy's impact this time was not so much paralytic as puzzling. "Ah," he said on entering the room, "here we have the government in exile." It was a felicitous start, but where was the get-up-and-go? One of those present, a local shoe manufacturer, said he'd spoken a lot to his workers and been impressed by the strength of their hawkishness. In the circumstances, didn't McCarthy think it a good idea to take a poll before coming into the state? "No, I don't think so," said McCarthy, "I think it would be very discouraging." It was an honest and shrewd enough answer—the national polls were showing Johnson 5-to-1 ahead of McCarthy, and there was no particular reason to assume New Hampshire differed from this pattern. But it was hardly the kind of response to make cautious, if uncomfortable, politicos come out ardently for his challenge.

McCarthy, clearly, was still not enamored of the idea of raising the standard in New Hampshire. On the way back to the airport that night, Hoeh, sitting in the back of the car beside Jerry Eller, glumly listened to the candiate being interviewed by David Halberstam, the writer. To a question about his campaign intentions, McCarthy replied that he was still of a mind to stay out of New Hampshire. Fortunately, the interview was for publication months later: if it had readied the press at that stage that McCarthy was definitely not entering New Hampshire, the tenuous base of support for his candidacy in that state would have collapsed totally. Hoeh, utterly despondent, turned to Eller and asked if there was still a chance. Eller advised him to contact Blair Clark, the man who, a few days earlier, had been appointed McCarthy's campaign manager.

Hoeh did that and more besides. With Studds he mapped out a crisp thousand-word memorandum, setting out the factors in favor of a McCarthy candidacy and the type of campaign that would be most effective in the state. The document was generously tinged with optimism. (The tyro President-launchers, for instance, estimated campaign costs at $55,000. The eventual figure was a little over $175,000.) But insofar as one can comprehend the convoluted workings of McCarthy's mind, it seems that this document and the ministrations of Blair Clark were the crucial influences on his decision to enter New Hampshire. Because it was seminal to his campaign, some passages in the memorandum are worth quoting:

There is nothing to be lost—and a great deal to be gained—by coming into New Hampshire:

a) Given the general impression that it is a "hawkish" state and a "conservative" state—plus Senator McIntyre's [Democratic Senator Thomas J. McIntyre] extraordinary prediction that McCarthy would get 3,000–5,000 votes (i.e., less than 10 per cent), anything better than that can be hailed as a stunning performance (and we can do considerably better than that).

b) The Senator would reaffirm the seriousness of his national candidacy by his willingness to enter against odds (e.g., JFK in West Virginia).

c) A victory here—which we think we ought to shoot for—and which seems to us far more within the realm of possibility than it did a month ago—would have major national repercussions.

There has been a clear, panic reaction to the threat of McCarthy's candidacy among the party hierarchy in this state—and with real reason. Many prominent Democrats have quietly refused to serve on the LBJ Committee.

If we are to move on the Senator's behalf, we must get going yesterday. e.g.: In the city of Keene, a McCarthy committee, with 90 adult

volunteers, has already located office space for headquarters and is
awaiting word from us to install phones and begin operations. Similar
efforts throughout the state need rapid encouragement.

An effective campaign here is *manageable*—and the attached
12-day schedule hits over three-quarters of the Democratic primary vote.
[The schedule contained an analysis of how much time McCarthy should
spend in New Hampshire's main population centers—Manchester,
Nashua, Concord, Berlin, Portsmouth, Rochester, and Keene.]

Blair Clark was easily impressed by such arguments. He had lived
in the state for two years and he too felt that McCarthy's personality was
perfectly adjusted to the quieter reaches of New England. He was not
an expert—but then an expert would probably have polled New Hampshire and decided it was a dead loss from the outset. He did, however,
have a rare talent among those connected with the McCarthy operation
at this stage: an ability to communicate easily with the candidate, without offending the susceptibilities of the lesser staffers.

As manager, Clark never really stamped his personality on McCarthy's campaign. Considering the operation's freewheeling development, it
is open to question whether this could have been done by anyone. Clark
hardly bothered to try. But in an enterprise of extreme volatility, where
mutual character-assassination seemed the most popular form of staff
leisure-hours activity, Clark did emerge with his head above the ruck.
"There were more coups in that McCarthy Washington office than in
Saigon," lamented one staffer.

Clark survived—and with a minimum of slurs upon his motivation,
personality structure, and general comportment. He was, by the reckoning of most insiders, a pleasant man with pleasant instincts. This in itself
was no mean achievement.

Like most of the campaign staff, he had come into the enterprise not
out of any particular affection for, or even knowledge of, Eugene McCarthy, but because it seemed the only alternative to a year of hopeless
impotence. He possessed, too, the useful independence of the rich; and,
for motivation, two sons of draft age whom he was reluctant to see thrown
into the Vietnam meat grinder. Clark's own career as a newspaperman
and a CBS executive had brought him into close contact with politics.
His range of acquaintants and friends was wide. Robert Lowell dedicated a book of poems to him. Jack Kennedy had been a close friend.

But as far as politics was concerned, Clark was not a professional.
Although he had only met the Senator a couple of times, he had decided
to send a modest tender of his support when McCarthy announced his
candidacy. In his letter, Clark mentioned the fact that he had worked as

a press aide for Averell Harriman in his successful 1953 New York gubernatorial campaign, and that he had managed to convey the impression that his multimillionaire candidate had been born in a log cabin. McCarthy apparently thought this an amusing enough reason for volunteering one's services and asked Clark to take charge of the campaign. At that stage of the game, it was a shrewd enough choice (not that competition for the job was particularly intense, at least outside the ranks of the peace-movement activists, most of whom tried the candidate's patience.) Clark had a natural "in" to the New York circuit of liberal campaign-fund givers—which was essential as the costs of New Hampshire escalated. And, most important, his freedom from rigid preconceptions about campaign management allowed the operation to evolve along unorthodox lines. (This quality, a virtue in New Hampshire, was to have less desirable consequences later, in other states.) Above all, Clark deserves the credit for levering McCarthy into New Hampshire, an accomplishment which Al Lowenstein subsequently considered one of the great contributions to the politics of 1968. Clark himself is diffident about it: "Some of the history books will say that I persuaded McCarthy to go into New Hampshire on a train journey from Washington to New York just before Christmas, and they'll be wrong. I made the journey and put the case, but you don't persuade McCarthy to do things like that: he decides himself."

Back in New Hampshire, the Hoeh-Studds group had virtually given up hope, though they continued to hide their pessimism from the press. Then, on January 2, Clark flew to a private meeting with Hoeh at the Wayfarer Hotel, on the outskirts of Manchester, and told him to get his people ready: the Senator would announce something within forty-eight hours. While they were having dinner, Hoeh was paged to take a call from Washington. He returned to inform a startled Blair Clark that it was McCarthy who had called. He was coming in, and Hoeh could announce the decision to the press in the morning.

The New Hampshire press, dominated by the Manchester *Union-Leader,* the only paper with a state-wide circulation, did not greet the news with much enthusiasm. It would be an understatement to describe the *Union-Leader*'s position as right of right. An idea of its ethos may be deduced from the fact that one of its leading political commentators is currently at work on a book entitled *Thirty Years of Appeasement—* an appraisal of United States policy in the modern world. The next most prestigious paper, the *Concord Monitor,* was well balanced and fair, but it was locked into advocacy of Romney's liberal Republican stance. With negligible coverage in the big out-of-state papers that had some circulation in New Hampshire, like the *New York Times* and the *Boston Globe,* and a local press ranging from hostile to cool, it became rapidly apparent that few votes would be won via the conventional pace-setters of public opinion.

McCarthy's local activists decided to set up headquarters in Concord. Manchester, a bigger and more central community, would, in a normal campaign, have been the logical location, but it was thought that the blue-collar sensitivities of that town might be affronted by an incoming force of student volunteers. Concord might not be a haven of peace sentiment, but its residents tended to be more affluent and hence more used to the foibles of educated youth. Hoeh and Studds rented a cavernous warehouse, formerly used for electrical supplies, on Main Street and started in a quiet line of business. Their total initial funds were four hundred dollars—two hundred and fifty of them from an uncle of Sandy Hoeh's.

On January 25, a full three weeks later, McCarthy made his first campaign visit to New Hampshire. As it was almost eight years to the day since Jack Kennedy had started his campaign in that state, outside Nashua City Hall, the organizers, predictably, decided it would be a nice idea to start outside Nashua City Hall. After some prodding, McCarthy consented to being maneuvered up against a bust of Jack Kennedy to deliver his opening spiel. It was a beautiful day, cold but crisp. The television cameramen got some good shots. Then McCarthy lumbered off for some handshaking in the shopping center. "He seemed a nice enough man," said one matron who received the treatment, but she couldn't quite recollect the candidate's name. It was all very low key. Later in the day, McCarthy's party found itself fifteen minutes ahead of its advance man; later still, they lost the advance man. A few seeds were planted for the subsequent tripartite controversy between the Senator's personal staff, the national campaign staff, and the local organizers. But nobody seriously blew his cool; nor, for that matter, did anyone blow very hot. It was the beginning of a social revolution in American politics; but, like many such moments, its historic quality was not immediately apparent to the naked eye. At the time, there seemed little to suggest that the local Democratic leadership's prediction that McCarthy would be lucky to get ten per cent of the vote could be much in error.

Although he was too loyal to admit it, throughout the month of January, Al Lowenstein had privately become steadily more depressed by the inertia of his candidate. Even his enormous reserves of energy began to be drained by his having to cover for McCarthy with outraged peace-movement comrades. One of them, a wealthy New York liberal, Mrs. Ronnie Eldridge, accused him of making "a serious historical error." Lowenstein's efforts to mobilize student support for McCarthy in New Hampshire would, she argued, keep McCarthy afloat when he richly deserved to sink. The only thing was to go and beg Kennedy to run. Lowenstein was more than half inclined to agree with her. His position, however, was highly delicate. As long as McCarthy was in the race, Lowenstein did not feel he could honorably press Kennedy to run. But he did meet Kennedy several times to discuss "the situation." He strove to preserve the fine line between tendering advice to his friend Kennedy, which he did feel free to do, and actually cajoling him to run, which he felt would be disloyal to his commitment to McCarthy. But this line tended to get badly smudged. At one of their meetings early in January, it disappeared altogether. Kennedy, with a hint of self-pity, was professing his helplessness. He told Lowenstein how his aides had consulted the various power-brokers in the party, Mayor Daley among them. But the advice they received had been virtually unanimous: it was not Kennedy's year, his chance would come in 1972, and any attempt to tinker with this timetable would simply result in splitting the party. This apologia was too much for Lowenstein. After a long silence, he surrendered to a violent desire to tongue-lash the Senator: "The people who think that the honor and future of this country are at stake don't give a shit what Mayor Daley and Chairman X and Governor Y think. We're going ahead and we're going to win, and it's a shame you're not with us because you could have been President, but it's too late now, and that's where it's at!"

But the breach was healed; both parties felt it had to be. And their subsequent discussions revolved around the conditions under which Lowenstein would shift his support from McCarthy to Kennedy. On January 24, the day before McCarthy's first campaign trip to New Hampshire, the two men met again in Kennedy's apartment at United Nations Plaza and roughed out half a dozen conditions under which such a change of allegiance would be justified. Most of them hinged on a failure by McCarthy to bestir his campaign efforts. Kennedy had, at one stage, lamented, "If you only had a good candidate like General Gavin . . ." Before the end of the month, Lowenstein had passed on some of these stipulations to McCarthy (as Lowenstein conditions, of course, not Kennedy ones). Whether they were instrumental in bracing the campaign is not absolutely clear. But McCarthy did become a more diligent campaigner. His original intention to spend only ten days in New Hampshire was revised. Eventually, he devoted fifteen days to campaigning in the state.

But February failed to produce any sign that the various elements in the McCarthy organization were capable of welding themselves into a coordinated unit. If there was to be a surge, it certainly would not be the result of one of those proverbial well-oiled machine operations. In a campaign organization with an average age of not much over thirty, there was a natural search for authority figures: but in vain. McCarthy himself was too aloof from detail, while Clark was distracted much of the time by national considerations: shell organizations, at least, had to be mounted in other primary states. After Clark, the next most important figure was Curtis Gans, Director of Operations. Gans was a man of shrewd political instinct. He realized, for example, that too much emotionalism on the antiwar issue could prove counterproductive. He was at pains to build up McCarthy as a Presidential personality, rather than as a symbol of protest. He had, however, little talent for organization or taste for delegating authority. Soon after his arrival in New Hampshire, he and the Hoeh group fell into a state of mutual antipathy. Ironically, Gans, though often credited with the creation of the "children's crusade" for McCarthy, was almost paranoically nervous about the students' impact on the voters. The local organizers, by contrast, were all for making the students a campaign motif—anything to get attention.

Another early national appointment was Seymour (Sy) Hersh, aged thirty. An ex-Associated Press reporter at the Pentagon and the author of a book on chemical and bacteriological warfare, Hersh was drafted to make some sense of the Senator's dismal press relations. There was a certain nobility in McCarthy's cavalier disregard for journalistic obsessions about deadlines. Many reporters approached his campaign with irreverence and were inclined to question whether he was a "serious" candidate. But if the press was being obtuse, there was still no good reason for antagonizing the reporters. Hersh's job was to expedite the flow of information, to ensure that McCarthy delivered the speeches he said he would so the journalists could get early releases, and, it was hoped, to make the candidate more accessible.

It was a tough task. But, then, Hersh did not expect it to last long. Blair Clark, when he recruited Hersh early in January, did not even attempt to disguise the object of the enterprise: "All we want to do is get Kennedy in." (The "we" was the staff, not McCarthy. One thing guaranteed to elicit a flash of spirit from the Senator was a suggestion that he might be a stalking horse for anybody.)

Hersh, unlike Gans, had few difficulties in working with Hoeh's group. But he had other problems. To do the job well he depended on frequent access to the Senator, a dependence that brought him into collision with the third locus of authority in the McCarthy operation—the candidate's personal staff, most of whom were way over the other side of the generation gap. Throughout the campaign, McCarthy's personal retinue tended to make a rigid distinction between their roles and that of the new-found claimants to his attention. "We work for Senator McCarthy," his secretary told a campaign worker. "You work for McCarthy, the Presidential candidate." As if this explained everything. The most important figure in the Senator's personal entourage was Jerry Eller, who had been McCarthy's legislative assistant ever since he entered politics. By shielding the Senator from his more volatile advisers, he took a lot of the flak that should more appropriately have burst around his master's head. But protection, undeniably, often extended to an irritating fussiness about detail. After one particularly heated row over scheduling, Hersh said to a group of reporters, "Gentlemen, I'd like you to meet Jerry Eller, who's been helping the Senator on and off with his coat for twenty years."

The original financial angels in New Hampshire were Blair Clark himself; Martin Peretz, a wealthy young Harvard academic; Arnold Hyett, the owner of a shoe company in Boston; and—much the biggest contributor—Harold Stein, of the Dreyfus Fund, who picked up the tab for the television advertising and mailing costs.

Stein spent a disconcertingly large amount of time watching his investment in action—even drafting his own ad man, Julian Koenig, of the New York firm Papert, Koenig, Lois, Inc., which had done political work for the Kennedys. Another Stein find was a sharp young Doubleday editor called Larry Freundlich, one of the small army of wordsmiths deployed on Bobby Kennedy's political testament *To Seek a Newer World*. Stein hired Freundlich with a view to lending him to McCarthy, only to find that McCarthy's own small team of writers were underemployed. The Senator had a characteristic almost unique in Presidential politics: an ingrained aversion to prepared texts. Stein's money was crucial at this early stage, but the internal rumors that he was trying to muscle in on Blair Clark's territory, to "professionalize" the outfit on behalf of Bobby Kennedy, were less than helpful. Stein did, in fact, stick loyally with McCarthy through the year, but it seemed rather Machiavellian at the time.

Despite the tension in its upper echelons, and its appallingly late start, the McCarthy campaign in New Hampshire ranks as one of the best of the year. In a situation verging on chaos, the local organizers, who best appreciated the mood of the electorate, had few qualms about standing up to, or maneuvering around, the obstinacies of the feuding national groups. They might not be ultraprofessional themselves, but they soon saw the pointlessness of being in awe of the national staffers—or, for that matter, their candidate. This led to a series of small, but by no means infinitesimal, victories which undoubtedly contributed to the over-all effectiveness of the campaign. Some are worth recounting:

McCarthy, true to his policy of fidelity to the issues, refused to make political capital of his Catholicism. Sixty-five per cent of New Hampshire's ninety thousand registered Democrats are Roman Catholics. So, nothing daunted, the local staff ascertained when he was attending Mass privately and leaked the occasion in advance to local press photographers.

Envisaging the possibility that the Senator might be inveigled into a stunt, his personal staff "forgot" to pack the candidate's ice skates. The local staff borrowed a pair, and McCarthy, clearly enjoying the break from his speech-making routine, spent twenty energetic minutes on the Concord rink playing hockey with a group of semipros. He won the puck in three face-offs, and "McCarthy on Ice" broke the glacial indifference of the national news magazines.

A late-night party for student volunteers in mid-February was declared off-limits to the press by the national staff. The local staff revoked the order, and for some of the newsmen present it became a turning point in their perceptions of the campaign. There was scarcely an angry radical in sight. They were all so well scrubbed and polite, the kind of children of which the American middle class—and most reporters consider themselves members—could be proud.

Julian Koenig, Stein's ad man, was all for hard-hitting, emotional advertising on the war issue. The subject of burned babies was discussed. The locals persuaded him to cool it. And Koenig did come up with one of the best slogans of the campaign: "New Hampshire can bring America back to its senses," which conveyed the right impression while subtly flattering local pride. This, with "There IS an Alternative," became McCarthy's principal billboard motif in the state.

All this was collectively fruitful, but hardly enough to bring a ten-to-one outsider into contention. What did turn despondency into elation was the Tet offensive, beginning on January 31. Initially, it was feared that news of this event might provoke a hawkish spasm. But as the days passed and the accumulation of information revealed the full extent of the damage to the American cause, the public reaction was not so much visceral as questioning. "For the first time," said Gerry Studds, "a large proportion of the country was capable of being convinced that the government had lied to them." It was a situation that could afford cool understatement, and this was an area in which McCarthy had few peers. Thus, in a speech at the Alpine Club in Manchester:

> In 1963, we were told that we were winning the war. In 1964, we were told we were winning the war. In 1964, we were told the corner was being turned. In 1965, we were told the enemy was being brought to its knees. In 1966, in 1967, and now again in 1968, we hear the same hollow claims of programs and victory. For the fact is that the enemy is bolder than ever, while we must steadily enlarge our own commitment. The Democratic Party in 1964 promised "no wider war." Yet the war is getting wider every month. Only a few months ago we were told that sixty-five per cent of the population was secure. Now we know that even the American Embassy is not secure.

An unlooked-for consequence of Tet was the arrival of Dick Goodwin. Speculation at the time suggested that Goodwin had been cunningly insinuated into the operation to oversee Kennedy's interests. He did, of course, but his initial motivation was uncharacteristically impulsive. At home in Boston, Goodwin read about the bombing of the temples in Hue and decided the situation demanded more of him than mere private proddings of Bobby. So he threw his typewriter into the back of his car and motored up to the Wayfarer Hotel in Manchester, where the McCarthy wordsmiths were closeted. Goodwin's arrival in New Hampshire—and he was the first real pro to come on the team, however equivocally—had an immediate bracing effect on the McCarthy staff's self-esteem. "With these two typewriters," Goodwin told Sy Hersh, "we're going to overthrow the government."

Although Kennedy resolutely abstained from saying anything flattering about McCarthy's initiative, it was already clear that McCarthy was receiving more covert assistance from other Kennedy friends. Ted Sorensen had visited the state in January and urged a vigorous "write-in Bobby Kennedy" group to stop its activities. The group was headed by Eugene Daniell, a fiery old radical lawyer who, at the time of the Great Crash, had lobbed a stink bomb into the New York Stock Exchange. Daniell complied with the request, thus unifying the local antiwar forces; and he became one of the most trenchant critics of Kennedy's candidacy after McCarthy's showing in New Hampshire. ("It's like one dog stealing another dog's bone," he said.) Even Kennedy's chief contact man in the state, William L. Dunfey, a hotel tycoon and a former Democratic state committee chairman, while not coming out for McCarthy, was privately free with helpful tips for the Hoeh group. On Dunfey's advice the McCarthy camp tightened up its delegate-slate policy—entering only 24 pledged delegates for the 24 available spots. The Johnson group, gross with overconfidence, had allowed more than 40 names to be listed, which resulted in a wasteful scattering of pro-Administration strength. When the votes were counted, McCarthy found himself possessed of a bonus of 20 delegates, despite his narrow eclipse in the popular vote.

The crassness of the regular local Democratic leaders was actually a major factor in the McCarthy campaign's rise. And the first evidences of this neatly coincided with public bewilderment over the Tet offensive. The organizer of the Johnson write-in movement was a cheery, but not terribly imaginative, businessman called Bernard L. Bootin. Bootin had resigned as head of the Small Business Administration in Washington in the summer of 1967. His ostensible reason was to return to private life, but Bootin was soon hard at work assessing his old chief's prospects. (In the early period, naturally, Robert Kennedy was taken as the potential adversary.) Lining up the leading Democrats was no problem. The Democratic governor, John W. King, had excellent loyalist credentials; he was hoping to round off his career with a Federal judgeship. Senator McIntyre was absolutely sound on Vietnam. All that needed to be done was to ensure that the voters turned out. However, in their loyalist zeal, Bootin and King made the mistake of acting like old-style machine Democrats in a state that had little taste for, or tradition of, the politics of *force majeure*.

The device that caused most resentment was the "pledge card" drive. These explosive little documents, which the voters were asked to fill in and return to local headquarters, contained three sections, each having a serial number. One was to be retained by the voter as a reminder; the second, which contained a simple pledge to write in President Johnson's name on March 12, was to be held by the local organization; the third was to be detached and sent to the White House as an express affirmation of the individual Democrat's loyalty. Receipt of a completed pledge card entitled the loyalist to a free portrait study of Johnson and Lady Bird by return post. A mind did not have to be darkly suspicious to detect overtones of Big Brotherism in this enterprise. And when Governor King declaimed, "Now is the time for Democrats to stand up and be counted—or be counted out," he may not have been referring to those serial-numbered pledge cards, but no one could be quite sure.

It was a gift. The McCarthy staff photocopied the pledge card and disseminated it in poster form under the slogan WHATEVER HAPPENED TO THE SECRET BALLOT? (Some voters had actually thought the pledge cards *were* ballot papers.) McCarthy himself, on his second campaign visit to New Hampshire early in February, used it with loving deftness. It rather reminded him, he said, of the way they put a brand on cattle in Texas; he saw it as a test of the independent spirit of New Hampshire and hoped the voters would react against such a device. McCarthy kept the issue alive throughout the campaign, though the pledge cards themselves mysteriously disappeared. Bootin, in an agony of embarrassment about the whole affair, later said that thirty thousand had been sent off to Washington; the White House issued a statement to the effect that no pledge cards had been received, or were ever likely to be.

If McCarthy was fortunate in the caliber of his opposition, he did, nonetheless, slowly establish that he was no mean candidate. Indeed, perhaps the key influence on the campaign, and the one most under-valued at the time, was McCarthy's own style. The shrewder members of his new entourage began to realize why McCarthy had been winning elections while they were still in short pants.

He could still be maddening—as when he turned down an op-portunity to appear on "Meet the Press" because he was miffed at not being the number-one selection. "I think," muttered Clark, when he heard of this decision, "we have a fraud on our hands." Yet, at the same time, McCarthy did exhibit a talent for hauling morale out of the pit. At one particularly low point in New Hampshire, Sy Hersh gloomily showed the candidate a copy of that morning's *Union-Leader* with a barbed cartoon on the subject of McCarthy's campaign theme: a bearded hippie entering McCarthy headquarters, waving a picture of Ho Chi Minh and saying, "There is an alternative." McCarthy looked up from the paper and said lightly, "Well, he is an alternative, I suppose." In the context of the times, when the opposition was resorting to mindless but unnerving appeals to patriotism, it was enough to brighten several staffers' day. Hersh, for instance, had been advised that he might find himself unemployable in Washington after his New Hampshire detour. It was heartening to be with a candidate who did not scare easily; in fact, he did not scare at all.

McCarthy on the campaign trail was a revelation. There was no Kennedyesque hysteria, yet he kept making a good impression. He never bullied a voter, though he could, when an audience seemed suitable, be waspish. One night in a country-club section of Manchester, a woman lamented the possibility of an election choice between Johnson and Nixon. "I know," said McCarthy, "that's like choosing between vulgarity and obscenity, isn't it?" But his most effective appearances were frequently among the "gut" Democrats in the factories and workingmen's clubs. The name helped—"McCahty, you say. You've got my vote." The staffers wondered how many thought the Senator's first name was Joe.

The most important thing about McCarthy was his method of raising the issues. He did not make listeners retreat into a patriot shell by declaiming on the "immorality" and "brutality" of the war (though he believed it was both), nor did he lay into the President's personality. (This disappointed Goodwin, but McCarthy understood that dislike of Johnson did not have to be underlined.) With most audiences, McCarthy's technique consisted of a careful analysis of what the war was costing in lives and money. He would then ask people to make "a reasoned judgment" on whether it was worth it, and he would cite a list of military authorities who thought it was not. He would say cannily, "We can sympathize with the President's problems and respect his intentions, but . . ."

The result was that, despite his fundamental criticisms of the Administration, the polls showed that he was not considered "radical"—a dangerous label in American election campaigns. Nor was he, of course. One of his earliest campaign speeches in New Hampshire dilated on the conservative theme of constitutional separation of powers. Johnson, he argued, was "blurring the distinctions of government." It was difficult for any voter who met him—and about fifteen thousand did in the course of the campaign—to cast him as a traitor or a revolutionary. For readers of the *Union-Leader,* the contrast between the reports and the reality was all the more startling.

While McCarthy supplied the all-important respectability to the enterprise, the students came through with the energy. Back in November 1967, Robert Kennedy had discussed with Professor Galbraith the kind of campaign McCarthy ought to wage in New Hampshire. Kennedy was very emphatic on one specific point, urging Galbraith to tell McCarthy, "Make sure this is a grown-up enterprise. He'll have more Dartmouth undergrads than he could or should use, so let him look out for that." That a campaign could be "grown-up" and yet make lavish use of student volunteers was not part of the conventional political wisdom. Yet when the students came, by hundreds in early February and thousands for the final two weekends of the campaign, there was plenty of work for them. Mailing lists had to be composed virtually from scratch—not only of the ninety thousand Democrats, but also the hundred thousand registered independents (independents are allowed to vote, provided they register as Democrats or Republicans on polling day). Lists of registered voters, separated by sex, were available, but their addresses had to be pin-pointed by cross-reference with the city directories. After some internal agonizing, it was decided that students could be turned loose as canvassers, with carefully prepared instructions on how to go about it. Few encountered hostility. Many were almost overwhelmed by the response of individual voters.

One group of forty French-speaking students from Yale plunged into the French working-class areas of Berlin armed with pamphlets listing their candidate's attributes under such heads as *"Le Sénateur Eugène McCarthy se presente," "McCarthy au sujet de Vietnam,"* and *"McCarthy parle des citoyens agés."* Of the cities in New Hampshire, Bootin considered Berlin the most rock-solid for Johnson. McCarthy took it. The LBJ men, ever unwilling to believe that voters make decisions on issues, rationalized the loss as the consequence of the Paul Newman vote. Indeed, the movie actor had made an impressive pro-McCarthy campaign stop there. "Why does McCarthy need you?" bellowed a heckler. "He doesn't need me," said Newman, "I need him."

But the student canvass in Berlin and in other areas had established another factor that is often overlooked in high-powered dissertations on media politics: nothing flatters a voter more than personal contact. By the time polling day came around, McCarthy's student volunteers had rendered this compliment to over three-quarters of the potential electorate. The Johnson people could see its effect but, without a highly motivated counterforce, were powerless to do anything about it. "What can you do?" Governor King groaned to an aide. "It's all these kids."

The students came from over a hundred different colleges, from as far west as Michigan and as far south as Virginia, though the hard-core regulars were from Harvard, Yale, Boston University, and Dartmouth. Their dedication was prodigious, and sixteen-hour working days were not unusual. Perhaps because the New Left maintained its barrage of criticism of McCarthy, only a small minority were committed radicals. Those that came tended to be adaptable, particularly in sartorial matters. Under the ruthless direction of Sam Brown, the campaign's "student coordinator," arrivals were subjected to a careful weeding process: "straights" —boys who were clean-shaven and wore suits, and girls with minimum décolletage and maxi-skirts—were allowed out in the wards on personal-contact visits; "nonstraights," a majority at first, were consigned to the routine jobs out of the public eye. One bewhiskered student, making the supreme sacrifice, borrowed a razor and whipped off his beard before presenting himself for reclassification to alfresco duties. The prissy but practical slogan, "Neat and Clean for Gene," was born. "My campaign may not be organized at the top," McCarthy told a reporter, "but it is certainly tightly organized at the bottom."

Aside from its impact on the New Hampshire voters, the student crusade had one other significant consequence on the development of Democratic party politics during the rest of the year. The students came because of the antiwar issue, but most of them developed personal loyalty to the candidate. The campuses had always been considered as Kennedy's base. He had been nurturing this constituency for years; he lost it in a month. McCarthy seemed to embody all the academic virtues of wit, integrity, and wisdom without the most obnoxious of academic vices, pomposity. He was frequently described as "beautiful," the word of the year. And long before the votes were cast, Bobby Kennedy joined Lyndon Johnson in the demonology of many volunteers. "He's a moral slob," said a Cornell senior. "In our crowd, we're circulating a dump-Kennedy-in-'72 letter."

By the end of February, all but the most head-in-the-snow reporters had realized that something strange was happening in New Hampshire. The Elmo Roper poll, published at this point in *Time,* had been based on responses three weeks earlier; it was eons out of date. Bootin and company were exhibiting signs of panic. Unlike the McCarthy camp, they were getting regular private poll data supplied by the New York firm Quayle Associates, and the evidence of defections was mounting. Revising earlier predictions, Bootin remarked that McCarthy could not get more than twenty-five per cent of the vote. Nobody mentioned the ten-per-cent figure any more. On the advice of the polling firm, which reckoned that McCarthy's peace commitment was not fully understood in New Hampshire, the loyalist Democrats turned up the patriotism knob to full blast. Carefully modulated, a-vote-for-McCarthy-is-a-vote-for-Hanoi might have worked. In the event, its crudity shocked many Democrats. Radio slots urged them not to vote for "fuzzy thinking and surrender." On March 6, a full-page advertisement in the New Hampshire newspapers reminded them "the Communists in Vietnam are watching the New Hampshire primary." Governor King labeled McCarthy "a champion of appeasement and surrender." The faithful Senator McIntyre weighed in with a reference to McCarthy, the friend of "draft-dodgers and deserters." It was too much, and too late. McCarthy charged the opposition with McCarthyism (Joe's brand) and found public sympathy flowing his way.

Meanwhile, news of McCarthy successes was coming in from out-of-state. In California, his supporters secured the much-prized number-one slot on the ballot by gathering thirty-five thousand petition signatures. In his home state of Minnesota, the Senator's followers had demonstrated a technique for picking up delegate votes in nonprimary states. In Minnesota, delegates are selected partly through the mechanism of the local caucus of party faithfuls. The McCarthy workers packed the early caucuses (in years past, some of these had been run by only four or five party regulars) and snatched fifteen delegate places from the professionals.

Against these morale-boosters for the McCarthy operation, the Johnson men had nothing but more blood, sweat, and tears for their own loyalists. The President was closeted with his top civil and military advisers, and news leaked that they were considering sending another two hundred thousand men to Vietnam. New Hampshire could hardly take kindly to this new development. Because most of its communities are relatively small and close-knit, it was a state already deeply conscious of the toll of the war; most residents knew, or knew of, a family that had lost a relative in Vietnam.

Five days before polling, Bootin, knowing the latest Quayle findings, raised the ceiling on the McCarthy vote yet again. "It would be a disgrace," he maintained, "if McCarthy gets less than forty per cent of the vote." But it still was not high enough for Bootin and all who served under him to escape humiliation. Just to make life more unbearable, it snowed—hard—on polling day. It was weather to favor the more highly motivated voters, and there was not much doubt about which camp had those. At the Johnson headquarters in Manchester, three small rooms above a law office, a disconsolate McIntyre aide looked out the window at the factory workers, heads down, trudging through a minor blizzard. "There they go," he complained, "all our voters . . . straight home to the television."

All the action was over in the Wayfarer, where three hundred of McCarthy's youthful volunteer army watched the votes coming in, cheering each McCarthy gain to the echo. One of the original Hoeh-Studds group, Sylvia Chaplain, an attractive middle-aged lady with a "Goodbye Lyndon" button pinned to her dress, got up and made a speech. "I was a rather tired liberal, I admit. But I'm not tired any more. You young people have given me new strength." It was that kind of occasion. The biggest cheer, of course, was for McCarthy himself, who made an impromptu midnight speech. "People have remarked," he said, "that this campaign has brought young people back into the system. But it's the other way around: The young people have brought the country back into the system."

It was hard to know what was going on in the candidate's mind. If he felt surprised by what he had started, he did not show it. Lowenstein, in the gaggle of people behind him on the platform, seemed ready to burst with happiness. Goodwin, unsmiling and looking slightly bored, stood with arms folded and surveyed the eager young faces (perhaps pondering how to get them equally enthusiastic about Bobby Kennedy). When the applause for the candidate died away, a young shining-faced girl turned to a friend and said, "He's so humble." Humble or not, McCarthy was now a serious candidate.

Meanwhile, New Hampshire Republicans had a virtually unchallenged front-runner in Richard M. Nixon. Two weeks before polling day, his principal opponent, George Romney, had decided to write off an investment of a million dollars in his Presidential aspirations and withdraw from the race. It was not covert butchery in a smoke-filled room, or even the result of a sudden access of modesty on the candidate's part. It was euthanasia: rational self-destruction.

Romney's opinion pollsters, the technicians who had guided him through his boom years in Midwestern politics, had informed him that Nixon was leading him 70.3 per cent to 11.3 per cent among New Hampshire Republicans, and they could see no prospect of any startling change. Their sixty-year-old candidate, a Mormon, who had first achieved national prominence as the man who had dragged American Motors out of the red with a messianic effort to convert America to the compact car, had already tried everything and failed. His campaign had been built to the most precise specifications—but the product was Ford's Edsel, not Romney's Rambler. The voters just would not buy him.

Romney's problem, one not uncommon in American politics, had been his inability to make the jump from state to national politics. A candidate for national office is subject to relentless exposure in a way that no governor ever is. Campaign reporters live in close proximity to the candidate, and cherished standards of "objectivity" can slip if they find the job tiresome. McCarthy was hard to forgive because he mocked them, but he was at least amusing. Romney's condition, however, was incurable; he was boring, and this, combined with his jejune approach to international affairs and his somewhat ostentatious piety, had been his undoing.

In fact, he never really recovered from his clumsy remarks on Vietnam in the summer of 1967. At that time, Romney alleged that his confusion on the subject was largely due to his having been "brainwashed" by the President. This was true, of course; most Americans had been. But it did not inspire respect for the toughness of Romney's mental equipment. The press, almost gleeful at the opportunity, crucified the unfortunate governor. In New Hampshire, Romney's efforts to re-establish himself sometimes assumed an almost manic aspect. He had a tendency to draw voters on with his handshake and enfold them in a bear hug. The technique frequently had the opposite of the desired effect. Romney became part of the nation's folklore as a political buffoon, and no amount of costly advertising could remedy an image like that.

Asked by reporters whether he thought Romney's "brainwashed" *gaffe* had dealt the death blow to his chances, McCarthy replied, "Well . . . er no, not really. Anyway, I think in that case a light rinse would have been sufficient." McCarthy's press aides, appalled at the possible effects of this remark on Republicans who, bereft of a dove candidate in their own party, might write in McCarthy's name, pleaded with reporters not to use it. They dutifully complied; though few would have done the same for Romney.

With Romney safely back in Michigan, Nixon was denied the kudos of a potent victory ceremony. He rolled up 79 per cent of the Republican vote in the primary, but did this really mean that he had shed his loser's image? He was, after all, without opposition.

Nixon's campaign was well financed—almost five hundred thousand dollars was spent on reaching New Hampshire's 190,000 registered Republicans—and clinically well organized. "Nixon's the One," the campaign slogan which endured through the year, appropriately suggested a reluctance to fuzz the voters' minds with issues. The improvements in Nixon's style since 1960 were much commented upon. He seemed more relaxed, smiling easily and frequently, but the substance, if anything, seemed even thinner than of yore. In his set-piece rallies, he would promise "to end the war and win the peace," but the methods by which this desirable outcome could be achieved were left unspoken. An aide proudly described The Speech (Nixon rarely deviated from the same text) as a "prose poem," and it did have a comfortable kind of rhythm. But like rain on limestone, the words fell on the ear and then mysteriously trickled away. Nixon is a consummate master of the art of speaking much and saying nothing. Apart from frequent declarations of the need for "New Leadership," it was apparent that the new Nixon had decided to steer clear of specifics, at least until somebody forced him into debate.

The only man on the Republican horizon likely to do this was Nelson Rockefeller, Governor of New York. All through 1967, Rockefeller, a two-time contender for the Republican nomination, had faithfully backed George Romney, proferring advice, manpower, and expertise. The New Yorker had waxed, publicly at least, almost lyrical on Romney's qualifications as a champion of liberal Republicanism. But doubts had crept in. Asked privately in January what he thought about Romney's damaging impulsiveness, Rockefeller suggested, "You'd better ask a psychiatrist." Such reflections and other odd signs of restlessness on Rockefeller's part obviously eroded Romney's gratitude to his quondam mentor. When he withdrew from the race, Romney pointedly declined to have any part of a draft-Rockefeller operation.

Rockefeller himself, however, lost no time in hinting at his possible availability. While publicly deterring voters from writing in his name in the New Hampshire primary, a generously financed drive in this direction arose from the ashes of the Romney candidacy. Rockefeller write-ins wound up as 11 per cent of the primary vote, not nearly enough to evince "spontaneous" grass-roots support for his nomination—but a start had been made. Meanwhile, pressure on Rockefeller to run was mounting at more exalted levels of the party. After New Hampshire, it was no longer a question of whether Rockefeller would make his third entry into the Presidential lists, but when.

ACT IV

The Tide of Fearful Faction

1

The Restless Tiger

"Only those who dare to fail greatly can ever achieve greatly."

—Robert F. Kennedy, *To Seek a Newer World*

"It is absolutely necessary that rebellion find its reasons within itself, since it cannot find them elsewhere. It must consent to examine itself in order to learn how to act."

—Albert Camus, *The Rebel*

There are well over two thousand political reporters in Washington, and at any given moment a good half of them would give their right arms for the same thing: half an hour with the man of the moment. No leading Senator, no Secretary of State or Defense, could possibly spare the time to see all the journalists who would like to see him. And so there have grown up several little informal clubs of journalists in Washington who, every month or so, invite a great man to lunch, or even—for great men's schedules tend to be crowded—to breakfast. The usual convention is that those present may report what is said, even, if they wish, in their guest's exact words, so long as they do not reveal that he is their source. There is an element of fiction in this, and sometimes even of comedy; there are days when half the leading political correspondents in the country arrive at identical conclusions, ostensibly by independent sucking on their pipes. But it is a useful fiction, for both sides, and it is therefore not likely to disappear in a hurry.

It didn't take any exceptional journalistic perspicacity to see who was the man of the moment in Washington in the middle of January 1968. For months, every journalist in the city had been doing his best to read the contradictory scraps of evidence about Robert Kennedy's intentions into a coherent pattern, and to make up his mind whether Kennedy would decide to run or not. So it was quite a feather in the cap for Godfrey Sperling, of the *Christian Science Monitor,* when he was able to tell the members of his background group that Kennedy would have breakfast with them, in the President's Room in the National Press Club, on January 30.

Kennedy was in a dark and brooding mood. How did he feel about the pressure on him to run? one of the journalists asked. "Badly," he said with a quick, wry grin, "badly." What did he think about the McCarthy campaign? "I think it is being helpful to President Johnson." Well, was he going to run? "No, I can't conceive of any circumstances in which I would run."

He talked starkly about the things that had gone wrong: "I feel that the war is one of the greatest disasters of all time." He talked about racial tensions, about the generation gap between young people, "with their drugs and sex," and their parents. "They just don't have any kind of respect for older people," he said with amazement. That wasn't the way he had been brought up, or the way he was bringing up his ten children. "I think these problems are going to intensify. There is a strong feeling among middle-class whites against the Negroes. In New York City, the Democratic leaders have a strong feeling against the Negroes. They just don't like them."

And then for a moment he talked wistfully about the campaign he would have liked to run. "If someone could appeal to the generous spirit of Americans to heal the race question, this is what the campaign should be about. You must appeal to the generous spirit of Americans. This is what a campaign is about." He added, less than generously, "McCarthy is unable to tap this spirit."

"Well then," one of the reporters asked, "if you feel so strongly about some of these issues, why don't you take a stand and run despite the possibility of defeat?" It wasn't just a matter of opposing the President, he answered heavily. There was the Democratic Party to think about, and the Republican candidate. "My running would automatically elect a Republican by splitting the Democratic Party, and Democratic candidates would be beaten all over the country." Then why not support LBJ? Everybody laughed.

Another questioner pressed the point. "Aren't principles more important than political victory?" "If I thought there was anything I could do about it, I would try to do something."

Recognizing a major story when they saw one, some of the journalists pressed Kennedy to make an exception to the usual rule and find a form of words that they could put in his mouth, "on the record." "All right," he said, "in no conceivable circumstances would I run." His press secretary, Frank Mankiewicz, who had been hoping for months that he would run, managed to persuade him to modify that absolute negative to "in no *foreseeable* circumstances." That was as far as he would be moved. And so, the next morning, the *New York Times* reported quite calmly, on page 19, that "Senator Kennedy told a group of reporters breakfasting with him: 'I have told friends and supporters who are urging me to run that I would not oppose Lyndon Johnson under any foreseeable circumstances.' "

It sounded both inevitable and final, but it had not been the one, and it was not to be the other. Less than two weeks before, Robert Kennedy had come within inches of taking the opposite way out of the dilemma that had been perplexing him for so long. On January 19, he was in New York to make a round of speaking engagements in suburban Westchester County. That day, the President had announced the appointment of Clark Clifford to succeed Kennedy's close friend, Robert McNamara, as Secretary of Defense. Kennedy had been deeply perturbed about the war for months. Now he was aghast. "He might just as well have appointed Attila the Hun!" he muttered savagely to two friends in the car with him. Both the friends—Jack Newfield and Mrs. Ronnie Eldridge—were passionately in favor of his running, and to them he rehearsed the arguments of caution and calculation.

Before he would run, he said, one of three conditions would have to be met. He would have to be convinced that Lyndon Johnson was actually psychotic. Or he would have to be asked to run by the Senate doves—men like George McGovern, Frank Church, and J. William Fulbright, who were afraid that his candidacy would hurt, not help, their own campaigns. Or, thirdly, he would have to be urged to run by "one more politician of the national stature of Unruh." Jesse Unruh, speaker of the California State Assembly, was the most powerful Democrat in the largest state. He was one of the first "practical politicians" to come out in favor of Kennedy's running. The news that he had taken a large bet on the question with a fellow professional, at the state Democratic committee meeting in Fresno a couple of weeks earlier, had powerfully stimulated rumors that Kennedy was going to run. (Unruh says he never did collect.)

And on the strength of Unruh's case—reinforced by the judgment of another Californian, Fred Dutton, a Washington lawyer who had served in John Kennedy's Administration and who had become very close to Robert Kennedy since 1966—a poll had been commissioned and carried out by the Kennedy pollster, John Kraft. It showed that Kennedy could do very well in the California primary. There was Unruh, and there was Harold Hughes, Governor of Iowa, ex-truck-driver, ex-alcoholic, and an excitingly practical liberal, also urging him to run. Still Kennedy wanted more. He mentioned no names to his friends that day. But it is not too hard to guess the "one other national politician" he had in mind: Richard Daley, Mayor of Chicago, and the last remaining boss in the Democratic Party who might be able to "deliver" the convention vote of a major state. Daley had idolized John Kennedy. He had his reservations about the younger brother, but he had reservations about Vietnam too. He could see what harm the war was doing to the party. If Daley could be persuaded to consider the unthinkable and join the rebellion, then, with New York, California, and Illinois, the unthinkable might not be too risky.

That same evening, at a cocktail party in New York, Kennedy ran into Melina Mercouri, the Greek actress, for whom politics is a matter not of subtle calculation but of epic simplicity. She has been known to slap a man in the face for disagreeing with her about politics. In her most Sophoclean manner she swept up to Kennedy and said, "You don't want to be the man of whom history will say, 'He waited too long'!"

Robert Kennedy was capable of responding to the impassioned entreaties of his liberal friends with cool political calculation. That did not mean that he was necessarily impressed by those who used cool and calculating arguments against his running. That same weekend, as it happened, he was much moved when his wife, Ethel, after listening to the cautious arguments his brother's former speech-writer, Theodore Sorensen, made against her husband's running, burst out contemptuously: "With all your high-flown statements about morality, how *can* you say he shouldn't run on political grounds!"

Whatever the reason, that night in New York, January 19, he did come very close to making up his mind to go. At dinner with his brother-in-law Stephen Smith, chief manager of the family finances, and young Carter Burden, from his New York office, he turned to Smith and said laconically, "I think I'm going to cost you a lot of money this year!"

On Sunday, in a television discussion, he edged closer toward an open break with the Administration on Vietnam. He denounced the policy of insisting on "unconditional surrender" and called for a bombing halt and a negotiated peace. Then something happened. He had always been afraid that if he did run he could be destroyed by some utterly unforeseeable, uncontrollable act of fate. With his family's history, it was an understandable preoccupation. What happened between the dinner with Smith and Sperling's breakfast was something very remote indeed. It was the seizure by the North Koreans of the U.S. electronic espionage vessel *Pueblo.* In logic, there was not perhaps much reason why the *Pueblo* incident should have made Robert Kennedy change his mind. But the next day he made it plain to Allard Lowenstein that it did. For it was a reminder of other uncontrollable things that might happen, and that could put it in Lyndon Johnson's power to destroy him.

At Sperling's breakfast that day in the Press Club, the reporters were passing to and fro scraps of tape torn from the wire machines—the first reports that heavy street fighting had broken out in Saigon and other South Vietnamese cities. The Tet offensive—"the most important historical event of 1968," in the view of John Kenneth Galbraith—had begun. Twenty-four hours later, Robert Kennedy realized that he had made what one of his friends called "the mistake of his life." Had the breakfast been a day later or the attack a day earlier, those who were closest to him at the time agree, Kennedy would have made no such statement, and very probably he would soon have been a candidate. In the long perspective of his decision whether or not to challenge Lyndon Johnson, the events of January were only one episode. But it brought into play all the complex thrusts and strains, for and against, that held him immobile, in paralyzed equilibrium, for so long.

Like some young prince of the Renaissance, Robert Kennedy liked to think that all human experience was to be tasted and enjoyed. He lived at the center of a vortex of the most varied and surprising people, from whom he sought excitement, instruction, fun, and advice. The Oxford philosopher Isaiah Berlin was a friend of his, and so was the pop singer Andy Williams; the crew-cut astronaut John Glenn and the shaggy revolutionary Tom Hayden were equally likely to be found at his table. Any occasion—a plane journey, a dinner party, a quiet weekend on Cape Cod—was likely to turn into an anguished debate on the future of the country and of his own political career. Sometimes, like a French monarch granting the privilege of the greater or the lesser levée, he would continue these discussions even while he dressed or undressed. On one occasion his faithful Boswell, Newfield, and Richard Goodwin were invited to advise him while strapping him into his cummerbund for a

dinner to which neither had been invited; nobody in the Kennedy circle
would see anything odd in that.

As we shall see, it sometimes happened that a chance conversation
with a relative stranger struck a chord in Kennedy and affected the ebb
and flow of his hesitations, just as Melina Mercouri managed to touch a
nerve of quixotism. But at the heart of the vast concentric circles of his
friends, counselors, and acquaintances there were three groups whose
advice on the great question—to run or not to run—was so regularly
taken that it took on the settled structure of a debate.

There was the family. That meant especially his brother Ted; his
sisters Jean and Pat; Jean's husband, Stephen Smith; and above all his
wife, Ethel. There was the undefined but always articulate round table
of Camelot, his brother's friends and advisers. And there was his own
staff. Beyond these groups there was a handful of others who could claim
to be close enough for one reason or another to be "Kennedy men":
Richard Goodwin, Fred Dutton, William vanden Heuvel, and two journalists who had worked for him in the Justice Department, Ed Guthman
of the *Los Angeles Times,* and John Siegenthaler of the *Nashville
Tennessean.*

It was the measure of Robert Kennedy's own personal tilt to the
left that his staff was always far more radically inclined than his elder
brother's. Many things combined to influence his personal evolution.
Inside government, he had acquired a deep suspicion of the military and
intelligence establishments, especially as a result of the Bay of Pigs. His
move to New York after he was elected Senator brought him into touch
with the traditionally radical intellectuals of New York City, whose style
he enjoyed. His travels made him aware of poverty and alienation
abroad, and of the contrast, which he found shameful, between the
revolutionary ideals of American tradition and the reactionary image
that the United States had acquired in the world. In the Justice Department he had come face to face with the racial crisis in America, and in
New York the ghetto and its angry leaders were part of his constituency.

But above and beyond the particular circumstances of his experience, this change from the hard young Irish investigator that he was in
his twenties—his radical friends call it his "conversion"—was all of a
piece with his character. As the runt of an intensely physical and competitive family, as the underweight Kennedy who made the Harvard
football team, he had had from his earliest childhood an almost obses-
sional drive to prove himself. That drive took him not merely up moun-

tains or down the Colorado River to prove his fitness and courage, but into the ghettos and *barrios* to prove his humanity.

From the moment Lyndon Johnson took the oath of office as President, there were many who looked to Robert Kennedy as the eventual restorer of the House of Kennedy. That was a very different thing, however, from suggesting he not wait until 1972 but contemplate the unheard-of audacity of challenging an incumbent President of his own party. Significantly, the honor of being the first to urge that course fell to one of the young men in his Senate office, none of whom had worked for President Kennedy. The very day after the mid-term elections of 1966, Adam Walinsky laid on his desk a memorandum urging just that, and containing the words, "Lyndon Johnson is a lame duck."

This may have been the first formal presentation of the case for running against Johnson, but Kennedy had discussed the hypothetical possibility at least a month earlier. On October 1, 1966, and again on October 16, he had had long talks with Goodwin, who argued that, quite independently of Vietnam, the President's popularity would decline and Kennedy's would rise, because people hated Johnson's personality, not merely his style or his policies. On the other hand, Goodwin emphasized that Johnson would stop at nothing to defeat Kennedy: "He would dump Humphrey and even stop the war if necessary to defeat you."

For the whole of 1967, all Kennedy's staff assistants in his Senate office—Walinsky, Peter Edelman, Joseph Dolan, Frank Mankiewicz, and, after he joined in the summer, Jeff Greenfield—were heart and mind in favor of his running. They argued that the President could be beaten; but they laid more emphasis on the idea that, even if he could not, the moral imperative to stop the war and to divert the country's resources and energies back to the racial and urban crises was so urgent that Kennedy must run even if he could not win.

Almost equally to a man, the older generation of Kennedy men urged caution. The Young Turks suspected and disliked the veterans of Camelot. Their affluence rankled, for one thing. Arthur Schlesinger's memoir, *A Thousand Days,* and Ted Sorensen's *Kennedy* had been best sellers. Sorensen had a large retainer to advise, of all things, General Motors. And Pierre Salinger had bounced in and out of a series of business ventures, all of them at least financially sucessful. But ideology and a generation gap were involved, as well as envy. "Those New Frontier cats were out of the fifties," one of the Young Turks said, pronouncing the decade with wonder and distaste as an old, ill-favored thing.

"Don't forget that JFK campaigned in sixty on Quemoy and Matsu and that Cold War crap, and on some mythical polls about how our prestige was down in Europe."

The Young Turks were not altogether fair to the men of Camelot, whose caution was in most cases not the result of cooling ardor so much as of longer exposure to the conventional wisdom of Washington, and indeed to the traditional caution of the Kennedys themselves. "Bob always used to take the same line with any of his friends who called and asked his advice about running for office themselves," one of them recalled. "The first question he would ask would always be 'Can you win? If you can win, then you should run. If you can't, don't.' "

The older generation of Kennedy's friends were telling him no more than, in one mood, he was telling himself: that he had every chance of being the nominee in 1972, that an incumbent President "couldn't" be disloged, that to challenge Lyndon Johnson would look like, and would be made to look like, the "ruthless," "arrogant" greed of a man who claimed a hereditary right to the Presidency, and would therefore split the Democratic Party from top to bottom. Some of them argued, too, that the country was drifting so far to the right that *no* Democrat could win in 1968. None of them gave much thought to the argument that Kennedy should run even if he knew he had no chance of winning. That would not have been "pragmatic," which, with "tough-minded," was the favorite epithet on the New Frontier. Besides, they thought they knew their man better than that.

From the men in the family—from his brother Ted and from Steve Smith—he got much the same prudent political advice as from his brother's friends. With the women, it was different. Later, when Schlesinger joined their side of the argument, Kennedy told him: "You and my wife and sisters are the only ones who want me to run" (which should perhaps be a warning against exaggerating the weight he gave to the young tearaways like Walinsky, Hamill, Edelman, Newfield, and Lowenstein). Ethel Kennedy was a woman who luckily had been able to identify her own happiness completely with the happiness of her husband and her children without losing a certain slightly unsophisticated sharpness of mind and an unshakable toughness of character. Jesse Unruh calls her "the one of the Kennedy women with *real* class," and guesses that her advice, and possibly that of his sisters, counted for more with her husband than all the arguments of all the intellectuals. For her, it was a simple matter. She wanted him to be happy. She thought that in his heart of hearts he thought that he ought to run, and that he would not be happy if he didn't. Therefore, she wanted him to run. . . . At her Christmas party, on December 23, a young guest plucked up his courage and asked if Bobby would run. She grinned and crossed her fingers, and said, "I hope so!"

The truth was that the arguments between his advisers always reflected the conflict in Kennedy himself. At forty-two, he had not yet been forced by life, or had not yet consented, to make those final choices which set a man's character in what we call maturity. His personality could only be described by listing pairs of opposites, all of which might be true, but which still did not add up to a final or a satisfying answer to the question: What sort of a man is this, and how will he act? The slim figure, high color, untidy hair, and springy, nervous movements made him look boyish; and so did a sly smile which would sometimes broaden into a devastating grin of complicity. Yet if you looked at his cool blue eyes you saw that he was a man whose experience had not left him unaware of the tragic injustices of life, or of the potentialities of human beings for evil. He was widely regarded as ruthless, yet he could be both sensitive and vulnerable. He was gay, and also fatalistic; cynical, but also idealistic: impulsive by nature, and calculating by habit. "He hadn't decided what kind of person he was," says one of his admirers. "He was the existential man," says another, "he was defining himself by his actions." He felt the need to live up to a code of chivalry. Show him a mountain, and he would want to climb it. But present him with a choice with infinitely ramified consequences for himself, for his friends, for a political party, and for the country: what would he do then?

In the summer of 1967, as we have seen, he was going out of his way to endorse a President whom he privately suspected of insanity. In September, neither Lowenstein nor Galbraith could shake his conviction that to challenge Johnson would be self-defeating because it would be set down to ambition and would split the party. On November 2, he learned that McCarthy was going to split it anyway. On that day, he dined with Arthur Schlesinger, who had just learned of McCarthy's probable decision from Joe Rauh. The next morning Schlesinger sat down and summarized the case he had made in a long letter.

"McCarthy has definitely decided to go," Schlesinger wrote.

> It would be a fatal error in my judgment to say anything which would be construed as your backing Johnson against McCarthy. To do so would be to convince a lot of people, especially the young, that you prefer politics to principle. . . .
> If it would be fatal to back Johnson, it would not seem to make

great sense to back McCarthy. If you are going to do that, you might as well run yourself. . . . Until recently, I have argued against the idea of your trying anything in 1968. My main ground has been that, while you might conceivably get the nomination . . . the fight would shatter the party . . . [and] result in making Nixon President.

I am now having second thoughts about this argument. I think the country is feeling increasingly that the escalation policy has had a full and fair trial . . . and that we must therefore have a new President.

I think that events are moving faster than one could have supposed three months ago, and the situation may be highly fluid in another three months. I think that you could beat LBJ in the primaries and that you have surprising reserves of strength in the non-primary states. And if all this should lead the Republicans to nominate Nixon, so much the better. . . .

If you were to decide to go, it would have to be done in a way which would not reinforce the theory of ruthless ambition or the theory that you are indulging a personal feud against the President. Ideally, you ought to be asked to run by a group of leading Democrats. In this connection, I tentatively wonder whether you should not have a talk with McCarthy. I know well that he has not been high on the Kennedys through the years; also that he is a somewhat indolent and frivolous man. On the other hand, he evidently cares deeply about the Vietnam mess. It is still probable that he might be willing to stand aside and support you. . . .

This last guess of Schlesinger's was wrong. McCarthy and Kennedy did talk in November, and their meeting was a comedy of misunderstanding. But for the rest, it was a persuasive analysis, and Kennedy's political conscience must have flinched from certain phrases: "to convince a lot of people, *especially the young,* that you prefer politics to principle." That was the last thing in the world he wanted to do.

Schlesinger was still in a minority. In November, a first council of war was held. Pierre Salinger, in New York for a few days, invited to a meeting in his suite at the Regency Hotel on Park Avenue about two dozen people, including some who were by no stretch of the imagination members of the inner Kennedy ring. But Dutton, Sorensen, Stephen Smith, Ted Kennedy, Kenneth O'Donnell, and Dick Goodwin were there, and so were some practicing politicians—John Burns and Jack English from New York, Pat Lucey and Ivan Nestigan from Wisconsin. None of the Young Turks was asked, and Goodwin was the only person who spoke out in favor of Kennedy's running. Kennedy himself was not there.

There was another meeting on December 10, after McCarthy's announcement. This time it was at Bill vanden Heuvel's home, and the attendance was slightly more restricted. But once again, the Walinskys and the Edelmans were not invited. Goodwin and Schlesinger spoke for Kennedy's running, and Ted Kennedy and Sorensen deployed all the familiar arguments against: that an incumbent President had never been denied the nomination, that Kennedy would split the party if he ran, that this would guarantee Nixon's election. Dutton was silent and uncertain; Kennedy said unhappily at one point that Schlesinger was morally right, but that Sorensen was politically right. Later, he was to say that he was reminded of the cabinet meeting at which the Bay of Pigs adventure was approved: he felt that he ought to run, but the weight of expert opinion among the friends whose advice he had come to trust seemed too great to go against; and the question was posed in terms that made the answer inevitable. For most of the survivors from Camelot, the question was still not "How can we save the country? but "What will be best for Bob's career?"

Yet Kennedy was not the only one whose conscience was troubling him. Pete Hamill, who had left the *New York Post* to go and live in Ireland and write a novel about Che Guevara, had seen quite a bit of Kennedy during the fall. He is a vehement young man, a bomb thrower by nature, and he was deeply suspicious of the JFK men. So he was astonished to discover, when he ran into Kenny O'Donnell in Boston in the first week in December, that O'Donnell too had changed his mind. Something peculiar was happening in the country, O'Donnell said; "Bob had better get out and run in sixty-eight or he can forget about seventy-two." O'Donnell had been John Kennedy's appointments secretary and the guardian of his political secrets, a grimly loyal black Irishman. He was also Bob Kennedy's oldest hero, the football captain who gave him his letter at Harvard; and now O'Donnell too was disgusted by the war and thought that Kennedy had no alternative in honor but to run.

Another weight had been picked out of one pan of the scales and dropped into the other. And so it went on. There were no more big formal meetings, but Bobby's life had become one continuous debate. Everybody he talked to became an advocate in it. Almost everything that happened became converted into an argument pro or anti. With McCarthy in the field, and with the brightest and best of the young people in his own New York and Cambridge rallying to him, Kennedy became more sensitive than ever to anything that seemed to make his hesitation a matter of cowardice. And by January that was what people were calling it. As he performed the cliff-top quadrille we watched at the beginning of this chapter, the very journalists who had smothered him and his brother with flattery now seemed to be enjoying his predicament. "Artful dodging," said *Newsweek,* slyly reminding him that his brother had written a book called *Profiles in Courage.*

He was hurt by the characters which the cartoonist Jules Feiffer invented in January called the Bobby Twins:

> "We're going in there and we're killing South Vietnamese, we're killing children, we're killing women—we're killing innocent people because we don't want the war fought on American soil" [says the Good Bobby]. "Do we have that right here in the United States to perform these acts because we want to protect ourselves? I very seriously question whether we have that right. All of us should examine our consciences on what we are doing in South Vietnam."
>
> [To which the Bad Bobby replies:] "I will back the Democratic candidate in 1968. I expect that will be President Johnson."
>
> "I think we're going to have a difficult time explaining this to ourselves!" [says the Good Bobby].

That was shrewd enough. But both Bobbys were upset when, at Brooklyn College, where Kennedy went to deliver a lecture in memory of his brother, he was met by cruel placards:

BOBBY KENNEDY: HAWK, DOVE, OR CHICKEN?

That touched his honor, and hurt his pride. It was also an ominous signal of political danger. One of those who had argued against his running at the December 10 meeting understood the double thrust—political and personal. "He hated to see the constituency he had built up so carefully among the young, and which had had so much effect on his own development as a person, turning to someone else. That really hurt."

On January 31, the morning after the breakfast at the Press Club, Pete Hamill was listening to the B.B.C. as he was getting up to face his typewriter for another day in his rented house in Howth, on the misty northern horn of Dublin Bay. When he heard what Kennedy had said, he laid Che Guevara aside until he had hammered out a long letter to Kennedy. Hamill is a romantic of the tough school. He likes boxing and he loves courage. He is also a gifted writer. What he said to Kennedy, with a bluntness that Arthur Schlesinger does not use, and with a frankness which only something close to disappointed love could excuse, was that a generation of Americans had looked to him as the only man who could restore their faith in their country, and that he had betrayed their trust.

On Thursday, February 8, Kennedy flew to Chicago, where he had breakfast privately with Mayor Daley and spoke at a "book-and-author lunch" sponsored by the *Chicago Sun-Times.* It was the strongest speech he had yet given against the war. "Our enemy," he began, "savagely striking at will across all of South Vietnam, has finally shattered the mask of official illusion with which we have concealed our true circumstances, even from ourselves." Relentlessly, he ticked off the illusions and set out his version of the truth. "We must actively seek a peaceful settlement. We can no longer harden our terms whenever Hanoi indicates it may be prepared to negotiate, and we must be prepared to foresee a settlement which will give the Vietcong a chance to participate in the political life of the country . . . the best way to end casualties is to end the war . . . it is the truth that makes us free."

That night, in the plane going back to Washington, he seemed set free from the gloom that had covered him all week. His mood was so cheerful that Frank Mankiewicz was emboldened to show him some of the letters he had left unread. One of them was the letter from Dublin. Kennedy was so upset by it that when the plane landed at Washington he went straight home without a word to anyone.

At the beginning of January, Kennedy had asked his staff aide Joe Dolan to do a paper on the requirements for entry in each of the state Presidential primaries. Shortly after that, he had Dolan and Steve Smith do a telephone check with Kennedy agents in each of the primary states. In January and again in February, John Kraft came up with encouraging polls from California. But the news from Wisconsin, the state with the second primary (after New Hampshire), was not so hopeful. The chief Kennedy man there was Pat Lucey, a bookish Irish real-estate man in Madison, the state capital. In late January, Lucey got a call from Smith asking him to go to New York to talk to Bob about running. "I went there armed with a Wisconsin state poll which had just been taken. It showed Johnson with 80 per cent and McCarthy with only 13 per cent. That was before Tet. I told Bob very strenuously not to run because I thought Johnson would kill both him and McCarthy. Bob was terribly torn. He kept telling me that Schlesinger and others were urging him to run, and that Ethel was very strong for him running. I said practical politics said that he shouldn't. I didn't see Bob for a while after that, but I heard from Steve Smith several times. Then, a week before New Hampshire, Steve called me and said, 'My tiger is getting restless!' "

He was indeed. On Sunday evening, March 3, Frank Mankiewicz called his boss at home to remind him to watch a television program Jack Newfield had made about the Bedford-Stuyvesant ghetto, a subject near to Kennedy's heart. "You'll have to watch it for me, Frank," he said. "We're having a sort of a meeting out here." It was Kenny O'Donnell's birthday, and he was there, along with Fred Dutton and Ted Sorensen. They talked late; so late that Kennedy didn't get into his office the next day until around noon. That was the day the Senate Foreign Relations Committee hearings on Vietnam began, and the television set in the Senator's office was tuned in to them as his private debate went on. From time to time he or his aides would check another opinion with a long-distance phone call: to Ted Kennedy, to John Siegenthaler in Nashville, to Burke Marshall in New York. Dutton was now arguing the case for going in. He had seen the third of Kraft's polls, done for Jesse Unruh, and it seemed to show more plainly than ever that Kennedy could win California. Sorensen was still against. He even argued against Kennedy's idea of going out to be with his friend Cesar Chavez, the leader of the California grape strike. Chavez was due to end a protest fast the next weekend. But Sorensen was losing the argument; perhaps had already lost. The weights were being picked up and put into the other pan at an accelerating rhythm: the scales were beginning to tilt.

On February 29, the Kerner Commission reported. Kennedy's neighbor in McLean, Virginia, Senator Fred Harris of Oklahoma, had been the man on the Commission who insisted that the report face up to the facts of white racism in America. He had, in fact, done a good deal of the writing of it. He and his American Indian wife, LaDonna, had become close friends of the Kennedys'. So when the President—to whom Harris remained loyal—snubbed the report, that was just one more sign to Kennedy that he was incorrigible. The same day, McNamara left the Pentagon, leaving Kennedy more pessimistic than ever about the future of the war. (Symbolically, McNamara's departure was pure farce. He got stuck in an elevator with the President, and the public-address system broke down!)

As the duty to run seemed to grow more imperative, the danger seemed to diminish. The press was now in full cry after the Administration on the issue of the war. American troops were in danger of a Dienbienphu at Khe Sanh, and the Communist flag waved stubbornly from the citadel of Hué. The voters seemed to be changing too. Kraft's polls made California look promising. Pat Lucey began to change his tune about Wisconsin. And Bill Dunfey, Kennedy's lieutenant in New Hampshire, was making some strange predictions about what might happen there. The war was so unpopular, he said, that McCarthy might end up with over thirty per cent of the vote. A week before the New Hampshire primary, in fact, Kennedy was ready to go. The discussions went on. But now the question was no longer *whether,* but *how:* how to announce, and how to campaign once he was in.

Before the end of the week, Steve Smith and Joe Dolan had been packed off to California to help Jesse Unruh pick a slate of Kennedy delegates. On Friday, March 8, Ted Kennedy was given a far more delicate assignment: to tell Eugene McCarthy that Robert Kennedy might be on the point of stepping in to harvest his crop. Ted Kennedy thought this would be a mistake, and he never made the call. He said later he was afraid McCarthy might have used it against his brother in the closing days of the primary campaign. It wasn't until Robert Kennedy got back from California, late on Sunday, that he discovered that McCarthy had not been warned. And it wasn't until Monday that he asked Richard Goodwin to break the news. Goodwin was understandably not enthusiastic about this assignment. His standing in the McCarthy camp was still doubtful, precisely because he was suspected of being a Trojan Horse for the Kennedys. And McCarthy was not an easy man to approach on behalf of the Kennedys at the best of times. The upshot was that it wasn't until Tuesday evening, March 12, the very night of his triumph, that McCarthy learned it might be taken from him. The delay did nothing to improve relations between the two candidates.

The night the New Hampshire votes came in, Kennedy was in New York to speak at a United Jewish Appeal dinner. Afterward, he went out for a late meal at "21" with Arthur Schlesinger and Bill vanden Heuvel. He was not particularly surprised by the result—Dunfey had warned him to expect something like this. Nor was he visibly upset. It was simply that it made his decision more urgent than ever.

On the Monday afternoon before the primary, Steve Smith's office had called the faithful to a grand and final strategy meeting in his apartment set for four o'clock Wednesday. There was a deadline. If Kennedy was to get into the California primary, and it was his best hope, he must announce by Monday, March 18.

Yet even at this late stage, Kennedy's vacillation was not over. That, at least, is the most convincing explanation of one of the most ambiguous transactions of the whole year: the puzzling affair of the "peace commission." No one can claim to be sure what happened. It was like a deadly and ingenious game, in which each of the three players knew only his own intentions. The stakes were undeniably high: nothing less than the issue of war and peace and the disposition of the office of President of the United States. And the three players were the three most powerful politicians in the Democratic Party: Robert Kennedy, Richard Daley, and Lyndon Johnson.

The story begins with the breakfast meeting of Daley and Kennedy in Chicago on February 8. Surprisingly for those who think of him only as an iron-fisted, wooden-headed bully, Daley had been deeply troubled by the war for months. He knew that it was bad politics; that it could divide the Democratic Party and perhaps cost it not only the Presidency, but also elections nearer home. Daley's loyalty to the Democratic Party is as absolute as his loyalty to his city or his church, so he has a natural antipathy to the sight of Republicans holding patronage jobs in Cook County—or jobs, such as state attorney general, with broad powers of investigation. But there was a second, more personal, reason for his opposition to the war. Some years before, he had helped to get a place at Harvard for the son of one of his friends. The boy had done exceptionally well, graduated high in his class from the Law School, gone to Vietnam—and been killed.

So Daley disliked the war. But he remained a loyal party man. He had always made it his rule not to interfere in national politics—at least, until national politics came to his doorstep. (He hated Washington. When he had to go there, he always flew back on the last evening plane rather than spend a night there.) And so he was torn. He supported Lyndon Johnson, but without real warmth. He had worshiped John Kennedy. But his feelings for Robert Kennedy were a little different. "The Mayor wasn't specially keen on Bob," says one of the few men who was a close friend of both. "He had been Attorney General, and politicians think of the Attorney General as a kind of cop. Daley doesn't like cops. [!] There'd been a couple of investigations. . . . And he couldn't understand his sympathy with the black militants. And another thing: Daley is so organization-conscious that he couldn't understand a Democrat taking on a Democratic President of the United States!"

"Why," says Skeffington, the Irish mayor in *The Last Hurrah,* "that brings us to Man's Best Friend. The compromise!" Daley's instinct was the same. And so, over breakfast, he had sketched out a politician's solution, one that would at the same time offer some genuine hope of an end to the war and relieve Robert Kennedy of his desire to rend the body of the beloved party. Couldn't Kennedy perhaps get together with the President and agree to hand the question of the war over to arbitration, like a Chicago strike? The idea was put in very general terms. Kennedy promised to think it over, and Daley promised to mention it to the President, which he did very shortly afterward on the telephone.

It so happened that Theodore Sorensen had legal business for General Motors on which it was always useful to know what the White House was thinking. He had therefore fallen into the habit of chatting occasionally with an old acquaintance who was assistant counsel to the President, a tall and exceptionally clean-cut young man called DeVier Pierson. Almost alone of the old Kennedy hands, Sorensen went out of his way to keep up civilities with the Johnson regime, and it was natural for him to mention to Pierson that it would be pleasant to stop by the President's office one day and say hello. On Saturday evening, March 9, when Sorensen was in Washington for a dinner of the Gridiron Club, Pierson told him that the President would see him on Monday.

The two apparently contradictory accounts which the two parties gave afterward of how Sorensen came to see the President are therefore both literally true. Kennedy's office said that Sorensen went to the White House "at the President's invitation," and the White House said that he "asked to see the President." Each statement was true. Neither was the whole truth.

Sorensen saw the President alone. (Two members of the White House staff escorted him into the Oval Room and then left the two men by themselves.) From this point on, the Kennedy and Johnson versions of what happened differ rather radically. The story put out by Kennedy's office is that the President asked Sorensen—as he was in the habit of asking almost every visitor—what he would do about the war, and that Sorensen, totally ignorant that anything of the kind had been discussed between Kennedy and Daley, suggested an independent commission "as a means by which the President could signal the concerned citizens that this nation's policy would not remain unalterably fixed." The White House, on the other hand, maintains that, while the general idea of the President's consulting people outside government was discussed, no one made any mention of a formal commission.

According to the White House account, Clark Clifford received a call from Edward Kennedy on Wednesday, March 13, the day after the New Hampshire primary, and the two men arranged for Clifford and Robert Kennedy to meet the next morning. The Kennedy version is that the White House called Sorensen about a meeting. Both sides agree that Clifford, Sorensen, and Robert Kennedy did meet Thursday morning, March 14.

The President's men insist that Kennedy linked the idea of a peace commission with his own candidacy: they contend he said that if a way could be found to change American policy in Vietnam, it would no longer be necessary for him to run. Sorensen then described the plan for a commission and suggested possible members: Edwin Reischauer, a professor of Far Eastern affairs at Harvard and a former United States Ambassador to Japan; Roswell Gilpatric, a lawyer in New York who had been McNamara's deputy at the Pentagon; Kingman Brewster, president of Yale; Carl Kaysen, who had worked for President Kennedy in the White House and was now Director of the Institute for Advanced Study at Princeton; two prestigious but dovish retired generals, Matthew B. Ridgway and Lauris Norstad; . . . and Senator Kennedy. Clifford says he then asked Kennedy whether any other Senators would be on the commission. Kennedy suggested Mike Mansfield, a friend of the President's but one of the earliest and most inveterate opponents of American involvement in Vietnam. "No Republicans?" asked Clifford, and Kennedy suggested two: John Sherman Cooper of Kentucky and George D. Aiken of Vermont (whose attractively simple solution to the Vietnam problem was on record: "Declare a victory and bring the boys home!").

Kennedy's friends do not deny that this was the substance of this conversation, but they maintain that the names were only tentatively suggested, and they maintain that the men proposed were moderates, not doves. Kennedy did admit telling Clifford that if the commission "were more than a public-relations gimmick, if both the President's announcement of the commission and its membership signaled a clear willingness to seek a wider path to peace in Vietnam, then my declaration of candidacy would no longer be necessary." His friends insist that this was no threat. But that was what it looked like to the President. One White House aide was present when Clifford reported back to his principal. "When the President heard the terms," he says, "he rejected the whole idea immediately. It looked like utter, cold political blackmail. Maybe it wasn't intended that way, but that was what it looked like."

The next day, the White House press secretary, George Christian, skillfully leaked the story to *Time* and *Newsweek* and to CBS—he denies it, and other Johnson men blame Kennedy's office, but the evidence is against them.

What is the true meaning of this episode? Did Daley betray Robert Kennedy to Lyndon Johnson? Or did Kennedy seize an opportunity to use a public-spirited suggestion of Daley's? Did Johnson spring a trap on Kennedy, or did he react with justifiably injured pride? Was Kennedy blackmailing the President, or was he honorably exploring one last possibility of discharging his commitment to peace without splitting the Democratic Party?

Neither Johnson nor Kennedy has told the whole truth. It cannot be true that Sorensen suggested the peace commission out of thin air, as the Kennedy version maintains. Nor can the President have reacted with quite the injured innocence which his staff attribute to him, since Daley had warned him what to expect.

No doubt the motives of all three players were as mixed as the situation was obscure and dangerous for each of them. But there is one clue to the meaning of the affair from Robert Kennedy's point of view. After Sorensen had seen the President, Kennedy called Daley to say that he was under tremendous pressure to run, and that he might have to yield to it. He asked what had come of the idea they had discussed back in February. Daley told him he had mentioned it to the President. After he put down the phone, Kennedy turned to a friend and said, "I don't care what they do to me with it, I said I would walk the last mile for peace, and I'm going to do it!"

Stripped of its rhetoric, this can only mean one thing. Divided to the last between his passionate feelings about the war and his sense of his own destiny on the one hand, and his fears and calculations on the other, Kennedy was still reinsuring. In the very act of putting his fortunes to the hazard, he was exploring a tortuous last way out.

That Thursday night, he said afterward, when Clifford telephoned the President's refusal to appoint the commission, "it became unmistakably clear that as long as Lyndon B. Johnson was President our Vietnam policy would consist of only more war, more troops, more killing, and more senseless destruction of the country we are supposedly there to save. That night I decided to run for President."

By an absurd coincidence, he had invited a group of twenty New York State weekly-newspaper editors to dinner that evening at Hickory Hill. To leaven what promised to be a sticky evening, he had asked some of his most high-spirited friends to meet them. They rather overdid it. At one point, Kennedy overheard Renée Carpenter, the astronaut Scott Carpenter's divorced blond wife, arguing the case for legalized marijuana, tongue in cheek, to a scandalized group of editors—Republicans to a man. "Shh!" he said with a big grin, "you'll spoil everything!"

The phone rang several times. It was Clifford, throwing down the gauntlet. The last time it rang Kennedy said cheerfully to one of his youngest guests, "You'd better take it this time. It'll be the President of the United States." But it wasn't. The incident of the peace commission was closed. As Fred Harris left, he looked at his friend hard and said, "You'll do what you have to do." Kennedy knew what he had to do.

There still remained the question how to say it.

Oddly, at least for those who find it difficult to believe that impetuosity and calculation can coexist in the same person, Robert Kennedy found it as hard to keep his secret as a child with a birthday present for his mother. Cornered in a Senate corridor the day after the New Hampshire primary, he blurted out the phrase which he later considered his greatest political mistake: "I am reassessing my position." So soon after New Hampshire, it was too crude to pass without infuriated mockery from the McCarthy students, who showered him with bitter telegrams. That evening, when the grand conclave assembled in Steve Smith's apartment in New York, someone turned on a television set, and the counselors of caution watched in horror as their man as good as declared his candidacy on Walter Cronkite's news program—or so it seemed to them in their anguish. "What the hell's the point of holding this meeting," said Ted Kennedy, "when he's already made up his mind!" And on Friday morning, Bobby asked a *Kaffeeklatsch* in Brooklyn to "help in the effort I am going to undertake." On the way to the airport, he told Mankiewicz laconically, "You'd better get the caucus room for tomorrow."

That meant the historic high-ceilinged Senate caucus room where the Fulbright hearings had first aroused widespread public sentiment against the war and where John Fitzgerald Kennedy had stood under the television lights and said, "I am announcing today my candidacy for the Presidency of the United States."

All Friday afternoon and evening at Hickory Hill, as the speechwriters worked over their drafts, the schism that had divided them in the previous months of debate—and that was to divide them in the campaign to come—reappeared: the rift between Camelot and the Young Turks. The staff wanted the speech to stress the new politics of moral commitment and concern. Al Lowenstein worked for passages that would soothe McCarthy's supporters. (McCarthy himself was beyond the reach of conciliation. At Kennedy's request, the two candidates had met on Wednesday afternoon in Edward Kennedy's office, but it had been a stiff and unhappy occasion. On Friday night, at the suggestion of some of McCarthy's people, Teddy flew off to Milwaukee to see McCarthy again with a rather vague plan for an alliance. He arrived after McCarthy had gone to bed and was received frostily. A few hours later, he was back at Hickory Hill, shaking Arthur Schlesinger awake, mistaking him for Ted Sorensen, and muttering sleepily, "Abigail turned it down!")

The Camelot men were staying at the house, and that gave them an inside track. After the others had gone home, Sorensen worked some of his famous Ciceronian touches back into the draft, and also a passage that simply outraged the Walinsky group: "At stake is not simply the leadership of our party and even our country, it is our right to the moral leadership of this planet." That was the rhetoric of John Kennedy's time, and to Walinsky, Edelman, and Greenfield it was a rhetoric that had led America into an unjust and destructive war, "one of the greatest disasters of all time." *Their* Bobby, the Good Bobby of Jules Feiffer's cartoon, would never say something like that. But Bobby did.

The young speech-writers were back at Hickory Hill by half past seven on Saturday morning, but the Old Guard had been up before them. Sorensen, Schlesinger, and vanden Heuvel were down at breakfast with the Kennedy brothers by seven. Back in January, vanden Heuvel had written a seventeen-page memorandum against Kennedy's running and now he girded himself for one last attempt. He was thinking not as a political adviser but as a friend. He was alarmed by the passions which had already begun to seethe in New York, by the envenomed hostility of the McCarthy people. "I was afraid that if he did go into the primaries he would be engulfed in a whirlwind of hate. Nobody disagreed—except Bobby."

The announcement scene itself was an archetypal Kennedy occasion —family party, pep rally, and historic drama in one. Nine of the Senator's ten children were there, and the babies, while adorable, were understandably not at all times riveted by what their father had to say. He had had his hair cut a little shorter than he had been wearing it, and he wore a dark blue suit with a Brigade of Guards tie. The speech went out of its way to conciliate both McCarthy—his campaign was praised as "remarkable" and "valiant"—and the President. The man himself might be irreconcilable, but Kennedy was still concerned not to seem driven by the devils of personal dislike and ambition. Besides, there was no point in alienating any of the loyal regular Democrats unnecessarily.

Kennedy summed up his reasons for running. He spoke of "inexcusable and ugly deprivations"—in Mississippi and Watts, on Indian reservations and in eastern Kentucky—of the war, and of the anger and alienation of the young. That was the language of the radicals. But he ended with Sorensen's peroration about "the moral leadership of this planet." The first question from the press asked whether Kennedy was seeking the endorsement of Gus Hall of the American Communist Party, who had apparently said something nice about McCarthy. Contemptuously, Kennedy trod on that one, and turned his heel on it. He was not able to dismiss the next question so easily. "There has been speculation," it began—the press has its conventions, like the bench or the bar—"that this is opportunism on your part, that McCarthy had the courage to go into New Hampshire and how after his success . . ." Uproar. That was not the kind of question you ask at a family party, or a pep rally, or to mar the solemnity of a historic occasion. "Do you mean I have to repeat that?" Kennedy said. "A lot of nasty things." But people were going to say a lot of nasty things.

It was too late to draw back. But it was also perhaps too late period. The irony was clear. The contemplative McCarthy, mired in complexity, had known how to act. The supposedly existential Kennedy, who sought to create himself by action, had hesitated too long.

2

The Charisma Machine

"Why now, blow wind, swell billow, and swim bark!
The storm is up, and all is on the hazard."

—William Shakespeare, *Julius Caesar*

"The contest in 1968," Robert Kennedy told a student audience at Vanderbilt University in Nashville on March 21, "is not for the rule of America but for its heart." The same day in Sacramento, his partisans, led by Jesse Unruh, filed a slate of delegates for the California primary on June 4, picked with the utmost cunning to outmaneuver both the President and Senator McCarthy.

There were always two sides to a typical Kennedy operation; it was, perhaps, the trade mark of the Kennedys' instinctive understanding of politics. There were—to borrow Max Weber's terminology—the "charismatic" side and the "bureaucratic" side: image politics and backroom politics. It had been true in 1960. All the grace and dash of John Kennedy's public appearances would not have brought victory without the nitty-gritty in the back rooms: the noses counted, the arms twisted, the friends of friends called up, and the IOU's called in.

In the Kennedy campaign of 1968, the public, charismatic side preponderated far more than in any of the family's previous efforts. For the first time, for one thing, a Kennedy was running with a minimum of support from the party regulars. Mayor Daley, king ram and bellwether of the breed, might have reservations about the President, but it took him only three days after Kennedy's announcement to say flatly that the President could not be beaten. And this in spite of no fewer than three phone calls from Robert Kennedy and one from his brother Ted pleading for an endorsement. The South was solid in its hostility.

In the scramble to say something derogatory about Kennedy, Robert
Vance, chairman of the party in Alabama, distinguished himself with the
remark that Kennedy's campaign "would draw about as much attention
as an intra-party dispute in Czechoslovakia." (What newspapers had
Vance been reading?) The Northern party regulars, except in New York
and California, were on the whole just as cool. And the young, the radical, the committed were temporarily furious with Kennedy for apparently
trying to cash in on McCarthy's victory in the primary Kennedy had,
as it seemed to them, not dared to enter; "the buzzard," they called him
unpleasantly. Lastly, Kennedy's hesitations meant that his campaign was
not carefully planned—as all previous family efforts had been—but
hastily improvised. These facts dictated the strategy that was hurriedly
forged that weekend in Robert Kennedy's Washington office and in
Steve Smith's office on the thirtieth floor of the PanAm Building in
New York.

The essence of the plan was to get the candidate out on the road
as quickly as possible while Smith and Ted Kennedy got the organization
into gear in New York and Washington. New York and California, the
two biggest states and also the two where feeling against the Vietnam
war ran highest, were the priority targets.

Kennedy's first speeches were to be made at universities. That
would enable him to do a quick once-over of every geographical section
of the country without risking hostile receptions; to prove that he could
attract enthusiasm in the Midwest and the South as well as the liberal
East and the volatile West. It would give the media striking images to
project. And it might well woo back at least some of the younger generation and take the wind from New Hampshire out of McCarthy's sails.

For Kennedy started out with the extra disadvantage that he
must fight on two fronts. On the New York and New England campuses,
and among intellectuals in New York and Boston, the manner of his
entry into the race had provoked bitter cynicism and scorn. This was the
time of bitter jokes and unkind cartoons, like one which appeared in the
Capital Times of Madison, Wisconsin: it showed a toothy Bobby making
his leering apologia in front of the television cameras:

> Initially I decided not to run because it might divide the party and
> I didn't want to be called an opportunist.
> However, New Hampshire changed all that and I must reconsider.
> It is now obvious that the party is severely divided . . .
> Enough for me to take advantage of it!

Even Allard Lowenstein, who had been sympathetic enough to his friend's predicament to help draft his announcement speech, thought that the timing of it was the worst political mistake of Kennedy's life. And Kennedy knew it. All through the months of his hesitations he had kept Lowenstein's name off his office calendar; he realized that every time he was known to see Lowenstein, there was the danger of a crop of rumors. After the announcement he asked Lowenstein what he thought of it. Lowenstein said something about its being unfortunate that everybody would think he was trying to steal McCarthy's victory. "Oh, come on, Al, baby!" Kennedy said. "Can't you find something more original than that to say? That's what all the papers are saying. I tell you what, you find something nice to say and we'll meet, and I'll let you keep me off your office calendar!" Steve Smith, who thinks Kennedy was right not to go into New Hampshire, nevertheless thinks his brother-in-law "tortured himself" about the manner of his announcement afterward.

Kennedy, however, knew that in less sophisticated places than New York or even Madison—at Kansas State University in Manhattan, Kansas, at George Wallace's own Tuscaloosa, which Kennedy had helped to integrate, at Vanderbilt—he would have little to fear from enemies on the left. He went to those places in the first week of his campaign, and he was rapturously received. So while Smith stayed in New York, getting the campaign organized, going through the card files, raising money, hiring an advertising agency, and doing all the other things that needed to be done, the candidate went into orbit.

On Saturday morning, March 23, he left New York for California and one of the most dazzling campaign progresses in the memory of the oldest reporters in the business. The trip had been swiftly but brilliantly "advanced" by Pierre Salinger and Dick Tuck—both veterans of 1960—on the advice of Jesse Unruh and Fred Dutton, one of them certainly the most powerful and the other perhaps the ablest Democratic politician in California. From the moment the candidate stepped out of his plane into pandemonium on the crowded upper deck of the San Francisco airport, the unseen hand of inspired professionalism could be felt. Since the local Kennedy people had planned to greet the candidate at the foot of the airplane steps, Tuck and Salinger were appalled. The squealing girls and the hired *mariachi* band would be lost in the open air. So the arrival was moved indoors, where it duly generated the required hysteria. It was equally obvious that money was to be no obstacle. An extra Boeing 727, complete with stewardesses, Bloody Marys, and sandwiches was prepared at a few minutes' notice to take an overflow of half a dozen reporters for a ten-minute flight to Sacramento.

But there was nothing contrived about the reception Kennedy got. At the first stop, he lost the first of a long series of cufflinks and was almost pulled from his moving car by the frenzy of the grabbing, grasping hands. At the little airport in San Jose, there was a warmth in the atmosphere like California sunshine after the chills of New York. Mexican musicians plunked gravely at the chords of *"Cielito Lindo,"* while Kennedy went hand over hand along the crowd that lined the airport fence, some of them blond teen-agers with sun-bleached hair and some of them black-eyed teen-agers who spoke to him in Spanish. "Beautiful, beautiful!" murmured a television film director. "Cut!"

At Salinas airport the next morning it was wilder than that. Dick Tuck was tense as Kennedy's plane banked down in a slow curl over the white Pacific beaches and the emerald green of the golf courses on the Monterey peninsula. Then he saw the crowd and broke into a grin. "Salinger's mother lives here," he cracked. "She must have brought her friends." They were standing three deep on the roof of the airport building and milling all over the runways. Kennedy gave his little speech. He began, as always, by introducing his two sisters—Pat Lawford, tall and duchessy in manner, out of nervousness, and Jean Smith, smaller and more self-possessed. He used some of his little repertoire of jokes. There was one about his brother Teddy's being sent off to buy campaign buttons and putting his own name on them, but the ones that went down best were the self-deprecating cracks about himself. (He always got a laugh for calling himself "ruthless.") And then he would turn serious, as he did that morning at Salinas airport.

The rhetorical device he used was a list of social injustices strung together with a single phrase, or variants of a single phrase. He would reel off all the things wrong with America: hunger in Mississippi, discrimination against black veterans home from Vietnam, squalor in the ghettos, and misery for Mexican migrant workers in the San Joaquin valley. And after each point would come the same tag line, "And I don't think that's very satisfactory here in the United States!" Then he would end, somehow with enormous charm and appeal, by saying, *"That's* why I run for President of the United States, and *that's* why I come here and ask for your help!"

The line of attack sounded radical enough, but—consciously or not —it appealed to middle-class chauvinism as well as to the social radicalism of those who actually suffered from the injustices he denounced. And there were times when he trod close to the edge of demagogy. Over and over, for example, he talked about how terrible it was that American boys were dying in "bottomless Asian swamps" when the Vietnamese themselves were not conscripting eighteen-year-olds. And he went on saying this for some days after it was pointed out to him that the Vietnamese were in fact conscripting eighteen-year-olds.

But perhaps only the reporters noticed such points of detail. What the crowds seemed to love was not the political substance but the style. There was the line about Beaumont, Texas, for example. The teen-agers would squeal "Beaumont, Beaumont!" and Kennedy would give a sharp little grin and do it for them. Apparently the President had been rash enough to say, in rebuttal of the charge that the government of South Vietnam was corrupt, that there was corruption in Beaumont, Texas, too for that matter. "I don't agree with the President of the United States that there is corruption in Beaumont, Texas," Kennedy would say wickedly, as if the President might know all about that. "I stand up for Beaumont!" And they loved the George Hamilton joke too. "I know we're doing well." Pause. Then grin. "Last night George Hamilton called up and asked for my daughter's phone number."

And he was doing well. The crowds swelled. Outside the oldest building in Los Angeles, in the little plaza in front of the eighteenth-century mission church of Nuestra Señora la Reina de los Angeles, worshipers were holding up babies to see their champion, and hanging from the branches of the liveoaks. In Watts they were standing on the roofs of automobiles, denting them with their weight. And at Griffith Park in Hollywood they were perched on the floodlight pylons, sixty feet above the heads of the crowd.

As a progress, it was more than royal. The abiding memory it left on all who saw it was of the sheer intensity of feeling of those volatile, emotional Californian crowds, the men in sports shirts and the women in loud, solid colors, the young people barefoot, the boys in beards and the girls in ponchos, Bermuda shorts, or miniskirts. And a slim figure perched on the back of a car, swaying precariously at the apex of a pyramid of reaching hands. They seemed to want to touch him more than to listen to him. Whoever could explain what those hands were reaching for, it seemed, might be able to understand and perhaps to heal the American malaise. But it did not follow that the object of this adoration must be elected President. For the gesture was personal rather than political. It had some of the yearning that was once poured out before the great queens of Hollywood, and, before that, was paid as tribute to royalty itself. It was real, that yearning for the young prince of the House of Kennedy; but it was also close to hysteria. It seemed to have more to do with psychopathology than with politics.

"Abigail turned it down!" said Edward Kennedy, a few hours before his brother's announcement on March 16. What Senator McCarthy had just turned down—with his wife's approval, though scarcely at her dictation—was a secret plan for carving up the primaries and forming a common front against Lyndon Johnson.

It was not the Kennedys who initiated it. As we have seen, the Kennedy and McCarthy campaigns sprang from the same soil. Of the three men who had lunched together at the Quo Vadis so long before, Arthur Schlesinger was now an adviser in Kennedy's campaign. John Kenneth Galbraith, while still on the best of terms with Kennedy, was soon to campaign for McCarthy in Wisconsin precisely because he felt he had committed himself too far on McCarthy's behalf—raised too much money for him, apart from everything else—to withdraw with decency now. And Richard Goodwin, who had been one of Robert Kennedy's closest counselors, was now the key man in McCarthy's campaign.

The young volunteers might be passionate in their loyalty to McCarthy and bitter against Kennedy, but there was always the feeling among their elders that the McCarthy they were so loyal to was a figment of their own imaginations, a Platonic ideal of a McCarthy who did not bear a very close resemblance to the infuriatingly flesh-and-blood Senator McCarthy whom senior people in the campaign had to deal with. It was an axiom that the higher one went in the hierarchy of the McCarthy campaign, the more likely one was to find people whose loyalty, if it came to a choice, was not to the candidate but to the cause. Richard Goodwin was of that group, and so was Curtis Gans.

It had always been expected that if Kennedy announced, Goodwin would leave McCarthy's service and enter Kennedy's. Goodwin had very fairly and frankly explained this to McCarthy in a Chinese restaurant in Washington, when Blair Clark first brought them together. And McCarthy recognized this with something as close as he gets to a compliment. Goodwin, he said, was a professional; he might be traded from the Cards to the Braves, but he could be trusted not to give away the Cards' signals.

On March 14, the Thursday before Kennedy announced his candidacy, Curtis Gans talked to Goodwin on the telephone. "We decided,"

Gans puts it, "that the stakes were just too high to fight about it." Goodwin flew down to Washington and checked into the Georgetown Inn. Several times on the telephone he and Gans discussed the idea of sharing the primaries, with the idea of registering the biggest possible combined vote against the President and the war, and not risking cutting into it by internecine fighting. Goodwin talked to Ted Kennedy. Gans talked to Blair Clark, who was in Wisconsin with McCarthy. Time was running out. It was agreed that Ted should fly out to discuss what kind of compromise could be worked out with McCarthy. Late on Friday night he left Washington—in a jet chartered on Blair Clark's personal credit card. As the plane headed west for Green Bay, where McCarthy happened to be speaking that night, Goodwin and Gans went over the details of possible deals. Goodwin was for letting Kennedy win in Oregon in return for an uncontested run in Nebraska: Gans, who knew more about how well McCarthy would do in Oregon, thought it would be better the other way around. Ted Kennedy said he would "have to talk to Bobby," but he was seriously interested, they could see. (It is odd how often and how easily in this story those who profess themselves the most determined champions of "open politics" slip into the smoke-filled rooms and puff away with the best.)

They went to the Holiday Inn and called McCarthy's hotel. They got Sam Brown on the phone, and he talked to Mary McCarthy. "Dad's asleep," she said. This was a characteristic touch. McCarthy had been warned that Ted Kennedy was on his way, had agreed to see him, and had then gone to bed, though not without tipping off the faithful David Schoumacher of CBS, who was therefore waiting with a camera as Kennedy and Goodwin stepped out of the elevator and disappeared into McCarthy's suite. For if McCarthy was willing to hear what Kennedy had to offer, he was not in a mood for making any deals. He listened to what Kennedy had to say, but in the end Kennedy went back with empty hands.

The truth was that Wisconsin already looked good to McCarthy, and he could afford to take a high line with the Kennedys. Asked whether he would accept an "accommodation" with Kennedy a couple of days before the chance of one turned up in so melodramatic a form, he smiled wryly and said, "We could talk about an accommodation the day after California; that's the way it was in New Hampshire." A month earlier, one of the loyalist Democratic politicians in Wisconsin told the *New York Times,* "There's no question of McCarthy winning here. The only question is whether he can produce more than a hundred and fifty thousand votes, say, and hurt Johnson as a matter of political prestige." At about the same time, the state chairman, Richard Cudahy, consulted his county chairmen, and, on being assured by most of them that there was indeed going to be no problem in carrying the state for the President, proceeded to do very little more about it. But by the time McCarthy made his first appearance in the state, on March 15, fresh from his New Hampshire triumph, the Johnson Democrats realized they had misjudged the state of feeling in Wisconsin. They began to poor-mouth furiously. The morning after New Hampshire, Cudahy announced that the President was the "underdog"! Actually the first McCarthy canvass, taken a few days later, gave McCarthy thirty-seven per cent of the vote, so Cudahy was crying before he was hurt. But the factors in McCarthy's favor looked very considerable. He could no longer be dismissed as a mere "protest candidate," and nobody need feel that a vote for him would be wasted. Moreover, he had an important technical point in his favor. Republicans are allowed under Wisconsin law to "cross over" and vote in the Democratic primary. With Romney out of the race, all the interest was now on the Democratic side. Dozens, if not hundreds, of thousands of Republicans might be expected to vote for McCarthy simply in order to embarrass the Democratic President.

But what might be expected to help McCarthy most of all were the character and traditions of the state. When people in Wisconsin are Republican they are very, very Republican, but when they are Democrats they tend to be progressives. The Democratic Party in the state is not dominated by anything resembling a machine, except in the Polish wards on the south side of Milwaukee. Most of the leading Democrats in the state—Senators Gaylord Nelson and William Proxmire, Congressmen Henry Reuss and Robert Kastenmeier, for example—were either sympathetic to McCarthy or uncommitted. They all belong to the dominant Stevensonian tradition in the party, which in turn owes a good deal to the University of Wisconsin. That institution pioneered academic involvement in state politics in America, and for many years the involvement has almost always been on the liberal side. The undergraduates had been "politicized" when campus police clubbed a group of demonstrators in October 1967, and thousands of them were ready to enlist as McCarthy's infantry. Many graduates and faculty were also liberal Democrats who sympathized with McCarthy. On March 17, for example, the Sunday night after Ted Kennedy's abortive talk with McCarthy, a meeting of the Shore Wood Village Democratic Club, in one of the most expensive suburbs of Madison suggested how the wind was blowing among politically active Wisconsin Democrats. The meeting was held in a handsome, split-level private home. A young attorney and alderman, who was to put the case for the President, was soon reduced to stumbling incoherence by Arnold Serwer, a journalist on leave from *The Progressive,* the local left-wing monthly, to work for McCarthy, and by some University of Wisconsin professors. One critique of the Administration's gold policy was so learned that the Johnson man could say nothing in reply beyond a gulped "thank you." What was particularly noticeable was the appearance the alderman gave of defending the President only because he thought he had to. He was going out of his way to be friendly to the McCarthy workers. Here was one humble soldier in the President's armies who seemed to smell defeat on the wind.

The smooth progress of McCarthy's campaign was interrupted by an incident, trivial in itself, which suggested some of the strains that might develop if Senator McCarthy were ever to look like a serious contender for the White House. There had been tension for some time between Curtis Gans, who was now in effect managing the campaign in Wisconsin (while the nominal campaign manager, Blair Clark, managed the candidate), and Sy Hersh, the press officer. Hersh's assistant, Mary Lou Oates, was—like Gans himself—a veteran of civil-rights work in the South. Unlike Gans, she and several other young campaign workers felt that Senator McCarthy ought to be making a special effort in the Milwaukee ghetto. "We were trying to maximize the vote against Lyndon Johnson," Gans told us. "That means that we were not making any particular effort in the Milwaukee ghetto, which has a small part of the Wisconsin vote. That upset some of our staff."

On this point, there was a highly emotional meeting on March 25. Forty young staff people crowded into a hot room. One of the senior people—not Gans—spoke more bluntly than was perhaps wise. "We need those Polish votes to get Milwaukee," he said, "and the Senator's not campaigning in the core"—that is, the ghetto—"or the Poles will think he's soft on Negroes." There were angry shouts of "White racist!" and "Back to the Resistance!" from the young militants, and the meeting broke up. Many tempers were lost, and Hersh and Mary Lou Oates resigned.

Several personality clashes were involved, everyone was exhausted; when tempers cooled, it was obviously absurd to suggest that the McCarthy campaign was being run by racists. It is also possible that both politicals and militants exaggerated the hostility of working-class Milwaukeeans, especially of those of Polish descent, to Negroes. But it was certainly true that Negroes were a small minority in Wisconsin and that Mayor Henry Maier was a good deal more popular in Milwaukee than Father James Groppi, the militant civil-rights leader there. What had happened, for the first time but not the last, was that the McCarthy *crusade,* last hope within the system of the militants for peace and civil rights, had come into contact with the McCarthy *campaign,* a political operation aimed at winning the Democratic Presidential nomination.

The Hersh-Oates resignations, however, caused hardly a shudder in the McCarthy operation, which was, in Gans' words, "beautiful, like a machine, it was lovely to watch, it almost worked by itself." The candidate spent almost three weeks in the state, and if he sometimes shocked the volunteers by his insistence on getting a good night's sleep, he campaigned harder and more regularly than in New Hampshire. ("Guess where the Senator is?" asked a young volunteer one night, coming into the crowded headquarters. "Eating?" suggested a girl worker. "No, in bed!" "Well, it's ten-thirty-nine." "What d'you mean, it's ten-thirty-nine? He's got fifteen calls to answer, he left a staff meeting at ten-thirty." Utter disgust.) The University of Wisconsin provided an army of volunteers, stiffened by New Hampshire veterans. And the Wisconsin progressives—lawyers, professors, and middle-class housewives—worked well with the national staff. ("Housewife Power" was one of the great discoveries of 1968: idealism plus frustrated energy plus free time is the formula for a political explosion.) Above all, there was money. In mid-March, a difference of five dollars per thousand on a printing bill was reason enough to take a lower quotation. By the end of the campaign, six hundred thousand dollars had been spent. Howard Stein undoubtedly helped to raise major sums. So did Galbraith and Blair Clark himself, and small contributions poured in. One letter with five dollars came from York, England. But the main reason for the opening of the floodgates was undoubtedly Robert Kennedy's entry into the race. There are those who believe that money was sent from pro-Humphrey sources anxious to stop Kennedy. That is possible, even plausible, but the most that can be said after careful investigation is that there is no definite evidence either way. In any case, the pro-Johnson forces found themselves decisively outspent. Their budget for Wisconsin was seventy-five thousand dollars, and in the end they overspent by about fifteen thousand, so that McCarthy, the threadbare outsider, actually outspent the regular party by more than six to one! The McCarthy television, in particular, was devastatingly effective, and so were the full-page newspaper ads, stressing the personal choice between two men: "McCarthy is *the best man* to unify our country."

Too late, the White House woke up to what was happening. At the beginning of the first week in March, reinforcements were thrown in: in addition to Leslie Asplin, the Pentagon systems analyst who had been sent to run the President's campaign, a task force of professionals began to gather: Neil Staebler, the former Michigan state chairman; Kenneth M. Birkhead, from the Department of Agriculture; Robert J. Burkhardt, the New Jersey chairman. Every night, they were on the phone to James Rowe or Marvin Watson with gloomy news. Finally Larry O'Brien flew out, looked around, and returned to break the bad news to the President himself.

O'Brien's visit was from Tuesday until Friday, March 29. The next day, a McCarthy canvass found sixty-three per cent who said they would vote for McCarthy, and the Johnson men were privately foreseeing 200,000 Republican cross-overs. A telephone check that Gans ordered on Monday, after the President's withdrawal, showed a 7-per-cent dropoff in the McCarthy vote, and there is other evidence that this was about right. The President acted just in time to forestall a catastrophe, with an adverse vote of at least two to one. As it was, the result was shattering enough. Six weeks before, 150,000 votes for McCarthy would have been a moral victory. He got 412,160. The President got 253,696. And Robert Kennedy, who was not a candidate, got 46,507. (Richard Nixon got 79.4 per cent of the Republican vote.)

Exactly four months had gone by since the night of poignant farce in Chicago when Eugene McCarthy had punted a Dixie cup against the wall in his frustration as he waited for Lowenstein to introduce him to the liberals of America as their savior. For all his strengths and virtues, McCarthy had not then been their first choice to oppose the President. That prerogative was clearly Kennedy's. Even when he forfeited it, most liberals who were honest with themselves would have to admit, McCarthy had not even been their second or third choice. His campaigning, though demonstrably effective, had so oscillated between the eccentric and the lackadaisical that, as one of his chief associates asserts, "There wasn't one of us who didn't ask himself some time in January whether we didn't have a fraud on our hands." If such a candidate, campaigning in such a way, could outpoll an incumbent President of his own party by more than three to two and, to put it at the lowest, contribute powerfully to his withdrawal from the race, then indeed the storm was up.

It was understandable that many observers, seeing what McCarthy had achieved and seeing the panache with which—it seemed to them— an altogether more experienced, more attractive, and more serious campaigner had swept through California, concluded that McCarthy had indeed merely blazed the trail for Robert Kennedy. In the mass media in particular, coverage of Kennedy's opening tour of California upstaged McCarthy's campaign in Wisconsin; and President Johnson's withdrawal drowned his actual victory. *Newsweek,* to single out one example almost invidiously among so many, reported that Kennedy had made "amazing progress" in rounding up delegates in the week after his return from California. To do them justice, few of Kennedy's advisers made the same mistake. And Kennedy himself, though he might be carried away by the fierce excitement of the struggle for which he had been preparing himself for so long, had few illusions.

On the plane from San Francisco to Denver at the end of the California safari, there was a sort of Kennedy staff meeting. The same division that had been so clear in the long months of hesitation and that had flared briefly in the excitement of the announcement over "the moral leadership of the planet" was still very obvious. The younger people— Walinsky, Edelman, Greenfield, Pete Hamill—were intoxicated with the enthusiasm of the California crowds and delighted with Kennedy's unashamed pitch for minority votes among the young, the blacks, and the Mexicans. And some of the older heads—Fred Dutton and Mankiewicz in particular—while aware that winning the nomination would not be all kisses and wine, felt they were going about it in the only possible way. But there were others, Pierre Salinger most obviously, but also Sorensen, Steve Smith, and the candidate's brother, who asked, "Can you really campaign in Indiana the way we campaigned in California?" They were more aware than the younger people that there were in any case two campaigns, the primary campaign and the national post-convention campaign. In the primaries, they said, O.K., you might win by relying on the minorities and the antiwar vote, but how much did those crowds mean? "Why were those crowds there?" Salinger asked in the plane during that trip. Yeah, said others, and who stayed away, and why? The consensus inclined toward caution. Let's poll those towns, was the feeling, and find out just what those crowd scenes mean.

The one thing everyone agreed on, as one eyewitness recalls it, was that the immediate strategy was simple: "Get that son of a bitch out of the White House." When the extraction was self-performed, exactly a week later, nobody realized more clearly than Kennedy how difficult his situation was. He had come into the battle in order to be the giant-killer. Once he had entered the lists he hardly expected serious competition for that role from Eugene McCarthy. And—as he had so clearly understood when hesitating to run—any Kennedy campaign was bound to be a personal challenge to Lyndon Johnson.

On April 2, the whole picture shifted like a kaleidoscope. It was McCarthy who had slain the giant. Hydra-like, the giant now seemed on the point of growing a new head in the shape of Hubert Humphrey, who spent that day telephoning virtually all the major Democratic politicians in America and asking them not to commit themselves to Kennedy just yet. It was highly significant that on the next day, April 3, for the first and only time in his campaign, McCarthy did exactly the same. For six or seven hours without a break, Goodwin and Gans dialed the numbers— ex-Governor "Pat" Brown and national committeewoman Anne Alanson in California, Midwestern governors, Eastern mayors. It was a most uncharacteristic lapse into strenuousness and the old politics for McCarthy. And for Kennedy it was a reminder that he must now fight on two fronts—neither of them the one he had prepared for. The ogre had vanished in a puff of smoke. But what was most disconcerting of all was that suddenly it was not merely unprofitable to attack Johnson; it might become positively dangerous.

On Tuesday, April 2, the day of the Wisconsin vote, Robert Kennedy was in Philadelphia. The three parts of his day might have been devised by a novelist to illustrate the difficulties of his new situation. In the morning, he spoke to a packed house of students and faculty in the basketball arena at the University of Pennsylvania. The house was liberally sprinkled with McCarthy buttons and favors, and when Kennedy rose to speak the cheering was speckled with watchful, hostile silence and even occasional jeers. This was the first Eastern collegiate audience he had met as a candidate, and for the first few minutes it must have confirmed his own worst fears that he had lost his own natural constituency.

It was the kind of test that brought the best out of Kennedy. He did not hesitate to answer quite sharply the questions which seemed to him unfair, and he defended the draft, which took some courage. But it was not the substance of what he said that won the day so much as the style. He stood in the cockpit of steeply banked tiers of students, a complete master of the style they themselves were trying to achieve: informal but authoritative, involved but cool. As he left, dozens of students were taking off their McCarthy buttons, and hundreds were arguing earnestly about what he had said. To one observer at least, it seemed certain that by the time of the convention Kennedy would have regained his following among all but the most radical students.

If the university in the morning was a tour de force, the midday motorcade through the downtown business section was a triumph. The candidate stood on the roof of a car at the corner of Chestnut and Market streets, in the midst of some of the most conservative institutions in America. Nobody could hear what he was saying. Ticker tape floated down from the trust-company windows, and the crowd was jammed together for blocks in every direction. It was the California rapture in three-button suits; again, it might not be politics, but it was phenomenal in intensity.

The evening was something else again. Kennedy spoke at the Jefferson-Jackson Day dinner in the Philadelphia convention hall, a monstrous building well papered with city employees and the party faithful by Mayor James Tate and the regular Democratic machine. Kennedy angled blatantly for an endorsement from Tate, which was civilly but bluntly withheld. He was introduced by Senator Joseph Clark, and Clark too was willing to pay him any compliment except the one that mattered. He couldn't even win an endorsement from Congressman William Green (son of the former boss of the city), who was personally inclined to support Kennedy, though he wrestled for it in a hotel room after the meeting for an hour or more. And every time Kennedy mentioned Lyndon Johnson in his speech the party faithful did a surprising and disconcerting thing: they stood up and clapped.

Projected onto the national scale, the lessons of Kennedy's first full day of campaigning since the President's withdrawal were not encouraging. The President had obviously succeeded in blunting Kennedy's two sharpest issues—the war and the President's own personal unpopularity. Kennedy's magnetism might be as highly charged as ever, but with the students and the intelligentsia he was still on the defensive. And the party regulars, the very men who had put his brother in the White House, were apparently neither convinced that he could win nor particularly keen that he should.

That night, on the plane to Washington, Kennedy warned his euphoric supporters not to underestimate Hubert Humphrey. And by the end of the week Humphrey was confiding to his staff that he thought Kennedy had failed to seize the nomination in his first rush. In California he had proved that he could excite the emotions more than any other politician in America, but Lyndon Johnson's last stroke and McCarthy's victory in Wisconsin had robbed the California expedition of decisive effect, and reduced Kennedy to the status of one among three aspirants for the throne to which he had seemed the heir apparent. And the storm was still rising.

3

The Double Incumbent

"Two voices are there; one is of the deep,
And one is of an old half-witted sheep,
And Wordsworth both are thine."

—J. K. Stephen, *"Lapsus Calami"*

Even the beginning of the Humphrey campaign contrived to be tinged with anticlimax. Almost four weeks passed between that Sunday morning when Lyndon Johnson appeared like a fairy godmother at his apartment and Hubert Humphrey's announcement that he was a candidate. And it was typical of the man that when he did announce what had been obvious for so long, he had to tack on to his carefully prepared speech a *gaffe* that had his opponents chortling for weeks. Yet it was also typical of Humphrey that there were both shrewd and honorable reasons for the delay, and that by the time he did move he knew he had the nomination halfway into his pocket. For the Vice-President was all paradox: the most innocent of manipulators, the shrewdest buffoon in politics. Even before he left the American Ambassador's residence in Mexico on Monday, April 1, the day after the President's withdrawal, Humphrey had received more than fifty phone calls beseeching him to run. (He returned only one of them, from Margaret Truman Daniel, daughter of the former President and wife of the managing editor of the *New York Times.*) When he got back to Washington he disappointed a crowd of several hundred people and several dozen journalists who were waiting at the airport by driving straight home without the dramatic announcement they expected. And he spent the next day talking on the telephone to politicians from all parts of the country, telling them that he couldn't yet say he was running, but that if they would hold their hands for a while they would not regret it.

Humphrey's personal impulse, of course, was to go. He had been painfully adjusting himself, amid the minor humiliations of his position as Vice-President, to the probability that he would never be President. A dozen times in those months before Johnson's withdrawal he had tried to prepare his wife Muriel for the crowning disappointment. "I'll never run for President," he would say. "I'll be sixty-one in nineteen-seventy-two. There'll be nearly ten years of the Johnson Administration behind us then. People will want a change." And Mrs. Humphrey would answer tranquilly, understanding that it was himself he was trying to convince as much as her, "Yes, Daddy. Anything you want is all right with me." But it is not likely that these exercises in psychic self-defense had been entirely successful. No man can go as far in politics as Humphrey had gone without being infected with the virus of Presidential ambition: not even a political Sherpa Tensing can stand on the North Col for four years without beginning to experience something of a Hillary's yearning to stand on the peak.

To adjust to the possibility that the dream of a lifetime may not come true is hard enough. To cope with the sudden possibility that it may come true after all is infinitely harder. And then there were practical reasons for caution, too. At the office, one of his staff made the point. "For heaven's sake, Hubert, don't jump into this thing without knowing what you're doing. You got clobbered before."

"Goliy," said the Vice-President, "you're right!" He had been clobbered in West Virginia in 1960, and one reason had been lack of money. At least if he was to go again in 1968 it would not be with an economy-class ticket.

One of the ironies of history was that where in 1960 he had been swamped by Kennedy money, now he could have all the money he wanted if he ran against a Kennedy. On Tuesday evening, after a brief chat with the President in which he carefully refrained from asking directly for his help, Humphrey flew to New York for a dinner at the Waldorf-Astoria. It had been arranged by Gardner Cowles of *Look* magazine, for his advertisers, but after dinner Cowles took Humphrey upstairs for a private chat with some of his rich friends. Besides the two Cowles brothers, Henry Ford II was there, and Sidney Weinberg of Goldman, Sachs. After a long talk they adjourned to the New York apartment of Dwayne Andreas, a wealthy friend of Humphrey's from

Minnesota. No one was asked for a specific pledge, but everybody present urged Humphrey to run. The interesting thing is that at this very time many of the same men were also urging Nelson Rockefeller to run. There were many who felt it was that important to stop Kennedy.

Only a few hours after this flattering tribute from capital, there came an imposing appeal from labor. George Meany, the seventy-four-year-old head of the AFL-CIO, came close to an endorsement and urged Humphrey into the fray. "In no other way," Meany said publicly, "can the American public be reassured of an effective spokesman and advocate for the programs needed to continue the social and economic progress of the last eight years and unite the American people behind the defense of freedom and democracy in the world." In private, Meany was almost angry with Humphrey for not declaring immediately. The next day, at the Steelworkers' convention in Pittsburgh, the union's president, I. W. Abel, greeted Humphrey with "Go, Hubert, go—we are with you!" When Humphrey pitched into Richard Nixon in his speech, union stalwarts were jumping up and down in the aisles. "I'm getting interested," said Humphrey with a grin as the well-orchestrated applause boomed out to him. But that was all.

That same afternoon, Martin Luther King was shot. If Humphrey had been on the point of announcing, he had to delay now. But there was in any case another reason for caution. Before coming into the race, Humphrey had to be sure that he was not simply hurling himself under the wheels of a Kennedy bandwagon. The first question he had asked when he stepped off the plane from Mexico was "Has Bobby got it locked up yet?" One of Humphrey's staff said, "Everybody expected Bobby to put on a blitz. When politicians began calling from all over the country, saying, 'Bobby's pushing me, I have to know whether you're going to run,' we knew that the bandwagon wasn't happening. We couldn't tell them that we were running, but we were able to say, 'Hold off a bit longer, and you won't be sorry.' " Humphrey believes that Kennedy lost the nomination in those first few days.

"Hubert's going to be able to put together an incredible coalition," said Johnson's man in California, the lawyer and Democratic national committeeman Eugene Wyman. "He's got top management, top labor people, he's got the labor vote, the solid South, and the important Negro leaders." It was true, but hardly incredible. What did Meany and the money men, a Southern segregationist like John McKeithen, Governor of Louisiana, and Carl Stokes, the Negro mayor of Cleveland (the latter two declared early for Humphrey) have in common? It might not be obvious, but it was real enough. Each of them in his own world stood for the established powers that felt threatened by the swirling currents of radical dissent which Robert Kennedy was trying to ride into the White House. "I've got every establishment in America against me," Kennedy told a reporter in his plane the night Humphrey dined at the Waldorf. It seemed a strange and even an unseemly complaint, coming from a Kennedy. But there was a degree of truth in it.

Whoever felt threatened by the new voices of dissent, or challenged by them in his interest in the *status quo,* or hurt in his pride, thirsted for revenge. That was what made so many people in Washington so eager to see Hubert Humphrey take up the cudgels. Even so gentle a person as Mrs. Katharine Graham, owner of *Newsweek* and the *Washington Post,* was heard to say in ringing tones in a Washington restaurant, "The trouble with Gene McCarthy is that he thinks he's Jesus Christ!" The Southern governors felt threatened by George Wallace, and the Northern Negro leaders felt threatened by Black Power. The union officials felt threatened by a new and arrogant assertion on the part of the liberal Establishment that "the young and the well-educated ought to rule America." "That sort of baloney is all very well for conning money out of rich women with baggy tits," said one normally urbane union official to us about the McCarthy campaign, "but it just isn't politics!" Perhaps the most typical expression of the mood of those who looked to Humphrey was a lushly written parody of Dr. Pangloss by the veteran liberal Eric Sevareid, published, significantly, in Cowles' *Look,* in the same issue with an admiring profile of Humphrey. "The world still moves our way!" cried Sevareid, and *Look* called his effusion "an answer to the cynics who claim our nation is doomed."

Whether he liked it or not, Humphrey was cast from the beginning as the champion of ruffled national complacency, the man who would rebut the hurtful suggestion that all was not for the best in the best of all possible Americas. It was a role for which he might have been type-cast. In his Pittsburgh speech he shouted, "Deception, doubt, and despair— that is the litany of those who would sell America short!" That was the stuff to give them. And so on April 27, having tested the water with his toe for three weeks and six days, he stood on the platform in yet another of those hotel ballrooms which punctuate this story—this one in the elephantine Shoreham Hotel in Washington. He had a grin on his face like the little boy who had the cream cake, a thousand of the faithful in front of him, and a carefully prepared text in his hand.

He began by thanking Fred Harris and Walter Mondale, the two young Senators who were cochairmen of his campaign. And then, following the instinct of a lifetime, he told the people in front of him what he thought they wanted to hear. "Here we are," he caroled irrepressibly, "just as we ought to be, the people, here we are, in a spirit of dedication, here we are, the way politics ought to be in America, the politics of happiness, the politics of purpose, and the politics of joy. And that's the way it's going to be, all the way, from here on in!"

It was not a slip of the tongue. "My credentials?" he asked in the prepared text. "Well, they may be rather simply stated: loving family . . . teacher . . . mayor of my city . . . Senator from my state . . . Vice-President of my country . . . grateful husband and proud father . . . believer in the American Dream . . ."—here the audience of professional politicians, Federal office-holders, and labor officials, dreamers all, rose to its feet—"and the concept of human brotherhood."

There were those, like James Reston, who were delighted by the idea of "the politics of happiness." Others felt that it was not an altogether felicitous slogan for a Presidential campaign in a year that was clouded by deep and violent national divisions, by assassination, and by war.

"Hubert the Happy," wrote Marya Mannes unkindly,

> Goes yackety, yackety,
> Yackety, yackety, yack.
> If anyone tells him for God's sake to knock it,
> He cheerfully yacketys back.
>
> If he stopped yacking, he couldn't go anywhere,
> Poor little Hubert, he couldn't go anywhere—
> That's why he always goes
> Hoppity, yackety,
> Hoppity,
> Yackety,
> Yack.

Humphrey's garrulity is the one characteristic on which his admirers and his detractors agree. Lyndon Johnson has described him as "a man who prepares for a good solid thought-provoking speech by taking a deep breath." And a journalistic admirer has put the same thought more tactfully: "The locus of interest—the self, really—of Humphrey becomes harder and harder to find, let alone to respond to, when the subject matter multiplies and the rhetoric overwhelms." His public speeches, and especially the impromptu bursts with which he loves to embroider the prepared texts, are astonishing rag bags of pulpit rhetoric and folksy chatter, of original thoughts—both Humphrey's and those of other think-ers—and hardrock clichés.

But to appreciate the full virulence of Humphrey's compulsion to talk, it is necessary to experience his conversation. Interruption is un-thinkable. But that is not unusual with politicians. What is disconcerting is the feeling that one is being talked to with so little thought for who one is or what one originally asked. A specific question about the prob-able number of votes available for some bill, for example, becomes the text for an uplifting discourse that could be transcribed and read to a high-school civics class in Minneapolis.

It can sound mindless. Yet Humphrey is an intelligent man. Few Senators have ever spread themselves over so many subjects and still managed to achieve his grasp of detail. As a stand-up, hip-pocket di-plomatist in the Senate, a technician in the wooing and wheedling and all-around negotiation with which majorities are put together in that unstructured chamber, he has had no rival in the last ten years and only one master: Lyndon Johnson, who paid him the supreme compliment early in his time by saying, "I wish I had the training of that boy," and had his wish come true.

Humphrey can be made to sound superficial and undirected, and yet few men in American politics have achieved so much of lasting sig-nificance. It was Humphrey, not Senator Dirksen, who played the crucial part in the complex parliamentary games that were needed to pass the Civil Rights Act of 1964. It was Humphrey, not John Kennedy, who first proposed the Peace Corps. The Food for Peace program was Humphrey's idea, and so was Medicare, passed sixteen years after he had first pro-posed it. He worked for Federal aid to education from 1949, and for a nuclear-test-ban treaty from 1956. These are the solid monuments of twenty years of effective work for liberal causes in the Senate. "Most Sen-ators are minnows," Johnson liked to say. "Hubert Humphrey is among the whales."

Yet by 1967 the arch-disarmer had turned into an arch-apologist for the war, who was given to trotting around Vietnam looking more than a little silly in olive-drab fatigues and a forage cap. The man whose name had been a by-word in the South for softness toward Negroes had taken to lecturing black groups about how the Irish and the Jews and even the Cubans had made it in America without Federal grants, so why couldn't they? The wild-eyed reformer had become the natural champion of every conservative element in the Democratic Party.

Humphrey's friends and apologists argue that he was trapped by his position as Vice-President. This is untenable. For one thing, his dicta, particularly on the war, went far beyond what solidarity with an Administration or loyalty to a President demanded. Again and again Humphrey insisted that he believed in the war. One should do him the credit of believing him.

"Ah," say his friends, "but he didn't really mean it: he was trapped." Joe Rauh, for example, one of his oldest friends, told us in an interview, "Hubert just had blinkers on. I said to him once, 'If you were President, we'd be out of this war in ninety days.' He said, 'No.' He really thought the war was right. But he was only thinking it through from A to B because of those blinkers he'd put on out of loyalty to Lyndon Johnson. If he'd let himself think it through, he'd have been against the war. But as it was, you have to say that he stayed and out-Johnsoned Johnson. You have to have forgiveness, though, because he is a really fine and noble man, and it was loyalty that made him do it."

One key to the mystery lies in the fact that, like many another leader of the Democratic left in both Europe and America in the generation that grew up with Stalin, Humphrey is deeply and sincerely anti-Communist. Neither his original purging of the Marxists from the Democratic Farm-Labor Party in Minnesota, at the outset of his career, nor his sponsoring of the Communist Control Act in 1954 were mere gestures to avoid being outflanked by the Republican Red-hunters of the day. They may have been illiberal, but they were from the heart.

Humphrey was undoubtedly influenced both by Johnson and by the power and bonhomie of the Senate long before he became Vice-President. The rather pathetic gesture of modeling his home at Waverly on the LBJ ranch suggests how much he held his leader in awe. (President Johnson gave the Humphreys the plans for the guest house on his ranch to copy.) And to feel the subtle machinery of the Senate respond to his hand, to bask in the acceptance of that clubbable society—these are heady delights for any man, and for the country boy from Huron, South Dakota, who loved all his life to be loved, they were intoxicating.

For this, surely, is the key to Humphrey, and the only basis on which his undeniable achievements and his occasional fatuousness can be reconciled. There is a revealing anecdote in Robert Sherrill's and Harry Ernst's unflattering biography, *The Drugstore Liberal.* During the 1966 campaign, it seems, Humphrey went on a hedge-hopping stump tour of Minnesota. At each stop he greeted the notables lined up to meet him and asked them which church they belonged to. If the man said he was a Methodist, Humphrey (who is a Congregationalist) would say joyously that he was a Methodist too. If the next man said, "Baptist," Humphrey would say he was a Baptist. After he had told Episcopalians he was an Episcopalian and Lutherans he was a Lutheran, one of his fellow campaigners took him to one side and said, "Gosh, Hubert, you're going to get caught up in this. You can't tell everyone you belong to their church." Humphrey is alleged to have looked puzzled. "Why not?" he said. "I'm a Christian."

Nothing that Humphrey did in 1967 caused more distress and anger among the liberals and the blacks than a picture that was taken of him arm-in-arm with Lester Maddox, the abusively segregationist Governor of Georgia. Apparently this came about not through cynical political contrivance but on a sheer impulse of Humphrey's. The next morning his press secretary, Norman Sherman, pointed out what a disastrous reaction there would be.

"What are you talking about? I never did that. I was just polite to him, that's all," said Humphrey.

"Yes, you did, Mr. Vice-President."

"No, damn it, I did not."

Sherman said nothing, but placed the *New York Times* in front of Humphrey. There on page one was the picture of Humphrey with Maddox.

"Gee," said Humphrey after a minute, "I guess I did, at that."

"Humphrey likes people like an alcoholic likes booze," says a Senator who has known and liked him for many years. "The warmth is not affected. It is real. He really enjoys the endless round of contacts. He is always willing to speak to any group. For twenty years he's been speaking to the Boilermakers and the Hodcarriers and the Kiwanis and the Rotarians. He spoke, and spoke, and spoke, and spoke.

"He's always been willing to spill his energies in any project, any good cause. But after twenty years, it's taken its toll. At fifty-seven, he gets tired. And twenty-five years of this endless politicking have robbed him of something else—of the contemplation, or the reflection, you need if you're going to be a serious political leader. They've taken away his freshness, turned it into a kind of sterility. There's very little poetry in him: he says very few things you want to remember, let alone quote."

Humphrey's friends lay heavy stress on his practicality, his effectiveness. "In this country," one of his staff explained to us carefully, as though this were some peculiarity of the American way of life, "you've got to please people to get things done. You can have a simon-pure liberal make a great speech about civil rights, but Hubert Humphrey can

sit down with people like Senator Russell and Senator Stennis and get
agreements with them!"

> "I can call spirits from the vasty deep."

> "Why, so can I, or so can any man;
> But will they come when you do call for them?"

Anybody can sit down and compromise with his opponents. The question is not whether he can get agreement but what kind of agreement he can get. And the serious charge that can be made against Humphrey is that his constitutional craving to be liked, reinforced by years of learning how to "get along" in the Senate, has brought him close to, if not actually past, the point where compromise ceases to be a tactic and becomes an end in itself.

"You know it's a peculiar thing around here," he told a Senate subcommittee on disarmament in 1960, "you can get an extra billion for a B-70 bomber program, but it's difficult to get ten dollars for disarmament." And then he added, "I happen to think we want both"! "Both, please," said Winnie-the-Pooh, when asked whether he wanted honey or condensed milk on his bread; and then, so as not to sound greedy, he added, "but don't bother about the bread."

Humphrey himself is proud of his ability to get things done. "People say to me," he says, " 'Whatever happened to that liberal program you stood for?' I say to them, 'We passed it. Does that upset you?' " It is a remark that breathes the very spirit of the Johnson Administration. There it all is, in two dozen words: bragging, defensiveness, and crass incomprehension both of the nature of political dissent and of the mood of America. Who ever thought that the duties of a liberal in politics were discharged when he had worked his way through a shopping list of reforms drawn up years before? Who ever thought that America's problems could be solved, once and for all, by introducing a partial Medicare bill and a guaranteed minimum wage for some, though not all, workers? Apparently Hubert Humphrey did. And, while few would formulate complacency quite so baldly, something like Humphrey's view was almost orthodox in Washington among those who had considered themselves stanch liberals since the New Deal.

"Because of the great leap forward in economics," Humphrey's friend Richard Scammon, the psephological sage and former director of the Bureau of the Census, told us, "economic questions have been eliminated in American politics." This was not Senator McCarthy's view. "He always felt," Blair Clark said once, "that the ghetto question was a question of money, a question of redistribution." It was not Senator Kennedy's view. Interestingly enough it is not the view of Joseph Califano, President Johnson's key aide in all matters relating to the Great Society legislative program. In public, Califano has drawn attention to the vast catalogue of social legislation which the Johnson Administration has passed. In private, he has made it plain that he is well aware of the limitations of the liberal, legislative approach, as opposed to fundamental shifts of economic resources, in solving the problems of poverty and urban decay. There were many others in Washington who well understood that the passage of the Johnson-Humphrey program did not amount to the enactment of the millennium. But they were not strongly represented in the team which Humphrey had recruited to staff his campaign.

"Humphrey's weaknesses are the obverse of his qualities," another friend of his in the Senate told us. "He is incapable of being tough with people. Consequently he is the worst organizer in the world. He always asks six or eight people to do the same things, and the worst of it is that he's never had really good staff." In the supreme moment of his political career, this was as true as ever.

In theory, the structure was tripartite. There was United Democrats for Humphrey, the official campaign, run by the two attractive young Senators Harris and Mondale, with Orville Freeman, Secretary of Agriculture, John Gronouski, just back from a term as United States Ambassador in Warsaw, and the economist Robert Nathan in key roles. The treasurer was Richard Maguire, a veteran of the 1964 campaign.

Then there was the Vice-Presidential office, and Humphrey's official staff: William Connell, his executive assistant; John Reilly, his foreign-affairs adviser; John Stewart, writing speeches mostly on domestic policy; Bill Welsh, a highly respected political operative from Capitol Hill; Ted Van Dyk, who acquired considerable influence from his situation at Humphrey's side on the road; and the press secretary, Norman Sherman, an ebullient but sometimes flustered intellectual who once ran a bookshop in St. Paul.

And then there was Citizens for Humphrey, run by a group of Humphrey's old cronies: the Washington lawyers David Ginsburg, James H. Rowe, and Max Kampelman; and, on the financial side, Robert Short, owner of the Leamington Hotel in Minneapolis, where, by a curious coincidence, the press and traveling party always stayed whenever the candidate visited his home state. Rowe and Kampelman are the two among Humphrey's friends who have always pushed him to the Right. They are, for example, credited with influencing him at the time of his sponsorship of the anti-Communist legislation of 1954. It has also been stated for publication by Joe Rauh that Kampelman was one of several of the Humphrey circle who were undercover CIA agents. According to the *Washington Post,* "only criticism of some of Kampelman's past business activities . . . kept him from playing a major, open role in the [Humphrey] campaign." Those activities have included at different times organizing a bank whose most famous transaction was an unsecured loan made, on Kampelman's reference, to Bobby Baker; and being a director and stockholder in the first American company to sell used machinery to India with financing from the Agency for International Development, which put up four million dollars for the deal.

The Humphrey organization, in fact, was permeated, circumvented, and confused by a horde of old pals, old pols, eager beavers, and office seekers. Humble technicians concerned with such details as preparing campaign advertising, scheduling, or even writing the words to come out of the candidate's mouth, never knew who was authorized to convey the candidate's decisions to them. Some of these numerous helpers were high-minded and disinterested; others very possibly were not. But it was a fact that countless other figures crowded the overcrowded campaign hierarchy. They included high Federal officials like Freeman, Secretary of Labor Willard Wirtz, and United States Ambassador to the United Nations George Ball; Minnesota businessmen like the feed-grain man Dwayne Andreas, and Jeno Paulucci, the owner of Jeno's Italian and Wilderness Products; union men like Al Barkan, of the AFL-CIO's Committee on Political Education (COPE); Humphrey's personal physician, Dr. Edgar Berman—one of the pioneers of open-heart surgery, now described as "more than just a doctor, a sort of spiritual counselor"; functionaries of the Democratic National Committee; and veteran operators on loan from the staffs of friends on Capitol Hill. There was an elaborate pyramid of task forces and research groups and committees, studded with academic names like those of Samuel Huntington from Harvard and Zbigniew Brzezinski from Columbia. And there were old political friends like Marvin Rosenberg, who called himself "the Vice-President's eyes and ears in New York for many years." Many of the Citizens group, in particular, had long kept up to Olympic standards in giving off an impressive air of familiarity with the great in general and Hubert Humphrey in particular: for years this had been one of the most useful accomplishments for a Washington lawyer to master. So it was hard to be sure just who really had the candidate's ear, and harder still to know who spoke with his voice.

The great question from the beginning of the campaign was whether, or to what extent, Humphrey would disassociate himself from Johnson. It was on this issue, above all, that the internal divisions within his unwieldy general staff centered. There were those—cochairmen Harris and Mondale among them, for a start, and most of the younger members of the Vice-Presidential staff—who were pressing Humphrey to shake off the burden of his loyalty to the Administration and issue some statement that would show that he was "his own man." (This phrase was worked into so many briefings that it soon became a cliché in the thoughtful columns.) The only issue, of course, on which it would be both possible and profitable for Humphrey to become "his own man" was the war.

Some felt so strongly that Humphrey must disassociate himself from the President that they urged him to resign the Vice-Presidency; John Loeb, the banker, who had been a heavy contributor to the Johnson-Humphrey campaign in 1964, was one of these. Another suggestion was that Humphrey should resign all but the constitutional functions of his office.

Others, such as Connell and many of the Citizens for Humphrey, dismissed the Kennedy and McCarthy campaigns out of hand as unimportant minorities and considered the war as unworthy of attention when compared to the serious political task of accumulating delegates. Humphrey had declared on April 27. By May 1 it was calculated that he had nine hundred delegates; indeed, long before he announced, CBS in its wisdom credited him with a thousand!

Pennsylvania showed what could be done. Four days before Humphrey's announcement, on April 23, the third most populous state went to the polls in a Presidential preference primary. The only name on the ballot was Eugene McCarthy's, and he received 428,259 votes. There were 65,430 write-in votes for Robert Kennedy and 73,263 for either Humphrey or Johnson. One might suppose from those figures that all or most of Pennsylvania's 130 convention votes would go to McCarthy. Not so. The 130 votes were distributed among 160 delegates (a convention seat is a political perquisite, and the more it has to hand out, the happier a state machine is). Of those 160 places, 52 were simply handed out by the state committee, dominated by pro-Johnson bosses: Mayor James Tate of Philadelphia, Mayor Joseph Barr of Pittsburgh, I. W. Abel of the Steelworkers, and "young Bill" Green. Only one of the 52 appointees was for McCarthy. And since in the Pennsylvania primary, voters separately express their preference among the candidates and choose delegates who are not identified as supporters of a candidate, the

McCarthy delegates got a far lower vote than McCarthy. The net result of this obfuscation and confustigation was that Humphrey, who was not even a candidate when Pennsylvania held its primary, and was outvoted 8 to 1 by McCarthy, nevertheless got hold of 135 out of 160 seats on the delegation and, in the end, two-thirds of its vote.

With a few more states like Pennsylvania, perhaps Humphrey could have afforded to ignore the war altogether. But in fact a curious episode in mid-June was to reveal just how enmeshed he was in his dilemma from the beginning.

On June 14 a New York radio station interviewed Bill Moyers, who had become the publisher of the Long Island suburban newspaper *Newsday* but had been Johnson's right-hand man, and was being widely tipped for an important role in the Humphrey campaign. "The problem is," Moyers said in the interview, "whether or not Humphrey can free himself from the incrustations of the last four years and emerge as the Humphrey who really wrote the script for most of what Eugene McCarthy and Robert Kennedy have been saying this year." And he went on to urge Humphrey to say publicly what, Moyers said, he felt privately: "that present policies are inadequate, present personalities are inadequate, that we must move away from where we have been, we must liquidate the war in Vietnam in one way or another, we must rearrange the economic structure to provide for the poor who have been left out."

Moyers, who had resigned from the White House staff because he felt these things so strongly, passionately hoped that Humphrey would do what Moyers said he would. He had talked to Humphrey three times in two weeks, but he had no specific private knowledge that Humphrey was going to make a public statement to disassociate himself from the Administration. Nor, in the original interview, did he say so.

Understandably, a number of reporters called him up, and informally over the telephone he gave the impression that he did have inside knowledge and was making a firm prediction. The *New York Times,* for example, reported that Moyers had said on the phone that Humphrey would "emerge on his own within the next week or so." Moyers is apologetic about his role in the episode. "It was gratuitous," he told us. His motives were the highest: he was trying to edge Humphrey in the direction which he thought best not only for the country but for Humphrey too. But the result was disastrous.

A few days later Senator Mondale was defending his candidate's record as a liberal. Mondale was for Humphrey, he said, precisely because he was the most liberal of the three candidates.

"Except on the war," one of us said to him.

"That's right, except on the war. He was trapped."

"But since the Moyers incident he can't disassociate himself from the Administration?"

"That's it. That's just it. The Moyers business is the worst thing that has happened yet."

The central issue which only Humphrey could decide for himself had, in fact, been defined. It was to remain the central issue for the rest of his campaign, until he resolved it. Would he or would he not dissociate himself from "Johnson's war"? If he did not, he could probably still win the nomination. The question was whether, without doing so, he could win the election.

4

Venture into the Interior

"With Ethel, kids, and Freckles, he will barnstorm Hoosier-
land;
He will conquer Indiana with his hearty Irish band.
And if it costs a million, and his last reserves of gall—
That will not daunt the driver of the Ruthless Cannonball."

> —Parody on "The Wabash Cannonball," Indi-
> ana folk song, composed by reporters during
> the 1968 Indiana primary

French Lick Springs is a small resort town in that southern part of Indiana which almost takes on the character of Delta country. It was once a famous gambling center, and around the turn of the century, when its main hotel was owned by a prominent politician named Tom Taggart, it became a favorite place for Indiana Democrats to meet and talk things over. There was a meeting there in 1924 to rally support against William McAdoo, the fiercely segregationist Presidential candidate, who was endorsed by the Ku Klux Klan. (That year, it was reckoned that the majority of the Indiana state legislature consisted of members supported by the Klan.) French Lick is no longer a gambling town, because someone started enforcing the state laws rather strictly. But it remains a gathering place for Indiana Democrats, and in 1968, French Lick figured in a decision which precipitated one of the more colorful primary battles and helped to affect the direction of the Presidential campaign.

On the evening of Saturday, March 16, Democratic county leaders from all over Indiana gathered for dinner at the hotel in French Lick. They had been conducting a weekend workshop, and now at dinner they were to be addressed by Vice-President Humphrey, a popular figure with them. But even the prospect of this treat could not dispel the gloom that lay over the company. This was because of the prospects for the state Presidential primary, May 7.

It was the Saturday after the cataclysmic event in New Hampshire, which had sent a shudder through every good organization man in the Democratic Party, and especially those in the primary states. No sooner had the professionals begun to get used to the idea that conceivably the much-despised McCarthy might have to be regarded as a serious danger than the even more appalling possibility of Robert Kennedy's candidacy had been raised. And that very Saturday morning, Kennedy had announced for President. He had not said he definitely would run in the Indiana primary along with McCarthy. But he had hinted that he might, and the diners at French Lick feared the worst. It was not so much that they did not like Kennedy—although many of them did not. Even important Indiana Democrats such as Senator Birch Bayh, who liked and admired Kennedy a great deal, liked him outside Indiana. This was because of the situation the Indiana Democratic Party was in.

Indiana is not good Democratic country. The physical sweep of the state, from Lake Michigan to the Ohio River and the borders of Kentucky, incorporates most of the basic elements of American political life. In the north, around the steel town of Gary, racial tension smolders miserably in some of the nation's grimmest industrial deserts. The central belt, with the exception of Indianapolis, is small-town America, and the south is the beginning of the South. But the over-all mixture—which includes a splash of fierce local chauvinism—is significantly more conservative than the national whole. Since 1936, no one but Barry Goldwater has been enough to make Indiana go Democratic in a Presidential race.

However, Presidential Democrats are usually labeled as liberals. The citizens of Indiana do not object to electing Democratic candidates in state-wide races, providing that such candidates are not egregiously liberal. With hard work, they can be persuaded to vote for the two Democratic Senators, Bayh and Vance Hartke. Both men take, cautiously, a good many liberal positions. They can also be persuaded to vote Democratic in the gubernatorial contest, and in 1968 the Governor of Indiana was a conservative Democrat, Roger D. Branigin. The governorship is a matter of rather more urgent concern to Indiana Democrats than the Presidency, because the governor directly controls about seven thousand jobs in the state bureaucracy. And among these seven thousand there are appointments which control other appointments, so that the governor indirectly controls another eighteen thousand or so jobs.

Indiana, in other words, is a patronage society in an excellent state of preservation—one, furthermore, where the general rise in salaries has not so hopelessly outstripped state salaries as to make people too proud to fight for patronage jobs. Each appointed official in Indiana "kicks back" two per cent of his salary to the Democratic Party of Indiana—that is, assuming the Democratic Party is the in party. And kickback money is not all of it, because when you have twenty-three thousand people who depend on the party for their daily work, you have a comforting number of hard-core political activists when and whenever they are required.

There is, of course, a drawback to most good things. The trouble with the life-giving governorship of Indiana is that it comes up for election every year, so in 1968 it would coincide with a Presidential election.

Governor Branigin had been re-elected in 1967 by the largest margin a Democrat had ever recorded in Indiana, but nobody was foolish enough to imagine that it was therefore going to be easy in 1968. Branigin, having served four terms, was no longer eligible, and any new Democrat running for governor would face the likelihood of a considerable Republican shift. Also, it appeared that Richard Nixon would be the Republican Presidential candidate, and the state of Indiana was known to be very fond of Nixon. Nixon would win Indiana against any conceivable Democrat: but there was one Democrat against whom he was likely to win by a tidal wave, sweeping away the gubernatorial candidate and much else besides. That Democrat was Senator Robert F. Kennedy, whose personality was ideally constructed to remind the conservative voters of Indiana of that difference between Republicans and Democrats which the Democrats were encouraging them to forget. However well he might do in a primary among the state's minority of Democratic voters, Kennedy would be smashed in the autumn by voters who might well go on to punish the party for having the sauce to nominate him. Therefore, the organization Democrats of Indiana did not wish their state to do anything to help Kennedy with the nomination—in fact, they all wanted to do something to hinder him. But by state law, Indiana's sixty-three votes at the Democratic National Convention had to go, on the first ballot, with the preferences of the voters in the Presidential primary. As things stood, it seemed that the winner of the primary, if he came in, would be the unsuitable Kennedy. And if he did not come in, the winner would be the equally unsuitable McCarthy. There was no one else in the field, and it was all too clear, after New Hampshire, that Lyndon Johnson was not going to expose himself to any unpleasantness. The only hope, therefore, seemed to be to project a favorite son into the race to beat off the insurgent challengers and corral those sixty-three votes for the President's future use.

There was an obvious man for this role: Governor Branigin, who had nothing to lose. Fighting a primary to save an incumbent President the trouble is an honorable and rewarding task. For instance, in 1964, Governor Matt Welsh had taken on the nasty job of standing off George Wallace in the Indiana primary. Subsequently, he was appointed to the commission which, when required, adjudicates water-border disputes between America and Canada. The work, which is not thought to be onerous, or even frequent, pays $28,750 a year.

Branigin, however, was reluctant, despite the fact that he had been promised $130,000 from the Democratic National Committee to ease the strain on the state party budget. Branigin is a touchy and independent man and, being personally a millionaire, he did not give a damn about lucrative retirement jobs. Neither did he wish to be an ambassador. Worst of all, there had been a cutback on Federal highway funds which had not disposed him well toward the White House.

When the diners gathered at French Lick Springs, there were only twelve days to go to the deadline for filing papers in the Indiana primary, and there had been no sign from the Governor. At that moment, in fact, he was in a train on his way to Florida for a vacation.

When the Vice-President arrived at the hotel, he conferred at once with Gordon St. Angelo, the Indiana party chairman. St. Angelo said that he thought Branigin ought to run—"It was a matter of a man showing his respect for the Presidency and the country." Humphrey decided to make a final appeal to Branigin by telephone.

Naturally, this was difficult, although at one stage the resourceful men of the Secret Service considered having the train stopped so that Humphrey could talk to Branigin. At last, the call got through to Branigin at his hotel in Fort Lauderdale—by which time dinner in French Lick had started, with the Vice-President and St. Angelo seated at the head table. Humphrey and St. Angelo took the call in a large, dusty storeroom behind the banquet room.

The Vice-President spoke to the reluctant Governor for a good twenty minutes. Branigin, it seemed, doubted he was the best man for the job. Humphrey assured him he was. The question of the highway funds came up. Humphrey said soothing things. Then Humphrey handed the phone to St. Angelo, who said to Branigin, "I don't think you have any choice." Branigin capitulated.

Humphrey went back to the dinner and made a speech and at the end he announced that Branigin would run. The emotion which greeted this announcement was touching. People jumped onto tables and cheered hoarsely.

Just fifteen days after he was persuaded to take on the noble task of defending the President, the President removed himself from the battle. Standard-bearer Branigin was only told by the White House that his standard was not required a few minutes before President Johnson's famous withdrawal. When St. Angelo rang Branigin, a few minutes after the telecast, he was still fuming. The Governor said, well, he was going to leave his name on the ballot, come what may, and see what he could get out of it, for himself and for the state.

The day after the broadcast, Gordon St. Angelo got a call from Senator Edward Kennedy and went to meet him in Chicago, a short flight from Indianapolis. Teddy's question was an obvious one: was it, by any chance, possible that Governor Branigin might consider retiring from the primary race, leaving Kennedy free to demolish McCarthy alone? The answer, of course, was that the Governor, along with every other professional in the country, had worked out that sooner or later Hubert Humphrey was going to be a candidate, and that it would be worth sticking around to see what sort of price Hubert had to offer. In other words, they were going to make it tough for Kennedy all the way.

Still, no time had been wasted hanging out the "No Welcome" sign for Bobby. In response to some brisk work by St. Angelo with telegrams and telephones, all but one or two of the ninety-two county chairmen came out formally for Branigin. This loyalty no doubt owed something to the Indiana custom by which the county chairman of the in party runs the auto licensing for the county, which may be worth forty thousand dollars a year and rarely less than fifteen thousand dollars.

Kennedy had grave doubts about the wisdom of going into Indiana. At noon on the Thursday after Robert declared, Teddy Kennedy called one of the family's most rugged political retainers: Gerald Dougherty, a Boston lawyer with steely blue eyes and a knobbly Irish face. Would he go and make a reconnaissance?

"I am a nuts-and-bolts man," Dougherty says in frank self-description. "I don't get involved in issues and policies. I didn't have any particular view on Vietnam. I have the feeling, now, that they had already decided not to go in, but they needed someone to look. I can see why they would have chosen me, because it's a sort of joke around here—I'm known as a kind of Gerry Bad Nose. I work at arithmetic, and I'm always saying no, don't do it."

Kennedy retainers do not dally when doing the clan's bidding, and at three a.m. next day Dougherty flew into Indianapolis with one companion from Boston. They were met, in a snowstorm, by Michael Riley, the twenty-eight-year-old chairman of the Indiana Young Democrats, with two friends aged twenty-two and twenty-three. Spontaneously, these young men had telephoned Ted Kennedy and offered to help. They constituted the Kennedy people's first working contact with the grass-roots enthusiasm that could have been tapped so many months earlier.

The immediate problem Dougherty and his young friends faced was that the following Tuesday, March 28, was the deadline for filing papers in the primary. And each candidate's name had to be accompanied by a petition of 5500 registered Democratic voters, of whom there had to be at least 500 from each congressional district. "So we needed those fifty-five hundred signatures just to keep the option open," Dougherty recalls. "And between Friday night and Sunday noon, we got them."

Dougherty and Riley got about fourteen young workers to help them—but they got no help from the professionals. "In Massachusetts," said Dougherty later, "there are always politicians—some—to help out. There, they just pulled the shades down.

"We needed maybe ten thousand signatures to get five thousand good ones. In Lafayette County, they challenged seventy per cent of the names, trying to get us off the ballot. We bussed students in from Chicago to Gary, two buses, and got all the signatures in an afternoon. We brought people in from Ohio and from Louisville, Kentucky.

"The first day we sent out our lists by bus, by Greyhound. Well, that worked for six hours, and then *they just stopped arriving.*"

However, the signatures, against the resistance of the machine and the weather, were coming in. The network of helpers was expanding rapidly—and at this point Bad Nose Dougherty began to be moved by the extent of popular feeling. "It was," he recalls with a certain wonder, "just people working—all sorts of people. I had eighteen, twenty seminarians out in the northeast getting signatures in the snow. It was one of those things you see movies about." It was the first close-up contact of a Kennedy hard-noser with the remarkable passion for change which moved through America in that spring.

On Monday morning, Dougherty flew to Washington, convinced that Kennedy should go into Indiana. There was a conference which lasted most of the day with Ted Kennedy, Stephen Smith, and Theodore Sorensen. People were slightly amazed to find Dougherty coming back with tales of popular enthusiasm rather than dismal arithmetic, and Ted Kennedy was sufficiently impressed to cast his vote for Indiana. Smith, and even more Sorensen, seem to have been cautious.

Chiefly, and not surprisingly, they were worried about what had happened to John Kennedy in Indiana in 1960, where he had been badly beaten in the Presidential race. Perhaps the state just didn't like Kennedys? But at the end of the day, the candidate himself joined the meeting and decided to go into Indiana. His final reasoning was: It's difficult to run against the President and then say, "I'll run here, but not there and not there." They arranged for Kennedy to go to Indiana for the first time the next Thursday, and eight thousand people came out to meet him in Indianapolis.

Indiana was not hopeless territory for Kennedy. There were black voters in Indianapolis and Gary, and there were large bands of white working-class voters: the blue-collar workers, of recent European origin, known unpleasingly but unavoidably as "ethnic voters." He could start, therefore, with a decent base of the working-class white-Catholic and Negro support natural to an Irish Democrat—plus a considerable bonus from his celebrity status. And for all the talk about New Politics, for all the hippie beads and quotations from Camus, Robert Kennedy could play the ethnic-politics game with considerable professionalism. He did not, for instance, miss the Polish Dyngus Day spring festival at South Bend, Indiana. This is the observation of the death of Saint Stephen and is taken as an excellent excuse for drinking large amounts of beer and eating Polish sausage called *szynka*. The Senator was to be found in the West Side Democratic and Civic Club, consuming *szynka*, reminding the people of his own successful trip to Poland, and singing the traditional greeting "*Sto Lat*" with energy, if no great artistry. He carried it off better than Gene McCarthy could have done.

One much-advertised danger for Kennedy was the tension said to exist between the black and white working class, in Gary particularly. This was the country where George Wallace had made hay in 1964, and it was understandable that people should argue that a candidate with so strong an identification as the black man's candidate could be in trouble. But this was largely a chimera: in fact, in most opinion-poll "trial heats" during the year, Kennedy ran rather better against Wallace than any other Democrat.

The greater difficulty in Indiana was the white middle class, with its frequently harsh and conservative attitudes. Indiana is unregenerate Midwest, lacking in the bourgeois liberal traditions of the cultivated middle class on the coasts, lacking even the sophisticated influence of a great metropolis like Chicago. Its university tradition is markedly less radical than, say, Wisconsin, Berkeley, or Columbia. Committed liberals were going to vote for Gene McCarthy, and a lot of the orthodox Indiana Democrats at the wealthier end of the party spectrum were going to vote for Branigin. In this state, the image of the charismatic savior-rebel which Kennedy had carried to California in his first campaign trip could be simply ruinous. It was a situation which dictated the rather strained, liberal-conservative style Kennedy now began to develop for campaigning in the Midwest. It made some of his staff and supporters squirm, but when one saw the kind of reception he got at the Indiana University Medical School, it was hard to argue that he did not need it for survival.

This was a fairly characteristic Kennedy performance in Indiana, and it was, of course, a bold decision to talk to medical students about the need for medical reforms. Democratic politicians talking that sort of language to medical audiences can expect to run into a Pavlovian response of "socialized medicine!" And indeed, this was a restless audience, with a lanky youth holding up a blue balloon with REAGAN written on it. Kennedy left himself a bolthole in his speech by declaring that he did not think "the spending of more money" would cure the problem. All the same, his grim recital of facts—that twelve nations have higher life expectancy than America, that fifteen have better ratios of hospital beds to population, that the cost of medical care is rising seven times faster than the standard of living—did not especially delight his audience. They were even less delighted and began to groan and hiss when he suggested to them, entirely accurately, that they were members of a privileged class.

The response was indeed Pavlovian. Kennedy handled it first by facing it down and lecturing the students bluntly on their "social obligations." "Where does the money come from for these programs you suggest?" a student demanded. "The Federal government will have to make some available," Kennedy said. "Money implies control," the student shouted, to which Kennedy replied, "Barry Goldwater lost that struggle four years ago."

Kennedy's essential technique was to project startling differences in outlook by running variations on a few basic themes. His fundamental statement of belief on poverty and the ghetto again employed the decentralization mystique—but its essential core was the idea that somehow big business could be tempted to revitalize the ghettos. This theme could be elaborated, for a black audience, into a statement of the need for black people to run their own lives, make their own way—almost a speech for black separatism. Subtly varied, the same theme could be made palatable to entirely different audiences such as the Real Estate Association of Indianapolis. When addressing these prosperous folk over lunch at the Howard Johnson's motel, Kennedy's stress was all on the massive tax concessions and depreciation benefits that would be available for ghetto developers if his ideas went into practice. The formula that the "Federal government must produce tax incentives to harness the vast resources of private enterprise" was repeated six times in fifteen minutes, to the great pleasure of the audience. Jobs were the answer, he said, producing the uncharacteristically callous remark: "We must turn the poor into a resource, not a burden." The over-all impression of the speech was that it was one most Republicans could have made. Unfortunately for Kennedy, most of the real-estate men probably decided it would sound even better from a real Republican.

His staff tended to defend these speeches by describing Kennedy's belief that "you had to be able to talk to the businessmen as well, because that's the kind of country this is." No doubt Kennedy's obsession with national unity was genuine. But it was also true that he badly needed to capture some white middle-class votes in order to put together a coalition which would look as though it could win in November. He needed to do this not just in the Indiana primary, but also in the national opinion polls, in order to impress the organization men of the Democratic Party with the strength of his electoral appeal. Such speeches were clearly part of the attempt to do so.

His trouble was that he was pursuing the wrong kind of middle-class votes, the ones that needed code words about "law 'n' order." ("I was, for three-and-a-half years, chief law-enforcement officer of the United States," Kennedy said over and over again.) There was something wrong with the dynamics of his popularity: and this was largely due to the awkward existence of Eugene McCarthy. But on April 28, nine days before Indiana voted, a detailed survey by the Gallup office revealed, starkly, the weaknesses in the pattern of Kennedy's support.

Examining the national electorate and dividing it up by age, by religion, by education, and by membership or nonmembership in trade unions, the survey showed just how closely Kennedy was still locked into his basic "ethnic-and-black" constituency—and how McCarthy's presence hampered his efforts to break out into wider support.

Among voters aged twenty-one to twenty-nine, Kennedy held an unassailable lead over Humphrey: 41 against 16 per cent. But in this group McCarthy came close to Kennedy, with 32 per cent. Moving up the age bands, Kennedy's support declined dramatically: among voters aged thirty to forty-nine, he dropped behind McCarthy, 27 to 35 per cent, while Humphrey improved to 23; among voters aged fifty and over, Kennedy dropped to 25 per cent, well behind McCarthy's 32 and Humphrey's 29 per cent.

Cutting up the vote by education also produced sharp alterations in Kennedy's popularity. He was strongest among people with grade-school education: 36 per cent of them supported him. But this dropped to 29 per cent among people with high-school education *and down to 18 per cent among the college-educated.* Eugene McCarthy's famous remark that "the better-educated people vote for us," was only the truth, for his pattern of support according to education was exactly the reverse of Kennedy's. He had only 23 per cent of grade-school people, but 34 per cent of the high-school people and *44 per cent of the college-educated.* (Humphrey's support showed little variation, running sadly 24–24–26 up the education ladder.)

Kennedy's strengths showed up when the division was made by religion. He was ahead among Catholics, with 36 per cent to McCarthy's 30 and Humphrey's 24. Among Protestants, Kennedy fell to 26 per cent, behind McCarthy's 33 and only just ahead of Humphrey's 25 per cent. Again, he led among labor-union families, with 31 per cent to McCarthy's 29 and Humphrey's 27.

He had, in other words, converted no one. And this was revealed still more brutally in a rather more unusual set of questions that Gallup used. These divided up the national vote into those who approved of LBJ's Vietnam policy and those who disapproved. As might be expected, this division made all the difference to McCarthy. Among people who approved of Johnson's policy in Vietnam, McCarthy scored only 26 per cent. But among those who disapproved of the war policy, Mc-

Carthy's support rose to 41 per cent. A similar process, but in reverse, applied to Hubert Humphrey. Among people who disapproved of the war policy, Humphrey got only 16 per cent. Among those who approved, he more than doubled his support to 36 per cent.

But for Robert Kennedy, the issue of the war—remarkably—*made no measurable difference at all.* Among people who approved of Johnson's war policy, he scored 28 per cent. Among those who disapproved, he scored 28 per cent. It was, to say the least, a strange situation for a peace candidate. And, Kennedy had been campaigning hard for more than a month, with massive publicity.

The significance of the Gallup survey could be put this way: that Kennedy's support was coming from people who supported him out of personal loyalty, virtually regardless of the stand he was making on the war. No more dramatic illustration could be imagined of the damage that Kennedy had done himself by allowing McCarthy to become established ahead of him as the antiwar candidate. Nor could anything more thoroughly justify the men like Walinsky and Lowenstein who had urged him to run.

Kennedy even received some advice from the "old hands" on his staff to stop talking about the war in tough Midwestern states like Indiana. This he declined to do. But he spoke about it cautiously, saying, in effect that he would do something about it but that what he would do would not be a surrender. ("We can do better in Vietnam.") He was trapped. For long-term advantage, he needed to speak out more firmly on the war—especially if he was to make a proper impact in the Western primaries, where peace feeling was strong. But he could be badly damaged in Indiana by intemperate peace-mongering.

One of Kennedy's assets was the condition of McCarthy's campaign in Indiana, which was lurching toward the nadir it reached shortly afterward in Nebraska. Later, McCarthy was to say, "Probably, we should never have gone into Indiana, and if we had to, we probably shouldn't have done anything more than play baseball." (A set of pictures that resulted from a casual baseball game between the Senator and a group of newsmen produced just about the only favorable publicity McCarthy received in the state.) Although McCarthy's campaign in Indiana started well before Kennedy's, it did not have the corpus of effective local organizers which had made New Hampshire and Wisconsin work, and would soon do the same in Oregon. Gordon St. Angelo later claimed to have "infiltrated" McCarthy's organization: and indeed, Dan Fasig, an Indianapolis attorney who played a leading part in it, maintained excellent relations with the regular Democrats.

Curtis Gans, the national organizer in charge of the Indiana campaign, devised the so-called "rural strategy," which was later the target of much ridicule. This consisted of getting McCarthy out into the small towns—where, as a result of poor scheduling, he not infrequently got lost. It did not make a good impression on citizens to have the Senator lean out of his car window to ask where he was. No doubt it was this sense of disorientation which led him to say, from the steps of the courthouse in Gas City, "Here, in New Hampshire, you like to talk about the big issues." In the end, McCarthy did not do particularly well in the small towns against Branigin and Kennedy. And his strong performance in the suburbs of Gary indicated that there were lost opportunities in similar districts in Indianapolis.

What McCarthy did do in Indiana was begin to develop his radical position in a way that would stand him in good stead later. He began to talk more and more about the need to replace officials like Dean Rusk and J. Edgar Hoover. And he recommended the recognition of Communist China.

Confronted with Kennedy's talk of national and international issues —and McCarthy's rather cool-toned but developing radicalism—Governor Branigin's response was unhesitating parochialism. While they talked of war and poverty, he ran as a country boy against city slickers, referring throughout to McCarthy and Kennedy as "tourists." His headquarters in the Claypool Hotel, in Indianapolis, was fitted up as a "traditional" Indiana grocery store, christened Branigin's Corner, and staffed with people pretending to be cracker-barrel philosophers. Indeed, there were actual cracker barrels lying around. The Governor's campaign consisted largely of rustic imitations—which nobody seemed to think were discredited by the fact that he was a Harvard Law School graduate who had made several million dollars as a corporation lawyer.

A campaign journey with the peppery little white-haired gentleman was a slightly surrealistic experience: a step back into the grand old vaudeville tradition of American politics, when the candidate was expected to put on a good rousing show but not, for God's sake, to say anything serious. Governor Branigin had little to say to reporters except ritual denunciations of Kennedy and McCarthy, and when questioned about his stand on the issue of the campaign, was likely to say, accusingly, "You're trying to put words into my oral cavity!"

He did not waste much time in Indianapolis, which, having a substantial Negro population, was bound to go to Kennedy, anyway. The Governor made for the small towns with names like Peru, Floyd's Knobs, Gas City, and Brazil, which were his natural political environment.

The small towns of central Indiana look very much like each other, and they look even more like film sets. The streets are always straight and lined with shady trees. The houses are wooden and painted white, with no fences of any kind between house and house or between house and footpath. Most towns seem to manage a town hall or a courthouse on the highest point of land, constructed along vaguely classical lines with pillars and white stone. There is always a war memorial, celebrating victories from Tippecanoe to Iwo Jima. And one frequently comes across old men who say "by cracky" and spit with power and precision onto the pavement.

The Governor started a characteristic swing early on the morning of May 7, in Logansport (population twenty-three thousand) where he gave a speech perhaps as serious as any he gave in the campaign:

> We are in a very unparalleled situation here in America. There is this big conflict now on. I feel we shouldn't follow the course of appeasement, although I'm no saber rattler.
>
> I think President Johnson has done the right thing. He has retired so that he could negotiate a better end to the war. Many people think he dropped out because he thought he couldn't win another election, but I prefer to think he put his country first.

After the speech, Branigin asked what the legal situation would be if he, Branigin, led the state delegation to Chicago in the event that one of his rivals won the election. This drew the first homely witticism of the day: "I'm a lawyer, but I'm not going to speak for myself . . . and have a fool for a client."

At Peru, he was greeted by a fifty-strong choir of Moral Rearmament boys and girls wearing badges saying: UP WITH THE PEOPLE. The group was very clean and white, but contained two black children, seemingly so that a song about the multiracial society could be included in the repertoire. Singing was conducted for half an hour, with much massed arm-waving, fist-clenching, and vaguely military gestures of various sorts. One number, rendered with great energy, went:

> "Freedom isn't free!
> Freedom isn't free!
> You gotta pay a price:
> You gotta sacrifice!
> Freedom isn't free!"

The multiracial song was even more intriguing. One of the black children was a little boy being put to bed, and the other was his father. To a high, sugary tune, the lad asks, "Daddy, what color is God's skin?" To which Dad, and the chorus, reply crisply:

> "It's red and yellow—
> It's black and white!
> Every man's the same in the Good Lord's sight!"

Branigin, grand little trouper, appeared literally to dash a tear from his eye at this, before making tracks for Wabash ("First City Lit by Electricity"). After a short account of his ambition to serve the state as favorite son, he offered one of the most remarkable dissertations on Vietnam given in the whole year:

> None of us like war, and I hope it's over soon. But don't let's leave five hundred thousand boys and girls out there without an honorable settlement. Don't be weak and give in. Let us have no appeasement. We must be strong but not cruel.
>
> This is a sad war. The only war that was a happy one was World War One. People used to dance in the streets to see the boys go away. I was fifteen then, and I remember the songs . . . "K-K-K-Katy," and "How You Gonna Keep 'Em Down on the Farm, Now That They've Seen Paree?" But we haven't been happy in a war since then.

Exit, to cheers. The next stop was Huntingdon, where, met by the Boy Scout bugle band, Branigin declared emotionally, "The Boy Scout Handbook—next to the Bible—is the finest book that ever existed!" All this made a long day—during which the Governor seemed to have taken a good many jolts of I. W. Harper—and by the time the caravan reached Fort Wayne, he was tiring. Not that Branigin allowed this to inhibit his relentless pursuit of the local angle. If Wabash had been "the most delightful city in the whole Hoosier State," Fort Wayne was "the Hoosier jewel." Energetically, the Governor sought out jewel-like local qualities: "You have produced a great trustee for Indiana and Purdue universities. . . . You have produced—a great stream-pollution expert."

Before a slightly baffled crowd of about three hundred at Concordia Senior College, the Governor spoke for a rambling hour or so, concluding with a surrealist reflection on civil disorder. There had been riots in America, he conceded—but not just in America. England had the same trouble: "We've heard of the cyclists and the mobs running over Runnymede!" Nobody cared to ask the Governor what he meant, for fear of the accusation of "putting words into his oral cavity."

Branigin's performance might have looked artless and folksy—but of course it was not. The formula was a well-aged one, especially in the South and Midwest: a mercenary organization to mobilize the people, and an entertaining pitch by the candidate avoiding, so far as possible, substantive issues. Issues, after all, are liable to put as many people off as they turn on. The aim is simply to help people to remember the name when the election workers conduct them to the polls.

Contrary to theorists of the "Golden Age" of American politics, it was not cold-eyed admen in the mass-media age who discovered the political advantages of divorcing style from content. That manipulative proposition has been known since the first time a pair of thumbs were hooked into a pair of galluses. Of course, the politics of hokum go along fine with mass-media techniques, and so it was not surprising to find, standing behind Branigin the spurious folk hero, Robert Montgomery, one of the sharpest admen in Indianapolis and a veteran of the 1960 Kennedy campaign. Montgomery, who had also done the media work for Branigin's successful attack on the governorship, was an explicit admirer of the Branigin technique. "Running for governor, he didn't make a political speech. And so far as I know, he hasn't made a political speech this time. But, I'm happy to say, no one has noticed the omission."

Insofar as the Governor did have an issue, it was the proposition that the state should not sign away its votes to any one candidate. The argument was dressed up with lavish quantities of Hoosier patriotism. In this, the Governor was much helped by the most powerful newspaper in the state, the *Indianapolis Star,* an organ of shattering conservatism, one of the few papers in the country ever to stay consistently to the right of the Manchester, New Hampshire, *Union-Leader.* The *Star* is owned by Eugene Pulliam of Phoenix, a stanch Republican, friend and promoter of Barry Goldwater. The Democratic governor, however, gave every sign of pleasure at the support the paper gave him.

It was a local journalists' joke that "the only way Kennedy could get on the *Star*'s front page would be by getting shot." This was not quite true: the Kennedy name could make the front page any time some local Branigin supporter cared to unleash a particularly preposterous attack on him. On April 30, for instance, there was a very fine specimen headed: "McHale Raps Kennedy's Use of Racism, Religion."

This turned out to be about Frank McHale, a former Democratic National Committeeman, fearing for the purity of "Hoosier politics." The *Star* reported:

McHale said Kennedy brought up racism by telling Indiana University School of Medicine students, most of them white, that Negroes carry the major portion of the struggle in Vietnam.

"That statement just isn't true, but it promotes racism, and that's apparently what he's trying to do," McHale said.

He added: "We in Indiana haven't made distinctions counting our men who have died in Vietnam. The courageous Indiana Negroes who have died have died shoulder to shoulder with their white comrades.

"Why is King Bobby trying to downgrade the efforts of the white soldiers who have died?" McHale continued.

McHale concluded this performance by invoking Robert Kennedy's own brother against him, saying that the late, beloved President John F. Kennedy would be "ashamed" to hear of his brother's behavior. The *Star* vigorously propagated the Branigin mythology, in which the election was dramatized as a contest between sturdy Hoosier folk virtues and degenerate but well-heeled carpetbaggers. The entire xenophobia was encapsulated in a cartoon, printed on May 3, which showed a stern-faced, pipe-smoking old gentleman wearing an expression of contemptuous independence and a vest labeled DEBT-FREE INDIANA. He was seated on a bench, and in the background an enormously hairy Kennedy could be seen making wild, demagogic gestures. (Kennedy had had his hair cut before coming into the state, but that never fazed the *Star*.) "Debt-Free Indiana" was surrounded by a small crowd of people pushing television cameras and microphones at him, and these people were labeled up as a fairly complete version of the demonology of the farther right. There were "Liberal Press," "National TV," "Walter Crankcase," "Bunkley and Hinkley," and "Assorted City Slickers" (which seemed odd in a newspaper owned by a multimillionaire, published in a large city, and backing another millionaire for office). But perhaps the finest stereotype was a buck-toothed, top-hatted figure in morning dress, looking precisely like a dated Communist cartoon of an evil capitalist, labeled "Eastern Extremists." This large team was saying en masse to D.F.I.: "Come now, surely you don't want to live like a cornball all of your life!"

The flaw in Governor Branigin's operation was, sadly for him, the fabled Indiana machine, which he had neglected and antagonized throughout his four terms as Governor. Had he not done so, it is just conceivable that Branigin-style politics might have damaged Kennedy really seriously. As it was, the machine stayed loyal to him out of self-preservation, but with no enthusiasm.

Meanwhile, the Kennedy operation was acquiring fresh manpower by the day and the hour. "People were crawling out of the woodwork to help us," recalls Dougherty in a tribute to his first experience in "participatory democracy." Unlike in the McCarthy campaign, however, the zeal was helped along by cash payments: usually a dollar fifty an hour. At the height of the campaign, there were some four hundred people working for Kennedy, in addition to his national staff. Most of their efforts were aimed at mobilizing Kennedy's solid potential vote, rather than trying to contact new converts—and in view of the time available and what the private polls said, this was clearly the right approach. As Dougherty puts it: "It was a mechanical thing, a matter of grabbing people and getting them out to vote, dragging them out by their heads."

Normally, a native machine is hard to beat at this. Apart from knowing the right people to bring out on election day, an efficient machine operator knows the even more important secret of which people *not* to bring out because they are liable to vote against you. Only years of local investigation—spurred by the knowledge that a job hangs on it—produce that kind of intimate knowledge.

But the professional politicians of Indiana fought reluctantly for Branigin. It was felt that he was high-handed and arbitrary. Worse. He did not seem to have mastered the very formal set of rules about the reciprocity of favors by which the professionals live. In fighting for him, they were motivated, for the most part, by nothing more than a fear of the electoral consequences of a Kennedy victory. In only one part of the state did the professionals conduct their fight with real zest: Lake County, the county area of Gary. But the motivation here was hatred of Kennedy, not love of Branigin.

Gary is a spectacularly unattractive town, founded at the turn of the century purely for the convenience of U.S. Steel and named after the corporation's chairman of the board of directors, Elbert H. Gary. Built on the flat, sandy shores of Lake Michigan, the town makes no concessions to aesthetics, and the monotony of the landscape is relieved only by clusters of chimneys, oil-storage tanks, and power pylons. It is tough, as well as unlovely, and quite a good place to get beaten up in. (One of the more colorful beatings of the year occurred around the time of the election, when a gang of teen-age boys led by a five-foot, two-hundred-pound Lesbian pulped a local priest with a baseball bat in his own churchyard.) Yet this place consistently attracts good reporters—and the attraction is reflected in the quality of the Gary *Post-Tribune*—because

Gary has long been a fabulous center of political corruption. "There are enough news stories in this town to last you forever," says Terry O'Rourke, the *Post-Tribune*'s city editor.

The town's population is about half black and half white. (The whites are divided into classic ethnic communities: Croatians, Serbs, Germans, and Poles. Many are only first- or second-generation Americans, and ancient European feuds, like that between the Serbs and Croats, still persist.) Most of them are industrial workers, and so Lake County is classic Democratic territory. The Lake County boys are almost as good at "improving" the vote for those they favor as Mayor Daley's more notorious operators in nearby Chicago. It is said that there is a small shack on the main street of Gary from which eleven ghostly Mexicans have voted reliably for many years. They are also famous for making the most of the financial opportunities once their men are in office.

Early in 1960, Robert Kennedy arrived in Gary and met with the Lake County leaders. He explained that his brother Jack, a good Irish Catholic from Boston, was running for President and would be in the Indiana primary. He was already doing well, but it would be helpful in terms of impressing convention delegates if he could get a very good vote in Indiana. Kennedy realized that this was not easy, as Jack would be unopposed in the primary and interest would be low. Therefore he had come to ask for help in rolling up as good a total as possible in Lake County.

The Lake County boys were favorably disposed toward the Kennedys, and they did all they could. Jack Kennedy got a very respectable vote in the Indiana primary. Robert went on to become Attorney General. But in 1963, Federal agents moved in on the Mayor of Gary, George (Cha-cha) Chachiris, and arrested him for the crime of failing to pay income tax on the graft he collected. It seemed to the Lake County boys that this was the height of ingratitude and boorishness. (Threatening noises were also made at other citizens of Gary, but Cha-cha was the only man arrested and jailed.) It was, of course, entirely consistent with Kennedy's sternly moral views on the sanctity of public life that Chachiris should be jumped on. But, as the Lake County boys saw it, Kennedy had been happy enough about their political integrity when he wanted their help.

There was no hope of beating Robert Kennedy in Lake County in 1968, since the blacks would vote for him almost unanimously and so would most of the blue-collar whites. Further, Kennedy had the tacit support of Gary's black mayor, Richard Hatcher, who had won office independent of the white machine. But the Lake County boys were determined to hold his vote down as far as possible.

This was neatly shown in the arrangement of the ballot papers for the primary, the result of much thoughtful work by John Krupa, secretary of the Election Board and a prominent figure in Lake County politics. Indiana has a complex primary ballot, on which not only the Presidency of the United States is at stake, but such attractive posts as judgeships, coronerships, and treasurerships, along with seats in the House of Representatives and in the state legislature. In areas of Democratic hegemony, such as Lake County, the primary election is the major focus of energy, since once a candidate is assured of the Democratic nomination, success in the election follows virtually as a matter of course.

On this complex ballot, artistic variations in the order in which candidates' names are listed can have great effect on the voters' behavior. To prevent such artistry, a new law was passed in time for the 1968 primary, stating that all candidates should be listed in alphabetical order. This law, as interpreted by the Lake County experts, produced a fascinating ballot. The configuration of the voting machines used allowed no more than four names to be listed vertically on the ballot. Thus, in a notional ballot, they might appear thus:

County Dogcatcher
(Vote for Two)

Appleseed	Earhole	Inkstain
Brownjug	Fantan	Jellybaby
Comfort	Gumshoe	Kupcake
Dimsin	Hotspot	Lickspittle

Clearly, it might be useful to be on the top line, since voters, confronted with the task of choosing twenty-three names out of a hundred and thirty-six (as was the case on the Lake County Democratic Primary ballot in 1968), are likely to take the easy way out. At first glance, it might seem that one's chances were a function of alphabetical distribution of names over columns of four. But in 1968 it was possible to do better—after all, the law does not say that *each* vertical column must contain four names. One thus got some interesting combinations of names and empty spaces. For instance:

Judge
Criminal Court
(Vote for One)

John H.
McKENNA

Richard L.   Norbert
HOWARD   WLEKLINSKY

Paul B.
HUEBNER

George
KRSTOVICH

It may be superfluous to explain that the Lake County organization was favoring John H. McKenna for the criminal-court judgeship.

Although these devices showed that the Lake County boys had not lost their skills, they were not themselves usable in the Presidential primary. There being only three names for the Democratic slot, artistic permutations were useless. Other techniques were required.

There was always harassment. When the first busloads of Kennedy students from Chicago appeared in Gary to contact voters, Lake County officials did their best to frighten them away with dark talk of injunctions that were about to be issued. "Accidents" frequently happened to Kennedy literature, and sometimes to McCarthy literature. And, of course, there was no cooperation from local officials in such matters as helping to check voter registration and the like. (Perhaps the nastiest jab—which effectively neutralized Kennedy's eve-of-poll television program—was not a Lake County product. The Kennedy team had a film to run that night, showing, among other things, Kennedy shaking hands with a man in an American Legion hat. Five minutes before the Indianapolis courts closed at five p.m., the Legion secured an injunction against the film on the grounds that it involved the Legion in politics. At ten p.m., the Kennedy lawyers managed to get a special hearing of the Indiana State Supreme Court. After some argument they got the injunction lifted. But, as one of them said bitterly afterward, "What do you do with a political film at midnight?" It could have been a coincidence, but it was difficult to forget that Frank McHale, the stern Hoosier Democrat who had been so critical of Kennedy's views on the Negro in Vietnam, had once been a member of the American Legion national committee.)

In the end, it came down to seeing what could be done to affect the

way the vote came out. The conditions of voting in Indiana came as
something of a surprise to Kennedy's Eastern hands. "I don't know
what kinds of laws they've got out there," said Gerald Dougherty, "but
it isn't like Massachusetts. We have polling stations in solid places, like
schools and firehouses. There . . . they were just moving them about
all the time—from a garage to a barbershop, from a barbershop to a
garage." The idea, naturally, was to disrupt the teams of amateurs who
were getting the vote out for Kennedy. But finally, it seems, the valiant
efforts of the local professionals were simply borne down by weight of
people. "It was a waste of manpower," said one Kennedy man. "But
we had enough people to watch every polling booth from four-thirty
a.m.—and we did."

Of course, it was harder to discover what was happening to the
voting machines themselves in Lake County. There were several dark
tales of machines' being found with substantial Branigin totals racked
up before polling had even begun on May 7. Just how much of
this went on is difficult to estimate.

Probably the various harassments organized by the machine-men
did have some slight effect on Kennedy's total—and that was bad
enough, for he needed every vote he could scrape together. Still, the
votes that came in looked, at least at first glance, like a solid enough
win: Kennedy got 328,118 of the 776,513 Democratic votes cast, or
42.3 per cent. Branigin got 238,700, or 30.7 per cent, and McCarthy
got 209,695, or 27 per cent. It was a horrid disappointment for Governor Branigin, although the result had been foretold by the private
polls Robert Montgomery had organized for him. "He just couldn't
believe people liked the Kennedys that much," said Montgomery later.

But it was a messy result. For one thing, the control Kennedy
gained over the Indiana delegation was somewhat slippery: the national
convention delegates had to follow the voters' preference only on the
first ballot, being free after that to follow their own inclinations. As the
delegates were to be picked by the party regulars at the state convention
in June, no one was in any doubt about what those inclinations would
be—they would be for Humphrey. Indeed, the real victor of this exercise
in participatory democracy was the candidate who did not participate.
Kennedy's desire to avoid a clash with McCarthy in Indiana had been
a sound one, for the two insurgents had chiefly damaged each other.
McCarthy, obviously, had been damaged the more, but he had not been
eliminated: indeed, he had improved somewhat on the support the opinion polls had found for him. (Harris and NBC-Quayle had both put it

at twenty-four per cent.) The sad thing, from the viewpoint of a liberal Democrat, was that the voting pattern made it look as though either Kennedy or McCarthy, fighting alone, might have beaten Branigin. Naturally, Kennedy led easily in industrial areas like Gary—but McCarthy did better there than might have been expected. Lake County went: Kennedy 58,259; McCarthy 42,839; Branigin 23,330. McCarthy won the white executive suburbs of Gary—where, interestingly, Wallace had polled well in the 1964 primary. (There was some evidence throughout the year that elements of McCarthy's support came from "alienated" middle-class voters prepared to support almost any new figure.) "I'm pleased," said Kennedy. "I think it's better to win than to come in second or third." But McCarthy replied, "We have tested the enemy. We know his techniques, we know his weaknesses." Only a few weeks ago, the enemy had been Lyndon Johnson and the war.

When it became clear that Kennedy had won, a festival atmosphere took over in the Kennedy suite. Calls, congratulating him, began to come in, and he had just taken one from Pat Lawford in California when McCarthy came on television, being interviewed. Kennedy, cigar in mouth, started across the room to the TV set, and when he was halfway there, McCarthy began to explain that it wasn't winning that mattered. Kennedy stopped dead, staring at the screen. "That isn't the way I was brought up!" he snapped.

Kennedy knew that he had not broken the strange, newly forged loyalty that bound so many people to McCarthy. In the small hours of May 8, with virtually all the returns in, he went out with a group of staff men and reporters to get something to eat. Not surprisingly, there seemed to be only one restaurant open in Indianapolis, and there Kennedy encountered two young McCarthy workers, looking as weary as he did himself. There was a brief, low-pitched conversation—Kennedy asking, sadly, why they could not support him. (He always seemed hurt by evidence of hostility from those who he thought were on the same side.) But it was not the time for communication. As the two young workers left, Kennedy gazed after them wistfully.

The extra irony of such an incident was that the middle-class liberals who were turning away from Kennedy were turning away from the man who above all others could moderate the hostility between black and white which threatened the Democratic Party at its base in 1968. There were all sorts of rational reasons for a coalition of the McCarthy and Kennedy forces. But this was a contest of heroes in which rationalism had no place.

One week later, the Nebraska primary showed a simpler, but similar, pattern. In this rather surprising environment (where John Kennedy got his lowest vote in 1960), Robert Kennedy had perhaps his best-run campaign, apart from South Dakota. McCarthy was at his weakest, with almost no organization except around the university at Lincoln. Kennedy's plain but efficient operation was run by Pat Lucey, his chieftain from Wisconsin. With a small Democratic registration (the final vote was only 162,611), Lucey was able to reach every voter at least four times with literature and telephone calls: it was a textbook job. Even so, McCarthy managed to hold onto 31.2 per cent of the vote, while Kennedy took 51.7 per cent. Again, it was not a knockout blow. Pierre Salinger claimed, ebulliently, that the result "finished Gene McCarthy as a credible candidate"—but that only showed that Salinger did not know what was happening in Oregon.

Nobody could have looked more pleased about the result than Senators Fred Harris and Walter Mondale. Appearing together in Washington, they blandly produced an estimate that their man Humphrey now had 1265 votes promised to him on the first ballot, only 47 short of nomination. This, they felt, was rather more significant than a popular primary election in Nebraska.

But even these cool accumulators of pledges admitted to a little concern in private. With Oregon and California still to come, passions and emotions were being aroused which could easily damage the delicate structure of the Democratic coalition. The contests within the party were polarizing sharply—and those who feared that the process was just beginning were correct.

If the Democrats were in such bad shape, what did the Republicans have to offer? In the Indiana primary, running without opposition, Richard Nixon had attracted 508,362 votes. His lonely eminence gave a fine sense of party unity when contrasted with the brawl on the other Indiana ballot. But in Nebraska, things were not quite so simple. It is one of those odd states where a man's well-wishers can place him on the ballot without asking him. Along with Harold Stassen and an Indian cowboy named Americus Liberator, the name of Ronald Reagan appeared on the Nebraska ballot. Governor Reagan's position was that he wasn't a candidate but that it would be "presumptuous" to swear away *any* interest in the Presidency. And on May 14, to his ostensible surprise, he managed to acquire 42,703 of 200,476 Republican votes cast (21.3 per cent), which represented quite an inroad on Richard Nixon's 140,336 (70 per cent), especially as it was supposed to have been done without any campaigning. As we shall see, Reagan's claim not to have campaigned was as disingenuous as his surprise at the result: but no matter what, the Nebraska vote manifested some dangerous strains and rivalries within a Republican Party which at last seemed ready to come into its own.

There was another reason for Kennedy to feel uneasy as the trail moved west. On May 3, just before the Indiana poll, the Paris peace talks were announced. Everyone knew that the political substrata were moving, somehow. No one knew quite what the result would be.

ACT V

The Republican Phoenix

1

The Field, Ten to One, Bar One

"They're somewhat like the lowest of forms of plant and animal life. Even at their highest point of vitality there is not much life in them; on the other hand, they don't die."

> —Eugene J. McCarthy, on the nature of the Republican Party

"We know who our nominees will be. . . . I'm happy to be able to say the Republicans have all their bloody infighting to look forward to."

> —John Bailey, Chairman of Democratic National Committee, January 8, 1968

While the Democrats were having their slugfest, the Republicans presented a prim, almost smug exterior. Some felt the complacency entirely justified: An appearance of unity would, it was argued, be the most powerful of assets in 1968. All the Republicans had to do was hold themselves aloof while the Democrats destroyed themselves. Surely, at the end of the day, the voters would rally to the party that, through all the turbulence of the year, had contrived to keep itself intact.

Or would they? Nothing alienates voters more rapidly than the suspicion that a party feels it has their votes in its pocket. Republicans had good reason to be wary of this—from their viewpoint—atavistic tendency in the electorate. Most of the party's leaders were old enough to remember Thomas Dewey's campaign against Harry Truman in 1948—and the consequences thereof.

So with the complacency went a certain undertow of anxiety. Moreover, there was a school of thought that envied the Democrats their tribulations. Conflict makes news, and news was a commodity the Republicans badly needed. The Democrats might be fighting dirty, but at least they were fighting; in contrast, Nixon was merely shadowboxing. He could chalk up a seemingly impressive string of primary victories— but where was the opposition? Since Romney had failed to answer the opening bell in New Hampshire, there had been precious little to get excited about.

Back in the fall of 1967, everyone was predicting that the Republicans would be the headline-making party in election year. At that time, the chances of an effective challenge to Lyndon Johnson's renomination seemed impossibly remote, whereas the Republicans were exhibiting a luxury of choice—with Romney, increasingly dovish on Vietnam, looking capable of provoking Nixon, still a hard-liner on the war, into a tough fight for the nomination. And behind these two stood a whole range of glistering personalities—John V. Lindsay, Mayor of New York, and Charles H. Percy, the youthful liberal Senator from Illinois, who might be lured into contention. Yet here they were, in the spring of 1968, with scarcely an issue raised or a hair out of place. Nixon was not only the One, he appeared to be the only one.

By this time, the Republican Party was so well inured to irony that nobody seemed much aware of yet another odd twist. After the Goldwater debacle—when the party of Abraham Lincoln saved itself from electoral annihilation by taking the five Deep South states (South Carolina, Georgia, Alabama, Mississippi, and Louisiana; if George Wallace had run for the Presidency in 1964, Goldwater might have ended up with only one of the fifty states in the plus column, since the only other state he carried was his own, Arizona)—there was not much left in the way of historical paradox.

The number of time-honored rules broken by Goldwater is, perhaps, best illustrated by a passage from George H. Mayer's standard history, *The Republican Party, 1854–1966.* In the preface to the second edition, Mayer felt compelled to answer critics who had taken him to task for explaining the party in terms of personalities rather than structure and ideology:

> Only during the formative years of an American party, when it is developing a reliable base of popular support, is such an [ideological] approach of any major usefulness. Once this task is accomplished, however, principles tend to be an embarrassment. They cannot be abandoned or ignored except at the risk of offending the faithful. On the other hand,

they cannot be implemented in consistent fashion without disrupting the varied pressure groups that constitute the backbone of a successful party. So after the period of *Sturm und Drang,* the spotlight shifts from principles to leaders who keep the party afloat by personal charisma, adroit handling of patronage, and the manipulation of ephemeral issues that attract the voters.

In 1964, Goldwater bucked the problems of balancing pressure groups, heeded the voice of the faithful, excised the ambiguities from the Republican credo, fought an ideological campaign—and paid the penalty. Goldwater's coattails dragged Republicans down from every tier of the party's hierarchy. In the Senate and the House of Representatives, the Republicans woke up to find themselves weaker than they had been at any time since before the war; farther down the line the devastation was even more severe. Almost five hundred seats in state legislatures were engulfed in the Democratic tide; Republicans emerged in control of only seven of the fifty legislatures. To compound the bitterness, some of the most notable exceptions, like Romney and Lindsay, had survived by dissociating themselves from the national ticket.

Like most severe defeats, however, it offered an unusually fine opportunity to rebuild. That the Republicans moved up with such remarkable speed is partly a tribute to their own organization, and partly a commentary on President Johnson's rapid decline in public esteem. Helped by a low Democratic turnout, the Republicans came back in fine style in the mid-term elections in 1966—a phenomenon that amazed all the pundits except one Richard Milhous Nixon, who, while not a candidate, had campaigned vigorously on behalf of those who were (earning debts of gratitude that were to prove invaluable two years later).

Most spectacular of all were the gubernatorial gains. Of the fifteen Republican governorships in contention in November 1966, all but two— Maine and Kansas—were held; and Republicans captured no less than ten states from the Democrats, leaving them in control of half the country's state houses. Attractive deductions could be, and were, made about the significance of this new holding. The electoral votes of states with Republican governors amounted to 293—23 votes more than a Presidential candidate would need for a majority in the Electoral College.

In the House, the Republicans more than recouped their losses in 1964, and their ranks in the Senate were inflated by some intriguing new personalities: among them, Mark O. Hatfield, a former university professor and two-time Governor of Oregon; Edward W. Brooke from Massachusetts, the first Negro to enter the upper chamber since Reconstruction times, and Charles Percy, a product, according to Arthur Schlesinger, Jr., of "the black art of public relations," but a doyen of the progressive Republicans nonetheless.

Goldwater, naturally, had little to do with the Republican renaissance. Even Reagan, considered by many to be Goldwater's heir apparent, had asked him to stay clear of his campaign in California. And a visit by Goldwater to Mississippi had failed to delight the local Republicans on account of their quondam hero's warm commendation of the benefits of integration. All traces of Goldwater's influence had been expunged from the Republican National Committee, which under the fussy but diligent chairmanship of Ray C. Bliss of Ohio was fashioning an effective instrument of persuasion for 1968. Bliss turned the RNC into a forcing house for technical instruction; ideology was no part of his concern. He prides himself on being a technician in the least glamorous, but essential, aspects of party activity: registration drives, women's organizations, setting up research and public-relations facilities—the whole area covered by the term "political nuts and bolts." No less than twenty thousand party workers were corralled into Bliss-sponsored seminars on these prosaic subjects.

All this was excellent groundwork, but no guarantee of a happy outcome in 1968. The Republican *annus mirabilis* of 1966, while it had braced the party's self-esteem, had affected fundamental voting allegiances less than most people imagined. In the electorate at large, Republicanism was still a minority sentiment. A Gallup poll of that year asking voters whether they considered themselves Republicans, Democrats, or Independents had produced a 27–48–25 percentage split. This still indicated a handy margin for the Democrats (though the margin narrows if one takes into account the readiness of many Southern Democrats to vote Republican in national elections).

Another problem was a by-product of the Republicans' 1966 success. Freed from the constraints of overriding national ideology, the candidates around the country had been able to run their campaign more or less as they pleased. Thus Reagan could ride an extreme right-wing tide to victory in California; while, to the east, liberal "problem-solvers" like Nelson A. Rockefeller in New York, John H. Chafee in Rhode Island, and George Romney in Michigan were consolidating their appeal. Come 1968, however, these powerful and disparate personalities would somehow have to subsume their differences and swing behind a new leader. The Republicans had many new, and reburnished old, names to conjure with as Presidential and Vice-Presidential hopefuls, but most of them represented a bad case of the horrors for one or another section of the party.

No section of the party was more problematic than the South. Up in the big Northern industrial areas, Goldwaterism may have seemed like a bad dream, but in many areas below the Mason-Dixon line, it was viewed as just about the best thing that ever happened in national politics—at least until the votes were counted. The once-solid South was now in a state of political flux, and few things were more unpredictable than Southern Republicanism.

Long before Goldwater, Republican sentiment in the South (commonly defined as the eleven states of the old Confederacy, with Oklahoma and Kentucky tacked on) had been on the upsurge. The first watershed had been the Eisenhower candidacy in 1952. Prior to that date, a Republican in the South, if one could be found, usually fell into one of three categories: eccentric, carpetbagger, or Negro. There were pockets of Republicanism among isolated communities in the Blue Ridge Mountains, which had originally abjured slaveowning, opposed the Civil War, and continued to vote against the separatist party regardless of any change in its political ethos. But for the most part, there was little to disturb the one-party rule of—primarily segregationist—Democrats. The purpose of most Republican state organizations was to reap the benefits of Federal patronage in the event of a national Republican administration. These "post-office Republicans," naturally, had no interest in expanding their parties, a process that could only diminish the value of the potential pickings.

After Eisenhower's election, the party's national chieftains decided to establish a more secure foothold in the South. A special division of the Republican National Committee mounted an organization drive, entitled "Operation Dixie," with a view to flushing out the patronage satraps and building up a solid party with grass-roots support. The industrialization of the South, bringing with it new executive talent from the North who found nothing alien in the idea of voting Republican, was another factor in the evolutionary change of Southern Republicanism.

In the big cities, the Republican Party became the party of the upwardly mobile. Without being out-and-out integrationists, these new Republicans tended to be softer on the race issue than their Democratic counterparts. They might not relish integrated schools, but the Deep South techniques of keeping the Negro subservient—a combination of free-lance violence and "Southern justice"—offended their sensibilities. In 1957, when Eisenhower sent troops to Little Rock to enforce school integration, the executive committee of the Georgia party startled Southern sentiment by commending this move. Besides, the Negro vote was an emergent factor that a vote-hungry party could hardly ignore. In 1960, Nixon got fifty-eight per cent of the Negro vote in Atlanta.

Then, four years later, Goldwater received less than one per cent of the Negro vote in that city—an indication of the change wrought by Goldwater Republicanism in Dixie. In the Deep South particularly, the party had become the home of some of the region's most outstanding segregationists. For evolution, Goldwater had substituted counterrevolution. Republican gradualists in race relations were suddenly swamped by men like Strom Thurmond in South Carolina, who had led the breakaway Dixiecrat movement in 1948, and Howard (Bo) Callaway in Georgia, a textile millionaire with, until 1964, a penchant for backing segregationist Democrats.

The pattern was anything but consistent, however, and the 1966 elections provided a few straws for the cause of moderate Republicanism. In Arkansas, for example, Nelson Rockefeller's brother Winthrop— with the family's racial liberalism toned down but by no means eliminated—won a thumping victory in that state's gubernatorial election. Over in Tennessee, another Republican moderate, Howard Baker, Jr., came through strongly to win a seat in the Senate. But these victories were balanced by others that pointed in a less benign, and ultimately more significant, direction.

The most characteristic of these came in Florida, where the flamboyant Claude R. Kirk, Jr., another former Democrat, won the governorship with a campaign that leaned heavily on the racist code slogan "Your home is your castle—protect it." Kirk made made much of the fact that his moderate opponent actually accepted assistance from three former aides of the opprobrious, South-whipping Bobby Kennedy. In 1968, it was clear that moderate Republicans in the South were in for a thin time. Two factors made this inevitable: the challenge of George Wallace, and the general reaction to President Johnson's relentless sponsorship of civil-rights legislation. Republicans now had a sizable holding to protect in the region; and if they were to keep it, a hard-line attitude on race might be the only course available. In this way, they could lambast the Democrats and hope to take some of the edge off Wallace's appeal. Yet all the Southern leaders knew that an explicit "Southern strategy" of the kind Goldwater had pursued was likely to be counterproductive. This time around, it had to be something more subtle.

What were the implications of this attitude for the Republican
Presidential-nomination process? Naturally, few tears were shed below
the Mason-Dixon line when George Romney, that most unsubtle of men
and an ardent civil-rights advocate in the bargain, dropped out of the
race. (Yet in a curious way, the South owed him a debt of gratitude.
By pre-empting the liberal challenge for the nomination for so long,
Romney had made it virtually impossible for more durable figures like
Lindsay and Percy to get into the race.) There was, it is true, the
specter of Romney's mentor and the South's bête noire, Nelson Rockefeller, which might have to be fought off—but the New Yorker, even
with all his millions, might find it difficult to get into contention at so
late a stage. Nixon was another matter; he might not inspire the South,
but at least he was flexible. The South, however, was in no hurry. The
basic instincts of the more astute Dixie Republican leaders was to stay
loose and uncommitted: they would have to be courted, and they knew
they would be. Growth had given the Southern Republicans a new awareness of their strength. Since 1952, the region's share of voting strength
at the convention had risen from 19 to 26.7 per cent; collectively, they
were in the happy position of wielding 356 convention votes, more than
half the number required for nomination. This time, they were going
to be used shrewdly.

The Nixon people had been warned. Early in May, Martin Feldman,
a New Orleans attorney who acted as general counsel to the GOP in
Louisiana and who had been watching Nixon's interests in Louisiana all
year, put in what he thought was an urgent long-distance call to Nixon's
campaign manager and law partner, John N. Mitchell. Feldman told
Mitchell that it seemed to him that the whole slant of Nixon's campaign
strategy was in error. Headquarters appeared hypnotized by Rockefeller,
yet he knew from experience in his own state, and from friends in
neighboring states, that the man to really worry about was Ronald
Reagan, the right-wing Governor of California.

Mitchell was reassuring, almost complacent: "I can see why you
would think that, Martin, but you don't have the broader picture as we
do up here." After all, the danger did not seem great. Reagan was still,
officially at least, not a candidate. He could not, therefore, openly recruit
delegates. But Feldman was right: it was Reagan, not Rockefeller, who,
in the end, constituted the more direct threat to Nixon's power base.

What sort of man is Ronald Reagan? And what sort of technique
turned him from a disregarded neophyte governor into a conceivable

Presidential candidate? Ronald Reagan's qualifications for the highest office in the land seemed exiguous at best. He had capped a career as a film actor with a late, albeit spectacular, entry into politics—moving, in the fall of 1966, straight into the governorship of what is now the nation's most populous state. By the time of the Republican convention in Miami, he had been in office little more than eighteen months and had incurred some powerful animosities in that time. A "Recall Reagan" petition drive was a conspicuous feature of California politics 1968— under California's bizarre election laws the Governor can be forced to undergo another election if enough voters are prepared to request it in writing. This drive was to collapse on the eve of the convention, short of the 780,000 signature target, but no fewer than 440,000 Californians had appended their names to this curious document.

Such an indictment might be expected to take the gilt off any office-holder. But then Reagan is no ordinary political phenomenon. He is, as Goldwater was, a symbol of the old values of God, Home, and Country. His appeal is visceral. The most perceptive of Reagan's biographers, Bill Boyarsky, said of him: "Reagan's importance is not as an administrator but as an evangelist warning of the destruction of the American Dream."

To those Americans who inhabit the Dream—the verdant suburbs —he is especially consoling. He is for lean government, low taxes, and flag-waving patriotism. He is against civil-rights legislation, university radicals, and expenditure of government funds in the ghetto. He is Goldwater mutton, dressed up as lamb. But the dressing is all-important. Goldwater, a man of considerable personal sweetness, was also something of a buffoon. People laughed at, not with, him. Reagan, on the other hand, is a wonderfully smooth performer. A dream candidate for those Republicans—and there were many—who thought that the policies in 1964 were right but that the personality was wrong. As a medium for the message, Ronnie was without peer.

Ronald Wilson Reagan was born on February 11, 1911, in the small town of Tampico, Illinois, the son of an Irish shoe salesman and a vigorous do-gooding mother of English-Scottish ancestry (she used to give readings to captive audiences in the town jail). Sympathetic studies of the man make much of this small-town origin: how its simple virtues and sturdy individualism shaped his attitudes to Big Government, and so on. Reagan himself, when writing of his childhood environment in his autobiography *Where's the Rest of Me?* (published in 1965), wallowed briefly in nostalgia: "There were woods, and mysteries, life and death among the small creatures, hunting and fishing; these were the days when I learned the true riches of rags." (Reagan has since learned the true riches of riches, wisely plowing most of his 1950s television income into real estate. After his election as Governor, he sold a large slice of his Malibu ranch to Twentieth Century–Fox studios for about two million dollars.)

As a youth, he loved to be outdoors. For seven summers he worked as a lifeguard, an occupation which Reagan later claimed taught him much about human nature, and by his own count saved seventy-seven bathers from drowning. Almost all of them, apparently, rendered him scant thanks, and most, he says, denounced him for hauling them ashore. "I got to recognize," he says, "that people hate to be saved."

Other lessons were in store for the young man. When he was graduated from Eureka College, Illinois (majoring modestly but adequately in economics and sociology, and earning school letters in football, basketball, and track), Reagan encountered an America in the throes of the Great Depression, when millions of his countrymen (including his own family) were in desperate need of economic salvation. He became and remained for over twenty years an ardent Democrat, a proponent of Roosevelt's New Deal and Truman's Fair Deal and the enlargement of government that was their inevitable concomitant.

Reagan's first job after graduation was as a sportscaster. Working out of Des Moines, Iowa, he became known as "the voice of the Chicago Cubs" and rapidly achieved the reputation of being one of the best baseball commentators in the Midwest. For the handsome sportscaster, Hollywood was a logical step in 1937. Reagan failed to become a great star, but he stayed at work, making eighty films in all, of which *Knute Rockne* (1940) was about the least perishable. His range as an actor was small, but he had a simple, reassuring style. He was good-looking—broad shoulders, sparkling teeth, wavy brown hair—but he never came on overbearing. It was no surprise when he was given the part of playing Shirley Temple's first grown-up boyfriend in *That Hagen Girl*. Bosley Crowther, the *New York Times*'s film reviewer, called him a "fellow who has a cheerful way of looking at dames."

Apart from his exploits as a celluloid all-American boy, Reagan showed unusual ability at finding his way around the specialized Hollywood power structure. By the end of the war, he knew the scene better than almost any other actor. He did his military service in Hollywood, as a personnel officer and narrator for the First Motion Picture Unit of the United States Air Force, a unit known as the Culver City Commandos, which churned out training and morale-boosting films. In 1947, Reagan, always an active member, was elected president of the Screen Actors' Guild, a position he was to hold for six terms.

When he took over the Guild, Hollywood was in a hysterical condition. The question of Communist Party membership was obsessing Congress and the motion-picture industry was one of its prime targets. Reagan lined the union up firmly on the side of the inquisitors.

The Guild officially condemned all members "who have been named as past or present Communist Party members and in appearing before the House Committee on Un-American Activities refused to state whether they are or ever have been members of the party." Reagan could muster some feeling on this issue. He had just resigned from the board of the Hollywood Independent Citizens Committee of Arts, Science, and Professions, which had been exposed as a "Communist front organization." He felt badly duped: "One day I woke up, looked about, and found it was Commie-dominated."

There are those who claim that Reagan's allegiance to the New Deal philosophy was insincere, that there had always been a right-wing conservative inside screaming for liberation. They cite his style—"always a Boy Scout"—his aversion to the income tax, and his readiness to cooperate with the House Un-American Activities Committee. But this is probably wisdom after the event. The explanation is simpler: that the real Reagan, like the celluloid Reagan, inhabits a world composed of "good guys" and "bad guys." Reagan, naturally, prefers to be a good guy. During the Depression and war years the Democrats had a firm hold on the good-guy image for a young man making his way. Then, after the war, everything became complicated. The ranks of the good guys were infiltrated with bad guys; so the one-time good guys became suckers, a very bad role in real or fantasy life. Reagan felt that he was made to play it briefly, and he did not like the action. He had no intellectual depth, no feeling for the complexity of human affairs. He simply wanted to know where the good guys were so that he could be one again.

The good guys may have moved to the other side of the political spectrum. No matter, Reagan's narrow, but concentrated talent, would be placed in their service. Thus the years of flailing about among the movie world's Communists, while painful, helped Reagan to a new view of the world and a new sense of his place in it. He sees this period as a crucial one: "Light was dawning in some obscure region of my head. I was beginning to see the seamy side of liberalism."

There is no reason to question Reagan's sincerity as a New Dealer, just as there is no reason to doubt his later ardor in the right-wing cause. He is plastic rather than perfidious.

The date when Reagan started to come over is not one he can pinpoint himself. But 1952 seems to have been a catalytic year. He voted for Eisenhower and married Nancy Davis (Reagan's first marriage, to the actress Jane Wyman, ended in divorce in 1948). Miss Davis, a graduate of Smith College, was a young actress of pronounced views, most of them borrowed from her father, an eminent Chicago neurosurgeon and one of the strong men of the American Medical Association. Reagan was subsequently recruited by the AMA for its campaign against the evils of "socialized medicine." The actor's smooth voice warned of the horrors ahead—"Medicare for the aged is a foot in the door of a government takeover of medicine."

But the refinement of right-wing Reagan really came during his work on the famous General Electric lecture tour, a job he held for eight years, from 1954 to 1962. His G.E. contract (starting salary a hundred twenty-five thousand dollars, rising to a hundred fifty), required Reagan to host the television production "General Electric Theater" and to spend twelve weeks a year touring G.E. plants throughout the country. It was a standard deal: the sight of a "celebrity" telling true tales from movieland, it was expected, would enliven both workers and management. But Reagan, to the surprise of his employers, decided to strive for something better—and instead of gossip gave them theory on such topics as "Losing Freedom by Installments" and "Communist Subversion in Hollywood."

Most of it went over well, though at one point Reagan, warming to his theme of governmental excess and citing the Tennessee Valley Authority as a classic example of Federal overinterference in the private sector, caused a tremor on the G.E. board. TVA happened to be a fifty-million-dollar customer for G.E. equipment. Reagan, flexibly, dropped the reference when G.E.'s chairman, Ralph Cordiner, suggested that its excision "would make my job easier."

It was the basic G.E. lecture-circuit patter, honed to a fine edge and rechristened "A Time for Choosing," that launched Ronald Reagan as a political figure. This speech, a smooth blend of free-enterprise heroics and excoriation of government expenditure, was delivered on national television in the closing weeks of the 1964 campaign, and it evoked tremendous response. More than five hundred thousand dollars in party contributions were attributed to that one telecast. There were many Republicans who felt that Reagan was wasted as a cheerleader while Goldwater was out there fumbling passes.

Shortly after the Republicans' electoral debacle, some very big California money began to coalesce behind the actor. Early in 1965, The Friends of Ronald Reagan came into existence with a group of ultra-reactionary businessmen at its core. The key figures were four erstwhile Goldwater supporters: Henry Salvatori, its most vigorous member, a developer of oil exploration and drilling equipment, and a backer of the Anti-Communist Voters League; the late A. C. Rubel, of Union Oil; Holmes Tuttle, a Los Angeles auto dealer; and Walter Knott, an amusement-park operator and a longtime fundraiser for right-wing causes.

Such a group was easily able to disabuse Reagan of any doubts he might have about his qualifications for high office. Reagan's career was at a standstill—he had moved on from "General Electric Theater" to hosting for "Death Valley Days"—and he could hardly expect to win new plaudits in the film business at his age. In any case, Salvatori's requirements for the type of man who should lead the country were not especially demanding. In one of his rare interviews, granted to Doris Klein of the Associated Press soon after Reagan won California, he outlined them. "People criticize Ronnie for having no political experience," he said,

> but he has a great image, a way to get through to people. Look at the Goldwater experience. His philosophy was sound, but he didn't articulate it moderately. The Governor has a similar philosophy, but he can express his thoughts. Look at John F. Kennedy. He didn't have much of a record as a Senator. But he made a great appearance—and he had a beautiful wife. So does the Governor. Nancy Reagan doesn't have to take a back seat to anyone. And the Governor has plenty of time between now and the nomination to make a record as an administrator. But I don't believe people in other states really care much about what's happening in California anyway.

Reagan's candidacy in California could not have come at a more felicitous time. His natural constituency, the white suburbs, was in a militant mood, alarmed by the riots in Watts and appalled by the turbulence of the Free Speech Movement on the Berkeley campus. It looked as if a firm hand was required, and Reagan promised one. The Democrats, for their part, displayed an infirmity of touch from the start. The incumbent Governor, Pat Brown, was tired after eight years in office. He got off a few good cracks about Reagan's "citizen politician" approach to the office ("I've never flown a plane before, but don't worry: I've always had a deep interest in aviation"), but he overdid the sarcasm. Reagan could not be laughed off. When the election returns came in, Salvatori's protégé had 993,739 votes more than Brown.

Reagan's record as Governor has, even by his own ideological lights, been less than outstanding. If he had any creative ideas about cost-cutting, he has yet to reveal them, although his administration made some early gestures, mainly on the advice of Republican Governor James A. Rhodes of Ohio, who had achieved a somewhat suspect reputation as a budget trimmer. "If California wants to be thirty-seventh in education, forty-ninth in mental health, and forty-second in public welfare, follow the Rhodes plan," said an Ohio Democratic State Senator at the time. Briefed by Rhodes, Reagan declared across-the-board ten-per-cent cuts in all spending programs, a move that had some public-relations value, but which made little financial sense in that it penalized efficient departments just as much as those which needed trimming. Eventually, even this simplistic technique buckled, and the ten-per-cent cuts had to be reduced to six.

Even with these "economies," there is no way to stop the cost of running California from going up. Too many new people arrive every day to overload the state's already tautly stretched services. In the summer of 1967, Reagan found himself obliged to ask the legislature for a billion-dollar tax increase to finance a record five-billion-plus budget. In a curious way this helped Reagan extend his appeal; Democrats in the state, like Jesse Unruh, grudgingly admitted that Reagan was beginning to grasp the financial realities, while out-of-state journalists examining the new actor-Governor phenomenon were able to say that he was not half as alarming as he seemed. The *Washington Star*'s Mary McGrory, no friend of reaction, saw "the Crown Prince of Goldwaterism" being transformed into "a moderate Republican."

But this is to see Reagan as something other than what he really is. He is a public-relations man, not a policy-maker. Many actors feel the need to break out of role-playing and take possession of the action, but Reagan apparently felt no such yearning in his long acting career. He was not director material. Nor is he as a politician. He is willingly at the mercy of the experts and interests backing him. He can sell the policy, but he cannot make it. If taxes have to be raised, he will raise them and make it look as palatable as possible by blaming his predecessors' "spendthrift" policies, just as easily as he can promise in a campaign to trim government action to the bone. In one case, he is responding to the prompting of the bureaucracy, in the other he is mouthing the sentiments of his reactionary backers.

Consistency is not a serious problem for one so new to the business. After making a reputation as a hawk, Reagan was to have no ideological problem accepting the relatively dovish platform prepared by the Republicans in Miami. It is not that he had learned anything new to change his mind. He was simply responding to a new set of background promptings. It is doubtful, in fact, whether, despite the frequency of his statements on the subject, he ever gave it any concentrated attention. "You've seen Vietnam on the map. It's about this big," he once told a colleague of ours, with his thumb and index finger forming a small O. "Now, how can that be a problem for the United States?"

Reagan's incuriosity about fundamentals is matched by a distaste for detail. The minutiae of government bore him. After being installed in his office (complete with newly bulletproofed windows) in Sacramento, Reagan astounded old executive hands by reducing the Governorship to a crisp nine-to-five-thirty job. His desk stays tidy all day, while he takes in information in the form of mini-memos (a technique used by Eisenhower) and keeps appointments tightly scheduled.

His memory is good, though Sacramento reporters are sometimes astounded by odd lacunae in the Governor's knowledge of state affairs and contrast this unfavorably with his readiness to make snap judgments on national issues. The same reporters, emerging from press conferences with the impression of having tied the Governor up on some detail, are often chagrined to see, on the evening television news programs, edited shots of Reagan displaying consummate mastery of the main issues raised at the conference. Playing to the camera, a technique which few politicians or reporters master, is Reagan's forte.

Some of the reporters who have watched Reagan closely have concluded that he is alert but fundamentally lazy. There is something in this, but it is certainly not a physical laziness. Reagan always moves with an air of bustling purposiveness. His speeches for Republican fundraising ventures are done on a virtually any-time, any-place basis.

The total phenomenon is a recognizable one. In Reagan's mind there is no contradiction between his personal sense of righteousness, his antiquated small-town philosophy, and his response to the pressures of the moment. It would not strike him as essentially bizarre that he should turn down a request to inspect the state's mental institutions more closely while making himself available for out-of-state fundraising jamborees. So he cannot be explained as a primitive, or a cynic, or a smart aleck. He is less sinister, but much more dangerous, than any of these. What resolves the contradictions is the realization that Reagan is totally devoid of any concept of objective morality. In short, he has no imagination. And so, to ask whether Reagan is good or bad is, in a sense, an irrelevant question. He is a force—whether for good or ill depending entirely on which direction he is pointed in and who is at the controls.

Soon after Reagan was elected Governor of California, Salvatori and his friends decided to point Reagan at the Presidency. The project was an elaborately circumspect one, requiring from the central figure considerable talent for what is known in the Presidency-hunting business as "honest lying." The method may not have been of Reagan's choosing —he likes to think of himself, in a frequent metaphor, as starting "prairie fires" of fervor—but then, he had no alternative. The method also required some undercover work which one of its prime movers later described as being "like something out of a James Bond movie."

Campaigning for the governorship, Reagan had, seemingly, boxed off his options for a Presidential challenge in 1968; his electioneering trail was littered with pledges to serve out his term as Governor and promises not to use the office as a stepping stone to something more august. Flexible Reagan may be—but no one could be flexible enough to get away from these pledges. If he was to become the next Republican Presidential nominee, he could not overtly seek the position; the position had to seek out Reagan. There are ways of making such things happen.

From the outset, Reagan had one basic advantage: he did not have to worry about his name not being placed in nomination. After the bloodletting over the gubernatorial primary, California Republicans wanted time for the wounds to heal. One certain way of opening up the scar tissue again would be to allow California's eighty-six-man delegation to squabble over who should be the national leader. The welcome suggestion that Reagan head this off by being a favorite-son candidate on the first ballot was actually made by the state's lieutenant governor, Robert Finch, a close friend of Richard Nixon's. In Finch's mind, at the time, the favorite-son candidacy was a formality, subject, like all such candidacies, to withdrawal on later ballots or even, if the situation warranted it, before the balloting began. For Reagan, the suggestion was a godsend: in one stroke it eliminated his most immediate problem—namely, how to ensure that his name would be placed in nomination without his being an open candidate for the Presidency. It also gave him a healthy eighty-six-vote base to build on.

In addition to conforming with his campaign pledges, the non-candidacy posture had another advantage: it helped to free Reagan from comparisons with the other candidates in the national opinion polls. For a politician like Reagan, cast in the Goldwater image, this was highly significant. The polls would almost inevitably have shown his nation-wide standing as inferior to that of a "moderate" candidate like Nixon or Rockefeller. (There is concrete evidence for this assumption: one of Rockefeller's secret weapons was a poll taken on the eve of the convention showing Reagan running against Humphrey almost as badly as Goldwater against LBJ in 1964. The intention was to flood the convention with copies of the poll if the situation ever polarized into a straight fight between Rockefeller and Reagan. It never did, so the poll was never released.)

This desire to stay off Gallup's and Harris's polling roster was the principal reason for the strenuous denials emerging from the Reagan camp every time a journalist so much as mentioned that something might be in the wind. An example of this came in June 1967, when David Broder, a highly perceptive political correspondent for the *Washington Post,* was attending the Western Governors' Conference in West Yellowstone, Montana. Broder happened to notice Reagan deep in private conference with some old Goldwater hands, notably F. Clifton White, the renowned New York campaign consultant who had masterminded the draft-Goldwater movement in 1964. Putting two and two together, Broder wrote in his lead the next day: "A number of key Republicans are now willing to bet that it is only a matter of time before Ronald Reagan has the third fully-fledged organization [the other two, at that time, being Nixon's and Romney's] in the battle for the Republican presidential nomination . . . and its operating head will be none other than F. Clifton White."

The story was robustly denied by all concerned. But the only thing Broder had wrong was the timing. It was another seven months before Clif White was formally unveiled, and then it was as an "adviser" to the California delegation to the convention. His services had been recruited by the ubiquitous Henry Salvatori of Los Angeles, a delegation member. And it was not to be until the convention, of course, that the Reagan candidacy was formally acknowledged.

Out of necessity, the Reagan for President operation was conducted on several levels. The first was anything but clandestine. Reagan had to free himself of his West Coast image and get himself known among

Republican Party people outside the state. Other, more shadowy levels involved the development of grass-roots sentiment for Reagan.

The public phase of the operation presented a logistic problem, but not much else. Reagan had a perfect excuse for traveling out of state— he was in demand. His "A Time for Choosing" speech in 1964 had marked him out as that most desirable of all guest speakers for local Republican groups: a man who persuaded the faithful to put their hands in their pockets. As Governor, his mailbag bulged with requests from Republican organizers all over the country to speak at anything from a fifty-dollar-a-head steak-and-eggs breakfast to thousand-dollar-a-head cocktail parties and dinners. Such functions not only offered the Governor a chance to broaden his appeal, but also brought him directly in contact with the kind of men who would be delegates at the convention. This was not the stage at which to light the match for the "prairie fire," but there was no harm in ensuring that the vegetation was good and dry and ready to blaze. Reagan became the country's most peripatetic Governor.

By January 1968, Reagan had raised the impressive sum of $1.5 million for the Republican Party, putting party officials throughout the country politically in his debt. In the year before the convention, he made no fewer than a dozen fundraising swings. From New York to Arizona, from Washington to Florida, Reagan carried the message of the need for new leadership, national regeneration, and (with a modest self-deprecating smile) of his own *non*candidacy for the office of President.

For Nixon, who knew what Reagan was up to, it was all something of a pain. He could hardly demand that Reagan come out in the open and fight, when the Governor was stressing unity all the time. (Reagan solemnly informed questioners that for him to campaign in the primaries would only create "divisiveness," the thing he most wanted to avoid.) Thus the Republican front runner had to confine himself to a few veiled cracks—"the Governor appears to be becoming a more active noncandidate"—and let it go at that.

At fundraisers, the Reagon persona could be very potent indeed. In his somewhat old-fashioned attire (his suits tend to be of the high-padded-shoulder variety, his trousers wide but not flared), he seems to embody the message, to those who might need reassurance, that it's still possible to be square and sexy. His talks, delivered in a soft earnest voice, were spiced with the kind of gags that his business audiences liked

to hear. His specialty was clothing ignorance and prejudice with a semblance—sometimes even a facsimile—of wit and down-to-earth common
sense.

Here are some examples from a fundraising swing in May through
Louisiana, North Carolina, Florida, Illinois, and Ohio (raising a reported seven hundred fifty thousand dollars for the Republican parties in
those states):

On Robert Kennedy—"Sometimes I think the reason Bobby's so
concerned about poverty is that he never had any when he was a kid."

On President Johnson—"We can't really blame the President alone
for the mess we're in. A mess like that takes teamwork."

On crime and inflation—"You have to admire the Administration's
anticrime program. They're making the money so cheap it's not worth
stealing."

As the election year progressed, Reagan seemed less and less inclined to dilate on the virtues of his governorship and more and more
concerned with conveying his stance on national issues. Thus Reagan at
a fundraiser in New Orleans in May: "This nation is totally out of control." And, then, an extended burst about the enemies in the nation's
midst:

> Civilization simply cannot afford demagogues in this era of rising ex-
> pectations. It cannot afford prophets who shout that the road to the
> promised land lies over the shards of burned and looted cities. It cannot
> afford politicians who demand that Social Security be tripled; that the
> national duty in Vietnam be discarded to provide huge make-work pro-
> grams in the city slums with money diverted from Vietnam; that no
> youth need honor the draft; that Negroes need not obey the law; that
> there will be pie in the sky once the country gets moving again.

It was the old free-swinging style of the California campaign trail,
replete with the broad, cudgeling less-than-half-truths which are themselves the hallmark of the demagogue, the creature Reagan claimed to
be against.

True or not, this was the kind of rhetoric many people, unnerved
by black militancy and violence in the society, wanted to hear. What was
obvious irresponsibility in the mouth of George Wallace passed as
smooth reason in the low-key tones of California's Governor. Reagan
was building himself a limited, but emotional, national constituency.

A delegate constituency could not be so easily assembled, though in
F. Clifton White the Reagan operation had acquired the best-regarded
delegate-hunter in the business. White, at the age of fifty, had become

something of a legend. He is a tall, somber-looking man with a penchant
for bright bow ties that go oddly with his saturnine appearance. His
Goldwater operation wrought something of a revolution in American
politics—he was the architect of the strategy of packing caucuses in the
nonprimary states with party militants (a technique which, as we have
seen, the McCarthy insurgents used very successfully within the Democratic Party in states like Minnesota). Many middle-rank Republican
officials had come into politics as a result of this operation. So when
White started his wanderings around the states early in 1968, becoming
almost as peripatetic as his noncandidate, he had a lot of old friends to
go to.

White is an unusual kind of campaign consultant. For one thing, it
is not his full-time job, though he keeps on a steady lecture tour on the
subject with his old friend and fellow professional Joe Napolitan, who
was to become consultant for Humphrey's Presidential campaign. He
describes himself as a "public-affairs consultant," which means he spends
much of his time advising corporations on their relations with the political structure. He will enter the political arena direct only if a campaign
tickles his fancy. The campaigns that do that are invariably well to the
right.

Even for a man of White's talents, the task set by the Reagan camp
was a formidable one. Political intelligence, to be of any use, must be up
to date. And White had been off the national scene for three years. Power
structures had changed, and in some cases the ins of 1964 had become
outs. Moreover, White was up against probably the most sophisticated
delegate-intelligence system ever assembled—that of Richard Nixon.
White was one man against a small army. Old friends helped, but in
some states, inevitably, White found himself going to the wrong people.
Butch Butler, a Houston oil man who chaired Texans for Reagan, was
grateful for White's help but lamented: "It's no good. He's working the
wrong side of the street."

White's other problems were his terms of reference. The whole
scenario was a reverse of the Goldwater plot. The Arizonan could take
the convention by storm, but Reagan had to proceed by stealth. Instead
of the role of proselytizer, White had to assume the objective façade of
a taker of soundings. Reagan, he had to say, was not, repeat not, a candidate. There were, however, a number of California delegates who were
hot for him to run and who believed that the sentiment was shared
around the country. Evidence of this sentiment, White would then go on
to say, could have some impact. This did not, of course, mean that every-

body should come out for Reagan on the first ballot. That would clearly be too much to ask. But determination to stay loose, say, behind a favorite-son candidacy on the early ballots, would be almost as useful. If there were enough popular expressions of support for Reagan around the country, then it might, just might, be possible to persuade the Governor to run.

White would then go into a few personal reminiscences about the Reagan personality. How he had met Ronnie back on the G.E. circuit and found himself "kind of impressed with his philosophy." How, when he was organizing for Goldwater, he had found Ronnie just about the very best citizens'-group chairman in the country. How much he admired what Ronnie was doing out in California. It had to be, as White said later, "an ultrasoft sell."

Anything less oblique could have been disastrous. And Reagan's backers were made all too well aware of what polls could do to their man when, on April 16, the *Los Angeles Times* State Poll, conducted by Don Muchmore, published a highly significant set of figures. Among California Republicans, Reagan's popularity as a Presidential choice, never great, was declining fast. Nixon had a 54-per-cent rating as against 35 per cent for Rockefeller and only 8 per cent for Reagan. The Governor's figure had slipped from 19 per cent in a similar poll conducted in September 1967. There could be no more telling reminder of the unwisdom of the open route to the nomination. If Californians did not want Reagan, what must the rest of the country feel?

Fortunately for Reagan, the Muchmore poll is little read outside California. Nixon and Rockefeller would see it, of course, and take heart that there was not much to fear from the extreme right—and this suited the Reagan people admirably. A false sense of optimism in the other two camps was an essential ingredient of the strategy. A good Reagan showing in the polls might tempt Nixon, in particular, to harden up on commitments in the South, and that would be the end of things.

Ironically, on the very day the Muchmore poll was published, the travel-stained White arrived in Los Angeles to deliver the results of his "sounding" operation. Meeting the members of the California delegation behind closed doors, White felt able to inform them that there was indeed much sentiment for their Governor around the country. Among the things that had most particularly impressed him had been "a rather significant increase in the number of self-generated state and local citizens-for-Reagan committees in such states as Minnesota, Kansas, Colorado, and Idaho." The South, he was confident, was also sympathetic. Yes, all

in all, F. Clifton White felt that Reagan would make an excellent showing as a national candidate.

The Governor's attitude to all this was—had to be—one of amused
tolerance. At a press conference the next day, Reagan spread his hands
and said, "It's a free country. They know my feelings, and there's not
much I can do about it." He reiterated that he had done all he could do
to discourage all attempts to promote his candidacy. There was just no
holding them back.

Just how sincere this assurance was can be ascertained by an
examination of the third, and most clandestine, level of the Reagan for
President operation. The key figure here was a much younger man than
White and much closer personally to the Governor. Tom Reed had, at
the age of thirty-two, been one of Reagan's closest aides in his California
campaign: "Politically" he says frankly, "I am the Governor's creature."

A nuclear physicist by training, Reed, the son of a millionaire, also
made a million or two of his own in oil geology and real estate before his
attraction to politics merged into involvement. He was not a popular
man with the press, once telling a group of reporters that he thought
government should be the responsibility of young men like himself who
had made fortunes by their initiative in the business world. He was, however, extremely popular with the Governor, and for months after Reagan
assumed office, Reed's handsome, dark-haired figure was rarely far from
his side. He was officially the Governor's appointments and traveling
secretary—in fact, he was simply ubiquitous, Reagan's alter ego. Reed
has a sophistication and wit not usually found on the further conservative side of the Republican Party. But he leaves no doubt where he
stands. Asked when he became interested in politics, he says, "You
mean, when did I become a right-wing fanatic?"

Then, in the fall of 1967, Reed resigned from the Governor's staff.
He had, for the record, decided to return to private life. In fact, he was
about to start the "James Bond" phase of the Reagan for President
operation.

Reed's task, in essence, was to be the right-wing's Al Lowenstein,
a man with whom Reed shared one helpful characteristic: an apparently
inexhaustible supply of energy. Reed was to light the fires under the
faithful, which would in turn ignite the delegates, which, if their luck
held, would make the office come to the man in a blaze of surprise, and
glory.

Outside of the polls, there are only two ways of demonstrating
grass-roots support for a candidate: success in the open primaries or an

impressive array of active citizens' groups throughout the nation. Before the end of 1967, Reed was hard at work on both these fronts.

Reagan could not, as we have seen, run openly in the primaries (that would be "divisive"—i.e., destructive). On the other hand, he was reasonably sure that his name would be on a number of primary ballots. In some states, like New Hampshire, a candidate's name can be placed on the ballot by petition, even without his consent. In others, like Wisconsin, Nebraska, and Oregon, the law empowers state officials to place on the primary ballot any person they consider should be a candidate for President. The only way a man can get off is to swear an affidavit saying he does not wish to be President. Reagan was to side-step this problem by saying that, while he would discourage any activity on his behalf in the primaries, it would be "arrogance" on his part to remove his name from a ballot and deny his supporters the chance of voting for him. One could scarcely expect arrogance of so modest a man. Naturally, as an official noncandidate for the Presidency, Reagan could not be expected to make a spectacular showing in the primaries. If, however, a steadily rising graph of support was demonstrated in the primary votes, this would be a valuable card to play if he came out in the open later.

Lacking Ron to turn the voters on, Reed had to resort to the next most potent device available—films of Ron. His first move, then, in November 1967, was to assemble a small, but highly sophisticated film unit. Fortunately, two very competent operators, both with political experience, were available: Greg Snazelle, a San Francisco producer of TV commercials, whose career had taken off four years previously, when he started regulating his life to each whim of his zodiacal sign; and John Mercer, vice-president of the San Francisco advertising agency, Meltzer, Aron and Lemen Inc. Snazelle and Mercer must have had an acute sense of *déjà vu*. Two years earlier, during the California gubernatorial campaign, Reed had come to them with a problem. Reagan, it seemed, was going over big in southern California, but his impact in the north, a Democratic stronghold, was problematic. What the candidate needed was a more moderate image up there. In short, Reagan needed a schizophrenic campaign that could appeal to both sections of the state. Snazelle and Mercer were commissioned to do TV spots that would present Reagan in a more liberal spotlight; these were to be beamed exclusively at the northern voters.

The 1967–68 project was much more ambitious, and one that neither man (Mercer is a registered Democrat) could resist. It appealed to the professional in Snazelle—"Reagan was the first politician to come along literally tailor-made for the media." Both dropped all other work and got down to the task of crafting a Presidential image for Reagan. From the outset, Reed made it patently, almost paranoiacly, clear that at no stage must the Governor's name be associated with this venture. They would be allowed to shoot the Governor diligently working in his office or displaying togetherness at his Sacramento home. But if inquisitive reporters asked what they were up to, they were just "shooting footage for stock." Meanwhile, Reed would lay his hands on all the stock political film of Reagan he could find, and from these elements, they were to compose a half-hour campaign "biography" of the candidate.

Above all, it was essential that nobody should know that the enterprise had a California focus or that Reed himself was involved in it. All the overt action was to be initiated by Citizens for Reagan groups around the country, which Reed himself was to ensure would be firmly established by the spring of 1968 (those "self-generated" local groups to which White was to refer so glowingly in his April briefing of the California slate).

The official center of all operations was to be the citizens' group in Topeka, Kansas—ultimately set up under the chairmanship of Henry Bubb, a savings-and-loan executive and a veteran of the 1940 Wendell Willkie campaign—which would be responsible for disseminating all information about the rising star in the West. To complete the cover, Reed himself, in cases where secrecy was deemed essential, would appropriate a new identity—that of a Kansas businessman, John Kurwitz.

This led to bizarre absurdities—like Mercer and Snazelle receiving teletype instructions from Kurwitz (Reed) in Topeka, when they happened to know that the author was sitting in his office ten blocks away. When telephoning Reed, they would ask for Kurwitz, and the secretary would take their number; then five mintues later Reed would come on the line. Contact between the film unit and the Governor's staff was kept to an absolute minimum, though from time to time Reagan's personal press secretary, Lyn Nofziger, a forty-three-year-old former Washington newspaperman of extreme right-wing views, would drop by to oversee the operation.

The film, all agreed, should emphasize Nixon's weakest point—his loser image—while conveying the impression of Reagan as a great vote-getter. This had to be done with some delicacy if it was to be effective, and not boomerang. It was, therefore, with some reluctance that they decided not to use Reed's prize find, a full television tape of Nixon's breakdown at his press conference after his defeat in the California election of 1962 (the famous "You won't have Dick Nixon to kick around any more" diatribe).

The acquisition was not entirely useless, however. Early in 1968, some of the Nixon aides mused aloud about the advantages of their candidate's contesting in the California primary, but one of the things that deterred them was a suggestion from the Reagan camp that they might feel obliged to rerun that potent piece of footage during prime TV time if this came to pass. In the end, both sides compromised: neither Reagan's favorite-son candidacy nor his slate of convention delegates would be challenged in the primary, provided the delegation reflected all strains of opinion in the party. (The Reagan slate was actually composed of about one-third Reagan men, nearly half Nixon men, with the rest leaning to Rockefeller, a heterogeneous setup that was to produce awful complications at the convention.)

Eventually, the Reagan film group found what they regarded as a suitable formula. Among shots of Reagan the orator, Reagan the dynamic union organizer, Reagan the diligent executive (but not Reagan the actor), they had Reagan the slayer of the giant vote-getter Pat Brown. This made a happy sequence: Brown in 1958 triumphing over the Republican white hope Big Bill Knowland; Brown triumphing in 1962 over the best the Republican Party could wheel up, a former Presidential candidate, Richard Nixon (shot of a disconsolate Nixon making his concession statement); then the finale, a radiant Reagan toppling the mighty Brown by a margin of almost a million votes. The message could hardly be considered subliminal.

The finished product, bearing the title "Ronald Reagan: Citizen Governor," was packaged and ready to roll by March 1968. Nofziger vetted it, but Reagan himself did not. It might cramp his style, it was thought, in disclaiming all interest in such projects on his behalf. A request from his wife, Nancy, to see the film before it was used, also had to be turned down.

In theory, the film could have been used in all the primary campaigns. There were enough Reagan for President groups in embryo— or actually in independent life—who could have used it under their imprimatur. But in practice, it was decided to hold off until the later primaries. A low vote in the early engagements did not much matter, and would even be an advantage in that better showings later would look like a surge for Reagan. Up to a point, this is what happened.

In New Hampshire in March, no effort was made—Reagan picked up a minuscule one per cent of the vote. Before the Wisconsin primary in April, there was some local activity but not much in the way of media promotion—Reagan moved up to 11 per cent of the vote. Nebraska in May was another matter; a strongly conservative and hawkish state, custom-built for a Reagan drive. It was time for the unveiling of the film "biography," and Reagan surged nicely again—picking up an impressive 22 per cent of the vote. But the big effort of the secret bandwagon was to be made in the May 28 primary in Oregon, the last important one. (California came later, on June 4, but there were no plaudits to be won there, as Reagan was the only candidate. In the event, Reagan's vote in the California primary was less than that of the combined vote of the five Republican candidates competing for the Senatorial nomination, which meant that a number of Republicans who bothered to turn out for the polls did not bother to vote for Reagan.)

In the film unit, the prospect of the Oregon primary produced a flurry of extra work. The "biography," it was decided, had to be updated. Since the original version was made, events had moved on. The *Pueblo* crew had been incarcerated; Martin Luther King had been shot; and there had been a new upsurge of "law'n'order" rhetoric. Reagan's oratorical set piece at the end of the film was beginning to look dated. The suggestion was made that Reagan should as soon as possible make a speech, drawing on more newsworthy themes, that could be shot by Snazelle and substituted for the old footage. Reagan happily complied and invited the cameramen to the earliest possible venue, a fundraising dinner in Oakland, California. It proved a tough assignment for the film makers. The diners, about seventy in all, were less than attentive— "Everybody was smashed out of his mind," said one of the film-unit members, groaning at the memory. Reagan, used to larger, more solicitous gatherings, stumbled over his new lines. He was very unhappy about the whole performance.

But with subtle editing, and the insertion of canned applause, Snazelle came up with a version that he thought acceptable. Reagan was still worried—the professional in him was affronted by his own clumsiness—and he wanted to be sure the Oregon film was good. So he broke the original ground rules and saw the film himself before giving it the final O.K. By then, of course, Reagan was nearing the end of the "honest-lying" phase.

The Oregon operation had plenty of muscle and money. The citizens' organization, headed by Robert Hazen, a Portland banker and ex-Rockefeller supporter, included a brace of immediate past Republican state chairmen, party chairmen from two of Oregon's biggest counties, and the finance chairman of the state committee. The media budget was virtually open-ended (Reagan's rivals claim he must have spent two hundred thousand dollars in the state), and the "biography," shown *six* times, won critical acclaim as well as good ratings.

Mercer and Snazelle topped off the TV barrage with a series of sixty-second commercials based primarily on interviews with that legendary figure, the man in the street. "You know the kind of stuff," an insider said. "We got them to say things like 'Nixon's O.K. but he's a loser. Now that *Reagan* . . .'"

Short of making Reagan an open candidate, everything that could be done was done. But Oregonians are notoriously shy about voting for men who fail to look in on their corner of the Union. (One of Rockefeller's most telling themes in his victorious primary campaign in Oregon four years earlier had been: "He took the trouble to come.") Reagan's showing was not dismal—twenty-three per cent of the vote—but after optimistic pitches by his local activists about garnering thirty to forty per cent, it could scarcely be considered a mandate. Other activists around the country took what comfort they could from the figures. Butch Butler, the Texas oil man, for instance, reckoned Reagan had done as well as he could considering the nature of the Oregon political terrain, which, from his vantage point, looked like a "socialist state . . . where they spend Federal money like it was going out of style."

Reed and the other insiders were disappointed. Over-all, the grass-roots operation had been sound but had failed to yield sensational results. If there was to be a "prairie fire," it would have to start among the delegates. And the only place where that could happen would be where the delegates were still part "loose," and wholly insecure. Inevitably, that meant the South. And that, in the end, was where they rocked Nixon.

Hamlet on Fifth Avenue

"I do not know
Why yet I live to say 'this thing's to do,'
Sith I have cause, and will, and strength, and means,
To do 't. Examples gross as earth exhort me."

—William Shakespeare, *Hamlet*

There is something almost self-consciously discreet about the pair of old brownstone town houses on Manhattan's West Fifty-fifth Street, between the Italian Pavilion restaurant and Mr. Carmine the hairdresser, a few yards from Fifth Avenue. It is a busy block, yet a row of black limousines always seems to be able to find parking space in front of the blue-gray doors, which are kept locked. If you press the small polished brass button, a well-dressed Negro in a sports jacket will stick his head out and politely ask your name and business. An inquisitive passerby might be intrigued to know that a jerry-built corridor connects the houses with the corresponding house on West Fifty-fourth Street, Number 13, next to the Museum of Primitive Art. But the two brownstones are not a center for international vice or espionage. They are the New York City headquarters of the Governor of New York State, and they, and the house on Fifty-fourth Street, and, for that matter, the museum as well, are all part of the imperial private property of Governor Nelson Aldrich Rockefeller.

The Governor spent a large part of his childhood in the Fifty-fourth Street house, but he doesn't live there now; he has a magnificent apartment a few hundred yards up Fifth Avenue, looking out over the trees and rocks of Central Park. He uses the house now as a bolthole on the rather frequent occasions when he wants to evade the curiosity of the press, and as a private refuge. There is still a kitchen there, and a small dining room.

It was here, over lunch, a couple of days after George Romney announced his withdrawal from the campaign, that Rockefeller sat down with his two most trusted advisers to discuss seriously for the first time the question that the press and indeed the whole political world had been discussing loudly on his behalf for months: should he be a candidate in 1968?

The result of that conversation, and of its continuation in other places over the next few days, profoundly affected the outcome of the Presidential election. Yet this was not a party caucus or even an informal caucus of party politicians such as might have assembled at an earlier period of American history to discuss a nomination. Only one of the three men had ever been elected to public office, and he had leaped straight into one of the most important offices in the land with little help from the regular Republican Party organization. Two were the personal servants of the third, paid from his private pocket. And, incidentally, though it was the Republican nomination they were discussing, only two of them were Republicans.

Political parties in America have always and necessarily been loose coalitions of geographical and other interests. In the late nineteenth century and well into the twentieth they were often dominated by alliances struck between bosses, each of whose power was based in some state or city machine. On the Republican side, the party could be controlled by alliances between the likes of Quay of Pennsylvania and Hanna of Ohio; the Democratic nomination could be arranged between the Southern chieftains and the masters of Tammany. But here was a new reality: the party not as a broad coalition or even as an alliance between factions, but as a political kingdom to be disputed by private armies owing their allegiance not to some local machine, but to a nationally puissant family or individual.

Twenty-five years ago, an Oxford don called K. B. McFarlane rippled the quiet pools of medieval historical scholarship by describing a change that took place in the character of political loyalty in the fourteenth century. Before that time, feudal duty had been accepted as being almost as natural as loyalty to one's family. Men felt an unbreakable allegiance to the lord from whom they held their land, once they had put their hands between his hands and sworn the feudal oath: "to love whom he loveth, and hate whom he hateth."

But long before the outward forms of feudalism had been abolished, the old unquestioned and unquestioning relationship of lord and vassal was replaced by something more modern and more mercenary. Money replaced land as the cement of politics. Men began to attach themselves to the glittering princes of the later Middle Ages—to put on the collar of linked S's which was the badge of John of Gaunt, or to wear the livery of Warwick the Kingmaker, embroidered with the bear and ragged staff— not because they had to, but because they thought it would be to their advantage. They began to choose as their patron the man who could do them the most good, and, with a cynicism that would do credit to a twentieth-century public-relations man, they called their boss not by the plain and ancient name of "lord," but by a new piece of cant: they called him their "good lord."

"When a man asked another to be his 'good lord,'" McFarlane explained,

> he was acquiring a temporary patron. In this loosely-knit and shame-lessly competitive society, it was the ambition of every thrusting young gentleman—and also of everyone who aspired to gentility—to attach himself for as long as suited him to such as were in a position to further his interests. For those who wanted to rise in the world, "good lordship" was essential.

Since the lord, in his turn, needed lawyers to win his suits, country gentlemen with influence in the provinces to help him get his friends elected to Parliament, men of talent and women of charm to make his house attractive, and in the last analysis men-at-arms to fight his battles, so

> there accumulated a vast but indefinite mass of councillors, retainers, and servants, tailing off into those believed to be well-wishers.

These hangers-on McFarlane called the "bastard feudatories," and to the whole system he gave the name of "bastard feudalism."

The retinue of the great princes of the fifteenth century, he went on, resembled the factions or "connections" found in eighteenth-century English politics and described by Sir Lewis Namier:

> There was the same element of voluntary interdependence, the same competition for place, and the same absence of any separate fund of political principle. . . . A baron inherited rank and possessions to do with what he could. But he was dependent on the goodwill, the con-fidence, and the cooperation of [those] better-educated, more experi-enced, and more prudent than he was himself. Politics were a joint-stock enterprise and he and his advisers had got to make them pay.

Historical analogies, like old wheelbarrows, are apt to collapse if they are pushed too far. The modern American barons are not in politics to make them pay. But there is a startling resemblance between this late medieval prince, surrounded by his "vast but indefinite mass of councillors, retainers, and servants, tailing off into those believed to be well-wishers," and Robert Kennedy as he debated whether to raise the standard of rebellion with his friends, relations, employees, and political allies. The parallel occurred to the well-read Eugene McCarthy. "One of the things I object to about the Kennedys," he told one of us, "is that they are trying to turn the Presidency into the Wars of the Roses."

The serious point of the analogy is that the old, automatic allegiances of American politics, based on geography and on ethnic identification, have been largely replaced by a new kind of loyalty very much like "bastard feudalism." No longer does a clever and idealistic young man gravitate automatically into the sphere of a local leader such as William Jennings Bryan or Robert La Follette. He can join "the Kennedys," or he can attach himself to the retinue of some other "good lord" who can promise high adventure and reward. In the "loosely-knit and shamelessly competitive society" of contemporary America, just as in England of Chaucer's day, the straightest road to fortune for a "thrusting young gentleman" lies not in self-help, but in joining the retinue of a great man and hoping to rise with his "good lord's" fortunes.

Consider, as an example, the choices open to a bright and bouncy young man named Jeff Greenfield when he graduated with excellent grades from the Yale Law School in the summer of 1967. He was twenty-three years old and expensively educated, though with no money of his own to speak of. He had something of a talent as a satirical writer, but he had learned enough of worldly values not to dream of launching out on so hazardous and unprofitable a career as writing. There were, as he saw it, only three practical alternatives: he could work as a law clerk to a judge; he could go to work "on Wall Street"—accept one of the tempting offers with which New York law firms besiege the brightest graduates of the big law schools; or he could "go to work for someone in Washington."

As it happened, young Jeff Greenfield became the junior member of Robert Kennedy's speech-writing team. The appointment "worked out." Greenfield found that he could write the sort of stuff that was wanted, and he developed a fierce loyalty to his new "good lord." But it cannot be said that this allegiance was based on a "separate fund of political principle." Nor was it a permanent loyalty. After Kennedy's death, young Greenfield was, by the end of 1968, working happily and with the same fierce personal loyalty for a new prince, Mayor John Lindsay of New York—a Republican.

Now consider the same sort of history from the standpoint of "the Kennedys." A politician with whom they are on friendly terms is looking for a young man to write his speeches. He approaches one of Robert Kennedy's aides (this is after Robert's death) and asks him to work for him. The aide privately thinks this is a bit beneath his dignity, but it is important that the politician should be helped. He places a call to a contemporary who is teaching at the Yale Law School and asks him if he has any bright students to recommend. Names are suggested and then subjected to a catechism. "Is he *really* bright, Guido? . . . Can he operate? Do you know what I mean? No, well, I don't expect you do, we'll have to find that out. . . . Does he have a *practical* mind? He does? . . . Well, I'll come up and see him . . . if he's really bright. . . ."

The operations of the new "bastard feudalism" in American politics extend far beyond the hiring of personal staff. The Kennedy brothers have their men not only in the great universities and foundations, but also in industry, on Wall Street, in the television networks, and in the press, so that a long-distance phone call would be enough to find a job to reward a friend, to divert an embarrassing project for a magazine article or television documentary, or to raise millions for a political campaign. Harper & Row was in this sense the Kennedy publishing house, and there are Kennedy hostesses, and even Kennedy football players— like Roosevelt Grier—so that the hero worship of black adolescents is not wasted, but harnessed to add its little candle to the refulgence of the princely house. The duties which a "bastard feudatory" may be called on to perform are almost infinite in scope.

One day in the summer of 1968, a young State Department man who studied in England as a Rhodes scholar received a phone call from Milton Gwirtzman, a Washington lawyer "close to the Kennedys." Britain's Chancellor of the Exchequer was in town, Gwirtzman said, and had expressed a desire to meet Senator Edward Kennedy. The Senator wanted to seem knowledgeable about his distinguished guest and had asked Gwirtzman to brief him. Did the State Department man know anything about Roy Jenkins? On the spur of the moment he answered that Jenkins had written a book about Disraeli—which, as it happens, he has not, though he has written three distinguished books about nineteenth- and early twentieth-century politics. It is not known whether the Senator congratulated the Chancellor on his Disraeli book, but if he did, it is certain that Jenkins had no idea what an elaborate network had been called into play to impress him.

To the limit of his ability to attract or to reward, every major politician in America with national ambitions today tries to build up a nationwide entourage of "councillors, retainers, and servants, tailing off into those believed to be well-wishers." One of the first things that Lyndon Johnson, for example, set about doing when he first conceived national ambitions during the days of his power in the Senate was to construct just such a retinue, and he returned to the task even more energetically after his great victory in 1964. It was then to the advantage of such talented men as the Wall Street investment adviser Eliot Janeway, the Princeton historian Eric Goldman, the columnist William S. White, and the Los Angeles lawyer Eugene Wyman to be known as "Johnson men." And it is no reflection on them as individuals—only the natural consequence of the system—that few of them are as keen to wear the Johnson livery today. For in America today, as in fifteenth-century England, bastard feudalism is "a partnership to their mutual advantage, a contract from which both sides expect to benefit," and "lordship lasted only so long as it was found to be good lordship or until it was ousted by a better." Two key members of President Nixon's initial White House staff are evidence of this. Henry Kissinger's relationship with Rockefeller and Daniel Patrick Moynihan's friendship with the Kennedys have both been "ousted by a better."

There is only one princely house in American politics which can challenge comparison with the Kennedys in this power to attract and reward talent, and that is the House of Rockefeller. In terms of sheer financial resources, of course, the Rockefellers far outstrip the Kennedys. Joseph P. Kennedy was a speculator with the nerve and the cynical intelligence to salvage money where others did not dare to look for it: in Hollywood, in liquor, and in the shipwreck of American industry during the Depression. John Davison Rockefeller was something more than that; he was a major figure in the economic history of the world who made himself the master and almost the monopolist of one of the basic raw materials of modern civilization: oil. He and a handful of his contemporaries, as Walter Lippmann has said, were not just rich, they were richer than men had ever been or were ever likely to be again. "Before he started his enterprises, it was not possible to make so much money; before he died, it had become the settled policy of this country that no man be permitted to make so much money."

Nobody can say precisely how much richer the Rockefellers are than the Kennedys. The highest plausible estimate of the entire fortune accumulated by Joseph P. Kennedy is four hundred million dollars: each of the Kennedy children is said to have been given a trust fund of ten million, a figure which would be less than the *income* of each of the five Rockefeller brothers on the *lowest* recently published estimate of their wealth. The wealth of Nelson Rockefeller and his four brothers and sister has been guessed at from two to three hundred million dollars each to a collective family total of ten billion.

But if the Rockefellers have more money to reward their followers with than the Kennedys, they have less glamour to attract them. They earned their money in the days before Madison Avenue had persuaded the average American that wealth is a sign of virtue. The family tradition, dour, a little stuffy and defensive, still bears the scars of the journalistic flogging they were given by the muckrakers. They are more cautious, less piratical, more inhibited than the Kennedys. The family tradition draws on the Baptist repentance of old John D.'s later years, though the money comes from the ruthless acquisitiveness of his youth; and it has been further refined by the passion for beautiful things which so often succeeds the passion for money. The empire is ruled from quiet offices full of Oriental *objets d'art* and corridors lined with Braques and Légers.

Among them, the brothers own, administer, or control an astronomic profusion of investments, charities, enterprises, and possessions, from John D. III's precious china to Winthrop's prize bulls, and still thirst like moralist Alexanders for new worlds to improve. They own estates in Maine and *estancias* in Venezuela. They finance colonial Williamsburg and they lease nineteen skyscrapers in New York. Two of them are Governors; bored, Winthrop went out and put Arkansas in his carpetbag with the aid of the first computerized political campaign in American history. David, the youngest, is president of the world's second largest bank. But perhaps the most important of all their activities are the International Basic Economy Corporation, a sort of private Marshall Plan to Latin America which spent over 200 million dollars in 1967 and still made a modest profit; the Rockefeller Foundation, which had assets of 1287 million to spend on its modestly defined purpose, "to promote the well-being of mankind throughout the world"; and the Rockefeller Brothers Fund, with assets worth 193 million.

It was the Fund which sponsored the Special Studies Project in 1957, which produced reports, published as a book with the title *Pros-*

pect for America, which may be said to have erected the intellectual scaffolding for the military and foreign policy of the Kennedy Administration. Both Dean Rusk and Walt Rostow took part, and the over-all director was Dr. Henry Kissinger of Harvard. All the brothers, particularly Nelson, have always taken care to surround themselves with the best advisers that money can buy (which is not always to say the best advisers there are). Nelson Rockefeller keeps a staff of fifteen wise men as his personal consultants on public affairs. It is the Rockefeller style to move not with the intuitive impetuosity of a Robert Kennedy—even whose hesitations sprang from feeling and instinct—but with a measured, calculated thoroughness. Nevertheless, when, at the beginning of March, 1968, Nelson Rockefeller set himself to face the question of his candidacy, he chose to share his dilemma with only two of them: George Hinman and Emmett John Hughes.

Hinman is a quiet, gray-haired man in his sixties. Before he went to work for Rockefeller in 1956, he was a lawyer in Binghamton, in upstate New York, and he has the cautious shrewdness and the pleasantly old-fashioned manners of a country lawyer. His relationship to Rockefeller is rather like that of the "man of business" to a political duke in eighteenth-century England. Rockefeller trusts him absolutely, and so do the politicians he is sent to deal with.

Hughes is fifteen years younger and a more worldly and elegant figure. He wears his hair long, combed back at the sides from features surprisingly like Lyndon Johnson's but smoother. A Democrat, he wrote speeches for Eisenhower in the White House and then wrote, to the anger of many loyal Republicans, one of the most literate and penetrating of American memoirs about his experiences there, *The Ordeal of Power.* Since 1961, he has doubled as Rockefeller's "senior policy adviser" and as a columnist for *Newsweek.* He is one of those men who speak in prose.

The third man at that meeting is not so easy to describe. He has about him that impenetrable differentness that Scott Fitzgerald observed in the very rich, and which is also to be noticed in the royal. "Let me tell you about the very rich," said Fitzgerald, "they are different from you and me." "Yes," said Hemingway, "they have more money." And most Americans have thought Hemingway had the last word. But it was he, not Fitzgerald, who was naïve. The very rich *are* different for the good reason that their whole experience of life has been different. "They possess and enjoy early, and it does something to them," Fitzgerald went on to say. "It makes them soft where we are hard, and cynical where we are trustful, in a way that unless you were born rich it is very difficult to understand. They think, deep in their hearts, that they are better than we are. . . ."

Nelson Rockefeller has spent his whole life apparently trying to disprove that judgment without ever quite succeeding. He has been painstakingly faithful to the ideal of public service in which he was brought up. From 1940 to 1945 he worked in Washington, first as Coordinator for Latin American Affairs, then as Assistant Secretary of State. He played a role of some importance in the founding of the United Nations. He was Under Secretary of Health, Education and Welfare in 1953–1954, and in 1954–1955 he worked for President Eisenhower as a special assistant in the White House. He is a shy man, and it was not easy to learn the common touch. When he first ran for Governor of New York, it was noticed that he greeted everyone with "Hi, fella!" which, it was pointed out, was apt to annoy those who didn't happen to be called fella. Now he can ride a subway, kiss a baby, hug a grandmother, or eat a blintz as if he had been doing it all his life. But he hasn't. Look more carefully at the joyous grin, and you will often notice that the eyes above the extraordinarily wide mouth are not smiling. It is not only that he has learned to be cynical where others are trusting. He is also soft where others are hard. He was hurt by the public lewdness about his divorce and remarriage in 1963, and both hurt and puzzled by the irrational hatred with which he was greeted by the convention that nominated Goldwater in 1964.

Though some think otherwise, his second marriage has been successful. "Something happens in your life," he said in a quite uncharacteristic burst of introspection in the autumn of 1967, "and you lose ambition because you have a sense of fulfillment. There are things that happen inside. I'm not a psychiatrist or a psychologist. I can't analyze it for you exactly. But I don't have the ambition or the need or the inner drive, or whatever the word is, to get in again." On another occasion he said of the Presidency, "Emotionally, I just don't need it any more." It was, perhaps, a revealing because a double-edged remark: it came close to a retrospective admission that once he had needed it. But now, at sixty, he had his new wife Happy, of whom all one can say is that it is easy to understand how she got that nickname at school and never lost it. There were two new sons for a man whose beloved third son had been tragically lost on an archaeological expedition in New Guinea. And there was the exacting, urgent work of governing New York, a tormented society of almost twenty million people.

Hinman and Hughes felt that Rockefeller was sincere, at every conscious level, when he told them that he didn't want to run for the Presidency. "At no time—not even as a sudden outburst," Hughes insists, "did he even say, 'I guess I've got to run.'" Yet they also felt that he ought to run, that he ought to be President. And one can guess—though they would never admit it—that they knew that he felt this too in the depths of his impenetrable Rockefeller mind.

Hughes began the discussion by asking Rockefeller to bring him up to date on the Republican scene and to state the pros and cons of running. Then Hughes asked a second question. "Just as a yardstick, if you were to announce your candidacy on Thursday, how many of the leaders of the party would you count on to welcome you?" Rockefeller thought for ten or fifteen seconds and answered, "I don't think any of them."

This was the nub of Rockefeller's strategic dilemma. There was good reason to think that Rockefeller could be elected President if he could be nominated as the Republican candidate. But there was very little reason to think that he could be nominated, for while he was popular in the country, he was not popular with Republicans, and he was even less popular with the professional Republican politicians who would decide the nomination.

In November 1967, for example, a Harris poll showed Rockefeller with fifty-two per cent of the electorate, against thirty-five per cent for Johnson, but another report on the same day showed Republican county chairmen favoring Nixon over Rockefeller by no less than five to one. And it was county chairmen who would influence the choice of convention delegates and in many cases be delegates themselves. On March 16, Harris was to find that Rockefeller still led Johnson by forty-one to thirty-four per cent among all voters (where Nixon was tied with Johnson, thirty-nine per cent each); but among Republican voters (who make up only a quarter of the electorate), Nixon led Rockefeller by fifty-six to thirty-two per cent. The Republican Party, Harris pointed out, was faced with an anomaly: "Nixon today would sweep a nation-wide G.O.P. primary, but Rockefeller would be a much more likely winner against Mr. Johnson."

There are two reasons for Rockefeller's unpopularity in the party. The first lies in the character of the people who run it. "Have you ever seen a Republican convention?" Rockefeller asked someone who had asked him why he lost in Miami. What he meant was that the party is still controlled at the local level by members of the little local elites that have run America since the Civil War—small-town bankers and middle-sized industrialists and their lawyer and doctor friends from the country clubs, many of them decent people, but narrow and self-righteous. Theirs is an old feudal class whose power and dignity is threatened by every change, not least by the emergence of a new national elite that overpowers them. For twenty years, they have nursed a grudge against the Eastern establishment and what seems to them its liberal cant about expensive social programs at home and thankless internationalism abroad. And Nelson Rockefeller was the embodiment of the Eastern establishment.

The second reason lay in Nelson Rockefeller's own character and behavior. The party might be "paranoid," as one of his closest friends claims. But he had done little to soothe and much to arouse its phobias. In 1960, when the party leaders were so suspicious of him that one of them introduced him as Nelson Roosevelt, he seemed to have betrayed Nixon in the "treaty of Fifth Avenue." To the rank and file, Rockefeller seemed to show no interest in the party or its principles except every four years when the Presidential nomination came up. "Rockefeller dumped Nixon and me in 1964," one bitter professional grumbled to the *New York Times,* "so I just frankly don't see how any Republican can support him." "I hope the son of a bitch supports the ticket this time," another reporter was told. "He probably will . . . if he's on it!" And it was not only conservatives who resented what they saw as Rockefeller's selfishness.

"I keep reading that Governor Rockefeller has become the great spiritual leader of progressives within our party," growled a moderate Republican in Congress. "He's solving this, he's attacking that, he's proposing another thing. Well, bullshit! He's not leading *us.* He's got these gigantic research projects and fact-finding commissions coming out of his ears in New York. We've formed a research group, but we can't fund it more than one hundred thousand dollars—that doesn't scratch it! Rockefeller hasn't helped *us!*"

Not all the Republicans felt like that about him. The young men who had been elected as governors, Senators, and Congressmen in urban states understood Rockefeller's "liberal" record for what it was: not ideology, but intelligent realism. They too had to worry about slums, schools, strikes, traffic, air and water pollution, above all taxes. (Rockefeller was not on the record as a dove on Vietnam. Anybody who knew his record—conciliatory, rational, internationalist—might guess that he

would ultimately be for a negotiated settlement of the war. But so far
he had not said so.) These, if anybody did, were the men who might
support his candidacy.

One of this new crop of Republicans was openly enthusiastic
about Rockefeller's running—embarrassingly so, in fact, from Rockefeller's point of view. Spiro Agnew, the bull-necked son of an immigrant
Greek restaurant owner, seemed the epitome of the new urban liberals
in the party. He had emerged from total obscurity as an elected county
official in the Baltimore suburbs in a race for the governorship of Maryland which was disfigured at the primary stage by a wild-and-woolly
candidate named George Mahoney, whose slogan—"Your home is your
castle!"—was a barely concealed appeal to the racial nervousness of the
Maryland poor whites. Mahoney made Agnew look liberal, and in his
first months in office he was. Obviously ambitious, he was thrusting himself forward as a Rockefeller backer. At one point early in 1968 he came
up to New York to talk privately to the Governor. Rockefeller insisted
that he was not a candidate; Agnew went straight downstairs and told the
press, to Rockefeller's intense irritation, that he hoped Rockefeller might
run.

At the end of February, Agnew set up a "Draft Rockefeller" movement in Maryland; and a couple of days later, an old pro called Al
Abrahams set up a national "Draft Rockefeller" headquarters, which
may or may not have been financed by Agnew, but of which he emerged
as chairman by March 6.

In Rockefeller's inner political family, the debate was now engaged
in earnest. For almost all of the first weekend in March, Nelson and
Happy Rockefeller talked their decision through and around, for and
against, with George Hinman and Emmett Hughes in the great apartment at 812 Fifth Avenue. None of the four was flatly in favor of
announcing a candidacy, but none now ruled it out. A date began to
dominate the discussions: March 22, the latest day on which a candidate could enter the Oregon primary. By a peculiarity of Nebraska's
electoral law, a candidate who entered Oregon would be obliged to have
his name on the Nebraska primary ballot as well, and Nebraska was
almost the most conservative state in the country. There was another
complication: the Governor was now completely absorbed in New York
politics, and his instinct was to put off his decision until his battle with
the state legislature could be won. He kept grabbing at straws. Why not
enter the Oregon primary but only campaign for a couple of days? Or

why not organize a write-in movement? Patiently Hughes and Hinman
brought him to see that half answers would be the worst of all.

The crucial question was the one Hughes had asked straightaway:
Would a declaration be greeted with "deafening indifference"? That was
an overstatement, perhaps. On March 10, there was a carefully publicized gathering of supporters to test the wind. Seven governors came:
Agnew, brother Winthrop, Shafer of Pennsylvania (a critical state),
LeVander of Minnesota, Chafee of Rhode Island, Love of Colorado,
and McCall of Oregon. An eighth, Nils Boe of South Dakota, sent a
representative. There were three Senators, half a dozen Congressmen,
and a miscellany of other party notables, mainly from New York—like
Mayor Lindsay. As a muster, it was not negligible; but with no one from
the big Midwestern states or the South, or from the party leadership in
Congress, it was inconclusive.

The debate continued all that week. Discreetly, George Hinman
allowed some wheels to turn. Advertisements began to appear in the
papers, such as one paid for by Stewart Mott, a major shareholder in
General Motors, saying, "It's your move, Nelson Rockefeller!"—as if he
didn't know it. On Sunday, March 17, another group came to 812 Fifth
Avenue to urge him to run, this time a spontaneous delegation from
Oregon, where time was running short. On Monday night, Rockefeller
flew to Washington and dined at his house on Foxhall Road with Senator
Thruston Morton, the genial and much-liked moderate who had been
Republican national chairman. He asked Morton to manage his cam-
paign, if he made one, and Morton agreed to run it up to the convention.

There was not likely to be a campaign for him to manage. Just
before lunchtime, Emmett Hughes had read Rockefeller a draft statement for him to give on television on Thursday—a statement of his
reasons for not running. And in the early afternoon, Hinman had rung
up with the results of a poll which Lloyd Free, the Rockefeller house
pollster, had been commissioned to do in Oregon. As Rockefeller turned
back to Hughes from the phone, he was laughing. "I guess you really
are my guardian angel," he had said. "I've just got a poll where I've
slipped twelve points and Dick's gone up eight."

Nevertheless, he put himself to one more test. Morton and Senator
Hugh Scott of Pennsylvania, another staunch Rockefeller backer of old,
had arranged for their man to meet a group of Senate colleagues on
Tuesday morning. Sixteen or seventeen men turned up, which Morton
thought was a good score, but which depressed Rockefeller. What was

far more discouraging was the tone they took. No one expressed enthusiasm. But what really irritated Rockefeller was the attitude, articulated with painful frankness by Senator Hiram Fong, who has mastered
the ponderous tactlessness of a Chinese White Anglo-Saxon Protestant.
By all means let Rockefeller spend his money on a campaign, said Fong.
It would bring the party useful publicity and help to elect Dick Nixon.
That night, on his private jet going back to New York, Rockefeller
decided it was hopeless. The telecast was arranged for Thursday.

A comedy of errors remained to be played out. By one of those
absurd ironies that have a habit of changing the fortunes of war and
politics, Rockefeller's men proceeded to make a slip that turned out to
have more effect on the course of the campaign than anything they did
on purpose—and this in the very department of politics in which they
were acknowledged to be the meticulous masters. They made a historic
mess of their public relations. On Thursday morning the always-con-
siderate Hinman reminded Governor Rockefeller that he ought not to
make his negative announcement that afternoon without privately warning half a dozen of those who had most publicly committed themselves
to him. Before leaving the apartment to make final arrangements for the
broadcast, Hinman placed calls to some of them: to Thruston Morton
in Washington, to Harold LeVander in Minneapolis, and to Ted Agnew
in Annapolis. At this juncture, Ted Braun, a California public-relations
man who had won Rockefeller's respect by his advice at the time of his
divorce, arrived on the scene and began to argue that the telecast was
one of the most important moments of his political life, and that it was
essential to rehearse it.

The calls Hinman had placed were never made. And at almost
exactly the same moment, in Annapolis, another public-relations man
was giving Agnew advice. This was Agnew's day, he was saying. Rockefeller's announcement would be his doing as much as anyone else's. Let
Agnew take credit for persuading a major candidate into the race; let
him step into the front rank of Republican leaders. His weekly press
conference would coincide with Rockefeller's telecast anyway. Why not
invite the reporters into his office and let them watch the speech there,
and then subtly take some of the credit for Rockefeller's candidacy in a
few carefully spontaneous remarks? Agnew is a vain man, and it sounded
like an excellent idea to him. A color-television set was hired and installed in the Governor's office, and the press was invited. When Rocke-

feller said he was not going to run, eyewitnesses swear that Agnew's jaw dropped a full inch.

Agnew did not forgive Rockefeller. Months later, he was brought to believe that it had indeed been a sin of omission and not of commission. But at the time, he took it as a deliberate insult. At a political garden party in Maryland, several weeks afterward, the two men met. Rockefeller did everything short of going down on his knees to convince Agnew that the failure to make the call had been an oversight. Agnew was implacable. In any case, though Rockefeller didn't know it, it was already too late.

Thruston Morton happens to have a brother, Rogers Morton, who is a Congressman from Maryland and who differs from his brother in that he does not particularly like Nelson Rockefeller, whom he finds snobbish and a little insincere. Shortly after the New Hampshire primary, Rogers Morton came out for Nixon, and was rewarded by being named as his floor manager for the convention. He saw his chance with Agnew sulking in his tent, Achilles-like, and swooped. Agnew allowed himself to be persuaded to go to New York and visit Nixon. "They were pretty *simpatico*," Morton noticed. "That first meeting they talked about a whole lot of things, about the relationship of the Federal government to local government, all sorts of things. They found themselves pretty much in agreement emotionally. They had several meetings after that. . . ."

First Romney, then Agnew. Twice a crucial Rockefeller friend had become an enemy because of a slip, an obstinate something that looked like arrogance escaping out of his subconscious mind. It would be quite unjust to call Nelson Rockefeller an arrogant man at the conscious level. No man tries harder to disprove the charge. And yet, perhaps Fitzgerald was right. Perhaps a Rockefeller is not only soft where we are hard and cynical where we are trusting. Perhaps he can never quite forget that he is . . . well, not *better* than we are, exactly—but still a Rockefeller.

3

The New Tenant

"You'll like Dick. He's so square."

—Frances Hodgson Burnett, *Little Lord Faunt-
leroy*

In the aftermath of the contest in 1962 for the governorship of California, Richard Nixon's numerous enemies felt, with relief and pleasure,
that at long last they could consign him to the political ash can. Two
years earlier he had lost a Presidential campaign to a man who, when
the battle started, had been the less well-known candidate. Now he had
been routed in a gubernatorial contest by an incumbent Democrat who
had seemed—at least to Republicans—ripe for defeat. And in the famous
"last press conference" after the results came in, he had offended spectacularly against his own principle that "no politician is dead until he
admits it." Having admitted his own political death, it was a very good
question where Richard Nixon should turn next.

There was one obvious thing to do: go back to law practice with
Adams, Duque and Hazeltine in Los Angeles, the city which was as
nearly his home as any other place. Such an acceptance of lucrative
obscurity would have been entirely in the tradition of candidates who try
and fail in the contest for major office. The firm wanted him back—
Earl C. Adams, its senior partner, had offered Nixon work as early as
1946—and this was the option Nixon was generally expected to take up.
Another, less known, option was to return to Washington to become national chairman of the Republican Party. Nixon seriously considered
this, and no doubt he would have done the job extremely well. It calls
chiefly for diligence and inflexible party loyalty, qualities Nixon possesses

in full measure, although perhaps he lacks that talent for invisibility which the best party chairmen have.

But he had friends and advisers, such as Robert Finch and Raymond Moley, who did not accept the popular belief that Nixon's potential as a national candidate was exhausted. Therefore, they advised him against staying in California, the scene of his most humiliating disaster, and against taking the chairmanship, which would turn him into a party bureaucrat professionally debarred from having great ambitions of his own.

At the time, Nixon seems to have felt that his friends were exaggerating his capacity for regeneration. Nevertheless, the advice they gave him—to move to New York—was sound. And had the move not been made, it is hard to see how the subsequent accession to the White House could have been organized.

There were some good personal reasons for making the break. Nixon was surrounded by political depression in California, and his enthusiasm for further adventures was sapped by the way his children were teased at school: in New York, he would be only a one-time loser. And, although Adams, Duque and Hazeltine was a prosperous enough firm, Nixon would probably be able to make even more money in New York. It was time that he made some money, for seventeen years of public service had left him, at least by the standards and aspirations of the people among whom he moved, a relatively poor man. But the move also had important political connotations, which Moley articulated with great clarity.

Nixon's dilapidated state at the end of 1962 never seriously shook Moley's view, held for many years, that this was the man best fitted to rescue an America which had gone sadly astray. Moley, who had taught economics at Columbia University, had been one of the architects of Roosevelt's New Deal. But he broke with FDR and was one of the first men of stature to revolt against the philosophy of optimistic liberalism which became the orthodoxy of American politics as a result of Roosevelt's success. Today, Moley writes an occasional column for *Newsweek* from a position of marked conservatism; but, in his view, it is not he who has moved to the right since the thirties. Rather, it is America which has moved to the left—through a process of deceit and intolerable intellectual slovenliness. (Moley once remarked bitterly that he never knew Franklin Roosevelt to read a serious book.)

Moley, who comes from Ohio, believes that one of the important organizing principles of American politics is a struggle in which the combined forces of the West and Midwest are pitted against the entrenched power of the East. When he speaks of the Eastern Establishment, he does not mean so much the kind of intellectual and administrative elite to which we referred earlier, but rather, the old financial empires of the seaboard, and their dependencies. Bluntly, it is in the interest of the Easterners, who have already made it, to prevent or at least hamper the growth of economic power in the West which might rival and even surpass their own. One way to do this is to erode the economic freedom which was once the creative principle of American society and which served their own ends well in other days. The Eastern Establishment, Moley and many, many others less intellectually honest than he suspects, has its own reasons for wanting the Republican leadership kept in liberal hands.

Without subscribing to the lurid conspiracy theories of the right-wing fringe, Moley shares the belief of many Republicans that, in the past, the power of the East has succeeded in imposing unsuitably liberal Presidential candidates on the Republican Party—Wendell Willkie, the registered Democrat; Thomas Dewey, accused of "out-Roosevelting Roosevelt"; even Eisenhower, whose supporters brutally elbowed out good Robert Taft of Ohio. The unattractive qualities of the Eastern establishment could hardly be better incarnated than in the person of the quasi-Democrat, Nelson Rockefeller.

Still, the Easterners, however unsound, could not be ignored, and Moley believed that it was necessary to deal with them on their own ground. Therefore, Nixon should move to New York, demonstrate his intellectual capacities among the Easterners, learn their ways, and—insofar as it might be necessary to insure their qualified support—actually become one of them. At the right time, he would thus be able to appear with the unique advantages of being loved by the faithful of the West and Midwest, while being at least tolerated by the heathens of the East. In more fulsome language, he would be the man who could "unite all sections of the party."

It was an entirely brilliant analysis. What Moley saw was that Nixon was the only "natural" candidate of the West and Midwest who at the same time possessed the degree of flexibility necessary to disarm the East. Unlike the charming but feather-brained Goldwater, or the simplistic and indolent Reagan, he also possessed the professional qualifications and mental equipment to thrive in the classic forcing house of Eastern Republican leadership: Wall Street. Failing the advent of a miraculous candidate, such as Eisenhower, only a man like Nixon, adding to the gut loyalty of one section of the party the sophisticated tolerance of the other, could contrive the precarious miracle of a Republican Presidential victory.

In May 1963, Nixon announced that he was about to move to New York City, where he would join the old-established Wall Street firm of Mudge, Stern, Baldwin & Todd. In due course, he would become a partner. In the months after this, Nixon denied frequently that there was "any political motivation" in his move: he was interested in nothing more than practicing his profession on a "fast track." But if he was looking for nothing more than a track, Los Angeles is not all that sluggish. Perhaps a more revealing remark was the one he made later on the nature of the political life: "Once a man has been in politics, once that's been his life, he will always return if the people want him." Nixon may have set little store by his future Presidential prospects. But there could be no harm in moving himself to a place from which "the people" could fetch him, should they at any time wish to do so.

Nixon moved to New York on June 1, 1963, and set up house in an apartment at 812 Fifth Avenue, with twelve rooms and a fine view over Central Park. It was entirely suitable that this was the building containing the New York apartment of Governor Nelson Rockefeller.

Few politicians are more difficult to write about than the man who survived the complicated elimination game of Presidential politics in 1968. Nixon might seem a dull fellow, but he stirs passions, positive and negative, that run strong and deep. Since the early fifties, only the rather febrile—and not entirely spontaneous—Reaganism of 1968 has matched the trust, even love, that Nixon inspires among grass-roots Republicans west of the Alleghenies. Yet, as Victor S. Navasky once said with no great exaggeration, "You can't have voted for Richard Nixon and been a member of the New York intellectual establishment." He has been around so long, of course: the tortuous path of his career seems to pass through the center of most of the pressure points of post-war political history. He has not been off the front pages since 1948, and there are not many of that vintage around. Then too, he suffers from the lust for simplicity, the desire to deal in stereotypes, which disfigures political communication in America, as in most places. But as Nixon has spent a good deal of his own career making up, and selling with profit, definitive lists of Goodies and Baddies, there is a certain poetic justice in that.

His opponents have usually found in him a special dishonesty, a deviousness, summed up in the indestructible nickname Tricky Dick. The same perception, no doubt, gave wing to that outrageously successful slogan: "Would you buy a used car from this man?" (Ironically, from what one knows of Nixon's personal standards, he would be a rather good man to buy a used car from.) It seems odd that Nixon should be thought *especially* tricky, more so than is professionally necessary. After all, the political matrix in which we find him includes so sophistical a moralist as Eugene McCarthy and a man of such ideological ductility as Hubert Humphrey. The Kennedys' political operations, while they have been criticized, have never given rise to the same impassioned distaste as has been visited on Nixon. Yet, to make one's barely qualified younger brother Attorney General of the United States seems in some ways more cynical than anything that can be put to Richard Nixon's account: John Kennedy apparently did not take exception to Robert's admiring remark that such a maneuver took "the guts of a burglar." That mental climate seems to leave Richard Nixon among the innocents.

It is not always quite clear what sort of dishonor is supposed by opponents to attach to Nixon. There is often the suggestion that there is something financially dubious about his life, and indeed the Democratic Party has been looking for some impurity here for twenty years, off and on. The only substantial incident produced by this search was the "secret fund" case in the 1952 Presidential election . . . but seventeen years later, the aroma lingers on. And what, after all, were the facts of that case?

After Nixon's election to the Senate in 1950, a fund was set up which collected and disbursed, over a two-year period, just over eighteen thousand dollars to meet various political expenses of Nixon's. The contributors, as one might expect, were oilmen, bankers, and other ornaments of Southern California society. It was not against the rules of the game for Senators to accept such contributions to maintain political activity between elections. Conceivably, it should be—but that is another matter. Nixon would have been in trouble if he could have been shown to have used any of the money personally, but insofar as a negative can be proved, it was clear he had not.

Sometimes, in the retrospective arguments over this incident, it is hard to be sure whether the anger that is still deployed against Nixon derives from the nature of the fund itself or from the "Checkers" speech that he made in defense of it. If you read the transcript of that performance in 1968, it is not easy to see why it was so offensive. Nixon explained the nature of the fund and then—"to discredit any future smears"—told the world all about his private financial status. The property he owned was worth twenty-seven thousand dollars, he said—life insurance, plus equity in his house in California and his house in Washington. He also owned a 1950 Oldsmobile. No stocks or bonds. He owed forty-three thousand dollars, mainly on the houses.

Nixon seems to have been determined to tug on the audience's heartstrings, and this led him to the famous passage about the doggy. Perhaps what riled people was that he led off this bit by saying, "One other thing I should probably tell you, because if I don't they will probably be saying this about me too. . . ." Clearly, there was no actual compulsion to introduce Checkers, the little black-and-white spaniel which a Texas admirer had donated to the Nixon children. Even his worst enemies would admit that Nixon's price is higher than one dog. Still, he ground on, with mock-heroics about how he would not take Checkers away from the kids, no matter what they said about him. It was a bit irrelevant, and no doubt tasteless. Perhaps Nixon, mugging a martyred look, made it look even worse, but all the same it hardly seems the grossest of political offenses. Mrs. Nixon was dragged in too, via references to her "respectable Republican cloth coat" and the fact that "Pat is not a quitter. After all, her name was Patricia Ryan and she was born on Saint Patrick's Day, and you know the Irish never quit." (Nixon has remarked elsewhere that Mrs. Nixon never really recovered her zest for politics after this incident, but he does not seem to have reflected that no one was forcing him to wave his wife about as a kind of honesty charm.) It was quite true, as one critic subsequently wrote— William Costello in *The Facts about Nixon*—that Nixon did not discuss the ethical question of political finances generally. Could one really expect a practical politician to do so in that sort of position?

The emotional tone of the Checkers speech has clearly stayed in people's minds longer than the facts—such as they were—about the fund. Perhaps it was assumed that emotion, in the unyielding interrogator of Alger Hiss, must be synthetic—but there is much testimony that Nixon, for all his normal containment, is full of emotion. It is sometimes thought that emotions long pent up must be of the grander kind, but they may be something as commonplace as self-pity, which was the dominant tone of the speech.

Yet people do like Nixon, and they are not all villains. Indeed, for a politician, he has surprisingly few ex-friends who are now enemies. Some people start off disposed against him and come around to different views. For instance, in 1958 Earl Mazo, a journalist, was commissioned by Harper & Row to write a book about Nixon. Mazo says now that he planned it as a three-month hatchet job, and it took him fifteen months. He tried to check out all the available dirt on Nixon at that time and came to the conclusion that "half of it simply wasn't true, twenty-five per cent was half true, and twenty-five per cent was true but not important." For example, at the height of the McCarthy period, a Nobel Prize–winning scientist, Dr. Edward U. Condon, lost his job in the Bureau of Standards. Many scientists felt, partly because of what Condon said in an article for the *Bulletin of the Atomic Scientists,* that Nixon was to blame. On inquiry, Condon's lawyer, Henry Fowler, told Mazo that Nixon had nothing to do with the matter. And in fact Nixon went on record as saying that it was wrong that Condon had never been given a chance to clear himself. This does not mean that Nixon's role in the McCarthy period was blameless: it merely illustrates his talent for getting blamed for things he didn't really do.

In late 1960, when he was on the now-defunct *New York Herald Tribune,* Mazo spent a long time investigating the decidedly dubious voting patterns involved in the crucial Democratic victories in Illinois and Texas. Having gone a long way with the investigation and become convinced that there was serious evidence of vote fraud, Mazo received a call: Nixon wanted to see him. When Mazo showed up, he not unnaturally expected Nixon to give him some further evidence. Instead, he says, Nixon told him that it was intolerable that the Presidential election should be challenged in this way, especially as there was no evidence whatever that the Democratic candidate was in the slightest way involved. Nixon said bluntly that not only would he not help with the investigation, but he would use all his influence to get it killed, which he did. Mazo, after some ten years of intermittent study of Nixon, has two conclusions about the man which may produce varying degrees of surprise. One is that, within his own terms, he is a man of unbending honesty. The other—which may have significance later in this story—is that he is not a particularly astute politician.

Nixon's technique, however, sometimes makes even his supporters uneasy. And although there was much talk at the beginning of 1968 about a New Nixon, some of his campaign utterances followed a twenty-year-old pattern which made Alexander Bickel say that "it is necessary to monitor Mr. Nixon . . . as carefully as ever, especially when he deals in numbers." Specifically, Professor Bickel was complaining about a speech in which Nixon attacked the Supreme Court for erecting a "barbed wire of legalisms" which made the criminal's task all too easy.

Chiefly, Nixon objected to certain Court decisions which govern the admissibility of confessions and identification as evidence in criminal trials. The effect of these decisions is to make sure that arrested persons have proper access to legal advice: Nixon implied that, largely because of these scruples, no more than "one in eight major crimes committed now results in arrest, prosecution, conviction, and punishment." The source of the "one in eight" figure was the President's Crime Commission, but the Commission made clear a point which Nixon blurred: that the largest single factor in the total number of unpunished crimes was *cases where no arrest was made.* Clearly, rulings on the admission of evidence in court cannot seriously affect the number of arrests made. The Crime Commission found that the rate of convictions in cases brought to court is high: in other words, the reverse of the picture Nixon conjured up of criminals' walking blithely out of court after seeing the evidence against them disallowed on fiddling technicalities. (The case against which Nixon mounted his most serious attack was *Miranda:* it was therefore disingenuous of him not to tell his audience that Miranda was convicted, although his confession was disallowed as evidence.)

To hostile Nixon-watchers of long habit, such incidents fit into a pattern. Unlike some other politicians, Nixon is not often caught in great, thumping lies. But over and over again, people feel they have detected the same oversharpness of debating technique. The facts, as far as they go, are accurate: it is how Nixon puts them together that causes trouble.

Whatever the rights and wrongs of the matter, there is no doubt that there exists in America a durable reservoir of hostility toward Richard Nixon. Given the conditions of the Presidency and the modern world, that hostility could well expand with startling speed. And, as the history of Lyndon Johnson shows, it is not exactly an academic matter if a large and active proportion of the American elite comes to dislike and distrust the President. No one, indeed, is more conscious of the fact that he is a natural center of conflict than Nixon himself, with whom self-analysis is virtually a life style.

But Nixon's brand of self-analysis is apt to be as unusual as everything else about the man. For instance, there was the remarkable operation which ran through most of 1967, beginning shortly after Raymond K. Price, an ex-*Herald Tribune* journalist, joined the emerging Nixon political *apparat* in May. Price, although hardly a radical, was a considerably more liberal figure than those who had been close to Nixon before him. He had, for example, broken with the Republican ticket in 1964, when Nixon supported Goldwater—and, indeed, wrote the editorial in which the *Herald Tribune* shattered its ancient Republican traditions and recommended Lyndon Johnson.

Price joined Nixon—as a speech-writer, naturally. But one of his most important functions was in a long-drawn-out process in which he and his colleagues were asked to throw at Nixon every sort of criticism they could think of from every conceivable viewpoint. Price, whose hiring was described as "very much Nixon's own decision," was regarded as the man who could spark up this curious debate and see to it that divergent views were fed into the argument. One of the people who took part in the process said that it was "a lawyer's idea"—and it certainly sounds like it. Nixon seems to have been saying, Throw everything at me. Let's see what the worst of it is.

Supposedly, this was an uninhibited, even scarifying process, in which "Richard Nixon was taken apart politically and put together again." One is rather skeptical about this, because there is little perceptible difference between Nixon's positions before and after. (Some people say that the process contributed to the new self-assurance that was widely detected in the candidate of 1968.) But rather than the result, it is the approach which is remarkable: a kind of mechanized attempt at self-awareness.

We know that it was Richard Nixon's professed ambition, as he approached his Presidency, to unite his fellow citizens, to "bring them together." Yet, if things should turn that way, we also know that he is uniquely fitted, by his personality and his history, to divide them. There are, perhaps, tensions in the man himself which account for the traits and techniques which so alienate many of the people who would normally be counted among the best in American life. It may also be that, for the liberal middle class, Nixon represents, with unequaled skill and persistence, all of the forces and movements that they find most unattractive in their own country.

If there is truth in either or both of these propositions, we must be able to trace the facts back to his political and personal origins. And their development must be observable in his career.

Nixon's home town of Whittier—he was born just outside it, in the hamlet of Yorba Linda—was founded by Quakers in 1887, as a place where Friends could live according to the quiet traditions of their society in the California sunshine. When Frank Nixon settled down there, after knocking around as painter, potter, and roustabout, it was rather like a small Middle Western town transferred to the Pacific Coast. It is still a quiet place. The campus of Whittier College, in the center of town, sounds with bird song, and you can smell new-mown grass under the cedars. Children—black, white, Mexican, and Oriental—play peacefully together on the tree-lined streets. But today, Whittier is only a small oasis in the smoggy, treeless tangle of the Los Angeles urban area. Successive booms in oil, movies, and defense industries have pushed the city out greedily, fifty miles past Whittier into the desert. The traveler flashing past on the San Gabriel Freeway receives just one reminder of the Quakers: a billboard importuning him to buy a house in "the Home of Friendly Hills . . . only $54,000 to $63,500." The boomsprawl of Los Angeles, which, if it is not the spirit of modern America, certainly advertises itself as such, has turned the peace of Nixon's home into an enclave and its values into a sales gimmick.

The story of Nixon's family is that of the ordinary people of the old America—not the wealthy and established aristocrats of New England or the landowners of the South, but the ones who worked and fought and prayed their way across the continent. Both sides of the family were Quakers, settled in America before the middle of the eighteenth century. One ancestor fought with Washington, and another was buried on the battlefield of Gettysburg. The Milhouses took their Quakerism especially seriously. They moved out of the South because of their objections to slavery and helped runaway slaves along the Underground Railroad to freedom.

If ever anyone's people had earned the right to a land flowing with milk and honey, then surely the descendants of such pioneers felt that theirs had done so. And for many of the Quakers of Whittier, the land did provide them with the solid prosperity which the Friends wear with such notable grace. But the home in which Richard Nixon grew up was not, on the whole, a fortunate one. The shadow of poverty, if not poverty itself, was never far away, and sickness was often close by. Richard's father suffered from ulcers. Two of Richard's brothers died in childhood—one of meningitis and one of tuberculosis. For several years, his mother had to leave California to run a nursing home in Arizona, to give the tubercular brother desert air and to meet the doctor's bills. Richard himself nearly died of pneumonia when he was four; and when he was in high school, he suffered a bad attack of undulant fever.

Frank Nixon seems to have had plenty of energy and the usual strong but undifferentiated desire to succeed in some kind of business enterprise. Like most of the Americans who battered on the doors of economic opportunity during the first quarter of this century, he was willing to turn his hand to many different kinds of work. What he lacked was luck—and luck, for all the talk of character, ingenuity, faith, and adaptability, is really the common factor in most of the lives of the men who won in the economic lottery of the times.

Nixon Senior's lack of luck was never better exemplified than in his decision to open a filling station in 1922. Two sites were available to him, and, after much rational calculation, he chose the site at East Whittier. This was a pity: in 1923, oil was found on the other site, the first well drilled producing twenty-five barrels a day. Passing so close to wealth had a powerful emotional effect on the Nixon family—although it does not seem to have produced in any of them, least of all in Richard, even marginal skepticism about the qualities of an economic system whose rewards were distributed in such an arbitrary way. In the period just after the gusher discovery, Frank Nixon did display a good deal of anger and resentment—but it was focused rather on Washington, where the Teapot Dome scandal was just breaking over the Harding Administration, a matter of oil reserves being appropriated as a result of crooked intrigues in the capital. Frank Nixon became "increasingly livid" over each new disclosure, write Earl Mazo and Stephen Hess, in *Nixon: A Political Portrait*. "His diatribes against 'crooked politicians' and 'crooked lawyers' dominated the family conversation for weeks." It almost sounds as though Nixon Senior blamed the corruptions of Washington for his failure to become an oil millionaire.

It is certainly part of the Nixon family's received belief that it was during this rather angry time that Richard, then age twelve or so, set himself on the path to distinction. He told his mother that he intended to become "an old-fashioned kind of lawyer, a lawyer who can't be bought." And his younger brother, Donald, says that, already at this time or thereabouts, Richard saw himself going beyond law into politics. It is suggestive, in view of the later obsessions of Nixon's career, that he should be said to have decided his course at a time when the family environment was dominated by an image of danger, conspiracy, and corruption at the administrative heart of the nation. And from the start of his political life, Nixon's fighting stance appeared to be that of a man who considered the scales unjustly loaded against him. His most deadly attacks have frequently been delivered in a persecuted tone.

On his way to becoming an "old-fashioned kind of lawyer," Nixon spent a youth which was remarkable for diligence, and for reserve. The passions which burned within him were not allowed to show themselves except in an unchanging appetite for work and concentration. It was only years later, in one of the few revealing passages (in *Six Crises*) in all the thousands of words he has produced, that he quoted with interest Balzac's remark that politicians are "monsters of self-possession"— adding: "Yet while we may show this veneer on the outside, inside the turmoil becomes almost unbearable." But, unlike many ambitious and contained youths, he was not unpopular, and Whittier today contains many people—not necessarily his political supporters—who liked and admired Richard Nixon, and still do. His self-possession did not mean that he was alone: on the contrary, he was a student leader both at high school and at Whittier College. He represented the college in more than fifty debates and won most of them. And he was an academic success. Yet, characteristically, it was his one real failure that obsessed him most, and it still does. This was football, which remained, in 1968, one of the few nonpolitical subjects on which Nixon discoursed with real animation. (One of the things which seemed to give him quite disproportionate pleasure during the campaign was his endorsement by the great Bart Starr of the Green Bay Packers.) Nixon's troubles with football were virtually insurmountable, in that he was too light and had poor coordination. But this never stopped him from trying to become a first-string player.

Behind the self-possession, there appears to have been a great insecurity. Not that Nixon suffered from that kind of self-loathing which creates the most ruthless and dangerous class of ambition: his family background, in particular his mother, had provided him with values which made the core of his personality stable enough. It was simply that he was filled with a need to prove his abilities, to "make it" in a way that he and his family had not yet succeeded in doing.

To this end, he became a risk-taker early in his life, setting a pattern which ran through most of his career. At certain points, he would gather up what capital he had accumulated and risk it in an attempt to gain something more. Frequently, he stood a real chance of losing. When he found, on entering Whittier College, that the established student fraternity was beyond his reach—largely because he was too poor—he took a large part in organizing a successful rival fraternity. Within its terms, it sounds like a considerable social initiative for boys of seventeen and eighteen. No doubt, this helped him to be elected president of the student body in his senior year. He took an activist role in that presidency: instead of basking in the office, he challenged the moral hostility of the college establishment to introduce dancing on campus. It must have been quite a difficult battle in a Quaker college in 1933, but he won it. (Nixon himself didn't care much for dancing, and was not good at it.) He was a great one for excelling within the rules, one of which at Whittier was that the student president provide a country privy to burn on the end-of-year bonfire. It was thought distinguished to provide a two-holer, and Nixon set a record which still stands by coming up with a four-holer.

When he returned to Whittier with his law degree from Duke University, he took another chance. He put a lot of local prestige on the line in a ten-thousand-dollar company which was to freeze and market surplus oranges from the Whittier area. Current freezing and packing techniques had not yet been developed, and Nixon lost. But his first big risk after the war paid off, when he put half his Navy savings into the war chest for his campaign against the well-established local Congressman, Jerry Voorhis. Later, his risk in backing the word of Whittaker Chambers against Alger Hiss came off—but, of course, his 1960 decision to debate against John Kennedy failed. ("I can't understand people who won't take the chance of failure," Nixon said once.) Oddly enough, although it was Robert Kennedy whose admirers liked to describe him as an "existential politician" and a man of action, the much-despised Nixon was, on the record, nearer to this model. Unlike Kennedy, Nixon was not inhibited by the belief that no action should be undertaken unless victory could be assured.

But all of Nixon's risks were taken within a particular context. He played entirely within the rules: he never seems to have doubted the assumptions of the society which produced him. It is natural for successful politicians to be conventional fellows, at least in their maturity. Even so, one expects to find some moments of gentle questioning. To make the comparison again, Robert Kennedy, however orthodox his actions may have been, conducted within his own mind a steadily widening inquiry which led him to challenge more and more of the straightforward Irish-American values in which he was brought up. Nixon appears never to have questioned any of the verities of the American Way. Eisenhower might allow himself an occasional doubt about the use of atomic weapons in 1945, or a departing outburst against the "military-industrial complex." But not Nixon. His whole philosophy seems to have been summed up in a remark he made in the 1960 campaign, and repeated in 1968, that "I believe in the American Dream because I have seen it come true in my own life."

The dense and concentrated battle of Nixon's younger life seems to have been conducted without a moment of intellectual doubt. He supposedly learned French at Whittier and studied "the French classical philosophers." Maybe so, but no traces appear in his subsequent thoughts and actions. The nearest thing to a process of development is the fact that he left Duke Law School as a mild "legal liberal"—a result of the usual student's admiration for Louis D. Brandeis—and painlessly became less liberal as a result of what he saw in the Office of Emergency Management during the early war years. Even this is hardly complex: he just says that he thought the Federal government inefficient. All of that diligent intelligence, all that "almost unbearable" inner turmoil was confined within a framework of the utmost conformity.

If it is true that the ideal politician is an ordinary representative of his class with extraordinary abilities, Richard Nixon was never more exemplary of the thesis than when he finally "made it." This, it seems to us, did not occur during all his years of mixed political adventures before 1962, nor even in his elevation to the Presidency. Rather, it was in his period as a successful Wall Street lawyer, 1963 to 1967. Even during his two terms as Vice-President, Nixon was never entirely assured as a national politician. His standing with the public leapt erratically from high to low, and his patron, Eisenhower, never quite repaid the unswerving loyalty Nixon gave him. Ike equivocated in 1952 when Nixon was unjustly accused of corruption and again in 1956 over the question of retaining Nixon on the ticket. The cautious, unemotional Eisenhower seems to have detected some uncertainty, some lack of solidity in his eager acolyte.

And most certainly Nixon had not "made it" by the most important measure of the society whose values he so frankly accepted. He had made no money. He had been on the fringes of the greatest power and success, but he had depended on other men for his access to them. He had not even practiced his profession seriously in the big league: he had still not become, successfully, "an old-fashioned kind of lawyer."

Nixon was returning, quite specifically, to an old ambition when he went to Wall Street after the 1962 debacle. He had tried for a job there, as an honors graduate of Duke in 1937, and he has said since that if he had won the job he wanted with the Dulles firm, Sullivan and Cromwell, "I would have been there today, a corporation lawyer."

Nixon's success, second time around, was immediate: he found that Wall Street regarded him as a very good lawyer indeed, and many of his friends believe that a new assurance and poise in his personality date from that experience. Certainly one of the few things that have been enough to rouse him to anger since was the suggestion that contacts, rather than ability, made him a success.

Very swiftly, he began to make a great deal of money—at least two hundred thousand dollars a year—and this generated in him an intense and almost innocent delight. He was struck by how easy it was, after all, for him to make the stuff. One story he told his friends concerned a big corporation which came to him for advice about a plan to establish a division in France. They wanted his advice on the likelihood of political stability in France. Nixon, after some thought, told them simply that France would be stable while de Gaulle was alive, and he was much impressed to find that the clients were happy to part with twenty-five thousand dollars for this insight. For some time afterward, he went around celebrating the ease with which money could be made in corporation law, and his pleasure was not diminished when a more seasoned operator told him that he had been a fool not to charge a hundred thousand. It does not appear to have crossed Nixon's mind that there was anything curious about an economic system in which great corporations had become so superfatted that they could disburse small fortunes to acquire information available to the most casual newspaper reader.

Nixon accepted the prizes of the system unquestioningly. Apart from money, there was the matter of his admission statement. Having qualified already for the California Bar, Nixon did not have to take the full New York Bar examination: having satisfied the residential qualification, he had only to prepare a five-hundred-word statement on the question, "What do you believe the principles underlying the form of government of the United States to be?" Nixon submitted a draft on this subject without much reflection and was startled when the examining committee declared that it was so brilliant that they wanted to make it public. This unprecedented idea was debated, with much palaver, by the Supreme Court of the state, which finally decided that it should be read out at Nixon's swearing-in ceremony in Albany. After all the fuss, this, in its entirety, was the great work:

> The principles underlying the government of the United States are decentralization of power, separation of power, and maintaining a balance between freedom and order.
> Above all else, the framers of the Constitution were fearful of the

concentration of power in either individuals or government. The genius of their solution in this respect is that they were able to maintain a very definite but delicate balance between the federal government and the state government, on the one hand, and between the executive, legislative, and judicial branches of the federal government on the other hand.

By contrast, in the British system, the Parliament is supreme. In the present French system, the primary power resides in the executive, and in some older civilizations the judges were predominant. Throughout American history there have been times when one or the other branches of the government would seem to have gained a dominant position, but the pendulum has always swung back and the balance over the long haul maintained.

The concept of decentralization of power is maintained by what we call the federal system. But the principle is much broader in practice. Putting it most simply, the American ideal is that private or individual enterprise should be allowed and encouraged to undertake all functions which it is capable to perform. Only when private enterprise cannot or will not do what needs to be done should government step in. When government action is required, it should be undertaken if possible by that unit of government which is closest to the people. For example, the progression should be from local to state to federal government, in that order. In other words, the federal government should step in only when the function to be performed is too big for the state or local government to undertake it.

It is a little hard to see why so much fuss was made of this concise, if pedestrian, account of some crashingly unexceptionable opinions. Nixon, however, also added to his reputation by some altogether more serious legal achievements. For instance, his part in the Supreme Court appeal of *Time Inc. v. Hill,* a complex case involving rights of privacy and the freedom of the press, was thought by most lawyers to be highly competent, and Nixon was, no doubt justly, proud of it. Why, then, did he go along with the ridiculous charade about his treatise on government? The answer to this, and perhaps other, puzzles about Richard Nixon, may lie in the difference between operating intelligence and discrimination, a distinction he has given no sign of caring about.

Leaving aside for the moment the question of whether the qualities of a first-class advocate are those required in a President—and the question of whether those forces represented in the Wall Street legal world are those which have most concern for the American community—one can scarcely deny that the senior partner of Nixon, Mudge, Stern, Guthrie & Alexander was a long way from the ex-politician with a mortgage and a middle-aged car. He sat in well-stuffed black leather chairs in an office crammed with the trophies of a notable career. (Nixon seems to possess in full measure that politician's yearning for plaques, gavels, autographs, inscribed golf balls, and ornaments of every description, including, in his case, incredible quantities of elephants, a gold kukri, and a silver-framed photograph of Queen Elizabeth.) A staff of more than a hundred lawyers stood at the senior partner's beck and call. And, at the end of the day, a chauffeur-driven, air-conditioned Cadillac, provided not by the sufferance of the government but out of recognition of his own commercial worth, took him home to Fifth Avenue. There, by going up in a private elevator, he could avoid the misfortune of bumping unprepared into Governor Rockefeller. It is not that Nixon is mercenary, or even sybaritic. On the contrary, he seems always to have been a man of plain tastes and hard work. The luxuries of his new life were badges of virtue to a man who had never questioned the equation in which virtue precisely equals success.

The directness with which Nixon accepted this virtue-success equation was shown by the nature of the spiritual comfort he chose in New York: the heavily modified Dutch Reformed Church of Dr. Norman Vincent Peale. Nixon had been impressed by Peale well before 1960, but now he was able to show up fairly regularly at Marble Collegiate Church on Fifth Avenue. Dr. Peale has evolved what must be the most strictly functional brand of Christianity yet offered to Americans, and it is apt that Nixon should have an affinity for it. Peale is not one of your suspect evangelical doctors: he is a native of Ohio and has, like Nixon, perfectly good intellectual equipment, insofar as he chooses to make demands on it. His degrees in theology are not from some Southern Bible college, but from Boston and Syracuse universities.

However, like Nixon's other Ohio-born counselor, Raymond Moley, Dr. Peale believes that there is a certain danger in the East. While he was at Boston, he declares, attempts were made to convert him to "ethically patterned Christianity, designed to facilitate the rise of left-wing panaceas." Peale was able to throw off this influence and create his own "scientifically applied Christianity." The essential point about this faith is that it abolishes the tension between God and Mammon which exists, at least vestigially, in most Christian belief. Pealeism bluntly proposes that the proper purpose of prayer is to bring about worldly success. Dr. Peale advises his followers, virtually in so many words, to make God their business partner. "Take all your bills," he says. "Lay them out on the table. Then ask God what to do about them. Ask him for a definite plan of financing." Dr. Peale's talk teems with tales of how men have, by prayer, become oil millionaires and national television stars. You get what you want by praying for it, and if you pray right, God will give it to you. One day in the summer of 1968, he expounded the point that the Presidency itself was entirely open to this method—a sermon presumably turned that way for the benefit of Richard Nixon, who was sitting attentively in the congregation.

Dr. Peale's talks stress not so much the afterlife, or spiritual values, but rather the "positive results" that can be obtained here on earth by exploiting the relationship of godliness, or virtue, to success. Neither is there much said about moral duties or social obligations. Indeed, his point on racial matters is that black men, like all others, can pray for what they want and thus can pray themselves into the middle class. The only difficulty Dr. Peale raises is the threat that moral degeneracy poses to this simple process. He is appalled by the hairy, beaded, Spock-trained young, and when he speaks of them he says that "something terrible has happened to America"—the same phrase that Richard Nixon used at one point of the campaign trail. No doubt Dr. Peale felt, when he performed the marriage of those two flawless young Americans, David and Julie Nixon Eisenhower, that there was still good stuff among the younger generation.

It can, at times, look all very innocent and uncomplicated. The values expressed by Peale, and approved by Nixon, appear to be ones with which large sections of the American people feel at ease. Few liberals, perhaps, would care for the product—but are they challenging the crass style of expression, and the sheer bluntness of materialistic logic, rather than the underlying ethic of individual ambition and success?

It is not easy to be sure what is the true substance of the quarrel between Nixon and his enemies. There are nuances and shadings, certainly, and important differences at the margin. But why be so passionate about a nuance?

One reason, in a political system so closely concentrated upon individual personality, must be our human appetite for dramatic contrasts of hero and villain. The Presidential office in its modern form focuses on personality rather than the more diffuse target of party. The emotional tensions involved in the contest can be almost religious, and the form this lay religion tends to assume is Zoroastrian. As in that dramatic old Persian faith, so in American politics, national and international, there are armies of light and armies of darkness. Political opponents must play their roles as Ahura-Mazda, leader of light, or Ahriman, force of darkness. One may be only slightly better, or slightly worse, than the other, but within such a dualism there can be no subtleties. To take a case in point, John Kennedy did not fight a particularly noble or enlightening campaign in 1960: in fact, he went in for some vigorous Cold War mongering, peddled a dubious missile gap to the electorate, and when he did talk about the need for social reform frequently justified it as a necessary part of the struggle for world freedom. Kennedy's behavior in the McCarthy period was at best circumspect, and his ascent to the nomination was not an especially edifying operation. Yet, in the great documents of the Kennedy cult—*A Thousand Days, The Making of the President*—Kennedy was portrayed as a shining prince and Nixon virtually as a monster. Did Kennedy, by the standards that were supposedly being applied, deserve so much honor? Did Nixon deserve so much blame?

Nixon's credentials as a monster go back to what he calls his "fight against Communism" and his enemies call his ruthless exploitation of the Communist issue his pasteurized McCarthyism.

It is sometimes claimed that Nixon was not genuine in his anti-Communism, that he merely used the issue as a cynical device. Yet there is no serious evidence to support this thesis. But all the evidence points in another, and more disturbing direction: that Nixon's hatred for Communism, a movement he has seen in many strange guises, is the one real and genuine passion of his otherwise sterile political personality. Certainly it is the only issue which seems consistently to galvanize his prose style. Here is his account of the mob which prevented him from speaking at San Marcos University, in Peru:

> . . . Some of the younger students started to quiet down. But the older ones in the rear, the ringleaders, saw what was happening. They tried to whip up a frenzy again, egging the young students on, just as if they were driving them with whips. They shouted insults at those who shook hands with me. There were only a few leaders—the usual case-hardened, cold-eyed Communist operatives . . .

Nixon's swift recognition of the "usual Communist operatives" is intriguing, since, prior to this trip, his only known confrontation with an allegedly Communist crowd was at Pegu, Burma, in 1953. It is difficult to imagine where Nixon might have met a Communist in his life (unless you count Hiss, and, indeed, Chambers) before his trips to Soviet-bloc countries as Vice-President. It seems likely that at San Marcos Nixon was recognizing a stereotype which existed in his own mind, rather than making a perception of reality. But the strength of emotion involved is hardly questionable.

After the San Marcos clash, the demonstrators contrived another confrontation with Nixon outside his hotel in Lima. For a time, the Vice-President and his party were jammed in the crowd:

> Just as I reached the hotel door I came face to face with a man I later learned was one of the most notorious Communist agitators in Lima. I saw before me a weird-looking character whose bulging eyes seemed to merge with his mouth in one distorted blob. He let fly a wad of spit which caught me full in the face. I went through in that instant a terrible test of temper control. One must experience the sensation to realize why spitting in a person's face is the most infuriating insult ever conceived by man. I felt an almost uncontrollable urge to tear the face in front of me to pieces.

Quite a confrontation. What did the man with the "distorted blob" see in this dramatic instant? But these demonstrations were mild stuff compared with what happened in Caracas, Venezuela, where Nixon was in real physical danger (and reacted to it with impeccable courage). His car was stopped and surrounded by a hostile crowd, which, at one point, seemed likely to turn it over and set it on fire:

> It made me almost physically ill to see the fanatical frenzy in the eyes of teenagers—boys and girls who were very little older than my twelve-year-old daughter Tricia. My reaction was a feeling of absolute hatred for the tough Communist agitators who were driving children to this irrational state. . . . On the way back to the Embassy, I felt as though I had come as close as anyone could get, and still remain alive, to a first-hand demonstration of the ruthlessness, fanaticism, and determination of the enemy we face in the world struggle.

It was no doubt intensely unpleasant and dangerous. But as far as accounts go, the incidents seem to have borne the character of ordinary Latin-American mob fury, which has served in many causes apart from the Communist one and probably looks much the same each time. But the reality is not so important as what Nixon perceived.

The irrational anti-Communism of so many Americans of Nixon's generation is one of the central facts of modern political life—and one of the most dangerous. It is not intended to suggest that it was not rational for America to be anti-Communist, or that there were not plain clashes of interest and aspiration between America and the Soviet Union at the end of World War II. It is meant as a strictly limited point: that in their confrontation with Soviet and other brands of Communism up to now, many Americans, prominently Richard Nixon, have acted irrationally with regard to their own nation's interests. By an exaggerated view of the Communist threat to American life, they have helped to distort the climate of domestic politics and to prepare the way for costly and humiliating entanglements abroad.

In his first Congressional campaign, in 1946, Nixon displayed himself as an early believer in the domestic threat of Communism. He talked about "lip-service Americans," and claimed that Moscow was insolently trying to influence American voters on behalf of his opponent, Jerry Voorhis. The proposition that Moscow's detailed interests extended to an off-year election in the twelfth Congressional District of California certainly implied an almost superhuman efficiency on the part of the Russians: but, then, perhaps that was the picture Nixon had of them.

In fighting so ubiquitous an opponent, one clearly cannot afford to be too delicate in one's methods. Voorhis's denials of leftist backing and assertions of his own anti-Communist principles were not allowed to stand in Nixon's way. Just how much all the wild conspiratorial talk affected the election is not too clear: although Nixon won, the district was likely in any case to return to the Republican allegiance out of which it had been jolted in the thirties.

Even at the time, let alone in retrospect, the proposition that there was any *mass* threat from Communism was plainly absurd. America, like Britain, was a country in which the Communist Party had entirely failed to attract a working-class following. Therefore, the danger could come only from a deadly conspiracy aimed at the seat of government. And, of course, it was the Hiss case which was seen as dramatizing this proposition.

Partly, no doubt, it was the legal complexity and long-drawn-out drama of the case which made it loom so large in the public imagination. It became a symbolic conflict between those who saw themselves exposing a wicked conspiracy against American life and those who saw themselves trying to stop witch-hunting on the part of hysterical Yahoos. The social contrasts among the three main characters have often been pointed out: Hiss, the Eastern intellectual and public servant; Nixon, the small-town lawyer; and Chambers, apostate Communist and minion of Henry Luce at *Time* magazine. Battle was irretrievably joined long before it was seen that neither the pro- nor anti-Hiss forces were on ideal ground. Nevertheless, his liberal sympathizers were distressed and embarrassed when Hiss was found guilty of the perjury charge brought against him, and the other side was proportionately delighted. The case had made Nixon a national figure, and the feelings of his admirers were well expressed in a telegram from ex-President Herbert Hoover: "The conviction of Alger Hiss was due to your patience and persistence alone. At last the stream of treason that existed in our government has been exposed in a fashion that all may believe."

The case was taken as showing that there existed a large body of organized underground Communists in Washington. In fact it did nothing of the sort. What happened? Chambers was called before the House Committee on Un-American Activities on which Nixon served. Like most recanting Communists, he did not cut a very attractive figure. (Hugh Trevor-Roper once remarked on the unpleasantness of watching people "regurgitate at tedious length unattractive matter which one had not oneself felt inclined to consume in the first place.") Chambers said that before the war, before the Nazi-Soviet Pact, he had known Alger Hiss, a State Department official who was also a Communist. Hiss appeared before the Committee and, in a distinguished performance, denied that he had ever known a man "by the name of Whittaker Chambers." Nixon, the lawyer, noticed that this was not quite the same as denying that he had ever met his accuser. The Committee, assuming the role of a court with Nixon as prosecutor, pursued Hiss and, with further evidence from Chambers, broke down Hiss's denial. Clearly, Hiss had known Chambers; Hiss now, tardily, sued Chambers for libel because of Chambers' assertion outside Committee privilege that Hiss had been a Communist. Chambers produced further evidence: the famous "pumpkin papers," microfilms of the secret documents which he alleged Hiss had given him for transmission to the Soviet Union. It was all very melodramatic. But Hiss was brought to trial on a charge not of espionage, only of perjury. It took two trials to convict him. The whole business did not demonstrate very much—only that, during the thirties, Hiss and, allegedly, some other public servants sympathized with the Russians and, according to Chambers, passed information to them through him. Nixon, however, saw it as far more than that, and he set down his view in a remarkably congested passage of *Six Crises:*

> Whittaker Chambers . . . perhaps came closest to the truth when he wrote in *Witness* that the situation which involved Alger Hiss and himself was not simply "human tragedy." Here, "the two irreconcilable faiths of our time, Communism and Freedom, came to grips in the persons of two conscious and resolute men."
>
> In this sentence, he compressed whole chapters of world history: the rise, and—as some would argue—partial decay of the philosophy called "liberalism"; the parallel emergence of a liberal heresy called

Communism; the assumption of world leadership by two superpowers, America and Russia, each wedded to a competing faith and each strengthened and yet limited thereby; and finally the present confrontation of these two faiths and these two superpowers at specific times and places in every part of the world. The issue at stake, to put it starkly, is this: whose hand will write the next several chapters of human history?

One could hardly put it more starkly.

Nixon saw the Hiss case as a simple battle against the powers of darkness. It was a natural corollary to see all attacks on him as inspired by the Communist enemy. For instance, one of his earlier responses to the 1952 accusation of improper use of the "fund money" was:

> You folks know the work I did investigating Communists in the United States. Ever since I have done that work the Communists and the left-wingers have been fighting me with every possible smear. When I received the nomination for the Vice-Presidency I was warned that if I continued to attack the Communists in this government they would continue to smear me. And believe me, you can expect that they will continue to do so. They started it yesterday . . .

It was an absurd outburst. The accusation had received its most vivid start in the *New York Post* and was taken up with some enthusiasm by numerous other papers, and by the Democratic Party. This was rough but not unusual election tactics, and a good deal less absurd than Nixon's riposte that the whole thing was a Communist plot against him.

There were, of course, no Communists in the government, in the sense that Nixon and Hoover implied—that is, a group conspiring at the highest levels for major influence. The most laughable thing about the great crusade against "domestic Communism" is that, after three decades, nothing has shown up except some important but perfectly understandable spy rings, usually run by professional Soviet intelligence men. (Not that the failure to produce the Great Conspiracy has lessened the frenzy of the investigators who remain on the scene: after all, what better proof of the scale of the conspiracy *than* the very lack of evidence?)

The argument is not that there was *no* Communist threat to the United States, but rather that people like Richard Nixon had an exaggerated, almost delusionary view of it. The cast of mind, in any case, is shared by a large number of Americans—by a majority it sometimes seems, of the middle and lower-middle classes. And it is not only in foreign affairs that these Americans encounter subtle disappointments. The plain and simple precepts upon which they were brought up offer no explanation of why modern America should be so complicated, and sometimes so nasty. The urban jungle of Los Angeles which has swamped Whittier is largely the product of leaving individual initiative—in this case, the realtors'—largely untrammeled. But individual initiative is supposed to produce only good, and if that is so, one must either argue that the result is attractive or suppose that some other force is at work. Another unpleasant risk is that one's children may reject the environment created for them with such effort; Dr. Peale does not seem to exaggerate when he says "something terrible has happened."

From the viewpoint of those who are newly prosperous, there is another threat. Now that they, after some trouble, have won something in the game, there seems to be some attempt to change the rules. Faith in "individual initiative" seems to give way to talk about "social obligations." And, as it appears to many of them, much of this new talk comes from people like the Rockefellers, Kennedys, and Roosevelts, who did not have to make the stuff themselves. It had been made for them by ancestors with a rugged faith in individual initiative and very little interest in social obligations. Confronted with such a situation, one might well look for a scapegoat.

Communism makes a natural enough candidate. After all, its creed is the overthrow of capitalism, and it does exist. To many people, it seemed irresistibly plausible that America's ills were the work of foreign and domestic Communism.

Richard Nixon did not invent the anti-Communist crusade. The cry was used by several Republican hopefuls in the 1946 election, but it had been a damaging piece of rhetoric for many years before that. The atmosphere is not easy to re-create impartially. But a year or more before Nixon first ran for office, an Administration dominated by liberal Democrats was already deeply involved in the confrontation with Soviet power. Granting the nature of American society and politics, they were hardly justified in being surprised when the sharpening of the conflict brought with it some disturbing domestic developments.

Anti-Communism was by no means confined to the Republican Party when Nixon fought his most notorious campaign for the Senate against Helen Gahagan Douglas. The first "red smears" against Mrs. Douglas came not from Nixon, but from her party colleague Manchester Boddy during the campaign for the Democratic nomination—which took place only a few months after Joe McCarthy had produced his famous list. Boddy's smears against Mrs. Douglas were sufficiently comprehensive that Nixon did not need to add too many of his own. Some of the techniques he did borrow came from another Democrat, George Smathers of Florida. Smathers' dumping of Senator Claude Pepper in the Democratic primary looks in retrospect like the most vicious campaign of the year. (Smathers, in deference to his locale, managed to mix a little racism into the anti-Communist brew.) As Smathers' opponent was called the Red Pepper, so Nixon and his manager, Murray Chotiner, nicknamed Mrs. Douglas the Pink Lady. Smathers swamped his state with a booklet entitled *The Red Record of Senator Claude Pepper*. It was effective, and Nixon, who studied the Smathers campaign with great care, followed suit. This was the genesis of the famous distortion of Mrs. Douglas's voting record.

If Nixon did not invent the anti-Communist crusade, neither did he participate in its most ludicrous excesses. Certainly he was dramatic about it: he seems to have poured into anti-Communism all the passion and emotion bottled up inside him, but otherwise so rarely given play. On television in the 1952 campaign, he produced some remarkable histrionics while reviewing the great moments of the Hiss case. "Let me describe the room to you [where Hiss was interrogated] because it is here that you can see the Communist conspiracy in action . . . twisting and turning and squirming . . . evading and avoiding." It is the tone of an inquisitor describing the downfall of a witch.

But for all this, Nixon managed to avoid the fatal error. He may have been wildly uncritical in his assessment of the dangers of a "fifth column" in America, but, unlike McCarthy, he did not plunge across the line between mistaking the significance of particulars and manufacturing particulars wholesale. That diligent intelligence retained the ability to recognize a fact and to distinguish between evidence and fantasy. Nixon came close, time and again, to what Richard Hofstadter called "the paranoid style," but he never quite surrendered to it. Therefore, he acquired the political asset of being trusted by the zealots while being altogether more durable than their other heroes.

Nixon's style therefore appears as a mixture of fury, caution, and legalism. This is to be found in all those famous phrases which attempt to link Democrats, and especially liberal Democrats, with Communism: Dean Acheson suffered "color blindness—a form of pinkeye toward the Communist threat." "Real Democrats" were "outraged by the Truman-Acheson-Stevenson gang's defense of Communism in high places." He went close to the edge with his claim that Truman, Acheson, and Stevenson were "traitors to the high principle in which many of the nation's Democrats believed." He went close again with his 1954 claim that "the candidates running on the Democratic ticket are almost without exception members of the Democratic Party's left-wing clique which has been so blind to the Communist conspiracy and has tolerated it in the United States."

It was rough, and effective, stuff. And once the rhetoric and logic of a world struggle for freedom had been granted—which it was by Acheson and Truman, if not entirely by Stevenson—it was difficult to counter. If a country is involved in a total struggle and is, in John Kennedy's words, "the watchman on the walls of world freedom," the criticisms made of the nations' leaders will no doubt be made in apocalyptic terms. In a total struggle, one is entitled to expect total performance, or suspect malpractice.

But as one would expect, it does not seem to have been Nixon's denunciations of Communism, as such, which most enraged the liberals. It was his tendency to widen the target which they found intolerable.

Most of all, perhaps, Nixon was loathed for his attempts to link Adlai Stevenson to Alger Hiss. He pointed out, during the 1952 campaign, that Stevenson had testified to the excellence of Hiss's reputation, and said,

> It is significant that Mr. Stevenson has never expressed any indignation over what Mr. Hiss has done and the treachery he engaged in. . . . In my opinion, his actions, his statements, his record disqualifies him from leading the United States and the free nations in the fight against Communism at home and abroad. . . .

To liberals, it seemed unbelievable that anyone could make such an attack other than cynically. And yet—suppose that the concept of domestic Communism expressed here was just as chimerical and melodramatic as the process by which America's natural differences with the Soviet Union were dramatized as an all-embracing world struggle. This would not mean the concept could not be genuinely believed in. What it would mean—the nature of the belief being confused—would be that blows would land on surprising targets, which is what happened. It is noticeable that in all his millions of words on the subject, Richard Nixon has never given any clear account of what he means by "Communism," a movement which in any case is not easily defined. The fury of the attack, and the vagueness of the objective, make a curious contrast.

The whole continuing crusade, one feels, is independent of the existence of Communism. It is about the tensions of American society and, in particular, about resistance to attempts to modify it. With startling frequency, the "hotbeds of Communism" were found to be among the institutions of the wealthy and established. In the exchange that followed his attack on Stevenson, Nixon called Stevenson "a snob," which is perhaps nearer to the realities of the matter than the rhetoric about the free world.

None of this is to say that there were not established Eastern aristocrats among the crusaders, or to deny that among those who felt themselves oppressed by "something terrible" were other rich and comfortable men. But, in the main, the movement was made up of angry and disturbed people who felt that the America they deserved was being taken away from them by forces they did not understand. In truth, that ideal America did not survive into the complexities of the twentieth century —if indeed, it ever existed—but to consider such an admission would be to put one's own Americanism in question. It does not seem to be the case that Nixon cynically manipulated these people, but rather that he too felt angry and persecuted, and he gave those feelings remarkably cogent expression.

Here, he was aided by the intensely legalistic cast of his mind. He is at home in the world of legal dialectic, where you make your case with the materials at hand. Emmett Hughes, a member of the Eisenhower Administration, wrote of Nixon in government that he was "crisp and practical and logical, never proposing major objectives, but quick and shrewd in suggesting (or refining) methods—rather like an effective trial lawyer . . . with an oddly sleek interest in the law." There is an interesting example of this in Nixon's connection with the Bay of Pigs affair.

During the 1960 campaign, on October 20, John Kennedy demanded that the United States must help the anti-Castro forces to recapture Cuba. "Thus far," he said, "these fighters for freedom have had virtually no support from our government." This put Nixon in a difficult position, and not only because Kennedy had pre-empted a tough position he would have liked to keep for himself. The other reason was that Nixon knew that an invasion of Cuba was already being prepared.

What could Nixon do? He was not permitted to reply by saying, "Yes, that's exactly what we're doing," for that would ruin a secret operation. To agree in the abstract that it would be a good idea would seem weak and might alert the Cubans anyway. The only thing to do, he felt, was to "go to the other extreme: I must attack the Kennedy proposal because it would violate our treaty commitments." And so *Nixon* argued that, if America supported an anti-Castro invasion, "we would lose all our friends in Latin America, we would probably be condemned in the United Nations, and we would not accomplish our objective. It would be an open invitation to Mr. Khrushchev . . . to come into Latin America and engage us in civil war and possibly even worse." In *Six Crises,* Nixon records the bitterness he felt at having to argue against a program he favored. But he does not note, even as an irony, that his devil's advocacy was an almost exact forecast of the grotesque calamity that overtook American interests when Kennedy put Eisenhower's plan into practice. Nixon appears to be quite artless in his account of the matter: he was just making a case, and he used the best arguments available. This occurs again and again in his speeches. Like a trial lawyer, he does not specifically try to distort the underlying truth of the situation: it is simply not his concern. In the structured courtroom, this technique is acceptable. In political debate, where there is no impartial and all-powerful judge to impose institutional discrimination on the process, it is not the same thing at all.

This, then, was the man who began, during the mid-sixties, the painful task of reconstructing from his new base his position as the logical Presidential candidate of the Republican Party. Intelligent within the conventions of the world he had chosen to live in, he was also honest within the terms of his own rather narrow morality. We have listened to his admirers, some of them new ones, trying to convey the reasons for their affection: they describe nothing more than the abilities of a high-grade advocate and the qualities of a decent boss. To echo the manner of Don Juan's catalogue in *Man and Superman,* he was not so much serious, only solemn; not callous, only unimaginative; not vicious, only self-pitying; not upright, only conventional. And he was no longer passionate. The one real passion of his life, apart from the desire for measurable success, had been a negative one—the hatred of a mask of Communism. And now that fever had run its course, with the decline, at least for the moment, of the great drama of the Cold War. He was a burnt-out case. The turgid, heated language of the anti-Communist years did not reappear in the bland speeches of the 1968 campaign. All that remained was the lawyer's technique: the overdeft juggling of crime figures, or the careful involutions of one memorable speech in midsummer in which, by blurring the various implications of the desire for change in America, Nixon presented himself, among other things, as the heir of the New Left radicals.

How did Nixon go about rebuilding himself? What people and forces allied themselves with him? To put it at its simplest, they were the people who had always backed him. In 1946, his promoters included such men as Frank E. Jorgensen of the Metropolitan Life Insurance

Company, and Herman L. Perry, manager of the Bank of America in Whittier. His money, however, came most heavily from more localized business interests than these: when his famous, or notorious, fund was examined, it was found that thirty-six per cent of the money came from California real-estate men. There was nineteen per cent each from oil interests and from manufacturing and distribution interests.

In New York, Nixon was in a bigger league, and there were slight but important differences in the nature of his associates. They now possessed more of the flavor of the national, corporate enterprise than of Southern California entrepreneurship. Nixon's rise as a Wall Street lawyer was accompanied by seats on the boards of three major corporations: the Harsco steel-products group of Pennsylvania; Mutual of New York, the insurance giant; and the big Minneapolis-based mutual fund, Investors Diversified Services.

His initial introduction to Mudge, Stern, Baldwin & Todd was organized through Elmer H. Bobst (the Vitamin King), the counter druggist who became head of Warner-Lambert Pharmaceutical. It was Bobst to whom Nixon mentioned his desire to go to New York in 1963, and Bobst who introduced him to Warner-Lambert's lawyers, Mudge, Stern. Bobst, then in his seventies, had been a contributor to Nixon's campaigns for many years, and is said to have had a "fatherly affection" for Nixon. Certainly, he is a family friend of the Nixons, and his wife took a lively interest in the dynastic Eisenhower-Nixon marriage of 1968.

Members of the law firm, naturally, merely say that they were interested in acquiring a first-class new partner. But Nixon's allure was presumably heightened by the fact that his friend Donald M. Kendall, president of Pepsico, had indicated that if Nixon moved to New York the corporation would want him as its lawyer. Nixon's and Kendall's paths had first crossed in the fateful kitchen of the American exhibition in Moscow. Kendall's rise owed much to the fact that, when in charge of Public Relations at that exhibition, he persuaded Khrushchev to be photographed with a Pepsi bottle in his hand. Nixon's good offices in bringing about that coup deserved a return. Pepsico did indeed become a client of the firm—one more on an impressive list which includes General Precision Equipment, American Bulk Carriers, Mitsui of Japan, and General Cigar. The great Wall Street firms—and Nixon, Mudge, Stern is now one of the ten largest—are, of course, far more than professional lawyers: they are advisers, fixers, comforters, and ambassadors for the great business empires. Nixon, Mudge are, for instance, registered lobbyists in Washington for American Bulk Carriers. Apart from his abilities in litigation, Nixon clearly had qualities useful in the international division of American corporate endeavor, something particularly important for the far-flung Pepsico. He is said to have negotiated Pepsico out of trademark difficulties in Formosa: it would be surprising if there were a part of the Western world where businessmen would not have heard of, and paid respect to, the globetrotting Nixon.

However, the assurance of a position in mighty boardrooms cannot be automatically converted into delegate strength in the Republican Party. Here, Nixon's extraordinary capacity for hard work and harder travel took over. He had acquired, over the years of campaigning, credits and loyalties within the structure of the party which covered every part of the country and most of the available ideological persuasions. A typical, and important, one was that of ex-Congressman Robert Ellsworth of Kansas, an intelligent and practical liberal who, in 1968, became one of Nixon's most effective managers. "I began to admire him in 1960," says Ellsworth. "He came out to Kansas and campaigned for me. And as I got fifty-one point two per cent of the vote, and he carried the state by sixty-eight per cent, it's not too hard to imagine how I feel about him." Nixon maintained his contact with Ellsworth, and took him on a world trip in December 1966.

The Nixon operation, in the long, politically lean years between 1962 and 1968, was based frankly on the law firm. According to his colleagues there, it was only by "incremental stages" that they realized that they had a Presidential candidate in the senior partner's chair, although the beginnings of the conviction go a long way back. Leonard Garment, another partner, recalls that the feeling began to grow as far back as the traumatic period just after the assassination of John Kennedy. "We were struck by the fact that Nixon still showed up in the polls, that there was a solid basis of support for him." Nixon, indeed, elaborated this into a theory that he was in some odd way the beneficiary of the Kennedy years, that people thought he, not Johnson, should have been the successor.

There was a critical decision to make in 1964 about Goldwater. Nixon knew Goldwater would lose. ("He certainly did call that one right on the button," says Garment.) But the question was how hard to campaign for a sure loser? The disadvantage came clear in 1968, when, as Ellsworth said, people tended to associate Nixon with the Goldwater debacle. But Nixon decided, inevitably, that the only course was to demonstrate solidarity at a time when rivals like Rockefeller were drawing aside. In the end, Nixon campaigned harder for Goldwater than the

somewhat unprofessional Goldwater did for himself. And most of the
unfortunate image was washed away by Nixon's heroic part in the great
revival campaign of 1966.

One remarkable day in October 1966 exemplified both his involvement with the campaign, and his extraordinary stamina. At this time, the
crisis of the *Time Inc. v. Hill* appeal in the Supreme Court occurred, but
Nixon did not let that stop him. He spent Tuesday in court in Washington, but the case did not end that day. In his hotel room, Nixon dictated
an exhaustive memo on the case, which Garment, the chief litigator for
Nixon, Mudge, claims is one of the most remarkable pieces of legal
analysis he has seen. On Wednesday, the case continued another hour.
Then Nixon rushed to the airport to fly to San Francisco. During his
connection in Chicago, he made three phone calls to inquire about
Percy's Senate campaign. In San Francisco, he met three television
crews, drove to his hotel, and conducted a thirty-five-minute press conference. After sandwiches and coffee, he drove across the bay to Oakland to speak for a losing Congressional candidate. (He had already
shaved for the second time that day, concerned as always about the
famous "shadow.") He spent twenty minutes handshaking and auto-
graphing, then drove to Palo Alto, an hour away. Here he met his close
friend Robert Finch, who was running for Lieutenant Governor of California, and spent two hours discussing the campaign with him. He slept
for three hours, then took in a television interview before a fundraising
breakfast for Finch. He then flew to Bakersfield, where he spoke at a
rally for the (ultimately successful) Congressional candidate Bob Mathias
and gave a press conference. Then he flew to Burbank for another press
conference and a taping session, thence to Ontario in California, where
he addressed a rally for another eventual Congressional winner, Jerry
Pettis. He got back to New York on Friday morning, having slept for
only some nine hours since Tuesday morning. The investment of long,
tedious days in places like Sioux City, Iowa, which Nixon had already
visited four times on such trips, was to pay a golden dividend.

The people who gathered around Nixon as his Presidential intentions became clearer were once classified by one of their number into
"those who were too inexperienced to know how difficult it was, and
those who were too committed to care how difficult it was." Very approximately, the inexperienced centered on the law firm, and the committed
on the Nixon for President Committee which was set up in Washington in
March 1967. The dominant figure in this latter group was Maurice H.
Stans, a bridge between New York and California. A New York–based

investment banker, Stans had been finance chairman of Nixon's 1962 California campaign and was in Eisenhower's Administration as Director of the Budget Bureau.

The Committee may not have glittered, but it was a solid and well-distributed representation of Republican respectability. It included several more men from the Eisenhower Administration: Fred Seaton of Nebraska, Secretary of the Interior; John David Lodge, Henry Cabot Lodge's brother and ex-Governor of Connecticut, then Ambassador to Spain; Robert C. Hill of New Hampshire, Ambassador to Mexico; and Walter W. Williams of Seattle, Washington, chairman of Citizens for Eisenhower-Nixon in 1952 and later Under-Secretary of Commerce.

There was not likely to be any shortage of money. Elmer Bobst was backing the Committee, and so were the DeWitt Wallaces, the *Reader's Digest* family. The bankers, Stans and Williams, could raise funds without difficulty, and from the first, the Nixon campaign never pretended to be anything but well heeled. (Nixon once claimed in 1960 that the Kennedy staff had more money to spend than his people. No one outspent him in 1968.)

In short, the Committee was made up of people who had enjoyed Republican power in Washington and believed that Nixon was the man to re-create it. Some of the members were there perhaps more for their totemic qualities than their organizing abilities. But, then, Nixon being the man he is, a leader who likes to keep his enterprise under his own hand, the Committee was not expected to do too much of the crucial work. This devolved upon his personal organization in New York.

Most of the people who have been close to Nixon think that his politics and tactics in 1968 trace back in every respect to his 1960 defeat by John Kennedy. This analysis stands up, and not least in the matter of personal staff. Nixon felt that the party wheel horses around him in 1960 suffered by comparison with Kennedy's constellation of talented and often youthful retainers. He set about constructing a similar group within the rather more sober and conventional framework of Republican acceptability.

This was good politics, because people do observe in practice Machiavelli's maxim that "the first impression that one gets of a ruler and his brains is from seeing the men he has about him." Much of the feeling about a "new" Nixon derived from the fact that there were new people around him.

What the "new men" had in common was, on the whole, youth and a lack of involvement with the misfortunes of Nixon's past. Many of them, in striking contrast to the hacks of the Republican Party, were and are literate, amusing fellows. However, the impression which gained ground early in the year that the group had liberal and even radical overtones was misleading. The center of gravity of Nixon's constellation remained firmly on the right—and any liberal elements which were introduced were carefully balanced off.

There was, for instance, the liberal speech-writer Ray Price. Price, a cautious, amiable, pipe-smoking man, was regarded as a liberal chiefly because he had broken with Goldwater and because he wrote eloquent speeches for Nixon on the Nature of the Presidency, a favorite subject of the boss's. ("We should bring dissenters into policy decisions, not freeze them out. . . . Ours is the chance to see the American dream fulfilled at last in the destiny of man.") Price was a conservative at Yale and did some research for William Buckley's book *God and Man at Yale*. Since Yale, he had moved so far to the left as to write speeches for Senator Percy.

Lest Price's radicalism get out of control, he was balanced by the other and longer-established member of the speech-writing team, Patrick J. Buchanan, who started working for Nixon in January 1966, a year before Price. Buchanan is an affable fellow who was known to many reporters on the Nixon trail as Shoot-'em-in-the-legs because of a memorable suggestion he made for dealing with Negro rioters. Buchanan never pretended to be other than a conservative—"a true believer," as he put it. British reporters found that he simply could not understand even *why* the British government might have a quarrel with the white Rhodesians. He once cited his major formative influences as Aquinas, James Burnham, and Eric Hoffer.

One slightly older member of the staff, Leonard Garment, was frequently regarded as the archliberal of the Nixon camp. Certainly, Garment has a heterodox background for a Wall Street lawyer. He is Jewish and was born in a poor section of Brooklyn. He played a little jazz saxophone and was once in a group that backed Billie Holliday. That, however, does not make a liberal, and, as Garment says himself, "I made my decision some time ago. If I was particularly against business or had any specially radical thoughts I wanted to express, obviously I wouldn't be here."

One of the most interesting responses to the question of "Nixonian liberalism" arose when one of us talked to Alan Greenspan, who joined Nixon in 1968 as head of economic research for the campaign. "Sure I'm a liberal," said Greenspan seriously. "But I'm a nineteenth-century

liberal." Greenspan, head of a highly successful economic consulting firm
—and, again, youthful and extrovert—is, in fact, just that. He expressed,
at least before he joined the Administration, frank and unshakable belief
that the untrammeled forces of the market could save America.

Nixon did not have around him people like Goldwater speech-writer
Karl Hess, who once wrote that what made America great was the spirit
of men who "suddenly tire of palaver and reach for the rifle on the wall."
(Hess's personal odyssey in search of "liberty" has now taken him to the
fringes of the New Left.) The Nixon men are smooth, self-assured, and
competent. But insofar as there is ideology, it is strictly of the right:
Richard V. Allen, for example, whom Nixon chose to handle his foreign-
policy research is a multiple linguist with an exhaustive knowledge of
Marxism-Leninism and a firm belief in taking the hard line with the
Soviet Union. His intellectual pedigree is in the firm tradition of what
might be called the New Right: he went from the Georgetown Center for
Strategic Studies to the Hoover Institution for the Study of War, Revolution, and Peace. Allen could find much to admire, for instance, in the
California *ultra,* Max Rafferty, but, equally characteristically, could be
glad to see him defeated, not because he was wrong but because his
advocacy of the right-wing cause was so clumsy.

In other words, whatever the style, the ideological freight that the
Nixon bandwagon carried was strictly conservative. Later in the campaign, there was to be evidence that some items, at least, could be
jettisoned when the need arose. But the general structure was far too
well established to be altered.

But ideologists of any persuasion were scarcely the dominant
group in the Nixon operation. Most of all, the men who gathered together
were energetic, practical organizers, more like business executives than
politicians. John Sears, for instance, a young Nixon, Mudge associate
who was taken on to do delegate intelligence for Nixon, was in many
ways more important than Price and Buchanan. Sears, an agreeable
graduate of Notre Dame and Georgetown Law School, used to say cheerfully of his inquiries in the ramifications of the Republican Party, "I am
the one who knows where the old bodies are buried and where the 1968
models are." It was the operators, under the most powerful of Nixon's
law partners, John Mitchell, who dominated the Nixon campaign. The
story of how Mitchell, almost an unknown man in the spring of 1968,
emerged as one of the most effective yet curiously limited political managers in America comes later in the narrative.

There was one great and indisputable Nixon asset which underpinned the whole laborious enterprise of resurrection, and it can be illustrated with an anecdote. On Wednesday, April 29, 1968, virtually the entire bureaucracy of the Republican Party of Indiana was gathered in Indianapolis. The high point of the meeting was to be a ceremony in which all of the state's Republican Congressmen would announce jointly as chairmen of the state Nixon for President Committee. One of the observers present was working on George Romney's campaign, and he received a phone call which informed him that within an hour Governor Romney was going to withdraw from the New Hampshire primary and from the Presidential race. The Romney man informed the Indiana chairman, who without hesitation stood up and told the assembled crowd. Instantly, a loud and emotional demonstration of joy broke out. Men cheered, thumped the table, and waved things in the air in a spontaneous outpouring of affection for Richard Nixon. (Probably, Nixon was personally known to most of the men in the room, and in most cases would have been the only national figure the man could claim as a friend.)

The demonstration went on for some four minutes, and then, as though by a secret signal, it cut itself off and was replaced by an uneasy silence. In this silence, solid citizens stared at each other with expressions of newly realized horror, and then, hoarsely, one man gave voice to what everyone was thinking: "Now that sonofabitch Rockefeller's going to try to buy it," he said.

ACT VI

George Wallace, the Man Who Talked in Code

1

The Professional
Southerner

"Can a former truck driver who is married to a former dime-store clerk and whose father was a plain dirt farmer be elected President of the United States?"

—George C. Wallace's campaign brochure

The voice at the other end of the line was so loud that the man held the receiver a foot away from his ear. The angry words crackled into the room. "Who the hell am I going to vote for now? I couldn't vote for that goddamn Humphrey, or Kennedy, or Rockefeller, or that goddamn son of a bitch who's giving everything to the niggers. Christ a'mighty, they're *putting* those goddamn niggers to rioting. . . ."

The scene was one of the basement offices in a small modern office building on a tree-lined street in Montgomery, Alabama, from which George Wallace's campaign for the Presidency was being run. The time was the Wednesday afternoon of the week after Martin Luther King was shot. In Washington, an hour or two before, Congress had passed the long-delayed civil-rights bill which several times earlier in the year had seemed to be on the point of legislative death. And the strident citizen on the telephone was one of many who—in their outrage that even this small crumb was thrown to the blacks—reacted by hastening to express their support for Wallace's Presidential ambitions.

What was most significant about this overheard call was where it came from: not from Alabama, but from the backwater state of Delaware, close to a thousand miles to the north and east.

"You'd be surprised," the telephoner bellowed, "how many people right here in this state—ladies and gentlemen, not just anyone, *Masons* and people like that—would rather vote for George Wallace than for anyone else. I think he'd carry the goddamn state tonight. Goddamn it, if you can just get him on the ballot, I'm telling you he can be elected." By that time, George Wallace was on the ballot in Delaware.

April 1, the morning after Johnson's withdrawal speech, Wallace's announced candidacy looked like an April Fool joke. "We were panic-stricken," recalls Hamp Graves, the mayor of Eufaula, in Barbour County, Alabama, Wallace's home county, and a lifelong friend of his. "We knew that if Humphrey or Kennedy got in, we'd get a flogging that'd make all the rest look like no more 'n a wrist-slapping."

It was not only that. Wallace, the perpetual-motion candidate, was immobilized. Only two weeks before, his wife, Lurleen, the Governor of Alabama, had undergone abdominal surgery, and that was less than three weeks after her third operation for cancer in two years. As long as she was desperately ill, Wallace could not campaign. As long as he could not campaign, money was coming in at a mere trickle. And if she died, control of the state of Alabama would begin to slip from his hands: he would be like a general who had lost his base at the very moment when he set out to march into enemy territory.

The death of his old adversary, Martin Luther King, came like a miracle. The riots it touched off meant that the 1968 campaign would be fought on Wallace's chosen ground. The theme would be his theme: law and order. King's death, and the timing of it, made it inevitable that George Wallace, already the most assured and skillful Southern dema-gogue to appear on the national scene since Huey Long died in 1935, must now become the most dangerous third-party challenger for the Presidency since 1912.

He had come a long way. There is a shiny new courthouse in Clayton, Alabama, now, a monument to the eminence of the last county judge. But the inevitable Confederate monument still stands in the middle of the square, with its unnecessary motto: WE WILL NEVER FORGET! Like the Greek chorus in a Faulkner novel, lean old men with a day's growth of silver stubble and younger men with beer bellies and country muscles still stand for hours in front of the garage, sipping Dr. Pepper in the heat, and talking politics. An elderly Negro, jogging through the square on a mule cart, threading among the old Fords and the red pickup trucks with the rifle racks in the back window, still knows enough to keep his eyes down. Ask any white person outside the drugstore opposite the courthouse about George Wallace, and you'll get an answer: "I'm just about one hundred and *fifty* per cent fo' him!" Ask any Negro, and he will look at his boots as if he'd suddenly lost the power of speech.

"I think, over-all," says George Wallace's brother Jack, who succeeded him as the judge in Clayton, "you'll not find a better place to raise children than Clayton." You can see what he means. The south Alabama countryside is lush and the climate is mild, except for the burning heat at high summer. The judge can walk to work from a spacious brick house in an acre of ground, and, when the duties of his court allow, which is rather often, he can shoot deer on the waste ground opposite his door or catch fish in the lake a mile away. The white folks in a town like Clayton live on terms of easy friendliness, tempered by an old-fashioned respect for people of consequence. The judge can spend hours at his carpentry with peace of mind, while his wife drinks coffee with the neighbors and the children run wild.

Yet it strikes a visitor that the idyll of Southern small-town life, which lurks like a memory of paradise lost at the back of so many American minds, is a poisoned idyll. The bell Jack Wallace uses to call his children in to supper has a pretty tone, but it was cast as a slave bell. His ten-year-old daughter runs in with a charming lack of shyness to tell us that the cat is having kittens again in the cupboard by the back door. She seems to take it for granted that a heavy automatic pistol is kept next to the cat's basket.

The Wallace brothers did not inherit even this modest and flawed comfort. "There was no money," Judge Wallace remembers with pride, in his soft voice, "and if you had it in a bank you lost it. I guess you could say we were in poverty, not as a matter of attitude, but as a matter of economics. We had patched overalls on, but they were clean. We grew most of our own food, and in the summertime we spent a good bit of our time helping Mother shell peas and snap beans. There was very little you had to buy at the store."

It was the classic childhood of the Southern back country. There was the father, chronically ill and with only one lung, but with enough spirit to be constantly fighting and politicking and raising hell. There was the mother, spent by the drudgery of keeping the family going, but fiercely religious, fiercely ambitious for her children, and sternly authoritarian. "She'd whup the shit out of us," George's other brother, Gerald, remembers with love. There were Negroes, old retainers like Carlton McKinnis, and the Negro boys they fought and swam and

played marbles with, according to the Southern code which decrees segregation only from the age of puberty. And there was the whole proud,
hungry, Puritan ethos of that formidable class in the South who were
indisputably both poor and white but who never for a moment dreamed
of accepting the insulting undertones of defeat and hopelessness which
Northerners conjure up when they use the term "poor whites."

All the Wallace boys went to college, though their father died during
the first year George, the eldest son, was attending. "My mother took a
job at one of these alphabetical programs back in the Depression," Jack
says, "supervising a sewing room. Of course primarily it was a make-
work project, but in any event she made a living for herself and for my
young sister too. But that was the extent of her ability. So we went, and
George worked shoveling coal and waiting on tables in boarding houses,
and I dug ditches on the campus, laid steam lines for a new building one
time, picked up papers, did just the ordinary work for twenty-five cents
an hour. George did the same thing. We worked our room, board, and
tuition."

George worked his way through law school. He got through the
war, as a flight engineer in B-29s on bombing missions over Japan. ("It's
awful that folks have to drop bombs on other folks," he has philoso-
phized. "You know, Japan's a great little country, they're a great little
people.") He met and married Lurleen Burns, and lived with her in a
converted chicken house in New Mexico. ("We were in hog heaven," he
claims, compared to other places they had lived in.) He caught meningitis while in the army, and survived that too, though with a ten-per-cent
disability pension, which inspired a piece of Southern repartee not quite
fit to rank with what John Randolph of Roanoke said when somebody
called him impotent: "Sir, you pride yourself on a faculty in which you
are equaled by the meanest of my Negroes, and greatly excelled by the
jackass"; or Carter Glass's immortal insult to Huey Long: "I understand
that in the ultimate decadence of Rome they elected a horse to the Senate.
At least it was a whole horse." It was Senator Wayne Morse who brought
up the question of Wallace's nerves. "Well," said Wallace, "At least I
have a paper that certifies I have ninety per cent of my faculties, which
is more than Wayne Morse can claim!"

Many a man who had been through the ignoble miseries of those
years might have been glad to settle for a quiet life and the sure hope
of a glass of beer at the end of the day. Not George Wallace. He had
always known what he wanted to do in life. The British politician
Quintin Hogg has a theory that about each man there is a definitive anec-

dote, one that reveals the quintessential man more than any number of thousands of words of analysis. The anecdote of anecdotes about George Wallace is told in Marshall Frady's superb biography, and we cite it with admiration:

> A farmer in Barbour county remembers, "All through the war, people around here had been gettin' these Christmas cards from all kinda places—Denver one year, then the next year it'd be Guam or someplace like that—and openin' them up, they'd read, 'Merry Christmas, George C. Wallace.' I got 'em too, and I couldn't quite figger them out. I thought it was real nice of this young fella, so far away and all and yet bein' so thoughtful, but I wasn't quite sure I knew who this George Wallace was, and why he was writin' me. It seemed kinda strange. Anyway, when the war was over with and the local political races had done got started over the county, I was out in my field one fine spring afternoon plowin', and I happen to look up and see this young fella comin' across the plowed field from the road, like he had just popped up out of nowhere, steppin' real smart and lively across those furrows, already grinnin' and his hand already stretched out, and all of a sudden I knew why I'd been gettin' them nice cards every Christmas. . . ."

"George's great weakness," says his friend Hamp Graves, "is running. He's a compulsive runner. We all are in Barbour County. We've produced seven governors of this state and one lieutenant governor. There's an old saying: There's north Alabama, south Alabama . . . and Barbour County. Hell, you gotta be sharp, quick on your feet, to survive round here. It's the coffee-shop atmosphere. I can take you to, oh, the Pappas place, the Holiday Inn, the Town Terrace, the Town House, the Courtesy Grill, any of them round about morning-coffee time—any time, for that matter—and you'll see a little group of folks, a man with a million dollars to his name *waiting on,* I mean really *serving,* some man with scarcely a shirt to his back—because he respects his wit, his quickness. That's what it's like. If you come from round here, you cut your teeth in that ambiance."

Whole essays might be written to explain why the coffee shops of a backwoods county seat in south Alabama should be to politics in the age of the Kennedy Institute what the Stoa Poikile was to philosophy in Plato's time. And that is not altogether tongue in cheek. Strange as Southern political mores seem to an outsider, and hard as it is to believe that rational men could actually hold its philosophical premises, there is no getting away from the superior performance of Southern politicians. It all goes back, like everything else in the distinctive political culture of the region, to the old man on the mule. But for our purpose, the essay can be reduced to three axioms: (1) Because of the presence of the Negro, and the white man's stubborn commitment to maintaining supremacy, Southerners take their politics more seriously. (2) Because, since slavery, the South has, on the whole, been an economically back-ward region, politics has attracted a higher share of talent than else-where in America. (3) Because—and this too goes back to Emancipation and Reconstruction—the South has until recently been a one-party region, it has nurtured a tradition of professionalism in politics, a politics of faction, a politics of personality.

When George Wallace came out of Barbour County, the dominant personality in Alabama politics was Jim Folsom, a vast, warm, outra-geous man who ruined his career and his health with whisky but without ever destroying the affection in which he was held by most Alabamians. It was natural that Wallace should model himself on Big Jim. Folsom was a Populist, a most ambivalent political faith. It is the predicament of the mass of white people in the South that they are the men in the middle. To the North and to the rest of the world, they appear as a class of oppressors, holding down the aspirations of the Negroes below them. But in their own minds they are the oppressed, eternally cheated of their deserts by the conspiracy between the Southern Bourbon and the hypocritical Yankee with his freight rates and his guidelines. This is the cause of an enduring tendency to political paranoia like that of the Afrikaner in South Africa or the *pied noir* in Algeria. But Populism faces two ways. It demands a better deal for the common white man. Sometimes it seeks to include the Negro in its program of social reform. Sometimes it turns savagely against him.

Folsom was gently disposed toward Negroes; for ten years his protégé and imitator, George Wallace, pursued an undistinguished career as a state legislator and county judge, wearing Folsom's colors as, by Alabama standards, a racial liberal. After the 1954 Supreme Court deci-sion, however, Wallace began to parade his defiance of Federal inter-ference—long before the Federal authorities had noticed his existence. And, in the end, he broke with Folsom. It happened, according to an eyewitness, like this: Wallace was infuriated by Folsom's making an appointment in Barbour County without consulting him. In his rage, he was pacing to and fro in the lobby of the Jefferson Davis Hotel, which serves as a clubhouse for Alabama's legislators and lobbyists. He passed in front of the seat from which a veteran politician called "Foots" Clem-ent was observing the show. Clement asked him what was the matter.

Wallace told him. "You can't break with the Governor over a patronage matter," Clement said. "Go get yourself an issue." "What do you mean, an issue?" said Wallace. "Well, isn't there anything you don't go along with Jim Folsom on?" "Yeah," said Wallace, "he never was right on niggers."

In 1958, Wallace ran for governor and was beaten by John Patterson. To all appearances, a mediocre political career had reached its ceiling. "He didn't have nothing," says another of Wallace's Barbour County cronies, Billy Watson. "No law practice, no savings to speak of, nothing!" But Wallace was not ready to give up. "John Patterson out-niggered me," he complained to his friends. "And boys, I ain't going to be outniggered again!"

He has been as good as his word. On the day he was inaugurated as Governor, in January 1963, he stood on the steps of the State Capitol in Montgomery, where Jefferson Davis took the oath of office as President of the Confederacy, and cried, "In the name of the greatest people that have ever trod this earth, I draw the line in the dust and toss the gauntlet before the feet of tyranny. And I say, Segregation now! Segregation tomorrow! Segregation forever!"

"As Governor," Marshall Frady maintains, "Wallace proved to be, aside from his racial aberration, essentially a Populist." It is quite true that Wallace was, as Southern governors go, a big spender. He built schools, he built roads, he spent generously on health programs, especially—at his wife's insistence—for mental health. He also made strenuous efforts to attract badly needed new industries to Alabama. But Robert Sherrill, in *Gothic Politics in the Deep South,* is surely right when he insists: "In the last analysis, one must judge the degree of populism behind a welfare or a public-works program according to who pays for it. In Alabama it is the consumer who pays. . . . Paradoxically, he kept taxes off big business and industry, yet the money leaders fear and distrust him; he piled new taxes and debt on the people, and they love him."

It is true that Wallace raised the revenue for social programs not from taxes, such as the property tax, which fall heavily on corporations and on the rich, but from sales taxes on essentials like food and gasoline, which hit the poor disproportionately hard. Alabama has the lowest property tax in the United States and one of the highest levels of consumer taxes: the state sales tax is four per cent across the board, and most cities add another two per cent on top of that. Wallace also increased the car-license fee by a flat ten dollars, which hit the farmer with a ten-year-old Chevy just as hard as the Birmingham "Big Mule" with an air-conditioned Cadillac. It is also true that big business in Alabama is not happy with Wallace. In 1965, a group of industrialists clubbed together to put an ad in the *Wall Street Journal* pleading for "tolerance" and "moderation"—in the circumstances, an ill-concealed slap at Wallace. Industry is scared of Alabama's growing bonded debt, much of which Wallace has cleverly funded so that the full impact of interest and repayment will not be felt in his time.

But the resolution of this paradox is simple. Wallace may have a certain fondness for the businessmen's conservative ideology, and he certainly feels the poor country boy's resentment of the rich. But neither ideology nor resentment is the source of his policy. He is interested in power. Using a classic formula, he takes from each what each has to give: from the rich their money, from the poor their votes—and their money too, if they have any. William Bradford Huie, writer and champion of Negro rights whose family has lived in the state for generations and who still lives there himself from choice, has watched Wallace's rise closely. He brushes off talk of his populism and uses an uglier word. For Huie, Wallace is a new-style American Fascist masquerading as an old-style Populist. "Wallace has mixed exactly the same political brew as Adolf Hitler," Huie says, "in that he uses racism to power his machine. He attracts the poor white people with racism. But when he has got the poor white man's vote, he is not really the poor man's friend."

Wallace went to remarkable lengths to turn Alabama into the closest thing to a police state that has been achieved in the twentieth century within the jurisdiction of the United States. He established a seven-man Sovereignty Commission to protect Alabama from encroachments by the Federal government and by civil-rights organizations. This was a secret tribunal with powers to hire staff "to make and conduct special inquiry, investigation and examination for the Governor," including examining witnesses. It was expressly exempted from the obligation to record its proceedings. He also beefed up the State Highway Patrol, under tough Al Lingo, who has close links to the Ku Klux Klan, as a tough private police force, answerable to the Governor. He ran civil-rights groups out of the state. And he practiced unsystematic but occasionally most unpleasant intimidation. In some instances, Wallace himself may have known nothing of the intimidation practiced by his supporters. But we have learned of enough instances to be satisfied that both physical and economic intimidation have been regular parts of Wallace's system. Newspapers that have criticized him have lost valuable advertising from the state liquor monopoly. Individuals who have opposed him have had their barns burned or their cattle ponds poisoned. One particularly sly technique goes like this: A citizen writes a letter to a newspaper in support of Carl Elliott, a liberal Alabama Congressman whom Wallace opposes. Late one night there is a knock at his door. Two burly highway troopers are standing there, their faces impassive behind dark glasses, their hands on the butts of their pistols. They introduce themselves and say they are "just checking." Somebody has been writing nasty letters to the papers from this address. "Oh, you mean you really did write that stuff? Because there have been so many forgeries. . . ." They take ostentatious notes and zoom off into the hot night, leaving one more citizen wondering how wise it is to oppose the Wallace machine. "My principal case against Wallace," says Huie, "is that he brought the fear to Alabama. In the conditions that exist, it is dangerous to be against him."

One argument for caution in opposing Wallace in Alabama is his link with the Klan. He says he has no time for that organization, and he told us in an interview that the Klansmen are "just a bunch of thugs." But one of his first acts on coming into office was to parole, before they had served the legal minimum term for their offense, a group of Klansmen who had been convicted of castrating a Negro. "Ace" Carter, the Birmingham Klan leader, has raised funds for Wallace. So has Robert Shelton, Imperial Wizard of the United Klans of America. Whatever Wallace may say he thinks of the Klan, the Klan thinks the world of him. "I support the principles and what George Wallace stands for," Shelton told us in an interview at his comfortable lakeside home in the woods near Tuscaloosa. "George Wallace himself has an understanding of the conspiracies that exist, that's bringing about the destruction of Christianity, that's lowering the moral tone of the nation." And Shelton's office was crammed with Wallace literature—twenty thousand copies of one item—and even with bumper stickers saying WALLACE FOR PRESIDENT: STAFF MEMBER for distribution to Klan members as a convenient precaution against being stopped by the highway patrol!

Wallace does believe in segregation, of course. "Everybody does, when you get right down to it," he told the *New York Times,* perhaps partly as a tease. But he believes in power for himself more. He is a segregationist second, a demagogue first.

In 1963, he was talking to Alabama, so he waved the banner of segregation. In 1968, he was talking to the nation, so he changed his tune. For, in his first year as Governor, he made a discovery that lifted him in one heave above the whole long line of Southern demagogues (with the possible exception of Huey Long)—above Bilbo and Vardaman, Talmadge and Pitchfork Ben Tillman and the whole apostolic succession of stem-winders and spell-binders who mastered the trick of keeping a crowd of yokels listening to their promises for three hours in the sun, and then selling them out when they got to the Governor's mansion. Wallace in 1963 learned a trick that made him a hero, not just in Alabama, but in the whole South. The next stage in his growth came when he adapted that trick to give himself a following, not just in the South, but in the whole country.

Alabama in 1963 was convulsed by the confrontation between the Negroes, led by Martin Luther King, and the forces of repression symbolized by "Bull" Connor and his dogs. It was in an atmosphere of rising fear and anger that Wallace announced that if the Federal courts ordered that Negro students be admitted to the University of Alabama, then he would "stand in the schoolhouse door" rather than allow it. The courts made their order. Wallace made his stand. The Federal bayonets duly appeared through the trees, and the Negro students were duly admitted. At the time, it seemed to most Northerners, and to the Kennedy Administration, that Wallace had lost, that he had, indeed, made a fool of himself. Many Southerners, too, indignantly pointed out that, by acting like a mountebank, Wallace had been less effective as a defender of segregation than if he had chosen cunning and pliability instead of open resistance. But the defense of segregation was not Wallace's first object. He knew what he was doing, and he knew it had been successful.

Consciously or not, he was doing essentially the same as what his arch-enemy, Martin Luther King, had done in Birmingham. By avoiding compromise and deliberately seeking a showdown, by acting out a symbolic drama, he managed to turn a legal and practical defeat into a political victory. (It was not the first time. In 1958, the United States Civil Rights Commission demanded to see the records of Barbour County. Wallace impounded the records and turned them over to a grand jury. He then spread the word that he was forced to surrender by a threat of five years in prison, made by the Federal judge in Montgomery at a secret night meeting. And he campaigned on the story in 1962, telling every audience he spoke to, in every corner on the state, that he had been bullied by the "integrating, scallywagging, carpetbagging liar" of a judge. In fact, he had secretly surrendered the records to the Federal authorities all along in time to avoid being cited for contempt of court. He had discovered the formula: invite punishment by defiance, slyly avoid real unpleasant consequences, and then advertise your martyrdom.)

What he had divined was that there was a market for this kind of martyrdom because a large number of Southerners did feel powerless and humiliated in face of the threat of Federal interference and coercion. His next discovery was that powerlessness and its combustible political consequences were not confined to the South.

As early as January 12, 1963, two days before his inauguration as Governor, Wallace met the embattled diehards who were trying to defend segregation to the last in Montgomery. Roy Harris was there from Georgia, Leander Perez from Louisiana, Ross Barnett from Mississippi. Harris, in particular, who had helped to found the Citizens' Council movement, had been looking for a leader for the South's resistance ever since 1954. "We weren't about to sit back and watch the nation being brainwashed into believing that our way of life in the South was unconstitutional and un-Christian," Harris told us. "And we've been looking for a Senator or a governor to front up this movement ever since. Every time we thought we'd got one, he turned soft—trying to get some of the nigra vote." For Harris and his friends, Wallace was promising material, an exciting potential successor to Strom Thurmond. But Wallace had a better idea. There was no concerted attempt to get behind a Southern candidate in 1964. The Goldwater campaign divided the ultraconservatives. ("We took four states for Goldwater in 1964," said Harris, "and hell, we didn't even like him. He voted against the Civil Rights Act, and we just showed our appreciation.")

Wallace went his own way. After the "schoolhouse door," he began to get invitations to speak all over the country. Late one afternoon in the winter of 1963–64, he was in Wisconsin. It was hostile territory. Somebody wrote FUCK WALLACE on the frozen lake at Madison when he spoke at the University. But the last afternoon of his visit, a man called Wallace's suite at the hotel and said he had a plan for Wallace to run in the Wisconsin primary. It seemed a fantastic, hare-brained scheme. But as everybody knows, he ran—in Wisconsin, in Indiana, and in Maryland. He got 34 per cent of the vote in Wisconsin; 38 per cent in Indiana; 43 per cent in Maryand.

The 1964 primaries consolidated Wallace's position as *the* Southern leader. They planted in him the seed of a grander scheme: a Presidential campaign in 1968 that would leave him even more indisputably the master of Alabama because he had shown his power to counterattack the Yankees on their ground. Yet before he dared attempt anything so ambitious, he had to secure his base.

If Wallace was to achieve anything in 1968, he had to face two facts, and to find some way around the obstacle they presented: (1) His basic source of money was the State of Alabama. (2) Because Alabama law does not allow a governor to succeed himself, his control of the state would end in 1966. He tried to get the legislature to change the law. He pleaded, he orated, he threatened, and he used all the political muscle he could flex. The bill passed in the House, but it was too much for the senators. He was finished, his Presidential plans at an end, unless he could think of something, of somebody. And then, perhaps for the first time in years, he seriously thought of Lurleen. The marriage had not gone well. There had been four children, but Lurleen had tried to get a divorce. She was a sad, quiet, dim woman, kind but colorless. Perhaps her disease was already draining her energy. But it didn't matter what she was like. The people would vote for Governor Lurleen but they would get Governor George for another four years; why not, indeed, for another eight? There was nothing to stop George from succeeding Lurleen, if Lurleen could succeed George. The election was a formality. Poor sick Lurleen went to the Governor's mansion. ("You're goin' to have to sleep with that woman again now," said one of her husband's friends.) And George Wallace stayed in his two large offices in the Capitol. Framed on the wall was his commission, naming him as his wife's "Number One Adviser" in the Alabama Military Department in recognition of her "confidence in his patriotism, valor, fidelities, and abilities, as the highest-ranking officer in the State militia." He was more than that. He was the most powerful, because the most secure, politician in the history of the South since the fall of the Confederacy.

"There is an established custom in Alabama," a committee reported to Governor Folsom in 1948, "for highway contractors to make sizable donations to political campaigns. . . . While all of the contractors before the committee denied that there was any advantage in being on the successful side in a political campaign, yet the highway contractors are striving desperately to gain such a position. . . ." What the committee so decorously suggested in 1948 still holds good today. Not only highway contractors, but any businessman hoping to sell to the State of Alabama—road-machinery supply people, printers, insurance men, and so on—would have to reckon on dealing with George Wallace and his friends for at least eight years to come. For some, the prospect of losing all state business for so long must have been daunting.

Later, we shall have occasion to take a more detailed look at the various sources of Wallace's campaign funds. But the point of departure, the source of the original campaign chest, was the State of Alabama. Any Southern Governor has numerous ways of raising money. Businessmen are highly unlikely, for example, to refuse to advertise in the handsomely produced brochure celebrating a governor's inauguration. But the two really serious plum trees to be shaken are the contracting industry, and the state liquor monopoly. Wallace and his friends shook both greedily. (This, incidentally, casts some light on Wallace's Populism: school-, road-, and hospital-building programs can all be made to yield a multiple political dividend: votes from the people, favors from grateful legislators from the districts affected, profit for friends and favorites, funds for the campaign chest. Even the strange modifications made in the liquor-wholesaling system, as we shall see, masqueraded as reforms.)

Ironically, in view of Wallace's tirades against Federal bureaucracy, the largest indirect source of money may well have been the Federal government. The Department of Health, Education, and Welfare in Washington complacently assured us that no money leaked from Federal school-building grants. Anyone could have told them that it is common knowledge in Alabama that few of Wallace's vaunted school-building programs would bear strict auditing. The system is classic. The state government is allowed to "five-per-cent" a contract. That means that it is not bound to accept the lowest tender on contracts but may give them to any firm it likes, provided the price negotiated is five per cent below the lowest tender. This is a standing invitation to favoritism, and the five per cent can easily be made up by "additional work orders," not subject to tender, and carrying a hefty profit.

In 1964, the Bureau of Public Roads, a Federal agency, investigated the awarding of consultant engineering contracts for highway work in Alabama. The report disclosed that Wallace's crony (and, in 1968, his campaign-finance manager) Seymore Trammell, finance director for the State of Alabama, had a system going whereby a firm of consulting engineers that wanted to work on the highways in Alabama had to hire one of Wallace's friends as an agent. The precise kickback varied: sometimes it was as high as ten per cent, and in one case it was a flat eighty thousand dollars. Trammell dismissed the investigation as "nothing more than vindictiveness against Governor Wallace on the part of the Federal Administration in Washington." The investigation also showed that one firm of consultants had been constrained to hire Robert Shelton as a "public-relations consultant" at a fee of four thousand dollars on an interstate-highway contract.

Early in 1968, a company called Waugh Asphalt filed suit in Federal court which spelled out how Trammell's system worked in another department of the state's business. The Waugh firm is run by an asphalt contractor named Howard Alexander. He sued Trammell, the state purchasing agent, Howard White, and a long list of codefendants for $1,150,000. The suit alleged, in great detail, nothing less than a conspiracy in which Trammell made every asphalt contractor who wanted a contract from the State of Alabama kick back fifty cents to a dollar on every ton of asphalt supplied, or pay an equivalent amount in "political contributions" to Wallace's campaign. The action was settled out of court.

Will Rogers once said that the voters of Mississippi would vote "dry" as long as they could stagger to the polls. Alabama has inherited from the same idiosyncratic temperance tradition an Alcoholic Beverage Control Board which is a venerable haunt of corruption. George Wallace's first executive order as Governor was to abolish what he called "the evil practice of paying off political debts with commissions on sales of whisky to the State of Alabama." But under the guise of reform, he proceeded to introduce a neater system for the same purpose.

Shortly after this pious proclamation, Jack Brock, a former undertaker and—what was more to the point—former lobbyist for the American Federation of Labor in the days when Wallace was in the state legislature, started a business called Montgomery Wine. It had no employees, and indeed no telephone and no office. Brock operated it by himself, two or three days a week, from his own home. It had only one customer in 1967: the State of Alabama. But in the course of the year, it sold the state thirty-two thousand cases of whisky for more than two million dollars. Two unknown firms in Baltimore, called Montebello Liquors, Inc., and Majestic Distilling, Inc., neither of which had sold any liquor at all to Alabama before Wallace became Governor, suddenly mushroomed into the state's biggest suppliers of domestic gin, vodka, and bourbon. Thirty Alabamians were irritated to notice that unheard-of brands with names like Shooting Lodge Scotch, Old Setter Bourbon, and even Virgin Bourbon, appeared on the shelves of their local liquor stores in place of well-loved national brands, and sometimes at higher prices. Associates of the newly favored suppliers indignantly deny that there was any hanky-panky behind these odd events. "They are the most strait-laced people in the world," said Alfred Bernstein of Montebello about his clients in Alabama. Strait-laced or not, several of the new liquor suppliers found themselves named in a suit filed in Federal court in 1968, alleging that they "paid substantial monies directly or indirectly by way of commissions, fees, or otherwise, to one or more agents or persons" connected with Wallace's Administration.

By the middle of 1967, thanks to asphalt and highway contracts, Virgin Bourbon and a dozen other new variants on time-honored wheezes, George Wallace had a million dollars in his campaign war chest, enough to bring in more in contributions from the faithful once the standard was raised. He was ready for the march to the North.

2

Where Is That
Mason-Dixon Line?

"The boll weevil came East, and the cotton went West;
the Yankees came South, and the niggers went North."

—Southern proverb

"The basic philosophy of the people all over this nation
is similar. I receive just as enthusiastic a response to my
message in Oregon, or in the state of Washington, or in
California, as I do in Alabama."

—George C. Wallace, Jr., in an interview with
one of the authors in April 1968

George Wallace's success in the three primaries he entered in
1964 was the first inkling for most Northerners of the fact that water
flows both ways. For twenty years, the differences between North and
South had been diminishing. The natural assumption was that the South
was getting more like the North—and so it was, in many ways. What
had dawned on almost none of the leaders of Northern opinion before
Wallace drove the lesson home was that in important respects the
North was also getting more like the South.

Less than thirty years ago, when George Wallace was working his
way through the University of Alabama, he was, as a Southerner, a
citizen of what was still, three-quarters of a century after the collapse of
secession, very much a nation within a nation. Turn over the pages of
any of the massive books written to describe the South in those very
years—Rupert Vance and Howard Odum's encyclopedic studies in
human geography, the *Report on the Economic Condition of the South*

276

done for President Roosevelt by the National Emergency Council, above all Gunnar Myrdal's prophetic *An American Dilemma*—and you will find them crammed with evidence of just how different the South was from the rest of the country.

Average income, in the eleven states that had seceded plus Kentucky and Oklahoma, was then almost exactly half what it was in the rest of the country. The richest Southern state ranked lower than the poorest state outside the South. Standards of education and public health lagged even further behind. Indeed, the South then followed the classic pattern of an underdeveloped colonial country; its great wealth of natural resources was systematically exploited to enrich the North. Interest rates in Atlanta were more than half as high again as rates in New York, and it cost half as much again to ship goods from Atlanta to Chicago as from Chicago to Atlanta.

In politics, the South was still dominated by a one-party system. Culturally, apart from the more obvious traumas that had marked it as a region, it had almost wholly missed the characteristic American experience of immigration: if you left out Texas with its Mexicans, and Florida with its northern colonies, then, in 1940, fewer than one Southerner out of every two hundred was foreign-born.

But the greatest difference of all, and the fundamental cause of all the other differences, was that the South, alone of all the American regions, had a substantial population of Negroes. As recently as 1940, Negroes made up one-quarter of the population in every Southern state, whereas the only places in the rest of the country where they amounted to as much as one-twelfth were half a dozen cities—New York, Detroit, Chicago, Cleveland, Philadelphia, and Pittsburgh.

The great migration of American Negroes from the Southern farmlands to the cities—one of the great movements of people of the twentieth century, in scale as well as in consequences—began in the second decade of the century. By 1940, only one and three-quarter million had made the fateful journey to the North, but by the middle sixties, more than half of America's twenty million Negroes lived outside the South. For two centuries and more, the only communities on the mainland of North America where black men were anywhere near as numerous as white men had been remote plantation counties in the South. Suddenly, after the Second World War, ratios of one black to every four whites, one to three, even one to one, began to be approached precisely in parts of important and sensitive Northern cities: in New York, in Chicago, in the District of Columbia.

Step by step with this great black trek, there was a second, silent migration of white people out of the South. Sharecroppers and farm folk left east Texas, Oklahoma, and Arkansas for California. Mountain people left the Appalachians and Ozarks for the assembly lines of Detroit, Chicago, and St. Louis. And ambitious young men and women escaped from the narrow horizons of small Southern towns to the big cities. Lyndon Johnson, Dwight Eisenhower, Dean Rusk, and Jesse Unruh are all members of this unnoticed army, and so are bankers, novelists, professors, generals, and Supreme Court justices.

And, third, Yankees went South. Some were executives or technicians moving down with a branch office or plant. Some were employees of defense or space contractors. An increasing number were simply people who preferred to feel the sun on their backs, other things being equal. And things were getting more equal between North and South very fast. Natural wealth, government policy, and boondoggling made possible by the South's entrenched strength in Congress all helped the growth of industry. Industrialization brought a phenomenal growth in the cities. Atlanta, Houston, Dallas, and Miami, among others, sprouted from dreary provincial tank towns into autonomous regional metropolises, generating their own industries, their own investment funds, and their own political and social philosophy. The economic differential between North and South had everywhere been eroded by the middle sixties, and in the more fortunate corners of the South it had almost disappeared. In the very years when Bostonians and New Yorkers were laughing at Tom Lehrer's song, the Old South "where pellagra makes you scrawny" was vanishing into the same limbo as that older South of "whuppin' slaves and pickin' cotton."

As any Southerner will tell you, the North had always felt a potent compulsion to make the South over in its own image. But in the fifties and sixties, this was reinforced by the new political leverage of Negro voters concentrated at the fulcrums of power: in New York, Philadelphia, Cleveland, Detroit, and Chicago—swing cities in the decisive states in Presidential politics. And so, for the ten years from the Supreme Court's 1954 decision holding school segregation to be unconstitutional to the Civil Rights Act of 1964, Northerners had every reason to think that the South was becoming more like the North; that this was right, proper, and inevitable; and that a few more years of Northern pressure would iron out the last stubborn traces of Southern frowardness in racial matters.

George Wallace himself, staking everything on the assumption that

Northerners would react to the presence of large numbers of Negroes in their midst by adopting traditional Southern racial attitudes, seems sometimes to have been surprised at the correctness of his own assumption. In December 1967, for example, when he gave a speech to the Rotary Club of St. Louis—the kind of audience which, four years before, he could hardly have hoped to be invited to address—he was openly nervous beforehand about the kind of reception he would get. Again and again, though, his talk was interrupted with applause, and at the end he was cheered. In the plane on the way home, he seemed awed by his own success. "I didn't feel any hostility at all," he said. "No hostility. None at all. They really liked me!"

What made Wallace acceptable in the North as no Southern politician had ever been was not simply the fact that the North had changed, that there had been a massive reaction to Negro militancy and Negro rioting. That was Wallace's opportunity. He was able to seize it because he had learned to adapt to Northern sensibilities one of the oldest devices in the Southern politician's armory. He talked in code.

Speaker of the House Sam Rayburn once reproved a group of fellow Southern politicians by telling them that all their high-flown political vocabulary boiled down to just three words: "nigger, nigger, nigger." For a century, politicians in the South had learned to talk about states' rights, and constitutionalism, and the Southern way of life, and many another resounding shibboleth, in such a way that everyone knew exactly what they meant. Wallace now proceeded to export this regional expertise. In his Alabama campaigning, he had tempered and forged a single speech out of the lines that brought the most applause. (He posted cronies round the fringes of his crowds to watch the effect of his speeches; whenever a line proved effective, it would be welded onto the body of his performance, until, in the end, he had a single speech compounded of all the lines that brought the best response.) He now repeated this blacksmithery with a national, not an Alabama, audience in mind. There was no more "segregation now, segregation tomorrow, segregation forever!" Instead, Wallace would insist with furrowed brow that he was no racist. "I've never made a racist speech in my life," he began to say. The speech began to be so deeply inlaid into his brain that he would recite hunks of it even in private conversation. On any cue even vaguely related to race, he would trot out the figures for 1966, say, showing that most Alabama Negroes had voted for his wife. (This was perfectly true: they had voted for her in the general election, when the only alternative was an even more explicitly racist Republican

candidate and when many Negroes were candidates on the Democratic
ticket with her. In the primary, they had voted equally massively for her
opponent.) Unashamed racists like Roy Harris were not deceived.
"When you get right down to it," he announced cheerfully, "there's
really only going to be one issue, and you spell it n-i-g-g-e-r."

George Wallace never spelled it out like that. He was against the
Civil Rights Act of 1964, of course—but not because he was against
Negro rights. Oh, no: as he explained on "Meet the Press" in April 1967,
he opposed it as "an infringement upon the property-right system." "I
don't believe there is backlash in this country because of color," he said
in the same interview. "I think that's a journalistic expression. I think
it was coined by the news media. I think there's a backlash against the
theoreticians and the bureaucrats in national government. . . . There
isn't any backlash among the mass of American people against anybody
because of color. There's a backlash against big government in this
country." But then again he would say, "I'm not fighting the Federal
government. I'm fighting this beatnik mob in Washington that has just
about destroyed the Federal government." He and his followers were not
racists, Wallace would explain self-righteously. It was the "liberals and
intellectuals—intellectual morons"—who had made them out to be
racists. And one day, in the middle of 1967, he hit upon the sentence
that was to be an applause line in a hundred speeches because his audiences loved it so: "Our lives are being taken over by bureaucrats, and
most of them have beards!"

That was it! Never mind if a bearded civil servant in Washington
was as rare as a dodo. Wallace dealt in nothing so prosaic as literal truth.
He offered the poetic variety. And millions of Americans did feel that
bureaucrats in Washington, clean-shaven or not, were in some vague
but real way part of the same conspiracy as the intellectuals and the
students, and foreigners, and blacks, and Communists: all conspiring
together to trample on the small plot of the ordinary American's pride
and to let cold draughts of uncertainty into the cherished fireside of his
life.

Wallace drew the lines of class feeling with exquisite skill. On his
side stood the People. His movement, he said,

> is a movement of the people, and it doesn't make any difference
> whether top leading politicians endorse this movement or not. I think
> that if the politicians get in the way in 1968, a lot of them are going
> to get run over by this average man in the street, this man in the
> textile mill, this man in the steel mill, this barber, the beautician, the

policeman on the beat. They are the ones—and the little businessman
—I think those are the mass of people that are going to support
a change on the domestic scene.

And the enemy? Why, the people of power, the people with education: the "top politicians," the "bureaucrats," the "pointy-headed professors," the press and the national news media, "who are going to get
some of those liberal smiles knocked off their faces," "Federal judges
playing God," and the whole sneering, contemptuous army of the "sissy-
britches," the "intellectual morons" and the "theoreticians" who "don't
know how to park a bicycle straight."

The historian Richard Hofstadter has argued that, just as Americans
are uniquely convinced of the goodness of their own political system
and the perfectibility of human society under its aegis, so they are
uniquely vulnerable to a certain kind of political paranoia. The paranoid
individual starts with a conviction of his own superior gifts and high
destiny. Then, if his actual situation in life fails to live up to this conviction, it is too hard to modify it. It is far easier to look around for scape-
goats, to blame one's own shortcomings on the machinations of "them."
In a strikingly similar way, as Hofstadter shows, groups who were resentful or fearful of the way society seemed to be evolving at every stage
of American history have blamed their troubles on conspiracies, rather
than be forced to abandon their faith that all was for the best. (At times,
the tendency led to farcical fantasies: as late as the twenties, no less
a man than Henry Ford was blaming the nation's evils on the Illuminati,
who were to his mind a sinister secret society, but were in fact an
eighteenth-century Bavarian sect, no single member of which is known
to have landed in America!) As we have seen, the same mental processes
can be traced behind the phobia about domestic Communism which has
had so deep an influence on Richard Nixon's development.

To say that millions of Americans are the victims of a kind of political paranoia is not, of course, to suggest that they are paranoid as
individuals. On the contrary, many of the people who exhibit this
tendency in their politics are the solidest of citizens and the decentest
of souls in their private lives. An article in the late *Saturday Evening Post*
by Bil Gilbert in April 1968 made the point neatly. In it, Gilbert described a visit to an idyllic small town in central Pennsylvania called
Millersburg and, in particular, an evening spent talking to five ladies
who live there. The ladies expressed their fear of the "over-all Communist plot to destroy us." Gilbert asked them whether this fear was

a real and immediate thing in their lives, "like the furnace not working, or the plumbing going bad," and got this answer: "Well, it is all part of the same thing. Crime, the streets being unsafe, strikes, the trouble with the colored, all this dope-taking, people leaving the churches. It is sort of a breakdown of our standards, the American way of life."

This, Gilbert sensibly observed, can be made to sound like the most pathetic kind of lunatic-fringe raving, but it is not. The people who share the concerns of the ladies from Millersburg are not "paranoid kooks," he insisted, and he is surely right. "That Mrs. Baker and Mrs. Novinger should believe that there are people and forces working toward the elimination or drastic alteration of Millersburg, America, does not seem to me evidence of derangement," he wrote.

> There are such people and forces. Every year, communities like Millersburg become fewer. They are gobbled up by freeways and housing developments, sacrificed, rightly or wrongly, to the needs of a growing, mobile population. Also, as anybody inside or outside Millersburg knows, there are a lot of real and prominent people, ranging from Sinclair Lewis to Stokely Carmichael, who have made it quite clear that Millersburg is anathema to them.

Millersburg, Pennsylvania, is not so very different from Clayton, Alabama, though its traditions are such that it responds to different political rhetoric. George Wallace was able to march north because he had found a set of rhetorical keys which would open many political boxes in America in 1968. He knew how to denounce what was happening in such terms that those for whom the most important problem was the Negro Revolution—the racists like Roy Harris—believed he was merely spelling n-i-g-g-e-r in a new way, while millions of others who were not obsessed with race nevertheless felt he cared about the issues that troubled them. For whatever could be said in favor of the American political system in early 1968, one thing could hardly be denied: millions of Americans felt that no one in it spoke for them. To these people Wallace offered one of the most deftly demagogic of all his tirades. We quote the most superbly baroque version of a thought he expressed a thousand times:

> Now you take a big sack and you put LBJ in there, and you put Hubert Humphrey in there, and you put Bobby Kennedy, the blood-giver, in there, and you shake 'em all up. Then you put this Richard Milhous Nixon, who with Eisenhower put bayonets in the backs of the people of Little Rock and in your backs, and you put in Earl Warren, who doesn't have enough legal brains in his head to try

a chicken thief in my home county, and you shake 'em all up. And then you put in that socialist Nelson Rockefeller from the most liberal state in the country, and that left-winger George Romney, who was out in the streets with the demonstrators, and that Clifford Case of New Jersey, and that Wild Bill Scranton of Pennsylvania, and that radical Jacob Javits of New York, and you shake 'em all up. Then you turn that sack over, and the first one that falls out, you pick him up by the nape of the neck and drop him right back in again, because there's not a dime's worth of difference in any of 'em, national Democrats or national Republicans.

This connoisseur's piece of invective, fit to stand with the ripest achievements of Boss Crump or Senator Bilbo, was characteristic of Wallace's rhetoric in another sense: it was folksy, and it had an unmistakable, though muted, undertone of violence. ("I have said it before," Crump orated in an advertisement in 1948, "and I repeat it now, that in the art galleries of Paris there are twenty-seven pictures of Judas Iscariot—none look alike but all resemble Gordon Browning; that neither his head, heart, nor hand can be trusted; that he would milk his neighbor's cow through a crack in the fence; that of the two hundred and six bones in his body there isn't one that is genuine; that his heart has beaten over two billion times without a single sincere beat." Bilbo's periods were less polished but a good deal more violent.) For if, especially in his stressing of the issue of law and order, Wallace was angling for the same fish as Nixon, it has to be said that where Nixon used a dry fly, Wallace baited his hook with good old Southern country blood-red crawlers.

Wallace took a good deal of care to avoid actual incitement to violence. The original formulation of one of his favorite lines, for example, was, "If any demonstrator lies down in front of my car when I'm President, that'll be the last car he lays down in front of." Later, after the line had been quoted as evidence of his bloodthirstiness, he introduced a subtle modification. "If any demonstrator lies down in front of my car," he took to saying instead, "that'll be the last car he'll feel like laying down in front of." Nevertheless, the flavor of Wallace's language was unmistakably violent. Demonstrators, beatniks, and other dissenters were to be "drug before the courts by the hair of their heads and thrown under a good strong jail." For other types of political protest, "a good crease in the skull" was recommended. And as the year went on, the threats became, if anything, even more open. The country ought to be turned over to the police for two years, he actually said; and he got in the habit of telling hecklers to do their shouting now, "because after November, you're through!"

The document known as the Constitution of the United States does not recognize the existence of political parties, which were regarded by the framers as a lamentable impurity in republican politics. Still less does the Constitution enact a two-party system. But the living, small-C constitution goes to extraordinary lengths to discourage third-party candidacies in Presidential elections. Somewhat anomalously, this important national question is left to state law, and a third-party candidate who wants to be on the ballot nationally must first study and then comply with a ticket of different state provisions. In most states, a candidate must file a petition signed by a certain proportion of the registered voters. Sometimes the required proportion is fixed by reference to the total number of voters; sometimes it is related to the number of votes actually cast at the last Presidential or gubernatorial election. And, in practice, the height of the hurdle varies in proportion to the dominance of machine politics in a state. The number of signatures required varied, in practice, from 300 in Colorado and North Dakota to 433,000 in Ohio—a barrier which third-party candidates were definitely not intended to surmount. Finally, in certain states voters must do more than merely sign petitions. They must also reregister themselves as members of a new party.

Altogether, the vagaries of state law and the existence of rump parties obliged Wallace to adopt no fewer than six different names for his party: the American Independent Party, the American Party, the Conservative Party (in Kansas), the Courage Party (in New York), the George Wallace Party, and the George C. Wallace Party. In addition, there were states where Wallace's name appeared on the ballot as an independent candidate; states where it appeared without description; and still other states where the names of independent electors pledged to Wallace appeared without the candidate's name. Not for nothing is it said that the American system is a government "not of laws, but of lawyers."

The drive to get Wallace's name placed on the ballot in all fifty states—which, in the end, it was—was perhaps the most remarkable triumph of participatory democracy at the grass roots in the campaign of 1968, not excluding the McCarthy campaign. It was organized by four young attorneys, three of them—Joe Fine, Joe Di Carlo, and Stan Sikes—from Alabama, and Tom Turnipseed from South Carolina. They called the ballot drive among themselves "Mission Impossible." Altogether, at least 1,662,000 signatures were legally filed, and another 391,203 voters in Alabama voted for Wallace in the primary. The Wallace campaign claims that a total of 2,717,338 signatures were obtained, and even after due allowance has been made for fraud or accidental duplication, it is a sobering total.

Five months before he officially announced his candidacy, Wallace's friends began working to get his name on the ballot in California. That was one of the states that demanded that voters reregister as members of a third party: specifically, that 66,059 Californians register as members of the American Independent Party. It was openly regarded by political journalists in California as an impossible task. Yet by January, it had been done. In Georgia, Wallace's supporters had no difficulty in collecting twice as many signatures as they needed.

At first sight, those two states might look like corroboration of Wallace's claim to be a truly national candidate, appealing to the same constituency of the disenchanted in every part of the country. But on a closer look, even the earlier stages of the ballot drive, successful as it was, foreshadow what was to be a fatal failure. Like Robert E. Lee, Wallace could penetrate deep into Northern territory, striking fear into Yankee hearts. Yet his operation—like Lee's—never quite managed to rise above the status of raids. In the South, the Wallace insurrection was an authentic and largely spontaneous movement. Outside the South, though it had plenty of support—even, at times, what could be called mass support—it was not self-starting, and the support never came in any significant degree from elected politicians. The movement had to be initiated by Wallace's Alabama myrmidons, and, as we shall see, they had their own reasons for being in no hurry to hand over control to local enthusiasts. The contrast between the California and Georgia petition drives illustrates all these points.

It was vital to get on the ballot in California, vital and forbiddingly difficult. California's subsoil was rich in generous kooks, right-wingers, and transplanted Southerners—all of whom could be tapped for far larger amounts of money once Wallace got his name on the ballot there. By mid-1967, Wallace had accumulated about one million dollars in his war chest, and he decided to gamble a good deal of that on California. He took charge of the operation himself and virtually transported his wife's state government to the West Coast. Mrs. Wallace's press secretary, Ed Ewing, went with him, for example; and so did a planeload of other state officials, Alabama lawyers, and other helpers—including no fewer than sixteen Alabama state troopers as bodyguards on one trip. There was some criticism, even in the Alabama press, of such lavish

use of the taxpayers' money on behalf of the Presidential ambitions of
the Governor's husband. The *Lee County Bulletin* of Auburn, Alabama,
was unkind enough to remind Wallace that Alabama folk, while as
"good and refined and cultured" as anyone else were also "as under-
educated, as poor in income, as plagued by lack of adequate physical
and mental health programs as most—and more so than many!" So
Wallace was delighted when he was able to replace a state airplane
with one ostensibly "lent" by a sympathetic Dallas millionaire.

Wallace was even more eager to get all the volunteer help he could.
His old pals from Barbour County rallied round manfully. Seymore
Trammell, his finance director and a Barbour County boy himself, met
a group of them in the Holiday Inn in Eufaula in the early fall of 1967.
Trammell laid it on the line. George had decided to go, and he needed
help, financial help, and bodies. Jimmy Clark, a state senator, made a
long face. "Hell, I can't afford it," he said, "but it's a damned poor man
who won't put his money where his mouth is!" Somebody else looked in
his wallet and fished out fifty dollars in cash and wrote a check for two
hundred and fifty dollars. Everyone else did the same. "We're not a rich
set of folks," said one Eufaulan. "But we really scraped for George."
Official returns later showed that 51 residents of Eufaula, with a population of 8300, scraped more than $11,000. Many another small town
in Alabama did as well.

"California," remembers another, "that was George's Rubicon. I
tell you, Alabama was just about deserted. The whole state just lit out
for California. Why just from round here"—ticking them off on his
fingers—"there was Henry Gray, he's a cattleman round here; and
Charlie Blondheim, he's an architect in town, went to MIT; and Billy
Houston, at the Citizen's Bank—he took his two-weeks' vacation and lit
on out there. . . . And the district attorney, he went, and the son of the
manager at the Holiday Inn. I tell you, there wasn't a lawyer left in
town."

"You didn't have any choice," another man recalls of those epic
days. "Just round about then, they'd start calling you up from Montgomery—that's if you weren't in California already—and they'd say, 'Go
to Montana' or Indiana or someplace, 'and get us on the ballot there.'
Wasn't no use saying, 'I can't.' They'd say, 'The hell you can't. Get on
out there.' So you went. . . ."

During most of November and December, Wallace stormed through
California, peeking over the top of a curious bulletproof structure known
as a "lectern" and raking in signatures and contributions. He himself

blurted out that the whole effort in California cost three hundred and
fifty thousand dollars. Later, his headquarters put the total at "from
one-half to three-quarters of a million dollars." "We never thought California would eat money like that," one of Wallace's friends said with awe
in his voice. "We knew it was going to be a tough one. That was one
reason we started there. We knew if we could get on the ballot in California we could get on it almost anywhere. But it still shook us." By the
middle of January, 107,000 Californians had reregistered, and the Rubicon had been crossed.

It cost only twenty thousand dollars to collect twice as many signatures in Georgia. (Even that was dear by the standards of Kentucky,
where a mail campaign brought in the required 10,000 signatures in no
time for a total expenditure of eighteen dollars and thirty-five cents!)
There was no need for airplanes, bulletproof lecterns, or bodyguards
in Georgia, and indeed no need for the candidate. The whole business
was quietly put together by the men who had been running the state for
years. "Every campaign I've ever been in," Roy Harris told us, "we
started at the top and worked down, with organizations in each Congressional District and county and even down to townships and militia
districts. Well now, that costs money. This time we didn't need to do
any organizing like that." Harris got together with a number of his
old friends, carefully choosing *ex*-officeholders who would have nothing
to lose by being active for Wallace, and called a convention for April
4 in the Henry Grady Hotel in Atlanta. There was Marvin Griffin, an
ex-governor; Peter Zack Geer, an ex-lieutenant-governor; Randall Evans,
Fred Hand, and Roy Harris himself, all ex-speakers of the Georgia
House; and a couple more "good old boys" from different parts of the
state, all veterans of many years in state Democratic politics. In a sense,
the Wallace campaign was an opportunity for this older generation of
courthouse politicians to take revenge on a world that had turned its
back on them since the Supreme Court's redistricting decision in *Baker
v. Carr* and the consequent abolition of Georgia's nefarious county-unit
system. (Nominations for the governorship, the Senate seats, and certain
other offices in Georgia had previously been determined not by popular
votes but by "unit votes" alloted to each county. Populous urban counties
like Fulton [Atlanta] were deliberately underrepresented in the allotment
of units to safeguard the hegemony of the small, conservative, rural
counties.) "They reckoned the redistricting would kill us," said Harris,
"me and the people like me who grew up under the county-unit system.
Well, sir, they're the ones who are in trouble now!" In many Northern

states, it would not have been unfair to apply the much-abused catch-word, New Politics, to the Wallace campaign. In Georgia, the Wallace campaign was the Old Politics, naked and unashamed.

The old politicians like Fred Hand who organized the Wallace drive in Georgia were astonished by the response they got from the grass roots. Roy Harris checked with his friend Ben Fortson, the secretary of state, and found out that they had to file a charter for the American Independent Party. He did that. Then, to Harris's astonishment, about six thousand people showed up for the convention, on April 4—far too many for the hall. But that took care of the petitions problem straightaway. "A feller" had come over from Montgomery with some sample petitions "in his vest pocket." Harris got his printer—he publishes a vehemently right-wing paper called the *Augusta Courier*—to print 50,000 petitions and got the folks at the convention to circulate them in their home towns. The law required 100,000 signatures; before Harris and his friends knew where they were, they had 210,000. They cut out 30,000, and that was that. "That was all the campaigning we've done," said Harris cheerfully. "You know all those Wallace stickers and buttons you see? Well, we've been *selling* them." The Wallace headquarters at the Henry Grady was selling bumper stickers for a dollar, a Wallace record of no obvious charm for a dollar-fifty, and so on. Everything was going like hot cakes.

Unlikely as it might seem, the old courthouse crowd, who had been barking segregation and Southern resistance to increasingly indifferent Georgians for years, now found themselves at the head of an authentic popular movement. "It scares me," said Harris frankly, "it's not my kind of politics." An anonymous Georgian explained what made people feel that way about George Wallace. Straightening up from beneath a truck he had been fixing, he said, "I don't intend to vote for anybody up in Washington again, and I'll tell ya why. When I get to thinkin' about how hard I work, and how damn greasy I get, and I start thinkin' about how much you-all take out of my pay packet for taxes and all, and I see those people settin' on their porches spendin' my money, why, I get so damn mad I just say to myself, I ain't never goin' to vote for them sons o' bitches again!"

By the spring, George Wallace couldn't wait to see how many voters in Indiana and Oregon—"this man in the textile mill, this man in the steel mill," the barber and the beautician and the cop—felt the same way. In Montgomery in April, he was pulling polls out of his pockets which purported to show that automobile workers in South Bend or teamsters in St. Louis were solidly for him. Steadily the "Mission Impossible" boys ticked off the states where Wallace would be on the ballot. In early March, it took just seven and a half minutes to get on the ballot in Nebraska, and New Jersey, deep in enemy country, fell almost as easily a few days later. On February 29, the Louis Harris poll had an ominous shock for the readers of its Northern-liberal newspaper clients: "It is entirely possible," Harris led off, "that former Vice-President Richard Nixon could draw even with President Johnson in a two-way contest for the White House, only to find that the third-party candidacy of former Alabama governor, George Wallace, has robbed him of his chance for election." And in an interview with one of us a few days later, Harris admitted that he suspected that Wallace had not yet reached his peak in the North, where, Harris said, "low-income whites are even more alienated than Negroes."

This was all before the dramatic weeks of early April. Everything that happened in the spring—the President's withdrawal, the assassination of Dr. King, the riots, even the first faint prospect of a negotiated settlement in Vietnam—tended to increase Wallace's appeal for the millions of voters who feared Robert Kennedy, or were appalled by the riots, or demanded victory. The very feeling that this was a wild, whirling year in which anything could happen and any protest might attract followers, favored Wallace, and his standing in the national polls began to climb. Still he did not make the final move.

The reason, of course, was Lurleen's health. Wallace had announced, on February 8 at a press conference in Washington, that he was "running to win." That same week he had paid for half-hour film and videotape programs in selected Northern and border markets. Then Lurleen had to go to the hospital. She had already undergone surgery for cancer in Houston in July 1967, but Wallace insisted that she wanted him to go ahead with his Presidential bid. "Honey," he says he told her one night after one of the California forays, "I don't think we ought to do it," and she said, "Well, I'll be mighty disappointed if we don't." She had to have another cancer operation on February 22, and Wallace, who had never seemed particularly close to her when she was well, went to Houston with her. She began to recover and came back to Montgomery, a frail, wan woman who really was extraordinarily popular. Secretaries would stop in the corridors of the Capitol and say, "Have you heard, she's much better." Then, on March 12, just as George was about to start campaigning again, in Texas, she had to have another operation, this time for an abscess. May 7 was the day of the Alabama primary.

Wallace was the candidate on the Democratic ticket. ("I'm an Alabama Democrat," he explained once, "not a national Democrat. I'm not kin to those folks. The difference between an Alabama Democrat and a national Democrat is like the difference between a Communist and a non-Communist.") That night, he planned to make a last statewide telecast —not to make sure of victory, for that was sure enough anyway, but to drive the nail right home for the benefit of the "distortin' news media." During the day he heard that Lurleen had taken a sudden turn for the worse, and he canceled the broadcast. That night she died.

It had not been a particularly happy or successful marriage, as we have seen, but Wallace had come to depend on it perhaps more than he realized. Once, after his wife's death, a friend saw him arrive exhausted in a hotel room and, without thinking, begin automatically to dial a number in Montgomery, only to drop the receiver suddenly, his face white and his hand shaking, as he realized there was no one there to hear his day's news. Politically, too, there were problems. The government of Alabama, which was to have been his political and logistic base for the next six years, suddenly passed to a stranger. The lieutenant-governor, Albert Brewer, while a Wallace supporter, might nevertheless be counted on to develop hankerings after independence sooner or later, and Wallace could, in any case, no longer confront potential rivals or contributors with the certainty that they would have to deal with him for the foreseeable future. But Mrs. Wallace's death settled one thing: there was no longer anything to prevent George Wallace from setting out in search of his political destiny.

His first tour, starting on June 7 and lasting eleven days, did not leave the South. It was essentially a fundraising expedition, and as such it was successful. In other respects, it was not impressive. In Atlanta, for example, the headquarters was a shambles. Arrangements for dealing with the press were chaotic, and security, despite a force of twenty-seven Secret Service men, signaling by their presence his status as a full-fledged national candidate, was deplorable. One of us walked unchallenged into his meeting and could easily have shot the candidate from a range of a few feet in spite of the bulletproof lectern. The auditorium was half empty, and the candidate was late. But everybody stood and sang "Dixie" *fortissimo*, and there were periodic standing ovations throughout The Speech.

The question was how the same performance would go down without "Dixie," north of the Mason-Dixon line. A month later, the answer was that, up to a point at least, it would go down very well.

Of course, there were heckling and scuffling, often enough. After one particularly vigorous scrimmage, in Minneapolis on July 4, President Johnson himself was moved to say a few words about the spirit of 1776. But all the time, Wallace was getting on the ballot in one Northern state after another. By the end of July, the score had reached thirty-nine.

His campaign settled into a pattern. He traveled in a propeller plane, which condemned him to relatively short and predictable hops, and reporters spoiled by the Nixon and Kennedy trips grumbled about the cold food and Dr. Pepper in place of hot meals and free Bloody Marys. The entourage was almost a hundred per cent Alabamian: thick amiable fellows with short hair and excellent manners who politely refused to talk about issues, and amiable young ladies with long skirts and lacquered sausages of platinum-blond hair who chattered happily about anything and everything, to the great relief of the press. Wallace himself hates flying, and he spent long hours morosely silent, in a front seat, with his feet up against the wall, stirring only to march down the aisle prudently to the men's room before each landing.

On July 26, Wallace spent a typical day in Rhode Island, deep in the heart of hostile territory—or so anyone would have assumed before 1968. His visit was timed to coincide with the collection of the five hundred signatures required in that state on the petition. Five hundred was a cinch: Joe Di Carlo took care of that in four days. And apart from a temporary office at the Sheraton in Providence over the weekend, that was the extent of the Wallace organization in Rhode Island at this stage.

Outside the hotel, a small crowd had gathered. Leaflets warning all and sundry of Wallace's evil schemes had been distributed by Resistance, an organization originally aimed at opposing the draft; but people seemed more curious than hostile. Wallace appeared and shook hands with almost everyone in sight, which was not difficult, and skillfully seized a hapless black boy of about twelve, clutched him fervently by the shoulder, and held him triumphantly in front of a television camera in this pose, grinning ferociously.

His first date was with a local television station which had offered an hour's free time to any Presidential candidate willing to undergo a telephone interview with all comers. Wallace opened smoothly with a dig at Governor John Chafee, who had been rash enough to predict that Wallace wouldn't get fifty signatures in Rhode Island and had then, the previous day, signed a round robin at the governors' conference supporting a pact against him: "Am I a threat, or not?" Most of the people who called in were hostile, but Wallace smoothly and skillfully fielded their questions and said many things that sounded sensible and moderate to the average voter, mixed up with some predictably appalling stands on other issues. Welfare? "A waste of money. Alabama doesn't have welfare programs. Able-bodied men work there." McCarthyism? "He wasn't all wrong. I'm tired of folks being killed by Communists when there are Communists in the Defense Department and college professors call for a Communist victory and college students wave the Vietcong flag." Fair housing laws? "I'd repeal them."

The Wallace rally that evening was in a hall owned by the Shriners, at a place called Rhodes-on-the-Pawtuxet. The manageress said it cost only a few hundred dollars to hire, and they'd had Secret Service there all day, looking for bombs. Outside, there were youths dressed in sheets, satirizing the Klan with anti-Wallace placards. Inside, well-scrubbed, healthy-looking students with open faces were selling Wallace literature and buttons and straw boaters with red, white, and blue ribbons. Quite a lot of them were Rhode Island kids who attended Southern colleges. (Where is that Mason-Dixon line?) A Providence boy who was to be graduated from Ole Miss in a year said he was going straight into the Marines as a second lieutenant. "The draft doesn't bother me," he said proudly. "I love the South, *and* Wallace."

The warm-up program dragged. A country-and-western band. Then the Taylor sisters, Mona and Lisa, with "Are You for Wallace?"—more in the tradition of the old wooden country church. And then suddenly, amid cheers from the majority and resolute booing from some thirty-five young blacks, he was there. He was able to announce, Wallace said, that they'd gotten their five hundred signatures in the first five minutes. Cheers and boos. Then serious, angry yelling from the black hecklers. He let it happen. And then said, with no introduction at all, "I want to talk about racism." There was a sudden flourish of banners from the black contingent, cheered by perhaps half a dozen whites: "Send Wallace Home to Europe!" "Racism Must Go!" After a few minutes of this, with the television crews shoving their way about the hall trying to get their footage, and Wallace standing smirking on the platform, he said, "Go ahead! After November, you people are *through*!" And he told them how his wife had received all the black votes in Alabama, even in Selma. At this, one black man rushed up to the front of the hall, almost literally apoplectic with anger. He frothed and writhed and shrieked for several minutes, again on camera. And then Wallace said *these* were the people the "pointy-heads" wanted to run everything—and that did it. The blacks gave one roar of outrage, and the hall became a great melee. The police and the television crews charged into the thick of it, and after a good deal of punching and swearing and no serious injuries, the blacks retreated from the hall, chanting their slogans, only to file back in again a few moments later.

Wallace greeted them with some pious observations about freedom of speech and then called for the indictment of those college professors who were calling for Communist victory. That led to his line about anarchists who lie down in front of the President's car, which he delivered in the unbowdlerized version to gales of laughter and applause. "They'd find it was the last car they lay down in front of." A pause. And then, menacingly, "Try me and see!"

This was a strange brew with which to try to charm Northern voters, and the pundits and commentators should not perhaps be blamed for being so slow to take its vendor seriously. Some newspapers, indeed, played down their coverage of Wallace as a deliberate policy, like parents who refuse to look when their child is doing something naughty for fear it might encourage him to show off. In the end, it was probably the polls that were decisive. They could no longer be ignored. Wallace rose, not steadily, but inexorably. Ten per cent of the electorate in October. Twelve per cent in December. (This is Harris.) Fifteen per cent in a Nixon-Johnson race in late March. Nineteen per cent with McCarthy running against Rockefeller—two "pointy-heads." By mid-July, sixteen per cent with McCarthy against Nixon, and seventeen per cent in the more probable conjuncture, Nixon against Humphrey. In Gallup, eleven per cent in late February, fourteen per cent in early May, sixteen per cent in mid-July. And perhaps the most chilling thought of all was tersely put in George Gallup's report on May 7: "If the Presidential election were being held today, the strong possibility exists that third-party candidate George Wallace would deny either major party candidate the electoral votes needed to win."

If, for the first half of the year, the press and the politicians had been slow to take Wallace in earnest, suddenly in July they began to overcompensate for their mistake. Television crews began to burrow through the crowds at Wallace rallies looking for trouble. (They can hardly be blamed for giving the public what it wanted. As a leading British current-affairs television producer likes to say to his reporters, "Don't forget we are in the bad news business!") Reporters began to throng to Wallace's meetings, and columnists alternately puzzled over his program—usually quite missing the code to what he was saying—and pontificated about his significance.

Then, in July, two well-intentioned efforts were made to neutralize him. The details of these two stop-Wallace plans, one endorsed by the *Washington Post* and the second proposed by two leading Congressmen, will be discussed later. But by the eve of the conventions, George Wallace had already established certain facts: He would be a national candidate. He would have serious support in the North. "Law 'n' order" was supplanting Vietnam as the prime issue of the campaign. And none of the candidates in the two major parties could any longer afford to ignore the existence of the man from Alabama.

ACT VII

California:
Right Back Where
We Started From

1

Oregon: The Twenty-eighth Election

"I am not one of those who think coming in second or third is winning."

—Robert F. Kennedy, Portland, Oregon, May 29

If Robert Kennedy had had any choice, he would not have entered the Oregon Democratic Party primary. But Oregon does not offer Presidential candidates a choice. As soon as newspapers and television announced his candidacy, his name, by state law, went on to the ballot for May 28. He could have it removed only by swearing an affidavit saying that he did not wish to be President—which of course was out of the question. There was never a good chance that he could win the state, and perhaps he might have mounted simply a token campaign there, but he had an unbroken record of twenty-seven Kennedy victories to preserve.

A magazine recently made an inquiry into the vacation habits of the American people. The people of forty-nine states said they liked to go out of state for their holidays. The people of Oregon replied that their favorite vacation state was . . . Oregon.

Oregonians have much to be chauvinistic about. Their state is a very beautiful one, mountainous and heavily timbered. Outside the few large towns, the aura of the old West and the Oregon Trail is still alive. People take conscious pride in their individualism, the fact that they are still on their own. They are conservative, but it is a mild and liberal conservatism.

From the start, it was McCarthy's state. (Indeed, if America consisted of a union of fifty Oregons, the skeptical and easygoing McCarthy would no doubt make an excellent President of it.) Oregon's huge college population was for McCarthy, and the prosperous small farmers liked his quiet ways and the country air he could assume. His oblique, complex speeches were to the taste of people who liked to think of themselves as swayed by reason rather than emotion. Most of all, McCarthy at last had an organization behind him that knew the state, knew what the people wanted, and knew how to get through to them. This, it must sadly be made clear, had little to do with the national staff of the McCarthy campaign.

The Oregon movement was established before McCarthy declared his candidacy by a group of people who simply wanted, at first, to do *something* about the war. Midway through 1967, they saw that antiwar feeling in the state, fostered by Senators Hatfield and Morse, was so strong it could sustain a Democratic candidate on that plank alone. On October 29, they had their first formal meeting.

In a certain sense, it was not a "protest" meeting. This was a gathering of quiet, determined people: well-to-do, middle-class Americans with a little political experience. It was held at the YWCA in Salem, the state capital, and the conveners were Howard Morgan, a former state Democratic chairman, and Blaine Whipple, a former journalist turned real-estate broker. ("The only Democratic real-estate man in America," he calls himself jokingly.) Eighty people were asked, and all but five showed up.

The decision was taken to invite someone to run in the primary, and although several names were mentioned, only two were discussed seriously: Robert Kennedy, the natural choice, and McCarthy.

Whipple, a tall, bespectacled man of thirty-eight, recalls that Kennedy was discussed at length. "But we had to drop him fairly quickly, because he kept saying he supported Johnson's stand on the war. So we were left with McCarthy as the only possible candidate, although quite a few of the people knew very little about him at the time." The meeting sent a delegation of three to see McCarthy in Washington. "He didn't commit himself then," Whipple recalls. "But he didn't turn us down, either. In any event, he had declared in a month—on November thirtieth—and I think we can claim that we were one of the first groups to convince him he should run."

McCarthy did not show up in Oregon until February 1, 1968. He came in on a commercial flight, Whipple booked him into a motel near the Portland airport, and he and Howard Morgan had dinner with him before taking him to a party at Whipple's house. It was fortunate that the enthusiasm of the Oregonians was at a high level, because McCarthy might well have dampened it that night.

Slightly worried by McCarthy's nonchalant approach to campaigning, Whipple offered to show him how he should tackle the Oregon primary. "I had all sorts of facts and figures on population and income and that sort of thing, and I offered to take him through them." McCarthy gave the reply that was to become something like a private slogan throughout his campaign: "I should remind you that you are the people who asked me to run. I am what I am, and I won't be changing. You will have to make your decisions on what you will do in this campaign on what you know of me already." It was scarcely a call to battle, and he said the same to the fifty guests at the party. "It's all up to you. You must accept me for what I am or forget this romance right now." McCarthy then left and did not reappear in the state until May 10.

As a matter of fact, the McCarthy campaign probably benefited from the leader's absence—or more particularly, from the absence of his well-meaning but ill-informed national staff, who were engaged in running two disastrous campaigns in Indiana and Nebraska during April and May. Left to itself, the Oregon campaign, now formally led by Morgan and Whipple, established fifty headquarters throughout the state and began to use the student population to get the news across that there was a peace candidate available. They sent canvassers to places which had never seen a political worker, and they even sent out canvassers on horseback—which, though it may not have impressed the farmers, made the front pages in the city.

It was a campaign in which local knowledge was deployed sensibly —which is something of a rarity, judging by the standards of 1968. Whipple and Morgan handled McCarthy's scheduling and planned his radio and TV advertisements, thus avoiding one or two near errors by the out-of-towners who did come in. "They had one great idea," Whipple recalls. "They wanted to run one five-minute ad which used quotes from Hatfield and Morse condemning the war. They hadn't realized that this sort of ad would alienate the Democrats who were going to vote against Morse in the Democratic primary and would also give the impression that Hatfield, a Republican, was telling Democrats how to vote. They're very independent voters up here, and they wouldn't have liked that one bit."

Despite McCarthy's stern remarks in February, the Oregonians even managed to bend him a little toward the media. Their great triumph was to insert him, somewhat unwilling, into a canoe which he paddled down the Willamette River, scoring a *Life* magazine cover out of it.

Kennedy's problems in Oregon derived from hurry and—surprisingly, in view of the legend—his poor political-intelligence system. He chose Congresswoman Edith Green to run his campaign, mainly because she had run his brother's successful primary campaign there in 1960. The Kennedy staff also calculated that, because Mrs. Green always won well in her district, she must be popular in the state. They miscalculated badly. Mrs. Green, a prickly ex-schoolteacher, was not at all popular— or even very well known—in Oregon. Young Democrats referred to her nastily as "the Madame Nhu of Oregon." Her success in 1960 owed much to the fact that John Kennedy's only active opponent was Wayne Morse, running as a favorite son. Humphrey, although still on the ballot, had been shattered in the West Virginia primary a few weeks earlier and was no longer campaigning. Away in Washington a great deal of the time, Mrs. Green did not develop an organization and failed to deliver even her own district to Kennedy.

At the end of April, one of Kennedy's own men from New York, William vanden Heuvel, went to Oregon to look over the situation. Within twenty-four hours, he had telephoned Kennedy to say, "This is where they're going to take us." A poll taken on May 1 confirmed his pessimism, showing McCarthy with 29 per cent, Kennedy with 28 per cent, and Johnson (still on the ballot, but out of the race) with 27. The mathematics were all too clear: the Johnson voters would not vote for their leader's greatest enemy, and it was likely that a big bloc of them would go to McCarthy.

Kennedy's reaction to the impending possibility of defeat in Oregon was a strange one, and it would be hard to imagine any other politician acting in the way he did. On May 21, a week before the Oregon primary, after a speech at the San Francisco Press Club, he answered a journalist's question by saying, "I think that if I get beaten in any primary, I am not a very viable candidate." He later explained that he hoped that this would make people realize how important it was to vote for him; but it was an answer that was to plague him at almost every press conference until his death.

As the two Western primary campaigns tightened up, Kennedy and McCarthy shuttled almost daily between the two states. Everyone was tensely aware that the Oregon result could crucially affect California polling one week later. One or the other—maybe both—of the candidacies was likely to be destroyed. And, as the showdown approached, tensions began to form between the McCarthy and Kennedy camps which were to make reconciliation all but impossible.

McCarthy's first major attack on Kennedy sprang out of a near disaster for his own campaign. On May 21, he flew into Coos Bay, Oregon. On the plane, he was talking to E. W. (Ned) Kenworthy of the *New York Times*. Unguardedly—he was very tired—he said there might be circumstances in which he could support Humphrey, although he wouldn't take a Cabinet post. In cold print, it looked as if McCarthy were signaling that he was coming round to Humphrey, but McCarthy was probably talking entirely in hypothesis—i.e., "I could support Humphrey if he changed his policies drastically." To many supporters, it looked as though McCarthy was quitting, and this was very much how people in California saw it. Gerald Hill, chairman of the California Democratic Council and now cochairman of McCarthy's California campaign, after being on the awkward end of a series of outraged telephone calls from fundraisers and others, set out for the Canterbury Hotel in San Francisco, where McCarthy's new manager, Thomas Finney, was staying. Bursting through a varied crowd of acolytes, Hill cried, "This is a disaster!" Finney cut him short, saying, "He's compounded it by talking about Cabinet posts." They agreed that the days of the "low-key" McCarthy speech would have to be closed: only a fighting speech from McCarthy, setting himself apart from all the other candidates, could save the situation.

There was an opportunity next evening at the Cow Palace in San Francisco. And the need for a strong speech fitted in perfectly with the desires of McCarthy's two young speech-writers, Paul Gorman and Jeremy Larner, who for weeks had been pressing their candidate to come out with firmer and more radical definitions of his position. Gorman was already working on a speech for the Cow Palace, and, thus encouraged, he began to strengthen it considerably. According to Hill and most other McCarthy people, the speech, which McCarthy gave again in Oregon a few days later, was intended to "end the rumors that Gene was playing footsie with Hubert." But most Kennedy supporters saw it as a savage attack on their man. And they had something to go on.

Essentially, the speech argued that the war in Vietnam, rather than being an isolated incident, grew out of a systematic delusion about America's proper role in the world—and that John Kennedy, and Robert Kennedy, and Hubert Humphrey, were all champions of that delusion.

The early passages contained a number of elegant jabs at Kennedy's candidacy:

> When I said I would enter the New Hampshire primary, at the beginning of the year, there were other candidates, particularly one from New York, who said he did not want to divide the party. I thought the time had come to divide the party if it was not already divided. . . . The Vice-President, at that time, was calling for unity and saying that this was no time for dissent. . . .
>
> I felt—and I don't mean to exaggerate—that this was a time when every politician ought to take some chance on his future, for the good of the country.

McCarthy now worked up to deal with Senator Kennedy's famous spaniel, Freckles, which had been much in evidence on the West Coast:

> After New Hampshire, things began to change. The Senator from New York said he was now going to enter the contest, and his explanation was a little involved, but a part of it was that he had stayed out of New Hampshire because he thought his entrance would not permit a clear test on the issues—that personality would have been an important factor. . . . Here in California [Oregon], I have not been able to understand how bringing Freckles out really helped to make it easier to choose on the basis of the issues. I could have brought my dog—and I think that in a straight contest between Freckles and my dog, that Eric would win—but . . . I think I can campaign against both the Senator from New York and his dog.

McCarthy then moved on, via a crack at Humphrey ("The Vice-President has taken a stand recently of having no real position. Yesterday . . . the substance of his speech was that if people wanted a miracle worker, not to vote for him. I don't think that opens up much by way of choice."), to matters of policy:

> Involvement in Vietnam was no accident: it did not happen overnight. We did not wake up one morning and find ourselves with half a million men in that part of the world, just by chance—it was not a landing in the dark—not exactly. It was no departure from the kind of diplomacy which we had been following up to that time . . . it was written in the past, if we had only seen.

American foreign policy, McCarthy claimed, was still in the Dulles Cold War tradition—still driven by "the idea that somehow we had a great moral mission to control the entire world." This conception had been built into the institutions of foreign policy, the State Department and the CIA; and out of "a sort of University of the Cold War" came leaders who have been guiding our policies ever since the early fifties.

To pretend, he said, that Communist China did not exist might have
been all right for a year or two after 1949, but to ignore it for twenty
years was to carry the thing too far. "Nothing has happened in the last
twenty years—in the last two administrations—to move on toward any
kind of better understanding or better communication between that
country and the United States." Dean Rusk, he added, was always warning that by the year 2000 there would be a billion Chinese, but "he
doesn't admit there are any now."

> [The] foundation [of American foreign policy] has remained the same
> as it was in the early fifties and in the sixties: containment and a con-
> tinuation of the Cold War . . . some new sails on the ships, some new
> rhetoric—instead of containment it is counterinsurgency—but no dif-
> ference in the policy, essentially the same diplomacy assuming for itself
> the role of the world's judge and the world's policeman.

This was a direct attack on the Kennedy Administration—and on
its concept of counterinsurgency. The reason it hurt, of course, was that
it *was* a valid point. John Kennedy had not done a great deal to change
the basic thrust of American foreign policy. McCarthy went to say that
the blame for Vietnam could not be fastened on Lyndon Johnson alone,
and then he attacked by name a whole series of Kennedy foreign-affairs
appointments:

> I suppose that the justification of that war, all the rhetoric and folly of
> the earlier years, received its fullest endorsement, its fullest expression,
> from the advocation of it at the present time from the Secretary of State
> Dean Rusk, Mr. Walt Rostow, McGeorge Bundy, and William Bundy.
> . . . Any man who played a prominent role in developing the policies
> of the early sixties, I think, can be called upon to explain his role in
> those policies, and not just in those policies but in the development of
> the process. . . . The policies are not the product of specific misjudg-
> ments—they grow from a systematic misconception of America and of
> its role in the world.
>   I am not convinced that the Senator from New York has entirely
> renounced those misconceptions, nor is the Vice-President prepared to
> say that the process is wrong, as well as what it produces. If they did,
> in the case of the Senator from New York, I would find it very difficult
> to explain why he would use an endorsement from the former Secretary
> of Defense who was one of the principal engineers of those policies.
> I have not yet heard him criticize, in this campaign at least . . . the
> role of the military in this nation, nor the Department of State, nor the
> Central Intelligence Agency.

Kennedy even suffered a flick of the lash for that unfortunate phrase
in his declaration statement, the one which had made his younger staff so

unhappy. "We continue to call upon America to assume the moral leadership of the planet, at least some of us do. This is an echo of John Foster Dulles," said McCarthy.

McCarthy wound up with a tough declaration that he would make no deals with other candidates, and would not surrender. It was an effective and eloquent speech, and it touched on big questions. When McCarthy delivered it for the second time, at the vast Portland Coliseum on May 27, even so battle-stained a reporter as Ned Kenworthy left the auditorium saying, "By Jesus, we've got a candidate at last!" But to Kennedy loyalists it was even more intolerable than McCarthy's joke that "Bobby threatened to hold his breath unless the people of Oregon voted for him."

McCarthy's fairly blunt criticism of John Kennedy was something very rare in public debate among liberal Democrats. But, more important, McCarthy cast doubts on the validity of Robert Kennedy's liberal sentiment, the famous "conversion" he had undergone. He did not for a moment step outside the conventions of straightforward, competitive politics, and for an ordinary politician and his followers it would have been a routine attack, but Kennedy was not an ordinary politician, and his followers were bound to him by a loyalty that could tolerate no attacks on him. Many of them felt a moral disdain for McCarthy, because he did not campaign with their own fierce energy. One day, in the Kennedy headquarters in Portland, someone mentioned to Stephen Smith that he had just bumped into McCarthy right outside. "How'd he look?" asked Smith. "He looked great, as a matter of fact," was the reply. "So he should look great," said Smith tightly. "He gets eight hours' sleep a night, doesn't he?"

In the last few days before the primary, Kennedy professionals arrived in force to look things over: Larry O'Brien, Pierre Salinger, and Pat Lucey. But now the private polls showed McCarthy two points behind Kennedy and gaining. "Of course, we all knew," says Lucey, "that McCarthy usually ran better than the polls. When I showed Pierre these polls for the first time, he looked as if someone had just thrown a bucket of cold water in his face."

Discussion within the Kennedy camp was now about whether the situation might be restored by having a television debate with McCarthy. McCarthy was willing and, on Friday, May 24, had announced that he had bought a half hour of Portland television time for Saturday night. He was prepared, he said—in the manner of a lord inviting an enemy to duel in the grounds—to extend his hospitality to Senator Kennedy for a debate in that half hour.

On Saturday, Adam Walinsky and Pat Lucey tried hard to persuade Kennedy to take up the challenge. O'Brien was neutral. After a lot of argument, Kennedy said, dismissively, "I don't want to talk to you any more. You'll have to talk to Larry." His chief reason for not wanting to debate was that he was exhausted—he had had only three hours' sleep, after a Friday night gala in California. Instead, Kennedy went down to the beach with Freckles and a large covey of photographers. The picture coverage which resulted was probably a mistake, in that the Oregonian voters already questioned the *gravitas* of the Kennedy campaign, and the beach frolics were likely to confirm their suspicions.

By polling day there was no real doubt what the outcome would be. Kennedy had some campaigning to do in California, so arrangements were made to fly to Los Angeles and shuttle back in the evening to accept defeat. The plane was crowded with his staff, as anxious and weary as he, and with reporters who were beginning to taste a new drama in the atmosphere. Most of the newsmen who traveled with Kennedy admired him, and some counted themselves as committed friends. But the spectacle of a losing Kennedy was a new, therefore interesting, phenomenon. The element of the voyeur present in almost every reporter responded to the dramatic possibilities of the idea that Kennedy's grand assault upon the Presidency might go down in disaster.

Joseph Alsop, the irascible columnist who has long been a friend of the Kennedy family, began to put the point to the candidate with remarkable bluntness. "Oregon looks bad. California is turning against you. You are going to destroy yourself politically. Why did you do it?" Kennedy shook his head and would not answer. "I don't want to talk," he said. "I want to sing with my friends." Bobby Darin, the singer and actor and a long-time Kennedy supporter, was sitting near by, with his guitar over his knees. Kennedy and he sang folk songs together until the plane arrived in Los Angeles.

At least, in Oregon, there was no great agony of waiting. The first computer projection came through fifteen minutes after the polls closed at eight p.m. It showed McCarthy taking forty-six per cent, Kennedy thirty-six, and Johnson (still trapped on the ballot) three. NBC said firmly that McCarthy had won. Kennedy was very gracious about it. He told his supporters in the ballroom of the Benson Hotel in Portland that he had sent a congratulatory telegram to McCarthy, pointing out that the great triumph was that between them they had collected a massive vote against the Administration. "The first person I met when I got out of the elevator," he said, "was a lady who asked me what it was like to be the first Kennedy to lose after twenty-seven elections. I told her Abe Lincoln's joke about the man who was being ridden out of town on a rail. Apparently, he looked at the crowd and said, 'If it wasn't for the honor, I'd rather have passed it up.' " The mourners moved quietly down to the gloomy Old Englysshe bar in the basement.

Usually, when the result came in in a Kennedy election, the retainers took part in an eager rush to get before the TV cameras, to join the phalanx on the platform as the leader made his speech. On this occasion, there was no such rush. "I guess," said Larry O'Brien, who never loses his sense of humor, "that you could have fired a cannon into the Benson ballroom and not hit any of us."

Naturally, the McCarthy people celebrated as if there were no tomorrow. Their headquarters, about two hundred yards from the Benson, in a grandiose building that had been a Masonic lodge, now presented a very curious appearance, with its cabalistic signs and symbols encrusted with McCarthy flowers and posters. In the main room, the flower children jumped up and down and danced to the music of a Dixieland band, cheering each progress count as it came over on television. In a side room, the adults anesthetized their eardrums against the noise with doses of vodka and bourbon.

Each set of figures was an excuse for a new cry of "We want Gene!" or "Gene sixty-eight—Hubert'll have to wait" or "Gene sixty-eight— they'll all have to wait." Under the screams, the band played on, churning out "Dixieland One-Step," "That's A-Plenty," and "When the Saints Go Marching In." Only once did a bandsman show any animation, and that was when an enthusiastic girl climbed onto the leader's trombone case to get a better view. "Lady," he told her, "primaries come and go, but that trombone case has to last forever."

McCarthy did not appear until ten-fifteen. He gave a rather nervous wave and waited for the screams to die down. "It's been a good night for all of us," he began. "As I said, after Indiana there was a shakedown. In Indiana we found our mistakes, and in Nebraska we found theirs. In Nebraska, I said that many wagons got to the Missouri, but the real test began when they crossed and started up the Oregon Trail. Here we have shown who had the staying power, who had the strength and the commitment. We had the best horses, the best wagons, and the best men and women. Now the second test is California." He added, with uncharacteristic obviousness: "California, here we come!"

Although the Kennedy political organization was as capable of incompetence as any other, people had not thought so. The result of the Oregon primary—the first electoral reverse for one of the Kennedy brothers in twenty-eight outings—came as a shock, and in the ensuing debate it was agreed that Kennedy had suffered damage to his "charisma." This feeling was clearly shared by the Kennedy staff, who were shaken far more deeply than was reasonable, considering that Oregon was neither the most important nor the most representative of states and that the margin of defeat was not large. Bitterness toward McCarthy climbed to a new peak. The normally cool and sensible speechwriter Peter Edelman, for instance, began to talk about McCarthy's being "irresponsible" and to accuse him of "cheerful iconoclasm." This, because McCarthy had suggested that Rusk and Hoover should be fired! Unaccountable campaign decisions were made in California, and plans and schedules began to alter with bewildering rapidity. Usually the *équipe* preserved a cool façade; now there were bursts of raw temper even from such poised figures as Adam Walinsky. On one hot and sweaty train journey, the normally jovial advance man Dick Tuck was found shaking a reporter by the throat and cursing him furiously.

Some explanation of this intemperate reaction may emerge from close examination of the word "charisma," so frequently applied to Kennedy's political personality. The word, used freely in political commentary at least since Eisenhower's victory in 1952, sometimes means nothing more than "glamour." Its simple dictionary meaning is "grace" or "God-given favor," but there is a more important meaning to the word as it was used by the German father of modern sociology, Max Weber, in his great unfinished work *Economics and Society* (translated in full for the first time in 1968). Drawing on examples as diverse as ancient Chinese empires, modern American capitalism, medieval Europe, and tribal African life, Weber argued that human society exhibits only three "ultimate principles" of domination, or command.

One is *bureaucratic,* in which obedience is given to a set of "rational" rules rather that to any particular person. Another is *traditional,* founded upon custom and habit, which prescribes obedience to some particular person. Obedience is given because it has always been given in the past. But personal authority can have its source in the very opposite, viz., the surrender to the extraordinary, the belief in *charisma,* i.e., actual revelation or grace resting in such a person as a saviour, a prophet or a hero.

Bureaucratic authority arises out of regular settlement of ordinary needs along rationalistic lines. Charismatic authority arises when there are special needs, which cannot be satisfied by the ordinary rules, but only by the bearers of special gifts of body and mind. Charismatic rulership, says Weber, "results from unusual, especially political or economic, situations. . . . It arises from collective excitement produced by extraordinary events and from a surrender to heroism of any kind." The matrix Weber describes here sounds very like that out of which Robert Kennedy's authority emerged. There was in America, and had been for some time, a feeling that there was a malfunction in society so gross and puzzling that no ordinary political operation could make any impact on it. (This, arguably, derives from the gap between perception and reality which we mentioned at the beginning of this story.) Robert Kennedy had been at the center of great collective excitements, had shown great heroism, and was one of a political family who were thought almost invincible when they set out to do something. (He had, with his brother, taken part in several great, if somewhat contrived, modern-dress miracles, such as the Cuban missile crisis.) He was therefore an automatic candidate for the role of charismatic rescuer, one which he filled in certain respects very well. For instance, Weber describes the staff a charismatic leader is likely have around him:

> It is based in an emotional form of communal relationship. The administrative staff of a charismatic leader does not consist of officials. . . . It is not chosen on the basis of social privilege nor from the point of view of domestic or personal dependency. It is rather chosen in terms of the charismatic qualities of its members. . . . There is no such thing as appointment or dismissal, no career, no promotion. There is only a call at the instance of the leader on the basis of the charismatic authority of those he summons. There is no hierarchy; the leader merely intervenes in general or individual cases when he considers the members of his staff lacking in charismatic qualification for a given task.

This reads like a contemporary description of the Kennedy following: that loose, heterogeneous band of people united only by their passionate commitment to Kennedy. It is also the "vast but indefinite mass of councillors, retainers and servants, tailing off into those believed to be well-wishers" of the late medieval lord. The formlessness of the Kennedy organization was notorious, and more orthodox politicians

complained that they never knew who was in charge of a Kennedy operation. A remarkable number of people contributed their share to the
Kennedy charisma: writers, artists, singers, athletes, executives, heroes,
academics, and other politicians. Men who held no formal salaried post
with Kennedy would drop whatever they might be doing and undertake a
mission for him at the sound of a phone call. As Edwin Guthman once
said, "I'm a Kennedy man. I'll go where he asks me."

There are several awkward things about charisma as a political
property, some of which may be best discussed later. But certain points
are relevant to the conflict in the Oregon and California primaries. One
is that:

> Charismatic authority is naturally unstable. The holder may lose his
> charisma, he may feel "forsaken by his God," as did Jesus on the cross;
> it may appear to his followers that "his powers have left him." Then
> . . . hope expects and searches for a new bearer; his followers abandon
> him, for *pure charisma does not recognise any legitimacy other than one
> which flows from personal strength proven time and again.*" [Our italics.]

In other words, the more closely a leader conforms to the ideal charismatic type, the more dangerous any reverse becomes. The magic cloak,
torn once, disintegrates. Politicians whose power depended less on one
principle of domination than did Kennedy's might be able to endure
numerous defeats: he could not. (Hubert Humphrey, shrewdly, realized
that if Kennedy were to lose in California his magic would be so comprehensively dissipated that he would be relatively little help to Humphrey
in the post-convention campaign.)

Not only is charisma unstable: it also tends to be inflexible and, in
a certain sense, intolerant. The followers of a charismatic leader consider
it the *duty* of others to recognize their leader—their own recognition
being "a matter of complete personal devotion to the possessor of the
quality, arising out of enthusiasm, or of despair or hope." To refuse
recognition is to deny, implicitly, the value of the commitment which the
followers have already made.

> When such an authority comes into conflict with the competing authority
> of another who also claims charismatic sanction, the only recourse is to
> some kind of a contest, by magical means or an actual physical battle of
> the leaders [or a primary election?] *In principle, only one side can be
> right in such a contest; the other must be guilty of a wrong which has
> to be expiated.* [Our italics.]

The anger Kennedy supporters displayed against McCarthy on the West
Coast was out of all proportion to the offenses alleged. The charge that

McCarthy's attacks on Kennedy went too far seemed absurd, coming from such self-proclaimed tough customers. The attitude was explicable only if it was founded on a substratum of moral outrage generated in some other way. McCarthy did not possess so many of the attributes of charismatic domination as did Kennedy. But he and his followers were challenging the legitimacy of Kennedy's charisma, and in Oregon they succeeded in damaging it.

It seems unlikely that a contest between two charismatic politicians —even under the rules of democracy—can ever end in accommodation and alliance. It can end only in the destruction of one leader. Ideological compatibility is not relevant: the nature of the competition polarizes personal antagonisms into a system of distrust which overrides all else. The practical consequence of this is that the liberal wing of the Democratic Party may find itself over and over again in the same condition as in 1968: that is, divided destructively among the followings of rival charismatic heroes.

In the end, it is unlikely that a charismatic insurgent can ever take over the party. According to Weber:

> As a rule, the party organisation easily succeeds in this castration of charisma. This will also remain true of the United States, even in face of the plebiscitary presidential primaries, since in the long run the continuity of professional operations is tactically superior to emotional worship. Only extraordinary conditions can bring about the triumph of charisma over the organisation.

Humphrey, the bureaucratic candidate, would probably have defeated Kennedy, had he lived, for the nomination (as the charismatic Teddy Roosevelt was overcome in 1912, an event which fascinated Weber, who had visited the United States a few years previously). But a degree of accommodation is possible between bureaucratic and charismatic authorities, since they do not challenge each other, intrinsically. Probably, maximum effectiveness for the party will always be achieved by a contest between one charismatic leader and one bureaucratic leader, with the latter winning. The presence of two charismatic claimants, such as Kennedy and McCarthy, creates tensions too explosive for the party structure to contain.

2

The King Must Die

"ANDREA: 'Unhappy is the land that breeds no hero.'
GALILEO: No, Andrea. 'Unhappy is the land that needs a
hero.' "

—Bertolt Brecht, *Galileo*

Nobody is quite sure whether Robert Kennedy was conscious for a few moments after Sirhan's two bullets hit him. The medical evidence is uncertain, and naturally the witnesses are confused.

But if he was conscious at all, it seems unlikely that he would have been surprised. He was prepared for the risk of violent death and had reflected a good deal about the possibility that he might be assassinated while campaigning. It does not seem to have been a morbid preoccupation, but simply stoic: his family's experience of the conditions of mortality being, of course, a strange one for prosperous Americans in the mid-twentieth century.

For most of us, the perils of existence have been a good deal tamed. Our families may be touched by the chances of disease, war, or accident. But short of nuclear disaster, most of us expect to live quite a long time in passable comfort, and with ordinary luck to end without too much distress.

The Kennedys lived lives spangled with altogether more violent extremes of splendor and agony. Power, vitality, wealth, and pride came to them along with death in war, wounds in war, murder, death by accident, maiming by accident, and the onset of diseases beyond the power of their physicians.

Robert Kennedy knew very well that there was violence in the American air in the spring of 1968, and that some of it was aimed at him. Because his political personality aroused such contradictory passions, he had always received a good many threatening letters. As the drama of his Presidential campaign mounted during April and May, the flow increased sharply. Many of the letters, not unnaturally, came from California, a state notoriously well endowed with cranks and bitter eccentrics.

On the night of Martin Luther King's death, after a speech in which Kennedy quoted Aeschylus, someone asked him, almost crassly, whether the death of King did not bring back terrible memories to him. "Well, that," he said. "But it makes me wonder what they might do to me, too."

The flow of angry letters was sufficient to make the FBI issue to receptionists in Kennedy's Washington office lists and photographs of people known to be dangerous—and the FBI would have liked to do more. But Kennedy would not tolerate any serious amount of physical protection.

He must have known—he was too intelligent and realistic not to have known—that the political techniques he was using in California added to his danger. The campaign was fought throughout at a high pitch of emotion: capitalizing on his glamour, Kennedy moved through huge and tumultuous crowds, drummed-up and stage-managed by careful and energetic advance men. Not only did the people surging around him at every appearance make protection difficult, it was also obvious that the passions of his campaign, projected by television, could well stir and confuse the excited and unhappy people who abound in the urban wildernesses of southern California.

But if Kennedy was willing to use the dangerous weapons demagogues use, he was not prepared to accept the cynicism that demagogues regard as normal. A George Wallace might shout that he was the friend of the people, protecting himself meanwhile from the people with ranks of hard-faced Alabama state troopers and keeping a bulletproof speaker's lectern in front of him. Kennedy would not do that. He declined to have armed mercenaries around him and would allow himself to be guarded only by friends.

Nevertheless, Kennedy did lean heavily on the magic of political emotion. And he never drew more deeply on his charismatic resources than in the last week of California. He was the kind of man who might square the use of demagogic techniques by accepting, directly, the physical risks involved. And it was generally true of him that if he occasionally played rough in politics, he was harder on no one than he was on himself. Therefore, whatever might be said about his political impact, there was to his life an enviable internal honor which was not surpassed by any of his rivals in 1968.

The reason, of course, that California had to be fought so intem-
perately was that his campaign was in trouble. It was not simply the
Oregon defeat and the unconscionable time that McCarthy took a'dying.
There had been, from the beginning, difficulties in "putting it together"
in California which arose from the nature and timing of the Kennedy
campaign, the nature of the McCarthy campaign, and the politically
refractory—not to say zany—nature of the state itself.

California, apart from matters of inevitable political calculation—
as the biggest, last-reporting, and most important of the primary states—
had a good deal to do with the emotional roots of Kennedy's campaign
for the Presidency. It was the focus of his connection with the Mexican-
Americans, for whom he felt a compassion perhaps more uncomplicated
and direct than he felt for any other underprivileged group in America:
a kind of compassion-in-action which entirely fitted his style.

On Sunday, March 10, two days before the New Hampshire primary
and in the midst of his crisis of reconsideration about the campaign,
Kennedy flew to Delano, California, to attend the festival marking the
end of a fast by Cesar Chavez, the militant leader of the Mexican-
American grape pickers. Delano does not represent the more glamorous
face of California. It is a sun-faded town of 14,000 people sprawled out
on either side of the long, hot ribbon of Highway 99, which runs the
length of the dreary but abundantly fertile floor of the Central Valley.
Yet Delano was transformed that day by an electric enthusiasm for
Chavez and Robert Kennedy. There were ten thousand people from the
valley in the town square. Kennedy was the only outsider—indeed, almost the only "Anglo"—who had been invited to the celebration.

Paul Schrade, state director of the United Auto Workers, who had
been deeply involved in helping the grape pickers since their first strike
in 1965, recalls: "The place went wild for Bob and Cesar. You took your
life in your hands being with them. Everyone wanted to shake their
hands, and talk to them, and there really was a chance we would be
beaten under by the crowd's enthusiasm." No other American politician
could have drawn the response that the grape pickers gave Kennedy—
chiefly because no other had done so much to deserve it.

The Central Valley is the home of California's richest industry,
"agro-business," worth nearly four billion dollars a year, outdoing even
the glittering aerospace industries spread out around Los Angeles. Within
this prosperous agricultural machine work a million Mexican-Americans
—men, women, and frequently children—known by the callous col-

lective "stoop labor." (They are suitable for it, said Governor Reagan in one of his less appetizing asides, because "they are built close to the ground.") More than eighty per cent of their families earn less than the thirty-one hundred dollars a year established as the Federal "poverty level" figure for families of four.

Led by Chavez and his National Farm Workers' Association, the Mexican-Americans—*chicanos,* they call themselves—had been fighting and are fighting now for the most elementary necessity of workers: union recognition. Under that banner, the fight has also been for less tangible but still important things: for the regeneration of a people—out of the decay and emptiness of a migrant laborer's life on land not his own, out of the physical squalor of the barrios—in a word, for self-respect. Chavez and his people, abused as Communists and degenerates, threatened with violence—and replying, on occasion, in kind—are acting out a gritty drama which seems to belong more to the 1930s, or even the nineteenth century, than to modern America.

To choose the grape pickers' side in this struggle does not require a radical or complex political philosophy. It requires compassion, some measure of courage, and a relish for direct action and plain loyalties. These values have drawn many young "Anglos" to stand side by side with the *chicanos,* and Robert Kennedy was one of them.

They are not, it should be said, a deeply popular cause with orthodox politicians. As migratory workers, few Mexican-Americans are registered to vote. Whatever the righteousness of their cause, it might fairly be said that it is not one that deeply concerns the mass of the American electorate: not so much out of callousness, but simply because it is peripheral. Where there might be serious mileage in being the man who could understand the blacks, and get their vote, a Presidential aspirant who championed the Mexican-Americans stood to gain relatively little except, perhaps, a reputation for involvement with turbulent and unwashed minorities. Had Kennedy really been the political calculating machine that some of his enemies thought, he would have reacted fairly coolly when his young assistant Peter Edelman began to argue the Mexican-American cause to him in early 1966.

In fact, he reacted with the avidity of a man who needed the good fight. He did not simply make admirable Senate speeches about the plight of migrant workers (as Eugene McCarthy had been doing since 1952). With a sense of drama that made him, in Schrade's words, "the only man in Washington the Mexican-Americans respected," he brought the Senate Subcommittee on Migratory Labor to hold hearings in Delano early in 1966. It was a high point in the battle with the growers and with the frequently ruthless allies they had in the power structure of the Valley.

There can be little doubt that the astringent questioning to which Kennedy submitted the growers and their friends in the hearings was a substantial aid to the embattled workers. Kennedy's most celebrated exchange was with Kern County Sheriff Roy Galyen, who, when pickets were threatened by men still in the fields, had arrested the pickets instead of the workers.

> KENNEDY: What did you charge them with?
> GALYEN: Violation of— Unlawful assembly.
> KENNEDY: I think that's most interesting. Who told you they were going to riot?
> GALYEN: The men right out in the field that they were talking to said, "If you don't get them out of here, we're going to cut their hearts out." So rather than let them get cut, we removed the cause.
> KENNEDY: This is the most interesting concept, I think. How can you arrest somebody if they haven't violated the law?
> GALYEN: They're ready to violate the law.
> KENNEDY: Can I suggest that the sheriff read the Constitution of the United States?

As in the prosecution of Jimmy Hoffa (whose union, by an intriguing coincidence, was collaborating with the farm bosses against Chavez), Kennedy was at his best with an enemy in his sights and a strong conviction of right in his heart.

The simple act of coming to the Mexican-Americans' aid when they needed it lit a durable flame of loyalty in the people of the Valley, and Kennedy returned the affection. And even in 1968, the relationship remained undisturbed by the sort of tensions which had for some time marked dealings between any white liberal and the blacks. There were no Brown Panthers to pre-empt the radical positions and accuse everybody else of moral cowardice or irrelevance. Arguably, the relationship was a little seigneurial for some tastes, but it was a genuine one. And among the delirious, worshiping crowd in the sun at Delano on March 10, it seems clear that Kennedy's last doubts about running for the Presidency vanished. (Paul Schrade, who was with him there, was convinced of this, and so are a number of other Kennedy supporters.)

Yet, at the same time, his California troubles began. An early mistake, later corrected, stemmed simply from a failure to be hard enough. American politicians, not least the Kennedys, work by the rule that one good (or bad) turn deserves another: normally, they are remorseless about picking up IOUs. Yet Kennedy was reluctant to enforce the return favor due him from Chavez.

Obviously, once he had declared, he had to scrape up every available vote in California, and this meant having the open and unequivocal support of Chavez to rally the Mexican-Americans. In detail, this meant that Chavez's name must appear on the list of convention delegates pledged to Kennedy. When two or three days had passed after Kennedy's declaration and his supporters in California had heard nothing from Cesar Chavez, Jesse Unruh began to get worried. On the Tuesday after the declaration, Unruh got Paul Schrade to telephone one of Chavez's assistants and ask what was happening. He was astounded to hear that Kennedy had called Chavez but had not asked him to do anything more than help to register voters. This was a useful and quite necessary job, but not enough. Schrade put in a call to Kennedy in Virginia; Kennedy said that when he called Chavez "Cesar sounded so ill I didn't have the heart to press him." Chavez was indeed ill, as a result of his fast—six months later, his vertebrae were crumbling from calcium deficiency, and his kidneys had become displaced. He also had political trouble: coming out for Kennedy would seriously damage his chances of getting desperately needed help from the national union movement, which he knew to be pro-Humphrey and anti-Kennedy. Schrade was unsure quite what to say. Then he said, "This doesn't sound like the hardhearted Kennedy we've all heard about." Kennedy laughed.

Kennedy's attitude was not really out of character. The man who was capable of the rather cumbrous Machiavellianism of the Peace Commission maneuver, or of distorting the record of Kenneth Keating when running against him for the Senate was, equally, incapable of coercing an admired friend to pay off on a political debt.

After a moment, Schrade asked Kennedy whether he in fact wanted Chavez on the slate. Kennedy said yes, he did. And so Schrade took the responsibility of telling Chavez immediately that it might be hard, but it was necessary, and it had to be done. When he put down the phone, Chavez called a meeting of his people in Delano, and at four a.m., he called Schrade back and said he would do it. In the end, the votes of Chavez's Mexican-Americans contributed most of the slender margin by which Kennedy beat McCarthy in California.

Schrade, when putting the pressure on Chavez, had considerable moral capital to draw upon. When he himself had declared for Kennedy, the day before, it had been a calculated defiance of the state and national labor leadership, and everyone in politics knew it. Schrade, a tall, silver-haired man of forty-three—who, like many Californians, looks ten years younger than his age—represents the most socially radical element of America's most socially radical union, Walter Reuther's United Auto Workers. Throughout the year, Schrade and a small group of his friends were the only important element of the American labor structure to do battle on behalf of an antiwar candidate. A few hours before he spoke to Chavez, Schrade had been in Detroit for a UAW board meeting. There, he found Reuther, the least conservative national labor leader, inclined toward Humphrey, along with the rest of his board. That very morning, both Johnson and Humphrey himself had called Reuther and emphasized that they expected the UAW's continued support for the Administration candidate. Schrade had to make it very clear that his was a personal decision, which did not commit the union, and he also had to promise that he would not spend California union money to help Kennedy. So, he was able to say to Chavez, "I know it will be hard. It was for me."

Only one other California union official, Tom Consiglio of the United Steelworkers, declared for Kennedy. And although his name went on the delegate slate, Consiglio was forced to say shortly afterward that he wanted to be "dissociated" from the entire Kennedy campaign. Allegedly, colleagues had been complaining that Consiglio's stand for Kennedy implied that the entire million-strong steelworkers' union was endorsing Kennedy. The charge, of course, was ridiculous and was itself evidence of the pressure Consiglio was under. "We tried to get a labor committee going," says Jesse Unruh. "But Meany said no. We tried desperately, but Meany's power was absolute." The tactical advantages of bureaucracy were showing up.

Kennedy's lack of the labor-union support that Democratic politicians normally rely on had two effects in California. One was that he did not get the unions' help in consolidating and turning out the blue-collar vote. But that, in California, matters far less than in a state like Indiana, where the labor and political machinery is more formally integrated. What union supporters might have been able to provide was money for the campaign, and this was much needed. Strangely, in view of the famous Kennedy millions, the California primary campaign got off the ground in a state of near-pauperism. (There was not even any money for the essential staple of any American political campaign—that is, a supply of buttons. Rather desperately, early campaigners painted bobby-pins red, white, and blue and tried to persuade suitably committed girls to wear them in their hair. The theory was that this would rouse people

to ask, "What's that in your hair? It looks like a bobby pin." To which
the girl was supposed to reply, "Yes, I'm for Bobby.")

Jesse Unruh, as one of his earlier actions, had directed an urgent
financial SOS to the East. Probably, most people would have expected
such an appeal to produce manna rather speedily—as Stu Spencer, a
famous merchandiser of California Republicans, said at the time, "The
Kennedys have a reputation for what you might call instant dollars."
Unruh probably knew better. Despite some ups and downs, Unruh had
been a loyal enough Kennedy supporter for a good many years. But he
knew that he was not a member of the Kennedy clan. Although the
Kennedys indeed applied "instant dollars" whenever a problem warranted it—beating Hubert Humphrey in West Virginia in 1960, elevating
Edward Kennedy to the Senate in 1966—the money had always been
strictly under the control of the family. In keeping with the tradition of
most rich families, they preferred their bagmen to qualify for the post
by ties of blood or at least marriage. This is one of the sound traditions
by which the rich stay rich.

But in this case, with so little time to get the California campaign
moving and with the intimate clansmen too heavily embattled in Indiana
and the East to be spared for Western matters, it was self-defeating
caution. "If they were going to trust Jesse to run the campaign," complained Paul Schrade's lieutenant, Marvin Brody, "they should've trusted
him with the cash."

Perhaps the Kennedy leadership felt that if the hastily erected Western satrapy were spoiled at the start, efforts to raise local money might
be discouraged. And no doubt they relied on Unruh's considerable reputation as a fundraiser for Democratic causes in his own state. Certainly
Unruh, not long after he became Speaker of the State House of Representatives—and therefore approximate overlord of the shifting aggrega-
tion of factions which is the Democratic Party of California—had made
a notable breakthrough in this direction. He had discovered that certain
California financial powers—notably financiers like Louis Warschaw of
Signal Insurance and Howard Ahmanson of the Savings and Loan Corporation—were willing to go against the traditionally Republican alliances of the big money in California.

But 1968 was not a vintage year for fundraisers. This was due in
large part to what Carmen Warschaw—Louis's wife, whose father
created Harvey Aluminum and is another political Maecenas—described
as the "Infernal Revenue." Mrs. Warschaw, a dynamic, dark-haired lady
who mostly looks after the family's politics, went so far as to say that

she and her husband had become entirely convinced that President Johnson was not going to run for re-election when they discovered just how harsh the revenuers were being over matters of political donations—particularly in the swing states of Illinois and California. The vigor of the oppression, indeed, was such that Ahmanson's public-relations subsidiary, Howfield Inc., which he found convenient for channeling political funds, had been forced by a court order to open its books for inspection.

There were other reasons for Unruh's bank-roll trouble. Earlier in the year, the fat cats had been levied fairly vigorously by the section of the party under national committeeman Eugene Wyman which had started out to organize on the presumption that LBJ would be running again. (Their slate of delegates, headed by Attorney General Tom Lynch, naturally transferred its allegiance to Humphrey.) And although many big political donors like to play "both sides of the street" in order to be in favor no matter who wins, Kennedy did not look a good enough prospect when he first declared. As Dick Kline, one of Unruh's staff, said later, "The big money-givers the Democrats rely on here—like Lou Wasserman of Universal Pictures—are not going to give money to, in effect, fight the President." After Kennedy's hefty win in the Nebraska primary, Unruh hoped aloud that some of the purse strings might loosen. But this was already May 14.

There was, of course, a reservoir of potential backers activated more by idealism and less by calculation—that is, the wealthy middle class, in particular the prosperous Jewish community around Beverly Hills and the show-business liberals of Hollywood (the "ideological money" Kline calls it). But the McCarthy campaign had been milking these people for the best part of two months before Kennedy declared. It was a vicious circle: because of the late start, it was hard to raise cash; and because there was a shortage of cash, it was hard to make up for the late start. The upshot was that the Kennedy campaign scarcely had a proper headquarters organization in Los Angeles until about three weeks before the primary. Looking back at the end of the year, a weary Unruh said, "It was a shambles."

The Kennedy national staff tended to underrate the danger from the McCarthy campaign in California. One reason for this was the spectacular size and emotional temperature of the crowds that Kennedy drew on his raid into California the weekend after his declaration. Among those looking at the sea of people in Griffith Park, Los Angeles, on Saturday afternoon, there was a tendency to say, "Well, that settles the idea that McCarthy's got all the enthusiasm." But that crafty observer

John Kenneth Galbraith, making a cooler reconnaissance of the state a week later, came to a different conclusion. He decided that McCarthy's campaign in California had better people behind it than Kennedy's—and that the battle was a long way from being over. While Professor Galbraith may have slightly magnified the difference in quality between the two camps, he did not go so far as the uncompromising idealists of the local Peace and Freedom Party. Examining the list of people Unruh had assembled into a slate of delegates, and ignoring the Paul Schrade–Cesar Chavez element, of which they thought well, they published a contemptuous broadside entitled "Hookers for Kennedy!"

The sting of the charge marshaled by Peace and Freedom's energetic polemicist, Farrel Broslawski, was that too many of the hundred and seventy-two people who were running for election as delegates under Kennedy's name were there not because of any commitment to peace and social justice—the banners under which Kennedy claimed to march—but because Jesse Unruh had put them there. And, indeed, many of them had been sufficiently unmoved by the agony of Vietnam to be prepared to back Johnson—until they were signaled to go for Kennedy.

The activating principle of Democratic politics in California is, to a greater extent than perhaps anywhere else in the United States, a Florentine striving between the followers of rival chieftains. And at the time that Robert Kennedy launched his Presidential attempt, the chief antagonists were the Unruh following and the Wyman following. One might well say, for instance, that the ruling political passion of the formidable Mrs. Warschaw was an aversion to Mr. Wyman, stemming from an incident some years earlier in which he had seen fit to deny a commitment she believed had been made to her. Taxed with defaulting, Wyman apparently said, reasonably, "Well, you didn't get it in writing, did you?" Mrs. Warschaw did not like this explanation, and to this day she presents to people with whom she does business ball-point pens specially engraved: GET IT IN "WRITING." LOVE, CARMEN. Her displeasure pursued Wyman across the continent to the 1964 Democratic Convention in Atlantic City, where she hired a pilot to write in smoke across the sky, GET IT IN WRITING.

When the Johnson slate had been made up, Wyman had conceded some places on it to followers of his rival chieftain, Unruh, and Mrs. Warschaw was one of them. But after the Kennedy declaration, her loyalties were transferred, and a public expression of this was arranged

by having her husband's name placed on the Kennedy list. This technique was reversed in order to allow Alfred Song, State Senator and
party vice-chairman, to make *his* stand clear. Although Song was also
trapped on the Administration slate his wife's name was placed on the
Kennedy slate. So Robert Kennedy's candidacy from the start was em-
broiled in the complex vendetta culture of California democracy. Unruh
had managed to hold some of his followers in reserve against a Kennedy
nomination. But his supplies had been depleted, and there were some odd
companions in the adventure. Willard Murray, a Negro who works for
Los Angeles' highly conservative Mayor Yorty, was there, and so was a
leading black liberal Councilman, Tom Bradley. One Assemblyman on
the slate, Bob Movetti, had been until recently in favor of the war and
had sponsored an antiriot bill that was generally thought to be aimed
against Negroes, but State Senator Mervyn Dymally, a Negro with strong
militant links, was also there. Cesar Chavez was on the slate, but so was
Jack Hovard, who had campaigned on a pro-Johnson platform in 1966.

Theoretically, there was even a case for saying that Jesse Unruh
was the wrong man to be running the Kennedy campaign. His name
rouses stern and contradictory passions in California, and he is too often
regarded as a member of the Order of Bosses only slightly junior to
Mayor Daley, the Iron Chancellor of Chicago. Possibly his physical appearance contributes to this. He is a short, extremely broad man. He has
a very wide jaw, with a certain saurian look about it, and in recent
years he had weighed some three hundred pounds, which was certainly
how a boss ought to look.

And it is true that Unruh is not exactly an idealist. Like a good
many Californians, he emerged from a gritty background of Texan rural
poverty such as breeds few idealists. Possibly he once had bosslike ambitions, but even a Daley would be daunted by the task of extending a
truly monolithic empire over the expanse of California. The chief reason
for this is simply mobility: to control people, you must know where to
find them, and voters, following the wild dance of real-estate values, shift
as freely as water over the great urban plain of Los Angeles. People
move on the average once every five years, and do not acquire their
political coloration from their community as they do in more settled
parts of America. In such a place there is no way to build the tightly
knit structure of *predictable* wards and precincts upon which Daley's
power rests in Chicago.

The politician's dilemma in this situation is beautifully exemplified
in the puzzling case of the San Fernando Valley, just over the Hollywood

hills to the north of Los Angeles. In 1945 it was country, where film stars kept sheep and small farmers raised chickens; then the aviation and electronics firms moved in, real-estate operators found the land cheap and available, and the summer heat was perfect for people whose dream was to spend most of their leisure time around a swimming pool. From four hundred thousand in 1950, the population has shot up to more than a million today.

Politically, the valley is divided into two Congressional districts, the Twenty-second and the Twenty-seventh. Each has a mixture of successful blue-collar workers, a cross section of middle-class professionals, and a sprinkling of really wealthy people. More than two-thirds of the families in the valley own their own houses, though they are exceptionally mobile, even for Californians. (Houses cost anything from thirty to a hundred thousand dollars or more.) The average income was ten thousand dollars in 1960 and is now higher. The population is overwhelmingly white and has undergone a remarkable quantity of education: nearly a quarter of the inhabitants over twenty-five have been to college.

In 1964, the Twenty-seventh District elected a conservative Republican to Congress—which seemed natural. But at the same time the Twenty-second elected a young liberal Democrat named Jim Corman. It was assumed that Corman's victory was a by-product of LBJ's landslide victory over Goldwater and that he would be removed in 1966. Far from it. Corman was re-elected with an increased majority, despite the right-wing tide that elected Ronald Reagan to the governorship.

This result so baffled the important International Association of Machinists, a powerful union with many members in the valley, that they commissioned a series of special polls to find out what was going on. Interviewers crawled all over the valley for several weeks and came up with—nothing. There was no observable sociological difference that would explain why two apparently similar communities would exhibit such divergent voting patterns. Confronted with such rampant individualism, what can a boss do?

Even if this problem were surmountable, California law presents a dense thicket of hazards to the party organizer. These were erected by the great Progressive reformer Hiram Johnson, working on the proposition that parties were sinful institutions—a not unreasonable thought, in the aftermath of the elephantine corruptions that pillaged California sixty-odd years ago. Accurately noting that patronage was the lifeblood of the party, Johnson devised a system that makes as many civil-service posts as possible in California elective rather than appointive. The principle is carried further than in any other major state and extends deep into the administrative process by making a great many executive decisions subject to referendum. Like its approximate contemporary, Prohibition, it was a Noble Experiment. But when one surveys the lively chaos produced in the attempt to legislate sin out of the American heart, one wonders, as with Prohibition, whether the disease might not be preferable to the cure. In the bewildering political landscape of California, political operators cluster around such focuses of power as they can discern: an essentially decent and reasonable man like Jesse Unruh, who has been Speaker of the House of Representatives, or the reactionary and secretive oilman Henry Salvatori, who has never been elected to any public office.

The practical result for the Kennedy campaign was that Jesse Unruh had no solid block of voting support to contribute, only a following of professional politicians—one of the more powerful ones, but far from dominant. And Unruh's support automatically brought with it the dislike of other factions. Partly this was because of his past actions in support of the Kennedy cause, imposing Pierre Salinger on the party in 1966 as a rather disastrous Senate candidate. Partly, also, antagonism was inspired by a belief that Unruh was interested in heading the Kennedy campaign in order to advance his gubernatorial ambitions. This suspicion, shared at times by some Kennedy henchmen, appears to have been quite unfounded. Unruh was animated throughout by his entirely accurate conviction, substantiated by private polls, that an Administration candidate would lose in California.

He was afraid that a Presidential debacle for the Democrats would help the Republicans to win a majority in the State House of Representatives—and this is precisely what happened. In his setback, Unruh (like ex-Governor Pat Brown) preserved the humorous stoicism that characterizes those who have tried to win California for the cause of moderate reform. "In the thirties," he says, "there was a party here called EPIC —Eliminate Poverty in southern California. I'm thinking of starting another EPIC—Eliminate Politics in California."

In a manner all too reminiscent of Weber's description of a charismatic leader's administrative staff, it was never entirely clear who was really in charge of Kennedy's California campaign. "It was won in the end on Bob's personal energy," says Unruh, "not by rational politics."

"We had a lot of conflicts with the national staff," says Dick Kline. "They wanted to get the candidate out among the Mexicans and in the black suburbs. We tried to tell them he was needed more in the middle-class white suburbs, because he was going to get the black and Mexican vote anyway. What they didn't seem to realize was that the picture of Bobby surrounded by frenzied mobs pulling his shoes and shirt off was a violent picture, and it wasn't liked by the white voters, who had been very frightened by the Watts riots three years before." "I don't think," adds Kline, underlining that curious, fatal underestimation of McCarthy the Kennedy people had, "I don't think the national staff ever understood why the West Side liberals in L.A. were so overwhelmingly for McCarthy."

At the beginning of May, there was an attempt to pull the campaign into shape. Stephen Smith's arrival on May 1 brought some personal efficiency to bear, and Smith also did a great deal to repair relations between Unruh and the Eastern staff. (The nature of these relations may be judged from the reaction of Pete Hamill, who returned from Ireland to work briefly as a speech-writer for Kennedy in California. Departing again in mid-May, he wrote a long and unfriendly article for the *Village Voice* about the Unruh men running the campaign. "They all had neat suits," he wrote. "And they all had neat hair, and they all had crisp shirts with button-down collars. And they were all pricks." It was, he declared, a case of "Rent a Volunteer with Pragmatic Compassion.") Smith's attempts to patch things up, though, were diverted by the impending disaster in Oregon. Ten days before the California poll, Smith disappeared to Portland to try to salvage the hopeless wreckage of Edith Green's Kennedy campaign.

None of this would have mattered so much had not McCarthy, in California, been propelled by one of the most effective organizations ever to align itself behind that unhurried campaigner. It was, of course, amateurish—but that was the point. The Kennedy campaign was, in contrast, ambivalent about the "new politics" it claimed to represent. The camp of the charismatic chieftain hankered for bureaucratic respectability. As, before declaring, Kennedy relied on old-line professional henchmen for advice, so in the campaign he relied on professional Democratic leaders in every state where he could get them. The McCarthy campaign, on the other hand, was forced to be almost pure "new politics," because it had virtually no chance of access to the old politics. One reason for this was simply fear of the White House. Mrs. Anne Alanson, California's Democratic national committeewoman, did come out for McCarthy, but she received a number of rather unpleasant calls from the White House as a reward. Another was McCarthy's own stated attitude to the perils of campaigning. On May 11, in California, McCarthy said, "My strategy is to walk through the Red Sea dry-shod. Any of you who want to follow before the waters close in are welcome to do so." McCarthy was, in the end, supported by just two more Democrats with some orthodox political standing: Pat Brown, Jr. (son of the former governor, who came out for the Administration slate) and the liberal Congressman Don Edwards.

But there were other sources of potential support. There has been much excitement about the California far right—although some of its specimens, in the end, have turned out to be rather papery tigers, like Max Rafferty and Shirley Temple Black—and this has tended to obscure the fact that California, the most middle-class state, has a substantial tradition of bourgeois liberalism and in its contrary way, an active radical fringe, to balance the reactionary one. (The Peace and Freedom Party managed to get seventy-one thousand voter signatures together to get onto the Presidential election ballot—although, as organizer Farrel Broslawski admitted, "I guess a lot of them figured it was a new folk-rock group.") So there was an organizational starting point for McCarthy in the California Democratic Council, led by Gerald Hill of San Francisco, who had been so important in getting McCarthy to run. The CDC is a pressure group within the California party that is Stevensonian-liberal in origins and heavily reliant on middle-class housewives in the San Francisco Bay area. In the usual matters of politics—handling patronage, power-broking with national leaders—it is, predictably, a weapon of variable efficiency. But in a year like 1968, united by the war as no other issue could unite them (the pedigree of the CDC's opposition to the war, going back to 1965, could not be questioned), the CDC members made a fairly formidable group.

California, as Unruh's spring polls had shown, was a strong peace state. Like everything else about the place, this is not explicable along obvious lines. After all, California receives about twenty cents of every defense dollar and has some of the most brightly plumaged hawks in the country, when such birds find it convenient to fly. And, in terms of casualties, Californians were not being hit terribly hard by the Vietnam war. But the prosperous white middle class of California had already seen the war as a danger to the swelling prosperity of the West Coast Golden Life. The fact that Richard Nixon was born in Yorba Linda shows that some remnants of the Puritan spirit survived the journey across the continent. But most of it long since dissolved in the California sun.

Consider Martin Stone, the millionaire industrialist who was Los

Angeles cochairman of the McCarthy campaign. The headquarters of his company, Monogram Industries, is set in the spacious streets of West Los Angeles. Monogram now has sales of one hundred thirty-five million dollars, a rise from six million six years ago, when Stone took over. Its most important single product is aircraft toilets, which Monogram supplies to seventy-five per cent of American airliners and virtually all corporation jets. And Stone has an even more direct stake in American hedonism: he also makes toilets for pleasure boats. Stone does not approach the direction of his company in a grim or cheerless spirit: most afternoons he is to be found running around the streets of Westwood in a UCLA sweater, followed by his golden retriever Charles de Gall-Stone. He was thirty-nine when he took over the McCarthy campaign, but he looked twenty-eight, with chunky, athletic good looks.

He is almost the ideal Californian, and he has been cited by *Business Week* as a "classic American success story."

But Stone is also a man who likes to exercise his social conscience. In 1965—this was before the Watts riots—he launched a training program for unemployed high-school dropouts, putting boys who had never had steady jobs to work as helpers at a sheet-metal plant. Monogram hired fifty-three boys, and fourteen are still on the staff. (The others went on to jobs elsewhere or to military service.) "I really didn't think it would be good business," Stone says, "but it was. After we started the project, we ran into a severe labor shortage, and the program gave us employees we wouldn't otherwise have had." There is no question of Stone's sincerity, although naturally the program did not make a very large impact on Watts.

Stone's reasons for opposing the war were straightforward. He thought the American policy "immoral," but opposed the war primarily because of the damage he saw on the domestic front. "Our system may fall if we don't correct poverty and racial inequality. . . . If the society around us goes to hell, the business community won't benefit."

Ideologically, Stone is by no means an orthodox liberal Democrat, although he worked for Stevenson and John Kennedy. His views on Federal expenditures, for instance, were scarcely reconcilable with those McCarthy was to put forward in California. "I start with the assumption that I don't like the Federal government. I have no confidence in its ability to do anything. . . . I'm a Democrat," he says, "but sometimes I wonder why." At times like these, Stone sounds remarkably like Tom Reed, another eupeptic, successful young California businessman who spent the year serving Ronald Reagan in the anti-Federal cause.

Reed was for the war; Stone against it. Presumably, it was a matter of personality, and it would be interesting for the future of peace to know which type is likely to dominate the new California business society.

Stone met McCarthy first at a Los Angeles dinner party in October 1967. They talked about the need for someone to run against Johnson, and McCarthy said he thought Kennedy ought to do it. Stone was approached six weeks later by Pat Brown, Jr., and Max Palevsky, the head of a successful computer company (who subsequently joined Kennedy). They wanted him to become cochairman of McCarthy's campaign because a businessman would balance Gerry Hill's left-wing reputation.

The operation certainly did not have the surface appearance of a normal Democratic campaign. It hardly could, when the CDC held political functions at the Playboy Club on Sunset Boulevard. The show-business peaceniks pitched in from the first, organizing such memorable fund-raisers as a party in Beverly Hills at which Noel Harrison, in Nehru jacket and beads, read selections from the candidate's poetry. What the Senator would have made of it is hard to guess: he was not there. But the admiration for him was entirely genuine. Leonard Nimoy, the television actor who plays the pointy-eared spacenik in "Star Trek," said, "I'd certainly like to be like McCarthy." And Eva Marie Saint said, "I'm for McCarthy because he was the first one to take up the crusade." It was all very beautiful: nowhere in the whole year were the "furry people" who backed McCarthy more charming, or more furry.

The cheerful hedonism that was to dominate the campaign emerged first when the newborn organization set about the wondrous complexities of getting onto the Presidential primary ballot. To do so, one must first make up a list of one hundred seventy delegates (the last two delegation seats are held, ex officio, by the state's two National Committee members), whose geographic distribution around the state is rigidly controlled. (The California Elections Code says that names of candidates "shall be so selected that the smallest number of candidates who reside in any one congressional district shall not be less than the integer of the quotient obtained by dividing the number of the names of candidates appearing upon the same nomination paper by the total number of congressional districts in the State, and that the largest number of candidates who reside in any one congressional district shall not be greater than twice that integer.")

The list must then be supported by the signatures of registered voters of the party equal to one-half of one per cent of the total vote the party got last time it ran a candidate for governor. This, for the Democratic Party in 1968, was 13,851 signatures. This is not an easy task, and the regular Democratic organization found itself unable to accomplish it when assembling the pro-Administration slate. (It hired a market-research firm to do the job in the end, using paid interviewers.) Further, there are restrictions on the time allowed for gathering signatures, the season in 1968 being from March 6 to April 5. However, the first candidate to complete this process receives the top spot on the ballot, which, in view of the mind-boggling complexity of the California ballot, is reckoned much worth having.

The method used by the McCarthy people was the idea of a San Francisco girl named Jo Sedida. Starting in January, they organized about five hundred all-night parties to be held throughout the state on the night of Tuesday, March 5. At midnight, some of the partygoers (chiefly graduate students) turned into political canvassers and began to collect signatures. The largest single operation was a party some fifteen-hundred strong at The Factory, a discothèque in San Francisco. By six a.m., the petition was thoroughly oversubscribed, with thirty-three thousand signatures. McCarthy was first on the ballot: a success that advertised both the potential support for a peace candidate and the fact that the cause could call on the help of a large number of people who did not have to get up in the morning.

California's enormous student body provided, in the absence of any other base, an almost inexhaustible supply of raw political manpower without which there could have been no real McCarthy campaign in California. Mary McCarthy, the Senator's eldest daughter, spent a good deal of time in the state, not infrequently being a more fiery and consistent speaker than her father, always prepared to throw a sharp dart at the Kennedy people ("They have the jumpers and squealers—we have the thinkers and doers."), and her brief speeches along these lines struck a considerable chord:

> We are in this because of self-interest. This is a wonderful country, and it belongs to us—not to Dean Rusk and J. Edgar Hoover. There is no reason why this country should be in a war that we cannot justify, and there is no reason why there should be poverty and discrimination in America. *We do not want to go to the beach with an uneasy conscience.*

Outwardly, the McCarthy campaign looked a shambles. The logistics of moving the candidate around, with an entourage of staff, reporters, cameramen, and general hangers-on, were never totally mastered. (On May 10, for instance, McCarthy's plane left Sacramento ten minutes early, leaving behind four staff members and six irate reporters from Northern California newspapers. The Senator then arrived nearly an hour early to speak in Griffith Park, Los Angeles. He finished his speech at four-twenty, the time he was supposed to start, and left as hundreds of people were arriving.) National political reporters, accustomed to associating crispness of travel organization with political viability, were inclined to be contemptuous. Whatever other difficulties might beset the Kennedy campaign, his personal entourage was nearly always on time.

Hard-nosed political observers were not much more impressed by, say, a visit to the principal McCarthy headquarters for the Los Angeles area. This was in a large, decayed building suitably handy to the campus of the University of California at Los Angeles. The basement had been turned into a populous crèche, in which young housewives—the other major element of the McCarthy force—could stack their offspring while getting on with a little stamp-licking. Occasionally, random children escaped above, where they were easily confused with the small people handling literature and running messages. The cultural spectrum, which in New Hampshire and Wisconsin and Indiana had been pushed well— and rather consciously—toward the crisp and demure, here collapsed entirely into the flowered, beaded, iridescent. The walls were as heavy with the more literate specimens of pop iconography as with standard political devices. McCarthy's distinguished Senatorial features smiled uncertainly through the shifting colors of a poster done in the psychedelic style, occasionally juxtaposed with the idealized, Christ-like face of Che Guevara. Most campaign headquarters made some attempt to look hip—most stiffly and awkwardly the Nixon headquarters in New York. But, naturally, the McCarthy campaign in California went the furthest. One wondered what McCarthy would have made of it, but even more what operators like Larry O'Brien would have made of notices like WE NEED MAMMOTH MOBILES AND OTHER SPIFFY STUFF. COME AND DO YOUR OWN THING FOR US. Or the poster which echoed *Marat/Sade:* THE NOMINATION AND ELECTION OF EUGENE MCCARTHY AS PERFORMED BY THE INMATES OF AMERICA'S EDUCATIONAL INSTITUTIONS UNDER THE DIRECTION OF THEIR OWN CONSCIENCES. (Although Pierre Salinger claimed, when the Kennedy slate was filed on March 20, that Kennedy would have "overwhelming" student support in California, in fact the McCarthy campaign never lost its hold on the campuses. In May, *Time* magazine conducted a "mock primary" among students, and McCarthy got 33,789 votes in the state, to Kennedy's 22,459, with 14,345 for Nixon.)

It was all very amateurish in the strict sense of the word, because the McCarthy workers were on the whole unpaid, while the Kennedy workers were paid. But it was not so much that the canvassing, telephoning, and leafleting done by the McCarthy students and housewives was necessarily all that effective—in such a political climate, probably nobody's could have been—but rather that there were very large numbers of them doing it. The fact that there were so many volunteers indicated that there must be many more who were prepared to vote. The McCarthy delegate slate contained very few regular California politicians; rather, it was composed of scientists, educators, actors, business executives, and local citizens who probably had at least as much, and maybe more, identification with their local subcommunities as any professional politicians.

In the end, McCarthy's campaign had some hundred and fifty local headquarters throughout the state, and these had been set up almost exclusively by spontaneous local initiative. They had not been called into existence by any central will, because there was no central will. Quite plainly, one could have found in the subclusters of the campaign some remarkable variations in ideological attitude. Certainly, such disparities as moderate Republicanism and the fringes of the hip left were discernible. Had it ever been necessary to mold the campaign into a coalition for actual action, some startling adjustments would have been called for. But that, at the time, was the least of problems, and the immediate accommodation of political variations was completed by the fact that McCarthy, as a rather newly minted national figure, was one into which people were able to read such intentions as they wished to read. COME, as the notice said, AND DO YOUR OWN THING FOR US.

Eccentric as it all looked, there was also some serious politics going on. And at the end of May, there was a clash between McCarthy and Kennedy—or, perhaps more accurately, between their teams of speechwriters—that did amount to a serious discussion of methods of dealing with America's urban crisis. Sadly, it was not understood or explained by the media, which seemed to have become so accustomed to lack of debate as to have stopped looking for it.

On May 28, McCarthy made a speech at the University of California at Davis. Written by Jeremy Larner, the domestic specialist on his writing team, it was intended to set McCarthy off from Kennedy domestically, as the Cow Palace speech had done in foreign affairs. It began,

According to President Johnson, "Americans are the best-fed, the best-paid, and the best-educated people in the world. Although we have only six per cent of the world's population, we have half of its wealth." The trouble is that when the President talks about "we," he is not talking about the people who live in the ghettos of our major cities, where they are locked away from the affluence of American life and treated as colonial people.

In passing, McCarthy criticized Humphrey—"The Vice-President speaks of a 'politics of happiness,' as though the young men of the ghettos should rejoice that the government has given them a few summer jobs to keep them off the streets."

But the speech soon developed into an argument against the measures that Kennedy advocated for dealing with the urban crisis. Kennedy's method, exemplified in his Bedford-Stuyvesant project in New York, was to try to improve conditions in the ghettos. This theory enjoyed a good deal of vogue, because it seemed to fit in with the new anti-integrationist attitude of black leaders. At the same time, the basic idea of keeping the black men *in situ* was not likely to disturb middle-class whites, and much talk about the role private enterprise might be encouraged to play made it sound as though not much tax revenue need be involved. It seemed quite a salable package. In fact, the concept is open to question. Despite the fashionable rhetoric about "integrationism" being an outmoded liberal attitude, the wastefulness of creating two separate communities—one black, one white—throughout the United States would be ludicrous. And, qualifications notwithstanding, that was the logic of the concept. "Poverty in America," said McCarthy, "is no accident, any more than Vietnam is an accident."

> Any policy for rebuilding our cities must take into account the growing isolation of the poor in America. It will be important to bring industry into the central city, to create new jobs and make sure Negroes can be hired. But developing our central cities will not in itself be adequate. There is not enough land, there are too many people, and there simply will not be enough jobs and housing. In these circumstances, to offer programs for the ghetto alone is another form of paternalism. For the crisis of the ghetto is bound up with the structure of our entire society. The ghetto will not be fundamentally affected until a new politics in America addresses itself to our society as a whole. . . .
>
> That is why I am disappointed by Senator Kennedy's overemphasis on rehabilitating the ghettos through private enterprise. Certainly private industry has a role to play in the cities, but that role can never be sufficient. The ghetto may have a few more factories and a few more jobs, but it will remain a colony, it will retain its economic and political de-

pendence as long as its citizens are foreclosed from participation in the life of society at large. . . . Private programs designed solely to rehabilitate the ghettos leave open to question our commitment to an integrated society. Rehabilitation financed by a profit-making outside organization can easily become paternalism.

The heretical thought had thus been uttered that perhaps private enterprise was not the anointed savior of the urban slum. The Senator questioned, in fact, the essential idea that reform should, of necessity, be a matter of commercial profit:

> The only way to reduce poverty is to attack it at its roots, to eliminate the conditions from which poverty springs. . . . We must build modern mass-transit systems to enable the ghetto unemployed to reach the jobs in the outer metropolitan areas. There is no reason, for instance, why it should take three hours each day to travel from Watts to the Los Angeles Airport area and back again. We must implement the riot-commission report on housing, which calls for six million units in five years. The people who will live in these units should be given the opportunity to work in building them. We must construct adequate medical facilities in our central cities.

It was not just the rhetoric of separatism that made such a speech run against fashion. For 1968 was also a year in which the Federal government and its antipoverty programs were highly unpopular, and here was McCarthy demanding Federal funding on a huge scale. There was, however, a difference. Where most of the Great Society programs had been strictly within the tradition of applying palliatives to existing poverty, McCarthy was beginning to talk about breaking out of that tradition, using Federal funds to redesign the metropolitan pattern and remove the causes of poverty. McCarthy's speech was not exactly a detailed program, but its essential social philosophy was bolder than any other statement of the Presidential campaign.

It infuriated the Kennedy camp. They regarded the ghetto problem, really, as their own property. It was the subject with which their leader was most closely identified. Who was McCarthy to airily announce that they were on the wrong lines altogether? When had he last been seen in a ghetto? Peter Edelman bashed out a hefty document, for issue on May 30, headed, "A Program for the Urban Crisis."

Kennedy did not give the document as a speech—understandably, since it was nine-and-a-half single-spaced pages. It was a tough-minded document and, in the Kennedy style, densely studded with fact. "The proposals outlined in this statement are specific and concrete. . . . They are not general propositions of slogans or vague goals or new civil rights.

They are part of a strategy for performance and for fulfilling the promises which we have made. . . .”

It recorded that an infant born to a Negro family is three times as likely as a white infant to die in the first year of life, and has the same chance of reaching twenty years of age as a white man does of reaching forty. It also recorded that his sister was three-and-one-third times more likely to be raped than the “average person.” The statement also went on to say that “no program to attack the problems of the inner city can be constructed in the isolation of the ghetto.”

But for all the plethora of facts, the document still represented the thinking in which the ghetto was to be improved—or, putting it less kindly, “gilded.” Its most detailed program was one for introducing low-cost housing into ghetto areas. Private investors were to be provided with long-term, low-interest public loans, to build or even rehabilitate cheap ghetto housing. Together with tax incentives, the paper calculated, such developers could get twelve to fifteen per cent back on their original investments (and apparently at very little risk). Altogether less detailed was the section which dealt with the isolation of the ghetto, which simply said that in order to open up suburban jobs to central-city dwellers, “special transportation” should be made available. This was a decidedly brusque treatment of perhaps the most intimidating of all the city problems—as brusque as McCarthy’s, if not more so. Also, the paper celebrated the concept of “special impact” programs, in which Federal funds should be pumped into especially afflicted areas to improve community facilities. Naturally, this passage mentioned Kennedy’s own special impact program in Bedford-Stuyvesant, New York: a project so well intended as to be difficult to criticize, but nevertheless as good an example as might be imagined of the irrelevance of improving particular communities to deal with a national crisis. (How many Bedford-Stuyvesant projects would be needed to make an impact on Chicago’s South Side— and if they did improve the conditions, would they lessen the isolation of black Chicago?) Perhaps Kennedy never realized how much the viability of Bedford-Stuyvesant depended upon his own involvement. It was hard not to suspect that many of the firms which took part in the project were there because of the glamour of doing something with Kennedy. At the end of the year, Kennedy’s friend and biographer Jack Newfield visited Bedford-Stuyvesant and came to the conclusion that the enterprise was running down. Without Kennedy there, corporate America had lost interest, he wrote.

The exchange was inconclusive, sadly: not even serious newspapers

seemed prepared to take up the argument at any length. But by the time
it came out, the events which led to another opportunity for argument
had been set in train. This was the television debate—which Kennedy
had decided against three days before his defeat in Oregon.

The morning after the Oregon result, Kennedy flew back to Los
Angeles. At the airport, he stayed inside the plane for some time with his
staff, while the reporters and cameraman waited for him in the airport
building. When he emerged, he looked weary, eyes hooded with fatigue.
But he was also rigidly uncomplaining and self-controlled. He had a
statement to read, and it began, "I have wired my sincere congratulations
to Senator McCarthy . . ." He went on to say that Hubert Humphrey
was now, clearly, the leading candidate for the Democratic nomination,
although he had not presented his views to the voters in a single state.
"If the Vice-President is nominated to oppose Richard Nixon," he said,
"there will be no candidate who has opposed the course of escalation of
the war in Vietnam. There will be no candidate committed to the kinds
of programs which can remedy the conditions which are transforming
our cities into armed camps. . . . It is hard to believe, after the recent
months of hope, that our political system will fail to offer people a chance
to move in a new and more hopeful direction." Then Kennedy said that
he was sure that Senator McCarthy believed that his own qualifications
for the Presidency "are superior to mine, as I believe I am qualified for
the office." Kennedy said that he would be glad to discuss that question,
separately or in joint appearances.

Immediately, he was asked whether the statement meant that
he was now prepared to have a television debate with McCarthy. He said
it did. "I am not the same candidate I was before Oregon. I can't claim
I am." In answer to another question, he hinted that he would not stay
in the race if he lost California. And, finally, he said he would not change
his campaign style for California.

And indeed, he did not. As soon as the press conference was over,
he stepped into an open car to begin one of the most tumultuous motor-
cades ever seen in Los Angeles.

Los Angeles, almost surprisingly, does have a center: "downtown
L.A.," a few foursquare blocks of congested business buildings, elderly
and curiously Midwestern in feeling. The ten-lane freeways that sweep
across the surrounding plain are loosely knotted about this old center,
and for any driver who becomes disoriented among the infinite ribbons
of concrete, downtown L.A. is always the easiest target to aim for. The
Harbor Freeway runs the eighteen miles north from the airport to down-

town L.A., and so was the one on which Kennedy's motorcade started out. Like the other freeways, it gives a feeling of flying over a city, rather than driving through it. The twenty-foot ramp of the freeway is enough to eliminate virtually all sense of variations of class and wealth among the communities over which it passes. There is nothing visible but shallow-pitched roofs, and a forest of television antennae and telephone wires. A mile or two away, on either side, the curtain of smog keeps pace with the car. About halfway north along the freeway, Watts lies to the right. From above, it scarcely looks any different from the other featureless subdivisions.

This time, Kennedy did not descend into Watts but came down into the area south and east of downtown L.A.—at least as poor a part of town as Watts, and heavily populated by Mexican-Americans. One week earlier, they had given Kennedy a rapturous reception—removing, as usual on these occasions, his cufflinks and whatever else they could break loose. A lad named Joe Murillo managed to remove both of the Senator's shoes, which he wore to school the next day. (They were size nine, with high arches to give extra height.) This time, the pitch of emotion was even higher. Time after time, the cars were halted by the crowds, not just in the Mexican-American residential streets but also in the business section of downtown L.A. Cheers, sobs, laughter, and cries of "Viva Kennedy!" bounced off the walls of the buildings. Women, with their lipstick smeared and hair disordered, galloped along beside Kennedy's car. People reached out to touch him: again his cufflinks vanished, and his shirt was soon soaked with sweat under the hot sun. Several times, Kennedy got out or was pulled out of the car to embrace people, to shake hands, to exchange hoarse greetings. (Rafer Johnson did his best to prevent the candidate from disappearing totally under the human tide.) It was enough to terrify any Secret Service bodyguard. But when a street patrolman, thinking he saw the Senator being carried away by the crowd, thrust through to see what was happening, Kennedy snapped, "We're all right. Can't you leave us alone?"

The congestion and subsequent acceleration of the motorcade in pursuit of its shattered schedule did not please the Los Angeles police, who slapped on a hundred tickets for traffic violations. (Kennedy liked to blame this on Mayor Sam Yorty, that nominal Democrat whose eccentricities had included backing Nixon against Jack Kennedy.)

But to Kennedy, the occasion was a source of fresh strength. He seemed almost literally to expand in the exuberance of the crowd. The hooded weariness vanished from his face, the resignation from his eyes.

The drive ended in the western suburbs, at the Beverly Hilton, where Kennedy received a standing ovation from a thousand of his campaign workers. He was scarcely recognizable as the man who had left that gray airport news conference. "If I died in Oregon," he said, "I hope Los Angeles is Resurrection City!"

On the next day, the Thursday before primary day, the Kennedy campaign returned to its emotional roots in the Great Valley. The trip was a traditional one, a six-hour whistle-stop journey from Fresno to Sacramento. (This country lies north of Delano, but it is the same flat, hot, rich, land, with the San Joaquin River wandering through it.) All the way, it is the country of the Mexican-American laborers and their masters. In each of the featureless, carbon-copy towns along the way —Madera, Merced, Turlock, Modesto, Stockton, and Lodi—the Kennedy advance men had turned out ample and enthusiastic crowds.

It was a journey in search of reassurance, rather than converts, for of each crowd of two or three thousand who swarmed around the train, nearly all were people who would vote for Kennedy, come what may. And although these are poor people who need to take their politics seriously, the entire 174-mile progress produced no flicker of serious political argument. Instead, Kennedy talked down to the crowds, using a curious litany which he had first tried out on fourteen-year-old schoolchildren in Oregon:

"I am here," he would say, "to give you my message because I know that Senator McCarthy and Vice-President Humphrey haven't given you theirs."

"No, they haven't"—from the crowd.

"What, Senator McCarthy hasn't been here?"

"No . . . o!"

"Doesn't he care for you?"

"No . . . o!"

"And doesn't Vice-President Humphrey care?"

"No . . . o!"

"That's shocking. You wouldn't vote for someone who didn't care, would you?"

"No . . . o!"

"But you will vote for me, won't you?"

"Yes! Yes! Yes!"

In Turlock, where they raise turkeys, he said, "I am running for the Presidency because my wife, Ethel, told me I would have to come to Turlock, the turkey capital of the world, and that is why I am running today." In another town, where he began with a serious speech about inequality and the need to provide employment for the disadvantaged, he broke off to offer these thoughts: "We're helping the farmer. My family eats more tomatoes than any family I know, and my wife and children all wear cotton clothes. I'm doing more for the farmer than McCarthy or Humphrey."

Suddenly, at the back of the crowd, some McCarthy supporters raise a banner, SOUTHERN OREGON.

"Southern Oregon!" shouts the candidate. "You wouldn't do that to me, would you?"

"No . . . o!"

"You're my friends, aren't you?"

"Yes! Yes! Yes!"

It seemed entirely apt that, in the town of Turlock, a man on a large black bull galloped up and down throughout the performance.

This was not the performance of any ordinary kind of politician soliciting votes. It was a charismatic chieftain, refreshing his own faith, and his followers', in his "gift of grace."

There was, anyway, little time left for campaigning and no time for Kennedy to start getting through to new kinds of people. At this stage, he did as well, perhaps, to stir up as much excitement as possible among his natural supporters—mobilize as many of their votes as possible, and hope they could give him a fat enough victory to keep his campaign alive through the summer.

Californians take their weekend days pretty seriously, so after some high jinks on the cable cars in San Francisco and a rather routine foreign-affairs speech at the Commonwealth Club on Friday, May 31, Kennedy had only one big moment remaining in the California campaign. This was Saturday evening's television debate: the encounter which McCarthy had been seeking, and Kennedy avoiding, ever since Indiana.

It was to be the only direct confrontation, in the whole year, between two candidates for the Presidency. Yet even so, it was not a true debate, as even those famous exchanges between John Kennedy and Richard Nixon in 1960 were not true debates. In this case also, the television men interposed themselves between the contestants, asking questions of each in turn. It was hard to see why they were so keen to minimize direct conflict, unless the network people—in this case ABC's "Issues and Answers" staff—somehow feared abandoning control of their medium to mere politicians, or feared that a less inhibited form might lead to unmannerly verbal brawling. McCarthy proclaimed himself somewhat unhappy with the format, saying that it could scarcely be called a debate. But the encounter did produce some direct clashes between the two men—and the process revealed characteristic weaknesses in both of them. McCarthy's performance, technically, was a bitter and admitted disappointment to the best members of his young staff. Kennedy's performance certainly should have been an ideological disappointment to his staff and followers, although nobody seemed prepared to admit it.

McCarthy, who was still manifestly enjoying the afterglow of having defeated a Kennedy, if only in a primary, had put on a great air of unconcern about the debate ever since the announcement of the proposition. Kennedy, however, followed his usual mode of conspicuous consumption of energy and devoted the greater part of Saturday to fierce and intensive briefing sessions with Walinsky, Edelman, and other advisers. It was all rather self-consciously like the "skull sessions" John Kennedy had run with his young men before the 1960 confrontations; and it seemed rather a lot for a relatively limited hour's discussion on television against a candidate who had been regarded with contempt until very recently. Certainly it hardly seemed worth canceling the morning's fixture, a breakfast with six hundred labor leaders from all over the state. This had been arranged only after an enormous amount of gritty and difficult bargaining by Kennedy's friends in the UAW, Schrade and Marvin Brody. In the face of the organized hostility to Kennedy from national labor leadership, it had been a remarkable triumph to arrange this gathering, and it might have been turned into one of the first cracks in labor's anti-Kennedy barrier. Instead, the Labor-for-Kennedy committee had to send out a thousand-dollars'-worth of hurried cancellation telegrams Friday night. The disgust among these valiant followers was almost tangible.

Although he took less time about it, McCarthy, despite his aversion to "details," had also been thoroughly briefed by Paul Gorman and Jeremy Larner. In particular, they had concentrated on the problems of urban decay and poverty—where they knew McCarthy's image was weakest and where they expected Kennedy's attack to be sharpest. They went back to the break-up-the-ghetto speech of May 28, at Davis, and went over the reasoning behind it. It was here, obviously, that the main clash would come.

Then, before leaving for the television studio, McCarthy spent a quarter-hour or so in discursive chat with Robert Lowell. Not all the

McCarthy staffers were persuaded of the advantage of having America's premier poet permanently built into their political operation. In a campaign not marked for hardness of nose, some people felt that the plasticity of Lowell's distinguished organ was altogether excessive. Among such people, there was a tendency to feel that Lowell distracted McCarthy from the political ordeal before him.

The scene outside the studio, when the candidates arrived shortly before six p.m., reflected the momentary dominance the McCarthy campaign had achieved. The crowd was entirely pro-McCarthy, except for a small group of blacks who apparently wished to tax Senator Kennedy about the question of black representation on the panel. A McCarthy organizer with a bullhorn told the crowd to cheer furiously when their man arrived, and to fall into silence for Kennedy. McCarthy arrived, looking distinctly pleased with himself, via the front door. Kennedy arrived a little later, via a side door. Like good professionals, they showed no sign of their personal antagonism while they were arranged around a table with the moderator, Frank Reynolds, and the two-man panel—ABC's political editor, Bill Lawrence, and Congressional correspondent, Bob Clark. McCarthy looked composed, almost to the point of inertia. Kennedy looked rather edgy, and as usual, on the screen he looked almost a decade younger than he looked in the flesh.

The order of questions had been decided by flipping a coin, and the first one was addressed to McCarthy. "If in fact you were President, what would you do at this time that President Johnson is not doing in order to bring peace in Vietnam?"

The question opened up a slight but significant difference in attitude between McCarthy and Kennedy. "I think these are the important positions that have to be taken," McCarthy said.

> One is a de-escalation of the war; and secondly, a recognition that we have to have a new government in South Vietnam. I am not particularly concerned whether it is called a coalition or a fusion or a new government of some kind. And we have to recognize that that government would include the National Liberation Front. I think this is prerequisite to any kind of negotiations that may move on to talk about what the nature of that new government might be.

Kennedy's comment was more aggressive than had been expected:

> I would pursue the negotiations in Paris. At the same time, I would make it quite clear that we would expect Saigon, the government in Saigon, would begin their own negotiations with the National Liberation Front.

I would be opposed to what I understand Senator McCarthy's position is, of forcing a coalition on the government of Saigon, a coalition with the Communists, even before we begin the negotiations.

I would make it quite clear that we are going to the negotiating table, not with the idea that we want them to unconditionally surrender, and that we expect that the National Liberation Front and the Vietcong will play some role in the future political progress of South Vietnam, but that should be determined by the negotiators, and particularly by those people of South Vietnam.

I think that is terribly important that we accept that, because without accepting that, what we are really asking for is unconditional surrender, and they are not going to turn over their arms, lay down their arms, live in peace, if the votes and the government are going to be run by General Ky and General Thieu.

The next point: I would demand privately and publicly, an end of public corruption, the official corruption that exists in Vietnam, a land-reform program that is meaningful so that they can gain the support of the people themselves. . . . I would end the search-and-destroy missions by American troops and American Marines and let the South Vietnamese soldiers and troops carry the burden of the conflict.

It was a curiously cobbled and not particularly honest piece of debating. By implication, Kennedy seemed to try to make McCarthy look as though he was caving in to the Communists. Yet he himself made proposals which appeared to be essentially the same as McCarthy's, but dressed up in more hawkish language.

McCarthy, naturally, counterattacked on this point:

I didn't say I was going to force a coalition government on South Vietnam. I said we should make it clear that we were willing to accept that. . . . Now if the South Vietnamese want to continue to fight, work out their own negotiation, that is well and good. But I don't think there is much point in talking about reform in Saigon, or land reform, because we have been asking for that for five years and it hasn't happened.

There were some further reflections on the pointlessness of the Administration's bombing policy in Vietnam, on which there was little contention between the candidates. And then there was a little blood. Bob Clark said to McCarthy:

Senator McCarthy, the McCarthy for President Committee . . . has been running full-page ads in California papers in recent days saying that Senator Kennedy must bear part of the responsibility for the decision to intervene in Vietnam. The implication seems to be that, even though he has been a war critic for the past three years, he should be ruled out as President because of his participation in that decision in the Kennedy Administration. Is that what you mean?

MCCARTHY: I don't think we said it should be ruled out at all, Bob. He has said that he would take some responsibility for it. The question is, how much responsibility? I was talking more about the process. I said that one of the things we ought to talk about is the process by which decisions were made with reference to this war, because one of our problems has been to find out who decides and who is responsible, and on what kind of evidence did we have this escalation?

This was the same accusation that McCarthy had leveled against Kennedy ever since the Cow Palace speech: that Kennedy was enmeshed in the history and the thinking which had produced the disaster in Vietnam. The Kennedy camp resented this tactic bitterly and passionately believed that the charge was unfair—as passionately as Lyndon Johnson felt that credibility-gap stories were unfair to him. In both cases, however, the sting of the charges was that they were not entirely unjustified.

An extra dimension of resentment in the Kennedy camp was added by the feeling that McCarthy, had he been in power in the brave days of "counterinsurgency," might have acted just as Robert Kennedy had. There was something in this, for Gene McCarthy in the fifties had not stood further aside from the Cold War than most other liberal Democrats.

But with this advertisement, the McCarthy people had gone too far, and Kennedy, who had been quietly boiling off-camera, burst in: "[The ad] also said that I intervened in the Dominican Republic. . . . I wasn't even in the Government at the time!" There followed one of those flurried interchanges that sound confused on television and are not a great deal clearer in print:

KENNEDY: Now how did they get that?
MCCARTHY: Well, I think that what they did, I had—
KENNEDY: I wasn't even in the Government at the time.
MCCARTHY: Well, you weren't out very long.
KENNEDY: But I—
MCCARTHY: I don't want to fault you on that.
KENNEDY: And then it ran again today.
MCCARTHY: We stopped it—it may have run in two papers, but I don't think it ran twice.
KENNEDY: I saw it again this morning. I wasn't involved in the Dominican Republic, I wasn't even in the Government, and I criticize this.
MCCARTHY: What I said was that this was a process, what was involved in our going into Cuba, involved in our going into the Dominican Republic, and also into Vietnam and that I wanted to talk about

the process. In any case, I had not seen the ad. When I saw it, I said, "Stop it," and they stopped it as soon as they could.

KENNEDY: I appreciate that.

By now, the viewers, who presumably were rather hazy about the Dominican Republic, must have been wondering what was going on. But McCarthy was not done yet. He had a countercharge to produce, having made it clear that his own offending advertisement had been censored:

> McCARTHY: Which is not quite what happened to the voting record of McCarthy which was distributed across the country and is being mailed out in this state right now.
>
> REYNOLDS: Would you like to respond to that?
>
> KENNEDY: I don't know to what he is referring.
>
> McCARTHY (*smiling genially, and reaching back*): I have it in my pocket.

This was one of a number of somewhat unfortunate leaflets that were put out in one or two states, the original model being apparently the work of Dr. Martin Sheppard of New York. Most of them distorted McCarthy's record vis-à-vis Kennedy by ignoring a period when he had been absent from the Senate due to illness, and by making much of the fact that he had once voted against a bill to outlaw the poll tax. (There had been a genuine tactical difference among the liberals who were trying to abolish the poll tax, and McCarthy, along with several other impeccable opponents of poll tax, had gone against the bill at the request of Attorney General Katzenbach, who had said, correctly, that the poll tax would be declared unlawful by the Supreme Court and argued that the ruling would be more effective than an ambiguous statute.) Wherever such leaflets had appeared, the official Kennedy people had denied all connection with them, but the McCarthy people resented their appearance just as much as the Kennedy people resented the attempt to involve their hero in the Dominican escapade. McCarthy was encouraged by the television not to produce his evidence—perhaps it was as well they *were* in control—and the discussion was led back to Vietnam, and thence to domestic affairs, and at first it seemed there was no important difference between the two men. Both of them adumbrated their concern for America's black minority. There would be no prospect of preserving civil order, Kennedy said,

> unless we have some communication with those who feel that they are suffering from injustices. I have gone into the ghettos, I have talked to the Indians or Mexican-Americans or whatever group, and said, "We

can't solve these problems overnight, this cannot be solved by violence and lawlessness, but what we can do is to start at least providing jobs and employment for people. . . ." In some of these areas the unemployment is thirty and forty per cent. In some parts of the United States it is up to eighty per cent. I have been to Indian villages where it is up to one hundred per cent.

I think we have to provide jobs, with the government being the employer of last resort and the bringing the private sector in in a major way and hiring people, doing away as much as possible with the welfare system, the handout, the dole, and getting people jobs, just by giving the private sector tax incentives and tax credits.

McCARTHY: I think I am in general agreement. . . . I think critical to all of this is our really giving genuine hope to people who live in the ghettos or who live in poverty. . . . And unless we do that, I think we have to face the prospect that no matter how much repression we have, there will be protests, there will be some violence in America.

But now a difference did begin to emerge—McCarthy was talking about the cure in terms of public-housing programs with Federal funds, and Kennedy was returning to his proposition that the work could be done by the private sector of the economy, aided chiefly by tax incentives. McCarthy was complaining about the Congressional cuts in housing funds, which had reduced the suggested program of the President's Commission on Civil Rights by ninety per cent, when Kennedy came in with

I don't think those housing programs are going to be satisfactory, any more than the housing programs that we have had in the last twenty years. Public housing has not been adequate and 221-D-3 [Federal-funded medium-income housing, generally regarded as a flop], which is the other major housing program, has not built the housing where it is necessary in the United States. I think a far less expensive way is to bring in the private sector and have them do it.

That, said ABC's Bob Clark, was an interesting point. "I think it points up a difference in your basic programs for housing." Curiously, McCarthy said, "I don't think it does, no." But in fact it did, within the next few minutes. Kennedy agreed that his proposal was to rebuild the ghettos and to improve conditions for black men in rural areas. "You keep people where they are at the present time," said Kennedy. It was certainly not a radical position: perhaps Kennedy advanced it so firmly out of an oppressive feeling that he was being cut off from support among the white middle class. McCarthy now put forward a considerably more radical position, which, in the nonexistent world of ideal politics, should have made a powerful appeal to Kennedy's most loyal supporters among the underprivileged. Paradoxically, each man was now appealing to the other man's natural constituency. McCarthy said,

> I would say we have to get into the suburbs, too, with this kind of housing, because some of the jobs are in the city and some jobs are being built there, but most of the employment is now in the belt line outside of the cities, and I don't think we ought to perpetuate the ghetto if we can help it, even by putting better houses there for them or low-cost houses.
>
> What we have got to do is to try to break that up. Otherwise, we are adopting a kind of apartheid in this country, a practical apartheid. And I see that some industry can go into the ghetto, but some of the housing has got to go out of the ghetto so there is a distribution of races throughout the whole structure of our cities and on into our rural areas. But so far as who builds is concerned, I think there is no question but what it has to be a private-sector sort of an effort, and it means funding, I think, five billion or six billion a year, eventually, for this kind of housing in the same way that we have funded four billion to five billion a year for the interstate highway programs, or the same way we funded for the rural-electrification program back in the thirties.
>
> But it has to be there so that men can plan, the construction industry can adjust, the building trades can adjust, and to be there not for one year and then go down, not there while interest rates are low and then disappear when interest rates go high, but clearly funded so as to carry over a period of five to ten years so the housing needs of this country are met.

It was the message of the Davis speech. McCarthy was proposing reforms quite outside the mythology of private enterprise, reforms which, in theory at least, addressed themselves to the actual distribution of American wealth. But was it practical politics? Kennedy, plainly, did not think it was, and he came in with a brutal attack:

> I am all in favor of moving people out of the ghettos. We have forty million Negroes who are in the ghettos at the present time. We have here in the state of California a million Mexican-Americans whose poverty is even greater than many of the black people. *You say you are going to take ten thousand black people and move them into Orange County.* [Our italics.] The people who graduate from high school, which are only three out of ten of the people—or of children who go to these schools, only three out of ten graduate from high school, and the ones who graduate from high school have the equivalent of an eighth-grade education. So to take them out of where forty per cent of them don't have any jobs at all—that is what you are talking about. If you are talking about one hundred people, that is one thing. But if you are talking about hitting this problem in a major way, to take these people out, put them in the suburbs where they can't afford the housing, where their children

can't keep up with the schools, and where they don't have the skills for
the jobs, it is just going to be catastrophic.

I want [them] to move as other groups have moved in the United
States, that as they get the job and get the training, then they themselves
can move out into other areas of the United States and will be accepted
and will find jobs and employment.

But that does not exist. That does not exist. Those are not the
conditions we are facing in this country at the present time.

It was not an attractive outburst: no matter what gloss might be put
on it, it looked like a crude attempt to appeal to the prejudices of the
white suburbs, to put into McCarthy's mouth the proposal to "take ten
thousand black people and move them into Orange County." McCarthy
had said no such thing, and even if the Kennedy researchers did feel that
their opponent had been talking radicalism without going into sufficient
practical detail, that was no excuse for so blatant a perversion of the
record.

What was really extraordinary was that McCarthy let the attack
pass. "He isn't a man for confrontation," said one of his speech-writers
later, with a mixture of affection and resignation. He could have deployed
a little righteous anger, both at Kennedy's distortion of his own position
and at the strange contrast between Kennedy's famous concern for the
black man and his willingness to use white prejudice as a demagogue's
device. Having thus gained the floor, McCarthy could have pointed out
that he was not proposing haphazard shipments of ill-equipped Negroes
into the suburbs, but rather carefully planned movements of people to
areas where developing suburban industries were creating jobs. He could
have pointed out that many of the jobs being created in the suburbs did
not necessarily require a high-school education, and that such movements
could help to alleviate one of the most difficult problems of the ghettos,
namely congestion. But he did not carry it through. He replied to
Kennedy:

There are an estimated two hundred and fifty thousand jobs available,
but there aren't people within reach. I didn't want to raise—I thought
that you really—when this question was first raised, that this was not
your clear position of concentrating that much on the ghettos.

One could only conclude that McCarthy had not been listening to
what Kennedy had been saying for several years. Few things in politics
could have been clearer than Kennedy's commitment to amelioration of
ghetto life as a solution to the urban crisis. And Kennedy emphasized his
position bluntly in a follow-up to McCarthy's feeble counter:

I want to do the things in the suburbs, but what I am saying is, in order to meet the really hard-core heart of the problem, we have to face the fact that a lot of these people are going to have to live here for another several decades, and they can't live under the conditions they are living under at the present time.

A television debate on a complex subject tends, for most people, to resemble a boxing match in which one is not shown the interchange of blows but must judge from the expressions on the boxers' faces which one is winning. Apparently, California viewers thought on the whole that Kennedy "won"—at least, that was the tentative evidence of an inquiry by Los Angeles pollster Don Muchmore.

But, in reality, the McCarthy and Kennedy positions never engaged with each other, intellectually—although few things could have had a more salutary effect on national politics than a thorough working out of the two viewpoints. Perhaps this might have been possible, but, in the frustrating manner of television discussions, it sheared off in another direction at the moment when genuine conflict—as against nit-picking altercation—was possible. Bill Lawrence asked Kennedy whether it was true, as Drew Pearson was suggesting, that Kennedy, when he was Attorney General, had authorized a wire-tap on Martin Luther King's telephone. Looking straight into the camera, Kennedy went into an obvious set piece:

> I was involved as Attorney General, had the responsibility for, the national security of the United States. Under an agreement that was made by Franklin Roosevelt in 1940, the Attorney General was given permission to give approval of a wire-tap—I never gave any permission for bugging. Nobody was given, nor was permission asked for, in any case. It was given, permission to wire-tap, in cases that involved the national security of the United States, where the Director of the Federal Bureau of Investigation and others felt that the national security of the United States was threatened.
>
> I have never discussed individual cases, and it would be a violation of the law if I did, no matter what the political benefits might be for me.
>
> But what I do want to say is, as far as Martin Luther King is concerned, he was a loyal, dedicated American who, in my judgment, made a distinct contribution to this country.

It was scarcely a convincing rebuttal. McCarthy did not comment on what Kennedy had said but developed another of his favorite points, about responsibility in Washington, which led to a mild disagreement with Kennedy. McCarthy reiterated his belief that J. Edgar Hoover should be replaced as chief of the FBI, saying that the agency had "run long enough under one head, and we ought to have another look at it, with a new director, because there are enough indications of practices there that I think should be challenged."

Having passed up the chance for a major debate on American social policy, Reynolds now remarked that there did not seem to be very many differences between Senator McCarthy and Senator Kennedy. "Where do you disagree?" he asked. McCarthy said there was probably disagreement on "Dean Rusk and on Robert McNamara and on some of the persons in government." Everyone set off happily in pursuit of this subject—except, that is, Kennedy, who complained that he always said he was not going to "deal in personalities." Indeed, when Bill Lawrence pressed him on the matter of appointments in the event of his becoming President, he said, "If I am elected President of the United States, you can watch and see."

Of course, it was a fact that most of the officials liable to come under discussion were appointments he and his brother John had made. Kennedy, in another contrast to the impression of him as a ruthless politician, felt a certain personal loyalty to these men—a feeling that he was partially responsible for them—which made it impossible for him to attack them. An unscrupulous politician would not have hesitated to attack an old friend who had become so unpopular as Dean Rusk. Neither could a consistent radical have failed to attack an old friend who was as hopelessly wrong as Rusk was by any radical analysis. Kennedy's refusal to do so is excellent evidence that he was neither unscrupulous nor radical. But it left him in the position of saying that in the American political system it was somehow improper to talk about cabinet appointments while on campaign. Rusk, he said, "has been a very dedicated American, committed to performing a service to the United States. I happen to disagree with the policies that he is espousing in very important areas of this country . . . but I don't question his integrity." Nobody, of course, had questioned his integrity—only his policy.

Lawrence now returned to the point with another direct question about Rusk: did Kennedy think Rusk had been there too long?

> KENNEDY: No, I think with all the problems that are affecting the United States, with the internal problems that we have and the problems around the rest of the world, to talk about it in terms of personality of whether somebody has been there too long, I have made it quite clear that I think I disagree with him, but I say he is a dedicated American. . . . I think to try to answer it on the basis of who you are going to

fire and who you are going to continue in office— Obviously I have a direct difference, quite clear difference, with the Secretary of State. I doubt very much that he would want to remain under those circumstances. But I don't want to be playing games with people's reputation, or what I am going to do with them or not do with them. . . . If you have a President of the United States who disagrees with the Secretary of State, I don't imagine they would stay together very long.

McCarthy made some more mileage on this subject, although he might have handled his flick at the late John Kennedy more kindly:

I think we give Cabinet members too much protection. You say, "He is a dedicated man, he is serving the country." They ought to be held responsible for policy mistakes and for position mistakes. I think your brother was too kind to a number of people after the Bay of Pigs, myself. I think he was. I think that this builds a certain weakness into the American government, I think. You say, "Well, this man was appointed, therefore we have to protect him." I think cabinet members ought to be more expendable than Senators, really. Where they make mistakes, as in the British Cabinet system, you say, "Well, all right, you made a mistake, and now you go." If a man makes a mistake now, you can't let him go. He is built in. You are likely to be let go if you are successful. They say, "Well, you have been a great Secretary, good-by."

That was, effectively, the end of the argument. Each man was given a "couple of minutes" to state, uninterrupted, the reasons why he thought he ought to be President. Kennedy spoke first, and stressed his experience in the Cabinet, his experience as Attorney General. "I was involved in the three great questions that affect our country, the problems of peace, the problems of the races getting along together, and the problems of the development of—the problems of riots and violence in this country." He saw America, "as Thomas Jefferson said, standing for the last best hope of mankind, which we are in this country. We have dealt with the problems of riots when I was Attorney General, and we also dealt with the problems of equal justice."

McCarthy mentioned his twenty years in the House and Senate, and the fact that he had served on nearly every one of the important committees in that time. And,

since nineteen forty-nine, we have been involved in the problem of civil rights. Not only that, but the problems of migratory workers. I was the first, back in fifty-two, to begin to raise a question about them. . . . I think when they begin to look at my record they will say "Here is someone who has been concerned about us for a long, long time. He may not have received any publicity, but he saw what our needs were. . . ."

McCarthy put forward some characteristically involuted reflections on the nature of leadership:

> I think there is something to be said for a President or a Presidential candidate who can somehow anticipate what the country wants, especially when what they want is on the side of good and justice, and to provide not real leadership in the sense of saying, "You have got to follow me," but at least to be prepared to move out ahead somewhat so that people of the country can follow.

Afterward, most of the partisans in each camp were convinced their man had "won." Rafer Johnson (who, apart from making sure Kennedy did not vanish in crowds, was himself a prospective Democratic Congressman) said exultantly, "The Senator [Kennedy] murdered him." Kennedy himself was supposed to have said of McCarthy, "He didn't do his homework." In the McCarthy camp, the general feeling was that the uppity little Bostonian had been taught a lesson, and only the speechwriters saw it as a missed opportunity—especially as, on this occasion, McCarthy *had* done his homework. "I guess by the time it got to that point," said one of them later, "he had decided he'd won and had stopped listening."

The shooting of Robert Kennedy early in the morning of Wednesday, June 5, came as a shock, but not as a surprise. When the first news rippled through the crowd in the Ambassador Hotel, the reaction was one of horror, but not of disbelief. "They killed him!" people said. Scarcely anyone needed to ask who had been killed. (One of the few who did have to ask was Arthur Placencia, one of the six uniformed policemen who ran into the hotel at word of trouble, and wrenched Sirhan out of the hands of the people who were holding him down. Kennedy, according to Los Angeles police chief Tom Reddin, had refused police protection. When Sirhan had been "given his rights"—asked if he wanted an attorney—and removed from the bloodstained kitchen passage, Placencia turned to Jesse Unruh, and asked, "By the way, who did he shoot?")

The Ambassador Hotel is not a suitable locale for tragedy—and certainly not in the view of its executives, from whom, on the morning after Kennedy's death, it was remarkably difficult to extract even a recognition that so raw and cruel a process had commenced on their premises. It is an old-fashioned place, with heavy carpets, chandeliers, palms, and dark wood where the new hotels wear bright synthetics. Opposite, on Wilshire Boulevard, is the Brown Derby restaurant. One of the night clubs in the hotel is the Coconut Grove, the haunt of fashion frequented mainly by teen-agers who look, in its Oriental magnificence, as awed as if they strayed on to the stage during a performance of *Aïda*.

The Ambassador, in fact, seems to have more to do with the faded myths of the thirties than the bright, preposterous surface of present-day Los Angeles. But its cavernous halls and ballrooms are well suited for political functions, and on the same night another primary victor was celebrating there. That was Dr. Max Rafferty, a stern opponent of all forms of permissiveness, except where the right to bear arms is concerned. He had just beaten the liberal Thomas Kuchel for the Republican Senate nomination.

The geography of the assassination was simple enough. Kennedy made his speech in the Embassy Room. He stepped down behind the dais to walk through a kitchen passage to give a press conference in a smaller room adjoining. In the passage, Sirhan Sirhan was waiting, with his silly little gun. It was only a .22, and the experts say that you need at least a .38 to kill a man effectively. (Indeed, Dr. Henry Cuneo, one of the men who operated on Kennedy's wound, said that had the small bullet which hit Kennedy's head gone only one centimeter more to the rear he would have lived.) But there was more to it than that, of course. As the man said in *A Coffin for Dimitrios,* "What matters in an assassination is not who pulled the trigger, but who paid for the bullet."

Kennedy spent most of his last day at the Malibu Beach home of John Frankenheimer, the film director. In the afternoon, he surfed with his children. Twelve-year-old David Kennedy got caught in an undertow, and his father had to dive in and pull him out, acquiring in the process a large bruise on his forehead, probably from striking the hard sand. Around three p.m., there was the first news of the polling, when CBS, having taken samples of early precincts, projected the possibility of a forty-nine-to-forty-one Kennedy victory. But he was too experienced not to know that the CBS projections, which tended to come out first, were sometimes misleading, and that it would be emotionally wasteful, if nothing else, to start thinking of victory before the more cautious computer experts at NBC had given the word. So he took a short nap, and went back to his suite on the fifth floor of the Ambassador at about eight o'clock.

Downstairs, in the Embassy Room, the excitement was uncomplicated. There were many young people in the tight-packed crowd, and from eight p.m. at the latest none of them doubted their man had won. They just wanted him to come down and speak to them. But up in Suite 512, the outlook was more complex. It was almost certainly a win—but it was hard to gauge how good a win it was. The California voting pattern, sharply divided between the northern pole, around San Francisco, and the southern, around Los Angeles, makes judgment difficult. Early, it became clear that McCarthy, as expected, had won the north, as he had won the somewhat similar territory of Oregon. Equally, it was fairly clear that he had not won it by enough to offset the advantage Kennedy would get in the south, particularly in Los Angeles County. But Los Angeles County usually comes in late, and this night came in later than usual. To add to the difficulties, the computer in Fresno, handling the vote from the Central Valley, was not working properly, and a team of technicians had to be flown in to reprogram it. The delicate question was the effect of the victory on McCarthy and his followers. Every word, and every action, would have to be aimed toward closing the wounds that had been opened in March and had been widened since. This was the turning point for the strategy Theodore Sorensen had outlined ten days earlier: "reunite the liberals in June, reunite the Democrats in August, and reunite the country in November."

There was a crucial test approaching in New York on June 18, and no one knew better than Kennedy that, although it was his own state, he had some passionate enemies there. After the Oregon primary, McCarthy had filled Madison Square Garden for a wildly enthusiastic rally; there were plenty of people there who would fight a bitter delaying action against Kennedy on the slightest excuse. If he was to be in trouble in New York, it would be hard to challenge Humphrey elsewhere.

As Kennedy watched the returns come in on television, he promised to "chase Hubert's ass all over the country." But he knew that such a headlong pursuit would sway few professional politicians.

Nobody thought that evening that there was any chance of a personal accommodation with Eugene McCarthy. The bitterness was too deep for that. But, as Sorensen murmured, "We hope that some of his people might come to us after this." Chiefly, this meant Allard Lowenstein, who was now running in the New York primary for the Fifth Congressional District. In the last few days of the California campaign, Kennedy had said several times how important it was that "Al Lowenstein wins his primary."

By eleven-thirty, it was clear that Los Angeles County was going to Kennedy by a big enough margin to make victory entirely secure. And it was also clear that everyone knew as much about the final results as would be known that night. And so Kennedy decided to go down.

How long Sirhan had been waiting is not clear, but one of the kitchen helpers saw him in the passage at about eleven-forty-five.

Just before Kennedy went down, he asked Richard Goodwin to call Lowenstein in New York, but the connection could not be made before it was time to go. William Doherty, one of his organizers in South Dakota, rang through with late news of the smashing victory Kennedy had won in the simultaneous primary there. "It's marvelous how the Indians are coming out for you," said Doherty. "They've voted eight hundred and twelve for you, eleven for McCarthy, and four for Humphrey." "That's marvelous," said Kennedy. "I just wish we hadn't taken Oregon away from them." Shortly after that, he went down, arriving on the dais just after midnight.

Senator Kennedy was not alone in foreseeing the possibility that his campaign might end in assassination. Twelve days earlier, the San Francisco underground paper *Express-Times* had published an article by Marvin Garson (husband of Barbara, playwright of *MacBird*) cast in the form of an interview with the ghost of the assassinated President McKinley. "Don't waste your vote on Kennedy," Garson made McKinley say. "They're going to kill him." This was not a completely startling proposition to people who had seen the Kennedy campaign through Indiana, Nebraska, and California. There had often seemed a special edge of danger to it, a dimension of passion which is not part of ordinary politics.

In the Embassy Room, it was as though all the fierce tension of the past few weeks had been crammed and concentrated into that one space. There were, perhaps, fifteen hundred people there. The crowd's emotion had been feeding on itself for four hours, in the heat and the glare of the camera lights. There were television sets scattered around the room, switched to different channels; and each time a new projection came over, the people jammed around the sets carrying it roared with joy, and the roar would be answered by other sections of the crowd. Long before Kennedy appeared, the point had been reached where it no longer mattered whether the words coming over the television said the victory was large or small, or the prospects good or bad. Each response was a reflex to the name: Kennedy! There was a three-man rock group on the stage, but the sound of the instruments was only rarely audible above the clamor of the crowd. Eventually, the group gave up the attempt to sing and led a simple chant, which was picked up with fierce intensity: "R-F-K! R-F-K! R-F-K!"

And then Kennedy was there. His teeth gleamed startlingly white in the television lights and his tanned skin glowed. He looked, as he sometimes did, more vital, more handsome than any film star: the personification of brilliance and success. This last political moment went beyond politics: Kennedy was at once broker of power, magic leader, desired sexual object, protagonist of aspirations, liberator and hero. Societies have spent a long time separating such roles, and here they were reunited. There was too much in the vessel—*how great an act to spill it!* It did not matter any more how Kennedy saw himself. It was how the people saw him that mattered. If people could love so much, someone surely must have an equivalent hate.

Kennedy spoke coolly and carefully. It was a short and magnanimous victory speech, which it needed to be if the politics of the next few weeks were to have the chance of success. "I think we can end the divisions in the United States. What I think is quite clear is that we can work together in the last analysis. And that is what has been going on within the United States over a period of the last three years—the division, the violence, the disenchantment with our society; the division, whether it's between blacks and whites, between the poor and the more affluent, between age groups, or in the war in Vietnam—that we can start to work together." It was not a finely turned speech. This was not the moment for one. But as a last testament, it was a fair enough summary of the best things he had wanted to say. There was an ironic echo of the things he had wistfully said—five months before at breakfast with the reporters in Washington—a campaign ought to be about.

"We are a great country, an unselfish country and a compassionate country. And I intend to make that my basis for running—" The crowd drowned him out for a moment. "We want to deal with our own problems in our country and we want peace in Vietnam. So, my thanks to all of you, and it's on to Chicago and let's win there."

Then, struggling through the banks of cameramen, he was gone. The crowd relaxed; the tension went out of them. The moment with the hero had been enough, and for them the experience of the night was concluded. But there was still Kennedy's press conference to come. The two of us who had been watching the speech suddenly realized that it was not going to be all that easy to get to. It was to be held in the Colonial Room, an annex flanking the entrance to the Embassy Room. It was clearly impossible to get there through the body of the crowd, now pressing slowly toward the bottleneck of the entrance. Kennedy had vanished toward the little passage which connected the rudimentary backstage of the Embassy Room to its annex, but he was being followed by another dense column which seemed likely to block that access. The Ambassador is a warren-like place, and if you go out through a pair of steel doors which open from the backstage area, you can get down a shallow flight of steps, and run round to the front entrance of the hotel. Then a brisk sprint along a sunken passage, lined with costly shopfronts, and up a curving stairway, brings you out onto the broad main lobby outside the Embassy Room.

At the top of the stairs, we saw that there was something wrong with the people. There should have been an easy, gratified throng pouring slowly out of the Embassy Room. But the flow was disjointed: people were running hard, and others were stumbling softly into each other in a daze. There are big leather banquettes in this lobby: several people were slumped across them. Here and there, a figure slipped limply to the ground. Shock ripples oddly through a crowd, and although words may start it, the movement soon outpaces them, transmitted by lightning comprehension of the broken gestures, the blank expressions, with which disaster is acknowledged. *"What happened?" "They shot him— Kennedy's been shot."* For most people, *they* had shot him. Few made it singular: it was an impersonal executioner. Clearly, it was necessary to get there, and see.

There were still a lot of people in the Embassy Room, mostly standing, staring about them. It was a question of where was the epicenter of the shock: and it seemed that this was somewhere behind the flimsy screens that led from the dais to that kitchen passage. In the manner of these occasions, people were performing odd tasks which they had clearly devised for themselves. In disasters, people need to do this: it is sensible to give oneself something to do when the unbearable has occurred. People were moving about, very calmly, and telling other people to move back please, leave the room, so that there would be more air. It was a sad gesture, of course, because if there were people with gunshot wounds behind the screen small changes in the oxygen content of the hall were not going to make much difference. (Later, one realized that this apparently aimless chain of officiousness probably stemmed from Ethel Kennedy's appeal, in the little passage, for people to move back from her husband's body.)

Just beside the little stage, lying on a table, was a woman in bloodstained clothes. The blood is always so much more splotched about than you would think from pictures or movies. It is very hard to tell where people have been hurt. A black doctor was bending over the woman: he seemed to be telling her she was going to be all right. Someone said she was Mrs. Kennedy. But although she looked about the same build, she was not. So one moved on toward the passage. (That reflex is built into the task. The story was that Kennedy had been hit. Others wounded were incidental: any reporter will understand that there is no other way of looking at it.)

And then, after some maneuvering, and sliding past people, there it was. The cluttered passage was still densely packed with people, and a hoarse-voiced waiter was describing for a radio microphone how he had seen Kennedy get shot. It was very claustrophobic, like an alleyway deep in a ship, with the same coarse paint, naked metal, cooking smells, and yellow light. William Weisel, the ABC television producer, who had been hit while walking just behind Kennedy, lay on the floor very still, with a knee drawn up. It seemed that Kennedy, wounded at least twice, and Paul Schrade, also wounded, had just been carried out. Weisel had apparently been hit in the abdomen. After a few minutes, stretcher-bearers appeared and carried him out too. It was quite easy to see where Kennedy had been when he was shot. It was exactly on the diagonal between the ice cabinet and a long steel-topped row of heating cupboards. It was opposite the entrance to a second passage, entering at right angles, through which they had carried him away. There was a good deal of blood on the floor, which seemed very dark in the poor light, and there was a KENNEDY-FOR-PRESIDENT hat lying in it. On the wall by the ice cabinet, perhaps five feet from where Kennedy had fallen, five words were scrawled in crayon, which have not yet been satisfactorily explained but which in their absurd appropriateness heightened the irrational sense of ritual symbolism: THE ONCE AND FUTURE KING.

3

The Grief Machine

"One is never so happy or so unhappy as one imagines."

—La Rochefoucauld, *Maxims*

Circumstances conspired to make the period between the wounding of Robert Kennedy and his death as unpleasant as possible for everybody concerned. It was no one's fault particularly; it was just the natural functioning of impersonal publicity machinery. Kennedy was taken at first to Central Receiving Hospital, but, after a brief examination, it was clear that his only chance of survival lay in delicate brain surgery. Therefore he was transferred to Good Samaritan Hospital, which has a special expertise in that branch of medicine. The ambulance arrived at Good Samaritan a little after two a.m. Following it, only a few minutes later, was a Bell Telephone truck, zipping up the hill outside the hospital with a crew of technicians to rig temporary phones for the army of reporters. Within a few hours, a press room had been rigged up in an annex to the hospital; batteries of cameras with snaking cables were set up outside the entrance of the hospital, and its façade was floodlit by the glare of television lights. More than one person said, "I wonder if we aren't getting too good at this."

There was a large gap between the demand for news and the supply, which was not surprising because there was little the Kennedy staff could do except read medical bulletins. Each time Frank Mankiewicz or Pierre Salinger, stunned but tightly controlled, appeared with one of these bleak communications, he became the center of a jabbing circle of microphones, and had to blink into the hard lights and lenses behind them. The arrival or departure of a friend or relative at the doorway of

Good Samaritan immediately became a dramatic nugget of information, snatched up and disseminated with electric speed.

At two-thirty a.m., Frank Mankiewicz said that six surgeons were about to start operating. As it had been known that Kennedy had been wounded at least once in the head, there had not been much anticipation that he could recover. Mankiewicz's precise description of the wound made it seem impossible. "He has one superficial shoulder wound and one very critical wound—the bullet which entered the right mastoid bone on the right ear and has gone to the mid-line of the skull. That bullet is lodged in his brain."

At four-forty-five a.m., the second announcement merely recorded that surgery was continuing and might go on for another hour or two. The surgeons finished around five-forty-five—and the county medical examiner said later, no doubt rightly, that it had been very fine and skillful work. But the bullet, striking the spongy mass of the mastoid bone (the lump behind the ear), had scattered numerous fragments of bone and metal throughout the right side of Kennedy's brain, and the damage was too much to repair. If the small bullet had struck the bone a more glancing blow, Kennedy would have been alive and out of hospital in a few weeks. The luck that was not with Kennedy was with Paul Schrade: by an equally small margin, the bullet that hit the top of his skull failed to do vital damage, and he recovered completely—as did the four other people wounded by the eight shots Sirhan fired: William Weisel; Ira Goldstein, a nineteen-year-old Continental News Service reporter; Mrs. Elizabeth Evans, a Kennedy campaign worker; and Irwin Stoll, a campaign supporter, aged seventeen.

At seven-twenty a.m., Mankiewicz said that according to the doctors, the next "twelve to thirty-six hours would be a very critical period." Just before noon, Eugene McCarthy arrived at the hospital. The dimensions of his defeat by Kennedy had now become clear, and the count (after some fluctuation which briefly put McCarthy ahead in the small hours) was near to the official computation of 46.3 per cent for Kennedy, 41.8 for McCarthy, and 11.9 for the Lynch slate. Nobody, however, was much interested in percentages: it was being said by the media that Kennedy had been struck down at the moment of his greatest political triumph. In view of the closeness of the margin, this was not quite true. But then the media are in the drama business.

Tragedy and reconciliation, for some reason, are thought to go together, but on this occasion no such thing was possible. As Robert

Kennedy lay dying, the breach between his supporters and McCarthy's widened further, irrespective of the fact that despite their disputations they had aimed for many of the same goals. The intensely personal character of their political rivalry made it inevitable. Whatever McCarthy said or did, the Kennedy people, in their grief, could respond to no gesture from the enemy; he was alive and their hero lay dying. And, tragedy or not, the McCarthy people could not forget that they had just been defeated and that, until the shots were fired, Kennedy had been scheming to rob them of support. Jeremy Larner, McCarthy's chief speech-writer, had been invited to have breakfast with Kennedy the morning after the vote. He had declined, but Paul Gorman, the foreign-affairs speech-writer, had agreed to see Kennedy.

McCarthy had to go to the hospital—and something had to go wrong. What happened was that because McCarthy mentioned that he had to catch a plane to Washington and the traffic was bad, his police escort began to use sirens. The McCarthy people thought the police would turn the sirens off before getting to the hospital, but they did not. (There was no communication between the cars, so there was no way McCarthy could get the police to stop.) Apparently the incident rankled with the Kennedy supporters. At the hospital, McCarthy saw only Goodwin and Salinger. (Complaints about his alleged transgression with the sirens came back to McCarthy swiftly, and at the end of the year he commented sourly, in a *Boston Globe* interview, "When you get into that kind of response, you figure it is best not to try and prove anything any more.")

During the long afternoon and evening, there was no hint of hope. And when Mankiewicz walked to the press annex a minute before two a.m. on Thursday, June 6, his expression made his announcement plain in advance. Kennedy had died at one-forty-four a.m.—although one of the doctors said later that for all intents and purposes his wounds had extinguished his life some hours before medicine acknowledged the fact.

Around his bed at the end were his wife, Ethel, his brother Edward, two sisters, Jean and Patricia, his sister-in-law Jacqueline, and his brother-in-law Stephen Smith. And, of course, a priest. The three oldest children—Kathleen, Joseph, and Robert Jr.—had earlier seen their father as he lay unconscious on his deathbed. In this, as in most other details of the next few days, the Kennedys were helped to deal with death by the unflinching, ritualistic traditions of Irish Catholics unshaken in their faith. Their stoic dignity in performing the ceremonies of mortality was characteristically courageous.

It was harder to respect the funeral in its aspect as a public observance. Perhaps this was because the careless machinery of the cortège killed two people in New Jersey; but in general, these organized outpourings of grief, such as Churchill's funeral in Britain, or John Kennedy's funeral, suffer from the fact that under their coating of solemnity and good taste, it becomes impossible to distinguish between real and counterfeit emotions. When Kennedy's body was brought back to New York from Los Angeles, one of us was at the airport to see it arrive. Standing with a group of reporters, he noticed that they almost all watched the event on a specially rigged television screen. The actual coffin was passing behind their backs scarcely any farther away than the small-screen version. On these occasions, the tenuous connection between journalism, written or visual, and the real texture of events usually ruptures completely. A style takes over in which cities always pay hushed tributes, widows always give comfort to strangers and friends—in which, inevitably, New York received the dead Kennedy "with the sorrow and affection due a native son."

Those who still tried to record what they actually observed, rather than merely to register respectable emotion, seemed all the more valuable. One such was Russell Baker in the *New York Times,* with a cool and humane description of the crowd waiting to file past Kennedy's body at St. Patrick's Cathedral:

> The people who waited in a line twenty-five blocks long, eight abreast at many points, were neither shattered nor awed for the most part. They were a cross-section of everybody, including the shouters and jumpers and touchers who had been attracted by every campaign of all three Kennedys. A few were obviously in mourning. Some had obviously put on their Sunday best. But most were dressed "sensibly" for hot weather, as a crowd might dress for an outdoor political rally in midsummer.
>
> Five blocks from the cathedral the line moved with agonizing slowness. . . . The reason may have had something to do with the business of cutting into the line that was going on up near the cathedral. One woman from the Bronx, who seemed to reflect the general lack of awe for the occasion, boasted, "I've just snuck across the street and cut the line. I've got guts like he had."

On Saturday, June 8, the Requiem Mass was held. The list of those who attended demonstrated, for the last time, Kennedy's capacity for attracting into one personal coalition some of the most apparently disparate people and causes in American life. (This is not quite to say that all the people who attended his mass were his followers: indeed, some had been his opponents at the time he was killed.) This list of mourners seemed to make up a picture of the Kennedy world as they saw it themselves. It was a remarkable blend of aristocrats, American and British (Averell Harriman and Lord David Cecil); intellectuals (William Styron and Robert Lowell); athletes (Roosevelt Grier and James Whittaker); radicals (Michael Harrington and Julian Bond); conservatives (Douglas Dillon and Joseph Alsop). There were some figures who appeared incongruous at first glance, such as the reactionary Senators James Eastland and Russell Long. But the coding system of the guest list made it plain that they were there as Senate colleagues of the dead man, whom it would be difficult not to invite. The group of Kennedy family and friends who handled the listmaking decided that, in the case of some VIPs who expressed a desire to take part in the ceremony, incongruity outweighed importance. Mayor Yorty, George Wallace, and Billy Graham all wanted to join in and were refused.

Still, those listed as friends made a marvelously eclectic assortment: for instance, could Barry Goldwater and James C. Hagerty, Eisenhower's uncommunicative press secretary, have any other friend but Kennedy in common with Tom Hayden? Intriguing figures popped up here and there throughout the list. Gianni Agnelli, the boss of Fiat, and Sir Frederick Ashton, the British choreographer. Governor Roger Branigin, who had done so much to brake Kennedy's momentum in Indiana. Milton Friedman, the high priest of laissez-faire. Kenneth Keating, the man who had lost his Senate seat to Kennedy. Senator Roman Hruska of Nebraska, foe of gun laws. Floyd McKissick and James Meredith. William Manchester, the quarrel over *Death of a President* forgotten. Tommy Smothers of the Smothers Brothers, and General David N. Shoup, the tough Marine who had denounced the Vietnam war.

Generally, it was closer friends who were invited to ride on the train that took the body to Washington, and here there was a good sprinkling of people from show business: Kirk Douglas, Kim Novak, Shirley MacLaine, Jason Robards. There were also Cesar Chavez, John D. Rockefeller IV, Leonard Bernstein, Truman Capote, Isaiah Berlin, Allard Lowenstein, Carl Kaysen. And, of course, apart from the working press there was a copious number of journalists and commentators, including Stewart Alsop, Rowland Evans, Joseph Kraft, Richard Harwood, David Brinkley, Sander Vanocur, and Jimmy Breslin. Indeed, as the train moved through the industrial landscape of New Jersey, with the coffin laid on chairs at window level in an observation car at the end, the distinction between mourners and communicators of mourning among the thousand or more passengers more or less completely broke down.

It was a journey organized with all the characteristic efficiencies and inefficiencies of the "Kennedy Machine." Press releases were crisp and to the point, liquor was free—and the train left New York almost an hour behind schedule. The accident occurred at Elizabeth, a drab station fifteen miles from New York. There was the same muted crowd—half black, half white—as elsewhere. A Negro woman waved what looked like a yellow Kleenex. None of the white people responded, except that some of them pointed movie cameras. Another train, northbound, flashed past. "They've killed a woman. Oh, my God, they've killed her," someone shouted. From the train, keeping to its undeviating thirty miles per hour, it was impossible to discover what had happened.

Later, it emerged that in the crush, some fifteen people had spilled onto the track, not perhaps realizing that northbound trains were still running. Mrs. Antoinette Severini, a widow, and John Curia, a widower, died. Five other people were hurt, none seriously, although further along, at Trenton, an eighteen-year-old boy was badly burned when he touched an overhead live wire. The Penn Central officials, sensibly, stopped all northbound traffic.

The funeral train was slowed down, and then a brakeshoe malfunction developed which slowed it even further. The mood aboard the train (most of the coaches were without air-conditioning, and the sweat was pouring off the television-equipment bearers) was by now one of glum horror. Ethel Kennedy moved along the train, with her son Joseph, exchanging greetings, thanking people for coming. Their bearing and composure, amid this nightmare which seemed to be extending itself into infinity, was beyond admiration. "He's a real Kennedy," someone said.

The train, which had been scheduled to make the journey to Union Station, Washington, in four and a half hours, took just over eight, arriving at 9:08 p.m. Long before then, most of its human freight had slipped into a deliquescent, boozy gloom. If there were any on board, apart from the immediate family and friends, who could still summon up a sensible human feeling, they must have been among the most startling emotional athletes of their time.

Insofar as these occasions have value, it is to provide some reasonably dignified catharsis for national sorrow: in this case, the collapse of organization quite canceled out that worthy purpose. The afflicted train limping through urban America became a moving focus of absurd mor-

bidity, thoroughly mixed with banality by the communications media
and disseminated throughout America, to no beneficial result. Aboard
the train, those who could not contrive the resource of black humor vied
with each other in maudlin exaggerations about the national predicament.
The country, men agreed, was "shot to hell." An agency reporter, staring out of the window, said solemnly, "I saw a woman back there in the
woods. She was all alone, looking very still and dignified. I bet the
moment we passed some degenerate came out from behind a tree and
bumped her off."

In the dark, going through Washington on the way to Arlington
National Cemetery, there were moments of redemption. The procession
stopped for four minutes beneath the half-lit bulk of the Lincoln Statue,
while a Marine Corps brass choir and two local choirs sang "The Battle
Hymn of the Republic," arguably still the most moving and durable of
all songs of national spirit. About three hundred of the campers from
Resurrection City watched in silence. On the other side of the Potomac,
in Virginia, hundreds of onlookers lit candles along the way through
the cemetery. At last, at ten-thirty, the funeral service began. It took
about fifteen minutes, and then the members of the family stepped forward, each to kiss the coffin in farewell. The gesture was a belated reminder that at the center of the news event there were real people, with
real sorrows.

The destruction of Robert Kennedy evoked, naturally, a powerful
wave of mourning and emotion. As in the case of the death of Martin
Luther King, shops, offices, and stock exchanges announced periods of
respectful closure, and the leaders of national opinion ascended to
their pulpits to pronounce upon the state of the land.

It was no doubt proper that they should find the outlook a sad one.
But all the same, the zeal displayed for sounding all-inclusive tocsins
might well be thought excessive, and something of a disservice to America.
For instance, there was James Reston in the *New York Times* declaring
that there was "something in the air of the modern world; a defiance
of authority, a contagious irresponsibility, a kind of moral delinquency
no longer restrained by religious or ethical faith." Showing that eager-
ness, marked among American pundits, to convert the specific American
experience into that of man at large—a tendency which perhaps annoys,
say, thoughtful Swiss or Cambodians—his article was headed "World
Morality Crisis." Although Reston did note that there had not been a
world war for some years (a good thing), there was a "plague of lawless-

ness and violence . . . sweeping the globe." There was more in the same manner—rather like Senator Frank Church's cry after the King assassination: "We are steeped in violence. It is the curse of the land."

Reston and many pundits who followed his line seemed ready to lump the disparate phenomena of political assassination, riots, student unrest, civil-rights killings, national war, and private murder into a single corpus of dismay. This not only produced a sense of general confusion and near panic, but also raised doubts about the essential seriousness of the comment. Complaint made too inclusive becomes meaningless—like railing against the condition of human nature or the sun's distressing habit of setting each evening—and has the appearance of ritual cleansing, rather than criticism aimed at specific problems. The beating of the breast diverted attention from the complexity of the issues and certainly from the interesting fact that in most respects America has become less, not more, violent in recent years. This is a trend so well established that it would be difficult to reverse, but the construction of an alarmist atmosphere could do a good deal in that direction. Reston, of course, is no campaigner for alarmism. But words like his seem all too likely to help to heat up the atmosphere to the advantage of people less scrupulous than he.

For instance, ten days after Robert Kennedy was shot, Governor Ronald Reagan made a speech on the matter of "law'n'order," which in normal times would surely have gone some distance toward discrediting him as a candidate for national office. As it was, it passed almost without criticism. Addressing twenty-five hundred Republicans at a hundred-dollar-a-plate dinner in Indianapolis, Governor Reagan enlarged on the "philosophy of permissiveness" and the "sick society." By way of illustration, he said that "in this week of tragedy, six policemen in Chicago have been killed in the line of duty." As Chicago is not far from Indianapolis, it was not surprising that he left his audience convinced, in the words of one observer, "that Ronald Reagan, if not indeed Matt Dillon, was needed in the White House, speedily."

As a matter of fact, during the whole of 1968 up to the time that Reagan spoke, there had been *two* policemen killed in Chicago in the line of duty—a matter for regret, but something less than the massacre the Governor described. During all of 1967, five Chicago policemen died on duty. But Reagan and his staff did not seem put out by their *gaffe*. A press secretary in Sacramento said that the Governor was "prepared to stand by the text," whatever that meant. He said he did not know where the figures came from. It was clear that the "law'n'order" controversy had entered the realm of mythology, at least as far as the politics of 1968 were concerned. (Eugene McCarthy was the only candidate who totally refused to take part in the game, and indeed refused even to use the words "law and order," on the ground that they had become code words for repression of the blacks.)

The first point that needs to be made is that manifestations of violence and disorder are not necessarily interrelated. Confining inquiry, for the moment at least, to the United States itself, at least five different kinds of phenomena can be discerned within the general area of alarm: mass urban rioting, political assassination, murder and general crime, civil-rights killings, and academic unrest. Each was subject to different trends, and any connections between them were not simple.

First, mass urban rioting is so familiar as to be almost a tradition—although a declining one. Riots were a frequent occurrence, and at a frequently spectacular level of violence, in the nineteenth century. This was particularly true during the second half of the century, when the expansion of cities got under way properly. But the phenomenon was already well established in the first half of the century; Alexis de Tocqueville, writing in 1835, devoted one of the more gloomy footnotes of *Democracy in America* to the subject:

> The United States has no metropolis, but it already contains several very large cities. Philadelphia reckoned 161,000 inhabitants, and New York 202,000, in the year 1830. The lower ranks which inhabit these cities constitute a rabble even more formidable than the populace of European towns. They consist of freed blacks in the first place, who are condemned by the laws and by public opinion to a hereditary state of misery and degradation. They also contain a multitude of Europeans who have been driven to the shores of the New World by their misfortunes or their misconduct. . . . As inhabitants of a country where they have no civil rights, they are ready to turn all the passions which agitate the community to their own advantage. Thus, within the last few months, serious riots have broken out in Philadelphia and New York. Disturbances of this kind are unknown in the rest of the country, which is not alarmed by them, because the population of the cities has hitherto exercised neither power nor influence over the rural districts.
>
> Nevertheless, I look upon the size of certain American cities, and especially on the nature of their population, as a real danger which threatens the future security of the democratic republics of the New World; and I venture to predict that they will perish from this circumstance, unless the government succeeds in creating an armed force which, while it remains under the control of the majority of the nation, will be independent of the town population and able to repress its excesses.

Not long after Tocqueville wrote, modern police forces began to be formed in the cities of Britain and America: a response to the problem of urban order that may be looked upon as the independent force he thought would be necessary (although it was not always armed). But it was a long time before the passions of the American city began to be moderated, a peak of fury being reached in the New York draft riots of July 1863. The riots lasted three days, numerous fires were lit, a thousand or more people were killed, and one enthusiastic mob roasted a Negro alive on Broadway. The offices of the *New York Times*—which favored the draft—were threatened. In response, a Gatling gun was set up in the foyer and manned by the proprietor, while the members of the editorial staff were stationed on the roof with rifles.

Two years later, thirty-four Negroes and four whites were killed during riots in New Orleans. Reconstruction riots in Memphis, Tennessee, killed forty-six Negroes, and another in Colfax, Louisiana, killed a hundred Negroes and white Republicans.

Apart from these great outbursts, there was a continuous background of urban violence and disorder, which did not begin to be mitigated until well into the twentieth century. (Incidentally, talk of the "frontier tradition" as the fount of violence can be very misleading. The major focus of violence has always been the big cities: while there was perpetual danger to life and limb in the great cities of the East, cow towns like Abilene, Wichita, and Dodge City were relatively safe.) And it is curious that the nostalgia for the "good old days" appears to be focused, hazily, on the late nineteenth century, precisely the period of maximum personal danger to the ordinary citizen in civil life. What, one wonders, would a modern "law'n'order" enthusiast make of such contemporary accounts of American urban life as Jacob A. Riis's *How the Other Half Lives*?

Between the great explosions of the nineteenth century and the riots in Watts (1965) and Detroit and Newark (1967), there were, of course, others. When an East St. Louis aluminum plant hired black workers in July 1917, there was a particularly terrible riot in which thirty-nine blacks and nine whites were killed and more than three hundred buildings destroyed. Then there was the famous week of rioting in Chicago in July 1919, when thirty people were killed. (Two American sages pronounced on the causes of that turmoil in Chicago: Walter Lippmann said that it was the consequence of social injustice, and J. Edgar Hoover, then an ambitious young Department of Justice lawyer, said that it was the work of Communist conspirators.) And there was the Detroit riot of 1943, in which twenty-five Negroes and nine whites were killed. There was also rioting in Harlem in 1943 in which six people were killed and over five hundred injured.

The riots in 1967 in Detroit (forty-three people killed) and Newark (twenty-five) were particularly horrifying because they were so well described by television. And examination of the absolute number of casualities make the 1967 Detroit riot appear to be a larger castastrophe than the one in 1943. But when the casualty figures are examined comparatively, bearing in mind the size of the city and the extent of the racial problem that was the cause of both riots, Detroit 1967 does not represent a break with the general trend of decling civil disorder. Not only did Detroit grow enormously between 1943 and 1967, its black population also increased as a proportion of the total. (From around ten per cent before the war, it rose to sixteen per cent in 1950 and twenty-nine per cent in 1960, and by 1965 it was thirty-four per cent and still rising at tremendous speed.)

The earlier riots (including the antidraft riots, which were, broadly, Irish versus blacks) were, quite blatantly, attacks by white civilians on blacks. But it is doubtful whether the riots of the sixties really represent any remarkable change as far as blacks are concerned, since their most frequent starting point has been friction between white policemen and blacks (as demonstrated in John Hersey's *The Algiers Motel Incident*) —and in this sense the only difference is that the whites have put on police uniforms. In their most significant aspect, the riots are all similar: that is, far more blacks than whites are killed in all major instances. In view of the ratio of casualties, it is curious and ironic that *whites* should feel menaced by *blacks*.

Given the profound social imbalances in American cities and the many opportunities for disaster, it is a remarkable thing that there has been so little mass violence and that on the whole the tendency is toward containment. This real situation presumably runs counter to the wishes of black revolutionaries and in favor of white conservatives: it is odd that these opposed groups should share the same delusion that mass violence is increasing. Indeed, there is evidence to suggest that riots by blacks will occur less frequently in the future. For instance, Chicago, which is measurably the most segregated of the great cities, has been relatively quiescent, while Detroit, in which the ghetto is far more broken up, far less monolithic, has been a center of turmoil. For if the twenty-year process of isolation and psychic destruction of the urban Negroes continues, as seems likely, then rioting on the present pattern will decline: it was another remark of Tocqueville's that revolutions are made by the half-satisfied, not the despairing. The paradox is that if genuine progress is made toward alleviating the condition of the blacks—whose predicament, it must be emphasized, is qualitatively different from that of other minorities—it may well, in the short run, result in more, not less, disorder.

Outbreaks of mass urban violence are not necessarily connected with the assassination of prominent citizens. That is, although the killing of Martin Luther King *did* touch off race riots, the killing of President Garfield did not. Indeed, these two acts were of essentially different kinds. Successful and unsuccessful attempts on the lives of Presidents and other prominent (white) politicians have been made relatively rarely, and by varied types of assassins, acting on distinctly heterogeneous and often quite delusionary motives. On the other hand, Martin Luther King's death fits into a well-established pattern in which black men and their allies—some obscure, some well known—have been killed by recognizably similar people for recognizably similar reasons. (The great exception is the assassination of Malcolm X in 1965.) These killings are a part, often an explicit part, of a white disciplinary structure constructed against the Negro—essentially, a Southern disciplinary structure.

For instance, Emmett Till was killed in Alabama in 1954 because he allegedly whistled at a white girl. Four small girls were killed when a bomb blew up a Negro church in Birmingham, Alabama, in 1963. Medgar Evers, the desegregation leader, was shot outside his house in Mississippi in 1963. Colonel Lemuel Penn, a black U.S. Air Force officer, was killed in 1964 by Georgia Klansmen, apparently infuriated by his rank. Also in 1964, three young civil-rights workers (two white, one black) were killed by Klansmen in Mississippi. In 1965, Mrs. Viola Liuzzo, a white civil-rights worker, was killed in Alabama. If the authors of all these crimes were brought together in one room, they would have a good deal in common. Some of these killers may have been deranged, but their motives, although evil, were similar and comprehensible. Their crimes were designed to discourage the emancipation of Southern Negroes.

A very different result would be obtained by assembling in one room the killers and would-be killers of Presidents. Lincoln was killed by a crazy Southerner with aristocratic notions who believed that he was striking a blow for the defeated Confederacy. James Garfield was shot in 1881 for purely personal, if eccentric, reasons: his assassin believed that Garfield had denied him an office he deserved. William McKinley was shot in 1901 by an anarchist who at any rate professed intricate ideological reasons, and Lee Harvey Oswald (if, indeed, it was he who shot John Kennedy) was said to be motivated entirely by psychological resentment against the eminent. Brought together, this group of assassins would probably try to assassinate each other. To add the unfortunate man who tried to kill Franklin Roosevelt (but succeeded in killing Mayor Cermak of Chicago) in 1933 and the man who gunned down Huey Long in 1935 in the denouement of a personal feud would merely compound the confusion. And the demented anti-Zionism of Sirhan Sirhan has nothing to do with any of the other motivations.

Assassinations of the great have such a shocking impact that it is easy to overlook that four killings of American Presidents over a period of a century does not really represent a trend. (During the same time, there were five assassinations of roughly comparable figures in France [President Carnot, 1894; Jean Jaurès, 1914; President Doumer, 1932; Foreign Minister Barthou, 1934; Admiral Darlan, 1942]—and there have been several attempts at General de Gaulle. Indeed, there were nine known attempts on the life of Queen Victoria during the "tranquil" years of the nineteenth century.)

Assassination is only a particularly noticeable type of murder, and assassinations and civil-rights killings must be seen against the general background of occurrence of violent crime. It appeared to be the stated view of almost all major politicians during the 1968 campaign that violent crime was increasing at a frightening rate—indeed, at times this belief appeared to have decisive effects on the course of political events. Presumably, it may therefore come as a surprise to most voters to learn that American murders rates are *not* increasing dramatically.

Murder in America is, as in most countries, overwhelmingly a domestic event, in the sense that most murderers kill members of their own families over private quarrels or resentments. The connection with great political and social movements is not very direct. Since World War II, the United States murder rate has hovered between 4.5 and 5.0 murders per 100,000 population: higher than Britain and France, but lower than Mexico. There was a slight upward movement in 1967 to 6.1, but this was still below the rate of 7 murders per 100,000 in 1935. So far, the rate for the sixties remains below that for the thirties.

The fact that the murder rate remains essentially stable, with a slight tendency to decline, should be a stumbling block to those who argue that crime is increasing at a dizzying rate. The difficulty is that most categories of crime are subject to "reporting error": that is, the definition of a crime such as "assault" varies from time to time and from place to place. Particularly, it is altered by social status. Putting it crudely, a man used to the brutal conditions of slum life may not think very much of being roughed up in a bar. It is part of the small change of life. To a man used to the gentler conventions of middle-class existence, it may very well be an intolerable assault, for which he demands brisk retribution by the police. But if crime, especially violent crime, is indeed increasing as fast as Nixon claimed during his Presidential campaign (up by a hundred seventy-five per cent in the District of Columbia "since Dwight Eisenhower left office"), then it is hard to see why murder rates have not also increased dramatically. The situation is actually very complex, and while there is probably some gross increase in crime, it is difficult to be sure just what it amounts to. Certainly, considering the huge arsenal of firearms available in the United States (two hundred million, enough to arm every man, woman, and child), it is remarkable that the American people kill each other so infrequently. One thing that is sure: granted the explosive nature of the issue, there could be no subject less suitable for simplistic electioneering. In the words of Professor Alexander M. Bickel, of the Yale Law School, "No society will long remain open and attached to peaceable politics and the decent and controlled use of public force if fear for personal safety is the ordinary experience of large numbers."

Mass urban disorder may well continue to decline, relatively, and murder rates may also continue their general decline. But it may well be that modern politicians aspiring to the Presidency will face special dangers, and that assassinations will more frequently occur than in the past.

The charismatic politician, relying on his special mechanisms of emotion and magic, will be especially endangered, since his method stresses above all things the *uniqueness* of his particular personality and by implication promises that assassination will produce more exciting results than in the case of a man who is merely the replaceable representative of a bureaucratic organization.

Two kinds of cause contribute to the increasing danger of the Presidency. One is the continuing tendency to personalize and dramatize the Presidency, making it overshadow all other offices in the land in a manner certainly not envisaged in the Constitution. This process, which began with Franklin D. Roosevelt out of sheer political necessity, was developed by both John F. Kennedy and Lyndon B. Johnson. Not only did Johnson tend to draw all executive power into his own hands, he also added some remarkable royalist touches, carrying into apparently informal situations the protocol custom by which only specially favored persons should walk on his right-hand side. In these circumstances, the Presidential role as combined Chief Executive and formal Head of State is constantly dramatized until the President begins to appear as the personification of the political process.

The second contributing cause is television's tendency to increase the "penetration" of political images—if not of political information—in the public mind. The attention of everyone, lunatic and normal citizen alike, is concentrated on the one man.

Some suggestive evidence of the dangers of the modern Presidency is to be found in the increase in the number of "White House cases." These are deranged people locked up for threatening to kill the President. During the eight years of the Truman administration, there were only seventy-five "White House cases," or fewer than ten a year. During the Eisenhower administration this rose to about seventeen a year, and then to thirty-five a year under Kennedy. Under Johnson, it rose to about two hundred a year. The number of people arrested, and not always confined, for threats to the President rose from eighty in 1963 to four hundred twenty-five in Johnson's first year in office. That this increase came immediately after President Kennedy's assassination would indicate that discussion of Oswald's means of achieving notoriety was a contributing cause. (Some of the increase, naturally, may have been due to the extra vigilance of the Secret Service, whose strength went up from three hundred fifty to five hundred seventy-five after Kennedy was shot. The Service's file on potentially dangerous persons throughout the country has also increased from around four hundred sixty in 1963 to some eighteen hundred today. A computer is used to cross-reference their location with the President's movements.)

Moreover, the number of people apt to construct delusional systems for themselves is not likely to decrease in the United States. Apart from the traditional political paranoia, of the sort that makes Dwight Eisenhower out to be a Communist agent, for example, the level of clinical mental distress is unfortunately high.

At present, there are more than one million people in mental institutions in the United States, which is four times the prison population. Of these people, almost eighty-five per cent are "involuntary" patients—i.e., ones who are judged by the authorities to be likely to endanger themselves or others if allowed to go free.

To this extent, then, the problem of Presidential security has something to do with the political issues of urban life in America, since there is some evidence that the insecurity, competitiveness, and frustration of big-city life do more than anything else to produce high levels of mental disturbance. In 1961, a group of sociologists and psychiatrists from Cornell University studied a representative sample of the population in midtown Manhattan and came to the startling conclusion that only 18.5 of these people could be regarded as mentally "well." (Fifty-eight per cent suffered "mild" or "moderate" mental disturbance, and no less than 23.4 per cent suffered from "marked," "severe," or "incapacitating" mental symptoms.) They concluded, in cautious professional jargon, that "mental mechanisms which by psychodynamic derivation may be considered pathological may be a mode of adjustment to the urban environment." Or, as almost any New York cabdriver will tell you, "You don't have to be crazy, but it helps." It appears to us that tensions such as these are another expression of the social mechanisms that produced ready audiences for the nostrums of George Wallace.

In the line of this kind of analysis, the assassination of Robert Kennedy should not be regarded as part of some massive breakdown in the moral fiber of Americans as a people, and certainly not as an argument for stricter and harsher law'n'order. Sirhan's Arab nationalism can hardly be taken as any more than the trigger mechanism for his murderous rage—if only because there were far more sensible targets if he wanted to kill an American politician to help the Arab cause. But Sirhan was a classic example of an urban failure, intelligent yet inadequate, unable to come to terms with the baffling and competitive society in which he lived. Robert Kennedy's death, then, should be seen as a result of the interaction between the politics of personal power and intensely propagated charisma, and an urban society in which the tensions which bear upon individuals are particularly sharp. Both of those conditions have developed from trends that have been established for some time—but neither is irreversible.

There is one further class of disorder that is likely to increase and continue: namely, student dissent. This, in America, is quite opposite in motivation from mass rioting. It is not the product of random friction between unhappy classes. Rather, it is the product of the students' self-confidence—a confidence born of the economic security of the middle class (which is likely to increase) and of the students' sheer weight of numbers (which will also increase).

Although the most spectacular outbreaks of student unrest, such as the one at Columbia, are disruptive and perhaps damaging for the universities where they occur, this kind of challenge to authority may not be a bad thing per se. Rough and intolerant as the student rebels may seem, their revolutions have been far more dangerous to prestige, dignity, and sometimes the students' personal academic performance—which is their own responsibility—than to life and limb. And there is, one might argue, enough conformity and regulation in American life to make some general disrespect for authority worth having. When one considers the limitless orthodoxies of the great corporations for whom most students will eventually work, it does not seem a bad idea for them to have some training in heterodoxy early in life.

One of Robert Kennedy's greatest strengths—perhaps his greatest —was that, unlike almost every other professional politician, he gave constant evidence of learning and development. In his early days, he was not inclined to be tolerant of nonconformists. But as he went on, he learned to be, and he also came to deplore the simplistic demands for repression in the name of law and order (even if he did not feel it was practical politics to deny them as strongly as he would have liked). It would be sad, and silly, if the special tragedy of his death were used as evidence for the shabby proposition that there is a crisis of authority in America, and the even shabbier corollary that the iron hand is what the country needs.

ACT VIII

New Politics
and Old Pols

1

Two Case Studies in Insurgency

"May we know what this new doctrine, whereof thou speakest, is?

For thou bringest certain strange things to our ears: we would know therefore what these things mean.

(For all the Athenians and strangers which were there spent their time in nothing else, but either to tell, or to hear some new thing.)"

—*Acts of the Apostles,* Chapter 17, 19–21

obert Kennedy's friends and followers admired him not merely as a brilliant figure within the established tradition of American political leadership, but because they saw him as the prophet of a New Politics. None of them believed this more passionately than his young speechwriter Adam Walinsky. One winter afternoon, some six months after Kennedy's death, Walinsky sat in the living room of his house in a Washington suburb and explained what the New Politics meant to him. He talked about a new style, a new compassion and commitment, a new constituency of the young, the black, the poor, and some middle-class people. Above all, he identified the New Politics with youth. "Yes," he was asked, "but isn't the New Politics also a matter of technique?" He agreed. He mentioned, inevitably, Marshall McLuhan. And then he grinned. "Robert Kennedy always understood Guthman's Law: three minutes on the six-o'clock news is worth all the rest of the publicity you can get." (Edwin O. Guthman was Robert Kennedy's director of public information at the Justice Department and later his press assistant in the Senate; he is now national news editor of the *Los Angeles Times.*)

To Walinsky and to many others of the bright young men around Kennedy, there seemed to be no contradiction between a New Politics of commitment to radical social change and something quite different: a new sophistication in the use of modern political technology.

Every year in the United States there is a new Ford, a new Chevrolet, a new Chrysler, and a New Negro. At less frequent intervals, a New Woman, a New Child Psychology, and a New South make regular appearances. At the beginning of 1968, New Politics were in the air. Politicians talked about them. Journalists wrote about them. Pundits and academicians cranked themselves up to analyze them. The only trouble was that nobody agreed on what they meant.

Some greeted the New Politics as Wordsworth greeted the French Revolution: "Bliss was it in that dawn to be alive, but to be young was very heaven!" For them, New Politics meant the politics of "ordinary people who are fed up with the superficial and hypocritical politics of the two major parties." This was not a matter of anything so base as political technique. It was a mood, a style, a cause, and a commitment. There were more practical people, too, like Robert Kennedy's friend Fred Dutton, who felt that, though there might be short-term swings to the right, in the long run the future lay with a new radical coalition. It would be free from the narrow concerns of the older blue-collar workers with their own economic interests, free from the old ethnic obsessions, concerned at last with "the quality of American life." A new constituency was coming into existence, according to this school; an alliance, as Jack Newfield put it, of "campus, ghetto, and suburb."

It was doubtful how much validity, or even logic, there was to such theories. Pessimists noticed that all too often the economic and practical interests of these three groups were opposed. Some of the spokesmen for the New Politics seemed to confuse a temporary coalition, brought together by opposition to the war and to Lyndon Johnson, with a secular shift in the sociology of politics. But the fact was that on the left—and *to* the left—of the Democratic Party, especially among some of the most influential younger journalists, there was an unshakable faith that a new day was a-coming in 1968. The essence of the New Politics, for them, was contained in the lessons learned in the peace movement and the earlier civil-rights movements: that the old rules could be circumvented by action, mobility, drama, involvement, and confrontation; by learning all the ways in which determined People could wage guerrilla war against the Machine.

But for others the New Politics meant something completely different from this. "There are two essential ingredients of the new politics," wrote a Washington reporter for the *National Observer* named James M. Perry in a careful, and on the whole pessimistic, book published in January 1968:

> One is that appeals should be made directly to the voters through the mass media. The other is that the techniques used to make these appeals—polling, computers, television, direct mail—should be sophisticated and scientific.

Perry's book, entitled *The New Politics: The Expanding Technology of Political Manipulation,* described in detail the contributions made to the development of the technique of political management by such political-management firms as Spencer-Roberts and Whitaker and Baxter in California, by Joseph Napolitan, by Fred Currier and Walter De Vries in Michigan, and by Dr. William Ronan and the Jack Tinker agency in the Rockefeller campaign of 1966.

Perry drew an alarming portrait of a Presidential candidate under the new dispensation:

> The candidate's travels . . . will be scheduled by a computer. The campaign will be laid out by the critical path method. Polls will be taken over and over and analyzed and cross-analyzed. Spot commercials will be prepared weeks in advance of the election, and their impact will be almost subliminal. Researchers will read the polls and study the data from a "simulator"; the issues they develop will . . . be aimed like rifle shots at the most receptive audiences. . . . And the candidate? He will be out front, moving with a robot-like precision, being fed with data from the polls and the simulator. He will no doubt be articulate, and probably he will be handsome and vigorous. And he may or may not be qualified to be the next President of the United States.

This was presented as a would-you-believe-it warning of what some future campaign might be like. It was written in 1967. Yet, with the single exception of the simulator, every one of the techniques Perry listed was used by most of the major candidates in 1968.

In another book published in early 1968—*Robert Kennedy and the New Politics*—a Columbia professor named Penn Kimball, who is also Louis Harris's right-hand man, attempted a definition of the New Politics:

> the contemporary contest for political power characterized by primary reliance on personal organizations in preference to party machinery, emphasis on consolidating voters rather than on dividing them along

traditional lines of class or region, projection of political style above issues, and exploitation of the full range of modern techniques for mass communication.

There are four ideas, or criteria, contained in that definition. The first and third are closely connected and belong to what we have called "bastard feudalism." There is not the faintest reason why either should be correlated with compassion; they might be, or they might not. It is hard to see the originality of the second: national politicians in America have always tried to achieve consensus. As a matter of fact, some "new politicians," notably Kimball's particular subject of study, Robert Kennedy, have permitted themselves a good deal more dividing than, say, Johnson in 1964 or Eisenhower, to name two "old politicians." And there is one very good reason why the fourth criterion, the exploitation of mass media, should actually be negatively correlated with radicalism. The new political technology is very expensive. It depends on computers, public-opinion surveys, film, videotape, and other expensive toys. It also depends on the services of clever, highly educated and trained people to use these techniques. Such people don't come cheap. "The professional managers are mercenaries," Perry wrote of these very people. "They are willing to go almost anywhere for a buck." Not many of those bucks are to be earned by working for the young, the poor, or the black. Walter DeVries himself points out that Joseph Napolitan is the only one—of a dozen or more political "mercenaries" with a national reputation in America—who works for Democrats. And Perry suggests the reason is that, more than money, "these new technologists seek power. I suspect they get more satisfaction—more sense of power —working with a man of ability and potential than they do working for an institutionalized organization." In general, it is naïve to suppose that techniques which can be used only by those with access to enormous financial resources will often be available for any really damaging assault on the *status quo*.

The objection might be made at this point that the candidates who have made the most of the new political technology are not typically conservatives—though they do include conservatives like Ronald Reagan. More typically, they present themselves as liberals or moderates: Robert Kennedy, George Romney, Nelson Rockefeller. But these examples do not contradict the proposition that the New Politics of technology are unlikely to be found in the service of a New Politics of radical dissent. For moderate liberalism *is* the doctrine of the *status quo* in America, and it is not to be confused with radicalism. There is only one circumstance in which the poor, the black, and indeed the young are going to find computers, polls, and scientific campaign management used on their behalf: that is when a wealthy candidate appoints himself as their champion. The user of technology should not be confused with his clients. It is one thing to say that Robert Kennedy, who could and did afford to use "the full range of modern techniques for mass communication," felt a genuine concern for the disinherited. It is quite another to say that, because of this, the blacks of Watts or Bedford-Stuyvesant or the Mexican migrant workers acquired control of computers and pollsters and advertising agencies. And in politics, it is control that counts.

There were actually two brands of New Politics on display in 1968. Each represented a challenge to the old pols and to their established order. After Robert Kennedy's death, the old pols looked firmly entrenched in both parties. Newspapers, wire services, and magazines published "delegate counts" purporting to show that it was all over: headlines announced that Richard Nixon and Hubert Humphrey had the nominations of the two parties sewed up. But, with remarkable symmetry, the same development was happening in each party: a challenge to the old pols in the name of a New Politics. The brand of New Politics with which Humphrey was challenged was something very different from what Nixon had to cope with. The pattern of preconvention politics dictates that the same issues are raised, and the same tactics used, in state after state. Rather than follow the Rockefeller and McCarthy campaigns chronologically, it seems best to let two case studies illustrate the way two kinds of New Politics worked in the two parties. The Rockefeller advertising campaign and the McCarthy campaign in Connecticut illustrate the total difference between the two kinds of New Politics very clearly.

On April 30, in Albany, just under six weeks after his withdrawal, Nelson Rockefeller had announced his "active candidacy" for the Presidency. He said he had been deeply disturbed by the "dramatic and unprecedented" events of the past week and that he could no longer stand on the sidelines. He added that he had been urged to run by "men and women in all walks of life within the Republican party."

The phrase about walks of life conjures up a charming eighteenth-century vignette, in which respectful delegations of honest cobblers and blacksmiths wait upon our hero and remind him of his duty to save the country. It wasn't quite like that. "On March 22," the day after his withdrawal speech, says Emmett Hughes, "a group sprang up like flowers out of a rock and said to George Hinman, 'You can't let this happen!' " The prime mover was John Hay Whitney, with Walter N. Thayer at his side. Whitney, the angel of *Life with Father, Gone with the Wind,* and the somewhat less successful New York *Herald Tribune,* breeder of bloodstock and former Ambassador to the Court of St. James, had been left by his father, in 1927, the largest estate ever probated up to that time. His present wealth is estimated by *Fortune* magazine at between two hundred and three hundred million dollars. Thayer might be called his man of business, his George Hinman, a lawyer who has worked shrewdly and loyally for him in various ventures for twenty years.

Between them, Whitney and Thayer managed to round up on behalf of Rockefeller a good cross section of the old-money WASP business aristocracy, not just of New York—which would have been fatal—but of the country. There was a group in Chicago and even a little group in Texas. There were Gardner Cowles, whose family owns *Look* magazine and newspapers in Minneapolis and Des Moines; Ralph Lazarus of Federated Department Stores; H. J. Heinz, II; and Henry Ford, II. One of the most active was a Yale and Oxford graduate from Indiana called J. Irwin Miller, who runs the Cummings diesel firm.

Quite independently, a short while later, Rockefeller was approached by leaders of that other great financial oligarchy, the liberal Jewish business leaders in New York. These are not Republicans by habit and inheritance, like Whitney's WASPs. Some of them are Democrats. Others would classify themselves as independents. But there is a passionate liberal tradition in this world. Many of the leading Jewish businessmen in New York had already supported Rockefeller for governor, while contributing to the Kennedy and Johnson Presidential campaigns. What they said, in effect, through various intermediaries, was: "We would rather be with you than with Humphrey, but we have to be for someone who isn't Nixon. We have to know now, because if you don't go, we will have to go for Humphrey. Are you going to do it or not?"

The thing that most changed Nelson Rockefeller's mind between early March and late April, in the opinion of those in a position to know what he was thinking, was not Lyndon Johnson's withdrawal, or Martin Luther King's assassination, or the riots, or the international monetary crisis, although all of those events influenced his decision. The most important thing was that, for the first time, he felt he was being asked to run. For the first time in his life, he had widespread national support in the business world.

By the middle of April, Rockefeller was again seriously considering running. J. Irwin Miller set up a Rockefeller for President committee with a Minnesotan called Jerry Olsen to run it; this gave it a solid Midwestern flavor, but in the background George Hinman was pulling the strings. As soon as he thought his man was going to go, he knew exactly what to do next. He placed a call to an advertising man who happened to be in Clearwater, on the west coast of Florida, at a Humble Oil meeting. The move, as always with Hinman, was extremely logical.

"The situation is more fluid than some have thought," Nelson Rockefeller told the politicians and the reporters in Albany on April 30. "There has not been a crystallization of thinking to the point where we are faced with a closed convention." That sort of talk was all right for the record. What candidate is going to announce that he is engaged upon a forlorn hope? But afterward, as they mixed with reporters in the executive mansion and looked at the Picasso tapestries their boss has had made ("It's the only way I can get these great paintings!"), Rockefeller's professionals did not bother to keep up pretenses. They knew that Nixon had a long lead and that they had only one persuasive argument going for them. As a matter of preference, the great majority of Republican delegates would take Nixon if they could. Rockefeller's only hope was to persuade these men that picking him would make the difference between victory and defeat. His people had to put across the idea that Rockefeller could beat a Democrat and Nixon could not.

There were two ways of selling this case. The first, the orthodox way, would be the direct method. Rockefeller and his lieutenants would have to get out and make their pitch to the politicians. But, in fact, as Hinman and Hughes and Len Hall and Alton Marshall and the rest of them knew—as Thruston Morton and Bill Miller knew best of all, because they had just come back from a last-minute reconnaissance in six states—it was not going to be easy. It was not even going to be possible unless he could produce evidence.

Therefore, Rockefeller, like McCarthy, had to appeal to the people over the heads of the politicians. But he was going to do it in a different way. The central idea of his strategy was simple, bold, and rational. It was too late to bind delegates by primary victories. And it was unlikely that he would be able to persuade enough delegates directly. Therefore, he must use the media to influence public opinion—the opinion, it should be noticed, of Democrats and independents as well as Republicans. That would be reflected in the polls, and the polls in turn could be used as a compelling argument with the delegates. But the whole venture turned on whether, at the end of the day, the polls showed, not merely that Rockefeller was more popular than Nixon, but that Rockefeller could win and Nixon could not.

These were the two sides to Rockefeller's campaign: the orthodox campaign of direct delegate persuasion, and the effort to persuade indirectly through the polls. As soon as he announced, Nelson Rockefeller set out on a furious three months during which he met and talked to delegates in forty-five states. The Republican convention was due to begin on August 5. It was not long for a national campaign. He was most effective in what his staff called dehorning sessions: he would meet a group of delegates behind closed doors and try to assure them that he had not sabotaged Dick Nixon in 1960 or Barry Goldwater in 1964, that he was not a wild socialist spender in New York, that he was, in short, a loyal Republican and a regular fellow. He tried to persuade them, not to come out for him, but to stay loose. And up to a point, with the delegations from the key industrial states, he was successful. We are not going to describe these journeyings in detail, because it was the other side of Rockefeller's campaign that was both more important for him and intrinsically more interesting. The Rockefeller media campaign in 1968 is a classic study in the New Politics of technique. It deserves to be studied in detail, because it shows how the New Politics work—what they can do, and what they can't.

There are many media. Some can be paid for. Others must be played for in ways that are also not free. Three minutes of coverage on the six-o'clock news cannot be bought, but getting it may cost more than you would pay for three minutes of network prime time. The Governor must make news: He must be seen flying to exciting meetings, making speeches, shaking hands. He must put out a stream of statements, reactions, proposals to be reported on television and in the press. This aspect of the media war was the responsibility of Leslie Slote, Rockefeller's press secretary. Slote is a gregarious and agreeable man, but he is curiously lacking in enthusiasm for talking about the little tidbits of personal detail which are the spice of a reporter's material. This may well be a necessary precaution, since Rockefeller has always felt that his private life is nobody's business, and he defines privacy more inclusively even than the Kennedys. But it did mean that Rockefeller did not have the advantage the Kennedys have always enjoyed—a stream of gushingly favorable or at least fascinated free publicity.

That was why Hinman's call to Clearwater, Florida, was so important. The man he spoke to was Tom Losee, who runs the Houston office of America's second largest group of advertising agencies, McCann-Erickson, and who has worked in Rockefeller's political campaigns since 1958. Losee is a tense man with straw-blond hair whose sharp, nervous anxiety to impress you with his speed and toughness of mind would be a caricature of the Madison Avenue style if the qualities were not in his case real. When Hinman came on the line, Losee knew immediately what he was calling him about. Quickly, he flew to New York and greeted Hinman with, "What's cooking?" Hinman, whose manner was formed in a courtlier school than Madison Avenue, said carefully, "We don't know whether the Governor is thinking of going or not, but we rather think he may." Losee was not deceived. He got on the phone to a certain Gene Case. "Boys," he said, "here we go again!"

Case is a partner and the "top creative man" at a New York advertising agency called Jack Tinker & Partners, part of the McCann-Erickson/Interpublic empire. The agency is quite small and has a specialist reputation for original, intelligent advertising whose strength is that it tries to communicate with the consumer through a kind of dialogue, rather than by bludgeoning him. The account that made Tinker famous was Alka-Seltzer, for whom Case, among others, devised a campaign that was regarded in the trade as daringly cerebral. Tinker was hired by Dr. William Ronan, then dean of the School of Public Administration and Social Services at New York University, to do the advertising for Rockefeller's backs-to-the-wall 1966 campaign for re-election. The television advertising the Tinker people did for that campaign is regarded as a model. One commercial in particular, an interview with a large-mouth bass about water pollution, is regarded as a classic by the *cognoscenti.*

Losee had worked in that campaign with Ronan and the Tinker people, and in 1968, he was able to work with exactly the same team. It included five of the Tinker partners: Case; the art director, Bob Wilvers; Myron McDonald, head of the firm and a marketing man whose specialty is planning; Clifford Botway; and Dr. Herta M. Herzog, a lady sociologist from Vienna. Altogether, fifty people were available to work on the Rockefeller account.

They started work on May 1, in the trendily decorated Tinker of-

fices on West Fifty-seventh Street. Losee didn't have a completely free
hand: he was responsible to Emmett Hughes, in charge of media, and
Alton Marshall, Rockefeller's executive officer in Albany, a burly professional whom Rockefeller trusts as much as anyone. On May 30, with in
effect only the two months of June and July left, Losee and his people
presented a "concept," a detailed media plan, a budget, and actual specimen ads at a meeting at 22 West Fifty-fifth Street.

Their recommendations were based on a strategy paper presented
at that meeting. Typed on loose-leaf paper, it runs to twenty-nine pages.
As a sample of the shrewdest and most expensive advice available from
the professionals of the new politics, it deserves extended quotation.

The paper is described as representing "the consensus of Tinker
thinking concerning those aspects of the situation affective, particularly
of the public and, therefore, the polls and, therefore, the politicians
. . . the governors, the delegates, et al." After this rather jerky, row-
boat launch, the Tinker thinkers' prose sails away more smoothly: "The
American crisis," they assert boldly, "is not the war in Vietnam, nor
rioting in the cities, nor inflation, nor deterioration of respect among
our friends, nor any specific. It is a failure of leadership." The paper
goes on:

> WHAT IS A LEADER?
> A leader is bold, aggressive, positive, creative. . . .
> Despite the computerized complexities of modern life, the leader in
> his field is still the emergent hero. And America is, has been and (God
> willing) always will be hungry for heroes. Her treatment of them . . .
> from Lincoln to Babe Ruth to Martin Luther King amounts almost to
> canonization, so deeply is the need felt.
> Who among us is up to this?

No prizes offered for the answer to that one. But the answer doesn't
come for another seven pages, in the course of which Nelson Rockefeller
and his advisers are given a brief excursus on the other candidates:

> Eugene McCarthy . . . A Pied Piper who almost bridged the genera-
> tion gap until the visceral pyrotechnics of Kennedy interrupted the
> quiet communication . . .
> Robert Kennedy . . . A controversial figure. . . . In him, the recol-
> lection of a hero who fell in Dallas . . . shorter, more prolific
> progeny-wise, more enigmatic, less outgoing, but becoming more
> so . . . Kennedy's problem is to establish himself as a whole hero
> and not just as a sibling substitute.
> Richard Nixon . . . It is difficult just now to see him as *the* leader.

Having thus glibly slain his rivals, the Tinker men feel free to turn to their client. Without fear or favor, they press relentlessly on through the catalogue of his virtues.

> The only potential leader . . . the man with the guts to do the right things . . . a man from a famous American family. . . . His willingness to take action, after counsel, is perhaps his greatest strength in the current visceral contest. His vision of the world and its true momentum if one is permitted to divine it, is contemporary, ongoing, creative.

And so, at length, to the issues. One can picture the giant brains locked onto the world's problems, high above Fifty-seventh Street, the pipe smoke wreathing above the domed skulls, the final triumphant "Eureka!" and the salutes that greeted the following analysis as it fluttered from the flagpole:

> It is clear today that American society is divided between those who wish slower change and those who wish more rapid change. This dichotomy is more severe and more widespread than at any time in our history. . . .
>
> It is clear from Lloyd Free's preliminary report on American public opinion in early 1968, that certain of the Governor's positions coincide with those sought by the majority in many cases. It is also clear that when one cuts through the bafflegab of label rhetoric to real meanings, other of his positions can be seen productive of the actions and consequent results people really want. . . . What is really wanted is better "big government." . . . And in the heart of its Judaeo-Christian economic ethos, the American public really knows it is not going to get something for nothing!

Cutting, so to speak, through the bafflegab of label rhetoric, what the Tinker thinkers seem to have been trying to tell Rockefeller was this: that the best case he could make for himself was as a new leader, and that in pressing this case it would do him no harm to admit that he was a liberal. Rockefeller scarcely needed to be told this. The same idea had been expressed, much more clearly and succinctly, by Emmett Hughes in a private memorandum he wrote on May 19, summarizing points made in a conversation two days before:

> I believe it is essential, in the weeks and speeches immediately ahead, that you make *clear*—as *sharply* and *incisively* as possible—*the CHOICE that you are presenting to the Republican Party.*
>
> This means making clear—without any explicit dealing in personalities as such—that Nelson Rockefeller and Richard Nixon stand for *two profoundly different* views. . . .
>
> 1. Your entire candidacy rests on the promise of giving the Re-

publican Party a *choice*. It thus becomes our logical and central task
to make *forcefully* clear *a*) that there *is* a choice and *b*) *what* it is.

2. This becomes doubly true because Nixon does *not* want such a
choice defined. His haziness on issues may be natural, but it is not accidental. It is his deliberate *intent* to *blur* issues between you and him.
We must not conspire with him in doing this. . . .

3. This means that your public utterances essentially must be
aimed at *your standing in the polls—NOT the presumed preconceptions
of delegates.* Obviously the latter can and must be attended to *personally
and privately.* But the decisive favorable influence *on* the delegates *will*
be the polls. Or as Lloyd Free says: "The Governor is *not* going to win
delegates by sounding more and more like Richard Nixon. He cannot
out-Nixon Nixon."

The time is upon us for you to sound less and less like a philosopher—and more and more and more like a fighter.

What advertising agencies know about is advertising. There was
a remarkable contrast between the pretentious and amateurish advice
the Tinker people had to give on political strategy and the simple logic
of their actual media plan. It was aimed, they stated plainly, "at effective
influence on the national public-opinion polls." It should focus on a
number of key markets: "1. Representative of large and movable blocs
of delegates. 2. Representative of population segments potentially favorable to and therefore movable by clear and dramatic statements of the
Governor's position on the vital issues." They listed sixteen big northern
states, with one-third of the population and just over one-half of the
delegates to the Republican Convention between them, as "communication targets."

Tinker recommended three complementary assaults on public
opinion. The one most directly focused on the key areas was a campaign
of sixty-second spot television commercials for early- and late-evening
time periods in thirty key markets. These spots would be precisely aimed
at the very people most likely to react favorably when questioned about
Rockefeller by Gallup and Harris.

Tinker also recommended approximately three minutes a week of
national network television advertising for the seven weeks of the campaign. Correctly used, they argued, television "is the most emotionally
evocative of all media. Its topicality brings the futility of Vietnam into
fifty million homes nightly." Three network minutes a week, they calculated, would bring Nelson Rockefeller into ninety per cent of all American homes.

The most original advertising recommendation the Tinker people
made—and, in the end, perhaps the most successful—was not for tele-

vision, but for the oldest medium of all: newspapers. Tom Losee explained the rationale. "People see so much advertising," he said, zapping his head with his hands and making electronic zeroing-in noises. "Fifteen hundred, two thousand messages a day coming in. People think it's bullshit. Political advertising, to get through, has to be simple. It has to be dignified. Not that same old hack political gobbledygook." And so Tinker recommended that Rockefeller insert, in forty newspapers in the chosen key areas, "in referential, documentary black and white, the Governor's position on the key issues. As contrasted to the general non-positions of Richard Nixon." This was done. And as a final touch, the newspaper ads were bound together in a special supplement in the *Miami Herald* for the opening of the convention, so that each delegate would be confronted with a plain, bold statement of Rockefeller's position, signed in the hand that launched a thousand checks.

The entire media budget came to four and a half million dollars. In round figures, two million of that went on the television spots, one million on the network television, and a million and a half on the newspaper advertising. The advertising started in mid-June, and Losee and the Tinker people originally planned to bring it to a peak, not at the opening of the convention on August 5 but ten days earlier, on the day when the last Gallup interviews were being carried out. "Why spend money influencing people who have already been interviewed?" one of the admen put it. "The whole strategy of our campaign was to influence the polls."

The strategy was clear enough, but what about the tactics? What issues should the spots and the newspaper ads stress? At this point in the development of the Rockefeller media campaign something extremely interesting happened. It may not have affected the result, but it should be a warning against oversimple judgments of how the new scientific politics works. The theory presupposes remorseless pragmatism, unmoved by human emotions or ideological preconceptions: The polls identify the sections of the electorate that can be won; further polling determines which issues should be stressed to attract the winnable voters; and the media campaign then automatically addresses itself to those issues. That is the theory. But that is not quite what happened in Rockefeller's campaign.

The polling on which Rockefeller's media campaign was based had been done in February by Lloyd Free. Using a national sample of Gallup interviews, Free had asked people to say how worried they were about twenty-one problems or concerns he had listed on the basis of earlier polls. Their answers were graded on a four-point scale and used to draw up another list of problems worrying the American electorate, in order of intensity:

1. Vietnam
2. Crime and juvenile delinquency
3. Keeping our military defense strong
4. Rioting in our cities
5. Preventing World War III
6. Prices and the cost of living
7. Drug addicts and narcotic drugs
8. Maintaining respect for the U.S. abroad
9. Government spending
10. Communist China
11. Raising moral standards in the country
12. The threat of international Communism
13. Keeping NATO and our other alliances strong
14. Relations with Russia
15. Improving our educational system
16. Reducing poverty in this country
17. Negro racial problems
18. The problem of ensuring that lower-income families get adequate medical care
19. Air and water pollution
20. The trend toward a more powerful Federal government
21. Rebuilding our cities

Clearly, this list reveals an extremely conservative set of priorities in the minds of the voters. The right-wing concerns, numbers 2 through 13, all rate higher than the characteristically liberal concerns, numbers 15, 16, 17, 18, and 21. One would expect a campaign that took this profile of the voters' state of mind as its starting point to stress the need for toughness and preparedness in foreign policy and to put law and order ahead of social reform at home.

The logic of the list, pointing toward a conservative emphasis in the Rockefeller campaign, was reinforced by another consideration. As Free pointed out to Rockefeller at the Memorial Day meeting and on other occasions in private, it would be worthless for him to go after the votes of the poor and the blacks, or even their weight in the opinion polls. (Free was not making this point out of personal predilection. He happens to be a liberal Republican. To him, it was a matter of fact.) The Negro vote, he pointed out, was nine per cent of the electorate, and ninety per cent of it was likely to go to the Democratic candidate in November. Not only that: any support that might be won among Negroes or the poor was likely to be won at the expense of support from larger blocs of white Republicans or independents.

There was a third argument which cut the same way. The politicians —people like the lieutenant governor of New York, Malcolm Wilson, and Leonard Hall, an ex-Republican National Chairman—who were in charge of the delegate-wooing side of Rockefeller's operation viewed any emphasis on liberal issues in the media campaign as flatly counterproductive of what they were trying to do.

Yet, the Rockefeller advertisements were not conservative. They were, on the whole, liberal—some of them almost provocatively so. Free's sample might put "rebuilding our cities" as the last of the electorate's concerns, but one Rockefeller ad showed the candidate talking about urban renewal in Harlem and saying, "We have faith in the heart of Harlem, and we have faith in the people who live there." Most "unscientific" of all was a sixty-second film commercial that opened with a drum roll and a shot of a dark, wet slum street. Rockefeller himself read the narration, in that arresting, husky voice of his:

> Three thousand black men were among those brave Americans who had died so far in Vietnam.
> One hundred thousand black men will come home from Vietnam. What will they make of America, these men who risk their lives for the American Dream, and come home to find the American Slumber? What will they make of the slums where, too often, jobs are as rare as hope?
> This is Nelson Rockefeller, and I say they deserve more than this. I say they deserve an equal chance. They deserve decent housing. Decent jobs. And the schooling and training to fill these jobs.
> To those who cry, "We can't afford it," I say, "We can't afford not to do it."
> To those who cry, "Law and order," I say, "To keep law and order, there must be—

At this point, a black man looms out of the shadows and walks toward the camera, as Rocky says,

> justice and opportunity!

Justice and opportunity! That was not the first thought, apparently, evoked in many a viewer's mind by the sight of a strange black man walking swiftly out of the shadows on a dark street. "That ad was a flop," says Free candidly. "In fact, a lot of people, especially women, didn't like it at all. You see, you couldn't really tell who was coming toward you. It was a little alarming for many people."

The repercussions were immediate. Professional politicians from various points around the country got on the phone and "squawked like hell," as one of Rockefeller's closest friends puts it: "There was a big playback on that ad about the black soldier." "Our campaign was pretty schizophrenic," says another of Rockefeller's housecarls. "Sometimes our two organizations, the one aimed at the delegates and the other at the polls, were antithetical. If we put out something, say, a full page on the riots, that would appeal to Democrats and liberal Republicans in the northeast, Malcolm Wilson would go out of his mind in the Midwest—and you couldn't blame him." To their credit, the Rockefeller people were undeterred. "We had our charter," says Losee, "which was to go ahead and influence the polls. The politicians might scream like hell, as they did about the riot ad. But that was none of our business."

How did this confusion, this tug of war between heartless pragmatism and liberal instinct, remain unresolved so long? This was supposed to be a supremely professional operation of the new, nonideological politics.

But even at the level of pragmatism, Rockefeller faced a dilemma. Cold logic might dictate that he should concentrate his advertising effort on the issues that troubled the people, and that if the people wanted conservative talk, he must give it to them. But an equally unsentimental argument, as we have seen, cut the other way. As both Emmett Hughes and Free argued, Rockefeller could not hope to press his claims as a leader by trying to "out-Nixon Nixon." He must present "a choice, not an echo." And he must be himself.

The second reason for the unresolved dilemma lay in the kind of man Nelson Rockefeller is. He is not a desiccated calculating machine. On the contrary, he is emotional by nature, and, in particular, he is emotionally committed to the very issues that ranked so low on Lloyd Free's list of priorities: rebuilding cities, justice and opportunity for Negroes. "Nelson got tangled up in his emotions," says Free affectionately.

Finally, Rockefeller is a proud man. He might desire the Presidency. He might even, in some hidden corner of his Rockefeller soul, have some difficulty in repressing the thought that he had a right to it. But he was not going to stoop for it.

All of this is relevant to the future of the new scientific management in politics. It is never going to be easy to find candidates who combine the required force of character and intellect with a willingness to accept policies shaped by polls and computers. But a more specific lesson can also be drawn from the "schizophrenia" of the Rockefeller media campaign. It is that the "creative people" themselves will find it difficult to follow a grimly logical course. For one thing, some subjects make better film than others; it is easier to dramatize highly emotional issues of social justice. For another, people with the talent to manipulate the technology of mass media have ideas of their own. "What happened," says one of Rockefeller's political advisers, "was that the executives agreed with the policy indicated by the polls, but then the creative people gathered up the ball and ran with it. What they produced was pretty much what you'd expect from a group of New York intellectuals." Exactly: television films are not made by farmers in Iowa.

How effective were the New Politics, Rockefeller style? The campaign was, of course, extremely expensive. When Rockefeller was in Tulsa in June for the governors' conference, Les Slote managed to find an hour for *la dolce vita*. It gets hot in Oklahoma in the summer, and Slote was relaxing in the hotel pool, a cigar in one hand, a drink within range, with two pretty secretaries in bikinis to apply the sun-tan lotion. A reporter jocularly addressed him as a "cheap so-and-so." "Sir," said Slote, rising majestically from the water in mock indignation, "call this campaign what you will, but never call it *cheap!*" Few reporters were inclined to do so. Speculation rioted. In fact, the total cost was rather less than some of the more awed guesses: in the region of seven million dollars, all told, including the media budget, salaries, transportation, polls, communications, and rent—for the lavish Americana Hotel in Bal Harbor at convention time and for office space in New York and elsewhere. One close friend believes that each of the five Rockefeller brothers agreed to limit his contribution to seven hundred fifty thousand dollars. What value did they get for their investment?

"We actually did influence the polls," Tom Losee insists. Unfortunately, whether he was right or not depends upon which polls you read. The Harris series gives some support to his claim. For example:

May 16–18	Nixon 37	Humphrey 41	Wallace 14
June 10–17	Nixon 36	Humphrey 43	Wallace 13
July 25–29	Nixon 36	Humphrey 41	Wallace 16
May 16–18	Rocky 37	Humphrey 40	Wallace 17
June 10–17	Rocky 36	Humphrey 40	Wallace 15
July 25–29	Rocky 40	Humphrey 34	Wallace 20

In other words, if you are prepared to ignore all extrinsic factors that might have affected the candidates' standings and treat the fluctuations of the figures as a direct result of their media campaigns; if, too, you ignore any effect, positive or negative, that other candidates' media expenditures may have procured; then on Harris's figures it can be said that, whereas *before* Rockefeller's advertising campaign opened both Rocky and Nixon would have been beaten by Humphrey, *after* it Rockefeller led Humphrey by six per cent and Nixon trailed him by five per cent.

No such conclusion can be drawn from the two Gallup polls for which the interviewing was done between May 4 and 8 and between June 29 and July 3:

May 4–8	Nixon 39	Humphrey 36	Wallace 14
June 29–July 3	Nixon 35	Humphrey 40	Wallace 16
May 4–8	Rocky 40	Humphrey 33	Wallace 16
June 29–July 3	Rocky 36	Humphrey 36	Wallace 21

As we have seen, all Rockefeller's hopes were pinned on Gallup's third and final, eve-of-Miami, poll. They were to be cruelly disappointed. On July 30, George Gallup released from his sibyl's cave in Princeton the results of the poll conducted between July 20 and 23. In bold type across the whole sheet, the headline read: NIXON OVERTAKES HUMPHREY AND McCARTHY; ROCKY RUNS EVEN AGAINST BOTH DEMOCRATS. The figures showed Nixon seven points ahead of Humphrey at 40–38, where he had been 35–40; and Rockefeller still dead level against Humphrey at 36–36.

Bobby Douglass, an aide traveling with Rockefeller, describes the effect: "It was a terrific blow. We got it in the morning, in Washington. The press didn't catch up with it until we got to Pittsburgh that afternoon, on our way to Chicago. We decided to release our own polls to blunt the impact. But it didn't do much good. Nobody could understand what had happened. There were all sorts of suspicions in the heat of the moment, including the suspicion that Gallup had been got at, which was absurd. The Governor was fantastic. He never winced. He kept his cool, waiting to see what Harris would say. It was about one in the morning [of July 31] when we got advance notice of the Harris figures. You can imagine what an exciting evening that was!"

ROCKY TOPS ALL CANDIDATES, said the headline on the Harris poll when it appeared in the *Washington Post,* on August 1. The same day, Rockefeller headquarters released what they carefully called an Archibald Crossley poll—which was, in fact, done by Crossley for his friend Free and paid for by Rockefeller. It showed Nixon leading Rockefeller by two per cent nationally, but Rockefeller ahead in seven out of the nine key industrial states in which everybody realized the election was going to be decided. But by that time, it was too late. The damage had been done.

A flat contradiction between George Gallup and Louis Harris at such a critical moment was a landmark in the history of political polls in the United States. It was the first serious blow to their growing credibility since the disaster of 1948 when they predicted that Dewey would beat Truman. Realizing that the crisis for their profession was too grave for rivalry, Gallup and Harris put out a joint statement insisting that both of their polls were right—at the time the interviewing was done—and concluding, from an appraisal of the two candidates' strength in the big industrial states, that Rockefeller had the better chance of being elected. But what could explain so total a divergence over so short a period? The Gallup interviewing was done between July 20 and July 23, Harris's between July 25 and July 29. Lloyd Free suggested one explanation to Rockefeller: that Gallup's result reflected the endorsement of Nixon by General Eisenhower, still the most admired man in American public life. But Eisenhower's endorsement came on July 18. Could its effect have been at once so great and so short-lived? Privately, the pollsters concede another possible explanation. "Those of us who know anything about statistics know," Free told us, "that in the case of any given random sample poll, there are ninety-five chances out of a hundred that it will come within the limits of probability—that is, within three or four per cent of the true figure. It is easy to forget that that is another way of saying that there are five chances in a hundred that it will not." In plain language, one of the polls may have been plumb wrong. Which one?

It scarcely matters. For Rockefeller's whole effort had been staked on his faith that the polls would convince the Republican delegates that he could win and that Nixon could not. The flat contradiction between the two major polls meant that neither of them would convince the delegates of anything—least of all of something they did not want to believe.

The Rockefeller campaign can be seen as a rebellion by one section of the American upper class against the dominance of the middle class in the Republican Party. The candidate and his financial backers sprang from the great dynasties of the American business aristocracy. Their advisers—men like Hinman, Thayer, Hughes, and Free—had risen in the service or at least in the atmosphere of large-scale American corporate enterprise. Their instinct was to challenge the Republican leadership with weapons that had proved themselves in the corporate world—polls, computers, planning, advertisements.

But there is another section of the upper middle class in America that has little to do with the aristocracy of corporate business. Its life intersects with that of the great corporations at many points, but it has very different values. This is the aristocracy of education and intelligence. While the old pols of the Republican Party were being challenged by Rockefeller, in the Democratic Party, the McCarthy challenge was led by the intelligentsia, which also used the tactics and the weapons that came most naturally to it. This is what happened in every state where McCarthy had strength—in California, in New York, in the Middle West, in Oregon and Colorado. But it can be seen with the clarity of a laboratory experiment in the case of Connecticut.

Connecticut is the third smallest of the states in area, but the fourth most densely populated. Four-fifths of its two and three-quarter million people live in urban areas, most of them in the two sizable cities of Hartford, the capital, and New Haven, in industrial Bridgeport, and in the spreading, wealthy, New York suburbs in Fairfield County—Stamford, Norwalk, Westport. It is an industrial state with a high proportion of ethnically conscious first- and second-generation immigrants, and a high proportion of Roman Catholics. So it is not surprising that the Democratic Party in Connecticut has long been in the grip of a relatively genteel but deeply entrenched machine. And the machine has, for twenty years, been in the grip of a Hartford Irish lawyer named John Moran Bailey. Bailey won the chairmanship of the Connecticut party in 1948, and in 1960, thanks to having been the first of all the bosses to come out for John F. Kennedy, he became Democratic National Chairman as well.

Bailey's power was based on patronage—which successive Democratic governors cheerfully allowed him to dispense in return for the thumping majorities he delivered for them at election time—and on his control of the funds raised at enormous dinners to which contractors and others hoping to do business with the state, employees, and ambitious politicians were invited. In Connecticut he was known as King John, and on the national level he established himself as one of the great magnates of the old feudal politics.

On the eve of his greatest battle, Bailey walked alone into the lair of his enemies. It was at a McCarthy party in the Carleton Room of the Hotel America in Hartford, on Friday, June 21, the night before the Connecticut state convention. He found himself face to face with two of his most formidable adversaries, the playwright Arthur Miller and the novelist William Styron. Someone made introductions, and Miller asked, politely but with a finger pointed for emphasis, "Mr. Bailey, how do you keep all that strength?" Bailey pushed his glasses back on his forehead and took his cigar out of his mouth. "I just keep shaking hands," he said. Miller looked after him as he left. "He's really not the worst guy in the world."

But Connecticut was perhaps the worst state in the country, outside the South, from the point of view of those who sought at the beginning of 1968 to challenge the reign of the old politics. Bailey stood at Lyndon Johnson's right hand. And there had never been a challenge to his right as state chairman to pick whom he pleased to attend the convention. In January, he made the expected pronouncement. "The Democratic National Convention is as good as over," he said. "It'll be Lyndon Johnson, and that's that."

But that was not that. On April 3, Senator McCarthy was hailed by wildly cheering crowds in Bailey's own state as he pronounced the damnable heresy that "you only need a strong organization when you don't have people who can make independent judgments. . . . I think Mr. Bailey is like the Wizard of Oz," McCarthy went on. "When you pull the curtain back, there is only a voice."

On April 10, rather more than forty-four per cent of the Democrats who voted in primary elections in thirty-one large Connecticut towns—primaries that most residents of the state had never realized they could have—were for McCarthy.

On June 22, after a night of tense bargaining and extravagant excitement, almost a third of the delegates to the state convention in Hartford walked out in protest at Bailey's tactics. On August 28, out of the forty-four delegates who were with John Bailey at the convention in Chicago, nine voted for Senator McCarthy.

How was such a rebellion mounted? What sort of people dared to mount it? And how did the old pol respond to this frontal challenge from the new politics?

After it was all over, one of the McCarthyites summed up their strengths and weaknesses accurately, if arrogantly: "We didn't know much about politics, but we were pretty intelligent."

The chief ring-leader of this guerrilla insurrection among the intellectuals was a Protestant theology teacher named Reverend Joseph Duffey. Duffey first learned that McCarthy was going to be a candidate at an ADA board meeting in Washington. Although Lowenstein invited him to come to his Democratic Alternative meeting in Chicago, Duffey was not specially keen on going. He had been active in various peace groups, but he found himself disenchanted with the present mood of the

New Left: "I guess you could call me a sort of revisionist Marxist, but certainly I had very little sympathy with the Maoists." At the last minute, on an impulse, he decided to go to Chicago on December 2.

To his surprise, Duffey found there were about a dozen people from Connecticut there, and they decided to hold a caucus in the hotel. They were a highly educated, distinctly well-to-do group, and not particularly young: Duffey was 35, and most were older. Perhaps the most experienced was Mrs. Stephanie May. She was on the national board of SANE and had been an important organizer in the campaign for the nuclear test ban treaty. She was a transplanted New Yorker; the whole McCarthy campaign in Connecticut drew heavily on the New York suburbs. The major question at the caucus was whether what was wanted was another peace campaign or a political campaign. Duffey argued strongly that in an election year it must be politics.

A meeting was held on December 10, in Ezra Stiles College at Yale, one of the two magnificent new colleges designed by Eero Saarinen. Yale was the second great focus of the McCarthy movement in Connecticut. Already in the autumn, a Yale Law School student, Geoffrey Cowan, had been in touch with Lowenstein and Curtis Gans. Now he prepared a two-page study of Connecticut electoral law and read it out to the meeting.

There were about thirty people there, a slightly broader cross section than the group in Chicago the week before, but still middle-class. There were engineers, accountants, a few clerks, housewives, and teachers. To their great surprise (although most of them were to some extent active in local politics), they found that Connecticut could in effect have a primary. A new system for selecting convention delegates had been introduced in 1955 but never used.

The unit of local government in Connecticut is the "town." There are 169 "towns," some urban, most rural or suburban. In towns of under five thousand, Cowan told the group, the first round of selection of delegates to the state convention took place in caucuses, which began late in February. Any registered Democrat could take part. In the bigger towns, which was where the regular party had its strength, participation would not be so easy. Delegates to the state convention would be named by the town committee. The only way of challenging them was to pick a whole rival slate, pay a filing fee, get a petition in its favor circulated by a resident of that town, and get five per cent of the registered Democrats to sign it.

After the meeting, Mrs. May telephoned Washington and asked

national headquarters for some buttons. "Gee!" said the man she talked to. "That's a great idea! I'll have some made."

On January 13, the first McCarthy for President meeting was held at a restaurant in Cheshire, in the middle of the state. By this time Arthur Miller and William Styron had agreed to be sponsors, and Paul Newman had become an enthusiastic supporter.

They still couldn't get any literature out of Washington, so they sat down and wrote their own—biographical stuff about McCarthy, propaganda about the war, and a little leaflet, written by an engineer, called "The System: You Have to Know It to Beat It." They laughed a lot about the number of places in the law where it turned out that things happened "at the discretion of the chairman." That meant Bailey.

In the next few weeks, something very strange happened— the result, perhaps, of the Tet offensive. The insurgents began to be surprised at how much strength they had. Reports came in from one caucus after another in the smaller towns that they had elected delegates who were for McCarthy. And in the bigger towns people were organizing petitions and registering new voters. In New Haven, McCarthy people registered enough Yale graduate students to beat the Barbieri machine; the prime mover there was Chester Kerr, head of the Yale University Press.

On February 17, Senator McCarthy made his first appearance in Connecticut. It so happened, by coincidence, that that was the night of one of John Bailey's big fund-raising dinners in Hartford. It became a trial of strength. The insurgents and the regulars both tried to get as many people as possible to come to their show. In the end, Bailey's gigantic dinner attracted about 1800 people, but there were 2500 at the McCarthy rally in Westport.

Shortly afterward, a McCarthy for President office opened in Hartford on a shoestring. The McCarthy people were mostly quite well off, but they were not in a position to make the big donations that businessmen can afford. What money could be raised in Connecticut was mostly sent out of the state. "We had been discouraged by the national staff from doing anything in Connecticut," Joe Duffey says, "because it looked so hopeless."

In spite of the shortage of money, things began to look far from hopeless. Soon the required number of signatures had been certified on petitions in thirty-one of the larger towns. Now the question was how to turn delegates to the state convention, among whom the McCarthy supporters ultimately numbered 284 out of 958, into delegates to the

National Convention in Chicago. The McCarthy camp set up a committee which from April to June met weekly at a restaurant in Hartford to prime Joe Duffey, who went each week to negotiate with John Bailey. At first, there were just nine on the committee: Duffey, Mrs. May, Mrs. Anne Wexler, the vivacious wife of a Westport eye surgeon, and representatives of each of the six Congressional districts. But gradually it grew, partly because there was an unquenchable suspicion, not of Duffey's motives, but of his ability to avoid being cheated by Bailey. Duffey realizes now that the insurgents misunderstood Bailey's power. "They thought he was the boss, therefore he could deliver what he wanted. But after I had met him a few times, I realized that he too was locked in by his associates."

(There was another cause of dissension in the insurgent forces in April and May. Many of the McCarthy supporters would have preferred to be for Robert Kennedy, and Kennedy's entrance into the race produced great strains and some suspicions.)

"At the beginning of our weekly talks," Duffey remembers, "Bailey and I were sparring with one another. He would say to me, 'Don't worry, it's going to be an open convention.' I would tell him that we wouldn't be happy with less than half the delegates because after all we had got more than forty-four per cent of the votes in the primaries. And he would tell me, 'Don't worry, if you behave responsibly, we might have no objection to giving you one or two seats on the delegation.'

"I began to enjoy the stimulation of those Friday night sessions," Duffey admits with some surprise, "and I feel he enjoyed the drama and the competition too: that was one of the reasons why he was in politics. I felt I was learning something about human nature and also about the nature of power. In the beginning we had a certain paranoia and also a certain naïveté about Bailey's power. But as I talked to him, I began to understand that he had power only by exercising it as a broker, by seeing that as far possible people got what they wanted."

Shortly before the convention, the McCarthy people realized that *they* had something that Bailey wanted for *his* people. In the primaries, almost by accident, they had won some seats on the state committee, as well as at the state convention, and some of the leading figures of the party had been swept off the committee. In particular, there was the case of Miss Katherine Quinn, who had been on the committee for forty years. She more or less ran the state while Bailey was in Washington, and she was greatly beloved. She had, someone said, "been to a thousand wakes." The McCarthy firebrands saw her as a bargaining counter, but

Duffey, who had to do the bargaining, realized this could be dangerous. He knew that there were people on the other side who grudgingly recognized the merits of the insurgents' case; who would not go for McCarthy but who would vote for a resolution giving the McCarthy people a fair share of delegates at Chicago in the name of justice. For such people, it was a bombshell that Miss Quinn had been defeated, and if Duffey tried to exploit her fall, he would be a knight in tarnished armor.

Bailey, understanding this, played it for all it was worth. At the state convention itself, his crowd turned up wearing buttons saying "I Love Katie." Duffey tried to take the sting out of this counteroffensive by attempting to put Miss Quinn back on the committee. But Katie Quinn refused to be put back. The McCarthy people had stooped, without conquering. "It may sound absurd," Duffey mused to us, "but I did have the feeling that this was a case where we amateurs were playing the game a lot more crudely than Bailey would have played it."

The McCarthy levies were skillfully trained for the convention by Anne Wexler. They circulated copies of *Robert's Rules,* complexes of draft resolutions, and contingency plans. Quietly, they got fourteen of their people onto the thirty-seven-man rules committee, so that by the time the real business of the convention opened, it was clear that Bailey would have to deal with them. To the regulars, it seemed that someone was getting away with something, and their agony was well-expressed in a heart-felt cry from Robert Killian, state Attorney General:

> The rule of the majority [*in which he counted himself*] is the very fabric of our democracy. . . . The Elks have it, the Knights of Columbus have it, the American Legion has it, and gentlemen, as a man who was once a member of that great organization, I can say the Boy Scouts have it. Gentlemen, I recall that the Daughters of the American Revolution abide by the majority rule!

The insurgents had their first meeting with the Bailey forces on Friday afternoon. Bailey offered five seats on the delegation to the national convention, and said he wouldn't budge. Duffey said, "Ten," and they laughed. So then the McCarthy people offered to swap Katie Quinn for seats. There was a horrified cry of "Katie Quinn is not for sale!"

Bailey had sometimes said to Duffey as a joke that the whole thing would be worked out at midnight on the evening before the convention. But it was two a.m. when Duffey received the summons to come to Governor John Dempsey's suite in the Hotel America. "It was like something out of *The Last Hurrah,*" he said afterward. "The place was surrounded with strong-arm men, and I couldn't get into the inner sanctum until I had been O.K.'d. Bailey met me and said, 'I'll go to seven or eight.' " Duffey went back to his committee again, and the committee gave him a flat no. What was more, they now wanted him to run against Abraham Ribicoff for the Senate. Duffey called Ribicoff and broke this news to him; Ribicoff was extremely unhappy.

Duffey went back to the Governor's suite at about three a.m. The suite was crowded: the Governor himself was there, and Ribicoff, and what Duffey remembers as "all these hard-eyed men sitting around on beds." At one stage, a drunken woman came to the door. Someone barred her, but she bit the Governor's doctor on the arm, and he was hopping round giving out little moans.

Duffey explained that his people had been prepared for ten seats and that if they got less they would walk out of the state convention. At about four, having tried everything else, Bailey asked Duffey how much he made at the theological seminary and then offered him a job with the National Committee in Washington. "It was for rather a lot of money," says Duffey without resentment.

Duffey went away again, and Ribicoff called to say that the Governor was furious. Duffey told him there was nothing he could do about it, because even if he accepted less than ten seats, his people would walk out. Ribicoff was desperately anxious to prevent an open break, and the next day he actually got up and told the convention that the McCarthy people could have his seat. That still didn't add up to ten, however; so out they walked.

Rather to the Connecticut leaders' surprise, this heroic gesture was not at all appreciated by national McCarthy headquarters. On June 26, the Wednesday after the convention, Joe Duffey saw McCarthy in New York. McCarthy did not seem very interested in the details of the struggle in Connecticut, but he made it quite plain that he wanted those nine delegates. So Duffey wrote a letter to Bailey and called a press conference. He would take the nine delegates, he said, though he reserved the right to protest. He still wonders whether he was right. "If we had held back, we might have got more than those nine seats. We would have put Bailey under tremendous pressure. All the people who were running for office would have pressured him. I still wonder whether, after I talked to McCarthy, there wasn't a failure of my own will and patience. Perhaps the point was that both Bailey and I were locked into a system that couldn't bear so much participation."

Perhaps that was it. "The System—You Have to Know It to Beat

It." Or should the pamphlet have been called "The System: You Have to Join It to Beat It"? Joe Duffey and Anne Wexler and their friends achieved a great deal. They brought new people into politics, raised new issues, and shook the assumption that the old pols would always have it their own way.

"There is at least a possibility," says Joe Duffey cautiously, "that things will never be the same again." Just before Christmas 1968, a new Connecticut organization called the Caucus of Concerned Democrats met. Duffey and his friends were all there, and so was the New Left; so was a surprising sprinkling of party regulars. Already some people in Connecticut are hoping that what Duffey calls the "second- and third-generation educated" will be the new backbone of a Democratic Party in the state. Perhaps they will, perhaps they won't. But a New Politics? Certainly the lesson of 1968 in Connecticut would seem to be that the new politicians were successful in exactly the proportion that they learned to play the old game.

The Price of Loyalty

"Liberalism becomes a mockery when it is spineless and cowardly."

—Hubert H. Humphrey, *The Cause Is Mankind*

The night of the California primary, Hubert Humphrey was riding in from the airport to his hotel in Colorado Springs with his young aide Ted Van Dyk. They listened to the results coming in over the car radio. Van Dyk said, "I suppose, from our point of view, a McCarthy win or a standoff would be best." "No," Humphrey said, "I want Bobby to win big. Number one, there are too many party leaders opposed to him for him to have any real chance of winning the nomination. Number two, since Oregon, he can't use the argument that he went right through the primaries. And number three, he's a party regular in spite of everything. If he does lose the nomination, he'll get together with me, and work for me. Whereas, if Gene is my opponent . . ." He paused, and as the car whirred on in silence for a moment, heaven knows what small memories of McCarthy's stubborn deafness to pleas of party loyalty flashed through his mind. "Gene's my friend," he went on, speaking to himself now. "I've known him for twenty years. But if he wins tonight, he'll plague Bobby and me all the way to the convention." A few hours later, McCarthy was indeed his only opponent.

The Tet offensive, the President's withdrawal, the murder of Robert Kennedy—these can be seen, in retrospect, as the three great pivots on which the year turned. But to the rival candidates the campaign was like shooting down a wild and dangerous river at tremendous pace. The three events were like great bends in the river; there was no knowing what hazards the next stretch would bring. And at each bend, one of the rivals

402

was swept onto the rocks. The Tet offensive, indirectly but certainly, eliminated the President. After his withdrawal, the odds lengthened against Kennedy. Now, the question was what Kennedy's death meant for McCarthy and Humphrey.

To the extent that the McCarthy campaign was aimed at winning at all, rather than at simply protesting, it had always depended heavily on coming through a broken field at the convention. Blair Clark, for one, had always felt that McCarthy's only serious chance would come at a convention deadlocked between Kennedy and Humphrey. His theory, expounded to many a skeptical delegate and journalist, was that Kennedy and McCarthy between them would stop Humphrey, and that enough Humphrey people would then switch to McCarthy, in preference to Kennedy, to give him the nomination. As strategy, it had always had a somewhat gossamer look to it, and now Sirhan Sirhan's bullets had blown it away. McCarthy himself was in despair. "It's like someone gave you the football," he said at a private meeting with some *New York Times* people a week after the assassination, "and the field never ends. There's no goal line. No opponent. You just run."

On the other hand, Humphrey's chances of winning the nomination obviously improved. By the middle of June, the *New York Times* was giving him 1600 delegates—well over the 1312 needed for nomination. And there were only five weeks to go to the convention in Chicago. That figure might be worth little more than any of the other premature delegate counts the press came forth with, all year long, but there could be no denying that Humphrey was now in a very strong position indeed, that Kennedy's death had made him stronger. In Michigan and Ohio, for example, it came in time to save him from two bloody state convention fights. The week's moratorium on campaigning, a mark of respect for Robert Kennedy, also helped him, as the front-runner. "Of course, I'm as sad as anyone else," said a young volunteer at the Manhattan McCarthy for President headquarters the morning after Robert Kennedy's death, "but while the nation mourns, I'm terrified that Humphrey will steal away the nomination." In New York, where the primary was coming up on June 18, the moratorium gave Humphrey a welcome excuse for his almost certain defeat in that state. He promptly announced that he would not be campaigning there.

But already, as Humphrey, at his lakeside house in Waverly, pondered the changed circumstances, it was plain that his real problem was not the nomination, but the election—and, from that standpoint, Kennedy's death had compounded his difficulties. "It's a Republican year," grunted a union lobbyist, "and the Kennedy killing just confirms the trend."

Before his death, Robert Kennedy had indicated to Humphrey through third parties that if he were beaten in California, he would withdraw. Humphrey had believed him, and he also believed that even if Kennedy had won in California and then lost at the convention, he would have rallied loyally to the party's standard-bearer. Now Humphrey could no longer look forward to a charismatic campaigner helping him where he was weakest, bringing the young, the blacks, and the radical middle class back under the big consensus tent. There was some discussion at Waverly of offering a place on the ticket to Edward Kennedy, and—as we shall see—overtures were made and turned down. There were also overtures to the McCarthy camp.

The day after Kennedy's death, Humphrey and McCarthy spoke on the telephone, and there were later secret contacts through Eugene Foley, one of the Vice-President's supporters in New York, and Stephen Quigley, Senator McCarthy's brother-in-law. But not even the eternally hopeful Humphrey can have thought there was much chance of McCarthy's agreeing not to "plague me all the way to the convention." Within a week of Kennedy's death, McCarthy had virtually foreclosed the possibility by making scathing public statements about how "very difficult" it would be for him to back Humphrey if he were the nominee.

Humphrey had other worries on his mind. Kennedy's death sharply reduced the flow of money to his campaign, because many of the contributions to his campaign had been "stop-Kennedy" money. There were organizational problems too, not least the relations between the two liberal co-chairmen, Senators Mondale and Harris, and the staider wheels in the machine.

But the essence of the strategy decision Humphrey had to make was simplicity itself. He had to spring-clean his image, so to speak, and dress himself in a bright, new, washable campaign style. And before he could hope to do that, he had to define, for the world and for himself, his relations with the President and his position on the war. Already, McCarthy was hammering away at this. "It is now time for us to take our steel out of the land of thatched huts," he said in New York before setting out to resume his campaign after the moratorium. Humphrey did his best to find a formula that would make him look free from the President's leading strings without actually cutting them. "Hubert Humphrey as Vice-President is a member of the team," he told the National Press Club on June 20. "Hubert Humphrey as President is captain of a team—there's a lot of difference." It was hardly convincing. The question was what game the team was going to play.

It was a confusing period. McCarthy might feel that however hard he ran, the goal line never got any closer. But Humphrey would have been equally justified in feeling that however hard McCarthy was tackled, he always seemed to wriggle free and make a few more yards. On June 18, the McCarthy forces in New York, throwing in resources of volunteers, enthusiasm, and money with the grim enthusiasm of Marshal Foch on the Western Front, won a surprise victory in the state's primary. Out of 123 delegates to Chicago chosen that day, 63 were for McCarthy, against 30 pledged to Robert Kennedy—and presumably open to negotiation with a peace candidate—19 uncommitted, and only 11 for Humphrey. "The lesson of New York," wrote the *Washington Post,* which could hardly be accused of prejudice in McCarthy's favor, was that Humphrey was "measurably less popular with the voters of the party than he is with the party pros." It was indeed a famous victory, and one not confined to the delegate elections. On the same day the pro-McCarthy candidate, Paul O'Dwyer, a white-haired veteran battler for some of the less fashionable left-wing causes, stole away with the Senatorial nomination, eclipsing two much more highly fancied, and financed, candidates —Eugene Nickerson, a Kennedy protégé and the Nassau County Executive, and Representative Joseph Resnick, a multimillionaire manufacturer of television antennae. O'Dwyer, like McCarthy himself, had an engaging talent for making radical proposals sound like statements of the obvious. (He suggested, for example, that the best solution to New York's burgeoning crime and narcotics problem would be to issue free heroin to registered addicts.) Over in Nassau County, the ubiquitous Al Lowenstein survived charges of "carpet-bagging" to win the nomination for the 5th Congressional District against a liberal opponent backed by the local machine.

Inevitably, Kennedy's tragic removal from the race took some of the gilt off McCarthy's triumph. But the assumption, a common one among correspondents at the time, that Kennedy, had he lived, would have taken his own state comfortably was almost certainly a sentimental error. New York had been winding up an electoral low blow for its Senator for some weeks. For one thing, the state was almost tailor-made for the insurgent tactics of the McCarthy operation. Its primary system is so hideously complex that in most election years it is hardly used at all. Naturally the party regulars had become accustomed to hand-picking their own delegates. Petition drives by the McCarthy forces had, however, opened up the electoral procedures and guaranteed the voters a voice in the selection process. Elected delegates were chosen by ballot in the state's forty-one congressional districts (each district slate had three delegates). After a lot of bruising jockeying for position, the situation early in May was one in which thirty-six McCarthy-pledged slates had entered the lists, twenty-five were for Humphrey and thirty for Robert Kennedy (just to complicate matters, "pledges" were not binding: all delegates, in theory, were free, so there was no question of the "Kennedy" slates being withdrawn after the Senator's death). There were also a number of other slates classified as "uncommitted," though most of these were composed of Kennedy men in a neutral guise. Clearly, only the most highly motivated voters would be inclined to thread their way through this electoral labyrinth, and there was good reason to believe that a high proportion of those were for McCarthy. "That man," lamented a press officer in Humphrey's New York operation, "is everybody's second choice in both the Kennedy and Humphrey camps. But as far as the McCarthy people are concerned there is no second choice. There is only Eugene."

Ironically, resentment of Kennedy's candidacy was nowhere stronger than in his own state. The McCarthy people persisted in regarding him as a "Bobby-come-lately" to the peace cause; and their view of the Kennedy operation was not enhanced by its methods of slate selection. In some districts the New York Senator's adherents described their slates as "mixed" (i.e., composed of Kennedy and McCarthy elements), when it just was not so. Initially, there was some pretense of a common cause between the rival peace candidates. But by the end of May this had ceased to be the case. Mrs. Eleanor Clark French, millionaire sister of Senator Joe Clark of Pennsylvania, who with Sarah Kovner and Harold Ickes, Jr., son of FDR's cantankerous Secretary of the Interior, ran the McCarthy operation in the state, said after the Oregon primary, "If ever there was a honeymoon with Bobby, it's over."

The resentment of the Humphrey men was more esoteric but just as deep rooted. Kennedy had offended the most basic instinct of any party professional: the instinct for unity. Humphrey's slates were filled with old party hands, whose response to the political limbo period of March/ April—between the time Kennedy "announced" and the emergence of the Vice-President as a candidate—had been, in the parlance of the bewildered professionals, to "stay loose." To do that, they had to resist some vigorous arm-twisting by the Kennedy men. The process had left wounds that hurt the more because many of their friends had succumbed to the pressure. Traditionally, the only cure for rending the state party machine is the balm of victory. By the end of the primary period there were many New York regulars, inside as well as outside the Kennedy camp, who were beginning to suspect that all the suffering had been for nothing. Some had been hedging their bets all along. A neat instance of this was Jack English, the wily chief of the Nassau County Democratic machine and hitherto an ardent Kennedy supporter. English had chosen to pit an "uncommitted" slate against the McCarthy and Humphrey slates in his district, an equivocal position that was the envy of many old-timers. English could still privately pledge his allegiance to his Senator, which he did, but if, come state convention time, the House of Kennedy looked like falling, there was no ostensible reason why the chairman of Nassau County should be buried under the rubble. There were those who felt English rather overdid the ambiguity of his position, particularly when his congressional choice, Albert Vorspen, sensing the strong current of anti-Kennedy sentiment in his district, castigated Al Lowenstein for being "a friend of Robert Kennedy." (Lowenstein was backing the McCarthy slate locally against English's "uncommitteds.")

No such tensions inhibited the fervor of the McCarthy operatives. They felt they could get nothing from the regulars, and, pointedly, asked nothing. When O'Dwyer was pressed to clarify his position vis-à-vis the Vice-President's candidacy, he replied, "I would not support Humphrey. Period." The counter from John Fabrizi, chairman of the Association of Upstate Rural Democratic Chairmen, was equally explicit: "Then we won't support O'Dwyer. Period." Old-timers might be aghast at some of the more idiosyncratic features of the McCarthy operation. It was perhaps the first statewide campaign with a press office headed by a girl affecting a pink leather mini-skirt. But with over two hundred local offices functioning with the energetic manpower provided by an army of students returning to New York for the holidays, the McCarthy operation felt it could thumb its nose at the regulars. It was getting through to the voters, and at levels that no other campaign had previously attempted. One of the most ruthless vote-getting outfits in Manhattan was called Junior Students for McCarthy. Founded early in May, it was run by Nelson Gess, the son of an international lawyer at the United Nations, and Randall Stempler, the son of a lawyer with Twentieth Century–Fox. Gess was thirteen years old, Stempler was twelve. With the help of over a hundred like-minded children, and with an adviser in Charles Bell, formerly of the USAID staff in Vietnam, they made an intimidating squad. Their organizational high point was a dance at the Village Gate night club in Greenwich Village at which Margaret McCarthy, the Senator's twelve-year-old daughter, was the guest star. Almost two hundred micro-boppers came and drank Coke and ate hot dogs at a dollar a throw. But it was as canvassers that they were most formidable. Stempler understood why very clearly. "People don't mind talking to us about the war," he said, "because they think we're cute. With adults they might be embarrassed. Another thing is that we've got a great opening line. We just go up to someone and say, 'Do you believe in death?' "

Perhaps the effect of Kennedy's narrow victory in California would, had he lived, have made all the difference to his chances in New York. But this was by no means certain. The best evidence against such an assumption was the fate suffered by some of those most closely associated with him in life. In Manhattan's 17th (the Silk Stocking) District a Kennedy slate of Theodore Sorensen, Marietta Tree, and Robert Low was trounced by the McCarthy slate headed by Eleanor French. Where Kennedy's death made a major difference was in the next stage of the New York saga: appointment of the sixty-five delegates-at-large who would complete the composition of the New York slate.

This was the stage at which the McCarthy forces *did* have to ask favors of the machine. The delegate-at-large appointments were in the hands of the state democratic committee. Immediately after their June 18 triumph in the primary, Eleanor French and her friends lost no time in informing the state chairman, John Burns, that they thought the result entitled them to half of these votes. Initially, Burns, a Kennedy man, had been inclined to think the request reasonable (he had already displayed a conciliatory attitude by showing up at O'Dwyer's victory party, prompting the Senatorial candidate to the utterance, "So, the mountain comes to Mohammed!"). He would do his best. Without Kennedy's authority, however, Burns's power to dictate to the party regulars was virtually nil. Before the week was out he was overwhelmed with requests for at-large seats by the local county barons. The most intransigent demands were not from Humphrey's supporters. Those putting the screws on Burns—men like Joe Crangle of Buffalo, Stanley Steingut, the legendary Brooklyn boss, and Jack English of Nassau—had been Kennedy men. Indeed, the Humphrey national staff, nervous of an image that put them on the side of the bosses and brokers against the expressed wishes of the voters, tended to advocate conciliation. Both Bill Connell and Eugene Foley, Humphrey's personal representative in New York, urged a generous compromise. In this, however, they were singing a rather different refrain from Frank O'Connor, chairman of the Vice-President's New York campaign. (The McCarthy operation was to become famous for the contradictory signals put out by the various levels of its staff. However, at this stage, the Humphrey cause was fully its equal in this respect.)

The county leaders were moving in to fill what, to their way of thinking, was a dangerous political vacuum. Their argument was simply that the seats in the party's hands belonged to those who had a concrete record of favors rendered to the party. If the seats were turned over to the insurgents then the gratitude of those men whose services were needed to lubricate the party's regular operation might be destroyed. Monroe Goldwater, the law chairman of the state party, defending the prerogatives of the county leaders to a final say-so on delegate appointments on the "what-have-you-done-for-me-lately" principle, put the argument in its baldest terms. "We must have leaders," he said. "Call them bosses if you will, I don't give a damn. I've talked with three or four very decent McCarthy adherents. None of them have ever contributed over two hundred and fifty dollars to the party. I respect their intelligence, their sincerity, their integrity, but you can't run a campaign on that."

On the night of Thursday, June 27, a thoroughly chastened Burns met with reform leaders at Eleanor French's Manhattan home. He could promise only twelve to fifteen at-large seats to the McCarthy people. Mrs. French was adamant: anything less than twenty-eight—six less than the original request—would be totally unacceptable.

But when, on the following day, the New York State Democratic Committee met at the Commodore Hotel to ratify the at-large appointments, it was immediately apparent that Burns had decided that his only option was to side with the bosses. The McCarthy people were allotted 15½ votes and of these only 7½ were culled from names submitted by Mrs. French's group. Five of the six "McCarthy" delegates selected from Nassau County had actually opposed McCarthy in the primary. One of them was that political Houdini, Jack English. Two of the three "McCarthy" delegates put up by Steingut were totally unknown to the McCarthy campaign organization. While party oldsters such as James A. Farley, twice a Roosevelt campaign strategist and a man who had not missed a convention since 1924, sat like stone gods in lowering silence, the McCarthyites, understandably, broke all records, even by the exalted standards of New York reform Democrats, in their righteous indignation. The meeting at the hotel was held in a stuffy and crowded room, the natural ambiance of such occasions, and the feeling that for once the majority of the voters was behind them emboldened the liberals to operatic flights. "This day," sang Eleanor French, in a rich coloratura, "June 28, 1968, is a day which will go down in the history of Democratic state

politics as a day of perfidy!" The wicked duke in *Rigoletto* could not
have been more unmoved than the regulars. When Al Lowenstein
shouted, "You spit in the face of the notion that this convention is democratic," there were regulars hardened enough to laugh. "Boo!" shouted
others. "Sit the hell down!" Frank G. Rossetti, Manhattan County leader,
strode over to Steingut in the front row and snarled, "Are we going to
allow this rabble-rousing to go on? Chrissakes!" His problem was soon
solved. Lowenstein and Mrs. French and their outraged cavalry mounted
their white horses and galloped out of the room, shouting "Fascists!"
"Nazis!" and, more hurtfully still, since the aforementioned epithets were
obvious hyperbole, "Hacks!"

The gothic grandeur of the scene was not without prophetic significance. The Commodore Hotel, in microcosm, was a dress rehearsal for
the Chicago convention. Few, however, realized this at the time. The
hapless Burns was to say in self-defense, "If I ignored the people who
have helped me with the organization's work and appointed strangers
just because they were for McCarthy, I'd have a revolution on my hands."
But the McCarthyites, and most of the press, read it as a crude power
play by supporters of the Vice-President. Humphrey was harvesting his
delegates with boss rule, and the voters be damned. It was an issue that
was easy to project. Stephen Mitchell, Adlai Stevenson's campaign manager, who had just come aboard the McCarthy operation, bringing a
direly needed store of political experience, shrewdly pitched his harpoon
into the Vice-Presidential blubber. "It's obvious," he told a press conference in his inimitably pugnacious manner, "that President Johnson is
back in the saddle and he's leading the national convention like a mule
under halter."

Mitchell was not the only new face at McCarthy headquarters in
Washington. The ambiguous Tom Finney reappeared, bringing with him
a retired CIA agent named Tom McCoy, who aroused the sharpest suspicions of the young volunteers. And, on June 25, Richard Goodwin was
back with his cigars, his wisecracks, and his subtleties. The atmosphere
at McCarthy headquarters rapidly took on something of a girls' boarding
school and something of an Oriental court. Dark suspicions, wild accusa-
tions, and labyrinthine intrigues proliferated. Finney disliked Gans as a
radical and despised Clark as an amateur. Clark skillfully pitted Finney
against Mitchell. His attitude, someone said angrily, was "let everyone
do his thing, and flowers will bloom." If so, it was perhaps a more con-
structive attitude than some. The volunteers looked to Gans as their
leader. Gans was in disfavor with the candidate. The young radicals—

Sam Brown and his friends—tended to distrust Goodwin for his links with the Kennedys, and just about everyone suspected Finney for his links to the Administration—he was, after all, the law partner of the Secretary of Defense and a former White House aide. The candidate, meanwhile, cared for none of these things and more than ever preferred the company of his witty literary friends, Robert Lowell and the rest, to the tedium of political detail.

It would be the greatest mistake to dismiss the internal quarrels in the McCarthy campaign too lightly. They had their farcical side: for example, Gans was fired five times, Clark four times, and Finney three times, on one estimate. But they sprang from deeply serious differences of aims and attitudes, and indeed from a fundamental dilemma in the McCarthy campaign. For the idealists—the pristines, somebody called them: a solecism, but a neat one—the McCarthy campaign was a protest first and foremost. They considered it a protest not only against the war, but against the whole style of American politics, its compromises and its conventions. For such people, it would, of course, be nice to see McCarthy nominated. But if, in order to be nominated, he must sink to the small flatteries and sordid bargains of which the idealists thought the conventional political process was made up (most of whom had little or no experience of it)—well, then, so be it, the price was too high, the means would invalidate the end. To the realists, like Finney the lawyer-lobbyist and his friends, on the other hand, there was nothing wrong with the conventional politics, and this attitude was therefore ludicrous and indeed incomprehensible. McCarthy, for them, was a promising candidate, with an impressive fight record. If he were properly managed and trained, they felt, there was no reason why he shouldn't win the title in a poor year. All they asked was that he do the things a candidate usually did in order to be nominated. "He could have done a lot more to consolidate his support in New York and California," Finney said after the convention. "He could have talked to some of the people in Pennsylvania. *Nobody would have had to tell Jack Kennedy who to call!*"

The rank-and-file McCarthy workers rejected the idea that the nomination could be won by talking to enough politicians. In Chicago, in the fourth week of June, several hundred of them gathered to form yet another Lowenstein-inspired pressure group—the Coalition for an Open Convention. It was partly a bridge-building enterprise between McCarthy and former Kennedy supporters, but its particular objective was to find new ways of influencing the delegates. It was just that they did not believe that victory could be obtained by persuading the delegates from above, by talking to the Richard Daleys and the governors and those who were thought to influence them. Their idea was win over the delegates from below, stirring up a popular insurrection against "manipulation." There were all sorts of ideas—town meetings at which delegates would be called on to defend their position publicly, demonstrations, and so on. Some of them, including Gans and Sam Brown, were tempted by the idea of organizing a massive descent on Chicago, an idea which horrified the Finney school because of its probable effect on the delegates. As it became clear that the militant left was planning something similar, such ideas fell out of favor, and eventually the candidate himself asked his supporters to have nothing to do with mass demonstrations in Chicago. One idea did, however, endure up to and through the convention—that of a Fourth Party for McCarthy if he was rejected by the regulars. It was never official C.O.C. policy to advocate this, of course, but the Coalition gave fourth-party activists an organizational umbrella. The knowledge that such schemes were under discussion, combined with McCarthy's refusal to endorse the nominee of the convention in advance, did not please the party loyalists one bit.

The schism between the two wings of the McCarthy campaign was so wide that sometimes it seemed that they were working for two different men. Finney, for example, felt that McCarthy had "much in common" with Governor John Connally. When asked what he meant by that startling statement, he explained that Connally was in favor of limiting the action of the Federal government and McCarthy was in favor of limiting the activity of the President. On the other hand, those who had been brought into his campaign by Lowenstein and Gans persisted in treating their candidate as a man of the left, an identification which was made more plausible by the fact that Jeremy Larner and Paul Gorman did occasionally succeed in giving McCarthy's speeches a radical orientation—which might or might not conform to the Senator's own instinct.

It was, in any case, not easy to say which was the real Senator McCarthy, the idealist or the politician, since neither of the two showed great alacrity in stepping forward. On one occasion, it was felt by his staff that he ought to take a stand on the problems of world hunger and poverty. Two keen young staff members, working through the night, managed to produce an extremely creditable position paper. When they looked for the candidate to get his criticisms or at least his endorsement, however, he was nowhere to be found. A couple of days later, he was tracked down. He had flown to Minnesota for some dental work and then slipped off for a retreat at St. John's! The politicians found him at least as infuriating, if not more so. "I think Gene was rather schizophrenic," Finney says. "The level of his optimism fluctuated. A lot of the things that needed to be done were distasteful to him, and a lot of it was plain laziness." Whatever the explanation, the effect on even sympathetic delegates was all too often disastrous. To take a single example, Arthur Paini was a New Jersey delegate, forty-nine years old, police commissioner in his town, and chairman of the Democratic Party in his county. "I could have been swayed by McCarthy," he told us after meeting the candidate in July, "and I still could. But I was disappointed, I have to say. I mean, he was just so lifeless! I mean, you can't be dead on your feet if you're a Presidential candidate—we felt as though he didn't even like talking to people." And, of course, with the exception of people like Robert Lowell and Mary McGrory, that was exactly right.

There was nothing snobbish about this. McCarthy snubbed the high and the low impartially. On several occasions, he simply failed to return calls from governors who were known to be considering coming out for him but who had understandably let it be known that they wanted to be *asked*: these included Harold Hughes of Iowa. Twice McCarthy canceled appointments with Mayor Daley which had been set up for him by the prominent Catholic layman Patrick Crowley, a Chicago lawyer. The United Auto Workers were deeply troubled by the war and not wholeheartedly behind Humphrey. The mighty Walter Reuther, who could have been decisive with the ninety-six-man Michigan delegation and influential nationally, was privately interested in McCarthy. In late June, Reuther's man Leonard Woodcock, a McCarthy supporter himself, called McCarthy to say that a three-day meeting of UAW officials had been scheduled and that it was important for McCarthy to call Reuther and plan a strategy that might lead to an endorsement. McCarthy called Reuther once, but Reuther happened to be out. Five times in the next three days he returned McCarthy's call, but McCarthy had gone off on another retreat and couldn't be found.

"I think Gene's view of the thing was almost mystical," one of the realists told us with a shake of the head. "I think he really did want to change the character of American politics." That was all very well, said one of his most loyal and sophisticated lieutenants, but he was at the head of a six-million-dollar campaign, and he refused to make any strategic decisions. "He may have willed the end, but he just didn't want to know about the means."

And yet, the curious, the ironic fact, is that it worked, more than it deserved, perhaps, and certainly far more than the professionals believed possible. On July 20, McCarthy, the man who had shrugged off the polls in New Hampshire, was able to announce with obvious pleasure that the Harris poll due in two days' time would show him with a clear lead over Humphrey. If Nixon were the candidate, which seemed inevitable, Humphrey would lead him, 37 per cent to 35 per cent, but McCarthy would annihilate him, 42 per cent to 34 per cent. Less than a week later, on Kennedy ground, at Fenway Park in Boston, McCarthy drew thirty-three thousand, the biggest crowd for any candidate anywhere so far in 1968.

There were those who argued, from McCarthy's success, that his eccentric approach to campaigning was justified—that it was naïve to think it mattered whether or not he paid courtesy calls on Mayor Daley, because there were no circumstances in which Daley would endorse him anyway. (As a matter of fact, McCarthy and Daley did talk on the telephone several times during this period.) But there was at least one incontrovertible instance in which McCarthy hurt his own cause by his inexplicable unwillingness to make even the slightest concession to political etiquette.

After Robert Kennedy's death, many members of Kennedy's staff were desperate to find another candidate. McCarthy was simply unacceptable to them. They claimed to have been outraged by the "nasty" things McCarthy had said about their hero in Oregon and California, though it is hard to see that McCarthy said anything nastier about Kennedy than Kennedy said about him. But, whatever the reason, they wanted an alternative candidate, and the obvious choice was George McGovern. Even on board the funeral train, several of Kennedy's young men approached McGovern and pleaded with him to run. McGovern was slightly shocked and told them that if anyone emerged, it ought to be Edward Kennedy and that, in any case, he had accepted renomination for Senator from South Dakota.

The next day, McGovern got a call from two of McCarthy's friends, Joe Rauh and Tom Mechling, asking him to endorse McCarthy. But McGovern had, a few weeks earlier, been mildly nettled by a typical McCarthy performance. He had read in the newspapers that McCarthy was going to campaign in South Dakota. He felt it would have been polite of McCarthy to tell him this personally, but he nevertheless called McCarthy and offered to speak for him. McCarthy said, "Fine." Just as McGovern was leaving for South Dakota, he learned by accident from one of his aides that McCarthy had canceled the trip. No word from

McCarthy. So now McGovern told Rauh and Mechling that he had
the impression McCarthy "enjoyed being alone on the battlefield";
McCarthy had never asked for his endorsement, but he might give it
if McCarthy asked him. The message was passed to McCarthy. He
never did call.

Then on July 13 came the puzzling episode of the memorial dinner
for Robert Kennedy in Huron, South Dakota. McGovern himself was in
Sweden at the annual conference of the World Council of Churches.
Lo and behold, there appeared in this remote corner of the Great
Plains Jesse Unruh, leader of the largest of the Kennedy delegations
now looking for a new candidate; Kennedy's intimate adviser Ted
Sorensen; and a number of other Kennedy men. The sponsors and participants acted dumb. For example, asked whether the dinner was really
important, one of McGovern's political friends said, "I'm just a country
boy with hayseeds in my hair"—he shook his head as if to prove the
point—"but it seems to me it must be important, or all you big-time
reporters wouldn't have come all this way." It was obvious that at least
some of the free-floating Kennedy supporters would be very happy if
they could lure McGovern into being a candidate.

Within a couple of weeks, it began to appear that McGovern
was not altogether averse to becoming one. On August 4, at a secret
meeting with many of those who had been at the dinner plus some
other important liberal Democrats, at a motel at O'Hare Airport,
Chicago, McGovern seemed eager to go. "I love you, George," said
bluff Harold Hughes, "but you can't do anything for me!" Immediately
after that meeting, McGovern went off to the Black Hills with his
wife and family, rented a friend's cabin where he had been before
when he wanted peace and quiet, and thought his decision through.
On August 10, he announced his candidacy.

Bang went a certain number of delegates who could have been
McCarthy's for the price of a phone call.

June had turned into July, July was three-quarters gone, the
convention was less than a month away, and still Hubert Humphrey had
made no headway with either of his two problems. His campaign on the
road was still a near disaster, with angry demonstrations, thin crowds,
and snide reporters. And, on the war, his image was still as firmly
chained to the President's as ever.

On July 4, for example, he flew to Philadelphia for the traditional
Independence Day speech in front of Independence Hall. To a reporter

who had covered John Kennedy's eloquent and magnanimous address, calling for a new interdependence among nations, on that same spot and on that same occasion in 1962, it was a depressing expedition. One of us wrote in his notebook at the time:

> There is an unmistakable whiff of mediocrity about the Humphrey operation these days.
>
> There are some corny touches in the worst Johnson manner. At the airport before we left a remarkable object was waiting to be loaded and installed as a trophy in Waverly. It was an airline seat, upholstered in black leather and inscribed on a gigantic silver plaque:
>
> THE VICE-PRESIDENT OF THE UNITED STATES
> HUBERT HUMPHREY
>
> In recognition of his contributions to
> aviation development
>
> THE FLYINGEST PUBLIC OFFICIAL IN HISTORY
> FROM THE AIR FORCE ASSOCIATION.

The press party was noticeably scanty—two Swedes, two Italians, and a Belgian TV crew, but no CBS, and no big names, and both *Time* and *Newsweek* left after the first speech. The total press party was about 28, where Kennedy traveled with 70–100.

The police estimated the crowd outside Independence Hall at 20,000. I would put it at about 5,000, and this was the independent guess of several experienced local reporters. Many of these were obviously party hacks or city jobholders drummed up by Mayor Tate. The whole proceedings, complete with a Baltic girl in national costume reading in a toneless voice a prize-winning Liberty Belle essay about the religious persecution her relatives are undergoing in Estonia, had a disagreeable period flavor. I have never seen so many Secret Service men. They were swarming around the platform, they were on rooftops, they were "rogering" and "wilcoing" into two-way radios wherever one turned. And Tate had laid on *1200* police! There were two demonstrations while Humphrey spoke, one on each side of the platform. On HHH's right they were antiwar. They chanted, "Bring the troops home." I asked one girl whether she was for McCarthy, and she answered, "Not necessarily, but we prefer McCarthy to Humphrey." The other, smaller and quieter, demonstration was specifically pro-McCarthy, with signs saying DUMP THE HUMP, and ALL JOHNSON'S FORCES AND ALL JOHNSON'S MEN COULDN'T GET HUBERT ELECTED AGAIN! Some of the McCarthy people were circulating little pink leaflets complaining of the "stale air" around Humphrey, at which the Humphrey staff were unfeignedly shocked.

HHH then went to the Ben Franklin Hotel for a political lunch with Mayor Tate, who toasted him as "my very good friend and the very good friend of all big city mayors—uh, and of the whole American people."

Humphrey's theme was "down with the knockers!" "If I act like an optimist it's because the history of this country is on my side. We've always been able to make it!" Prolonged and frenzied applause from the guests, most of whom showed every sign of having made it financially, if not with each other for some years.

Humphrey's speech worked in almost every cliché known to politics, including specifically, "One nation, indivisible, under God" . . . "I have a dream" . . . and even "Let's get this country moving forward again!" and other copyrighted lines.

Outside, the McCarthy people, perhaps a hundred, were chanting in a fast rhythm, "Listen to the people, We Want Gene!" and one placard read HUMPHREY OR NIXON: TWEEDLEDUM OR TWEEDLEDEE! The Humphrey people are so angry this evening that there is some talk of a major speech denouncing anarchy! The Philadelphia police gunned the motors of their big motorbikes in an effort to drown the chants, and only succeeded in making them more noticeable, of course.

My impression is of a nice man, mediocre, uncomprehending, and a little desperate.

One area where Humphrey was unquestionably in good shape, and McCarthy could make little impact, was with the black community. Most black leaders who were within the political process at all soon endorsed him, and, on July 23, Humphrey gave a special press conference in New York to crow about another Negro endorsement: that of Diana Ross, of the Supremes. Wearing a shocking-pink silk suit and matching pill-box hat, and flanked by her two attendant goddesses, Mary Wilson and Cindy Birdsong, Miss Ross read through an obviously prepared statement, which explained that she had originally felt doubts about the Vice-President's policies on the war, but that after "hours of private discussion" she had become convinced that he was a "courageous man"—and here she leered at him from under her magnificent eyelashes, and he simpered bravely back. When a reporter asked her just what her differences with his war policies were, Humphrey got cross and said *he* was conducting this press conference.

That was bad enough. But an expedition to open a play street in East Harlem the next day was worse. New York City had a program in which anyone who raised thirty-four hundred dollars could buy the closing until Labor Day of a street to be used as play area. A small crowd huddled behind barriers. One single WELCOME HUBERT sign hung from the rows of tenements scarred with fire escapes and lapped by garbage. A loud-mouthed advance man bellowed, "The next President will be here momentarily—a courageous man, di-da, di-da," and the nice kind white ladies from Citizens for Humphrey handed out candy and balloons to the children. "Hubert loves children," boomed the advance man into the PA system, "that's why he's coming here today!" If you could believe that, as the Duke of Wellington said to the man who said, "Mr. Smith, I believe," you could believe any goddamned thing.

Then Humphrey arrived, to a fanfare from a group called The Versatiles. He shook hands with Joe Louis. ("Gosh," said a twelve-year-old. "Doesn't he look *old*!") "This is the new politics of Hubert Humphrey," the candidate said, "the politics of public service, of friendliness to all, of social service, of help." And he asked his committee in New York not to spend the money they had collected on television advertising but on play streets! He picked up a black baby for the benefit of the photographers. Another black child lisped a poem into the microphone and did the twist. Humphrey presented a camera to the most promising photographer in some program, shook some more hands, and disappeared. "The politics of happiness, the politics of joy." An evil smell still hung in the air. A black boy said, "They're always telling us what we want. They never *ask* us."

But Humphrey's main predicament was not his shortcomings as a campaigner. He had, in fact, shown himself to be an effective campaigner in 1964, and there was no reason why his ebullience should not once again come across as infectious and attractive, rather than hollow and embarrassing, once he could get his feet firmly planted on his own ground. Perhaps, from a strictly political point of view, what he said was not even so very important. But it was becoming desperately urgent, in the judgment of a majority of his advisers and friends, that he say something that marked him off from the President on the war. The difficulty was that there the number of possible positions for him to take was not infinite. On the contrary, Humphrey had painfully little space for maneuver.

To understand his dilemma a little more clearly, it is necessary to go back and see what had been happening in Vienam and at the peace negotiations, at least in outline. For events in Vietnam provided a sort of ground bass to the year's politics, so that any political melody that was not in harmony with what was happening in Vietnam and in Paris was likely to sound horribly out of tune.

The President's fateful decision at the end of March, to reject the various proposals of his military commanders for further escalation and to go to the conference table, was not the result of any fundamental change of heart about the political or moral justification of the war. He made the decision because he had new evidence about how badly the war was going. For many months, he had been sheltered from a true picture of the situation by the optimistic reports of General Westmoreland and Walt Rostow, whose function it was to funnel information to him from many sources—including military, diplomatic, and intelligence. Originally perhaps as much as a political device to disarm criticism as because he really wanted advice, he had had a blue-ribbon "informal advisory group" of nine members, an extremely eminent group: Dean Acheson; Generals Matthew B. Ridgway and Maxwell Taylor (the latter a co-author, with Rostow, of the report which led to the original commitment in Vietnam); Cyrus Vance, the President's trusted emissary on a number of delicate international missions; McGeorge Bundy, Douglas Dillon, the venerable General Omar N. Bradley, Arthur Dean, . . . and George Ball.

Ball had been the only member of the advisory group who was fundamentally critical of the President's war policy. But now, in March, after the manifest humiliations of the Tet offensive, things were different.

The group assembled for dinner at the White House with the highest officials concerned with the war—among them, Secretary of State Rusk; Secretary of Defense Clark Clifford; General Earle Wheeler, Chairman of the Joint Chiefs of Staff; and Richard Helms, Director of the CIA.

During dinner, the nine wise men questioned the officials closely —more closely, perhaps, than before Tet—not only on the war, but on the condition of South Vietnam and of its government, and on the effect of the war on the United States. Then the officials left, and the wise men were given three briefings. The first was by a State Department official, Philip Habib, who described the state of affairs in South Vietnam very frankly. He admitted that there was serious corruption there, and he reported the severe refugee problem. "He told it like it was," one of those present said. Then the group heard two different briefings on the military situation, one from an officer on the Joint Chiefs' staff, Major General William DePuy, and the other from a CIA expert, George Carver.

The nine wise men had been disturbed by Habib's account, but they were really shaken by the military briefings. In the past, they had only heard the Joint Chiefs' estimates of military strength, which counted only identifiable military units. Now they became aware that these were only a fraction of the forces available to the enemy, for the CIA's estimates, which included all military, paramilitary, and guerrilla strength, were considerably higher.

The next morning, the advisers gathered at the White House to consider what they had heard. They came to the stark conclusion that further escalation would be futile and that the President had no realistic alternative but to try seriously for a negotiated peace. After a pleasant social lunch, at which no business was discussed, they told him.

Their verdict came as a great blow to Johnson. He could scarcely challenge the experience or the patriotism of a group which he had personally selected for overkill in both respects; and he could not ignore their recommendations. Most of them, besides, had been his personal friends for many years. He did ask them where they had learned their facts and was told, "From Habib, DePuy, and Carver." It began to dawn on the President that the glowing estimates he had received from Rostow were not, perhaps, the whole story. He sent for the three officials separately and grilled them grimly in late-night sessions, but he couldn't shake them.

There were other factors. The Central Intelligence Agency had been accumulating more and more evidence of the unpopularity of the war among the South Vienamese themselves and also of the ineffectiveness of the bombing of North Vietnam. There is reason to believe that one new source of evidence on the first point came from the first polls carried out in South Vietnam with trained Vietnamese interviewers, which produced radically less cheerful results than previous surveys carried out in English by towering Americans. Far more important was the fact that the new Secretary of Defense brought a politically sensitive eye to the problem. Clifford was acutely aware of the meaning of the New Hampshire vote the week before, and of Robert Kennedy's entry into the campaign the previous weekend. Together, Clifford, the three experts, and the nine wise and unimpugnable advisers convinced the President, not that the war was wrong but that it had been unsuccessful.

On May 9, the peace talks opened at the Majestic Hotel in Paris, coinciding with four weeks of intensified fighting in South Vietnam. For some weeks, the talks at the Majestic were little more than desultory exchanges of stale charges, but on about June 15, there was a pronounced lull in the fighting in Vietnam. "The longer it goes on," a senior American official shrewdly pointed out to us a few days later, "the more pressure Humphrey is under to come out for a bombing halt. Yet his difficulty is that he can be crucified tomorrow if the North Vietnamese attack."

Like a sensible general, Humphrey probed various points on the perimeter before he set himself to decide whether he dare attempt a sortie. On June 23, for example, in a two-hour interview with the staff of the *New York Times,* he sought very skillfully to suggest that there was clear daylight between his position and the President's. It was a deft attempt:

> I have never been told what to say by the President. I have never cleared a speech with the White House. Some of my staff members on occasion have called up the State Department to see whether or not I was getting too far out on something. . . . There hasn't been much talk lately about a ceasefire. . . . We've almost become accustomed . . . to what the enemy calls talk-and-fight. I suggest that we talk.

But that horse, as Humphrey must have known, wouldn't run. Nor would another attempt he made, in a speech scheduled for delivery in San Francisco and, in the event, issued on July 12 as a statement because of illness, to divert attention from his Vietnam dilemma. In that statement, he suggested that East-West relations were more important than Southeast Asia and made some notably liberal remarks about China, including the suggestion that China should be welcomed into the United Nations.

But it was becoming all too plain that he could achieve his political objective only by a statement on Vietnam. And more than that: it was more and more obvious that there was only one statement he could make on Vietnam that would do the trick. He could talk about a coalition government. But that referred to the time after the war, eighteen months away at best, and who yet cared about 1970, with only a month to go before the 1968 conventions? He could talk about de-Americanizing the war, but everybody was for that—even Nixon. Only a call for a halt in the bombing of North Vietnam would establish his political independence and courage and liberal credentials beyond question.

Humphrey's foreign-policy advisers were, in any case, convinced that he ought to come out for a bombing halt. George Ball, though still Ambassador to the United Nations, was getting more and more interested in Humphrey's dilemma; perhaps it would be truer to say that he saw in it an opportunity to push ideas that he had long and courageously, but futilely, fought for inside the government. The other key influence was that of the foreign policy man on Humphrey's own staff—John Reilly, a quietly expert thirty-five-year-old graduate of Harvard and the London School of Economics.

Reilly had organized two task forces with overlapping membership from the academic world. Samuel P. Huntington of Harvard was the chairman of one, whose brief was labeled "Post-Vietnam." The other, under Professor A. Doak Barnett of Columbia, was supposed to be concerned with Asia as a whole. Huntington's task force worked on a White Paper on Vietnam. Reilly took it as the basis of a draft statement and showed it to a series of eminent professors—Barnett, ex-Ambassador Edwin O. Reischauer, Lucien Pye of M.I.T., Howard Wriggins of Columbia—and experts from the RAND Corporation, the Asia Foundation, and other outposts of the foreign-policy establishment. He also showed it to Humphrey's foreign policy "coordinator," Zbigniew Brzezinski—a significant touchstone, since he had had until recently a reputation for rather hard-line skepticism toward Communism but had now left the Administration and begun to criticize its policies. All of these experts accepted the Vice-President's proposed endorsement of a bombing halt.

On Thursday, July 25, there was a big meeting in the Vice-President's offices in the Executive Office Building. A dozen professors turned up at ten in the morning, with half a dozen of Humphrey's staff —Reilly, William Welsh, Ted Van Dyk, Orville Freeman to give political advice, the speech-writer John Stewart, and the Washington lawyer David Ginsburg. They started with Reilly's draft and reworked it. Then they adjourned for lunch while the draft was retyped, and in the afternoon Humphrey himself joined them. He listened without comment and then said he had two choices. He could either show the draft to the President or he could show it to Rusk and other State Department officials without showing it to the President. He was, in any case, apparently committed to some major statement on Vietnam. He had told several journalists that he was planning to make one, and he had even made a public pledge to issue an important Vietnam speech within ten days.

He never made it—not until it was too late. After some discussion, he went to the White House that night, only to find that the President was in conference with several other people. He cordially invited Humphrey to sit in. For two hours, Humphrey sat there with his declaration of independence in his pocket. At last, the meeting broke up, and Johnson—who knew perfectly well what was in the wind—suggested they meet again the next morning. But the next morning, both men were due out of town. The doves on Humphrey's staff wanted him to issue the statement anyway that Sunday. But Humphrey was too loyal —or too something.

He gave the draft back to Reilly and Ginsburg to rewrite. During the first week in August, he redrafted it himself at Waverly. By this time, the circle of those who knew about it had widened to include several of those who disapproved—Humphrey's aide William Connell, James Rowe, Larry O'Brien, who by this time was beginning to reckon that the nomination was safe and saw no reason to risk unlocking his sixteen hundred captive delegates. (O'Brien was not a man to let refined ideological arguments tamper with a winning formula. Still, his flexibility over the war issue was remarkable even by his standards. In the spring he had resigned from Johnson's Cabinet to assist Kennedy's antiwar campaign. After the New York Senator's death, he had been one of the first professionals to transfer his allegiance to Humphrey, where he lined up with those aides arguing against concessions to Kennedy's position on the war.)

By this time, too, another disturbing factor was entering the picture. In early August, American intelligence reports showed that the Vietcong and the North Vietnamese had their units up to strength and, in some cases, actually ready in attack positions for the long-dreaded "third offensive." High officials were in possession of specific evidence in captured documents that the assault was due between August 18 and August 20, though there was also reason to believe that Hanoi was being urged by other Communist capitals to delay the attack until after the Democratic Convention. Humphrey did not need to be told this by the President. He had access to the intelligence himself. He could visualize the nightmare only too well: Hubert Humphrey makes a speech calling for a bombing halt, and within days American boys are being killed with ammunition brought up to the front over the very routes which the bombers had—in theory—been blocking.

On August 9, he flew to the LBJ ranch with draft number ten in his pocket. To his astonishment, Johnson was quite unruffled and as good as said he couldn't have done better himself. For one thing, draft number ten was a somewhat emasculated document: it would have taken a Columbia professor to slip a razor blade between it and the Administration's position, someone who saw it said. And, in any case, Johnson had another ace in the hole. The next day, fresh from their triumph in Miami, Richard Nixon and Spiro Agnew visited the ranch, and Nixon came away saying that the bombing must go on. (Thanks to an over-garrulous Humphrey adviser, Nixon's foreign-policy advisers had penetrated the Victorian speech debate and were aware of what was under discussion. "There was very little they could say or decide without us knowing," a Nixon man told us proudly later. "We had them completely boxed in.")

What *was* Humphrey to decide? His dilemma was worse than ever. Could he loyally take issue with the President when the Republican nominee had accepted the President's position? Dare he break with the President at all? If he did, might he not be crucified by a third offensive? Hubert Humphrey could imagine only too well the grim satisfaction with which the President would drive in the nails. And—his advisers offered the balm of temptation—did he *need* to take such hideous risks? Surely the nomination was safe now.

His men had just picked up 110 delegates in three state conventions—Kentucky, Utah, and West Virginia. The secret delegate count had reached 1642, not including California or Texas. "We can win now, whatever happens," one of his co-chairmen told us that week, "without California or the South." If true, it should have been reason for taking a risk to improve his chances of the election. But Hubert Humphrey was not in the mood for heroic gambles.

He made up his mind—not to make up his mind. The issue was not dead, and it wouldn't go away, as we shall see. But the great opportunity had been lost. "Maybe Hubert Humphrey's situation is simply impossible," said a high official who knew what he was going through in early August. "Maybe his dilemma on the war is just insoluble. Maybe he is bound to be nominated, but he can't be elected."

ACT IX

Miami:
An Illusion of Unity

1

If Only They'd
Grown More Nuts

"He fixed thee mid this dance
Of plastic circumstance."

—Robert Browning, "Rabbi ben Ezra"

The deal was made on September 20, 1967. On that day, the Republican National Committee signed a contract with Miami Beach to hold its next national convention in that city. Cynics were later to say they deserved each other, that the coronation of Richard Nixon as the Republican Party nominee for the Presidency could not have taken place in a more appropriate setting—an offshore, subtropical island devoted to forgetfulness of the pressing realities of American life.

Back in the fall of 1967, however, it was simply a hardheaded business arrangement. The symbolism of Miami Beach was no concern of the Republican National Committee. They were going to Florida—for the first Republican National Convention to be held south of the Mason-Dixon line—because Miami Beach was making it worth their while. The unsentimental business leaders of the island had decided that the spin-off in prestige and incremental income (they had figured that each conventioneer must spend $35.42 each day) justified a generous financial subvention. Their bid was eight hundred fifty thousand dollars, a new record for such transactions, albeit a short-lived one. A few weeks later, Chicago secured the doubtful honor of mounting the Democratic Convention for just under a million dollars. Convention costs have rocketed since those days before the war when a little over a hundred thousand dollars was easily enough to secure the nation's most dramatic political forum. So too, however, have the fringe benefits. Though few people would go all the way with H. L. Mencken's judgment on political conventions—"the whole thing is simply an elaborate scheme for wasting time and money" —they do unquestionably produce a large economic fallout.

From a commercial point of view, the 1333 delegates who decide who is to carry the Republican standard into the Presidential lists represent only the tip of the iceberg. Behind them stand the alternate delegates (ready to spring into the decision-making process should any in the front rank fall ill, die, or just get lost), their families, the American press, the overseas press, the campaign staffs of the candidates—both real and potential—and varieties of other hangers-on. Thus, Miami Beach was braced for the impact of no less than an additional twenty thousand people from August 4 to August 9, when the 1968 Republican Convention came to town. It was a curious locale but not inappropriate. Miami Beach is a quintessentially American development. Its brief history runs through the classic cycle: pioneering days, boom, bust, birth, growth, and finally the full expression of the Dream.

At the turn of the century, it was spectacularly unprepossessing, a snake-infested mangrove swamp with only sparse evidences of human habitation. Alligators outnumbered people. Yet it had already broken several pioneering hearts and was about to rupture many another. The man who is credited with the first attempt to open up Miami Beach was a freebooting adventurer from New Jersey by the name of Henry Lum. It was in the year 1868 when Lum, a veteran of the forty-nine gold rush, first clapped eyes on this undistinguished piece of real estate three miles off the coast of Florida. From the rail of his schooner, he observed a few palms growing on the sands and, in the manner of those ebullient times, promptly conjured up visions of himself as King Copra.

Lum, a persuasive man by all accounts, inveigled a couple of other New Jerseyites to share his vision, and together the three men bought up most of what is now the Florida Gold Coast. In the space of ten years, they planted 334,000 coconut trees and then sat back waiting for the profits to roll in. They never came. For one thing, the copra market had suffered a sharp recession; for another, the trees themselves were lacking in an important respect. They did not have enough nuts.

A few desultory ventures with fresh vegetables and avocados for the Northern market kept the island inhabited, but its next point of take-off did not come until well into the twentieth century. It was another Northerner, Carl G. Fisher, from Indiana, a man who had already made a few million in the automobile industry, who detected a new frontier for Miami Beach. Instead of shifting the island's produce to the people in the North, he thought, why not bring the people to the island? The dream of Miami Beach as a resort for wealthy Northerners was born.

During the war years and the early twenties, Fisher spared no effort or expense in converting his holdings on the island into an earthly paradise. Men, money, and machinery—even a brace of elephants—were inserted into the gigantic enterprise of clearing jungle, dredging swamps, paving streets, cutting acreage into lots and selling them. These were the years of the great Florida real-estate boom, and Fisher's dream, unfortunately for him, came to be shared by many others who did not share his dedication to the laying of foundations. Up and down the Florida littoral, land was divided into building lots and sold for ten per cent down payment. Much of it was unlovely and undredged swampland, and most of the buyers never expected to live on it. But what did this matter when values were soaring and the eloquence of the speculators kept attracting shoals of new buyers? "The Riviera of America" seemed a sure-fire investment. But in the autumn of 1926, two hurricanes decimated the area. The more inclement of these winds killed four hundred people, made a shambles of Miami, and blew land values down to pre-speculative levels. Fisher, like everybody else, was badly scarred.

The collapse of the Florida land boom was a dress rehearsal for the trauma of 1929. In Miami Beach, Fisher paid a dreadful penalty for being before his time, and it was later and more cautious investors who were to make a killing out of the realization of his dream.

But even the hurricanes could not blow away its basic ingredients: year-round sunshine—February, the coldest month, has an average minimum temperature of sixty degrees—and the illusion, at least, of getting away from it all. Mainland Miami might grow—as it did to become a city of a million people—but it was scarcely capable of vaulting Bay Biscayne and polluting the island with metropolitan realities. By 1935, Miami Beach had recovered from the Depression. Water and electric power had been brought from the mainland, and two causeways provided easy transit across the bay. Time, taste, and unsentimental deployment of the fast buck did the rest.

There were those who claim that Miami Beach would have been better left as a swampland and that its history can be encapsuled as the substitution of sharks for alligators. But they are clearly not among the two and a half million visitors who come to savor its delights each year, paying hotel rates that range from eighteen dollars a day in summer (the off season) to ninety dollars a day in winter. Nor can it be denied that Miami Beach has been true to itself. Escapism had remained the cardinal imperative. Miami Beach has no factory, no railroad, no airport, and no cemetery (a considerable achievement, bearing in mind that Miami Beach's eighty-five thousand permanent residents have a median age of fifty-nine). The land area may be only seven miles square, but into this Miamian ingenuity has crammed 2518 apartment buildings and 369 hotels catering to every class of Hollywoodian fantasy. Even the names seem to be borrowed from old movies—Marco Polo, Casablanca, Ivanhoe, Eden Roc, Twelve Caesars, Monte Carlo, Moulin Rouge. In all of North America, only Las Vegas can compare with it for concentrated vulgarity. But there the similarity ends. Vegas's patrons seem to be in the grip of a ferocious, collective death wish. The quest in Miami Beach is for something different—insulation from life.

There are few snags in the idyll. It would, for instance, be rather better for public relations if it were not so widely known that the Mafia had invested heavily, and legitimately, in Miami Beach's oceanfront. And then there is the matter of the beach itself. At certain times, when the winds and tides are contrary, unscreened sewage from the island is washed back again, coating the shore with obnoxious solids. A critical sociologist might make points about private affluence abutting public squalor. But, then, every hotel has its own aquamarine swimming pool, and those who cannot afford them have no place on the island anyway. Miami Beach has long since perfected its defenses against the wrong kind of public. An offer by the Federal government a few years back to rebuild a brand-new strand was indignantly turned down by the hotel barons on the grounds that it would be free. It might, it was thought, attract a Coney Island type of person.

Apart from tourists, Miami Beach's biggest money-spinner is conventions. This, initially at least, seems surprising. For outside its air-conditioned palaces Miami can be enervating indeed. While admirable for making a torpid kind of whoopee by the poolside, the heat and humidity are sometimes such that it is difficult even to have, let alone then to exchange, an idea. The author Norman Mailer, who may know about such things, described the sensation of living and breathing in the Miami Beach atmosphere as "not unlike being made love to by a three-hundred-pound woman who has decided to get on top."

In the weeks prior to the Republican Convention opening, a few attempts were made to take the edge off Miami Beach's more rapacious aspects. The Chamber of Commerce implored all concerned not to gouge their august visitors—they might want them back another time. There were even a few halfhearted passes at cleaning up North Bay Village, whose prostitute population was reported to be, after Las Vegas, the highest concentration in the nation (Miami Beach is part of its catchment area). Buttons were dispensed bearing the legend I'M A FRIENDLY FLORIDIAN. And the state beverage department imported forty-five extra ·beverage agents to ensure that the barroom hosts did not get up to any pranks like overcharging the clientele or watering the liquor. But, for the most part, delegates and reporters had to take Miami Beach straight up.

The Rockefeller campaign took up its station in the Americana Hotel, with the "spiciest, splashiest, stark-nudest review this side of Paris" for company. Iowa's delegation in the Casablanca shared hotel space with a "Swinging Singles Club," offering "relaxing, down-to-earth, pillow-talk comfort." Everyone shared the Fountainebleau, the convention's executive and communications headquarters, and found out what really touches Miami Beach's heart. THANK YOU, FRANK SINATRA, read a plaque, FOR FILMING "TONY ROME" AT THE FOUNTAINEBLEAU.

The cultural shock for some of the more fastidious commentators was profound. Epithets like "a plastic paradise" and "our grossest national product" infested the columns of the national press. Miami Beach's architecture, a combination of modern monolithic on the outside and, most commonly, gilt baroque and rococo interiors, was called "modified bordello." Some were aghast that a national convention should be held in a location where the synthetic had so resoundingly triumphed over the real. But these were the early days.

Miami Beach did not entirely rely on its natural insulating equipment. Though nobody seriously suspected that the rowdy divisions in the country would beat against the sturdy walls of Miami Beach Convention Hall, nobody was taking any chances. The memory of what a "lone assassin" could do was still fresh. The aim, in the words of Miami Beach's burly police chief, Rocky Pomerance, was "to provide maximum security with minimum visibility." He achieved only half his objective. The convention hall itself took on the aspects of an armed camp, with gun-toting policemen manning its outer defenses—a six-foot-high chain-link fence erected specially for the occasion. A separate compound was erected for demonstrators who might step out of line. None did.

Security men in town actually exceeded the number of delegates. Miami Beach's own two-hundred-man force was supplemented by mainland forces from the City of Miami highway patrol, conservation control, and public-safety departments. Grafted onto these were no less than ten Federal investigative agencies, including the FBI, military intelligence, the Bureau of Narcotics, the Army (providing bomb-control experts), the Internal Revenue Service, and a hundred-strong group of Secret Service men to provide a round-the-clock shadow for the major candidates.

Within the convention hall itself, the GOP security staff devised an elaborate portfolio of tickets, passes, and badges to deter gate-crashers. No reporter whose livelihood depended on mobility around the convention hall could remember a more exasperating setup. But, then, none knew what Chicago's Mayor Daley had up his sleeve.

Chicago was to crystallize the deep ideological divisions in American society. Yet the convention at Miami Beach produced a more explicit statement of the American dilemma: the willful divorce of politics from social realities.

On the night of Wednesday, August 7, a few hours before Nixon's first-ballot triumph, Miami's inappositely named black ghetto, Liberty City, exploded in its first major riot; and Florida's Governor Claude Kirk was soon wading in with a promise of containment of the situation by "whatever force is needed."

By Friday night, three Negroes were shot dead and six hundred soldiers had been moved in to quell an orgy of looting and random sniper fire. A curfew was declared, the military sealed off the strategic blocks between Fifty-fourth and Seventy-ninth Streets; and another caldron of black despair and rage went slowly off the boil. Even the Negro leaders in Miami did not deem it fit to make any close connection between Nixon's smooth political operation ten miles away in the gilded cloud-cuckoo-land of Miami Beach, and the downtown rioting. "This is a Miami problem," said one, "home-grown, right here in our own little ghetto."

The two events might as well have taken place on separate planets. Yet Richard Nixon had just been moved one step nearer the White House by the power of men who were adamant against serious help for the black urban poor; men who saw the solution to social ills in the application of force, rather than money. For, despite the ballyhoo about Nixon's middle-ground candidacy, the vital point about Nixon's nomination was that he had only just squeaked in. And he did so with options dictated by a militant white South.

2

Suspicion of Arson

"Ronald Reagan, by his track record as a candidate, has demonstrated he is a politician of the first rank and has great potential for leadership."

> —Richard M. Nixon, Los Angeles, June 25, 1966

"So go to bat for the Cat in the Hat!
He's the Cat who knows where it's at!
With Tricks and Voom and Things like that!
Go! Go! The Cat in the Hat!"

> —Robert Coover, *The Cat in the Hat for President*

Throughout the year, Richard Nixon's political advance always contained an important element of *trompe l'oeil*. And this was never more pronounced than at the Miami Beach convention. Within minutes of his coronation, the nominee was telling the nation how effortless it had all been: "I won the nomination without paying any price or making any deals." It was good victory rhetoric, good television, and good propaganda for a party that now had no alternative but to recognize that Nixon was indeed the One.

Nixon's ability to get away with it, like most successful illusionism, was firmly grounded in people's preconceptions of what would take place. The pundits had been phrase-making about an inevitable Nixon victory all year, and it had come to pass. All the predictions—right down to Nixon's vote tally, at 692 only eight less than his camp's eve-of-convention prophecies—came as near true as makes no difference. People might be chagrined by this phenomenon (the Republican con-

433

vention, wrote Russell Baker in the *New York Times,* had been "planned in advance by six bores and a sadist"), but there seemed no denying it.

In fact, it had been anything but effortless. Nor was it inevitable. The king had. required a kingmaker. And the role was played—subsequent denials to the contrary notwithstanding—by that most Gothic of Southern politicians, Senator Strom Thurmond of South Carolina. It was his rough-hewn personality that turned many of the crucial skirmishes in the caucus battles that took place away from the convention floor and the prying eyes of the TV cameras. Without Thurmond, Nixon would have been in dire trouble; Nixon knew it, Thurmond knew it, and in classic Southern style, Thurmond exacted his price for it.

There is a theory that modern communications have eliminated the element of uncertainty in conventions. There is some evidence for this, in that multiple ballots, once a common phenomenon, are now extremely rare. The last time a Republican Presidential nomination went beyond the first ballot was in 1948, when New York Governor Thomas Dewey came through on the third ballot. Nixon himself, a connoisseur of convention maneuver, remarked early in 1968 that the days of multiple ballots were long past, because "people know the game too well." However, a political convention can still turn into a highly unpredictable organism. The presence of the media—there were six thousand journalists in Miami Beach —places a premium on public displays of unity, but it does not guarantee tranquillity. The tendency in most post-electronic conventions has been to push controversy farther out of sight—i.e., deeper into the caucuses. Intraparty strife abhors the light. Thus, the convention that the nation views on its TV screens has, at least until the final balloting, precious little to do with the real action. It is a curious piece of theater: a drama in which all the important struggles take place off-stage. Miami Beach fitted neatly into this pattern. The Democrats in Chicago, of course, were to provide a flagrant exception to the rule. But, then, Chicago was unique.

The fragility of Nixon's victory can be demonstrated by simple arithmetic. For a man who had run in, and won, all the primaries and who was pitted against two opponents who had spent much of the year protesting their uninterest in the nomination, Richard Nixon's final majority was agonizingly—almost insultingly—small.

To be nominated, it was necessary to collect 667 votes, an absolute majority of the delegates present. Nixon made 692, but he did not "go over the top" until the next-to-last state, Wisconsin, was called. It is true that he might have won a handful more votes if he had pressured Hiram Fong to release his 14 Hawaii delegates by dropping his favorite-son candidacy (an excuse for a lei-strewn extravaganza on the convention floor). But in the final moments before the balloting, Clifton White, Reagan's delegate-hunter, offset Fong's spare votes by tipping off a few old friends that it was all over—and they might as well stay in line and go with a winner. Thus, the 26 votes by which Nixon exceeded the magic 667 figure was a true reflection of the margin he had in hand. And at various stages in the preceding three days, many more than this number of Nixon votes had been in jeopardy.

Had these wavering votes, some of which were dragooned only a few hours before the balloting, stayed loose, the Nixon candidacy could have crumbled with unnerving rapidity. In the end, he garnered no less than 298 votes from 14 Southern and border states; yet for most of these delegates, Nixon was very much a second-choice candidate. Hence Nixon's willingness to placate Strom Thurmond.

Nixon's unique quality—the ability to be "acceptable" to all the wings of the party, Northern and Southern, Eastern and Midwestern—was a strength so long as passions were contained. But the plain fact was that Nixon was no one's beau ideal of Republicanism; while affection for him might run wide, it did not run very deep. Even those who were all-the-way Nixon men tended to couch their support in terms less than lyrical. Thus, Robert Robson, an Idaho delegate: "I'm not looking for much, just a man who makes a decision. I like Nixon. He wipes his butt the way I do." For those of more ideological bent, Nixon could never be other than a compromise choice—a candidate who lacked the capacity to excite but was a buttress against something worse.

To understand the weaknesses inherent in such a position, it is necessary to know something about the type of people assembled in Miami Beach, more particularly, the Southerners.

For the most part, the delegates to the 1968 convention were a somber, respectable-looking fraternity, deeply conscious that the eyes of an estimated thirty million American viewers were upon them. Walter Cronkite, sitting in his glass eyrie above the convention hall, gazed down upon them and pronounced himself much impressed by the improvement in their physical appearance over the years. He had attended conventions before television was invited and recalled, with a perceptible quiver, how delegates had lounged about gracelessly, their shirt collars unbuttoned, their feet ankle-deep in debris and discarded peanut shells.

Delegates tend to be older and wealthier than the average voter, and Republicans tend to be wealthier than Democrats. A study of the

1964 convention delegates established that their incomes were considerably above the national average—with the Democrats averaging around eighteen thousand dollars a year and the Republicans up in the twenty-one-thousand class. The Republican delegates assembled in Miami Beach—though only one in five was a survivor of the 1964 convention—did not look like men who had taken a cut. Most delegates are selected for length and tenacity of service to the party, particularly financial service. They are people who have already made their way in the world. Comfortable people. A survey of the 1968 delegates by the Ripon Society, a group of young liberal Republicans, confirms this impression of affluence. Almost half the delegates were businessmen, nearly a third lawyers, eight per cent housewives, four per cent teachers, and four per cent doctors. Four out of five delegates were Protestant, with Episcopalians, Presbyterians, and Methodists heading the list. Fifteen per cent were Catholic and two per cent Jewish. Civic organizations they belonged to included the Chamber of Commerce, the American Legion, the Masons, Elks, and Rotary in that order of frequency. The fact that eighty per cent had been to college was an indication of the inevitability of higher education for middle-class America: it was no guarantee of intellectual weight. The differences between this portrait and the national profile are fairly marked. Labor, the academic community, and the Negro (less than two per cent of the delegates and alternates were black) have very low representation at this level of the GOP.

If the delegates ever became excited enough to show their prejudices, then, they would be those of well-heeled suburbia. There were, however, good and sufficient reasons for not letting violent emotions off the leash in Miami Beach. The GOP had surrendered to an excess of zeal four years before and had ended up in an electoral cul-de-sac. This time around, the Democrats might tear themselves apart in front of the nation's TV screens, but most Republicans were intent on a different image. Yet there was bound to be tension between what heads dictated and hearts desired. And it showed on Monday, the opening day of the convention, when Barry Goldwater took the rostrum to make a speech. It was punctuated by thirty-three bursts of riotous applause—partly out of sentiment, like the gush of emotion for Adlai Stevenson at the 1960 Democratic Convention before the party rejected him for Jack Kennedy.

But, again like the ovation for Stevenson, it was also something else. The delegates were telling Goldwater that, despite the drubbing they had received under his leadership, fundamentally they still felt about America as he did. (Many did it more explicitly with "I'm still mad about Barry" buttons.) When the final frenetic burst of cheering died away, one Washington correspondent asked another, "Who says the Republican Party has lost its death wish?"

Clearly, any man who could channel this emotion into delegate votes would be in a strong position. Rockefeller could not do it: his advocacy of big government-spending policies cut across the grain of GOP prejudice. His only hope of success lay in tapping the delegates' long-deprived instinct for a winner and convincing them that only he could satisfy it in November. Nixon could not do it; he had been around too long to excite that kind of fervor; in any case, carefully crafted "consensus" appeal was not calculated to make the faithful fall about with excitement. Goldwater certainly could not do it; he was a reminder of past failure; besides, he had bowed out of the Presidential scene and was diligently seeking his old Senate seat.

There was, however, one man who could become the catalyst for a surge of fundamentalist fervor, a man who a few hours earlier had announced himself an open candidate for the Presidency: Ronald Reagan, Governor of California, whose secret and not-so-secret agents had, as we have seen, been busily promoting him for some time. No one had been surprised by the announcement—"It's like a woman who's eight and a half months pregnant announcing she's going to have a baby," said Governor David Cargo of New Mexico when he heard the news—but it was a symbolic act, and its effect on the delegates, particularly those from the South, had been electric.

Months later, Harry Dent, South Carolina's state chairman, who bore, with Thurmond, the brunt of the task of keeping the South solid for Nixon, still shuddered at the memory of that Monday evening: "The lightning struck. I have been in politics for I don't know how many years, and I have never seen anything like it."

Dent, however, could hardly have been surprised. Few people had done more than he to encourage Reagan to run. That he should have spent most of the year fanning Reagan's "prairie fire" into a blaze, and then three frenetic days at the convention doing his utmost to put it out, may at first seem strange. It had, nonetheless, a compelling Southern logic. All through the year, the more astute Southern politicians had been obsessed by two seemingly contradictory fears: first, that Reagan's secret bandwagon might run out of steam so that he would not run; and second, that it might go so fast that Reagan not only would run, but would also get the nomination.

The clue to this equivocal situation lies partly in the nature of

Reagan's appeal, and partly in the bitter lessons the South learned as a result of 1964.

Reagan had a reservoir of affection in the North (Rockefeller-Reagan was the "dream ticket" for many Northerners, as well as for *Time* magazine), but the South was his natural constituency. He was, quite literally, adored by the party's rank and file and by many of its chieftains everywhere below the Mason-Dixon line. Thurmond himself had been a Reagan fan ever since the Goldwater campaign. "I love that man," he would say. "He's the best hope we've got." He had been instrumental in giving Reagan his best exposure in the South, with a fundraising dinner in September 1967 at the Township Auditorium in Columbia, South Carolina. More than thirty-five hundred people paid a hundred dollars a plate to hear Reagan, while TV cameras beamed him live through the South. Whenever Reagan returned to the South, he was greeted by scenes of wild enthusiasm; his diligent advance men never had any problem assembling crowds and dispensing "Reagan for President" insignia.

If emotion ruled the Southern delegates, at least 300 of the South's 334 convention votes would have been in Reagan's pocket the moment he declared his open candidacy. But in 1968, all the GOP leaders in the South were suspicious of emotionalism. Although in 1964 nobody was sorry to have gone with Goldwater, it became clear in the course of the election campaign that the South had climbed on the bandwagon so early it was totally bereft of bargaining power. (Amazingly, despite Goldwater's opposition to the 1964 civil-rights legislation, the South still had a sneaking suspicion that the Arizonian might not be absolutely "sound" on race if he achieved office.)

The South has always been conscious that the convention setting is one in which it can be most effective—mainly because the ability to wield large blocs of votes is so often decisive there. Delegations from other parts of the country, where attitudes are conditioned by a variety of social factors (urban or rural, small town or metropolis) are prone to fragmentation. In the South, there is, when it comes to voting, only one social factor of any consequence: race. And in practical terms, this means that wherever the South has political leverage, it must be placed in the service of nullifying the civil-rights advance. Traditionally, this blocking action was pursued almost exclusively inside the Democratic Party, where the South's fondness for the unit rule made it even more effective. But Goldwater Republicanism, bringing into the party figures such as Thurmond and giving it for the first time a strong Southern base, changed all that. Squaring Southern interests is now just as much a problem for the Republicans as for the Democrats.

Very early in 1968, some key figures in the South decided that they could, given the right conditions, apply such leverage at the Republican Convention. The principal figures in this enterprise were three state GOP chairmen, Harry Dent, Bill Murfin of Florida, and Clarke Reed of Mississippi.

Together they formed what became known as the Greenville Group —so called because Greenville, Mississippi, was where the three, old friends and drinking partners, tended to get together. They were all agreed that 1964, heady while it lasted, had been a disaster. This time around, they were determined to hold fast to two principles: first, not to go with a loser, which might leave them exposed to a proselytizing civil-rights advocate in the Presidency; and second, to make sure that whoever got the Republican nomination would have to sweat for it and be well aware of the mind of the South before his coronation. Even before the election year opened, the three friends were impressing this broad view on other influential Southerners through the natural medium of the Southern State Republican Chairmen's Association.

This loose but pervasive outfit—its membership comprises Alabama, Arkansas, Florida, Georgia, Kentucky, Louisiana, Mississippi, the Carolinas, Tennessee, Texas, and Virginia—was susceptible to such reasoning. And a broad strategy of "hanging loose but hanging together" was agreed to be the South's best preconvention policy. Naturally, as the pressure for commitments from Nixon's camp mounted, this policy began to fray at the edges. But much of the original concept survived right down to Miami Beach: the South, as an entity, was never "locked up" by Nixon.

To have been so would have undermined the second element in the South's strategy—its determination to retain bargaining power. And for this the Reagan candidacy was an essential lever. In the months before the convention, the Greenville Group was among those most ardently urging Reagan to come out in the open and run. Yet all three members ultimately made private commitments to Nixon.

However, Reed was the only one of the three who took real pleasure in the prospect of double-crossing Reagan. He had an old score to settle. Back in 1966, Reed had found himself in a tough fight for the Mississippi governorship against John Bell Williams, a man who had already been a popular Congressman. Reed, struggling at around ten per cent in the polls, needed help badly. He appealed first to Reagan, but got no reply.

"It suddenly hit me that he wasn't interested. He didn't want to know a loser." But Nixon came and spoke—to some effect. Reed ended up with thirty per cent of the vote.

This episode was to haunt Reagan later in the convention. Before the convention, however, Reed was industriously putting the word to anyone who might have Reagan's ear—run, run. The thought of Nixon's coming through too handily alarmed even the grateful Mississippian. "I could see," said Reed, "that the harder Nixon had to fight, the more the South stood to gain. So we wanted a nice open convention."

For the South, a choice between Nixon and Rockefeller, a man who had been glad-handing his way through ghettos Kennedy-style, was no choice at all. And without Southern pressure, Nixon could lean over to appease the other militant wing of his party—the Northern liberals, men who wanted to raise the status of the Negroes, spend money on the cities, and generally conduct themselves in a manner inimical to the Greenville Group's conception of the South. It was a dire prospect.

On the other hand, there were risks involved in prodding the Reagan enterprise. There was no guarantee, once a Reagan candidacy came out of the hat, that the Southern GOP leaders could control their delegations. And if they could not, the whole strategy might fly apart. With Nixon's Southern base destroyed, they might end up with the anathema of Rockefeller or, not much more comforting, Reagan, a sure-fire loser in November. Still, on balance, the risk seemed worth taking.

In practice, there was no avoiding such a course; the grass roots were already crawling with Reagan activists. All over the South, Nixon men were taking out insurance with Reagan groups, just in case. In some instances, they actually enlisted Reagan supporters to put out isolated brush fires of Rockefeller sentiment, which occurred, naturally, only in Negro districts.

Louisiana provided the example of this *modus operandi,* as well as of the idiosyncrasies of grass-roots Republicanism in the South. In May, the Louisiana Republicans were confronted with a disconcertingly sharp increase in Rockefeller activity in New Orleans. The man himself had passed through and had been hugely feted at the airport. (The Nixon camp found out later that the Rockefeller people had advertised in the university paper that Rocky busses to the airport would be equipped with kegs of free beer.) It all seemed very perturbing—the district conventions were upcoming, and Bruce Bradley, one of Rockefeller's chief delegate-hunters, was stalking around town and seemed to be getting through to the Negroes. (Something the Nixon people never found out was that a private deal existed between Bradley and Reagan's delegate-hunter, Clif White, to share useful delegate intelligence on a national scale.)

The New Orleans Negro leadership had earlier tried to make a deal with the state GOP. The sequence, as related by Martin Feldman, Nixon's contact man in New Orleans and general counsel for the Louisiana Republicans, went something like this: Feldman was approached by Jesse Cook, a New Orleans Negro businessman, and told that if the Louisiana delegation was to reflect racial balance, there would have to be four or five black delegates on the successful slate. Obviously, New Orleans was the only place where Negroes could get elected, so would Feldman help in the area? Feldman was unsuccessful in trying to bargain the number down to one Negro. "I told him it wasn't a matter of race," recalled Feldman, in aggrieved tones. "In fact, I said to him, 'If you will take off that Rockefeller button and put on a Nixon one, I will personally guarantee you four delegates.' But he wouldn't budge. So we had to defeat him."

Thus, for two days before the district convention, local Nixon and Reagan forces joined hands to beat off this Rockefeller threat. New Orleans has two Congressional Districts, so four delegates were at stake. Feldman's tactics had a brutal simplicity: with Nixon money, he hired sixteen salesgirls and put them to work on a battery of telephones, generously donated to the cause by a local businessman. The girls then called every registered Republican in New Orleans except those in Negro neighborhoods. (Some exceptions were made for rich Negroes, on the assumption that even they might deem Rocky a dangerous socialist.) The beauty of the operation was that they pretended they were doing a poll of Republican opinion. Whenever they found a Rockefeller supporter, they just terminated the interview gracefully. Whenever they found a Nixon or Reagan supporter, they speedily urged him to attend his district convention.

The Rockefeller insurgents were beaten off, but in the process the Reagan people got a firm foothold in the delegation. (Seven of Louisiana's twenty-six delegates went for Reagan at the convention.) While all this was going on, Bruce Bradley, the man who started the flap, was, of course, diligently pursuing his double-agent role: feeding helpful delegate information back to Reagan's head-hunter Clif White. Thus, if this complex little struggle had a hero, it was Bradley rather than Feldman. The hopes of getting any Rockefeller delegates were always slim at best, but by throwing a scare into the Nixon camp, Bradley had succeeded in breaking up the homogeneity of the Nixon slate. From Bradley's view point, the next best thing to a vote for Rockefeller was a vote for Reagan.

The central fact about all the Reagan movements in the South was their disconcerting tendency—even when thoroughly infiltrated by Nixon men—to start throwing their weight around and assuming altogether too much independence. Inevitably, perhaps, the most bizarre expression of this came in Texas and is best exemplified by a telephone conversation which took place just a month before the convention between two friends, Senator John Tower, a Nixon man, and Butch Butler, the man who headed Texans for Reagan. As recounted (admittedly, in the glow of reminiscence) by one of Butler's staff, it ran:

> [J.T.:] Look, Butch. You've just got to cut it down. Quit being so damned successful.
> [B.B.:] You don't understand, John. I'm getting a whole lot of new voters. And whatever happens to Reagan, most of them will vote Republican in November.
> [J.T.:] But you're dividing the party.
> [B.B.:] Well, we'll all end up on the same side in the end. Besides, think of the publicity.
> [J.T. (*frenzied*):] You've got a whole lot of nuts in your outfit.
> [B.B.:] About the same percentage as in your group, I would guess.
> [J.T.:] I'm telling you, Butch, you'll hurt the party unless you clear out those nuts.
> [B.B.:] I would, John, I would. If I could be sure I wouldn't lose a few bolts at the same time. . . .

Tower's chagrin was understandable. He had recently been stricken with a severe case of that common disease among highly (and not so highly) regarded politicians in election year—Veep fever. For a while, it had seemed to him that if he could only deliver his delegation intact to the Nixon camp, their gratitude would be such that he could walk into the Number-Two spot. The trouble was that he no longer controlled his delegation; it was infested with Reaganites.

Ironically, the Texans-for-Reagan movement had been created almost exclusively by the Texas Republican establishment, whose antennae had given early warning of the danger of being outflanked on the right. In any case, they wanted to preserve options. The seminal meeting had taken place as long ago as December 18, 1967, when Peter O'Donnell, the Republican State Chairman, assembled fifteen party bigwigs and multimillionaires various at the Houston Club (they included an uncle of Tom Reed, the undercover Reagan operator).

O'Donnell laid it on the line: there was a grass-roots Reagan movement starting in east Texas, fueled by people who might politely be called hotheads—Birchers, *et al.* O'Donnell felt that if there was to be any kind of Reagan activity in the state, it ought to be steered away from extremes and, most important, be under their control. By the end of the Houston Club session, one of those present, J. R. (Butch) Butler, had been drafted.

Butler is not a man cut out to be anybody's creature; and, from the Texas Republican Party's viewpoint, it was not the wisest choice. He is not an untypical Texan figure—a one-time football star and a self-made Croesus who runs one of the biggest geological consulting firms in Texas oil—but his bluff, straightforward manner conceals a mind of Machiavellian complexity. He loves intrigue. An aide, displaying tremendous admiration, if a slightly uncertain historical grasp, once said of him: "In the Middle Ages, Butler would have been poisoned by the Medicis."

As Butler threw himself into the Texans for Reagan enterprise, some Borgia-like thoughts can hardly have failed to cross the leadership's minds. For the movement prospered hugely, too hugely. Not that Butler had any illusions about Reagan; he seemed to regard his candidate as a wonderfully effective, but blunt, instrument capable of being wielded by those with rather more savvy. "I know him thoroughly," Butler told a friend. "I've only met him three times, but I know him. He's a small-town boy from the Middle West. He's had a bit of success in a big and competitive world. He doesn't know how he got there, but he sure knows he likes it."

Reagan's unwillingness to declare was a hindrance; but Butler kept up an appearance of bounding action. At one point, he leaped on a plane for Massachusetts and offered the Number-Two spot on Reagan's non-existent ticket to Governor Volpe. A startled Volpe displayed interest but "reserved his position." Reagan must have been even more startled; Butler had not bothered to consult him on the subject. On one of Butler's trips to California, Reagan felt bound to warn him that his strategy required some circumspection. "I might have to repudiate you," said Reagan. Butler was unmoved: "It's a free country, even for governors." It was difficult to censure a man with such insouciant, freewheeling style.

When the Texas state convention came around in June, O'Donnell and Tower were less than delirious about the "control Reagan" strategy. They realized, said one of Butler's aides, "they had created a Frankenstein monster." At the convention itself, in Corpus Christi, the party's high command was hopelessly outmaneuvered by the Reagan forces. A simple investment of ten dollars for the organist brought on a wild demonstration for the actor-governor to the wheezy strains of "California, Here I Come." O'Donnell was furious, but the Reagan men got their money's worth.

When a resolution came up praising Reagan and urging him to become more active at the "national level," the GOP establishment decided its wisest course was to ride with the punch and let it go through. In the end, so as not to reveal how badly his delegation was split, Tower opted for, and got, the role of favorite-son candidate. This suited the Reagan people, as it denied votes to Nixon; at Miami Beach, however, Nixon needed first-ballot votes too badly to allow Tower this face-saver and forced him to release his divided delegation.

By the spring of 1968, it was impossible to determine the precise nature of Reagan's Southern support—how much was spurious, how much genuine, how much merely opportunist. Was the old Goldwater establishment really in favor of Nixon, or was the emotional appeal of Reagan threatening to prize it loose? One thing alone was clear: most of the Republican leadership in the South were obsessed with the threat of Wallace, and this alone could induce them to support a Reagan candidacy.

Even if it failed, they could at least face their home parties after such an attempt, claiming to have tried to get an effective counter to the fearsome Alabamian. Reagan as Vice-President might be enough; but then Reagan had made what amounted to a "Sherman declaration" about the Number-Two spot. ("If nominated, I will not campaign; if elected, I will not serve." —General William Tecumseh Sherman.) Was this genuine? Or was it simply tactical? One thing was clear: Nixon, tied up with his primary campaigning in the North, did not know the half of the trouble brewing down in Dixie.

But if Nixon was in the dark, so to a large extent was Reagan. If a date has to be put on the moment Reagan did most damage to his chances of the Presidency, it has to be Sunday, May 19, the day he met the Southern State Chairmen in New Orleans. For the Southerners, this was an important set piece, one they had been teeing up for some weeks. The basic idea was to have a collective look at all three candidates well in advance of the convention. Reagan and Rockefeller had already earned good marks by making themselves promptly available. Nixon, in contrast, had proved hard to get. "We had to *ask* for an audience," recalled Harry Dent. "I think Nixon took the South a bit for granted then."

Thus, when Reagan and the Southern chieftains met for dinner in his suite, the Rendezvous Room at the Roosevelt Hotel, he was confronted with a receptive audience. There were twenty-six in all—each chairman brought one guest (a pattern repeated with the other contenders)—and the mood, while friendly, was described by one of those present as "come on in or forget it." Reagan, tired from his fundraising exertions and irritated by the presence of Rockefeller in the same hotel (the New York Governor was scheduled for a similar confrontation the following morning), gave one of his rare lackluster performances. Still boxed in by fears of what the polls might do if news of his candidacy got out, Reagan protested too much his unwillingness to seek the nomination.

Many of his listeners actually believed him. (Reed of Mississippi did not—but then Reed was more ready than most to impute devious motives to the Californian.) Reagan said it would take a pretty formidable draft to make him run. This was not the kind of talk the Southerners wanted to hear; they wanted Reagan out on a limb, not themselves.

They were not foolish enough to expect an open declaration of candidacy there and then, but there were formulas—"I am not *now* a candidate," for instance—that would have enabled them to get the message, without compromising Reagan's public stance. Ironically, Reagan, so smooth in other respects, seemed ignorant of the subtleties of Presidency-hunting semantics.

Rockefeller was ebullient for the very reason that Reagan was depressed. He knew that his presence in the same hotel as Reagan would fuel speculation about a possible Rockefeller-Reagan ticket, which suited him fine: it would make Rockefeller's own candidacy more acceptable to the party regulars and at the same time reduce Reagan's credibility as the shining knight of the right who would never stoop to a self-seeking political deal. Just to increase the Californian's discomfort Rockefeller dropped in on Reagan for a chat on his way down to the breakfast session with the Southern chairmen. Afterward both men announced that they had spoken only generalities, though Rockefeller was deliberately cryptic: "Politics? Well, it could have been touched on." In fact, only generalities had been spoken, with Reagan concealing his fury at the New Yorker's nerve behind an icily polite mask. For Rockefeller, of course, the meeting was the message.

Rockefeller's subsequent performance before the Southern chairmen was impressive. None would vote for him, of course, but at least he was professional. The Rockefeller line was the "candid" one: I know you won't vote for me now, but can I appeal to you for unity and support after I get the nomination? In the meantime, gentlemen, your duty as I see it—"you, the backbone of the GOP"—is to stay uncommitted. The Southerners saw through it, of course: the longer they stayed uncommitted, the greater the chance that, under pressure from their own delegations, they would have to go for Reagan at the convention, which would stop Nixon and give Rockefeller a chance on later ballots. Still, it had been done competently. And there had been a lot of pleasure in observing the New Yorker picking distastefully at a breakfast of steak and hominy grits.

Nixon finally made it on May 31. The meeting—as crucial to Nixon's eventual success as the May 19 one to Reagan's subsequent failure—was held at the Marriott Motor Hotel in Atlanta, Georgia, and went on for three hours as Nixon fielded questions from all comers. Nixon understood all their sensitive areas: he was "sympathetic" on the Supreme Court, against forcing the pace of integration, and in particular opposed to bussing; explained ingeniously that he had endorsed the open-housing law only when it had become, he thought, unstoppable —pointing out that endorsement had given him the leverage to insert into the bill severe antiriot amendments; stood for stronger military forces; and was tough but vague on Vietnam. At this session, the subject of Nixon's Vice-Presidential selection was scarcely touched. No assurances were given and none asked. When the subject came up, Nixon turned it lightly by saying that whoever it was, it was not going to be anyone like his 1960 running mate, Henry Cabot Lodge. "Cabot Lodge would stake out some wild position and say that's what Mr. Nixon thinks. Then I would say, no that's not what Mr. Nixon thinks. Then Cabot Lodge would say, well, Mr. Nixon does think that, he just can't say so. That, gentlemen, is not going to happen a second time." (The Southerners, who have no natural reason to revere a Yankee Brahmin like Lodge, loved it.)

When the discussion homed in on practical politics, Wallace, not Reagan, became the key topic. (This concealment of the Reagan threat —partly, of course, because of Reagan's disappointing dinner date— seems to have been a major reason for Nixon's comparative ignorance of Reagan's potential strength.) The Southerners happily unburdened themselves of the message they had been vainly trying to get into Republican National Committee skulls for weeks: Wallace was doing some frightful damage. "If you're near the fire," said Reed of Mississippi, "you feel the heat."

Suddenly, Nixon, apprised that, in key states like Texas, Wallace was creaming off good potential Republican votes, became animated. What could he do? Everyone in the room agreed that the best stop-Wallace force was a galvanized Strom Thurmond. "Well, where is he?" asked Nixon.

The candidate, almost by accident, had stumbled upon the one man capable of holding off Reagan's late surge for the nomination. He had been in touch with Thurmond before, of course, but the South Carolinian, a man of colossal vanity, does not budge easily. This time, Nixon would not be simply asking for support but offering a great role. Thurmond was phoned directly after the Marriott Motel session and arrived in Atlanta by charter plane in time for another meeting the following day (June 1).

Nixon went through his Southern spiel and laid the flattery on with a trowel: "They tell me you are the only man who can defeat Wallace. Will you help us?" Thurmond, already half won-over, drove back in Nixon's car to the Atlanta airport. But he still needed clarification—not, as it happened, on the Vice-Presidency, a subject barely mentioned at this stage, but on a topic closer to Thurmond's combative heart: the nation's defenses against the Communist "menace." In the end, he extracted what he wanted from the candidate. Going on what he knew at that time, Nixon said that he was all for starting a comprehensive anti-ballistic missile (ABM) system as soon as he took office (a project opposed bitterly by such far from pacifist folk as Robert McNamara and Jerome Wiesner, on the grounds of its crippling cost and the inevitable prospect of a new arms race resulting). It was the clincher. Thurmond, reassured of Nixon's soundness on Communism, undertook to work vigorously against Wallace, and to hold his delegation steady. The crucial alliance had been forged.

In any event, it was a lot harder on Thurmond than on Nixon. When the South Carolina delegation met three weeks later to discuss policy, they were—all twenty-two of them—unanimous for Reagan. Thurmond had to pull out every stop to keep them in line, rehearsing a theme song that was to ring through the South from Miami Beach: "A vote for Reagan is a vote for Rockefeller. A vote for Wallace is a vote for Humphrey. We have no choice, if we want to win, except to vote for Nixon. . . . We must quit using our hearts and start using our heads. . . . I have been down this road, so I know. I am laying my prestige, my record of forty years in public life, I am laying it all on the line this time. Are any of you here making a comparable sacrifice? Do any of you have so much to lose? . . . Believe me, I love Reagan, but Nixon's the one." It was a great roar. South Carolina decided to go twenty-two for Nixon, though further "stiffening" was going to be required at Miami.

Thurmond's holding action came in the nick of time. In late June and early July, Reagan, now almost free from the fear of the polls, began to put on pressure. Key delegates from Southern states were flown to California to see the Governor. Reagan was now very impressive indeed. Harry Dent was in a constant state of anxiety over the condition of his delegates. ("They were just about ready to burst their britches for that man.") Then, in mid-July, Reagan took off for the most conspicuous phase of his noncandidacy. With Clifton White for company, he dropped in on the delegations from Texas, Arkansas, Virginia, Maryland, Indiana, Kentucky, Alabama, and North Carolina. At last, the South knew for certain that he would be in; it was no longer a question of whether, but when.

Reagan was still in no hurry. The original scenario mapped out by White was for declaration at the latest possible moment. The optimum situation would be a first-ballot Rockefeller-Nixon deadlock, because of a large vote for favorite-son candidates. Reagan could then be unveiled with suitable spontaneity as the man to lead the party out of the valley of irresolution. But this, given Rockefeller's late start, was too much to hope for. The momentum of an active Reagan candidacy was needed to stall the first ballot; but if the move was made too soon, it would give Nixon time to mount a counterattack.

Meanwhile, there were plenty of opportunities for exposure. Reagan was the first of the contenders to arrive in Miami Beach for the National Convention. On Wednesday, July 31, he gave verbal evidence to the Platform Committee, which had taken up residence in the Fontainebleau night-club café, the La Ronde Room, and roused this normally somnolent body to a display of enthusiasm. It was the only spontaneous display of emotion for a witness throughout four days of public hearings. Reagan's three most popular applause lines gave a clue to the subsequent underlying mood of the convention:

> We must reject the idea that every time the law is broken, society is guilty rather than the law-breaker. . . .
> It is time to move against these destructive dissidents [in universities]; it is time to say, "Obey the rules or get out." . . .

It is time to tell friend and foe alike that we are in Vietnam because it is in our national interest to be there. . . .

After a brief trip to other states to "drop in" on more delegations before they set out for Miami, Reagan was back on the beach by Saturday night and lost no time in staking out his natural constituency. In a television interview, Reagan made a shrewd play for Southern defections: "It's very difficult to disagree with most of the things that Mr. Wallace is saying," he said, and then hastily added that he was sure he must disagree with Wallace nonetheless. Then Reagan was off on a series of "by invitation" meetings with the state delegations that were beginning to silt up the swanky hotels along the Miami Beach littoral.

On Sunday, he was well received by Alabama, Georgia, Mississippi, Montana, Utah, and Wyoming—but still experienced some setbacks. Utah's tiny eight-member delegation decided, after a near commitment to him, to avoid controversy on the first ballot by going for Romney. (It was a futile gesture but a safe one; nobody in Salt Lake City could quarrel publicly with a vote for a fellow Mormon.).

Reagan's own delegation—composed of a mélange of Reagan, Nixon, and Rockefeller elements—was also, egged on by Nixon men, beginning to get fractious about all this glad-handing activity by its favorite son. It became clear that open rifts might develop among the delegates before his favorite-son candidacy metamorphosed into something grander. Reagan had to get them in line behind something formal, even if this meant declaring earlier than intended.

On Monday, Reagan had lunch in his suite at the Deauville with the ubiquitous Greenville Group—now privately committed to Nixon but still not inclined to discourage the Governor—and told them he intended to declare that afternoon. The Governor did not mention the ominous squeals inside his own delegation, but one of Reagan's aides said his decision to announce was based on a consultation that morning with Governor Rhodes of Ohio, a man he had in mind for the Vice-Presidency.

(The nature of Rhodes's role at the convention is perhaps open to more interpretations than any other. He was, and remained through the balloting, a favorite-son candidate, but it was never entirely clear whom he was holding for. Reagan clearly looked on Rhodes as a friend. The Greenville Group, however, was convinced he was an undercover Rockefeller man—and that he had prodded Reagan into declaring on Monday to generate some excitement and conceal the fact that Rockefeller's campaign had stalled badly. Eric Jones, Reagan's man inside the Ohio delegation, had still another view: Rhodes was batting for Rhodes, hoping that lightning would strike himself on a later ballot.)

At four p.m. Monday, Bill Knowland, an ardent Reagan man, emerged from a California caucus in the Deauville to make an announcement. The caucus, he said, had passed a resolution, taking note of the "growing demand" for Reagan to become an active candidate and coming to the view that "Such a declaration on the part of Governor Reagan would clarify the situation at the Republican National Convention. . . . The delegation hereby recognizes Governor Reagan in fact is a leading and bona fide candidate for President." A modest Reagan was on hand to say a few words before plunging off on another round of delegation meetings. "Gosh, I was surprised," he told the delegates. "It all came out of the clear blue sky." Ronald Reagan was an open candidate at last.

3

Trompe l'Oeil

"I think ideology is rapidly becoming anachronistic, irrelevant, and obsolete. To say this convention is ideological is silly . . . hardly worth discussing."

> —David Brinkley, to his co-commentator on NBC, Chet Huntley, on the 1968 National Republican Convention, Tuesday, August 6

Huntley nods agreement.

In most democracies, the search for new directions tends to be most obsessive inside the "out" party. Unburdened by the responsibilities of office, the "outs" have, in theory, the freedom to conjure with novel concepts and revel in unfamiliar ideas, in search of a strategy for "change." The United States in 1968 appeared to present a classic opportunity for this form of democratic action: a chance for the opposition party to look comprehensively at a system that suddenly seemed full of centrifugal and divisive tendencies. Seemingly nothing, but nothing, could have been further from Republican minds in Miami Beach. "America," declared Barry Goldwater, "is now ready to do what is right," and practically brought the house down. Yet it is impossible from a study of the convention proceedings to discover wherein that "right" lay.

To most Republicans, the electoral lessons of 1964 were more compelling than the social phenomena of 1968. In their eyes, ideology got you nowhere. And when raised at conventions it led, at best, to argument and unpleasantness, and at worst, to the commission of *the* party sin: betrayal of the cherished myths of unity. People did not have to agree; how absurd to think that, say, John Lindsay and Strom Thurmond could ever agree on anything. The important thing was that they should appear to agree.

451

Happily, the ideological vacuum had survived the deliberations of the 102-man Platform Committee, which, after its open sessions in the Fontainebleau's La Ronde Room, had retired, without any apparent sense of irony, to drafting sessions in the Voltaire Room. Under the tutelage of the veteran Senator from Illinois, Everett Dirksen (known to friends and enemies alike as the "Wizard of Ooze"), it had crafted a program of supreme meaninglessness.

It had not been altogether easy. The public testimony had been anything but consistent. On the day of Reagan's fulminations about "national interest" in Vietnam, for instance, the hero of liberal Republicanism, Mayor Lindsay, had declaimed the exact opposite. "The war," he said, "has estranged the majority of the American people from their own government . . . endangered our precarious economy, paralyzed our national will, and crippled our ability to deal with our critical domestic problems."

Dirksen, who had once incautiously remarked that he could well do without the committee's assistance in composing a "pungent" document of thirty-five hundred totally acceptable words, was obliged to deploy more wizardry than originally seemed necessary, but it all came out right in the end. So right that connoisseurs of such productions in the press were able to hail its Vietnam stance as dovish, while no hawk could reasonably complain about its contents. Failing in his objective of saying nothing, Dirksen had done the next best thing: he expanded the platform to ten thousand words and said something for everybody.

The Vietnam plank provides an instructive instance, since its original language had been subjected to what were described as "moderating" influences by Rockefeller supporters in the Voltaire Room. In its key sentence, the statement read, "We pledge a program for peace in Vietnam—neither peace at any price nor a camouflaged surrender of United States or allied interests—but a positive program that will offer a fair and equitable settlement to all. . . ."

Yet nowhere is there any indication of how this wonderfully desirable objective could be achieved. No mention of a bombing pause. Nor any mention of negotiating with the National Liberation Front. (A proposal by the liberal New York Senator Jacob K. Javits, that negotiation with the NLF be included, was specifically, and overwhelmingly, rejected.) Lest even this nebulous peace position be thought too pacific, the plank inserted an indictment of LBJ's Administration for its policy of gradual escalation, which had "wasted our massive military superiority and frittered away our options." It was, of course, therapy rather than policy.

Similarly, the platform proposed an assault on the "Crisis in the Cities," but the weaponry for such an assault was left studiously vague, though the role of private enterprise was thought to be crucial. The plank endorsed the civil-rights legislation on the books but reserved its strongest language for civil disorder and crime, promising "an all-out Federal-state-local crusade" on crime and militantly declaring, "We will not tolerate violence!"

Some detected a more loving craftsmanship in its wording on these matters than was displayed in the sections dealing with urban problems. And others felt that concern over the "starved" armed forces assumed too large a priority. (The armed forces were not as starved as all that. Since 1960, when the Republicans were last in office, defense spending under the Democrats had risen from forty billion plus a year to eighty billion plus.) The plank on "A Healthy Economy," for instance, generously pledged: "Such funds as become available with the termination of the Vietnam war *and upon recovery from its impact on national defense* will be applied in a balanced way to critical domestic needs and to reduce the heavy tax burden." But it could not be denied that the more disquietingly aggressive passages had been matched by genuflections in all the liberal directions. Dirksen had produced, as he said he would, a document "that any Republican can run on"—though in its dexterous quality of appearing to confront, while actually evading, most issues, it was probably better attuned to the personality of Richard M. Nixon than to that of either of his two rivals.

Yet to say that the 1968 Republican Convention was not concerned with ideology is to mistake appearance for reality. It chose not to discuss or crystallize ideological conflicts, but these were by no means absent. Even the simplest delegate at Miami Beach knew full well that while Reagan, Rockefeller, and Nixon could run on Dirksen's platform they would run on it in totally different directions. With such a diversified crop of candidates, who needed issues? Clearly the delegates thought it better to orchestrate unity themes in public, while the bitter struggle among these traditional political viewpoints—left, right, and center—took place in the decorous privacy of the caucus.

With all three on the scratch line, what were their relative strengths and weaknesses? The most uncomfortable was undoubtedly Rockefeller. His entire campaign had been projected beyond the delegates to the nation at large, in hopes that his showing in the polls would produce overwhelming evidence that he—and only he—could beat any man the Democrats chose to nominate. The polls had been good, but scarcely unequivocal; and the Gallup-Harris mix-up, though apparently resolved in Rockefeller's favor, had sounded the death knell to his chances of breaking much new ground before the first ballot.

Even his own (highly inflated) projections of his vote on the first roll call never exceeded 350. His basic strength in committed delegates was, more accurately, around 250, most of them from in and around his own Eastern bailiwick: New York, Pennsylvania, Massachusetts, Rhode Island, and Connecticut. There was, it is true, a concealed Rockefeller vote in delegations like those from Maryland, Michigan, Ohio, and New Jersey, all of which had pledged themselves to favorite sons. But since these also contained hidden Nixon votes, it was in Rockefeller's interests, on the early ballots at least, to leave the favorite-son blocs alone. Outside the industrial states, the traditional antipathy to Rockefeller showed no sign of mellowing in the Florida sunshine. When asked about the possibility of Rockefeller strength in his delegation, Louie Nunn, Governor of Kentucky, replied, "An awful lot of our delegates know that if they voted for Rockefeller down here they wouldn't be allowed off the plane back home." (Two Kentucky delegates did, as it happens, vote for Rockefeller and still contrive to return safely.)

Rockefeller himself as much as admitted that his peregrinations around the Miami Beach delegations were calculated more to reassure than recruit—"They can see I haven't got horns." There were a few new commitments in the offing—most notably that of Washington's governor, Dan Evans, whose convention keynote speech staked out an explicit peace position on Vietnam—but nothing that could be categorized as startling.

Rockefeller's men arrived in Miami privately afraid that it was all but hopeless. Yet after the convention George Hinman said, "Actually Rockefeller came very close. There *was* a chance after Reagan's entry split the conservatives. That's the only condition on which a moderate can go through." In short, Rockefeller's only chance of success depended, as it had for some weeks, on the sweet-talking talents of his ideological opposite, Ronald Reagan. If Reagan could chip away Nixon's Southern base and throw the convention open, then Rockefeller would be in business. On Saturday, August 3, a story in the *New York Times,* based on information supplied by Leonard Hall, Rockefeller's floor manager, was headlined: "Rockefeller Aides Fear Reagan Is Gaining Rapidly." A more accurate label would have substituted "Hope" for "Fear."

The Reagan outfit was not entirely happy with all this gratuitous publicity—coming as it did from a source which most of the delegates they were appealing to would find unappetizing. For them, predictions by Rockefeller's staff that Reagan might pick up a prodigious 300 votes on the first ballot were entirely counterproductive. All along, the Reagan strategy had been firmly grounded on the "poor-mouthing" principle, designed to make small gains look wondrously impressive. F. Clifton White's predictions, therefore, rarely topped 180 on the first ballot (Reagan got 182), though privately he was hoping for something nearer 250, more than enough to deny Nixon that crucial first-ballot majority.

As with Rockefeller, Reagan's cardinal weakness derived from his late entry into the race; he had only a meager base of committed delegates. Unlike Rockefeller, however, Reagan could expect that his proselytizing among the delegations could be converted into concrete votes. Outside the big industrial states, nobody thought Reagan had horns, though there were some in Miami Beach who seemed to think him capable of sprouting wings. His prejudices most nearly matched those of the average delegate. And the caucus setting was perfectly attuned to his talents. "There is nothing more impressive than Ronnie Reagan behind closed doors," according to South Carolina's Harry Dent.

Compared with his rivals, Nixon possessed assets that seemed almost impregnable. He had behind him a solid buttress of committed votes won in the primaries and by months of painstaking work on state party leaders around the country. Right-wing hearts might throb for Reagan, but it was Nixon who sought early, and won over, the conservative conscience of Barry Goldwater. The great party work horses were on his team: Ray Bliss, the party chairman; Gerald Ford, the House minority leader and permanent chairman of the convention; and the redoubtable Everett Dirksen. Those among the more spectacular figures in the party committed to him ranged from Mark Hatfield on the left to Strom Thurmond on the right. And their lofty endorsements were underpinned by a superlatively efficient delegate-hunting and -monitoring operation. Not that it differed in essence from that of the two other contenders—each had the *de rigueur* communications trailer outside the convention hall and constant walkie-talkie contact with the floor men inside—but neither could match Nixon's depth and range of contact.

"They were so good," said one delegate, torn between complaint and admiration, "they had these people at the end of each row, and you couldn't get out to the toilet without they followed you." In practical terms, Nixon had the manpower: a staff of three hundred compared with Rockefeller's two hundred and Reagan's eighty, and unmatchable intelligence sources. Whereas Rockefeller would be denied information by some delegations and Reagan by others, there was no delegation without a Nixon man on the inside. Most filed twice-daily status reports to be mulled over and acted upon by the Nixon command staff in the Hilton Plaza. An extra refinement of class was provided by Nixon's Navy—a flotilla of houseboats along the creek where delegates could meet Nixon delegate-hunters in conditions of luxurious repose. It was all very deft and decorous. As Clarke Reed of Mississippi, a veteran of a more rugged school of political persuasion, put it, "They would buy you a drink, but never a bottle."

With so much going for him, Nixon's main concern was to maintain an air of invincibility. Thus, while Reagan and Rockefeller sweated out the weekend delegation-hopping along the oceanfront hotels, Nixon was coolly and ostentatiously absent from the scene—mapping out his acceptance speech twelve hundred miles away, at Montauk, Long Island. When he arrived, as late as decently possible, at six-fifty p.m. on Monday, it was with the aplomb of a man who had come to claim the nomination, not to seek it. The demonstrations were all handsomely choreographed to buttress this impression. As his motorcade swung up to the Hilton Plaza, well-drilled teams of leggy dancers burst into well-rehearsed choruses of "Nixon's the One" to jolly along his supporters. (In the banal genre of campaign songs, it is perhaps the most banal. Full lyric: "Nixon's the One / Nixon's the One / Nixon's the One for me / We need Nixon—N-I-X-O-N / Nixon's the One for me!") Nixon's crowd scenes are methodical and well thought out. The attendant elephant who unwittingly stepped on a reporter's foot had been inserted into the festivities by Miami Beach well-wishers, not the Nixon organizers.

The psychology was good, but the structure on which this display of ebullience rested was not unshakable. Some weeks before the convention, Nixon staffers had thought, sometimes talked, in terms of a first-ballot tally of 850 for their candidate (the figure required for a majority was 667), but as the day of final reckoning drew nearer, the forecasting became more cautious. When the delegates assembled in Miami Beach, it was, for the record, around 700. Privately, Nixon's head-counters had realized that the achievement of even this figure, indeed the achievement of a simple majority, was anything but assured. To make prophecy reality, an elaborate process of political maneuver had to be carried out on two levels. First, a strategy for the South to prevent votes from ebbing away to Reagan. Secondly, a strategy for the North, where actual defections from other causes were required to push their man over the top. Of the two, the Southern strategy was much the more crucial.

The most compelling argument that Southern delegation leaders could use to keep their men in line was that only Nixon could hold off Rockefeller. But if Nixon failed on the first ballot, after all the ballyhoo about his having it sewed up, the rank-and-file delegates might assume that Nixon was not so safe after all. And if that hypothesis was made, then why should they not risk everything for the man they really wanted, Ronald Reagan? (There is some evidence that this would have happened. Governor Nunn of Kentucky, who held 22 of his 24 delegates for Nixon, intimated to a Reagan contact man that he would go for the California governor on the second ballot. Similarly, the Texas delegation, which split 41 for Nixon to 15 for Reagan, anticipated that these figures would be reversed if it went beyond one ballot.)

The chances of a breakaway in the South had suddenly, and nightmarishly, become a very real possibility. Reagan, now an open candidate, was going the rounds of the delegations, and his pitch was brilliantly seductive: they should let it go for a couple of ballots "just to get an open convention, so that all views get a chance to be expressed." This was backed by the disingenuous assurance that "nobody had anything to lose," because, sure, if nothing emerged by, say, the third ballot, then we can all go back and rally around Dick.

Reagan did not have to make much headway to prove really dangerous. Earlier on Monday, an uncharacteristically smiling Clif White had told reporters clustered outside Reagan's communications trailer, "All we need is just one break—one state switching to Reagan—and we've got him."

And that evening, Reagan was feeding on a formidable undercurrent of resentment over speculation about Nixon's probable running mate. Press projections had tended to cluster around the fashionable Northern liberals, whose vote-getting ability it was presumed would be essential if Nixon was to carry any of the big industrial states in November. Names like Percy of Illinois, Lindsay of New York, Hatfield of Oregon, and even (improbably) Rockefeller were being conjured with.

Nor was this entirely on the basis of wishful thinking. At a press briefing before Nixon's arrival, Herbert Klein had been asked what kind of Vice-President his boss might be looking for. Klein mentioned Hat-field and no one else. The information was untrue: Nixon was not look-ing at Hatfield. But Klein was presumably driven by the urgent need to woo Northern liberal delegates.

All this was intolerable to the South. On Sunday, a group of South-ern party leaders had sought, and obtained, an audience with John Mitchell to extract assurances on this very subject. Mitchell was guarded but gave them, in essence, what they were looking for: a promise that Nixon, the friend of the South, would not split the ticket—a vague as-surance which, the Southerners took it, excluded divisive liberal choices. But this private reassurance did nothing to abate the disquieting rumors around the convention hall. The South, true to its paranoid political style, suspected a double cross.

As the speech-making droned on, it became apparent that the real focus of action was not the podium but the small clutches of babbling Southern delegates dotted around the auditorium. Was Nixon's Dixie strength being eroded? What was happening, in fact, was not so much steady erosion, as random flopping around. Even some sections of the leadership were beginning to have reservations about their earlier com-mitments to Nixon. Jim Martin, the boss of the Nixon faction in the Alabama delegation, was frantic about the mood of his colleagues. At one point, he told a Nixon contact man that they might, after all, have to cast a ballot for Reagan. If Alabama did not show at least token sup-port for the one true conservative in nomination, there might be dire consequences—"We could get lynched when we get home." In other parts of the field, there were violent tremors among the Florida, Texas, Mississippi, and Louisiana delegates. Congressman James C. Gardner, boss of the North Carolina delegation, under pressure back home to en-dorse Wallace to help his own race for governor, told Thurmond flatly, "I'm for Ronnie."

At nine-twenty-five p.m. Edward Brooke rose to make a speech with racial justice as its theme. Urging the rejection of white separatism in the suburbs and black separatism in the slums, the party should, Brooke declaimed, "hold true to the course on which we have embarked —the course which leads to an integrated society of magnificent plural-ism." Such high-flown concepts were far from the delegates' minds. Long before Brooke sat down, he had lost his audience, his rhetoric a poor competitor for the news that Reagan was making gains. CBS had just completed its first thoroughgoing delegate count since Reagan's an-nouncement of open candidacy. It showed Nixon with 626 (still 41 short of the majority), Rockefeller 243, Reagan 192 (up 16), favorite sons and others 272. The "one break" Clif White had been looking for had not occurred, but Reagan was moving, while the others remained ominously static.

Thurmond did not have to wait for any head count to confirm the danger. He had already decided to cut the speech by his old friend Barry Goldwater, scheduled for ten p.m., and get on with the more important task of alerting the candidate. Soon after ten, Thurmond and Harry Dent were closeted with Mitchell and Nixon in the candidate's suite at the Hilton. It was, in the words of one of those present, "a panicky meeting." It was also the pivotal meeting of the convention, and the one that virtually ensured Nixon's nomination. Did it justify the charge that he had achieved it by "making a deal" with the South?

Was there indeed a specific deal? At this level of political operation, deals are not put in writing and sometimes not even into words. An understanding is enough, and this, in an hour-long session, is what Nixon and Thurmond achieved. Nixon was obviously stunned by the news of potential defections in the South. His strategy of dealing with the Southern party leaders, and only with the leaders, had left him ignorant of the strength of Reagan sentiment behind them. Until his arrival in Miami, he and Mitchell had seen Rockefeller as their main enemy. Because they were confident that, with tactics like tipping leftish Republicans for the Vice-Presidential spot, they had contained their New Yorker, they had relaxed. Thurmond rapidly disabused them.

The key point Thurmond made was that the delegates needed to hear the sort of thing that Nixon had told the chairman in Atlanta back in June. So the meeting developed into a sort of catechism, with Thurmond and Dent putting Nixon through all the articles of Southern faith. Two questions rose above all the rest: "guidelines" and the Vice-Presidency.

"Guidelines"—the term deriving from the Education Office's early regulations on school desegregation—has become a euphemism for the discussion of racial problems in the South. With all that civil-rights legislation on the books, nothing is more important to the white Southerner than the question of just how vigorous the President will be in enforcing it. Would Nixon, like Kennedy, be prepared to put in Federal troops if the pace of integration demanded it? Or would he deem the local authorities vigilant enough to ensure the effectiveness of such legislation— which means, of course, not very vigilant.

In semantic terms, the "guidelines" discussion boiled down to (a) local and states' rights, which Nixon declared himself to be very much in favor of, and (b) bussing as a means to integrate schools, which Nixon was against. He said he was for integration, but "freedom of choice" took first place. Whose freedom to choose this represented was, naturally, not under discussion. Thurmond was well satisfied with this approach.

The question of the Vice-Presidency was more complex. Thurmond was frank about the danger—"if they even think you are going overboard for one of those liberals, you can kiss half the South good-by" —but Nixon still tried to preserve options. He said he would consult all sections of the party, that he did not believe in split tickets, and so on. But in the end, he used the key phrase: his selection would be "acceptable to all sections of the party." And he assured Thurmond that he would be consulted before the final choice. To Thurmond, the word "acceptable," combined with a role in the consultation process, was enough. He would be the judge of what was acceptable to the South, and that eliminated all the popular Northern liberals, for a start.

Thurmond was charged, before he left the meeting, with the role of Reassurer-in-Chief. He was to go around the delegations to tell them everything was O.K.—if necessary, repeating verbatim what Nixon had told him.

In Thurmond's mouth, it was to sound very much as if he had a veto on Nixon's choice. This was not strictly true, but then in the game of Convention Bluff the exaggeration was hardly more than a peccadillo. In his miasmal, euphemistic chat with the candidate, Thurmond had convinced himself of one thing: Nixon was "not going to force anyone down the throat of the South." Next day, one critical delegation was to make Thurmond's private intimations to the candidate public and explicit. Florida declared that it would only place its thirty-three disposable votes with Nixon if they could get a pledge that Nixon's running mate would please the South. (The delegation numbered thirty-four, but Governor Kirk had come out for Rockefeller, in pious hopes of gaining the Vice-Presidency.) The delegation even went so far as to list some of the "unacceptable" candidates, Lindsay and Rockefeller among them.

But the counterattack was already moving into gear. Nixon's first full day in Miami began with an early-morning press conference, devoted mainly to foreign affairs. Nixon seemed intent on cultivating his "moderate" image. He could see the world entering an "age of negotiations," with the Communist bloc, once monolithic, beginning to break up. In this new atmosphere, negotiations with Russia, even with China, were possible. It was pure New Nixon.

But the important part of Tuesday morning's proceedings was his series of private meetings with the delegations, in which he produced, when required, several flashes of the Old Style. Unlike Rockefeller and Reagan, Nixon did not go to the delegations: they came to him. They came, in regional groups, to take coffee and buns with the candidate at the Hilton Plaza. It was Nixon's chance to massage the ego of the South, and he did it brilliantly. Taking the South in two groups, he ran over all the sensitive areas that he and Thurmond had thrashed out the night before. Fortunately, there is no need to rely on the fuzzy recollections of individuals about what was said at the second of these meetings (with Florida, the Carolinas, Kentucky, Virginia, Tennessee, District of Columbia, and Arkansas). An enterprising reporter on the *Miami Herald* persuaded one of the Florida delegation to tape-record the entire session. The transcript gives an insight into Nixon's backroom technique that can hardly be bettered, and for that reason alone more warrants quotation than anything in the hours of convention-hall rhetoric.

What was not known at the time was that the entire meeting had been carefully structured by Dent and Thurmond the night before. On their advice, Nixon had dropped his original intention of making a longish set-piece talk and consented to the idea of a question-and-answer session. Dent would ensure that the questions fell in the right areas.

Nixon's opening was short and pithy. A few pleasantries to start with: "I want to say first, that this afternoon between three and six, we are going to have our two girls . . . and we are having a little reception for all of you that would like to come. This afternoon, you can all come—with your wives, your girl friends, or, you know, with anybody else. (*Laughter*) Or bring your husbands!"

Then, straight into a general assurance that he was not taking any notice of nonsense to the effect that he should "forget the South" because it would be impossible to beat Wallace. He was going to be a "national candidate" and that meant campaigning in every region. "Look at Florida . . . North Carolina, Kentucky, Virginia, Tennessee, Texas. My friends, we polled them all. We can take every one of those states, and we are going to do it." (In the event, Nixon did take them all except Texas.)

On the vexed question of the Vice-Presidency, Nixon first made clear that his running mate would be determined by a process of consultation, and went on to say how embarrassing some of the speculations had been. "There have been some cockeyed stories that Nixon has made a deal with this one or that one. And I can assure you that some of those stories, which mentioned names, were, shall we say . . . difficult, as far as I am concerned."

He then set out the three qualifications he thought a Vice-President should have: an ability to be a good President; a good campaigner; and a man who shared his views. But it was the fourth qualification, uttered with great emphasis, that had the delegates clapping enthusiastically: "I want to say one final thing. I am not going to take, I can assure you, anybody that is going to divide this party."

Then it was question time, and the first, inevitably, was on bussing.

[A North Carolina delegate:] On the racial problem in the South. Can you say that you favor forced bussing of schoolchildren for the sole purpose of racial integration?

[A:] This is a problem in the North, too. This is nonsense to the effect that this problem exists only in the South of the United States. We're now learning that this is a national problem—and I'm going to talk national.

I don't believe you should use the South as a whipping boy or the North as a whipping boy. My feeling is this: I think that bussing the child—a child that is two or three grades behind another child—into a strange community . . . I think you destroy that child. . . .

We have got to educate them, and I don't believe in that manner of approach. And there is another thing that I would like to say with regard to the courts of this land. . . . I think it is the job of the courts to interpret the law, and not make the law. [*Applause*] I know there are a lot of smart judges, believe me—and probably a lot smarter than I am—but I don't think there is any court in this country, any judge in this country, either local or on the Supreme Court—and court, including the Supreme Court of the U.S.—that is qualified to be a local school district and make the decision as your local school board.

. . . Instead of talking about millions more for Federal jobs and Federal housing, Federal laws . . . I'm talking about building bridges to human dignity. I'm talking about remedial uses, about opportunities, about motivation. That is the way we get on with this subject [of education]—rather than simply in terms of, well, rather than try to satisfy some professional civil-rights group, or something like that, that we will bus the child from one side of the county over to the other.

It was all a bit incoherent, but Nixon's footwork had been sure. He was not a man to accelerate integration in the schools or even approve of the courts' attempting that task. He had comforted the South by making the problem national, and he had got in a crack about civil-rights groups.

[Q:] Mr. President [*sic*], the Florida delegation has asked . . . that you comment on open housing and Vietnam. . . .

[A:] Open housing . . . my position is the same as Gerry Ford's. I felt then—and I feel now—that conditions are different in different parts of the country . . . just like gun control ought to be handled at state level, rather than the Federal level.

Now, how did we get a Federal open-housing bill? [The candidate recalled how "open housing" was made a part of the 1968 civil-rights bill in Congress.] . . .

So I had a hard decision to make . . . and I talked to Gerry Ford about it—vote for it and get it out of the way or . . . so, I made that hard decision. In my view—and I think it vitally important—to get the civil-rights and open-housing issues out of our sight so we didn't have a split party over the platform when we came down here to Miami Beach.

I would have preferred that it be handled at the state and local level . . . the decision made in Congress, under the circumstances, was a sound decision and one that I approve. . . . .

My main concern was this: I want a united party. I know that when those Democrats meet in Chicago a couple of weeks from now, they're going to be hammering at each other. They're going to have majority planks and minority planks. We didn't have it, and the reason we didn't have it was that some of us made those hard decisions and got some of these issues out of the way—maybe not the way we all like it, but out of the way, acted on, and *now we can move in another direction.*

That had been a tricky one. But Nixon had made the central point clear: it was tactics, not conviction, that led him to endorse the open-housing legislation. And the tactics were designed to help the Republicans beat the Democrats—something any red-blooded party loyalist could sympathize with. Indeed, Nixon's personal convictions were opposed to Federal action in this area. Short of promising to repeal the legislation, Nixon could scarcely have gone further to conciliate the South.

Vietnam was less explosive, but again Nixon's approach seemed to consort oddly with his moderate statements in public. This was only a few hours after his "age of negotiations" press conference, yet for the purposes of instructing Southerners, the Communist world seemed to have turned once again into a menacing and monolithic structure which called for some belligerent missile rattling.

Nixon started by maintaining that his basic position on Vietnam

was a peace position. But it was peace through strength. Nixon recalled
how it had been done by the Republicans before.

> How do you bring a war to a conclusion? I'll tell you how Korea
> was ended. We got in there and had this messy war on our hands.
> Eisenhower let the word go out—let the word go out diplomatically—
> to the Chinese and the North Koreans that we would not tolerate this
> continual ground war of attrition. And within a matter of months, they
> negotiated. [Eisenhower, in his memoirs, claimed that he settled the
> Korean War by implying that he would use *nuclear* weapons if a truce
> was not signed]
>
> Well, as far as negotiation [in Vietnam] is concerned that should
> be our position. We'll be militarily strong and diplomatically strong. I
> think we've got to change our position regarding training the Vietnamese.
> . . . We need a massive training program so that the South Vietnamese
> can be trained to take over the fighting—that they can be phased in as
> we phase out.
>
> Critical to the settlement of Vietnam is relations with the Soviet
> Union. That is why I have said over and over again that it is going to
> be necessary for the next President to sit down and talk with the Soviet
> leaders—and talk quite directly, not only about Vietnam, you've got to
> broaden the canvas—because in Vietnam they have no reason to end
> that war. It's hurting us more than it's hurting them.
>
> We could put the Mideast on the fire. And you could put trade on
> the fire. And you put the power bombs on the fire . . . and you say:
> Now look here. Here's the world. Here is the United States. Here is the
> Soviet Union. Neither of us wants a nuclear war . . . they want some-
> thing else, but they don't want war.
>
> So they will say: "What are we going to do to reduce these ten-
> sions?" I believe in that way—that kind of diplomacy. We can get the
> Soviet Union to listen, not only to bring this war to an end, but perhaps
> to reduce the amount of stirring up they are doing in the Mideast and
> other places. . . .
>
> I'll tell you one thing. I played a little poker when I was in the
> Navy. I learned something—it was very expensive [*Laughter*]—I learned
> this—when a guy didn't have the cards, he talked awfully big. But
> when he had the cards, he just sat there—had that cold look in his eyes.
>
> Now we've got the cards. But we've got to strengthen the United
> States. What we've got to do is walk softly and carry a big stick. And
> that is what we are going to do.

It was rousing stuff, and it was warmly applauded. It all seemed to
fit in with the South's simplistic world view. That it savored of the
brinkmanship of the early fifties worried no one. Yet even Nixon must
have realized by now that the coolest poker-player's eye in Moscow
could scarcely guarantee much change in the Vietcong's will to fight.

But this was Nixon negotiating for delegate votes rather than peace, and a little Cold War fundamentalism rarely comes amiss in the South. The rest was pretty plain sailing: a pledge to open up a new front against crime—"against the narcotics peddlers, the numbers boys, and the peddlers of filth and all that"; a pledge to jack up the missile program; and a further statement of his determination to campaign in the South. The Southerners also took comfort from his criticism of Johnson's Supreme Court appointments. Although Nixon refrained from attacking Abe Fortas personally, his words amounted, in practice, to an endorsement of the grotesque tactics Strom Thurmond and his allies had used to try to block Fortas's confirmation as Chief Justice by the Senate.

All in all, it had been an excellent morning's work. Tom Stagg of Louisiana subsequently declared the spectacle of Nixon in caucus with the South to be "the greatest stand-up performance by a politician I have witnessed."

Meanwhile, Reagan was on the verge of being killed with kindness. The Nixon scouts had diverted Barry Goldwater from a projected fishing trip, and he was going the rounds sweetening the Nixon bait by saying what a wonderful Vice-President Ronald Reagan would make, and if he had his way, Ronnie would share the ticket with Nixon. Some delegates got the idea from this that Reagan actually would be the Vice-President—an idea of which Reagan hastened to disabuse them in telegrams to all the delegations saying it was not so. In private with delegates, he nailed the rumor even more firmly. He would not take it under any conditions: "Even if they tied and gagged me, I would find a way to signal by wiggling my ears."

Inevitably, Reagan's first move on Tuesday was an attempt to beard the Southern lion in his den, the palatial Versailles Hotel, where Strom Thurmond and the rest of the South Carolina delegates had taken up residence. The initial exchanges between Thurmond and Reagan, in front of witnesses, were friendly but unrewarding. Thurmond had given his word. And Nixon, surely—Reagan must understand—was at least acceptable. "Nobody's ever been able to pin any fraud on him." Reagan, undaunted, took Thurmond upstairs for a forty-five-minute chat *à deux*. It was the same story: Thurmond yielded to no one in his admiration of Reagan, but it just was not his year.

Reluctantly, Reagan had to go around Thurmond. His main targets were Mississippi, Florida, and Alabama. Unfortunately, by the time Reagan started working in earnest on the Mississippians, they had already had their flagging enthusiasm for Nixon braced by a boat ride with Strom Thurmond. To get through to them, Reagan had to try another authority figure: Clarke Reed, the boss of the delegation. Almost beseechingly, Reagan rang Reed with news of his plight. "I only want a chance," he said. "You've always said you wanted an open fight. O.K., release your delegates."

It was one of those delicious moments that political bosses, particularly Southern bosses, love to savor. Reagan had clearly forgotten about his failure to come to Reed's rescue in the Mississippi gubernatorial race in 1966. (It is possible he never knew about it, since his enormous mailbag of speech-making requests is sifted by aides before presentation to the great man.) But now Reed had Reagan's ear and full attention, and he did not waste them. Lovingly, he reminded the Governor of the time when he, Reed, had badly needed a favor and had got nothing. In the circumstances, he did not feel able to release his delegates. The full sweetness of Reed's revenge was distilled into a final piece of advice before he put down the phone on his petitioner: "Perhaps you had better try where you have a few favors owing."

Nor was there much to encourage Reagan on the left. The Rockefeller drive now seemed completely bogged down and was exhibiting the failures of coordination that are always a sign of ebbing confidence. There was no panic; just an air of lassitude. Typically, that afternoon, Rockefeller had arrived an hour late for an NBC broadcast, only to find the spot canceled. Another chance of exposure lost. Still, at five-twenty p.m., a gamely smiling Rockefeller confronted the press once again with his latest delegate count. It showed conclusively that Nixon could not achieve more than 550 votes on the first ballot.

"What about the second, Governor?"

"An erosion of about fifty votes in his strength."

"And the third?"

"The dam will break." By this time it was fairly obvious that the Governor of New York was either joking, or lying (honestly, of course), or that he just could not count.

It was already clear that the defection of Spiro T. Agnew, the Maryland governor, to the Nixon cause, would take most of Maryland's twenty-five delegates with him. Thus Rockefeller paid dearly in precious votes for snubbing Agnew back in March. Even David Cargo, New Mexico's governor, at heart a Rockefeller man, had seen the inevitability of Nixon and come out publicly for him. The *frisson* of uncertainty, of wild surmise, that had swept through the convention hall on Monday night seemed to have spent itself.

When the same cast assembled for the full convention session on

Tuesday evening, its mood was relaxed and tinged with smugness. Nobody had seriously lost his head. Unity was going to be preserved, after all. The delegates could sit back and enjoy the hamming of Everett Dirksen, presenting the report of the Platform Committee. For Republicans, Dirksen is first-class entertainment, and his performance that night was worthy of Lionel Barrymore. Starting with a merry quip—"I accept the nomination"—in response to the ovation that greeted his appearance, he gravitated through outrage—against the "tyranny of the looter, the blackmailer, the robber and the arsonist"—to partisan indignation— "this ballyhooed 'Great Society' . . . is not a fair deal or a new deal; it's rather a straight-out misdeal"—he closed, unblushingly, with a prayer that God would make "America worthy of his blessing."

Thurmond, who can hear this kind of stuff almost any day of the week in the Senate, lent only half an ear. Throughout Dirksen's oration and most of the evening's business, he was occupied with more important matters. He was stomping around the Southern delegations with Nixon's floor manager, Rogers Morton of Maryland. Their mission was to remind the Southerners of their duty to stay rock-steady.

That night, the head that almost wore the crown could sleep easy. All the delegate counts (apart from Rockefeller's dubious computation) showed Nixon hovering near the 667 figure. It seemed incredible, given the last-minute defections from other causes to go with a winner, that Nixon could fall short of his majority.

But Wednesday, the day scheduled for the balloting (it did not, in fact, take place until the early hours of Thursday morning), was not to be the easy, freewheeling day the Nixon camp expected. It turned out to be the most hectic of the convention, with new threats to "consensus" needing containment almost by the hour. The most dangerous of these came from Florida, seventeen of whose thirty-four delegates were women, most of them crazy for Reagan. Of all the Southern delegations, Florida was undoubtedly the most volatile, and its internal power struggles the most traumatic.

Oddly, the alarming stresses in the delegation of the host state had been late in coming to the attention of the Nixon camp. Partly, this was a matter of geography: the Floridians were not staying on the Beach like Yankee tourists. They were holed up in grand style at the Doral Country Club on the mainland, a temple of Southern living, with palm-lined lawns and cool interiors normally dedicated to the gentlemanly pleasures of poker and bourbon. Partly, also, it was a matter of overconfidence: Florida's preconvention commitment to Nixon had been made by Bill

Murfin, the state chairman and a member of the Greenville Group. Everybody thought Murfin would be able to deliver.

But the fact was that Murfin's own base was never secure. He had taken control of the party by what amounted to an old-fashioned *coup d'état*. Florida's Republicans have an unusual system, in which the state chairman of the party is elected by county organizations—and each county has the same number of votes, whether it contains two or two thousand Republicans. Murfin and his acolytes had exploited this system by careful forays into the northern counties, where registered Republicans are rarer than clockwork oranges.

This technique had, not unnaturally, made for animosities in the ranks. But the crux of Murfin's dilemma was that the people on the delegation who had helped him win control of the party were among the most fervent Reaganophiles.

To complicate matters still further, Governor Kirk, the other possible source of authority, had annihilated himself locally with his declaration for Rocky. (The decision prompted one member of the delegation to prophesy accurately: "That's Rocky's first and last vote from this state.") Kirk, however, was still trying manfully to wrestle for control. Firstly, he proposed that the delegates nominate him as favorite son, which was overwhelmingly turned down. His second, more crafty move, was to suggest that he, along with all the rest of them, vote for Reagan.

By Wednesday morning, the three-way tug of war between Kirk, Murfin, and Murfin's disenchanted helpmates was still in progress, though they were moving toward an agreement that if either the Nixon or Reagan forces mobilized a majority of delegates, the minority would fall in line. It was a tacit unit rule.

Before most of the other delegations were out of bed, the Floridian factions were already at work, maneuvering for support. The critical call was one from Murfin to his old friend Harry Dent of South Carolina. Murfin had just gotten some bad news: Bill Knowland and the primordial Max Rafferty, California's Republican Senate nominee, were coming over to pitch for Reagan on the first caucus of the day. Some of the women were almost hysterical for Ronnie, and the two California ultras might be able to push one or two of them over the top. Murfin came rapidly, if inelegantly, to the point: "If you want to stop this thing falling apart, you had better get Strom's ass over here before they turn up."

Strom arrived just ten minutes before the Reagan men and went into his routine. Unerringly, he overstepped his brief—at least one delegate swears that Thurmond used the words: "I have a veto over his [Nixon's] Vice-Presidential choice." It was an emergency.

By the end of Florida's morning session, there was still no change in the position: one for Rockefeller, fourteen for Reagan, and nineteen for Nixon. If Reagan was to swing the delegation his way, he needed three more converts. He tried.

At noon, he entertained sixteen of the Florida people in his suite at the Deauville. The flames started to leap again. When the Florida delegates assembled for their final private caucus at two o'clock in their club, they were in a highly emotional state. The room was not so much smoke-filled as tearstained. With their slender majority still intact, the Nixon forces had decided to press for the unit rule.

Murfin threatened resignation if they did not come into line. Several of the women were weeping openly, and, according to one survivor, "It wouldn't have been hard for a strong man to shed a tear."

Minutes before it was time to leave for the convention hall and the nominating speeches, they decided—with four abstentions—to hold together for Nixon on the first ballot. Still, Reagan would not give up. Installed with Clif White in his communications trailer outside the convention hall, the Governor valiantly tried to contrive a happy ending. Reagan's delegate-hunters would detach a couple of Floridians at a time from the proceedings in the hall and take them out for a highly personalized plea by the candidate. Naturally, the Nixon men had this operation monitored, and as soon as a delegate emerged from the trailer, they would take an arm and start in with counterarguments. Organizationally it was faultless, but it was hard on the nerve ends. At one point, a Nixon contact man detached himself from a covey of Florida delegates to shout to a colleague: "I tell you, these women can't stand many more trips to that trailer!"

While the Florida junketings were going on, Reagan also began to show some progress in his courtship of Alabama, where the state chairman, Alfred Goldthwaite, was strong for him. Around noon on Wednesday, it looked as if the Nixon strength, commanded by Jim Martin, might slip below the break-even mark of thirteen out of twenty-six. If that happened, the whole delegation might shake loose. At the same time, Martin was under pressure from Thurmond to make Alabama yield to South Carolina in the nominating session. Alabama, as the first state to be called, both for nominating and balloting, is naturally one that can have some psychological impact on subsequent events. But under

convention procedure, a delegation can yield its privilege to nominate
to another delegation of its own choice lower down the alphabet.

If Thurmond's state could lead off, nominating him as a favorite
son, there would be personal glory for Strom. It would also be a way
of getting Nixon's candidacy off to a good start, because after the
speeches on his behalf Thurmond would, of course, withdraw in favor
of Nixon and suggest that everyone vote for him.

The problem, from Jim Martin's viewpoint, was that such an
arrangement might drive even more Alabamans into the Reagan camp.
Even the Nixon men felt they had to do something—anything, almost
—to show they were really, deep down, more attached to Ronnie. So
Martin thought up a compromise: Alabama would yield, not to South
Carolina, but to California, "out of their deep respect for that great
conservative, Ronald Reagan." It was not much, but it was something
to show the folks back home, the unreconstructed grass roots to whom
Nixon was a dangerous radical. And for Martin, it meant the retention of
precious Nixon votes.

To hold the South against the Reagan raiders might not be enough.
To have a margin of safety, Nixon had to make at least one successful
foray of his own into the heart of the urban, industrial North. In theory,
the possibilities were Ohio with 58 votes, Michigan with 48 votes, and
New Jersey with 40. (Pennsylvania, with 64 votes, which Governor
Raymond Shafer hoped to deliver to Rockefeller, was also vulnerable.
But large defections in this state were in some degree contingent on what
happened earlier in the roll call. New York, of course, with its 92 votes,
was almost unshakably for its own governor.) All three of the possible
delegations approached the convention with most of their votes committed to favorite-son candidates.

Michigan's favorite son was its governor George Romney, and its
allegiance was fairly deep-rooted. He had, after all, been a viable candidate at the turn of the year. Now he was, by his own admission, "a
dead duck"; it would have been an excessively harsh fate to lose even
the token kudos of a favorite-son candidacy. Four stubborn conservatives from Grosse Point were untouched by the sad saga of Romney's
Presidential aspirations and broke away to Nixon. But the rest of delegates stayed behind Romney. Ohio, similarly, was well under the control
of Governor Rhodes, despite the activities of a pro-Nixon Congressman from the state, John M. Ashbrook, who kept going on TV and
making alarmist appeals to his fellow delegates. "The boat's moving out,"
said Ashbrook, "and we're still on the shore."

New Jersey was much the most vulnerable. And because of its position midway through the roll call, with some of the biggest delegations to follow, it was deemed of critical importance. The governor of New Jersey was not a Republican, so the role of favorite son was taken over by the state's highly respected liberal Senator, Clifford Case. This in itself made discipline precarious: a Senator lacks a governor's invaluable control over jobs and offices. Case had to rely on his personality to keep a hold on his delegates, and for some of them, his personality was too liberal by half.

Still, Case had seemed capable of keeping them together for one ballot at least. A few weeks before the convention, the New Jersey delegates had caucused, and thirty-eight of them decided this would be the optimum policy. Only two went for Nixon. One of the two, however, was the formidable Frank Farley, the so-called King of the Boardwalk: more prosaically, the boss of that tawdry mecca for mass fun-loving, Atlantic City.

The measure of Farley's influence showed in the fact that, soon after the delegation reached Miami Beach, it was twenty-four for Case and eleven for Nixon, with five delegates from Bergen County hanging loose. In response to this, the Rockefeller camp mounted a desperate operation to shore up Case's position. Rockefeller himself reserved his sharpest attacks on Richard Nixon for the benefit of the Jerseymen— "He hasn't won an election on his own in eighteen years." But Farley and the Nixon delegate-hunters offered more immediate ego gratification. All eyes were on New Jersey. If Nixon could be helped over the top, the state would be a kingmaker.

For Nelson Gross, the ambitious young attorney who ran Bergen County, this was a siren call. Gross, whose county contains over a million people, most of them in prosperous dormitory towns, was a rising force in the state and eager to put on political muscle. Apart from himself, the Bergen delegate preferences stacked up evenly—two for Rockefeller and two for Nixon. And Bergen exercised a unit rule. So Gross found himself in the useful position of having five votes in his gift. Apprised of this, Nixon had gone out of his way to flatter Gross at a Tuesday morning reception. He recalled how, in 1956, Bergen had been carried by 160,000 for Eisenhower, and he reckoned that, with the kind of leadership they had there now, Bergen could do the same for him. Emerging from this cozy session, Gross was heard to remark, "It's time Bergen took the lead."

On Wednesday, the New Jersey delegation caucused three times in a desperate effort to hammer out a common line. At one stage, it seemed that Case might get all but a handful of his delegation back in the fold. But the Nixon people were putting on the pressure too: the South was holding, did New Jersey want to be left high and dry? Gross finally made up his mind—"We don't want to wind up with a dark-horse candidate"—and entered his votes in the Nixon column. By the time a bad-tempered New Jersey delegation decamped for the convention hall, it had split down the middle, twenty for Case and twenty for Nixon. Farley's machinations had given Nixon his vital break in the North, but he had generated a lot of ill will in the process. "There wasn't an ounce of principle in it," growled a mortified Rockefeller delegate. Case was angry too, but not hugely surprised. He had expected Farley's instinct for the political main chance might lead him in this direction. "He has always been," said Case, "a very flexible guy."

At five-thirty p.m., as the delegates assembled for the nominating session, Clif White called all his regional aides to the communications trailer. It was time for the final count. He had done less well than expected. By his reckoning, Reagan had barely cleared 180, while Nixon appeared to be over the top, with 682 votes. But this number included about forty individuals in states like Alabama, Florida, and Mississippi, who still might be encouraged to defect. The strategy for the rest of the night, therefore, was to locate these potential converts and bring them to the trailer for some concentrated wooing. Even as he put it into effect, Clif White felt it was no more than a gesture.

For White's private arithmetic virtually mirrored that of the CBS News count, and this had bitten into the delegates' consciousness. Nixon's lead looked unassailable. The prospect, then, with twelve names to be placed in nomination, was of a long, noisy, and unexciting evening. (The nominees were the three main contenders, plus Case of New Jersey, Romney of Michigan, Rhodes of Ohio, Rockefeller of Arkansas, Carlson of Kansas, and Fong of Hawaii. Thurmond and Governor Walter J. Hickel of Alaska were nominated but withdrew before the balloting. The other candidate was the inevitable Harold Stassen, placed in nomination by his nephew J. Robert Stassen, a member of the Minnesota delegation.) As the *New York Times* described it, "Ten hours of thundering cliché, of enervating restatement of the obvious, of planned 'spontaneous' demonstrating—the American nominating process." And at the end of it, a ballot rendered, by the expertise of the media's previous delegate counts, about as invigorating as a game of bingo in which everybody has the same cards and everybody knows what numbers are going to come up.

The basic pattern is time-honored: a nominating speech, followed by a floor demonstration in which supporters of the nominee prance, chant, and wave placards, often with the assistance of mercenaries in the joy-making art (Rockefeller had hired the Philadelphia Mummers, whose leader shyly confessed to being "a pretty stanch Democrat"), a proceeding that might occupy anything from one to thirty minutes, depending on the status of the nominee and the stamina of his admirers. Once order is restored, seconding speeches are made.

For the record, the demonstrations for the three main contenders lasted twenty-nine minutes in Rockefeller's case, twenty-five in Nixon's, and twenty-two in Reagan's. An intensity recorder, however, would probably have put Reagan marginally in front. But the demonstrations are a poor index to the eventual result and an obvious strain on the portly delegates, whose average age in Miami Beach was forty-eight years. Three weeks later, in Chicago, the Democrats decided to dispense with planned demonstrations of this kind. It was generally held to be an excellent idea.

But the night was not without genuine incident. And again it was the South that provided it. Suddenly, the insurgents found themselves in possession of a new, and totally unlooked-for weapon—that evening's copy of the *Miami Herald,* with a boldly written story saying that Hatfield would be Nixon's Vice-Presidential choice. Few delegates had seen it before arriving at the hall, but around eight p.m. squads of Reagan floor men moved through the Southern delegations dispensing copies as if their political lives depended on it. See, they implied, Nixon is going to betray the South, after all. (A similar story, that morning, tipping that Nixon would pick a liberal, had been largely ignored. Back in May, on the occasion of Rockefeller's meeting with the Southern party chairmen, its authors, the syndicated columnists Rowland Evans and Robert Novak, had deployed such an Eastern establishment manner, and had flashed polls showing Rockefeller's strength so diligently to the politicians they were supposed to be interviewing, that they were widely assumed to be on Rockefeller's staff.)

For the next hour, it was like Monday night all over again. Clif White no longer felt he was going through the motions; this really might be the "break." The Alabama and Mississippi leaders located Dent and

Thurmond and said it was too difficult, they needed time to reorganize
and see how the other votes stacked up. They wanted to pass on the first
roll call.

Thurmond was furious: if the South wavered now, it would encourage the Rockefeller waverers to hold in the North. They would have
to get their delegations in line somehow; he knew for a fact the *Herald*
story couldn't be true.

In the end, it boiled down to the old put-up-or-shut-up line. Reed
pacified his Mississippians with this expedient—"I said I would put a
hundred dollars on my conviction that Hatfield would not be Veep.
There were no takers. I raised the bet higher, and higher. Still no
takers. . . ."

Bo Callaway, starting in the thousand-dollar class, cowed the
Georgians in similar fashion. It was no time for niceties. The most
impressive achievement was that of Harry Dent, who spotted Don
Oberdorfer, the man who wrote the *Herald* story, and dragged him in
front of a pack of doubting Louisianans. "Come on, I'll have three
hundred dollars with you your story is wrong." Oberdorfer declined
the wager. Louisiana was deeply impressed.

Thurmond, meanwhile, had grabbed a megaphone, the better to
project his derision at the idea of his allowing the South to be fooled.
Between bellows down this device, he found time to tell a television
reporter, "The South loves Reagan, but it won't break. It's just a matter
of calling the roll."

And so it was.

At one-nineteen a.m. precisely, the high-pitched voice of Mrs.
Bailey, the Convention Secretary, calls, "Alabama?" Fourteen votes for
Nixon, 12 for Reagan—so Jim Martin, after all his tribulations, has
managed to salvage a slender margin for his candidate. A mildly auspicious portent for the front-runner. The A's through D go as expected—
Arkansas holds behind its governor, Winthrop Rockefeller, as does California for Reagan. All the experts are waiting for Florida—32 votes
for Nixon, one (the Governor) for Rockefeller, and one (a man who
explained to his colleagues that he could not risk voting for a dangerous
radical like Nixon) for Reagan. The *aficionados* know it is all over.
Bruce Bradley, Rockefeller's deputy floor manager, had been prepared
to poll the New York delegation to give a little extra time for working on
the later delegations. Now he knows he does not have to bother. Illinois,
as everyone expects, is closer to the sentiments of Everett Dirksen than
to those of his colleague Charles Percy—50 of Illinois's 58 votes for

Nixon. Iowa, a curio—the Iowa delegates, so carried away by the social amenities of Miami Beach, had found themselves unable to organize a caucus for three days. They never did get fully organized: 13 votes for Nixon, 8 for Rockefelleer, 3 for Reagan. Maryland—a painful reminder for Rockefeller of what can be lost by hesitating. Agnew takes 17 votes with him into the Nixon column, leaving a rump of 8 for his one-time champion. Louisiana—Reagan detaches 7 of its 26 votes. Not enough. Michigan firm for Romney, with only 4 defections to Nixon. Mississippi now absolutely firm, all 20 votes to Nixon.

New Jersey and favorite son Clifford Case demands a poll of the delegation. Each delegate has to deliver his vote individually in front of the microphone. Nobody can avoid the spotlight. It is a last-ditch effort to shame some of the dissenters back in line. But the delegation's back is still broken—22 for Case, 18 for Nixon. Now everybody knows it's all over. A Rockefeller floor man goes over to Governor Rhodes to tell him that if he wants to go with the winner to please his fellow delegates, it's O.K. by him. Rhodes snarls, "Screw them." Ohio—56 votes for its favorite son, 2 for Nixon. There is one mild surprise left: Reagan's vote in Texas, expected to be up in the 20's, is only 15. But what can any Reagan vote do at this stage? At one-fifty a.m., Wisconsin casts its 30 votes for Nixon, as it was bound to do by virtue of a primary victory, and he is over the top.

The final scorecard: Nixon 692, Rockefeller 277, Reagan 182, Rhodes 55, Romney 50, Case 22, Carlson 20, Winthrop Rockefeller 18, Hiram Fong 14, Stassen 2, Lindsay 1.

In the end, it was as it was in the beginning: Nixon had it sewed up. But between the original concept and the consummation, there had been Strom Thurmond, and the need to placate him first on the score of his military phobias in Atlanta and second over the Vice-Presidential selection at the convention. Before turning to the actual processes by which Nixon arrived at his selection of a running mate, it is worth looking in more detail at the character of the kingmaker.

4

One Strom

"STROM IS FANTASTIC"

—Hand-painted placard waved by a member
of the South Carolina delegation when Strom
Thurmond's name was placed in nomination
as a favorite son at the 1968 National Republican Convention

War, said Clausewitz, is the continuation of politics by other
means. Politics, for the South, is the continuation by other means of the
Civil War. And it was Strom Thurmond's services in this cause, not his
Republican credentials and certainly not his charm, that made him such
a key figure at the convention.

After the event, the Nixon camp lost no time in pooh-poohing the
significance of Thurmond. This afterthought cannot be sustained by the
evidence. As we shall see, Nixon took pains to ensure that Thurmond
should feel that his part in the Vice-Presidential selection process was
crucial. For the fact is that, without Thurmond as an active proselytizing
force among the Dixie delegations, Nixon could not have achieved his
first-ballot victory. It was possible to stop Nixon in the South. But it
proved impossible to stop Thurmond—the South's most fanatical up-
holder of states' rights and segregation.

On the surface, the degree of his influence seems surprising. For
Thurmond, though representative of a certain kind of Southerner, is in
no way a typical Southern politician. Whatever their other faults, Southern politicos at the national level are rarely deficient in the saving grace
of humor. For most, it is an essential personality ingredient. Obliged to
fight in a political battleground where lip service to egalitarian principles
is the norm, they are daily confronted with the disparity between high

pretensions and brutal political realities. Given the choice implicit in such
a situation—laughter or tears—most, very sensibly, opt for the former,
an option commonly braced by heavy libations of Southern Comfort.
The South is the cruelest part of the United States; but, perhaps for this
reason, it can produce leaders with a sense of their own and their region's
absurdity.

Indeed, even that most devastating of electoral liabilities in the Deep
South—a suspicion of being "soft on niggers"—can sometimes be offset
by great masters of the comic art, like Big Jim Folsom, George Wallace's predecessor as Governor of Alabama. (Folsom once dismissed a
particularly crass piece of local anti-Negro legislation as "hogwash—it
reminds me of an old hound dog hollerin' at the moon.")

Nobody could ever accuse Thurmond of having a sense of humor.
His is a nature without nuance. He squares the contradictions implied
in leadership of the South by simply not seeing them. He is for states'
rights, pure living, segregation, Bible-thumping, and prune juice. He
is against fun, trade-unionism, alcohol, Communism, and tobacco, all
of which he treats as part of the same malady. A reserve major general
in the U.S. Army, he has been known to speak sympathetically of the
possibility of military rule in the United States. Robert Sherrill, a native
of Frog Pond, Georgia, in his marvelously perceptive book *Gothic
Politics in the Deep South,* gives the best clue to the climate of Thurmond's mind in his discussion of the South Carolinian's world view. It is,
he writes, "a Ptolemaic world of metaphysical absolutes. . . . It is a
world of pure blood. It is a world of one Eden, one Hell, one Heaven,
one Right, one Wrong, one Strom."

If mental health is an ability to correlate physical observation with
the workings of the intellect, then Strom Thurmond is stone mad. Unlike
other Southern leaders, he has no tinge of cynicism in his super-
patriotism. It is not, for him, a device to divert attention from the generous evidences of oppression in his own state. "Mississippi and South
Carolina," he once said, "are the two most democratic states in the nation"; *he* meant it.

But the essential point about Thurmond is not that he is absurd,
humorless, and irrational, but that, from the perspective of an ordinary
white Southerner, he has always been a man of principle. In Thurmond,
the savage impulses of the South find godly expression. It is this that
makes him such a fearsome political opponent. He is a holy warrior
with a record to prove it. (This reputation sometimes enabled him to
do things that few other Southern politicians would dare. As Governor

of South Carolina, he once ordered the arrest and trial of a white gang involved in lynching a Negro—at that time a highly original idea as far as South Carolina was concerned. But the flavor of Thurmond's attitudes is better conveyed by a case over which he presided as a judge, a trial of a Negro accused of raping a white woman. The jury returned a guilty verdict but asked for mercy; Thurmond lamented that he was thus prevented from sentencing the accused to more than forty years in prison.)

Thurmond was Governor of South Carolina when he engineered the Dixiecrat breakaway from the national Democratic Party on the issue of the 1948 civil-rights plank (the work of an uppity Minnesota liberal called Hubert Horatio Humphrey). And his leadership of the Democratic States' Rights Party in that year made him a figure of Southern fame and national notoriety. In national electoral terms, his Presidential candidacy was a futile gesture—the Dixiecrats took Mississippi, Louisiana, Alabama, and South Carolina and finished a derisory third—but in the South he became a man to reckon with. Other Southern leaders might disagree with his method, many of them being of the opinion that the way to keep the South the way they wanted it was to adopt a softly-softly policy in the national arena, but they now knew that many of their constituents were not averse to an occasional Gadarene.

Thurmond's subsequent record as a Democratic Senator (the only one ever to be elected as a write-in candidate) evinced a similar pattern. Inevitably, his humorlessness made him a loner in that assembly of clubmen. And this was compounded by his insensitivity to Southern legislative tactics. His great filibuster in 1957, while enhancing his grasp on grass-roots allegiances, was not an action that earned him friends among other Southern Senators, even though their racial perceptions were not much at variance with his. (It was, however, the occasion on which Barry Goldwater demonstrated *his* friendship by coming in twice during the performance with some minor remarks about the military-pay bill, giving Thurmond the opportunity to use the facilities of the men's room.) For most of the Southerners, the civil-rights bill was a bitter pill, but one they felt constrained to swallow. The majority leader, Lyndon Johnson, had made it marginally more palatable by the insertion of nonenforcement compromises. At the last ditch, they decided to let the legislation slip through without strenuous counteraction, the only effect of which would have been to draw attention to the fact of their defeat.

Thurmond's ill-timed filibuster made them all look foolish. To their constituents, it seemed that only Thurmond was standing up for the

South in its hour of need. Among his Senatorial colleagues, of course, Thurmond, not themselves, had been the betrayer of Southern honor. His filibuster produced a lofty, if elliptical, rebuke from the doyen of the Southern aristocracy, Senator Richard Russell of Georgia: "If I had undertaken a filibuster for personal political aggrandizement, I would have forever reproached myself for being guilty of a form of treason against the people of the South." Far from reproaching himself, Thurmond went on his way, aggrandized.

He is, however, most remembered in the Senate not for his filibustering achievements, but for a wrestling match. The occasion for this particular manifestation of the Thurmond technique was a meeting of the Senate Commerce Committee in 1964, where the appointment of a man unpalatable to Thurmond was being considered. Thurmond, therefore, hung around the door to the committee room, hoping to deter Senators from going in and making a quorum. One such was the liberal Senator from Texas, Ralph Yarborough, who shook Thurmond's hand on his way into the room and cheerily urged the South Carolinian to come on in. When Yarborough tried to loose his hand, he couldn't. Thurmond had it fast, and had taken the tease seriously: "I'll make an agreement with you, Ralph. If I can keep you out, you won't go in, and if you can drag me in, I'll stay there."

It was an unequal contest. Thurmond, though not large and sixty-two years old at the time, is a shape-keeper much addicted to push-ups. Yarborough is shaped like a Senator. For ten minutes, Thurmond held Yarborough pinioned to the floor, repeating the while: "Tell me to release you, Ralph, and I will." Ultimately, the committee chairman, Senator Warren Magnuson, had to come out and put an end to this unusual process of Senatorial reasoning. (Such tactics were not entirely alien to the traditions of Edgefield County, Strom Thurmond's birthplace. Among the many ferocious political figures associated with this area was Congressman Preston S. Brooks, the man who, back in the pre-Civil War era, caned Senator Charles Sumner of Massachusetts on the Senate floor to avenge Sumner's verbal attack on his uncle, Senator Andrew Pickens Butler.)

That year, 1964, Thurmond ceased to be the laughingstock of the Southern Democrats and became the pillar of Dixie Republicanism. His change of party, like that of many others in his region, was occasioned by Goldwater's "Southern strategy." It did not entail any ideological agonizing on Thurmond's part. Rather, it eased any he might have had; he had never been very much at home with the hold, fall back, and regroup legislative tactics of the Southern Democratic leaders. Goldwater Republicanism seemed to offer an opportunity to go back on the offensive.

Thurmond, like everybody else, was sobered by the electoral effects of Goldwaterism. But he stayed on to recast his state's Republican Party in an image that must have made Abe Lincoln revolve in his grave. In 1966, South Carolina's all-white Republican State Convention deliberated underneath a banner of the Confederacy. In the Senate, Thurmond's conduct continued to delight his electors and appall those who fondly revered the Senate as a great debating chamber. And in 1968 he came to the Miami Beach convention with the South fully and recently apprised that his fervor remained undiminished. In July, he had been one of the leaders of the Senate Judiciary Committee's assault on Justice Abe Fortas. Fortas was an intimate friend of President Johnson's. This was sin enough in Thurmond's eyes: back in 1966, Thurmond had described his old Senate leader as "a traitor to the nation and the South." More important, however, was the fact that Fortas had, as a member of the Supreme Court, always lined up on the liberal side of civil-rights questions. The fact that he was a lapsed Southerner—Fortas had been reared in Tennessee—only made the treason worse. The South, and some Northern Republicans, naturally wanted Fortas's nomination to the Chief Justiceship blocked in hopes that a more amenable appointment would be forthcoming when and if the Republicans took office.

Of all the performances during the committee's hearings, Thurmond's was by far the most memorable, surpassing even his own high standards of bully-ragging, pig-ignorance, and splenetic irrelevance. Knowing full well that Foras must refuse to discuss individual cases, on the grounds that it would rupture the constitutional distinctions between the legislative and judicial branches, Thurmond, nonetheless, spent four hours putting questions to Fortas in this area—a procedure that resulted in Fortas's refusal to testify being scrawled across the record no fewer than fifty times.

Thurmond had chosen as his target (any one would do, it was the consumption of time that was important) the court decisions that guaranteed the rights of criminal defendants. And it led down some strange rhetorical alleys. "Mallory!" bellowed Thurmond, at one point, "Mallory! I want that word to ring in your ears. Mallory, a man who raped a woman, admitted his guilt, and the court turned him loose on a technicality. . . . Can you, as Justice of the Court, condone a decision such as that?" *Mallory v U.S.* was decided in 1957, eight years before Fortas reached the bench. Thurmond's outrage knew no bounds at the thought of a defendant's rights sometimes resulting in the guilty going free. "Aren't you after the truth?" he asked Fortas. "What difference does it make if there is a lawyer present or not? What difference does it make if you get the truth?" Fortas observed that the difference might be the Constitution. At another juncture, Thurmond, near the nub of his complaint, asked whether Fortas agreed that the Supreme Court was "the principal reason for the turmoil and the air of revolutionary conditions that prevailed in Washington." Fortas, barely keeping his ice-cool, said, "No."

Thurmond's history as a liberal-basher made him a magnificent instrument for Nixon at the convention. Nixon, for all his back-room sweet talking, was, to the Southerners, suspect on race: he had once advised Republicans not to go prospecting for the "fool's gold" of racist votes. Nobody could pin such an alarming sentiment on Thurmond. If ever a man had a reputation for belligerent—if not entirely effective— militancy on behalf of the South, it was the frightful Strom. Yet there he was at Miami Beach, advocating the trimmer's course. If Thurmond could stomach compromise, then what Southerner could hold out against it?

In his set-piece sessions with Southern delegates, Thurmond, for the benefit of those few not entirely familiar with his services to the cause, would be introduced by his state chairman, Harry Dent, the theory being that Dent would sell Thurmond while Thurmond sold Nixon. In merchandising Thurmond, his fellow South Carolinian would dilate on his unswerving allegiance to Southern interests. Sure, it would require sacrifices to go for Nixon, but whose sacrifices could compare with Strom's?

And he was right. In the November elections, Nixon carried South Carolina, but most of the state Republicans running for office had a hard time. Thurmond's anti-Wallace, anti-Reagan stand had taken its toll. He may have been a kingmaker in Miami Beach, but back home there were many who felt that he had become that most treacherous animal in the bestiary of Southern politics: the crusader turned compromiser.

5

The Strange Death of
the Liberal Republicans

"I have a deep sense of the improbability of this moment."

> —Spiro T. Agnew, Vice-Presidential nominee,
> addressing the 1968 Republican National
> Convention

"It's some kind of disease."
"It's some kind of egg."
"He's a Greek who owns that shipbuilding firm."

> —Definitions of "Spiro Agnew" given by three
> Atlanta pedestrians interviewed on television
> the day Nixon announced his choice for
> Vice-Presidential candidate

"The man who would risk putting this country in Agnew's hands is, aptly, the man who puts the destiny of his immortal soul, presuming there is such a thing, in Billy Graham's hands, or Dr. Peale's."

> —Garry Willis, in *Esquire*

The mountains labored and produced: Spiro T. Agnew. A selection rapidly followed by some unhelpful Southern war whoops. "This is wonderful," crowed the boss of the Louisiana delegation, Tom Stagg. "It shows the South did have veto power." From the Northern wing of the party came little but an uneasy silence, punctuated by the sound of hurried telephone calls. Some, though not nearly enough, of the Republican Party's liberals were at last preparing to do open battle, but on a front that could not in logic be justified: contesting the Presidential nominee's right to have a running mate of his choice.

Nor could they even claim that Nixon had done it without consulting—if not heeding—all viewpoints in the party. The liberals knew they had been outmaneuvered. But how could they prove it? Even if they could prove it, what could they do about it? And, in the end, did they really feel strongly enough about it? Too many had gone along with Nixon's "nuts and bolts" strategy—victory first, ideology afterward—to wax hot now over what would seem to outsiders the obscurities of their candidate's running-mate selection. Why split the party over a lost cause?

Nixon, naturally, knew this better than anybody else. He had emphasized all along that his nominee would be acceptable to *all* regions; but what region felt so strongly as the South? Thurmond had braced the Mississippians by telling them that if Nixon let him down on the Number-Two selection, he personally would denounce the candidate from the convention floor. Nobody, in advance of the nomination or even after, had evinced such intransigence on behalf of the Northern liberals. The North might not be satisfied, but, ultimately, they would accept less than half a loaf. They had no choice. "Sure," said a laconic Nixon aide, contemptuously conceding one limitation on the North's indulgence, "the Bronx would have hated a Nazi."

Why all the fuss? The job of the Vice-President has not changed radically since Thomas R. Marshall, commenting in 1920 that it resembled a "cataleptic state," said that the Vice-President "cannot speak; he cannot move; he suffers no pain; and yet he is perfectly conscious of everything that is going on about him." The dog's-body qualities of the office, as Richard Nixon and Hubert Humphrey knew all too well, had survived down the years. Nelson Rockefeller's speculations about his Vice-Presidential potential—"I wasn't designed as stand-by equipment"—conveyed how unappealing the job was to men of independent stature.

What had changed, however, was the electorate's perceptions of the office. Even before Dallas—in fact, since the mid-fifties and the first of President Eisenhower's major heart attacks—Americans, brought by television into a new degree of intimacy with the Presidency, had been made aware how easily today's Number Two could be tomorrow's Number One. The duties of the Vice-President might seem more akin to those of a cheerleader than a policy-maker, but nobody could forget that, in the popular phrase, he was only a heartbeat away from supreme office.

Although this thought was sobering for all concerned in the running-mate selection process at Miami Beach, it was scarcely dominant. Nixon seemed healthy enough, and, being totally devoid of charismatic qualities, he made low-grade assassin bait. As far as anyone could predict these things, it seemed that if Nixon made it to the Presidency, he would live through it.

It was not so much Nixon's mortality that was the problem; it was his mandate. The don't-rock-the-boat policy had been a success—almost too much of a success. Nixon had campaigned all year and won the nomination without at any stage confronting the issues head on. Yet everyone knew that there were at least two Republican roads to the Presidency, either of which, because of his hitherto contentless "consensus," Nixon could take. The one to the left attacked the Democrats in the big industrial states and went boldly for progressive policies in America's great population and problem centers. The one to the right depended on detaching potential Wallace votes, particularly in the border states, capitalizing on the fear of violence in the cities, and doing nothing to disturb the ingrained conservatism of the Republican Midwest.

Which road would Nixon take? His choice of Vice-President, it seemed, would give the clue. In the end, this question, like so many others, was never squarely faced. The Republican Vice Presidential nominee emerged as philosophically insubstantial as the man who chose him. It was a price the party, and finally America, accepted in the name of "unity."

The selection of Spiro T. Agnew was an intriguing process: a classic example of the importance Nixon places on what *seems* to be done rather than what *is* done. Every section of the party was not only going to be "consulted" but, more important, everybody was going to be fully apprised of the process. (This trait was to become absurd after the election, when all sixty-two thousand people in *Who's Who in America* were flamboyantly solicited for their views on government appointments.) It is Nixon's version of the politics of participation. The advantage of it is that a body large and diffuse enough is never likely to come to complete agreement; the convener of such events, finding disagreement on all sides, is therefore able to impose the name, or policy, he originally had in mind.

The events at Miami in the early hours of Thursday morning can best be seen in terms of John Kenneth Galbraith's concept of the "no-business" meeting. This useful device—most notably developed by President Hoover in the midst of his economic troubles—consists of reassuring people that if enough wise men can be seen to be meeting, good news must follow. Such is not the case. The meeting itself is the news.

Nixon's theatrical discussions about a running mate were along these lines. Their function was to involve all those people Nixon judged to have influence within various factions of the party. Much ostentatious burning of midnight oil was involved; and the names of those consulted, some fifty in all, were released, with times of consultation, to a copy-hungry press. (A conspicuous absentee was Nelson Rockefeller. He was asked afterward by a reporter whether he had had any part in the oper-ation. The reporter thought he must have, since it was his understanding —an erroneous one—that one hundred leading Republicans had taken part in the process. "I guess," said Rockefeller, "that makes me, fella, the hundred and first.") In default of human drama, a charade suffices. For, despite all the to-ing and fro-ing, there is no evidence that the party leaders' long night's journey into day affected Nixon's choice in the slightest. In fact, the thought that Spiro Agnew would be his best running mate had been in Nixon's mind since June. John Sears, Nixon's dele-gate reconaissance man, subsequently told us that Nixon finally decided on Agnew ten days before the convention. He did not inform Agnew, so the option to change his mind was left open, but no arguments for an alternative selection that Nixon had not already anticipated were likely to come up.

As "no-business" meetings, however, the Nixon consultations in Miami Beach were impressive. At two-ten a.m. Thursday, Nixon had the nomination. By two-fifteen, sprawled in an armchair in the solárium off his Hilton penthouse suite, he was deep in talks with the vanguard of the army of politicians he and his staff were to "consult" in the course of the night.

The structure of this group, and the one which followed it, is interesting not only for Nixon's apparent assessment of who holds power within the Republican Party, but because each group was so precisely balanced. Everything was designed to whittle the options down to one man.

There were twenty-four people present at that first meeting, thirteen staffers and eleven outside political advisers. Nixon's Southern manager, Bo Callaway of Georgia, was carefully balanced against Minnesota Congressman Clark McGregor. Fred LaRue, Nixon's man in Mississippi, sat with Senator Roman Hruska of Nebraska. That was the pattern.

When Nixon opened by declaring, "I have brought no names to Miami" —a comment none of those present believed—it was inevitable that the meeting would oblige with the most disparate suggestions.

Nixon did the talking—the meeting lasted only fifteen minutes or so—as he defined what he wanted of his nominee: the unimpeachable virtues of competence and loyalty. As Nixon appreciated, however, many of the competent people were controversial. "I've had polls on these glamour boys," he said cuttingly. "If they help you in one place, they hurt you in another. If I want to win this, I'm going to have to win it on my own." (In fact, Nixon's private polls showed something even more curious than the damage inflicted by "glamour boys." They revealed that Nixon ran best with no running mate at all. Another name on the ticket destroyed the ideological vacuum that was Nixon's chief political asset.)

What names, Nixon wanted to know, had the convention thrown up? The candidates which emerged, however, ostensibly for further consideration, bore little relation to the realities either of what Nixon personally wanted or of what the party factions would accept. There were names like Reagan, Lindsay, and Hatfield, any of which could cause a revolt. There was a junior Congressman from Texas, who Nixon expressly said was too inexperienced but added to his list. Among the rest, was the name of Spiro T. Agnew.

The second house opened at two-forty-five a.m., before another well-structured audience of party satraps. There could be little doubt which section of the party this was. Twenty-two men settled down with cigars and tumblers of whisky, and only one—Illinois Congressman Don Rumsfeld—could properly be called a liberal. The clout lay with the South and West: Strom Thurmond himself, with Harry Dent; Florida party boss Bill Murfin; Governor Louie Nunn of Kentucky, a conservative even by the rigorous standards of the border states; a Congressman from Tennessee, William Brock; and from the West, the formidable contingent of Barry Goldwater and his Arizona allies Senator Paul Fannin and Congressman John Rhodes. The centrist counterweights were men like Governor Jim Rhodes of Ohio; Senator Jack Miller of Iowa; Eisenhower's Attorney General, Herbert Brownell; and, from California, Nixon's closest political friend, Lieutenant Governor Finch. The ubiquitous evangelist Billy Graham, a man who on occasions has brought spiritual solace to President Johnson, was also present. He urged that the group select "a man of high moral standards."

Everyone else had names. The list compiled by Senator Karl Mundt of North Dakota—once a lieutenant of Joe McCarthy's, now mellowed but scarcely modernized by the passage of time—was not untypical. Nixon had asked him (and most of the others) to sound out delegate feelings, and Mundt now had a fistful of names scrawled on a sticky envelope. On the right, the conservative choices: Reagan, John Tower, and Senator Howard Baker of Tennessee. On the left, names supposedly good for the ticket in the cities: among them, Lindsay, Romney, and the languid ex-Governor of Pennsylvania, William Scranton.

Thurmond's list was the subject of rather more attention. At its head, inevitably: Reagan. Failing him, Baker. Thurmond also confessed an affection for Senator Robert P. Griffin of Michigan, who had been in the vanguard of the attack on Abe Fortas in the Senate. Finally, almost as an afterthought, Thurmond mentioned two men in the "acceptable" category: John Volpe, the three-term Governor of Massachusetts and Agnew of Maryland.

Whom did Nixon want? At this stage, Nixon was not forthcoming with names, confining himself to sniping at the "glamour boys" whenever they seemed to be flying too high. But he had a few parameters. The man selected should have some knowledge of the cities, he suggested . . . probably a governor, since that would encourage the other twenty-five Republican governors to fight for the ticket . . . and what about the ethnic vote? The Republicans had tended to ignore those, but perhaps they should court them this time. . . .

Eventually, about eighteen names were flying through the haze of cigar smoke, only to be shot down by one faction or another. The battle lines can scarcely have surprised Nixon. Thurmond and Goldwater barred the liberals, while Rhodes, Miller, and Brownell cut down the extreme right-wingers. It was Rhodes, in fact, who most effectively punctured Thurmond's promotion of Ronald Reagan. "With Reagan on the ticket, we'd lose Ohio worse than nineteen sixty-four," he said. It was an awesome judgment: Johnson took Ohio by more than a million votes. It was also unsentimental, coming from a man to whom Reagan had offered the Vice-Presidency in the event of his nomination.

Predictably, they were deadlocked. A lowering of the sights produced less controversy, if not agreement. Two men seemed to fit neatly into Nixon's criteria: John Volpe, an Italian-American, and Spiro Agnew, a Greek-American—and both had been deemed "acceptable" by Thurmond. These two, with Baker of Tennessee, survived into the final rounds. Volpe, because of his administrative experience, so clearly seemed to have the edge in this trio that few of those stumbling off to bed at six a.m. had given Agnew much detailed consideration. "We thought it was clear," said one Southerner. "For the North, it was Volpe. For the South, it was Baker. Nobody looked hard at Agnew. We were all looking higher and lower."

So Nixon went to bed, the nomination in his pocket and his immediate task achieved. The "no-business" meetings had worked, and, with relative good will all around, each faction had been driven toward the center. Nixon had what he wanted, the semblance of unity. The remarkable thing is that, by breakfast time, Nixon should have been forced to consider shattering that unity. For an hour on Thursday morning, Nixon was under immense pressure to take John Lindsay as his Vice-Presidential choice.

When Nixon—his eyes puffy with fatigue—walked into the Jackie of Hearts Room in the Hilton at nine a.m. Thursday, the composition of the meeting dictated that this would be very different from the previous two. They had been factional; this was strategic—with advisers like Ray Bliss, Everett Dirksen, Gerald Ford, the bosses of the two Congressional campaign committees, Senator George Murphy and Congressman Bob Wilson, and Nixon's floor manager, Rogers Morton.

Significantly, the Deep South was not represented; instead, there were two of the Texas party bosses, Senator Tower and state chairman Peter O'Donnell. For this meeting was concerned with the simplest of practicalities: whose name on the ticket would win most votes? In that context, the South was irrelevant. Southern votes had won Nixon the nomination, but few believed that Southern votes—except perhaps those of Texas—would win him the election. Wallace would see to that. As for Strom Thurmond, he might have saved Nixon in Miami, but Ray Bliss had polls disputing whether Thurmond could even save his own state in November. So what profit was there in choosing a Vice-President to please the South?

On the other hand, Bob Wilson pointed out, his campaign committee had polls on the "fringe Democrats"—"the sort who call themselves independent but always drift the same way in the end," as one of Wilson's pollsters said later. This time, it seemed, they were fed up with the Democratic Party. A bold choice of running mate could cut into that bloc, Wilson urged. And that meant Lindsay.

Gerald Ford spoke up with Wilson. From his vantage point in the House of Representatives, Ford knew that the House seats the party desperately needed to take over would have to be won in the North. Which also dictated Lindsay—or Hatfield.

But Tower, the spokesman for the right, produced a counterargument. Was Wallace so unbeatable in the South? "Personally," Tower said later, "I reckoned perhaps half of Wallace's strength in some states might be sheared away by a determined assault from the right." But, Tower argued, there was only one man with the appeal to achieve that: Ronald Reagan.

O'Donnell, the other Texas boss, had a hand in proposing one of the more original scenarios. Why not accept the logic of Nixon's own view that no single nominee could appeal across the country? Decide which states were marginal but crucial and tailor the choice to those, he suggested. There could be no doubt of the most coveted states in that category, California and Texas. And the most appealing choices for them would be two men actually at the meeting: O'Donnell's good friend John Tower, or Nixon's good friend Robert Finch.

From Nixon's viewpoint, the meeting was a disaster. The conservatimes and liberals were united. They both wanted him to take a chance.

"Nixon didn't want to hear," said one of the participants later. "We talked about who would strengthen the ticket. And he kept saying that he didn't think a ticket with him on it could be strengthened. 'I'm going to have to win this on my own,' he kept saying." (Nixon, naturally, was reluctant to divulge the poll evidence that he ran best on his own.)

It was the compromise candidates again. Congressman Rogers Morton confided to friends later that maybe he had disappointed "the boss." Perhaps, when it came to a compromise, Nixon had imagined that he, Morton, would nominate his fellow Marylander Governor Agnew. In the event, Morton's desire to be helpful was somewhat dampened by the fact that Senator George Murphy had just nominated *him*. And more than one person at the meeting agreed that if a Marylander were required —Maryland being poised nicely between North and South—then Morton had far greater qualifications than Agnew.

Briskly, Nixon broke up the meeting, only to convene yet another one upstairs in his penthouse. His "advisers" were whittled down to six: three staffers, Mitchell, Haldeman, and Ellsworth, plus three survivors from the previous meeting, Morton, Tower, and Finch. "Well," said Nixon, "we seem to have come down to you three"—pointing at the three politicians—"or Ted Agnew."

"Frankly, I was slightly bored by this stage," said one contender. "I knew he didn't want any of us. Why not call Agnew? But we went on with the charade, going into the next room while we were discussed, all that business."

The unreality of the scene was heightened by the fact—unknown to most of the other participants—that, as Tower came upstairs, he had been asked by Nixon to phone Strom Thurmond. "If you had to choose between Volpe and Agnew, who would you choose?" Tower asked Thurmond. It was a rigged question: no other candidates were mentioned; and any fool knew that Thurmond would prefer the more "Southerly" of these two "acceptables." So Thurmond, too, was maneuvered into thinking that he had played a vital role while in fact merely endorsing a choice Nixon had already made.

"Well," Nixon said, "I think this meeting has accomplished about all that it can accomplish. Rogers," turning to Morton, "would you put in a call to Ted Agnew, and I'll speak to him."

At twelve-forty p.m. Thursday, Nixon walked into the American Scene Room of the Hilton to unveil his selection to the press. From his prologue, it seemed, incredibly, that Nixon might actually be about to nominate a man unpalatable to the South. They had, said Nixon, labored through the night—one in which he personally had had only an hour's sleep—to find a man qualified on three crucial counts. First, he had to possess the capacity to be a good President; second, he should have effective campaigning ability; and third—this with emphasis—he had to be a man "who could assume the new responsibilities that I will give the new Vice-President, particularly in the area of the problems of the states and the cities." And then came the name.

"Spiro *who?*" was a common reaction, even among some seasoned reporters. Despite the fact that he had placed Nixon's name in nomination, Agnew's personality had made little impact at Miami Beach. And only one leading correspondent, David Broder of the *Washington Post,* had predicted Agnew's selection in advance of the convention.

But the little that was known about him pleased the South. For Agnew's chief political distinction in the course of the year had been to start out as a racial liberal and arrive at midsummer, in the wake of the spring riots, as Mr. Backlash in person.

Spiro Theodore Agnew was born in 1919, the son of a poor Greek immigrant. The family name was Anagnostopoulos, which Spiro's father, presciently, shortened. The son completed the Americanization process, converting from Greek Orthodoxy to Episcopalianism, and embarked on a mild version of the Horatio Alger success story. Raised and educated in Baltimore, Agnew was studying to be a lawyer when his education was interrupted by the war. And he had, as the expression goes, "a good war" —attaining the rank of company commander in the Tenth Armored

Division. With the cessation of hostilities, Agnew went back to complete his legal studies at the University of Baltimore. He was already upwardly mobile. After a few years in legal practice, he changed his party allegiance to suit his new-found, albeit modest, affluence: from Democratic to Republican.

His rise, however, was not that of the rugged individualist so popular in American legend. Indeed, the one marked trait in his career seems to be a talent for merging with new backgrounds. It is the expression of frontier spirit adapted to the needs of a corporate society. His basic drive, therefore, seems not to have been for money or power, but for a somewhat more anodyne commodity: status. Predictably, he reacts most vigorously when his sense of personal status is assailed.

Agnew's activist interest in politics came late and did not get off to a particularly auspicious start. In 1960, for instance, the year Nixon first ran for the Presidency, Agnew finished fifth out of five in a Baltimore County judicial race. At that time, Republican may have been a respectable label in business, but it carried little weight in a predominantly Democratic state. Two years later, however, Agnew found himself County Executive of Baltimore County, a burgeoning area of suburban growth (population six hundred twenty thousand) which had suddenly grown tired of its feuding Democratic machine. And this was the springboard to the Maryland governorship—achieved in 1966, in contention with a Democrat who ran an explicitly racist campaign. Thus Agnew entered the big league with a progressive image which, with genuine fervor, he strove to burnish: bringing qualified Negroes into the Administration and ensuring the passage of the state's first fair-housing law. It seemed natural that he should be part of a draft-Rockefeller operation.

Then came what he took as two jabs to his vanity. The first, in March 1968, was over Rockefeller's initial withdrawal from the Presidential race, leaving Agnew out on a limb, with a bad case of bruised pride. Then came the riots after Martin Luther King's death. There were riots all over the country, but Agnew took what happened in Baltimore almost as personal insult. He had to call out the National Guard and ask for Federal troops to restore order. Convinced that he had done all that any man could reasonably do to alleviate black grievances, Agnew suspected a conspiracy. (Stokely Carmichael had visited Baltimore shortly before the outbreak.) To ventilate his rage, Agnew summoned a meeting of a hundred moderate Negro leaders and subjected them to a full-dress bawling out. Most of them had spent the preceding week trying to "cool it," and now they were being assaulted with the absurd charge of being parties to a conspiracy to riot (a charge which, as one commentator pointed out, would have made sense only if Agnew could establish that Carmichael had plotted King's assassination). Eighty of those present walked out on the Governor.

But Agnew lost no time in blocking out a new image. In subsequent speeches, he criticized the Kerner Commission for encouraging rioting by talking of "white racism"; announced himself in favor of shooting looters; and pin-pointed the cause of urban disturbances as "the misguided compassion of public opinion." By the end of April, his carefully nurtured appeal to the ghettos had vanished. The *volte-face* was visceral rather than ideological. What came to the surface was a feeling shared by many white immigrants and their children: a deep resentment that Negroes should claim through disorder what the Anagnostopouloses had saved and struggled for.

Without the fortification of a sense of history or any genuine philosophy of government, Agnew was naturally prey to such reactions. Outside his legal training, he had not read widely. Travel books and television are the main conduits of his information. His other interests were sporting: golf, ping-pong, and avid support of the Baltimore Colts. He is uncomfortable with intellectuals and with speculative ideas. Long before the convention he became very comfortable with Richard Nixon.

It is easy to see why Nixon was impressed. Agnew is what is known in show business as a quick study. First impressions are not always deceptive, but they are with Agnew. He is an imposing figure: six feet two inches, a hundred ninety-two pounds, and always well turned out. (The *Men's Hairstylist and Barber's Journal* placed Agnew on its best-groomed list.) He is blessed with a model politician's family of three daughters and one son, who, in 1968, was a Navy Seabee in Vietnam. He is, naturally, an apologist for the virtues of thrift and self-help, of which Nixon feels himself to be an expression. Moreover, he articulates a few interesting ideas about government—notably in his advocacy of new city building and in his oft-stated predilection for a system of equalized welfare payments. It takes some time to realize that these ideas, good in themselves, are free-floating, unrelated to any coherent thinking on social policy.

From Nixon's point of view, too, Agnew's political situation seemed beguiling. A Republican governor in what had been a strongly Democratic state; and a state neatly balanced between North and South, with a great city, Baltimore (sixth largest in the nation), within its boundaries. Stephen Hess, the liberal young Republican who, in the final stages of the campaign, was drafted to write speeches for Agnew, was at first incredulous at Nixon's selection. But on reflection he saw its rationale: "If you put all the conflicting Republican elements into a computer, and programed it to produce a Vice-President who would do least harm to party unity, the tape would be punched SPIRO T. AGNEW."

If, however, the same computer had been fed data from those most acquainted with his Maryland style, it would probably have come up with a different answer. Significantly, some of those most flabbergasted by Nixon's decision were members of the Maryland delegation. And Nixon's presentation of Agnew in Lindsayesque terms—as a man for the cities—astonished them most of all. "If ever there was a man of the suburbs," said George Hubbard, a delegate from Baltimore, "it's Spiro Agnew."

The revolt broke at eight-thirty Thursday evening, as the convention staggered into its final session. It was doomed, of course. Even *in extremis,* the liberals were incapable of uniting; and in a fine demonstration of prudent solidarity, the one man who could have rallied them, Mayor John Lindsay, was up on the platform nominating Agnew. The worst the dissidents achieved was to deprive Nixon of prime television time for his acceptance speech.

Licking their wounds afterward, the conspirators were inclined to blame Lindsay for the rout. Charles Goodell, the live-wire New York Congressman (now Senator) who became floor manager of the abortive coup, remains convinced that 450 delegates were ready to vote down Agnew. "It could have been a spontaneous uprising," he lamented. What Goodell and his henchmen forgot was that Lindsay, despite the picture in the *Miami Herald* earlier in the week showing him leaping boyishly into the surf, had no intention of creating any waves inside the Republican Party. Lindsay's eye was fixed on 1972.

Lindsay's own operations at Miami were well organized but discreet, befitting a party baron but scarcely constituting an assault upon the delegates. He had a seven-room headquarters in the Americana Hotel —organized by his deputy mayor, Robert Sweet, who arrived in Miami "on vacation" the week before. Nine walkie-talkies were smuggled onto the floor as a communications network. Claques in the audience were organized with the help of sophisticated ticket-swapping deals. And, in dozens of quiet meetings, Sweet sounded out delegates on their opinions of Lindsay for 1972 or even 1976. But it was a small-scale operation (much smaller than the twenty-four-man *équipe* which Lindsay's predecessor, Mayor Wagner, used to sport at Democratic conventions, for instance), and its intelligence services were poor. One Manhattan delegate whose offer of help had been rebuffed by the Rockefeller staff was amazed and flattered to be snapped up by Sweet and assigned the job of sounding out the Rhode Island and Connecticut delegations.

More for morale purposes than anything else, Lindsay's staff had constructed elaborate scenarios "proving" the possibility of Lindsay's nomination. (They all depended upon Rockefeller and Reagan deadlocking Nixon, battling through five or six ballots, and then turning in desperation to the Galahad from Manhattan.) None was remotely likely. And, in fact, Lindsay's main efforts for nine months or so prior to the convention had been to build a public identification with Rockefeller and a private understanding with Nixon, clearly anticipating a Nixon victory with himself, the liberal, demanded as Veep. Nixon nibbled: at Miami, Sweet had several talks with Nixon's man Charlie McWhorter on the prospects for the Veepship. And Lindsay and Nixon met a few times. But, assessing his chances in the light of Nixon's Southern strategy, Lindsay knew they were zero. It gave him a certain emotional tranquillity. "I am not covetous of the Vice-Presidency," Lindsay told friends. "But I would find it very, very hard to refuse if it were offered."

The only offer Lindsay got came from Goodell, trying to organize the revolt against Agnew. Lindsay never approved of the idea. Goodell's first approach he turned down flat. But, undaunted, Goodell went ahead and drummed up a certain amount of support. It was scarcely a single-minded enterprise: anti-Agnew conservatives like Senator Miller of Iowa and Scranton of Pennsylvania; pro-Rocky men like New York delegates Senator Jake Javits, Bill Miller, and Len Hall; pro-Lindsay activists like Rhodes of Ohio and Chafee of Rhode Island. Still, it was potentially a lot of votes.

Goodell cobbled together a deal. At the Veep nominating session, the delegations of Nevada (in the person of George Abbott) and Rhode Island (Chafee) would put up Lindsay against Agnew. But Abbott, sensibly cautious, told Goodell that he would only stick his neck out if it could be guaranteed that Lindsay would not chop it off. And there the scheme collapsed.

By the time a second emissary, Mac Mathias, then a Congressman and now a Senator from Maryland, a neighbor but no friend of Agnew's, reached Lindsay with the plan, the Nixon camp—superbly informed as ever—had castrated the movement by requesting Lindsay to nominate Agnew. Unless he wanted to wreck his painfully maintained persona as the "party man at heart," Lindsay had virtually no option but to accept (to be followed by a stream of seconders from all sections of the party). Even so, Lindsay wavered. "We need you," Mathias said. "Well, how many votes do you have?" asked Lindsay. He would not give the guarantee of running that Abbott needed.

For lack of anyone else, Abbott ended up nominating the ever-available George Romney (who, ironically, had just persuaded his delegates *not* to revolt). The result was derisory: Romney got 178 votes, Agnew got 1128. Few people were happy, clearly, but most delegates confined their revolt to the decorous limits of the Minnesota delegates: after a stormy caucus that morning, the Minnesota delegation unanimously reached a bold decision—not to applaud when Agnew was nominated!

With the liberals' revolt reduced to the level of a public sulk, the argument was over. There was nothing more to do but fall into line for a final enthusiastic burst of acclaim for the leader. Just before eleven o'clock, it came—with a five-minute ovation for Richard Nixon as he took the podium to deliver his acceptance speech, a speech that he himself characterized as the most important of his political life. This was not Nixon finagling for Southern-delegate support, or Nixon preaching to the converted on the primary campaign trail; this must be the Nixon who could inspire the country. The acceptance speech is more than a courteous thank-you; it is the first major address of the election campaign. And Nixon himself had given it an added piquancy by declaring that it was designed to let his audience see "the whole man."

If it did not inspire, the fault was not entirely Nixon's. Any man's statement of visions that night, with news of the violence in the Miami ghetto still filtering out, would have seemed somehow inconsequential. Nixon strove to reveal what was in his heart—and much of it seemed decent enough—but did it make a whit of difference to contemporary realities? Other deficiencies were more intimately related to Nixon's style. Nixon is not a man who naturally expresses himself in inspirational terms. His greatest flights often are reminiscent of something one has heard someone else do better before. All orators borrow rhetorical tricks from one another, but the best ones have a way of transmuting them and making them their own. With Nixon, the scars of the grafting operation still show. And those that come most easily derive from the exhortatory canon of the great coach—"And I say, let's win this one for Ike."

This is not to say that Nixon is a bad speaker. It is simply a surprise to find that, after so many years on the stump, he is not better than good. Unlike the Kennedys, and perhaps to his credit, Nixon does not choose to demonstrate his intellectual grasp by carefully culled quotations from the great thinkers of our, and other, times. He uses quotations sparingly, and usually out of the political tradition. The acceptance speech was flavored by three: from Theodore Roosevelt, Abraham Lincoln, and Nixon's personal political hero, Winston S. Churchill—"With Winston Churchill, we say, we have not journeyed all this way across the centuries, across the oceans, across the mountains, across the prairies because we are made of sugar candy."

But what was Nixon made of? Could a man who had escaped definition so long define himself? If he succeeded, then it is only possible to deduce that his personality is a conditioned political reflex. For, stripped of the inflation of style, it was the mixture as before: revealing a man who is most at home when required to exercise the talents of a prosecuting attorney—lambasting the Democrats. Least effective when advancing positive solutions—"I think it's time for new leadership," that universal placebo. And astute enough, while founding his appeal on patriotism and private enterprise, to wear a compassionate heart on his sleeve.

Still, it was not without interest as a clue to the direction Nixon's subsequent election campaign might take. After the ritual niceties, an obeisance to Eisenhower (who had had another heart attack that week), a commendation for his running mate—"a statesman of the first rank" —and warm congratulations for the losers in the contest for the nomination, he moved straight into a definition of his constituency.

> As we look at America, we see cities enveloped in smoke and flame. We hear sirens in the night. We see Americans dying on distant battlefields abroad. We see Americans hating each other; killing each other at home.
>
> And as we see and hear these things, millions of Americans cry out in anguish: Did we come all this way for this?
>
> . . . Listen to the answers to these questions.
>
> It is another voice, it is a quiet voice in the tumult of the shouting. It is the voice of the great majority of Americans, the forgotten Americans, the nonshouters, the nondemonstrators.
>
> They're good people. They're decent people; they work and they save and they pay taxes and they care . . . [and, as Norman Mailer was to point out, they watch their television sets].
>
> And this is their answer, and this is my answer to that question: When the strongest nation in the world can be tied down for four years in a war in Vietnam with no end in sight, when the richest nation in the world can't manage its own economy, when the nation with the greatest

tradition of the rule of law is plagued by unprecedented racial violence, when the President of the United States cannot travel abroad or to any major city at home, then it's time for new leadership for the United States of America.

A little jingoistic perhaps, but sound enough as rhetoric. But what would the new leadership do? Here, as always, Nixon becomes obscure, his oratory so evenhanded as to be meaningless. Thus, he can slash at the Administration's Vietnam policy, commend the loyal opposition (none more loyal than he), and pledge peace under leadership "not tied to the mistakes and policies of the past." Richard Nixon is rarely bowed down by logical inconsistency.

On the plight of the ghettos, Nixon speaks warmly of enlisting "the greatest engine of progress ever developed in the history of man"— American private enterprise. The fact that this "engine's" untrammeled development has contributed, more than any other force, to the creation of areas of urban blight is not deemed worthy of mention. It is enough for Nixon that he pledges to black America "a piece of the action in the exciting ventures of private enterprise." He promises policies that will guarantee this. He does not define them. He is thus left free to indict the Democrats:

> We have been deluged by government programs for the unemployed, programs for the cities, programs for the poor, and we have reaped from these programs an ugly harvest of frustrations, violence and failure across the land. . . . I say it's time to quit pouring billions of dollars into programs that have failed.

Where would Nixon be on the vexed, if largely mythical, question of law'n'order? Well—this with emphasis—he was going to appoint a new Attorney General (an unnecessary reflection; presumably he was going to appoint a whole new Cabinet), and this man would "open a new front" against crime. He respected the courts, of course, but "let us also recognize that some of our courts have gone too far in weakening the peace forces, as against the criminal forces, in this country."

But there was a crumb for the left, too.

> To those who say that law and order is the code word for racism, here is a reply: Our goal is justice—justice for every American. If we are to have respect for law in America, we must have laws that deserve respect. Just as we cannot have progress without order, we cannot have order without progress.

In foreign affairs also, there were phrases for all psyches. For those of militant temperament:

> And I say to you tonight that when respect for the United States falls
> so low that a fourth-rate military power like Korea will seize an Amer-
> ican naval vessel on the high seas, it's time for new leadership to restore
> respect for the United States of America.

For those more pacifically inclined:

> We believe this should be an era of peaceful competition, not only in
> the productivity of our factories, but in the quality of our ideas. We
> extend the hand of friendship to all people. To the Russian people. To
> the Chinese people. To all people in the world. And we work toward
> the goal of an open world, open sky, open cities, open hearts, open
> minds. . . .

Where policies are difficult to adumbrate, pipe dreams can be a
useful device. And Nixon used them. Borrowing from the oratorical
lexicon of Martin Luther King, Nixon pitched his sights eight years
ahead to the two-hundredth anniversary of the American Revolution.
The motif was "I see a day" (King's "I have a dream"). In all, Nixon
saw a day eight times. He saw a day "when we can look back on massive
breakthroughs in solving the problems of slums and pollution and traffic
which are choking our cities today"; a day when "Americans are once
again proud of their flag"; a day when "we will have freedom from fear
in America and freedom from fear in the world"; and a day "when life in
rural America attracts people to the country rather than driving them
away." He saw, in short, happy times all round.

Nixon believes that dreams come true. He is an expression of them.
Thus:

> I see [a] child tonight. He hears a train go by. At night he dreams of
> faraway places where he'd like to go. It seems like an impossible dream.
> But he is helped in his journey through life. A father who had to go to
> work before he finished the sixth grade sacrificed everything he had
> so that his sons could go to college.
>   A gentle Quaker mother, with a passionate concern for peace,
> quietly wept when he went to war, but she understood why he had to go.
>   A great teacher, a remarkable football coach, an inspirational
> minister encouraged him on his way. A courageous wife and loyal
> children stood by him in victory and also in defeat.
>   And in his chosen profession of politics, first there were scores,
> then hundreds, then thousands, and finally millions who worked for his
> success.
>   And tonight he stands before you, nominated for President of the
> United States of America.

Where would he lead those millions? There were hints that it would
be to the right: "the forgotten Americans," the emphasis on lean govern-

ment, and a crack-down on crime all seemed to point in this direction. But there was nothing conclusive. It was not easy, at this stage, to anticipate the full crudity of Nixon's "law'n'order" advertising campaign; the offensive, and sometimes dangerous, banality of Spiro T. Agnew; or the candidate's discovery, unnerving for those who think America is overarmed, of a "security gap."

It was still possible for an optimistic liberal to leave Miami Beach thinking that Nixon had done what he had to do to get nominated and was now a free man—free to put mending the cities before militarism. Nixon's widely touted pragmatism, it could be reasoned, must lead him in this direction. A few, however, refused to rationalize, and the most prescient tended to be the least influential. Chester Gillespie of Ohio spoke the most accurate epilogue to the convention: "The Republican party reckons it can do without the Negro. It feels it can win on the white backlash." Gillespie had no inside information about Nixon's maneuvers with the South. He was simply sensitive to mood. He did have one advantage in this respect: he was that rare phenomenon at Miami Beach— a black delegate.

ACT X

Chicago:
The Reign of Piety
and Iron

1

You Wonderful Town

"And there rises a shining palace . . . and thither come
all herds and fatlings and first fruits of that land for
O'Connell Fitzsimon takes toll of them, a chieftain descended from chieftains. . . . And by that way wend the
herds innumerable of bellwethers and flushed ewes and
shearling rams and lambs and stubble geese and medium
steers and roaring mares and polled calves and longwools
and storesheep and Cuffe's prime springers and culls and
sowpigs and baconhogs and the various different varieties
of highly distinguished swine . . ."

—James Joyce, description of Dublin cattle
market, in *Ulysses*

The personality who has been nominated "Man of the Year" by
such diverse groups as the Lithuanian American Association, the Cook
County Council of the AFL-CIO, and the Junior Association of Commerce and Industry is not, at first glance, the popular image of an
All-American hero. In appearance he resembles nothing so much as a
gangland boss. He is short and thick-set, with drooping jowls and a brow
that suggests a capacity for violent bad temper. When he is roused, his
normally gray complexion becomes a bright shade of magenta. He looks
altogether like a man who would be dangerous to cross. And so he is.
For Richard J. Daley, Mayor of Chicago, did not achieve his eminence
by any marked capacity to turn the other cheek. Admiring Chicago
politicians make a joke of it: ask any one of them the way to approach
the Mayor and the answer is always the same—on tiptoe.

But they say a lot of nice things about him as well. How he's the
finest chief executive the city ever had (one elderly alderman spends all
his time in City Council meetings muttering the invocation, "Thank God

503

for Mayor Daley, Thank God for Mayor Daley"), how you could not find a more loyal Democrat, how he's a fine God-fearing example to the community, and how everybody respects him. And they mean *everybody*. Lyndon Johnson personally advertised his esteem for the Mayor by informing the White House switchboard that all calls from Daley were to be put through to him, personally and promptly. While discussing his chances of securing the nomination, Robert Kennedy had said, "Daley is the ball game." Chicagoans get a big vicarious charge out of seeing the great humbled before their senior citizen. They had a joke about this too. When, predictably, "Daley for President" buttons started sprouting in the lapels of loyalists on the city's payrolls, the word was that the Mayor was embarrassed by such demonstrations of esteem. "The Mayor doesn't want to be President," went the punch line. "He just wants to stay here and send one of his guys down there to the White House."

The man himself is not much of a joker, though he accepts the flattering yarns spun about him as his due. He is inclined to be taciturn. His occasional rhetorical flights frequently fall stricken with malapropism. Daley-watchers collect them with loving care. The Mayor once said of his opponents, "They have vilified me, they have crucified me, yes they have even criticized me." At another time, striking a note of uplift, "We will climb to greater platitudes together." But Daley is nobody's idea of a figure of fun.

He can be loved or loathed but never laughed off. By the time the Democrats wound up their thirty-fifth quadrennial convention in Chicago, Daley, the man to whom John Kennedy gave major credit for his election in 1960, had become for many liberal Democrats the most loathed political figure in the country, and his beloved city was ineffaceably tagged with the image "Fort Daley." The convention had staggered through its business, but only after a display of indiscriminate police violence on the streets of Chicago dominated the nation's television on the night of the nomination. Daley's autocratic conduct at the convention and the brutality of his police tarnished the entire party. And when Humphrey remarked after the shambles of his nomination, "Let's quit kidding ourselves that Daley did anything wrong," he destroyed his first real opportunity to reunite the Democrats' splintered ranks. It was evidence that Daley could get away with virtually anything and still have his back scratched by the party's establishment. More particularly, it convinced many liberal Democrats that Humphrey, for all his earlier crusading credentials, was now almost beyond redemption. The Democratic nominee was a man who could not quit kidding himself.

McCarthy's friend Robert Lowell had said earlier in the year, "I fear, if we fail, the imposition of a new reign of piety and iron." Daley's Chicago fulfilled the prophecy. Yet when the delegates assembled on Monday, August 26, for the opening session of the convention in the International Amphitheater, it was difficult to quarrel with the most boldly expressed sentiment in the Mayor's address of welcome:

> I greet you as Mayor, but, if I can have a moment of politics, I would say it is an important sign of faith to the American people for this national political convention to be held here—not in some resort center, but in the very heart of a great city where people live and work and raise their families.

He was right, just as he had been right to insist that the city abide by its original million-dollar bid, accepted by the Democratic National Committee in October 1967, to host the convention; right to imply that the city's tribulations over industrial disputes among its telephone and transport workers were not enough to justify moving the event elsewhere; and, above all, right to resist the bland pressure of the television networks, which could, at a conservative estimate, have achieved economies of six million dollars had the Democrats, like the Republicans, held their forum in Miami Beach. Eugene McCarthy subsequently accused Daley of "arrogance" for his insistence on holding the convention in Chicago. But there was nothing wrong with the Mayor's fundamental instinct. If the convention could not be staged in the most polyglot and vital of American cities—one, moreover, that since 1856 had been the site of no less than twenty-three of the fifty-six conventions of the two major parties—the political process was in hopeless condition. For to cut and run from Chicago was to run from America.

There was, after all, no preordained imperative that political conventions had to be seemly occasions. Indeed, the tradition of such events, the Republicans in Miami Beach notwithstanding, was anything but decorous. Indeed, Chicago itself had hosted two of the most riotous conventions in American history. The 1860 Republican convention that nominated Abraham Lincoln drew, via Chicago's glamorous new railroad terminals, no less than forty thousand visitors to its emotion-charged proceedings. Lincoln's men packed the galleries while other evangelical foot soldiers loyal to his cause stacked fence rails and piles of lumber around the convention hall as visual evidence of their faith. A raid on the local whorehouses, organized by Chicago's Mayor Long John Wentworth, flushed out a covey of errant delegates but failed to cast a pall over the proceedings. The moment of Lincoln's nomination produced a scene in which, according to Lincoln's friend Leonard Swett, "Ten acres of hotel gongs and a tribe of Comanches might have been mingled . . . unnoticed."

Even this junket paled in comparison with the events of the famous "Bull Moose" convention of 1912—which, incidentally, contained some curious parallels to the Democratic scenario of 1968. Theodore Roosevelt, making his political comeback, arrived at the convention in Chicago's Coliseum with a great record in the primaries to pit against the incumbent William Howard Taft. Roosevelt had picked up 278 delegates on the primary trail compared with Taft's 48. But Taft, as incumbents will, controlled the organization and the loyalty of the party regulars. In retaliation, the Roosevelt forces put in challenges of fraudulent selection for 254 delegate seats. Taft kept control of the credentials apparatus and that was that, though Roosevelt's men went even farther in expressing their indignation than the supporters of Eugene McCarthy in 1968. While his politicos refused to take any further part in the floor discussions, the pro-Roosevelt galleries contrived to make it the most tumultuous convention on record. And it was in Chicago, again, that the defeated Roosevelt forces met two weeks later to establish the breakaway Progressive Party—the medium through which Roosevelt's cause of "standing at Armageddon and battling for the Lord" assumed political form.

While not anticipating a complete throwback to those rough-hewn days before television soothed, with exposure, the atavistic brow, Mayor Daley was apparently not beguiling himself with the thought that another soporific display of unity was the answer to the nation's problems in 1968. Here is another passage from his welcoming address, dilating on the various kinds of spokesmen calling for a better life in America:

> Some of them are impatient. Sometimes they make us uncomfortable. Some are reasonable and others are angry. They hail from all over the nation—farm, town, and city—to demand, to protest, and to dissent. But did you see them at the other convention?

So Daley expected—was even flattered by the idea of—a controversial convention. It would make a fitting contrast to the blandness of the Republicans' public face presented in Miami Beach. But there were limits to the degree of volatility that Daley deemed appropriate, and he specified them in the next section of his address:

> I do not refer to the extremists . . . who seek to destroy instead of to build—to those who would make a mockery of our institutions and values—nor do I refer to those who have been successful in convincing

some people that theatrical protest is rational dissent. I speak of those who came conscientiously because they know at this political gathering there is hope and opportunity. I speak of those who came because the instinct that brings them here is right.

The distinction was all-important. What Daley did not realize, or perhaps allow himself to realize, was the ferocity of the divisions within the party. He was unable to understand that many people, who in previous years could never have been categorized as extremists, were on the verge of being convinced of the irrationality of the political process. Their dissent had ceased to be simply a matter of the "other fellow's point of view"; it had become a demand that the "system" be made responsive to what many regarded as the popular will expressed in the primaries. And if this demand could not be accommodated, the institutions and values of the Democratic party deserved only mockery in their view. Daley's basic arrogance lay in his assumption that such a protest movement could be domesticated or, where this proved impractical, deterred from expression by a display of physical force. It was noble and fine to insist that the convention be held in Chicago, but it was the height of unwisdom to believe that a combination of force and careful stage management could produce a meeting that accorded with Mayor Daley's narrow canons of political propriety.

How he could ever have thought this possible is explained partly by the nature of the man and partly by the environment of his own beloved city. After thirteen years as its Mayor, Daley, at the age of sixty-six, was a profound believer in the efficacy of conventional political action. Chicago's tradition was wild, even violent, but Daley had, by his own lights, tamed it. Nothing irritated the Mayor more than the suggestion, made by some urban experts, that American cities had become so complex as to be ungovernable. Chicago's history, he thought, defied this analysis. It was a city that was slowly, perhaps almost imperceptibly sometimes, moving ever onward and upward. It was progressive.

Chicago was never saddled by nostalgia for a Golden Age. Ever since it evolved out of a frontier post in the early part of the nineteenth century, it had evinced a disposition for crude, ruthless energy. With the coming of the railroads, there was money to be made—pots of it—but only the fittest need apply. If the city was mean to its own, it was also touched with an aggressive pride that made it clear that it did not need any outsiders' advice on how to go about its business. And business at least was good. In 1873, less than two years after a fire had devastated a third of the city, the nation entered a financial crisis. Not Chicago.

Its banks, alone of those in the large cities, continued to pay out of current funds.

By the end of the century Chicago was well on the way to becoming the world's largest center for grain, livestock, and meat-packing. It was also the harbinger of violent, sometimes bloody, struggles between unionized labor and capital. The muckracking journalists of the early twentieth century took to Chicago as if it had been invented for them. The most famous of them, Upton Sinclair, anatomized in *The Jungle* the rough unconcern for labor that underpinned the fortunes made in the meat business.

The 1920s shifted the focus from the unions to the racketeers who found fulfillment in the Prohibition era. Chicago led again in providing underworld antiheros. Figures like "Scarface" Al Capone were not aberrations but expressions of a well-grooved tradition. A British journalist had his ears firmly pinned back by an indignant Capone after trying to elicit the gangster's sympathy by asking a question about his underprivileged origins. That kind of talk, if it got around, would have people figuring he was a socialist or something. He wanted the journalist to know there was no more fervent believer in the American free-enterprise system than Al Capone. The passing years have not been tender to Capone's place in history, but Chicagoans still evince a kind of shrugging indifference to manifestations of random violence. A few years ago a Negro alderman named Ben Lewis was shot and killed. The story is told of how an eastern magazine asked its Chicago correspondent for an article on the public outrage that must have been felt over this murder. The correspondent cabled back, "The feeling is that if he's an alderman he's a crook, and if he's a crook that's their business."

Chicago is often described as a melting pot, but the metaphor is misleading. Old national identities are tenaciously fostered there. It is said that more than forty languages are spoken within the city limits. And the city is able to sustain regular publications in Yiddish, German, Greek, Polish, Swedish, Italian, and Czech. Except in the suburbs, its neighborhoods retain a distinctive, sometimes embattled, ethnic quality. The elements that unite Chicago are a hard-nosed dedication to money-making, the Democratic "machine"—once the most notoriously corrupt in the country—and an ineradicable belief that anything New York can do Chicago can do better. Chicago, like most second cities, is hypersensitive about its image.

Daley understands the subtle pattern of resentments and accommodations in this ethnic patchwork. He is part of them. The son of a steelworker whose union activities caused him to be blacklisted in several Chicago plants, Daley has remained faithful to his roots. The Mayor still lives in Bridgeport, the largely Irish neighborhood where he was born, within hailing distance of the stockyards. He goes to mass every day, and he goes home to lunch every day. His Catholicism is the pre-ecumenical brand. A devoted family man, Daley abhors the sins of the flesh but is far from intolerant in other respects. The virtues he prizes most are loyalty and hard work; his career is grounded in them. Although he came up through the machine at its most corrupt, his strait-laced reputation has remained intact.

For a young man of conventional ideas, the machine was the only avenue into Chicago civic affairs. It did, and to an extent still does, have a valuable function. Constitutionally, Chicago is sundered into six major governmental bodies with an independence of each other that extends even to taxing powers. Cook County, which contains them all, is another unit, with hundreds of suburban governments as well. Chicago, itself is structured as a collection of fifty wards run by aldermen who, according to the strict letter of the law, have powers unbridled by mayoral authority. Without some authority binding these disparate elements together, the city would indeed be ungovernable. The missing ingredient is supplied by the Democratic machine and its bulwark, the Cook County Democratic Committee. When Daley became Mayor in 1955, he shrewdly retained his chairmanship of this all-powerful body.

The operations of the machine (Daley calls it "the Organization," but most Chicagoans cleave to the more old-fashioned, less euphemistic appellation) are complicated in detail but simple in essence. It is patronage in the service of vote-getting. Each ward committeeman controls about five hundred jobs, an asset which gives him an initial base of five hundred families on which to operate. Favors given naturally depend on favors returned, and the whole structure from ward committeeman down to the humblest precinct captain is rigorously judged by its output at election time. Daley himself first achieved status as a champion vote-producer in his own Eleventh Ward. Over-all, the apparatus controls about thirty-five thousand jobs and is reckoned to be worth a handy hundred thousand votes in a city-wide election. (In a tight election like 1960's, when John Kennedy carried Illinois by 8858 votes, the machine is capable of vote fraud, but it prefers not to have to resort to such tactics.) At the lowest levels, voters are sometimes encouraged by such devices as free chickens and canned peas before casting their ballots. The machine looks after its own. At higher levels, of course, there are more substantial perquisites. Daley has been given much credit for eliminating the more outrageous forms of graft, but "clean graft" still passes muster. Chicago's crime syndicate can dovetail its interests with that of the machine in a couple of wards, always provided it does not get greedy. Many ward committeemen make their money by selling real estate and insurance in their bailiwicks—activities that slot in neatly with their political duties. But Daley's well-founded reputation for personal and financial rectitude gives the machine a capacity to live with occasional aberrations down the line. The system ultimately depends on two things: a precise awareness of place among its members and a general feeling among most voters that it works.

Under Daley, both conditions have applied. He is not a dictator but a uniquely gifted balancer of interests. This sometimes requires dictatorial methods—like the device of the Ruly Crowd which is occasionally wheeled out at controversial City Council debates in order to keep out a potential Unruly Crowd. But Daley is the machine's servant, not its master, and most Chicagoans believe that the machine and Daley combined serve the community well. Daley's arrival in office back in 1955 caused palpitations among the business community, but that soon changed. Even rock-ribbed Republicans grew to like him. As the nation's leading convention city, Chicago has to sell itself, and most businessmen came to the conclusion that Daley sold it well. He pushed through programs in the downtown Loop area that turned it into one of the richest and most spectacular business areas in the country, while the Mayor's reputation as a Democratic kingmaker ensured a regular and massive flow of Federal grants-in-aid from both the Kennedy and Johnson Administrations. In 1967, he won re-election for a fourth term by taking every single ward and rolling up 74 per cent of the vote.

But Daley has his blind spots, and these are endemic in the successful operation of the machine. In the poor areas, the machine's ability to get out the vote depends in large measure on its welfare function— speeding up relief checks, giving jobs to breadwinners who fall on hard times, and a variety of small but remembered favors. It is no accident that the two Negro areas which succeeded in loosing the machine's vise-like grip in the 1966 elections were predominantly middle class.

Daley's hostility to the operations of the poverty program in his city was his reaction to the advent of a competing fund of largesse. And in 1967, when the Mayor thought that amending legislation was needed to give local government agencies control over Federal anti-poverty grants, his tame Congressmen in Washington were quick to act upon his wishes. The interests of the machine have to be preserved, but at a cost that masks the rising disaffection of Chicago's two massive Negro ghettos on the South and West sides. Back in 1940, when Daley was in the middle echelon of the machine, less than one-tenth of Chicago's population was black. By 1968, the net result of years of immigration from the South, Chicago's 3,500,000 population was 30 per cent Negro. Mississippi, Alabama, Arkansas, and Louisiana were driving their problem to Chicago. Daley had his programs, but they never matched the scale of the problem. Still, the black wards turned in large majorities for him; it was possible for the Mayor to convince himself that his efforts were appreciated. When Martin Luther King came to Chicago in 1966, declared it to be the most segregated city in the North (Cleveland had some claims on that doubtful honor, but Chicago could only have been marginally behind), and started organizing open-housing demonstrations, the Mayor was staggered by his intransigence. Ultimately King backed off, baffled not so much by the explicit racism he had discovered in the city but by his own inability to break the machine's hold in the ghetto.

Daley, naturally, was confirmed in his belief that the Mayor knows best. But King left something behind: the seeds of Black Power activism that eventually made the Mayor lose his self-control. And it fed on a deteriorating social situation which Daley's brilliant balancing act in City Hall had been unable to arrest. In an area that boasted the largest per-capita income of any industrial region in the country, the black poor were becoming relatively poorer, and opportunities for breaking out of the ghetto were receding. The sociologist Pierre de Vise, in a book published in December 1967, compared the plight of the average black Chicagoan to the average white and found that the Negro was younger by ten years, one-half as likely to be on a craft job, one-third as likely to be a sales person or manager, three times as likely to be a laborer, eight times as likely to be a domestic worker. Black families were one-fifth larger, had incomes that were one-third smaller, occupied dingier and more dilapidated houses but paid just as much rent as the whites. Even these figures, which incorporate the life styles of a sizable black middle class, cannot convey the despair at the core of Chicago's stinking ghettos. They are breeding grounds for militancy.

But most of the black faces around the Mayor are machine faces. Their own carefully established status is threatened most directly by manifestations of Negro militance. They say what the Mayor wants to hear. And Daley's violent reflex after the riots that followed Martin

Luther King's death won many plaudits among his black acolytes. When the Cook County men assembled in June for that most clubbable of occasions, the re-election of Daley as their chairman, the Mayor's name was placed in nomination by William L. Dawson, the octogenarian black Congressman and principal architect of the machine in the ghettos. Another Negro seconded the nomination and declaimed, "I don't give a damn about the new image of the Negro. When Mayor Daley said, 'Shoot the looters,' well, I'm for that program! If outside rioters come to Chicago from Detroit or Newark, they will be cut down with bullets on the South Side. I will make a list of people who don't want to be tough with those looters and have a field day with them."

Daley is better than his machine but still of it; and piety and iron have become its ethos. The Democratic convention was to give it a national showcase.

2

The Phantom Armies
of the Night

"If you're going to Chicago be sure to wear some armor in your hair."

> —Abe Peck, editor of *The Seed,* a Chicago underground newspaper

"Welcome to Chicago, the city of *The Front Page,* with an outstanding tradition of competitive journalism.

"Another tradition has been the excellent rapport between the Chicago police and working newsmen. You can be sure of our continued cooperation as you report to the nation about the 1968 Democratic National Convention."

> —Handout issued by Information Division of the Chicago Police Department

"Chicago police are going out of their way to injure newsmen, and prevent them from filming or gathering information on what is going on. The news profession in this city is now under assault by the Chicago police."

> —Chet Huntley, NBC news commentator, August 28

On the last evening of 1967, one of history's more pregnant New Year's Eve parties was held in the Greenwich Village pad of Abbie Hoffman. Hoffman, then aged thirty, is probably the most complex figure thrown up by the hippie subculture. With his long, curly black tresses and sharp, intelligent face he looks rather like a Semitic Charles I. He is said to be a veteran of sixty LSD trips and has the reputation of being pre-

pared to try anything more than once. Asked to define a hippie by David
Susskind, one of America's more pompous television interviewers, Hoffman, by way of reply, produced from a box a live and quacking duck.
In slightly more serious vein, Hoffman will claim that hippies, the most
flagrant symbol of the rejection of corporate America by the young, are
the true American pioneers; that the ideas of the dropout community on
free love, mind-expanding drugs, and the inutility of money will become
part of the conventional social philosophy thirty years from now. Hoffman
is possibly the least square man in the United States. At his fateful New
Year's Eve party, events were set in train that would lead him and his
friends into confrontation with possibly the squarest man in the United
States, Mayor Richard J. Daley.

To give some idea of the gulf between them, it is worth using
Hoffman's own description of the party as he related it to an investigator of the Chicago convention riots. (The fruits of this investigation were
published in the excellent Walker Report *Rights in Conflict,* presented to
the National Commission on the Causes and Prevention of Violence in
December 1968):

> There we were, all stoned, rolling around the floor . . . yippie!
> . . . Somebody says oink and that's it, pig, it's a natural man, we gotta
> win. . . . Let's try success, I mean, when we went to the Pentagon we
> were going to get it to rise 300 feet in the air. . . . so we said how
> about doing one that will win.
>
> And so, YIPPIE was born, the Youth International Party. What
> about if we create a myth, program it into the media, you know. . . .
> when that myth goes in, it's always connected to Chicago August 25.
> . . . come and do your thing, excitement, bullshit, everything, anything.
> . . . commitment, engagement, Democrats, pigs, the whole thing. All
> you do is change the H in Hippie to a Y for Yippie, and you got it. . . .
> you can study the media and you say well, the H is switching, now
> they're talking about Yippies. New phenomena, a new thing on the
> American scene. . . . Why? That's our question. Our slogan is why?
> You know as long as we can make up a story about it that's exciting,
> full of shit, mystical, magical, you have to accuse us of going to Chicago
> to perform magic.

Hoffman is a frolicsome but not unserious young man. Hoffman
himself and two other friends at the party, Jerry Rubin, a former newspaperman in Cincinnati, and Paul Krassner, editor of the underground
magazine *The Realist,* had all been civil-rights workers in the South—an
experience they found, if not stale and flat, largely unprofitable. Yet they
were still revolutionaries, in the sense of wanting to refashion a society
they despised. In conventional terms, the role of a revolutionary in the

United States, given the forces at the disposal of a potential counter-revolution, is spectacularly uninviting. The basic revolutionary text of Hoffman and his friends, however, was not Karl Marx but Marshall McLuhan. And with the creation of YIPPIE, they developed a new revolutionary premise for the electronic era: when the might of a society cannot be challenged, strike at its myths. Power in this situation does not proceed out of the barrel of a gun, but, in Hoffman's words, out of "charisma, myth, and put-on—the triple-barreled YIP shotgun." Given the gulf between most Americans' perceptions of their society and its underlying realities, this form of psychological warfare was a potent discovery which Hoffman and his hippie entourage were superbly well equipped to wage. They were in themselves mockeries of traditional American conceptions of clean-cut young manhood, yet their very bizarreness made them news. They lived with an awareness usually vouchsafed to politicians after years of bitter experience and sometimes never: the absolute noncorrelation between news value and moral values.

In the process of blasting off Hoffman's triple-barreled shotgun, they would clearly incur the contempt of much of society, but this was to be expected. (After all, revolutionaries in many countries risk something far worse than contempt.) It would be worth while if, in the process, the society they were at odds with could be made to look stupid or brutal. In Chicago Mayor Daley and his police were made to look, and were, both.

Back at the turn of the year, however, Hoffman was a cloud no bigger than a man's hand, compared with others on Daley's horizon. What Chicago feared was not a handful of long-haired verbal provocateurs but an army of dissenters which, according to the wilder surmises, might be a million strong. And with this went the dire prospect of an uprising in the ghettos, one of which extended to within a few blocks of the convention site.

The idea of mounting a gigantic demonstration of antiwar, anti-Johnson, antiestablishment, and antiracist sentiment to coincide with the convention was born within weeks of Chicago's successful bid back in October 1967. The power of the President's name alone was all that was needed to compose the traditional factions of dissenting liberals, old left, New Left, civil-rights moderates, and Black Power advocates. They all wanted to demonstrate opposition to what then seemed the inevitable: the renomination of Lyndon Baines Johnson.

The myriad peace groups had already had an impressive dress rehearsal. In October 1967, under the collective umbrella of the National Mobilization Committee to End the War in Vietnam, they had rallied fifty thousand people for a march on the Pentagon. It was Washington's largest antiwar demonstration. The march had been overwhelmingly peaceful, though there had been some violent incidents immediately outside the Pentagon. After it was over, the creator of National Mobilization, David Dellinger, a fifty-two-year-old Quaker who had served two prison terms in World War II for his pacifist beliefs, wrote in his magazine, *Liberation,* that the peace movement was on the way to forging "a creative synthesis of Gandhi and guerrilla." By December 1967 Dellinger and his two principal lieutenants, Rennie Davis and Tom Hayden, both twenty-eight, and both one-time leaders of the radical Students for a Democratic Society, were planning to transfer the concept to Chicago. The word was that it would make the Washington march look like a Sunday-school outing.

From the Negro community there was not much evidence of advance planning but plenty in the way of apocalyptic statement. On December 31, the *Chicago Tribune* reported that Dick Gregory, the Negro comedian and civil-rights activist, had notified President Johnson that unless racial conditions were improved in his home town, Chicago, he would lead demonstrations "which would make it possible for the Democratic party to hold its convention over my dead body."

The process of trying to draw these strands of anti-Administration choler together to produce a cohesive demonstration in Chicago began early in the new year. For the first time since the early sixties, when blacks and whites had last worked together in the civil-rights movement, it seemed possible that they might come together again in broad-based opposition to Johnson's policies. On March 23 and 24 several hundred representatives of antiwar, draft-resistance, New Left, and black-militant groups met at a YMCA camp in Lake Villa, a suburb of Chicago. The agenda was the convention and what to do about it. Views on the subject ranged from ignoring it altogether to "closing" it by militant action. SDS, which has its headquarters in Chicago, was inclined to the passive role; its spokesman feared that any vengeance for disruption in the city might be visited on their own organization after the others had gone home. But in so far as such an individualistic assembly could have a consensus it was for a massive "funeral march" on the Amphitheater. David Dellinger, who was entrusted with the task of cobbling the whole enterprise together, said after the meeting, "We are not going to storm the convention with tanks or Mace. But we are going to storm the hearts and minds of the American people."

Within a week, the lynchpin of the whole enterprise, Johnson's candidacy, was removed. From that time on the crusading slogan "On to Chicago" never had quite the same emotional impetus. And for some weeks, with Kennedy and McCarthy dominating the primaries, it seemed that the system might, after all, be capable of accommodating antiwar feeling. Only after Kennedy's assassination in California, when it became obvious that the party regulars were freezing out McCarthy, did talk of demonstrations revive. All major demonstrations in America depend for their foot soldiers not on a hard core of revolutionaries or even radicals, but on a broad swathe of the concerned middle class who are generally inclined to think well of their politicians but are willing to march or carry a placard, say a couple of times a year, if they think a particular situation has gotten out of hand. They were the kind of people who responded most vigorously to the particular appeal of McCarthy.

By early July, they had two potential avenues for protest in Chicago: Dellinger's National Mobilization, and the latest organizational product of Al Lowenstein's fertile brain, the Coalition for an Open Convention. Lowenstein's outfit set out with the target of bringing one hundred thousand "Clean Gene" supporters to the city. On a third front, Hoffman's now well-publicized Yippies were evolving plans for a Festival of Life— "to contrast with the festival of death in the convention hall."

There is no doubt that a hundred thousand marchers could have been assembled in Chicago had it not been for one factor: the increasingly belligerent and obstructive temper exhibited by Mayor Daley's administration. The Mayor himself had set the pace with his widely reported order, "Shoot to kill arsonists and shoot to maim looters," after the riots following Martin Luther King's assassination. Thereafter, it was never possible to get Negro leaders to evince much interest in projected demonstrations for Chicago. They were afraid that if these spiraled out of control, the police, while hesitating to use more than billy clubs on white middle-class students, might have little compunction about shooting blacks. Chicago's police force, like New York's, contains many devout admirers of George Wallace. Inevitably, Daley's outburst was interpreted as an implied rebuke of his own Police Superintendent, James B. Conlisk, Jr., who had earlier earned some liberal plaudits for the restraint exercised by his department during the riots. It seemed that the Mayor's thirst for "law'n'order" exceeded that of his own departmental chief, and the hint that an excess of zeal in preserving order might not come amiss rapidly filtered down the ranks. The expression of this new mood was not long in coming.

On April 27, the Chicago Peace Council sponsored a rally of sixty-five hundred war protesters in the Loop area. Similar events were staged in other big cities throughout the country, but Chicago's was the only one that became violent. Twenty demonstrators were injured in clashes that were, to put it mildly, uninhibited examples of police action. Superintendent Conlisk, presumably chastened by his earlier moderation, was on the scene witnessing the action without demur.

Subsequently, an eminent citizens' group looked into the circumstances of the incident. Though the group was liberal in complexion, its members could scarcely be classed as hairy radicals; it was headed by Dr. Edward J. Sparling, founder and President Emeritus of Roosevelt University, and included such dignitaries as a professor of neurosurgery, a professor of law, the president of an insurance company, and a brace of clergymen. Its report, published on August 1, concluded:

> Those [policemen] who committed acts of violence cannot be truly labeled "exceptions." For the presence of the Superintendent and his deputies indicates that the political system of Chicago, not merely individual officers, was at work that Saturday.
>
> The police were doing what the Mayor and Superintendent had clearly indicated was expected of them. If we are to erase the causes of the peace parade disorder, we must look to the responsible officials, and the dilatory and obstructive way in which they handled preparations for April 27.

Although some of those who drew up the report had been acquaintances, even admirers, of Daley in the past, City Hall greeted the report with a deafening silence.

Other intimations of a ruthless Daley line were coming through to the march organizers more directly. The Mobilization people, faced with the reluctance of the city officials to discuss the issue of permits for the desired march routes, had enlisted the assistance of the Community Relations Service in the Justice Department. They found a sympathetic listener in its chief, Roger Wilkins. Wilkins was impressed with the argument that the best method of avoiding chaos was to forge an understanding between the demonstration leaders and the city authorities. He perceived that the most dangerous of all situations would be one in which thousands of demonstrators descended on the city without any formally agreed channel for expressing dissent. Late in July, Wilkins flew to Chicago to put these arguments to Daley. He received what amounted to a brushoff. Before Wilkins was through his preliminaries, Daley cut him short with the observation that his was an orderly city. If there was going to be any trouble it would come from "outsiders" and his police were equal to that situation. There was no more to be said. This was not only mayoral arrogance; that familiar phenomenon of conflicting advice emanating from different Federal agencies had been at work. Wilkins' plea had to be set against the advice of the Secret Service that no march or demonstration be allowed near the Amphitheater. For Daley, choosing between advice that stemmed from the President's personal entourage and that of a Justice Department official was no choice at all.

Meanwhile, Lowenstein's Open Convention group, deterred by the prospect of violence, had changed its program from a march to a rally and requested the use of the Soldier Field stadium. Their permit application produced the revelation that the stadium had been booked for the entire convention week by the Democratic National Committee, with the expressed purpose of holding "Lyndon Johnson's Birthday Party" there (Johnson would be sixty on August 27)—a macabre function that, as it happened, never got around to being staged. Finally, on August 20, Lowenstein called the whole thing off with the angry comment that the authorities "seem determined to have a confrontation that can only produce violence and bloodshed." McCarthy himself had already advised his supporters to stay away—counsel dictated by tactical as well as humane considerations. The last thing McCarthy wanted was a convention polarized on the emotional but essentially meaningless "law'n'order" issue.

Over in their small but by no means insignificant corner, the Yippies were also showing signs of nervous tension. The enthusiasm of Hoffman's New York group had begun to fray the nerves of their counterparts in Chicago. With some difficulty Chicago's hippie community had established a scene in the Old Town district. They had built up a modest understanding with the local cops and with it some immunity from the "greasers"—groups of lower-middle-class lads whose idea of fun was thumping a hippie—but they also realized how fragile this immunity was. They were, in fact, in a most unhippie-like condition: up tight. Early in August the Chicago group circulated a letter, picked up by all the underground newspapers, to the effect that the festival of life could turn into "a festival of blood." It advised pacifically inclined out-of-town brethren to stay put. "The cops will riot," the letter warned. "The word has gone down—'Brutality be damned.' "

Nothing daunted, the New York Yippies continued to pile on the politics of the put-on—much of it seemingly calculated to offend Daley's sexual puritanism. The list of Yippie projects, by no means exhaustive, included ten thousand nude bodies floating in protest in Lake Michigan; the mobilization of Yippie "hookers" to seduce delegates and slip LSD

into their drinks; a squad of 230 "hyper-potent" hippie males assigned
to the task of seducing the wives and daughters of delegates; releasing
greased pigs in the Loop area; a mass stall-in of beat-up automobiles on
the expressways; the insertion of LSD into the city's water supply; Yippies dressed in black pajamas to dispense handfuls of rice to the citizenry;
and the infiltration of the right wing with crew-cut Yippies who, at an
opportune psychological moment, would exclaim, 'You know, these
Yippies have something to say.'"

They did have something to say, of course, but they were saying it
in a code that the literal-minded security authorities could not hope to
break. If it were not for its consequences in Chicago, the spectacle of the
Yippies' irreverent balderdash being pored over by hard-nosed investigators in the FBI, the Secret Service, and Daley's police department on
the hunt for clues to revolutionary intentions might have seized the nation with a paralyzing bout of mirth. The mind of the Chicago police
department, however, remained studiously unblown. An emergency guard
was placed on the city's LSD-threatened water supply, just in case.

Meanwhile, the Mobilization Committee, unable to inform its member organizations what kind of demonstration activity would be possible
in Chicago, was finding it difficult to drum up support. The city continued to set its face against any march proposal "within eyeshot" of the
Amphitheater; ultimately, the only permit issued was to the Mobilization
group for a rally in Grant Park on Wednesday, August 28—balloting day
for the convention. Grant Park, separated from the Loop hotels by a
knot of railway tracks, is four miles from the Amphitheater. The Yippies,
too, finally dropped their suit to hold a continuous festival in Lincoln
Park, an open parkland abutting the Old Town district—a mile from
the convention headquarters in the Hilton Hotel, and fully five miles from
the Amphitheater. They could use Lincoln Park without a permit during the day, but the normal eleven-p.m. curfew was to be rigidly maintained (though it had been waived in the past for functions that met with
the city's approval).

The city's obtuseness on permit applications, designed to deter outside protesters, was wondrously successful. A week before the convention opened, the *New York Times* ran a story about the demonstrators
saying that estimates of the turn-out "ranged from a probably conservative 50,000 to a seemingly inflated 'over a million.'" But the Mobilization organizers and, in theory at least, Chicago's police intelligence (since
it was receiving reports from FBI agents who had infiltrated the Committee's anything but furtive ranks) knew that even the conservative esti-

mate would be virtually impossible to achieve. A New York peace group, for instance, which had had to charter two hundred buses to ferry people to the Pentagon demonstration back in 1967, found that five buses were more than enough to accommodate volunteers for the Chicago jaunt. And it was increasingly obvious that the ghettos would not pose much of a problem. Some of the more powerful local Black Power leaders had expressed a fervent desire to leave town during the convention week. The most notorious of the South Side gangs, the Blackstone Rangers, also exhibited a strong instinct to stay clear of "Whitey's problem."

By this time, however, the security authorities clearly did not know whom or what to believe. Four days before the convention opened, Daley announced his attachment to the axiom "An ounce of prevention is worth a pound of cure." Daley's "ounce," it was revealed, would put Chicago's 12,000-strong police force on twelve-hour shifts, bring in 6000 Illinois National Guardsmen, and have on tap 6000 regular army troops complete with rifles, flame throwers, and bazookas. It was security in the paranoid style. In the event, the demonstrators who came to Chicago numbered at the outset no more than 2000 and, even at the peak of activity, on nomination day, did not exceed 10,000. Of this number the vast majority were peacefully inclined, capable of having their frustrations eased by the sop of a march. Scarcely more than a few hundred could be classified as revolutionaries, and their weapons were the psychological ones of obscenity and irreverence.

Freed of the problem of dealing with an unwieldy host, the city could have afforded to be flexible. A decision to let the Yippies camp in Lincoln Park, for instance, would scarcely have inconvenienced Chicago, since the Yippies were there all day in any case. And, while a policeman's psychology cannot be changed overnight, it is difficult to see how the "Battle of Chicago" could ever have been fought had it been made clear from the outset that loss of cool would not only play into the militants' hands but would also have serious disciplinary consequences. But Daley's security machine was moving on the premise that it was dealing with "terrorists"; like the American war machine in Vietnam, it felt it had an "enemy" to contain. And, as in Vietnam, bewilderment over establishing the precise identity of the "enemy" led to a lot of random busting of innocent heads.

It was tragic, but also absurd. During the days just before the convention, the Yippie leaders, aghast at the thinness of their ranks, amused themselves with bizarre late-night planning meetings for the benefit of their conspicuous police tails. At one point Paul Krassner asked a group of reporters whether they would like to meet his tail, and then led a posse of media men over to inspect an embarrassed loiterer outside Lincoln Park. "Why are you following me?" Krassner asked his silent detective. Then, "What did I have for dinner last night?" "I don't know," blurted the red-faced tail, all patience lost, "I don't work twenty-four hours a day."

In the four days before the convention opening, the world of Krassner and Hoffman moved toward that of Daley and his police department with predictable but nonetheless horrifying logic. On the night of Thursday, August 22, a seventeen-year-old American Indian, dressed like a hippie, was shot and killed by police a few blocks from Lincoln Park. Police claimed that the youth was fleeing after firing a .32-caliber revolver at them. It was an isolated incident, unrelated to any demonstration, but it hardened attitudes. On Friday morning, a group of Yippies arrived in Chicago's Civic Center and prepared to nominate a hundred-and-fifty-pound pig, called Pigasus, for the office of President. His platform, they said, was garbage. An unamused squad of police officers moved in, arrested six of the demonstrators, and carted Pigasus off to the Chicago Humane Society. A subsequent attempt to nominate a Pigasus replacement, Mrs. Pig, was also prevented by the police.

On Saturday, Lincoln Park began to silt up with Yippies and more conventional demonstrators. During the afternoon some practiced Karate and the *washoi*—a group maneuver evolved by Japanese student demonstrators for minimizing injury in riot situations. Police helicopters whirled overhead. The attitude of the police in the park fluctuated between amusement and contempt. There was some tension toward the curfew hour; Allen Ginsberg, the poet and pacifist, chanted his deep bass *om* to ease it. But the two hundred people left in the park at eleven p.m. were cleared by the police with little incident. There were muted portents of what was to follow: some sporadic shouting of "Pig" at the police, while a Chicago reporter who flashed his press card to a hustling police officer was told, "Fuck your press credentials!"

On the afternoon of Sunday, August 25, the final day before the opening of the convention, a hundred or so demonstrators fanned through the Loop area chanting slogans: "Peace now!" "Dump the Hump!" "End the war!" "Hey, hey, LBJ, how many kids did you kill today?" Over in Lincoln Park, about three thousand persons, most of them Mobilization Committee people, had come to watch the Yippies perform. Then, around five-thirty p.m., there was an ugly scene as the police halted the approach of a flat-bed truck, intended for use by the Yippies as a stage for their rock-group entertainment. The cops, it seemed, were spoiling the fun. Some of the watchers around the truck took up the "Fascist pig" chant. There were a few noisy arrests and, more ominously, some of the police were observed removing their badges. The mood had ceased to be equivocal; it had turned nasty. This time curfew would bring a real conflict of wills.

The Mobilization Committee marshals made themselves unpopular with the Yippies by advising against a confrontation. Hoffman, however, told a police commander that he and his followers were going to test their legal right to sleep in the park. The commander told him that anyone found in the park after eleven p.m. would be arrested. Hoffman replied, "Groovy."

It was, however, past midnight when a force of five hundred police officers moved against the thousand hard-core demonstrators who had resisted all appeals to leave the park. Some of the police were already over the edge. In the rampage of baton swinging, there were shouts of "Kill the Commies" and "Let's get these bastards." The fleeing Yippies rejoined with "Oink, oink" and cries of "The parks belong to the people." As the battle moved out of the park it became "The streets belong to the people." On Clark Street, Claude Lewis, a reporter for the *Philadelphia Bulletin,* took notes as police clubbed a young girl to the sidewalk. One of the officers turned, seized the reporter's notebook with one hand, and dexterously clubbed him over the head with the other. Photographers aroused even greater displeasure. Police complained that their strobe lights dazzled them, but their reason for their displeasure was simpler: they did not relish photographic evidence of their crowd-dispersal methods. By the time that night's demonstration was over, ten newsmen were on the inventory of the injured.

Thus even before the convention opened, the pattern of its subdrama—involving the police, the demonstrators, and the media—had set along abrasive lines. Only a change in Daley's implacable hostility to all manifestations of dissent could improve matters, and that, as every Chicagoan knew, was not going to happen.

3

Wheeling and Dealing
for Peace

"A man who wishes to make a profession of goodness in everything must necessarily come to grief among so many who are not good. Therefore, it is necessary . . . to learn how not to be good, and to use this knowledge and not to use it, according to the necessity of the case."

—Niccolò Machiavelli, *The Prince*

By the beginning of summer, all but the most antediluvian Democratic politicians had got the message: a Democratic Presidential nominee tied to Johnson's war policy would be the best possible guarantee of four lean years of Republicanism. McCarthy's buoyancy in the polls, the fact that he and Kennedy had garnered eighty per cent of the vote in the primaries, and the almost total disappearance of that once ubiquitous bird the hawk—all combined to suggest a change of national mood. But getting the message was one thing, acting on it was another. Johnson might be a lame-duck President, but he was not, at least until the Democrats found a successor, a lame-duck party leader. He had invested his massive ego in his conduct of the war, and he was not about to endure the humiliation of seeing the nominee of his party publicly trample on this policy while he served out the last six months of his term. At least, not if he could help it. The armed-camp aspect of Chicago was just part of the evidence that he could.

Nonetheless, for all Johnson's rigidity on the one hand and the moral righteousness of McCarthy's supporters on the other, the Democratic Party had not entirely lost its ingrained instinct for compromise. It had lost some of its best exponents—not least the President himself, who, until the war came along, had been perhaps its greatest temporizer and melder of conflicts since Franklin D. Roosevelt. But there were still a few astute politicians around who refused to see the party's plight in 1968 as one in which an irresistible force must collide with an immovable object. Their room for maneuver was pitifully small. But in the strange story of the "peace" plank for the party platform, they achieved a very high degree of excellence. Ultimately, their initiative failed, ground into extinction by a combination of Humphrey's pusillanimity, a crude Johnsonian power play, and a stroke of sheer bad luck. But it had been a close thing, and it left its imprint on the party's psychology, if not on its explicit program. If only as a case study of the system's attempt to accommodate a popular movement, this story merits extended mention.

Like most such maneuvers, it began outside the mainstream of the protest movement. Its originator, in fact, was a man with an almost uniquely embattled position within the system, John J. Gilligan, the forty-seven-year-old Democratic Senatorial contender from Ohio. Gilligan, a red-haired and gregarious product of a line of Ohio morticians, is not by nature an espouser of lost causes. During his spell as a Congressman, he had earned himself the reputation of being a tough but by no means inflexible liberal. (When a merchandising bill unpalatable to Procter & Gamble came before the House, Gilligan formed a legislative pressure group to remove its teeth: P & G's head plant is located in Gilligan's home town of Cincinnati.) Early in 1968, he scored a spectacular political success by upsetting Frank Lausche, until then regarded as the most indestructible Democrat in Ohio, in the Senatorial primary. His liberal credentials helped here, but so, more important, did the labor unions' resentment of Lausche's autocratic indifference to their interests. Labor generously funded Gilligan's campaign and felt he was their man. The assumption was not entirely correct. But Gilligan was certainly not inclined to go out of his way to alienate this solid base of support, especially after the riots in Cincinnati following Martin Luther King's assassination. Gilligan, appalled by the summary justice meted out to curfew-breakers (not rioters) in the ghetto, criticized the local courts, and the state's predominantly right-wing press descended on him like a ton of "law'n'order"-inscribed bricks. It was, from the unions' viewpoint, a mark against their candidate; he could not afford many of those.

Unfortunately for Gilligan's electoral prospects, the war had him in a gruesome squeeze play. His two college-age sons and his fifteen-year-old daughter, Ellen, were all passionate McCarthyphiles. Gilligan

shared their disgust with the war and was privately for Robert Kennedy
—privately, because the union leaders in Ohio, like those elsewhere,
had automatically transferred their loyalty from the President to Hubert
Humphrey. When asked whom he was for—it was always the first question on his campus visits—Gilligan would reply that he felt happy to be
a member of a party with three such fine contenders. Nobody knew
better than he the lameness of this response. But then nobody knew
better than Gilligan the strength of union bitterness against the two
anti-Administration candidates. When Kennedy motorcaded through
Cleveland, Gilligan sat—inconspicuously, he thought—in the rear of
the candidate's car. The following day, in Washington for an appointment with George Meany, Gilligan was snubbed by the irate AFL-CIO
chief. Bad mark number two.

After Kennedy's assassination, the pressure on Gilligan, as on all
other politicians, to endorse a Presidential candidate became more intense. He could understand his children's enthusiasm for McCarthy, but,
because of the wariness of his Senate colleagues, he could not share it.
He had higher hopes of a remotivated Hubert Humphrey, who, he knew,
was being urged by his campaign staff to break with the President's
hard-line policy. Then, on July 3, when he appeared with the Vice-
President on a television show in Cleveland, Gilligan had a chance to
see just how far this refurbishing process was from realization. It was
a dismal occasion; after the show, Gilligan took the Vice-President aside
in the dressing room and told him if he didn't snap out of it he could
kiss the Presidency good-by. Humphrey looked mournful. Gilligan, who
had liked and admired the old Humphrey, was left in no doubt that if
the Vice-President was ever to become, in the popular phrase, "his own
man," it would require the efforts of a lot of other men to help him.

Next day, sitting on the porch behind his home, Gilligan had his
idea: Why not do for Humphrey in 1968 what Humphrey had done for
Harry Truman twenty years earlier—i.e., get the candidate out on a
position that he could not take of his own volition but that could ensure
his election? (The analogy was not entirely accurate, but Humphrey's
piloting of the civil-rights platform at the 1948 convention did enable
Truman to enlarge his appeal in the North and, to some extent at least,
offset the platform's less fruitful electoral consequence—Strom Thurmond's breakaway Dixiecrat movement.) In practice, this meant divorcing, as far as possible, the issue of a Vietnam plank in the party
platform from the personalities of the rival candidates. Gilligan was
certain that the hostility of the party regulars would cut down McCarthy's

bid for the nomination. But if a peace plank could be presented as something separate from McCarthy's candidacy, and be presented by men acceptable to the regulars, it might work. It would be only half a loaf for the kids—McCarthy's policy without McCarthy—but at least the distinction would be made between the Republican and Democratic approaches to the war. Most of them would swallow their disappointment and work for the party. Gilligan reckoned that if the convention passed a peace platform and nominated Humphrey, the Vice-President would run on it. Gilligan's metaphor, vouchsafed only to like-minded friends, was: "It would be like throwing a child into a swimming pool. He'd swim." If a broad enough base could be assembled on the peace issue, there was even a chance that Humphrey might be emboldened to break with the President before the convention.

Gilligan phoned an old friend in Boston, Kenneth O'Donnell, and received a prompt pledge of active support. O'Donnell was a man whom party regulars understood and, in most cases, liked. And, in that uncertain period between the end of the primaries and the convention, he had one other inestimable advantage—freedom to maneuver. He was not running for office. Although he was an avowed opponent of the war, he was not tied to any bandwagon. After Kennedy's assassination, he had resisted the temptation to join other ex-Kennedy aides in mobilizing the candidacy of George McGovern—"George rang me, but I told him, 'You don't have any more chance than the man in the moon' "—and he was untainted by association with that disruptive student crusade. "Nobody"—this with a fierce glare—"could accuse me of being a wild and woolly McCarthy man." The next step was to muster as impressive an array of antiwar dignitaries as were available and work out a joint line.

On August 1, the main interested parties came together in Washington for a private lunch at the Carroll Arms, a time-honored venue for lobbyist entertaining just behind the Old Senate Office Building. It used to be one of Joe McCarthy's favorite watering places. There was, therefore, a certain historical appropriateness in the choice of site, for the men who met on this occasion were, in essence, trying to unravel the most disastrous consequence of McCarthy's impact on American foreign policy in the early fifties. The mix was basically: McCarthy staffers, plus former Kennedy and McGovern aides, with a sprinkling of dove Senators—Claiborne Pell and Wayne Morse. The McGovern/Kennedy men included Frank Mankiewicz and Ted Sorensen. The McCarthy men were Blair Clark and Joe Rauh. Others present were Gilligan, O'Donnell, and another influential Kennedy aide who had yet to find a

candidate, Fred Dutton. (A few weeks earlier, Humphrey had made a
vigorous attempt to recruit Dutton, who turned him down on the grounds
that he could not go along with Humphrey's Vietnam position. The Vice-
President, displaying a staggering lack of comprehension of the emotional charge in this issue, was genuinely surprised by Dutton's reasoning.
"Gosh," he said, "you *do* feel strongly about the war, don't you!")

From the outset, O'Donnell made it clear that their only chance—
a slim one at that—was to stay united. The other guiding principle had
to be flexibility. Intellectual honesty was all very well in its place, but
in composing a foreign-policy plank that would attract adherents currently outside the peace camp, it might be well to fudge the logic
of a rigorous antiwar position. This implied that the platform must not
be designed as a lever for any one peace candidate. Moreover, the
wording could not directly criticize the President or his past policies,
for then he and Humphrey would be compelled to fight back. This was
tough for McCarthy and even tougher for McGovern, an earlier critic
of the war, because they saw the historical perspective as important to
an understanding of the Vietnam debacle. Blair Clark, however, dutifully undertook to put the argument for moderation to McCarthy.
McGovern's supporters were more confident of their candidate's con-
currence; he did not have a vociferous rank-and-file constituency to deal
with.

One of the most remarkable aspects of this episode was the readiness of McCarthy's staffers to be conciliatory. In this, they totally belied
their reputation for intransigence among the party loyalists. The intransigence had always been in the main a lower-level phenomenon. And
McCarthy's inability to make any impression on loyalist delegates after
the primaries had had a chastening effect on his supporters. Still, as the
peace group with most delegate muscle, they might have been expected
to exert a little more authority in the Carroll Arms session. Clark and
Rauh, however, were shrewd enough to realize that the antiwar cause
would now be best served by the politics of party brokerage. When the
luncheon broke up, it was the three neutralists—Gilligan, O'Donnell, and
Dutton—who left with the key executive roles in the operation: Gilligan
and O'Donnell as cochairmen, Dutton as the man assigned to draft an
acceptable plank. Joe Rauh paid for the lunch.

They had just under three weeks before the opening of the Platform
Committee hearings in which to drum up support and coordinate a
strategy. Gilligan went back to Ohio to secure a place as his state's repre-

sentative on the Platform Committee, a move that immediately aroused the suspicions of his union supporters. To them, any association with a peace-plank enterprise looked like a conspiracy against Humphrey. Gilligan tried to couch it in terms that suggested a conspiracy *for* Humphrey, but it was an uphill task. At one stormy caucus of the Ohio delegation, he was described as "a Commie-lover." (Gilligan's initiative probably lost him the Senate seat: after the convention, the unions, outraged by his conduct, first blocked their campaign contributions and later cut them to the bone. Gilligan lost narrowly to his Republican opponent.)

At more rarefied levels of the party, hostilities tapered off and, on occasion, disappeared altogether. Dutton himself kept in regular touch with Humphrey's speechwriter, Ted Van Dyk. Another point of contact was provided by the Committee for a Political Settlement in Vietnam, a distinguished group of moderates headed by Clark Kerr, former President of the University of California, and including Walter Reuther (UAW funds primed the whole enterprise). Its Vietnam position —stop the bombing and begin a ceasefire—was a *via media* between the peace group and the Humphrey camp. Reuther was for Humphrey, and his aide, Jim Conway, provided a useful conduit for information exchange between the two groups. At yet another level, Ted Sorensen achieved an understanding with David Ginsburg, the Washington attorney entrusted with the frustrating task of drafting and redrafting the Vice-President's "break" position on Vietnam. Indeed, so close was their rapport that some of the McCarthy people suspected that Sorensen might be the Administration's Trojan Horse. Sorensen compounded this perhaps undeserved suspicion by a shy reluctance to confess any close contact with the Humphrey entourage. Unfortunately for him, at a gathering of old Kennedy hands in Ted Kennedy's house in Washington for the purpose of viewing a film about Bobby Kennedy which was later shown at the convention, a messenger arrived with the request: "Would Mr. Sorensen please contact Mr. Ginsburg on the matter he has been helping him on?"

Apparently beguiled by these contacts, Humphrey, in New York on August 17, delivered one of the most curious speeches of the year. Without indicating any personal dissatisfaction with the Administration's policy, the Vice-President startled his audience with the revelation that he and the late Senator Kennedy had held "remarkably similar views on Vietnam." He cited as evidence for this their agreement that a coalition government should not be "forced" on Saigon before negotiations.

This was a clumsy attempt to exploit the marginal, though not insignificant, distinction between Kennedy's and McCarthy's approach to peace negotiations.

Humphrey was not going to be allowed to get away with it that easily. Four of the men who had worked on Kennedy's Vietnam statements—Walinsky, Mankiewicz, Schlesinger, and Goodwin—rapidly composed a refutation and shot it off to the *New York Times*. They expressed "shock" at the Vice-President's "false and misleading" statement and, so that there should be no misunderstanding, recalled Kennedy's campaign references to "disastrous and divisive policies" which could be changed only by changing the men at the top. The point Humphrey had chosen to demonstrate his and Kennedy's togetherness was, they claimed, "exceedingly minor" and distracted attention from the main issue, which was, of course, Kennedy's contention that the United States must accept the principle of Vietcong participation in the South Vietnamese regime. The Vice-President would probably recall his response to this proposal when it was first formulated by Kennedy in February 1966. In case he had forgotten, the authors reminded him: he had variously described Vietcong participation as "putting a fox in a chicken coop," "putting an arsonist in the fire department," and "rewarding murderers and assassins." Nothing that the Vice-President had said since suggested that he had changed his mind on this score.

Irritation at Humphrey's public utterances was not, however, allowed to disrupt the process of assembling a peace coalition. In a sense, it facilitated them, for it showed that the Vice-President himself felt the need for, even if he did not yet have the courage to make, an understanding with the Kennedy forces. (His other objective, naturally, was to drive a wedge between the Kennedy men, who he felt were amenable to party discipline, and the McCarthy people, who seemed intent on changing the rules of the game. In this he was unsuccessful.) By the time the Platform Committee hearings started at the Washington Statler Hilton on Monday, August 19, the oddly assorted peace-plank forces had achieved a high degree of cohesion. They knew they had real leverage. Before the first session, they sounded out the 110 members of the Committee and arrived at an estimate that 39 or 40 were prepared to go along with a dovishly worded plank. This was more than enough for a minority report, which requires only 11 dissenting members, but that had been expected all along. What was impressive was the development of support among the party regulars. Fewer than a score of the commitments were from McCarthy men; others came from moderate figures like Philip

Hoff, Governor of Vermont, and Grant Sawyer, former Governor of Nevada and eventually Humphrey's campaign chairman in that state. Moreover, the prospects of prying other Committee members loose were still good, except among unreconstructed Southerners; the unofficial link between the peace group and Humphrey's staff was being almost formalized. Ginsburg had contacted O'Donnell and told him the name of the Humphrey committeeman calling the signals for his candidate: Wilson Wyatt, ex-Lieutenant-Governor of Kentucky. O'Donnell allowed himself the brief luxury of a vision in which the peace plank became the majority position.

The initial problem was simply to open up the Committee. It had become patent that its chairman, Representative Hale Boggs of Louisiana, a fervent admirer of Lyndon Johnson, intended to run the hearings with a tight rein. The list of witnesses for the first session suggested the pattern: they were all pro-Administration. Dick Goodwin exploded when he saw it and told a member of Boggs' staff that if a better balance could not be achieved, the peace group would walk out and hold its own hearings in another room at the hotel. It was largely bluff, but it worked. In the event, the peace group could hardly complain about the caliber of anti-Administration spokesmen Boggs called: they included George McGovern (who, unnervingly for the backroom conciliators, made a slashing attack on past policies by describing the Vietnam adventure as "the most tragic diplomatic and moral catastrophe in our national history" and went so far as to suggest repentance be recorded in the wording of the plank—"To correct error, it is first necessary to admit it."), Fulbright, Gaylord Nelson, Galbraith, Sam Brown, and— perhaps most effective—Roger Hilsman. Only a direct confrontation in private between Boggs and the two cochairmen of the peace group, led to the introduction of Rusk himself.

Both sides knew, of course, that committeemen were unlikely to be swayed by the rhetoric of witnesses, no matter how distinguished. The hearings were for public consumption. (And they were good ones, certainly better than the much-lauded debate on Vietnam which was to take place at the convention itself.) But any realignment of forces would depend on the backroom attempts to close the gap between Humphrey and the peace group. Unfortunately, events and the still awesome authority of Lyndon Johnson were not on O'Donnell's side. Lest anyone forget his position, the President underlined it on the opening day of the hearings in a speech to the Veterans of Foreign Wars in Detroit. There was no equivocation: his policy would remain unchanged until he left office. "It takes two to make a bargain," said the President, and the next move was up to Hanoi.

The next day, August 20, Soviet troops marched into Czechoslovakia. On the Committee hearings in Washington, the impact was melodramatic. At nine-twenty-seven p.m., just as Rusk had finished unburdening himself of the familiar justifications for administration policy and as Galbraith narrowly shaded Gilligan in a race to the questioner's microphone, Boggs rose to halt the proceedings. He felt obliged to read out the contents of a note just passed to him by a messenger, a press dispatch reporting the invasion of Czechoslovakia. With a wry—some claimed a relieved—smile, Rusk excused himself: "I think I ought to see what this is all about."

The consequences for the peace group went far deeper than the removal of Galbraith's favorite Aunt Sally. In a stroke, hard-line rhetoric about the Communist menace was restored to political respectability. And McCarthy's offhand realism in describing the invasion as "not a major crisis" was less than helpful. (McCarthy subsequently issued a statement deploring the cruelty of the Soviet action, a point he had earlier felt too obvious to mention. His original perception, however, that the invasion was something the United States could do nothing about and therefore did not merit the dramatics of Johnson's midnight convocation of the National Security Council, was entirely accurate, if impolitic. Indeed, much of the outrage was undoubtedly prompted by resentment that this unpalatable fact was being pointed out.)

The invasion virtually ensured the triumph of the hard-liners on the Platform Committee, and the blacker humorists among the political correspondents suggested that Kosygin had done it as a favor to Johnson. But Johnson was as chagrined as anybody by the new crisis—prior to it he had been secretly planning a summit meeting with the Soviet leaders to discuss methods of easing East-West tension. It was to have been the crowning achievement of his Administration. Now this grandiose ambition would never be realized.

By Thursday, when the Committee reconvened in Chicago for its final sessions, the lines between the peace group and the Presidential loyalists had hardened. There had already been indications on the plane journey to Chicago that Boggs was preparing to get tough. The peace group had been expecting to place three of its leaders—O'Donnell, Gilligan, and Bill Clark of Illinois—on the twenty-two-man platform-drafting committee. But Boggs told O'Donnell that only he would be on it. There were some protests, but the peace group no longer had the confidence to make an issue of their chagrin.

Meanwhile, draft peace planks were fluttering around like confetti. Dutton personally wrote seven, some of such extreme subtlety that it was thought that even a hawk might be beguiled into accepting them. One was tried on one of the Committee's most bellicose members, Senator Gale McGee of Wyoming. McGee was not bemused, or amused. "Play with the language all you like," he barked. "Some are saying get out and some are saying stick it out."

He was right, of course. Nevertheless, both the McCarthy and McGovern men were pushing as close to the middle ground as they could without being charged with betrayal. Inevitably, the process produced tensions. For the final drafting sessions in Chicago, Dutton was joined by a representative triumvirate, Goodwin for McCarthy, Sorensen for McGovern, and Gilligan for all comers. Gilligan acted as referee. "I'll say one thing about those Kennedy aides," said the Ohioan, recollecting a grueling experience, "they all hate each other cordially." The two polarizing forces were Goodwin, anxious not to see the final version so watered down as to be meaningless, and Sorensen, anxious to appease Humphrey as far as possible. Earlier drafts that had been aired with Humphrey staffers had produced three main friction areas: (1) the word "unconditional" in relation to a bombing halt; (2) description of the situation in South Vietnam as a "civil war" (this was viewed as a covert attempt to criticize previous Administration policy, in that Rusk's most repeated justification for the American presence was that it was helping to resist "external aggression"); and (3) the "imposition" of a coalition government on South Vietnam. Some of the Humphrey men had become frankly skeptical of the peace groups' moderating intentions on any of these points. When James Rowe bumped into Dutton in the Blackstone Hotel, where the drafting committee had taken up residence, there was almost total noncommunication. "Hell," said Rowe, "if we gave you guys a blank check you'd say there was something wrong with it."

Yet the final draft of the peace plank, which was unveiled at tenthirty Friday night, was not an intransigent document. In fact, it went more than halfway to meet the objections of Humphrey advisers and was softer in tone than a draft which McCarthy himself had submitted to the committee before the hearings started.

On the three points mentioned above, the peace group gave ground

on 2 and 3. The operative line on past policies read: "Discarding judgment about the wisdom of the past, we must now act to secure and
enrich our future by bringing the war in Vietnam to a swift conclusion."
There was no reference to a "civil war." On the desirability of a coalition government, the plank's recommendation was: "We will encourage
our South Vietnamese allies to negotiate a political reconciliation with
the National Liberation Front looking toward a government which is
broadly representative of these and all elements of South Vietnamese
society." Such negotiations, it was thought, would be "spurred" by the
knowledge that U.S. forces would withdraw as North Vietnamese regulars were withdrawn from the South. This was less explicit than McCarthy's original proposal that the United States take an active part in
establishing a coalition government by negotiation, which had led to
Humphrey's allegation that McCarthy would "force" such a regime on
America's Southeast Asian ally.

    But on the first point, there could be no real compromise. "Stop
the bombing" had become the symbol of the peace campaign as well
as the touchstone of American willingness for realistic negotiation. To
ditch it at this stage would have been regarded as blackest treachery.
Even so, the bombing-halt clause was cautiously worded; citing it as
the first step toward peace, the plank recommended "an unconditional
end to all bombing of North Vietnam while continuing to provide in
the South all necessary air and other support for American troops."
(In practical terms, this meant a very small declension of bombing raids;
it applied only to the North and, in accordance with the President's
withdrawal statement on March 31, these had already been sharply
reduced.)

    As soon as the text was released, Gilligan took off for a meeting
with David Ginsburg, who had been in Chicago since Wednesday working on Vietnam-plank drafts for the Vice-President with Humphrey's
administrative assistant, Bill Welsh. Just before midnight, the two men
settled down in a room in the Statler Hilton. The third man present,
William Geoghegan, was the room's regular occupant. As luck would
have it, Geoghegan, who had worked in the Justice Department under
Robert Kennedy, was a close friend of both Gilligan's and Hale Boggs'.
He was in Chicago as a member of the Committee chairman's staff. It
was one of those poignant moment in politics when a tiny group of men,
just below the top rank, feel capable of staving off disaster. Seemingly,
all the elements of compromise were there. They went through the
minority draft, clause by clause.

An "unconditional" end to the bombing was an obvious snag but not, Ginsburg thought, insuperable. He had just completed a draft plank of his own and was impressed by the narrowness of the gap between the two positions. After an hour's study, he announced, "There's not ten cents of difference between this and the Vice-President's policy." The meeting broke up hopefully; Ginsburg promised to let Gilligan know what Humphrey thought of the peace-plank language. He was inclined to think the Vice-President might be favorable.

It was all an illusion. Ginsburg never called Gilligan, not out of discourtesy but because he had nothing to say. It was out of his hands and, for that matter, out of Humphrey's hands too. The three men had felt like power-brokers, but the real power, that of Lyndon Johnson, had not been represented. Until Humphrey was nominated, Johnson had him cold. One false move on the Vice-President's part—and rumors that he might be tempted to move on the peace plank had been transmitted to the White House—and Johnson was perfectly capable of destroying the delegate base for his potential majority. Soon after he left Gilligan, Ginsburg was hard at work—not, as he had hoped, on "selling" the peace plank to his boss, but on Presidentially imposed refinements to its alternative.

The crucial meeting on Friday had been not in Chicago but in the White House, where Boggs and two other key convention personnel— Representative Carl Albert, the Permanent Chairman of the convention, and Senator Jennings Randolph of West Virginia, a pro-Administration member of the Platform Committee—had repaired with other Congressional leaders for a briefing on the Czech crisis. Johnson was at his most somber and statesmanlike. The news was grave: the Russians, according to his intelligence, were mobilizing on the borders of Rumania. Boggs asked the President what would be the effect of stopping the bombing of North Vietnam, and Johnson came back on cue by reading out a cable from General Creighton Abrams, Jr., the U.S. Commander in Vietnam. It predicted that a bombing halt would increase the DMZ capability of the enemy by five hundred per cent. There were doleful reminders of the intelligence hints, which had stretched Humphrey on the rack for over a month, that the Vietcong might be planning their third major offensive of the year. It was gloomy news indeed, at least for those still inclined to credit the President and his intelligence reports.

Boggs was among those who did. He returned to Chicago more resolute than ever. And his temper was not improved by the discovery that the liberals on the drafting committee had taken the opportunity of his absence to insert the recommendations of the Kerner Commission report. Johnson loyalists had put up a tough fight against this, as the report, which advocated massive spending programs to combat ghetto distress, had never elicited Johnson's approval.

When Boggs unloaded his dire intelligence from the White House, O'Donnell saw red. From where he was standing, it looked like a gigantic spoof, and as a veteran of such functions during the Kennedy years, he had an insider's perspective. "I told Boggs straight," recalled O'Donnell, "that I'd been to enough White House briefings for Congressional leaders to know they're mostly guff." It was not the language of persuasion, but, by Saturday evening, there was no longer much "give" in the situation. In the drafting committee, the level of debate descended to previously unplumbed depths; furious committeemen started challenging each other's military records.

That evening, Charles Murphy, a White House staffer who acted as Johnson's personal representative in Chicago, called at Humphrey headquarters on the twenty-third floor of the Hilton with a request for Ginsburg's final draft plank. He took it away without comment.

On Sunday evening, Murphy scheduled a private meeting with Boggs and the two Humphrey draftsmen, Ginsburg and Welsh. There was nothing illusory about this occasion. Murphy informed them that the language of Ginsburg's draft was unacceptable to the President, particularly on the issue of the bombing halt. Ginsburg had written: "Stop the bombing of North Vietnam. This action and its timing shall take into account the security of our troops and the likelihood of a response from Hanoi." The President thought that the bald statement of intent in the first sentence might give the wrong impression. The wording he preferred was: "Stop all bombing of North Vietnam when this action would not endanger the lives of our troops in the field; this action should take into account the response from Hanoi."

It was this version that Boggs flourished at the final session of the drafting committee, Monday morning, August 26. And it was a version that was not negotiable. Unlike the draft planks generated on all other issues, this one was not to be subject to textual revision by the Committee. There was no discussion, merely a series of resolutions to pass the peace plank and the pristine pro-Administration plank up to the full Committee for a formal vote. The whole procedure lasted fifteen minutes.

When the full text of the planks was released Monday evening, a few hours before the convention's opening session, there was no mistaking the distance between the two camps. Apart from the difference in language on the bombing halt, there were distinctions on the terms of de-escalation: immediate in the peace plank, but contingent on the South Vietnamese forces' ability to take on larger responsibilities in the pro-Administration version. And while this encouraged "all parties and interests" in South Vietnam to agree on the choice of a postwar government, it made no specific mention of the NLF. It did, however, contain several assertions of pacific intent and, like the peace plank, proclaimed a willingness to negotiate mutual withdrawal of troops with Hanoi. But it was rightly viewed as a thoroughgoing endorsement of Johnson's handling of the situation. The final platform vote was 35 for the peace plank and 65 for the majority position. The peace group had actually lost a handful of adherents over the week.

O'Donnell and Gilligan had clearly failed in their optimum objective. Humphrey had stayed locked in the Presidential embrace. But the attempt to build an anti-Johnson consensus had not been wasted. They still had a powerful issue, with broad support, to take to the floor of the convention. McCarthy himself, on Monday night, was perhaps relieved at their partial failure: he had been wearing the peace candidate's clothes too long to relish their seizure by Humphrey on the eve of the contest. His response to the majority plank was almost enthusiastic: "Now the lines are clearly drawn, between those who want more of the same and those who think it necessary to change our course in Vietnam. The convention as a whole will decide."

4

No Way to Break It

"As I was going up the stair
I met a man who wasn't there.
He wasn't there again today.
I wish, *I wish* he'd stay away."

—Hughes Mearns, "The Little Man Who
Wasn't There"

"The confusion accompanying most liberal reform movements is due to the fact that they are generally attempts to
make the institution practice what it preaches in a situation
where, if the ideal were followed, the function of the institution could not be performed."

—Thurman Arnold, *The Folklore of Capitalism*

The occasion was folksy: Lyndon Johnson with Lady Bird enjoying
a modest sixtieth birthday celebration at the Austin, Texas, home of his
daughter Luci. Baby grandson Lyn was naturally the center of attention.
Around dusk the homely scene became national property. Johnson had
decided to hold an impromptu press conference. There were pictures to
be had of the President, cradling Lyn in the crook of his left arm, as he
leaned over to blow out a candle on his birthday cake. "The great man
in an informal moment"—the kind of picture that always makes the
paper. The questions were those anyone might ask a President on a birthday which happened to coincide with the second day of his party's national convention. What did the President think of the convention? Did
he intend to go to any of its sessions? What was his principal birthday
wish?

The President seemed to be in one of his more expansive moods.

538

He felt that, thus far, it had been "a good convention with all viewpoints and sections represented," though he hastened to add that he had only the evidence of the television to go on. His own contact had been tenuous: "I haven't involved myself in rules, or platform, or personalities." And, by and large, he liked it that way. He was inclined to trust the party's instincts and, for his own part, remain relatively unobtrusive—though he allowed as how he was under some pressure from "the authorities" to "run up" to Chicago for an evening. Birthday wishes? Well, the President guessed there was only one answer to that: "I would like for all the boys to be able to come home and lay down their arms and live in dignity without fear. . . . If you could just mash a button, I guess you would want all humanity to live at peace with each other."

The convention that won the President's commendation was then well on the way to becoming the most riotous and ill-tempered in living memory, while the violence in Chicago's streets was showing signs of feedback into the convention hall itself. Nor was there any mystery about the reason for this turbulence: it was the suspicion that Johnson was mashing every available button to assure the endorsement of his hard-line Vietnam policy. If, by hinting at an intention to drop in on the convention, the President had hoped to subsume hostilities under a sentimental display of fealty to the chief, he was sadly mistaken. Indeed, its effect was quite the reverse. Experienced Johnson-watchers tended to be most wary when the President seemed at his most spontaneous. At the time, there was not much more than rumor to go on, but the word was that the President's "informal" call might turn out to be an elaborately stage-managed birthday celebration with, as its high point, Johnson himself making a personal endorsement of the majority plank on Vietnam.

Rumor was not far off the mark, though the full extent of the planned preparations for Johnson's advent only emerged piecemeal after the convention. (Among the exhibits in evidence: the construction of a Texan-sized birthday cake by a Chicago bakery; the reservation, by Mayor Daley, of the Stockyards Inn, where the aforementioned confection was scheduled for consumption; a hundred-twenty-five-thousand-dollar work of cinematic hagiography on the Johnson Administration, commissioned by the Democratic National Committee and entitled "Promises Made, Promises Kept"; and a cache of placards in a recess of the Amphitheater with inscriptions reading "Birthday Greetings" and "We Love You, LBJ.") No plan entirely survives contact with the enemy, however; and Johnson's enemies at the convention, though in the dark as to his intentions, were ready for almost anything. When Jesse Unruh, boss of the powerful California delegation, heard about Johnson's Austin press conference, he sidled up to John Burns, leader of the yet more powerful New York contingent, to put him in the picture: "I understand the Great Cowboy may come tonight. Well, we're waiting for him."

After some discussion, the loyalist authorities in Chicago relayed a more realistic estimate of the situation to the President. The discussion was not over whether but over how to tell him. Hale Boggs, the Platform Committee chairman, asked Carl Albert, the convention's permanent chairman, to do it. Albert was horrified at the burden: "How can I say that to him? I don't want to hurt his feelings." Ultimately, someone plucked up the courage. And Johnson made a small, but ignominious, historical footnote by becoming the first President not to attend a convention of his own party since 1944, when FDR declined the privilege because managing World War II was more pressing. For the anti-Administration forces, however, it was a victory of symbol, not substance.

Indeed, exponents of the conspiracy theory of history had no difficulty in defining the nature of the 1968 Democratic National Convention: it was a puppet show from beginning to end with the demoniac LBJ pulling the strings. The radical magazine *Ramparts,* in a generally perceptive report on the convention, described it as "an elaborate shuck, controlled in large part from the banks of the Pedernales." The theory has its beguiling aspects, even for those not normally afflicted by the paranoia of the left. For the evidences of the heaviness of someone's hand were everywhere.

For a start, there was the security. It could be argued, perhaps, that the *cordon sanitaire* around the Amphitheater was for the benefit of all concerned; that the roadblocks, the manholes sealed with tar, the serried ranks of policemen, and even the barbed-wire ring fence capable of being electrified at the flick of a switch were gruesome but necessary devices for the protection of delegates from hostile outside influences. A similar case could not be made, however, for the humiliating screening methods inside the hall, where delegates were required to bedeck themselves with elastic neckbands dangling plastic entry permits. The plastic cards were for insertion into hip-high validation machines, flashing green-for-pass and red-for-stop indicators (Instructions: "Upon arrival at the electronic credential reader . . . insert your correct daily credential—star end up —and push firmly. Your credential is now validated."), and the whole performance was overseen by blank-faced representatives of the Andy Frain security agency, whose services in the cause of in-house safety supplemented those of myriad other well-muscled figures from the FBI, the Secret Service, and the ubiquitous Chicago police department.

In terms of convention logistics, the oppressive security apparatus could only harm the antiwar, anti-Administration forces. They were the underdogs, the group most dependent on the traditional license of mobility around the convention floor to proselytize and cajole. And they, inevitably, showed most irritation. "I wasn't sentenced and sent here! I was elected," exploded New York delegate Alex Rosenberg, after two days of harassment by men who responded to every show of indignation with a maddening insistence that they were only doing their job. They were, of course; but the job was not necessary, unless it was viewed as part of an over-all plan to pacify the delegates before the advent of the chief.

Similarly, the limitations placed on camera crews on the floor of the convention were hardly justified by the argument of the convention's executive director, John B. Criswell, treasurer of the DNC. "Many people feel electronic media all but infringe the rights of the delegates." The *delegates?* As every television crewman knows, nothing pleases a delegate more than the opportunity to retail his views to the nation. But the convention floor, of course, was infested with anti-Administration views. Clearly, the only kind of television coverage the convention organizers liked was that focused on the platform, where the camera could pan across the image of loyalty: Hale Boggs, Carl Albert, and Senator Daniel K. Inouye of Hawaii, the keynote speaker and a long-time admirer of Johnson. Drop the focus a few inches and there, in the choicest seats just below the podium, loomed the stern-faced ranks of the Texas and Illinois delegations, at their respective heads the hard, handsome figure of "Juan John" Connally and Mayor Daley. A wave of Daley's hand was all it took to prompt the convention band to brassy renditions of "It's a Grand Old Flag" or "Happy Days are Here Again."

The voice of dissent had a tough time even to be physically heard. The militants in the Wisconsin, New York, and California delegations found themselves banished to the outer reaches of the hall, where they had to contend with poor-quality microphones and an acute hardness of hearing on the platform. This was the crudely overt part of the operation. There was a more sinister level too, located on the twenty-first floor of the Hilton Hotel, neatly poised between the Humphrey headquarters on the twenty-fourth and the McCarthy volunteer staff office on the fifteenth. There Postmaster General Marvin Watson, a sharp-eyed Texan, maintained a hawk's eyrie and two-way communication center between the convention and the President. Watson's entourage was small but exclusive. It included only the most trusted of Johnson hands, men like Joe Califano and Jack Valenti.

It all seemed very conspiratorial, but was it really necessary? Probably not. It had been clear all along that Humphrey's political muscle was all packed in Johnson's shoulders. The Vice-President had no money, no political base, nothing without Johnson's support. And he didn't have to be reminded. After the convention, some liberals argued that the peace plank, at least, might have been endorsed had it not been for the malign evidences of Johnson's determination to crush dissent. But their argument rested principally on the assumption that Humphrey, operating on his own, could have privately passed the word to his supporters that the peace plank was acceptable to him. This is to exaggerate Humphrey's capacity, or willingness, to take an independent line. Even without Marvin Watson looking over his shoulder, the Vice-President would not have been free. He could hardly have disseminated a subversive thought without news of it going straight back to Johnson. Humphrey's key whipper-in for labor was the AFL-CIO chief George Meany, an unreconstructed Cold Warrior. On Monday, Meany displayed his authority by having three hundred fifty union delegates and alternates to a lunch, at which they were strongly reminded of their duty to stay in line. A retaliatory lunch of Labor-for-McCarthy delegates, organized by Paul Schrade of the UAW, now fully recovered from the head wound he suffered at the Kennedy assassination, had fewer than fifty takers. In the South, the hawkish Connally with Texas's 104 votes to dispose of, was the lead figure. Both Connally and Meany were Johnson men first and Humphrey men a bad second.

Jack Gilligan, the inspirer of the peace-plank coalition, came to realize this better than anybody. "Humphrey was trapped," he said. "If he tried to get the word out to the unions or the South that he wanted our Vietnam plank, the only guys the delegates would believe were pro-Johnson. So the word would have reached Johnson before it did the delegates. Johnson would have gotten on the phone and said, 'What's this I hear, Hubert?'"

Humphrey, of all men, knew intimately Johnson's two most outstanding personality traits: the terribleness of his rage when crossed and his unwillingness ever to close an option. The combination of the two made for an appalling scenario for the Vice-President in Chicago, all the more so given the mysterious group on the twenty-first floor. If Humphrey took the advice of his dovish advisers and moved to accommodate the peace forces on Vietnam, might not the President, with a huge show of reluctance—but in the interests of national honor—allow his name to be put in nomination? And if that happened, where would it leave Humphrey? At the same time, Humphrey could hardly expect to detach votes from McCarthy's candidacy by a late dovish swerve. The thought of the vote he might drum up in such a situation was uniquely horrible to contemplate. It was no fun being a hollow candidate. "We felt the President was killing him, just killing him," said John Burns after the convention.

Still, Humphrey knew he had only one law to obey. By the end of the week, Humphrey may have seemed political kin to that Earl of Derby who, Lord Birkenhead once said, resembled a cushion that bore the imprint of the last man who had sat on him—but one imprint endured throughout the proceedings. Humphrey never deviated in his fidelity to Johnson's Vietnam policy.

Yes, it was Johnson's convention. But his influence was not essentially conspiratorial. It proceeded from his authority as head of the party machine, whose votes Humphrey needed, and hardly had to be made explicit. It was in no way dependent on the flagrant attempt to stamp his personality on the occasion. Indeed, there is some evidence that resentment of the Johnson/Daley/Connally axis in action, if anything, marginally swelled the peace vote. Nor can it be argued that the restrictions on the convention floor impaired the lobbying powers of the peace forces more than their own self-inflicted deficiencies. After the convention, Tom Mechling, who stocked the McCarthy headquarters with communications equipment, found that thirty of the sixty radio transmitters provided for McCarthy floor men had not even been picked up. Everybody was too busy losing his cool.

The key to understanding the convention is to realize that the petty chicaneries of the platform, the hassling on the floor, and the boorishness of Daley as impresario—in fact, all the things that gave the event the reverse of a democratic appearance—had little effect on its decisions. It was the exact opposite of Miami Beach, where an absence of incident masked very significant fluctuations in political fortune. In Chicago, the wealth and complexity of dramatic incident concealed the fact that there was very little real movement.

Perhaps the best evidence for this is the similarity between two key votes at the convention. The first was early Monday night, before irritation over the repressive apparatus had had time to build. Jesse Unruh had made the motion to defer until the next session consideration of credentials challenges—which, as we shall see, were the fulcrum of the McCarthy convention strategy. This would be the first chance to draw a line between the relative strengths of the machine and the insurgents. The final count was 875 for Unruh's motion to 1691½ against. The other vote, after two days of embittering floor fights and vigorous, sometimes hysterical, lobbying offered the last chance to draw the same line: the vote on the nomination. Humphrey rolled up 1760¼ to 826¾ for the various peace candidates. These votes would almost certainly have been the same had the whole enterprise been conducted with impeccable decorum on a small off-shore island. They may not have been an expression of the popular will, but they undoubtedly expressed the will of the delegates on the range of options with which they were confronted. (Had they, of course, been confronted with the real option of Edward Kennedy's candidacy, a political mirage with which we shall deal in the next chapter, it might have been another story. In that case Humphrey's authority as the leader of the regulars would have been put to the test.)

But if Chicago cannot be adequately explained in terms of skulduggery in smoke-filled rooms, neither can it be rendered coherent by reference to what had been the strongest tradition of American politics—the instinct for a winner. Humphrey came to the convention trailing ignominiously in the polls. Gallup had him 16 points behind Nixon, while McCarthy held up well only 5 points behind the Republican nominee. In Daley's own state, a *Chicago Sun-Times* poll published on the eve of the convention showed McCarthy ahead of Nixon and Humphrey losing the state by 10 points. The argument, common among Democrats, that anyone could beat Dick Nixon was beginning to look threadbare. When McCarthy arrived in Chicago on Sunday, the day before the convention, to be greeted by a rapturous crowd of students, he had no need to repeat the lessons of the polls. If the Democrats wanted a winner, then they knew where to find him. "All we're asking," he told his supporters, "is a modest use of intelligence."

McCarthy's ascendancy in the polls did not, however, impair the resolve of most delegates to reject him. In a curious way it may have increased their determination. For they were operating under a compunction as powerful as the instinct for a winner: the instinct for their own political survival. In this instance, it might be better served by going with a loser. Thus, the real explanation of Chicago is psychological rather than political. There were two kinds of political animal in Chicago and each, for a variety of reasons, was supremely ill-equipped to understand what the other was about.

It is no accident that the best reporting on the convention was done not by political writers but by craftsmen in more imaginative disciplines. One of these, Arthur Miller, had the additional advantage of being inside the operation as a McCarthy delegate from Connecticut. The core of Miller's analysis is contained in the following two paragraphs from an article in the *New York Times Magazine* in September:

> There had to be violence for many reasons, but one fundamental cause was the two opposite ideas of politics in the Democratic party. The professionals—the ordinary Senator, Congressman, State Committeeman, Mayor, officeholder—see politics as a sort of game in which you win sometimes and sometimes you lose. Issues are not something you feel, like morality, like good and evil, but something you succeed or fail to make use of. To these men an issue is a segment of public opinion which you either capitalize on or attempt to assuage according to the present interests of the party. To the amateurs—the McCarthy people and some of the Kennedy adherents—an issue is first of all moral, and embodies a vision of the country, even of man, and is not a counter in a game. The great majority of the men and women at the convention were delegates from the party to the party.
>
> Nothing else can explain their docility during the speeches of the first two days, speeches of a skull-flattening boredom impossible to endure except by people whose purpose is to demonstrate team spirit. "Victory" is always "forward," "freedom" is always a "burning flame," and "our inheritance," "freedom," "progress," "sacrifices," "long line of great Democratic Presidents" fall like drops of water on the head of a tortured Chinese.

Miller's perception went to the heart of the matter, but, perhaps because the bitterness of defeat was still fresh in his memory, he was too harsh on the regulars. And the harshness revealed some of the reasons why the party regulars found the new brand of delegate so difficult to stomach. It is true that they did not see issues in the same stark terms as the McCarthyites, but this did not mean they saw them only as devices for manipulating sections of public opinion. They liked the "game" of politics, of course, or they would not have been in it, but it would be wrong to suppose that they all believed this aspect of politics was an end in itself.

It is harder to generalize about Democratic regulars than Republicans, and Chicago had them in all their diversity—city machine men, Southern Bourbons, union loyalists, militant and moderate Negroes, and even intellectuals as complicated in their different ways as Miller. But there are some collective traits. In the North, at least, one of them happens to be an interest in issues. The Democratic Party did not become

the party of the Northern working class and of Northern liberal intellectuals by accident. The Michigan pollster Fred Currier, who has done
a lot of work for candidates of both political persuasions, is fond of
relating the differences in how they use his services. A typical Republican
comes to him with specific questions on what he should do to get through
to the electorate, listens intently to the advice, and then carries it out.
It is all done with great efficiency and dispatch. A typical Democrat, on
the other hand, is more likely to settle himself comfortably, loosen his
tie, and indulge in a long soul-searching ramble on what politics is all
about. It can take a couple of hours before he can be persuaded to divert
his attention to such important but uninspiring matters as the latest poll
findings. Currier, who is a Republican, concludes that working with
Democrats is more time-consuming but more fun. And there are academic studies which bear out such impressions. Herbert McClosky's
behavioral study on "Conservatism and Personality," published in 1958,
while it could find little difference between rank-and-file voter attitudes
in either party, did show a marked difference between Republican and
Democratic elites. Resistance to change was much less pronounced in
the latter group.

Still, in the final analysis, the Democratic regulars see all issues
within the framework of the need for party unity. And this was where
they began to part company with the McCarthyites at Chicago. For here
was a group of people who seemed to see an issue as above party.
Nothing rankled the regulars more than the refusal of the new politicians
to pledge support in advance for the nominee of the convention. And
the scarcely veiled threat that if the newcomers did not get their way
they might take the issue to the country with the vehicle of a fourth party
was almost incomprehensible. That was not democracy; it was anarchy.
Politics, after all, was about compromise, not a choice between getting
your way or going off in a sulk. The capacity to endure "skull-flattening"
rhetoric, about which Miller was so scathing, was just part of the price
that had to be paid for keeping the party together: If the bizarre coalition
of forces that was the Democratic Party could survive at all, then the
regulars took for granted that there had to be a gap between rhetoric
and reality. (Regrettably, this *ambiance* has a somewhat blunting effect
on intellectual reflexes. Thus, many regulars who were in no sense hawkish and were genuinely concerned about the war were easily persuaded
that the Vietnam-plank controversy was essentially semantic. After all,
the majority plank had all those agreeable phrases about "peace" and
"negotiation." So why not vote for it? It was possible to feel that one's

heart was in the right place and still not part company with one's friends. Mayor Daley, no untroubled supporter of the Vietnam war, in a later report on the Chicago street disturbances, gave his imprimatur to the conclusion that "the Convention demonstrated everyone wants peace and disagreement occurs *only* over methods.")

What felt like a moral crusade to the insurgents, then, looked like cussedness to the regulars. Especially when the insurgents made so little effort to disguise their contempt for the obtuseness of their opponents. (Al Lowenstein, at one of the preconvention hassles over delegate appointment in New York, declaimed to party stalwarts, "I implore you not to be so stupid.") The McCarthy people remembered the machine's crude devices for whittling down their delegate strength; the machine people remembered the precious places that had to be given up to McCarthy supporters which could have gone to loyal retainers of the party. The students might not know any better, but it was hard to forgive those who ran McCarthy's campaign. "They were squeezing off mayors with thirty years of service," Senator Inouye complained to one of us. "It's not right. And what's more, McCarthy himself knows it's not right." Inouye's moral passion on this score was every bit as strong as was Lowenstein's as an antiwar crusader. And for a very good reason: the party was the bedrock of his political morality; without it the most important issue in the world was irrelevant. This may seem absurd to ideologues, but the parties have to exist and to be serviced in years when the country is not sundered by ideological divisions, and they must exist at intrinsically dull and boring levels of activity, which would not, normally, tempt a solitary Ph.D. scholar from his books or a single political science professor to cough up a campaign contribution. People are unlikely to toil in such a humble vineyard without the occasional reward to boost their egos. One of the richest of all rewards for diligent, if unspectacular, service is a seat at the convention.

But more important than what the regulars resented was what they feared. Few of them ever put it into words, but it was fundamental: the realization that the novices might be a whole lot better at the game than themselves. The insurgents had, after all, guessed the mood of the country correctly before they had. They had demonstrated a bewildering familiarity with party rules which most regulars, if they had ever bothered to learn them, had forgotten long ago. And they were undeniably smart. What if they acquired a long-term taste for political action? The more confident regulars might talk airily about these people being wonderful recruits to the Democratic coalition; lower down the line, it looked as if the recruits were not joining the team but hustling the old one off the field so they could form their own. Congressman Milton Schapp, a Pennsylvania delegate and a regular who favored McCarthy, put it most explicitly when talking of his own delegation: "The last person they will vote for is McCarthy, not because they don't like him particularly—in fact quite a few think he would be better than Humphrey. But deep down they're afraid that if he wins the McCarthy supporters will replace them at the local level. If faced with the choice of losing the election or losing power in the local party, they would rather lose the election."

Pennsylvania provided one of the cruder examples of machine resistance to the insurgents. In the state's preferential primary in April, McCarthy received 428,239 votes (78.5 per cent of the turnout), against 65,430 for Robert Kennedy, and 72,263 for Johnson-Humphrey. The election was little remarked at the time—for the simple reason that it had virtually no effect on delegate selection. The state had two sub-Daley-style bosses: Mayor Joseph Barr of Pittsburgh, and Mayor James Tate of Philadelphia; and with I. W. Abel, the Steelworkers' president, that added up to a well-nigh impregnable machine. At Chicago, Pennsylvania split 103¾ for Humphrey to 26¼ for the peace candidates. The ability of the party organization to nullify the expression of dissent in the primary was founded on its control of delegates-at-large—52 of them, all in the loyalist mold, selected in January—and procedures for delegate election that are so archaic as to be impenetrable to the average voter. And the subtle matrix of relationships within the machine made it perilous to step out of line. For instance, one young union official who wanted to vote for McCarthy ultimately felt it was too risky. He was contesting a union election result and knew that the man who would mediate the dispute was pro-Humphrey.

But if Pennsylvania was outstanding in this regard, it was not especially idiosyncratic. Little more than a third of the convention's voting strength came through the primary system. Of the 3099 delegates in Chicago (wielding a voting strength of 2622, which accounts for the awkward fractional votes), no fewer than 600 were selected by state party organizations, and another 600 were elected, by various procedures, before the first campaign shots were fired in New Hampshire. Such delegates, very naturally, constituted the core of Humphrey's strength. Of course, every so-called democratic party in every country has its undemocratic features—there is no other way to preserve the security of the party's bureaucracy—but it might be argued that the provision for bureaucratic stability in this Democratic Party was unusually high. It certainly seemed so to those in the McCarthy camp coming upon it with a fresh eye.

In practice, relations between the insurgents and the regulars were not uniformly antagonistic. And the gradations were almost predictable, in that they responded to a curious but seemingly universal law: the smaller the acquaintance of the species professional with the species amateur, the greater the degree of animosity. The Southerners, for instance, who in many cases first clapped eyes on McCarthy activists at the convention, hated them cordially. Hostility was only slightly less strong in the big party-organization states like Ohio, Michigan, Illinois, and Pennsylvania. Similarly, where McCarthy delegates achieved only the tiniest foothold, their view of the party in action was almost unrelentingly bleak. Mary Epstein, one of a small group of McCarthy supporters in the Missouri delegation, reeled out of the head-count caucus on the peace plank, muttering, "You mean this is how the system works? I can't stand it." Further up the scale were delegations like Connecticut and New Mexico in which the McCarthy people, while some way from being dominant, were too numerous to be regarded as isolated freaks. A caucus was still in no sense a chance for private debate, simply a place where the lines were drawn. But there were, in less tense moments, some instances of banter between the two sides. At the far end of the spectrum were states, like New York and California, where the beginnings of mutual comprehension began to dawn. More startlingly, some of the machine men began to take on the coloration of the new legions. John Burns, the New York leader, clearly got a lot of pleasure out of his motley crew, which included McCarthy supporters like the columnist Murray Kempton, the folk singer Theodore Bikel, and the cartoonist Jules Feiffer. (Feiffer was less benign: "I said all along the system doesn't work. So I got in the system. And now I know I was right.") But perhaps the most radiantly transformed machine man was Jesse Unruh. Unruh, a man with a prodigious reputation for wheeling and dealing, had been moving steadily to the left ever since the phenomenon of Ronald Reagan burst upon the California scene. Still, it was a shock to Humphrey's lieutenants to find out how far the rot of incorruptibility had gone. Right down to the convention Unruh austerely resisted all attempts to secure his allegiance with large promises of favors to come; "Big" Jesse was a new man. (One might have suspected as much after news leaked out that Unruh had been seen holiday-making earlier in the year attired in Nehru jacket and love beads.)

In fact, the phenomenon of gradual accommodation was less remarkable than it seemed. It is fundamental to the nature of "bossism." A party boss rarely exerts dictatorial authority; his basic talent is balancing all the varieties of desire in his machine. As long as he provides satisfaction he can maneuver. But he can never attempt a maneuver—at least not if he hopes to survive—that undermines the self-image of his own supporters. As we saw in the case of the Connecticut delegation fights, John Bailey's inflexibility was not so much a personal thing as the sum of all the egos he had in his charge. Arthur Miller said at the convention, "The delegates would commit suicide if John Bailey told them to." Perhaps. But, in a certain sense, Bailey was committing suicide for his delegates. After all, Bailey was so high up the party ladder that he could probably survive even if McCarthy won the nomination—and survive on a potentially winning side. On the other hand, many of his delegates might easily be overrun by the new politicians. Unruh's new flexibility proceeded from the same set of circumstances as Bailey's old inflexibility; but Unruh was lucky enough to have an entirely new set of egos to massage. (Both men, incidentally, get precisely the same kind of wry, humorous pleasure out of their work. Had Bailey risen to power in California and Unruh climbed the ladder in Connecticut, the cause of peace in 1968 would almost certainly have numbered Bailey among the angels and identified Unruh with the forces of darkness.)

The new egos, though, were over-all in a distinct minority among the convention delegates. Even allowing for the signs of remotivation evinced by Burns and Unruh, all the preconvention prophecies had Humphrey way past the magic 1312 figure needed for nomination. The Vice-President had 1450 delegates as good as locked up. Could the figure be broken?

In theory, at least, there was one possibility. Humphrey's strength was the old Democratic coalition—the white South, labor, Northern Negroes, and city machine men—between whose elements little love was lost, but which was held together by considerations of shared self-interest. To the political tyros in the McCarthy operation, it seemed that if this coalition was dramatically confronted with its own internal contradictions it might—just might—collapse. After all, the main argument for its existence was its ability in normal years to deliver a comfortable nation-wide majority for the Democrats. But the polls were showing that the abnormal politics of 1968 might have eliminated this *raison d'être*.

The strategy, in fact, was to disrupt the habits of a lifetime for most regular politicians. It could not be a kid-glove operation. Jerry Eller,

McCarthy's legislative assistant, provided the pithiest description of the concept: "Achieve panic. Then win."

The chosen battleground was over credentials—that is, challenging the validity of the methods of selecting delegates in particular states on the grounds that they are not in conformity with the party's avowed policy. Every convention is preceded by Credentials Committee hearings for the purpose of adjudicating such disputes. The recommendations of this committee are then put to the convention for final decision. At most conventions, there are relatively few disputes; a strong reluctance to tamper with the methods of individual states is the norm of Credentials Committee procedure. The committee is drawn from representatives of all the states and a natural disinclination for dog to eat dog prevails. This time, however, that fiercest of mastiffs, the intellectual middle class primed with a sense of moral outrage, was about to be let loose on the committee. There was going to be unpleasantness.

On this front, the Kennedy men were conspicuous by their absence. For the credentials fight was, essentially, the reverse of the peace-plank operation. That had been constructed along lines which, it was hoped, would prove acceptable to old party stalwarts. But there was no disguising that fights over credentials constituted a direct attack on the power of the state party organizations, organizations which the Kennedys had manipulated to their advantage in the past and might well be able to manipulate favorably in the future. So while men like Sorensen, Gilligan, Salinger dutifully lobbed in pious declarations of the need for an open convention, they studiously stayed clear of the operation aimed at making it so.

Indeed, even within the McCarthy campaign there were some who shuddered at the potential consequences of such an attack. Tom Finney, who was trying to corral uncommitted delegates for McCarthy, was aghast at the multiplicity and venom of the credentials fights. How could he woo delegates in key states like Pennsylvania, New York, and Indiana while another part of the McCarthy operation was trying to take away their seats? It was proffering a handshake while clubbing a man with your left hand. "You've got to stop those kids," he told Tom Mechling, the head of McCarthy's delegate-intelligence bureau. "They're tearing this party up by the grass roots."

Mechling was inclined to agree, but what could he do? He had told Eller that the Senator would have to try to integrate his campaign. But Eller had replied that it was hardly necessary, as "the Senator always has about seven campaigns running at the same time." This was fine, of course, as a technique for state-wide campaigning. But as a method for trying to persuade a thousand or so prickly and self-important delegates to change their allegiance, it had acute drawbacks.

Mechling is not a student of Machiavelli. But he had an instinctive perception of the dictum, "Men must either be caressed or else annihilated; they will revenge themselves for small injuries, but cannot do so for great ones; the injury therefore that we do to a man must be such that we need not fear his vengeance." By this rule, the McCarthy operation's only hope of success was to caress and flatter the machine. Given the relative weakness of their voting strength they had no hope of annihilating the opposition; they could only inflict the kind of injury that would invite the machine's vengeance.

Yet there was no real possibility of choice. The very nature of the McCarthy campaign made it unamenable to control. It was not, after all, so much a campaign as a movement. It was impossible simply to ask that movement to stop at the end of the primaries and let the professionals take over. It might have been the wisest course; but who could tell at the time? The year had been activist, and great achievements had been wrought. How could one forbid McCarthy supporters to persist in their activism during the dying weeks of the campaign? One might as well tell a man striving for a four-minute mile that he could take seventy seconds on the last lap and still make it. A runner would know it couldn't be true. His instincts would tell him to pile on the pace even at the risk of blowing up in the home stretch. Something—anything—had to be done to advance the cause. And the only fight left was on credentials.

The task of doing the damage to the state party machines was not so much entrusted to as seized upon by the youthful wing of the McCarthy campaign. The key legmen in the operation were Sam Brown, Curtis Gans, and Dave Mixner, the twenty-six-year-old son of a migrant worker who earlier in the year had done sterling work on the caucus-packing front. ("I always made a point of knowing the rule book better than the pros. It's not difficult, a kid out of kindergarten could do it.") It was an enterprise without an effective executive, though its presentation was handled by Joe Rauh, the man who had paid for the original lunch of the peace-plank plotters but who had now gracefully backed off from a leading role in that more diplomatic operation.

Rauh was of the opinion that all the challenges should be concentrated on the Southern states, for the simple reason that they represented the most precarious part of the traditional Democratic coalition. Every

Northern regular knew that some Southern delegations bristled with out-and-out segregationists, many of whom would in all probability go with George Wallace in November. This put Humphrey in a bind. He needed Southern votes to feel safe about his majority, but if he rushed in to shore up his support there by opposing the challenges to Southern credentials, he might destroy his reputation as a civil-rights campaigner, in which case Northern liberals and Negroes might reject his candidacy. (The Democrats in Chicago had 212 Negro delegates, compared with the meager 26 at the Republican Convention in Miami Beach.) And Humphrey was on record with several barbs at Nixon's Southern strategy, dubbing his party "the Nixiecrats"; he had expressed a personal aversion to "clearing things with Strom." He would look foolish if he were forced into a compact with one or other of the Strom-like figures in the Democratic Party. On the other hand, if Humphrey failed to succor the South, there was a possibility that its votes might be diverted elsewhere, hardly to McCarthy at first, but perhaps behind favorite sons or even into an effort to renominate Lyndon Johnson. (By this time, the McCarthy camp was not entirely unhappy at the possibility of Johnson's name going forward. It might, in their view, destroy the credibility of both President and Vice-President. At the very least it would pose a ghastly problem of allegiance for the party regulars.)

The main reason for concentrating the credentials fight on the South, however, was public relations. The challenges could be presented not as an attack on machine politics or a device for advancing McCarthy's candidacy but as an attempt to root out racism in the party—and there were many regulars in the North who could go along with it. No cynicism is implied here: most McCarthy people were a priori against racism and needed no public-relations justification for opposing it. The question was which of the numerous aspects of the regular party organization which seemed undemocratic to the McCarthy supporters could be most effectively attacked?

In pressing the challenges, Rauh had a miraculously convenient weapon to hand: the official call to delegates for the 1968 convention which arose out of the credentials challenge of the Mississippi delegation in 1964. True to its compromising tradition, the party had then resolved its problems—and Rauh, it will be remembered, had been at the heart of the ambiguous business—by seating most of the segregationist Mississippi delegation and then putting in writing a bold determination to secure a racial balance at subsequent conventions. Many Southerners had naturally assumed that the return of tranquillity would make such embarrassing rhetoric a dead letter. But in the hands of Rauh, his team of merciless Young Turks, and the new breed of politically conscious Negroes in the South, it could come very much alive. There were two key passages in the call. The first abjured that Democratic voters in each state "regardless of race, color, creed, or national origin, will have the opportunity to participate fully in party affairs." Establishing that Negroes had had no such opportunity in states like Georgia, Mississippi, and Alabama was easier than falling off the proverbial log. The second key passage provided that each certified delegate be a "bona fide" Democrat who would participate in "good faith" at the convention: the "loyalty" issue, a useful stick for beating those who leaned, or were being pushed by the pressures at home, toward George Wallace.

Rauh's concept of making friends and influencing Northern regulars by a anti-Southern strategy was sabotaged from the start—not by the opposition, but by the indignation of McCarthy's supporters in Northern states. For most of them, it was their first acquaintance with the inner workings of the party bureaucracies, and their state of shock was in some ways comparable to that of Communist intellectuals in Western Europe during the period of the Stalinist purges. The comparison is not exaggerated. "We Can't Relax Now," affirmed a pro-McCarthy advertisement in the *New York Times* just before the convention, "Not while the killing goes on in Vietnam." In their eyes, lives were being wasted in Vietnam in a quest for the triumph of "democracy" that seemed to be lacking in their own party. In their outrage at machine methods, they scattered shot over the whole party. McCarthy groups in each state, of course, were entitled to put in their own challenges without deferring to a centralized campaign direction. Rauh vainly argued that while there were many abuses in Northern states, challenging credentials there would only alienate potential allies on the Southern fights. Besides, the Northern challenges were almost all complex; counterarguments were too easy. For instance, in Massachusetts, Johnson's withdrawal from the primary had left McCarthy in control of a delegation which contained many pro-Administration regulars. If the insurgents made an issue in Pennsylvania, then the regulars could come slamming back in Massachusetts. It might be a specious response, but then nobody imagined that the intellectual niceties would be observed. Rauh felt the same way about all the Northern challenges: "They aren't worth the gunpowder needed to blow them up."

Nonetheless, when the Credentials Committee met in Chicago on August 19, under the chairmanship of Governor Richard J. Hughes of

New Jersey, a man touted as a possible running mate for Humphrey, it was confronted by an unprecedented number of challenges, most of them inspired by McCarthy supporters and half of them directed against Northern state parties. In all, fifteen delegations were challenged, either in whole or in part. In the South, challenges homed in on Mississippi, Georgia, Alabama, Louisiana, Tennessee, and Texas. (In the case of Alabama, there were actually two rival challenging delegations; and to complicate matters further, the state chairman, Rupert Vance, filed a counterchallenge to all McCarthy delegates on the issue of the loyalty oath.) Challenges were also directed at the Connecticut, Indiana, Michigan, Minnesota, New York, Pennsylvania, and Washington delegations. (New York had already made some attempt to improve the racial balance of its delegation by appointing more Negroes and Puerto Ricans. In the process the McCarthyites had been partly increased—by five and a half votes —their share of delegate-at-large allegiances. The challenge before the Credentials Committee was ultimately dropped.) The pro-McCarthy delegation from Wisconsin was on the receiving end of another loyalty challenge.

Mississippi was no problem, but not much help either. It had made no attempt to put its lily-white house in order after the 1964 fracas and therefore had to go. Humphrey's staff recognized the case for the regular Mississippi Democrats as indefensible and collaborated with the McCarthy forces in challenging it. The challenge slate was a piebald mix of Humphrey and McCarthy supporters, but its leaders were mostly stanch Humphrey men like Hodding Carter, Jr., a courageous young newspaper editor. The Credentials Committee seated the challenges by an 84-to-10 vote.

Georgia offered an opportunity for real leverage. It had been a beautiful operation from the start. In late July, Mixner, Brown, and Gans had flown into the state to supplement the efforts of Julian Bond, a handsome young Negro legislator. Bond, the extremely articulate son of a well-known professor of history, was only twenty-eight but already a veteran battler of the state machine. In 1966, he had been refused a seat in the state legislature because of his opposition to the Vietnam war. He fought the case up to the Supreme Court and ultimately gained his seat. His project in the summer of 1968 was the creation of an alternative convention-delegate slate. With the help of the McCarthy staffers, Bond mounted a state convention at Macon on August 10, at which 41 challenge delegates, 21 white and 20 black, were elected. As an example of grass-roots democracy it had its gimcrack aspects, but when set beside the methods of delegate selection employed by the state party, it seemed almost pure.

Georgia's regular slate had been hand-picked by two men: the state party chairman, James Gray, and the governor, Lester Maddox. Both happen to be stanch segregationists in a state where a quarter of the voting-age population is black. They also happened to have very suspect loyalty credentials: in 1964, Gray headed a Georgia group called Democrats for Goldwater; Maddox, former proprietor of a "whites only" café, was on record with a denunciation of enthusiastic supporters of the Democratic Party as "either fools or cowards or traitors." To make matters worse for the Humphrey people, on August 17, Maddox, who, as we have noted, had been photographed arm in arm with the Vice-President, declared his own candidacy for the Democratic nomination, a move which brought national attention to the lunatic eccentricities of Georgia politics. Maddox's candidacy was designed to combat "socialist decay in the land."

The contrast between the ranting governor and the impressively lucid and cool Julian Bond testifying before the Credentials Committee had a compelling effect. Hughes knew enough to see when something had to give. "That man," he said of Bond, "is a symbol. We have to have him." So the compromise of splitting Georgia's votes between the insurgent delegation and the Maddox delegation went before the convention. It was crude but effective: to most regulars it seemed like a generous compromise, and it let Humphrey off the hook.

That was the limit of the committee's concessions to the insurgents. Any more would have to be won the hard way—in floor fights of the full convention. This time, Rauh was able to select his targets with more care. He would not press the Northern challenges before the convention. But the bruising struggles before the committee had already stiffened the regulars. (Hilda Stokely, a Negro delegate from New York, told a television reporter that "the McCarthy forces" were simply trying to "manipulate and distort" credentials challenges for their own ends.) Still, Rauh did his best; the minority reports submitted by the pro-McCarthy Credentials Committeemen all turned on the racial point—in Georgia, Texas, North Carolina, and Alabama. In that guise, the challenges went to the convention floor.

Ironically, the subject that caused Humphrey the most embarrassment was the seemingly less explosive controversy over the unit rule—the device making each delegation a bloc vote for its majority view—which is popular in the South but all but extinct elsewhere. This was the issue that revealed Humphrey's operation at its most inept and produced one of the most intriguing subplots of the year—an attempted alliance between McCarthy and the South. Humphrey, like most liberals, took a simple position on the unit rule: he was against it. But the question was when, not whether, it should be abolished. The Southerners wanted breathing space. Precipitate abolition of the unit rule, they claimed, would be like "changing the rules in the final quarter of the game." Privately, Humphrey agreed and gave Connally and the other Southern leaders the impression that this would be the line taken by his supporters on the Rules Committee. But then, inexplicably, on Wednesday, August 21, the day before the first Rules Committee hearing in Chicago, Humphrey headquarters released the text of a letter from the Vice-President to the chairman of the committee, Governor Samuel H. Shapiro of Illinois. The letter strongly advocated reform and recommended abolition of the unit rule at the 1968 convention and in the call to the 1972 convention. Connally blew his stack. And with good reason. Terry Sanford, the liberal former Governor of North Carolina, who was watching Humphrey's Southern interests, did not doubt Connally had been misled. "He was told one thing and then Humphrey did another. Bill Connell was telling him the unit rule wouldn't be abolished, and Fred Harris was telling others it would. Absolute conflict. All you can say is that it was without Hubert's knowledge." But it was no use pleading ineptitude. Connally felt betrayed. That kind of mistake should not be made with a man of his importance. The buttonhole of Texas National Committeeman Frank C. Erwin, Jr., ominously sprouted an "All the Way With LBJ" button. And Connally had a mind to go that way too.

Over at McCarthy headquarters, Dick Goodwin thought he heard opportunity give the faintest of knocks. Another McCarthy man, Hugo Sims of South Carolina, had already been going the rounds of Southern leaders asking them to put up proposals for the Vice-Presidential slot on a McCarthy ticket. Some wondrously baroque figures dropped into the hat: "Gorgeous" George Smathers, Louisiana's Governor John McKeithen, Governor Dan K. Moore of North Carolina.

Nobody was fooled, but it was a way of keeping dying hopes alive. Yet the Southern contacts all gave off the same emanations: Connally was not bluffing, he really was angry with Humphrey. So Goodwin was operational. Connally had just publicly lambasted McCarthy in the Platform Committee hearings, but that was no bar to discussion between two seasoned professionals, and Saturday evening Goodwin spent two hours with Connally. At a dinner party given by *The Progressive* magazine at a

Chicago restaurant that night, Goodwin, looking mysteriously optimistic, offered to bet any takers that McCarthy would get the nomination. Afterward he told another senior McCarthy staff man that there was just one complication: persuading McCarthy to take Connally on the ticket.

Goodwin's plan collapsed for two very good reasons. McCarthy, when he heard of Goodwin's initiative, was neither amused nor pleased. Even if he had been, it would have been futile. Connally had been using the affair as another ploy to fray the Vice-President's nerves. On Sunday, relays of Humphrey men were sent to mollify the Governor; and before the convention opened Connally was ushered into the presence of a deeply penitent Vice-President. The unit-rule thing had been a dreadful bureaucratic mix-up, Humphrey assured the Texan, but he would do his best to rectify the situation. Ultimately, even Humphrey could not change the convention's mood on this issue; on Tuesday night, it rejected the unit rule at all levels of the party by a vote of 1350 to 1206. On Connally's other phobias Humphrey could be more reassuring. The Governor could count on his staying firm on Vietnam; and the impertinent challenge to the Texas delegation would be opposed by his supporters.

And so to the voting. The insurgent forces just could not mobilize enough support. The minority recommendation on North Carolina went down by a voice vote; the Alabama challenge, muddled by the fact that there were two antimachine slates in competition and by the willingness of the regulars to sign a pledge as "bona fide" Democrats, was heavily defeated on a roll call, 1605 to 883½—which was about as expected. Rauh's real hopes were pinned on Georgia, a motion to seat not half but the entire Bond slate; and Texas, an attempt to split Connally's delegation by seating part of a racially mixed slate headed by Connally's archopponent, the liberal Senator Ralph Yarborough. Both were defeated: the Georgia motion by 1414 to 1041½; the Texas challenge by 1368 to 955. The strategy of disruption had failed. If the power of the machine could not be broken on issues that caused internal stress, there was no likelihood of its breaking on the principle of opposition to McCarthy. Rauh took it badly: "I thought you could really embarrass the alliance of Northern bosses, labor, and Southern reactionaries. I was wrong. 'You can't hold that alliance together,' I said. I was wrong. There isn't that much difference. The Northern bosses simply weren't embarrassed. We lost it in Michigan, Pennsylvania, Ohio, Indiana, and Illinois. The truth is that the guys like Daley, Barr, Tate, and Branigan are no longer ashamed of being in bed with Southern reactionaries."

It was a gloomy analysis; too gloomy, in fact. The alliance, if not broken, had been embarrassed. There had been some impressive movement in the ranks. The disparate elements in the New York delegation, for instance, had been welded together to cast their 190 votes unanimously for both the Georgia and the Texas challenges. The abolition of the unit rule had been a signal achievement, although it owed less to Rauh's operation than to Governor Harold Hughes of Iowa. (Hughes, who ultimately backed McCarthy, had earlier in the year chaired a commission on the democratic selection of Presidential nominees, and its cogently argued report had influenced many delegates.) But perhaps the outstanding achievement had been the start made on questioning the legitimacy of the segregationist Democrats in the Deep South. In any normal year, this range of reforms, combined with the spectacle of Governor Connally getting his back up, would have been considered a little short of revolutionary. But as a strategy for advancing McCarthy's candidacy it had been essentially counterproductive. It confirmed the impression of most regulars that McCarthy people were impossible to deal with; whatever their own internal dissensions might be, they felt, they had more in common with each other than with the insurgents.

McCarthy realized this better than anyone. His conduct both prior to and during the convention suggested the frame of mind of a man who knew it was all over but the shouting—and was instinctively dreading the shouting. He endorsed, but took no part in, the credentials and rules fights. He already knew that the regulars did not much like him and would like him less after close combat with his supporters. Perhaps he had come to think that the ritual cleansing of the party machine was more important than his own candidacy. There is some evidence that McCarthy at one time wanted to damp down his supporters' zeal in unseating regulars. In Oklahoma, for instance, his supporters had been demanding eleven seats, when, to their chagrin, McCarthy came into the state and said two would be quite enough—"All I want is representation for my views." But to pursue a policy of positive "caressing" of the machine, McCarthy would have had to spell this out and to some extent set his great authority against that of his wilder followers, which he was never prepared to do. Whatever McCarthy had thought, however, he knew in Chicago that the odds against him were impossibly long. He did not even bother to feign combativeness; of all politicians he is perhaps the least inclined to confuse activity with action. But if he was resigned, he could not manage to disguise his bitterness. Thus, at what, logically, should have been the crescendo of the peace campaign, its champion was at his most wayward and perplexing.

The response to his initial statement on the Czech crisis was perhaps what finally disillusioned him with the ritual of "going through the motions." When Galbraith phoned him to point out how serious its impact had been not only in strengthening his enemies but also on the morale of his supporters, McCarthy replied, "Ken, I expected all the other fools to call me, but I never thought you would." McCarthy, as we have seen, subsequently issued a statement deploring the "cruelty" of the Soviet action, but it was to be his final genuflection in the direction of conventional rhetoric. As an afterthought, it failed to take the edge off the unhappy consequences of his earlier statement. Any reluctance to join the chorus of righteous indignation was deemed at best indifference and at worst callousness. On the day the convention opened, those sudden recruits for the politics of compassion, Robert Novak and Rowland Evans, headlined their column: "McCarthy's 'Lack of Compassion' on Czech Crisis Shocks Friends." The story related how McCarthy's action had confirmed impressions some of his supporters had of his "insensitivity."

For McCarthy, being accused of "insensitivity" and "lack of compassion" by Republican journalists was indeed a hard lot. When, earlier in the year, he had shown almost unique sensitivity to the country's mood over Vietnam, most of the press had written about him in terms suggesting that anyone who took on Lyndon Johnson must be prey to some kind of psychological disturbance. A man with less self-regard would probably have shrugged it off, but McCarthy refused to grin and bear it. He visited only five delegations and presented himself on a take-me-or-leave-me basis. His performance before the California delegation in the Grand Ballroom of the LaSalle on Tuesday morning was typical.

It was a set-piece occasion, in which the three candidates—Humphrey, McGovern, and McCarthy—were to come together to present their cases to this influential, and large, delegation. The great confrontation that everyone had been demanding since Humphrey first entered the race was at hand. On the evidence of past performance, McCarthy should have been the most popular of the three. California had been the cradle of his candidacy, and now California's delegation was to host the showdown. It might be too late to influence the convention, but not too late to make Humphrey squirm in public. An unworthy thought, perhaps, but a common one among Californians at the time.

McCarthy was the lead speaker. To everyone's amazement, his first verbal assault was made not on the war, nor even on the Vice-President, but on George McGovern, the man who was running on the same antiwar position as his own. ("Running" may be an inappropriate term:

McGovern's candidacy was basically a device for mopping up peace support that might otherwise, because of irritation over McCarthy, drift back into the Humphrey column.) The previous day, when asked how his candidacy differed from McCarthy's, McGovern had incautiously remarked of his rival, "He has taken the view that a passive and inactive Presidency is in order, and that disturbs me. Solving our domestic problems will be much more difficult and that will require an active and compassionate President." So even McGovern had taken up the "lack of compassion" line.

McCarthy would not let it go. His remarks were perceptive but still faintly chilling: "Well, I think a little passivity in that office [the Presidency] is all right, a kind of balance, I think. I have never quite known what active compassion is. Actually, compassion, in my mind, is to suffer *with* someone, not in advance of him. Or not in public necessarily." McCarthy went on to recall his extreme lack of passivity on the campaign trail over the year, "raising issues all the way." It was not self-justification—nobody in that audience needed to be told what McCarthy had done for the cause. But rather it was an expression of contempt for those who doubted his seriousness as a candidate or his capacity to be President. The audience was not enthused.

Humphrey was Humphrey. He started by fielding an artful question on whether his position on Vietnam differed in any respect from the President's: "I did not come here to repudiate the President of the United States. I want that made quite clear." There was to be no change. The speech was a familiar mixture: The United States was "resisting aggression" in Vietnam, the negotiation "roadblock" was in Hanoi, but there were great hopes for "freedom" and "democracy" in Southeast Asia. After all, he put it, "when you look over the world scene, those elections [in South Vietnam] stand up pretty well, and the basis of the government today is a broader-based government."

Humphrey had pressed all the PR knobs for the policy, but he was speaking to an audience that questioned its basic intellectual structure. It would be child's play to demolish it. McCarthy seemed to think child's play beneath him. After listening to Humphrey's glowing periods with evident distaste, he refused the right of reply, contenting himself with a perfunctory "the people know my position."

It was left to McGovern to make the case. And he made it well. He pointed out that the South Vietnamese election the Vice-President had specially mentioned had a somewhat cloudy aftermath. The Presidential candidate Truong Dinh Dzu, whose children were being feted at McGovern's headquarters at the Sheraton Blackstone, had been sentenced to five years' hard labor for the very crime McCarthy and McGovern were freely committing: advocating a negotiated end to the war. But McGovern was a man without malice—recalling Humphrey's services to "civil and human justice" in America. He was clearly the hero of the hour, but when he sat down even Humphrey was smiling at what should have been the moment of supreme humiliation. The South Dakotan, when all was said and done, was a regular guy. From McCarthy there was final confirmation of irregularity. Before leaving the meeting, he reiterated his intention not to support a Democratic candidate "whose views [on Vietnam] do not come close to what mine are."

That evening McCarthy as good as conceded. Around ten o'clock, news came through to the convention, then girding itself for the unit-rule fight, that McCarthy had blown it. In an interview with the editors of the Knight newspapers he had wallowed in realism. The wire-service report had it that McCarthy estimated the combined strength of the peace forces at no more than 900 delegates. To a question on whether this meant that Humphrey had the nomination wrapped up, McCarthy had replied bleakly, "I think so."

Less publicly, the Johnson men in town were still watching out for their chief's interests. Just before midnight, Marvin Watson went up to Humphrey's suite in the Hilton to make sure everything was in order. Watson was perturbed by "rumors" that a handful of Humphrey supporters were putting the word about that it would help the Vice-President if delegates voted for the peace plank. This was probably not serious; Watson was sure that the Vice-President would find some way of disabusing them of this error before the balloting took place. It was to be Humphrey's final act of obeisance before his nomination.

Over in the convention hall, the last minutes of Johnson's birthday ticked away amid scenes of mounting confusion and choler. By one o'clock Wednesday morning, when it became obvious that the platform would try to ram through the Vietnam debate and vote that night, all restraint disappeared. The McCarthy people were not going to be cheated out of television prime time that easily. A podium decision to turn down the adjournment motion of Don Peterson, chairman of the Wisconsin delegation, was the signal for the chant, "Let's go home. Let's go home." Daley was on his feet, shaking his fist, and shouting for order; Carl Albert rapped his gavel furiously for silence. But two days of frustration inflated the lungs of the unruly. Eventually, Daley gave a disgusted signal—a slashing, imperious motion across the throat with his right hand—and

Albert recognized the Mayor's request for an adjournment. The peace forces had won a skirmish, but by this stage few expected to win anything more. The votes were just not there. Unless, of course, those rumors of the advent of a glamorous new champion were true. But without Edward Kennedy, as Richard Goodwin's professional realism recognized, "between the South and labor, there was no way to break it."

5

The Ted Offensive

" 'Is there any point to which you would wish to draw my
attention?'
'To the curious incident of the dog in the night-time.'
'The dog did nothing in the night-time.'
'That was the curious incident,' remarked Sherlock
Holmes."

—Arthur Conan Doyle, "Silver Blaze"

The only serious hope that sustained those Democrats who wanted
to deny Humphrey the nomination was the possibility that Ted Kennedy
might be a candidate. The great Austrian novelist Robert Musil had a
theory that the most important events in history are often the ones that
might have happened but somehow never quite did. By any standards,
whether you want to look at where power lay in the Democratic Party
in 1968 or to guess where it may lie in the future, one of the most significant incidents at Chicago was the curious case of the dog that didn't
quite bark.

Robert Kennedy, in the fall of 1967 and the first two months of
1968, *wanted* to run but couldn't make up his mind to do so because
most of the people whose judgment he trusted were telling him he
shouldn't. After his death, his brother Ted's situation was in some ways
exactly the opposite; he was being beseeched to run by some of the
powerful politicians in the Democratic Party. Some of them were telling
him that the nomination was within his grasp. The question was whether
he wanted it emotionally.

His brother's death had, of course, been a trauma. One day in late
July he went all the way down to Washington from Hyannis Port to sign

some important papers, stopped in his car outside his office, and turned around and went all the way back up to Cape Cod. "I just couldn't go in and face them all," he said. He was the head of the family now, ultimately responsible for its vast business affairs and for bringing up fifteen children, plus one still unborn. At thirty-six, he honestly did not feel himself qualified by experience for the Presidency, and he was acutely aware of the interpretation that many people would put on any attempt to assert a dynastic claim to the nomination.

Yet there is no more striking proof of how far the development which we have labeled "bastard feudalism" has gone in American politics than the way Ted Kennedy automatically jumped into the front rank of potential candidates. Both press and politicians treated him as such from the minute his brother died. The Kennedy henchmen turned instinctively to him: he had only to say the word and some of the most experienced and influential politicos in the country would be his to command. He himself never doubted that, young and inexperienced as he was, as the chieftain of "the Kennedys," he was "available" if he chose to be. (In its technical sense, as used by American politicians, the word "available" carries no implication that a man actually wishes to be considered a candidate: only that he has the attributes to be elected or nominated. Thus, at the moment at any rate, no Jew or Negro is available. Nor, normally, would a thirty-six-year-old Catholic freshman Senator from a smallish state be available—unless he were a Kennedy. The political magic of the Kennedy name, it was generally assumed, was a transferable inheritance.)

Ted Kennedy recognized, obliquely, the expectations that were placed in him when he went on television on June 15. On the lawn of his parents' house, sitting next to his mother and his paralyzed, seventy-nine-year-old father, he thanked the country for its condolences. "Each of us will have to decide, in a private way," he went on pointedly, "in our own hearts, in our own consciences, what we will do in the course of this summer and in future summers." He was aware, too—he could not but be aware—that in future summers, four summers and eight summers ahead, he might have other and better chances.

Early in July, he left for Spain with Robert Kennedy's oldest son, who was going to work on a *hacienda* for the summer there. Before he went, on July 2, there was a big meeting of three generations of the Kennedy retinue: White House veterans like Sorensen and Salinger; Bobby's friends—Robert McNamara, Burke Marshall, John Siegenthaler,

Fred Dutton, Peter Edelman, and Adam Walinsky; and David Burke and Dun Gifford, from Ted's own staff. They talked on an open patio overlooking the ocean. The purpose of the meeting was to plan a "living memorial" for Robert Kennedy. (Two further meetings were held for the same purpose later in the month. Each set off a frenzy of speculation.) In fact, after the meeting a small group including Sorensen, Burke, and Siegenthaler stayed behind to discuss Ted Kennedy's political future. It was decided that he should make a speech in which he would take himself out of national politics in 1968 but make a statement calling for a bombing halt in Vietnam. Since this might be construed as a slap at Hubert Humphrey, and since the men at the meeting seethed with bitterness toward Gene McCarthy, of whom "petty" was one of the kinder words used, it was also proposed to make a statement calling for urgent programs in the ghettos. This, the Kennedy loyalists felt, would be construed as a balancing slap at McCarthy.

Ted was back from Spain by the middle of July, and he spent the rest of the month incommunicado, fishing and thinking and sailing his rented sixty-foot yawl *Mira*. The politicians did everything short of actually slavering in their greed to see the magic name on their state tickets. It was noticeable that the loudest noises were coming not from the opponents of the war or from Robert Kennedy's liberals, but from the regular politicians. A Harris survey suggested that Kennedy as Vice-President would add five million voters to the Democratic ticket. At a dinner in South Dakota at which the McGovern balloon was floated, there was some talk of Teddy's running. That was on July 14. On the same day ex-Governor Michael DiSalle of Ohio got in first by announcing flatly that he would nominate Kennedy for the Presidency whether he liked it or not. And Senator Philip Hart of Michigan got off the remarkable judgment, "He's as fine a Kennedy as I've known, including John and Bob." A week later came three even more significant pseudo-endorsements: Governor Hughes of New Jersey said bluntly, "His candidacy would bring great strength to our ticket." Hubert Humphrey himself mused aloud in the course of a television interview about what a great personal friend of his the young Senator was. And Governor Sam Shapiro of Illinois grunted something about his being "a great American."

That made ears prick up. Shapiro is Daley's man. And sure enough, three days later, the great Mayor himself joined the chorus of supplication. Had he talked to Kennedy about the Vice-Presidential nomination? he was asked. "No, but I think the convention will draft him. I hope so." That night Kennedy telephoned Daley, thanked him for his kind thoughts, but made it plain that he was not interested in the Vice-Presidential spot. Daley asked him to think it over. Kennedy said he would but that he had made his mind up.

The pressure had now built up to the point where if some of the air was not let out soon Kennedy might find it impossible to go on saying no without looking haughty and ungrateful. And so on July 26 a short statement was issued from his office while he went out sailing. It expressed appreciation for the honor "many prominent Democrats" had paid him. "But for me, this year, it is impossible. My reasons are purely personal. . . . I have informed the Democratic candidates for the Presidency and the chairman of the convention that I will not be able to accept the Vice-Presidential nomination if offered, and that my decision is final, firm, and not subject to further consideration." He said nothing about the Presidential nomination.

It was August 21, almost the eve of the convention, before Kennedy gave the speech that had been planned on July 2. It was a sonorous text, and he read it with dignity. But it was also a bizarrely incomplete synthesis of two sides of the Kennedy tradition. Indeed, there were passages that almost sounded like a dialogue, through the mouth of the handsome young Senator, between the two antithetical schools of speechwriters and advisers which, as we have seen, had debated the issues of Robert Kennedy's candidacy: what might be called the radical, or Walinskian school, and the Ciceronian-chauvinist, or Sorensen, school.

Walinsky-Kennedy opens the debate by expressing concern for "the divisions among us." Sorensen-Kennedy ripostes by expressing regret that "so many of the young and the poor have felt impelled to defy the very basis of our system." And so it goes on antiphonally:

W-K: "For a while this year there was new hope that the voice of the individual could be heard . . . in a new politics of citizen participation."

S-K: "I am concerned, deeply concerned, about crime. . . ."

W-K: "But arms alone will never bring quiet or security to our streets."

S-K: "This is a nation of confidence and compassion and high purpose."

W-K: "This war is the tragedy of our generation!"

S-K (*cunningly seeming to agree*): "Old allies, and new friends, former enemies and present adversaries—all might have looked at our country with . . . the sure knowledge that this must be their model for the future. It was all here, but now it is gone. . . ."

W-K: "Extricate our men and our future from this bottomless pit of our dreams!"

S-K (*triumphantly*): "We will remain . . . as Lincoln said, 'the last best hope of mankind.' "

No wonder the politicians flocked to the standards of a young man who not only was rich and good-looking, and named Kennedy, but knew how to steer so steady a course between the Scylla of Yes and the Charybdis of No.

On Thursday, the day after the speech, Ted Kennedy let his staff know that he would prefer them not to go out to Chicago as they had planned. "He felt," one of them remembers, "that, whatever we did there, people would interpret our presence as an effort to work for his nomination. So we didn't go."

At this point the possibility of stopping Hubert Humphrey depended on a sort of parallelogram of four political forces: Daley, Unruh, McCarthy, and Kennedy. On paper, as we have seen, Humphrey was very close to the nomination, if not indeed, as Larry O'Brien was loudly proclaiming, over the top. But—as O'Brien knew better than anyone— many of those "firm delegates" of his were in fact all too loose. If the temperature could be built up with the excitement of a draft, some of Humphrey's support might melt. If the four forces were all to pull in the same direction, enough Humphrey delegates might be pried loose to give Kennedy the nomination. But if the forces in the parallelogram neutralized one another, it couldn't be done.

McCarthy knew he couldn't make it. He had something between five hundred and six hundred delegates. His commitment was against the Administration and against the war. His disdain for the Kennedy family was notorious. Was it conceivable that at this crisis his commitment might outweigh that disdain?

One hundred and seventy-four delegates, roughly half of them probably McCarthy's, were more or less under the influence of Jesse Unruh. California was originally, after all, a Robert Kennedy delegation. If Unruh were to shift to Ted Kennedy at the right time and in the right way, he might take with him not only the Californians but others as well—McCarthy delegates and some from Humphrey too.

Daley controlled one hundred eighteen Illinois delegates. He was now urging Kennedy to be a candidate for the Presidency. But only a month before he had been urging him to run for the Vice-Presidency. Was his new position the result of a decision that Humphrey could not win? Or was it a sucker trap, a ploy to get Kennedy to admit that he might accept the Presidential nomination, so that he could no longer turn down the Vice-Presidential one?

In practice, the game Kennedy had to play was even more difficult. It was not only that he could not reach for the nomination; he had to go through the motions of discouraging every attempt that was made to draft him. We say "go through the motions," because if his only concern had in fact been to make certain that his name was not even mentioned as a possibility, it would have been the easiest thing in the world to knock all such talk on the head. And that is not what he did.

Kennedy had asked his staff not to go out to Chicago, but then the Kennedys had always preferred to keep the most delicate assignments in the family. The main business of supervising the family's affairs has now devolved on Stephen Smith, and nobody who has met him will doubt his capacity to preside behind the discreet door marked "Joseph P. Kennedy" high above Park Avenue. He is a small, taut man of forty-one with china-blue eyes and a disconcerting habit of gulping for breath like a swimmer until the muscles in his face stand out, giving him a fierce look that is probably the result more of tension than of ferocity, since he is also capable of a sudden grin which makes his bark seem worse than his bite. He was, in any case, an ideal confidential agent for his young brother-in-law.

On the Friday before the convention Smith was in Chicago, seeing Daley "about quite another matter." That night he returned to Hyannis Port and reported to Kennedy that he had seen Daley and there had been no mention of the Presidential nomination. But on Saturday morning Daley called. He had been talking to a lot of people, people from Ohio, people from Pennsylvania, politicians from every part of the country who seriously wondered whether Humphrey could make it. Now, on the phone, he came straight to the point. Humphrey was in trouble, he thought, and Kennedy should be a candidate.

Kennedy said that was impossible.

"Well, then at least you ought to come out to Chicago."

"I can't do that."

"Then at least give some indication that you would accept a draft."

Kennedy said he couldn't do that either, but that Smith would be coming out—he was a delegate from New York—and would be in touch with him.

On Sunday morning, Jesse Unruh had breakfast with Daley in a private room at the Sherman House, where the Cook County Democrats have their headquarters, across the street from City Hall. Daley started to complain that Humphrey wasn't a winner. Unruh agreed. "Let's get another candidate," Daley said. Everyone present understood that that meant Teddy. Only two other possibilities were considered: McCarthy and Johnson. (Unruh respected McGovern but never regarded him as a serious alternative.) McCarthy was unacceptable to Daley. The President was unacceptable to Unruh. That left Kennedy, and Unruh went away convinced that "there was something going."

A few minutes after noon, Steve Smith checked into the Standard Club, a few blocks away from the Sherman House, and the first thing he did was to call Daley. The Mayor told him that he thought "the boys might decide to hold off for forty-eight hours." That was his little joke. He meant that he had decided to do something unprecedented. The Illinois caucus was due to meet that afternoon; each of the candidates was due to appear before it, and normally the delegation would then announce its preference. Daley had decided to give Kennedy forty-eight hours.

Smith reported to Kennedy and then called Daley out of the caucus to make absolutely certain that the Mayor understood Kennedy's position: it would really have to be a draft, and Smith was not going to be involved in starting it. Then he settled down with his telephone to count noses. All Sunday afternoon and evening, without breaking even for dinner, he hunched over the telephone, calling the men in every delegation who constituted the political patrimony of the youngest Kennedy. That night Mike DiSalle set up a Draft Kennedy office in his cramped and gloomy suite at the Sherman House. And that night Richard Goodwin called Smith. He said he had discussed with McCarthy in principle the idea of his stepping down in favor of Kennedy. McCarthy had given the idea some thought and suggested that the matter should be pursued further. Goodwin did more than pursue it. He pushed it. At one point he asked Smith, "Are you prepared to turn down the Presidency of the United States?"

That was what Smith didn't know. On Monday he went on with his telephoning. All morning delegates poured into the "Draft Kennedy" headquarters. By one o'clock about a third of the key Pennsylvania delegation, which was supposed to be for Humphrey, had called, and—stranger yet—an Alabama delegate strolled in and said he reckoned he could shake loose a dozen Southerners for Kennedy. The headquarters moved to a larger suite, and someone went over to locate a stockpile of twenty-five thousand two-tone Kennedy buttons left over from Robert's campaign. A Missouri delegate said he thought there was very little chance of winning with Humphrey, and a Nebraskan said, "This is what we've been looking for." Strangest of all, there was Al Lowenstein standing in the lobby, looking as pleased as punch. "Now we can stop worrying about America and start worrying over Britain's problems," he told one of us. For one of the best-kept secrets of the campaign was that this "Draft Kennedy" improvisation was one of Lowenstein's operations —not sanctioned by Smith or Kennedy but an effort to put pressure on them.

By the end of Monday afternoon, Smith had his answer. There were some people in almost every delegation who thought Humphrey couldn't be elected. New York would go for Kennedy. So would California. So would Illinois. If the name of Edward M. Kennedy were to be placed in nomination, he would get enough votes to stop Humphrey on the first ballot. And Mike DiSalle had promised to put his name in nomination. . . . Goodwin had asked the right question: Were they going to turn down the Presidency?

At nine o'clock that morning, from Hyannis Port, Kennedy had placed a call to DiSalle, and DiSalle refused to take it. All afternoon page boys toured the Hilton squeaking, "A long distance call for Governor DiSalle!" In the end Kennedy sent a telegram, and DiSalle finally called back and was told that Kennedy would not let his name go into nomination.

This was scarcely decisive. Anybody could see that you might not want your name to be put into nomination by someone who might be considered a cat's paw, and still not say no if it were put forward by Daley, say—or by McCarthy.

On Monday morning, as a McCarthy staff meeting was breaking up, McCarthy walked up to Goodwin and asked him, "What about this Teddy thing?" Goodwin said he did not believe that Kennedy would allow his name to go before the convention in opposition to McCarthy's, and he might not let it go at all. "Well," said McCarthy, "we might do it together." "After all," he added to Goodwin's astonishment, "experience isn't really important in a President. Character and judgment are the real thing. Of course he's young, but those fellows in the Revolution were young—Jefferson and Hamilton."

Three times, on Monday, Goodwin called Smith to ask how he saw things developing. The fourth time he called was at one o'clock on Tuesday morning. Smith's private hunch was that McCarthy was working for the Vice-Presidency on a Humphrey ticket, provided he could get an honorable compromise on the peace plank. "Would you accept the Vice-Presidency?" he asked Goodwin abruptly, and he thought he detected a significant pause before Goodwin answered, "I don't think so now." Goodwin suggested that Smith ought to come over and talk to McCarthy, and Smith said, "I'll let you know."

On Tuesday morning McCarthy again asked Goodwin what he thought about "Teddy." Goodwin was in a difficult spot. All year he had been suspected in the McCarthy campaign of being an undercover man for the Kennedys, and, although he worked loyally for McCarthy until his departure and again after Robert Kennedy's death, there was a sense in which these suspicions were not altogether unfair. So now he suggested that McCarthy himself should talk to Smith, and with characteristic ingenuity suggested a "cover." The platform fight was due to begin that night on the peace plank. Why not talk to Smith about that?

At about four-thirty on Tuesday afternoon Smith arrived at Goodwin's room a few feet from the elevators on the twenty-third floor. A considerable number of McCarthy staff workers and reporters were surprised to see Smith disappear into the McCarthy area.

The meeting that followed was one of the turning points of the whole year. It marked the climax, and the death, of that insurrection against the war and the leadership of the Democratic Party which had begun so many months before, and which had been sustained with such passion and tenacity.

There were only three people present. We have talked to two of them ourselves, and each of the three has had his account published in one form or another. Richard Goodwin has written his own version for *Look* magazine. What has been described as "Steve Smith's authorized version" has appeared in *New York* magazine under the byline of Peter Maas. And Senator McCarthy has delivered laconic comments in an interview with the *Boston Globe*. Since there are substantial divergences between Goodwin's and Maas's accounts, we think it best to print them both, and leave the reader to reconstruct this intriguing confrontation for himself. (Italics have been added to draw attention to the only two phrases which the two accounts, each of which purports to be nearly verbatim, have in common.)

GOODWIN

The talk began with pleasantries, and a quick agreement by Smith to cooperate on Vietnam.

Smith then said he wanted McCarthy to know that Senator Kennedy was not a candidate, and that neither he nor anyone else had lifted a finger on his behalf. Nor would they do so. His only role was to listen and observe, making sure that no one did anything that might be misinterpreted as a Kennedy desire for the nomination.

McCarthy listened calmly and then proceeded. *"I can't make it,"* he said. "Teddy and I have the same views, and I'm willing to ask all my delegates to vote for him. *I'd like to have my name placed in nomination,* and even have a run on the first ballot. But if that's not possible, I'll act as soon as it's necessary to be effective."

That was it, McCarthy had not been asked for support, and he had asked nothing in return. Both Smith and I walked from the room deeply moved. I thought of the snows of New Hampshire, the endless months of campaigning, the dedicated movement that had gathered around McCarthy banners—all now graciously and austerely offered to the Massachusetts Senator.

We were silent until we reached the elevator. "Let's keep in touch," Smith said, and left.

MAAS

McCarthy came in, hand extended, and said, "Hello, Steve." "You're looking well," Smith replied, "considering everything you've been through." They had met only once before, very briefly as he remembers, before this encounter.

McCarthy then said, "The situation is this. *I don't think I can make it.* What's Teddy going to do?" Smith said, as he had been saying to everyone else, "The Senator is not a candidate."

McCarthy continued, "Well, in that case, there is really only one course possible for me. *I would like to see my name in nomination.* I'll indicate beforehand that it will be perfunctory. Then I'll stand on the floor and take myself out, and I will urge my people to support Teddy."

Up until this point the meeting had been refreshingly direct, even gracious. Then McCarthy gratuitously added, "While I'm doing this for Teddy, I never could have done it for Bobby." *Time* reported that tears of gratitude came to Smith's eyes following McCarthy's offer. Smith later told me, "Somebody mistook it for all the spit in them."

"Would you think that with my support," McCarthy added, "Teddy has a chance?"

Smith agreed that he thought "it would be a real ball game," but he would have to check back with Kennedy about this new development. With that the meeting broke up. In all it had lasted about ten minutes.

"That story Richard Goodwin had is just about the way it was," McCarthy told the *Boston Globe*. "You see, I think all my people would have gone for Teddy, nearly all, and it was obvious that a good number of the people who were Kennedy people weren't going to go for me. . . .

I think it would have been close. I think he could have gotten 1,000 votes anyway."

The first comment to be made on this transaction—on either account of it—is that the new politicians seem to have behaved remarkably like the old. Here were McCarthy, the man who had campaigned all year against a closed convention, and Smith, the agent of two brothers who had appointed themselves as the champions of a New Politics of participation, coolly disposing of the Presidential nomination of the Democratic Party almost as if it were a block of stock in a private corporation. Their conversation would not have seemed too far out of place forty-eight years earlier, in the room in the Blackstone Hotel, on the other side of Balbo Street, in which the nomination of Warren Gamaliel Harding was decided. This was a smoke-filled room without the smoke. (Goodwin likes Panatellas; McCarthy and Smith are nonsmokers.)

In spite of the discrepancies in the quoted dialogue, the two accounts seem to agree on the essential point: that McCarthy did offer not merely to withdraw but to do so before the first ballot and therefore in time to stop Humphrey. That is the only meaning that makes sense of Goodwin's phrase, "as soon as it's necessary to be effective," and Smith and Maas are explicit on this point.

Then why did Kennedy turn it down? Maas appears to imply at first reading that the knightly code seemed to Smith to require Kennedy to decline the nomination because McCarthy had been nasty about his brother. It can be confirmed that Smith was deeply angered by what seemed to him a gratuitous insult to the dead. But on a closer reading, it wasn't as simple as that: even with his eye metaphorically full of spit, Smith still felt he had to check back with Ted Kennedy.

Did Kennedy, then, turn it down for the reasons that had been given publicly all along—because he was too young, too inexperienced, or too upset about his brother's death? No doubt all these things entered into it, but apparently this was not the whole story. Maas's account explicitly says that the decisive reason for Kennedy's decision was something else: "The Schoumacher report so muddied the waters that Kennedy, the next morning, called Vice-President Humphrey and irrevocably removed his name from consideration." In other words, for more than three hours after McCarthy's alleged insult, on Smith's own account to Maas, "Smith had been on the phone periodically with a Kennedy still struggling to decide what, if anything, he should do." So it wasn't the spit in Smith's eye. What about the "Schoumacher report"?

David Schoumacher, a CBS reporter, had covered McCarthy ever

since New Hampshire. At eight-thirty that Tuesday evening he went on
the air with a report that Smith had visited McCarthy and spent two
hours with him, asking for his support. This infuriated Smith, who immediately and perhaps correctly suspected a leak from the McCarthy camp.
He angrily telephoned Goodwin and asked for a retraction, and much
of the evening was spent in trying to get Goodwin to make an unambiguous *démenti* on television.

Yet even after Goodwin had made a second statement, Kennedy still
waited for many hours before he finally killed the last possibility of a
draft. It was not until Wednesday morning that he telephoned Humphrey,
Daley, and Unruh to tell them that he would withdraw his name even if
it were put forward, and dictated a statement to the same effect to be
given to the wire services by his press secretary. Only then was it certain
that he would not be a candidate, and therefore that Humphrey would
be the Democratic nominee.

What are we to make of this whole story? To begin with, there is
no reason to disbelieve Senator Kennedy and his friends when they say
they did nothing to encourage a draft. What cannot be so categorically
said is that "he didn't want the nomination." He did feel distaste at
the idea of picking up the prize his murdered brother had sought.
"This was Bobby's year," he told a friend. No doubt, too, he was afraid
of what people would think of him for picking it up. And no doubt he
questioned his own readiness for the Presidency. But, as his friends point
out, there were arguments that cut the other way. "He saw the resentment that would boil up if, indeed, he was summoned by his party and
turned his back on it," Smith told Maas. "He thought his brother had
given his life for that nomination," one of his aides told us; "perhaps
he owed it to him to seek it."

The truth is, it can be said authoritatively, that there were circumstances in which Kennedy would have allowed himself to be drafted. He
was in fact, "terrifically ambivalent." He understood that there is "no
such thing as a draft, that it's a circle, and that the situation in Chicago
was as close as you'll get to an actual draft," as Steve Smith put it to
us. Two considerations in the end were probably decisive.

For all his summer of meditation, the crown prince did not really
see in his own mind that the crown was his until Daley's telephone call
that Saturday afternoon. Instincts of correctness suggested he should do
nothing without a draft, and do nothing to encourage one. It was not
until later that he understood that in effect he was being drafted. But

that only happened when McCarthy made his offer. And the nub of the matter, the fitting climax to the tragedy of his brothers' relations with the man, was that when it came to the point, neither he nor Smith trusted McCarthy. "The tip-off to me," Smith has said, "was when he said, 'I'll stand on the floor and take myself out, but I can't nominate Kennedy.' Well, I always think in this life either you do or you don't."

"I don't think McCarthy's offer was genuine," echoes an older man, with experience of both politics and diplomacy, who is perhaps Kennedy's most trusted adviser outside the family. "He was asking Kennedy to trust him. And politicians can't trust one another on the floor of a national convention. It's like nations trusting one another at a disarmament conference. They just can't do it."

On Wednesday morning, Steve Smith met a friend in the lobby of the Hilton who had talked to McCarthy. "I wanted Teddy to take it," McCarthy is reported to have said, "and then be beaten. It would have broken the chain." The chain was not broken. A surprising and surely conclusive witness steps forward to clinch the point.

"I was in Europe," Mrs. Rose Kennedy said afterward, "visiting Eunice [Shriver, her daughter] during the convention. I didn't realize how strong the pressures on him had been until I got home. Then Teddy greeted me by joking, 'You almost had another candidate.' I felt he made the right decision for the obvious reasons. This was not the time. I have been worried about his safety, yes, but I feel he should go on in politics."

In his heart of hearts, Kennedy did not turn down the Presidency. He took a rain check on it.

6

A Throne of Bayonets

"In his master's steps he trod,
  Where the snow lay dinted;
Heat was in the very sod
  Which the Saint had printed."

—John Mason Neale, "Good King Wenceslas"

"A man may build himself a throne of bayonets, but he cannot sit on it."

—Dean Inge

So it was to be the survival of the unfittest. In the theory of political Darwinism, the obstacle course over which candidates for the Presidency have to compete eliminates all but the hardiest political animals. Sometimes this is indeed what happens. But not in 1968. Nixon won his nomination because he was the lowest common denominator acceptable to all the jealous factions of his party. He won, not because of the exceptional nature of his gifts, but precisely because they were unexceptional and unexceptionable.

Humphrey was on the brink of nomination because he had accepted the loss of his own political identity. That identity had probably been exaggerated in the past, it is true, but it had always gravitated to the side of the political angels. Now the quondam battler for liberal causes was, for want of any other force to further his ambition, being borne aloft by the powers of illiberalism. But the man who had availed himself of the President's piggyback to the nomination, with many a wince to his old liberal friends to suggest the discomfort of the ride, was not going to be set down in quite the same condition as when he got on. Humphrey was never a very big man. On the day he became the Democratic Party's nominee for the Presidency, he was almost infinitesimal.

It was all over by nine-thirty Wednesday morning, August 28, the time of Edward Kennedy's definitive public rejection of all efforts on his behalf at the convention. By the end of the morning, Jesse Unruh had retailed the bad news to the California caucus. And Mayor Daley emerged from the Illinois caucus in Sherman House to announce, poker-faced, that "after a long session in the typical spirit of Illinois democracy," the delegation had decided to cast 112 of its 118 votes for Humphrey. That left only two unanswered questions: Could the authorities who had ensured Humphrey's coronation be generous in victory; and could the forces ranged against them be gracious in defeat? The portents were not good.

On Chicago's two fronts—the convention hall and the streets—hostilities had escalated over the preceding two days. The turbulence over the seating of Julian Bond's Georgia challenge delegation accustomed delegates to the spectacle of strong-arm tactics on the convention floor (not, however, Governor Lester Maddox, who left town Wednesday morning fulminating against the Democratic Party's infiltration by "socialists, beatniks, and misfits"). And a CBS convention-floor reporter voiced the frustrations of his profession by dilating on the impossibility of his labors "with these gumshoes on my tail all the time." In the streets, the roster of media casualties mounted each day. Relations between the police and the Yippies were beyond the point of no return. Monday night, the Yippies erected a gimcrack barricade in Lincoln Park as a confrontation symbol at curfew time. Thereafter, any hippie type found after dark by the police was in danger of being Maced or beaten up; any squad car in the Old Town district ran the risk of having its windows smashed by a hail of bricks. At an "anti-birthday party" for Johnson in the Chicago Coliseum on Tuesday, Dick Gregory enlivened the proceedings with the intelligence: "I've just heard that Premier Kosygin has sent a telegram to Mayor Daley asking for two thousand Chicago cops to report for duties in Prague immediately."

Bobby Seale, one of the leaders of the Black Panther Party, arrived in town. The Black Panthers, a militant Negro group based in Oakland, California, pioneered the application of the term "pigs" to policemen. Seale advised demonstrators to "go barbecue some pork." In the early hours of Wednesday morning, a crowd of demonstrators opposite the Hilton bayed, over a phalanx of National Guardsmen, "Flash your lights if you're with us." Banks of lights on the fifteenth and twenty-third floors —the two McCarthy-staff floors—winked on and off in sympathy. The McCarthy kids, too, were being "radicalized."

Yet Wednesday started quietly. The convention debate on Vietnam was curiously free from hysteria. When the delegates were reassembled at one o'clock, it was with the air of men resigned to their fate. Humphrey was not going to budge. Although attempts to circulate Draft Kennedy petitions and other literature on the convention floor had been continually hampered by security officials on previous days, most of the anti-Administration delegates were not surprised to find on every seat a neat mimeographed "fact sheet" endorsing the majority plank. Preparation and distribution of this document had been handled by David Ginsburg, the man who five days earlier had informed Gilligan that there was not ten cents' worth of difference between the peace plank and Humphrey's own position. That was an age ago. Now it seemed, to quote the "fact sheet," the peace plank was "emotional, unreasoning, inflexible, unworkable— and a threat to any rational U.S. policy in Southeast Asia." It was, moreover, "a barely concealed attack on the President and recent administrations," while its call for an unconditional bombing halt was "completely misleading" and its proposals for political reconciliation in Vietnam "an effort to blackmail. . . ." If there were still any doubts about where Humphrey took his stand, these were rapidly dispelled. Congressman Clement Zablocki of Wisconsin, one of the pro-majority plank speakers, announced that he had been authorized to tell the convention that "the Vice-President fully supports the majority plank."

The debate itself was unprecedented—three hours of alternating set speeches by advocates of each side—but intellectually modest. True to their policy of allaying the qualms of the regulars, the peace-plank coordinators assembled a list of speakers calculated to comfort them with echoes of the Kennedy years. O'Donnell, Sorensen, and Salinger were the main advocates. Salinger evoked the warmest response with "If Senator Robert Kennedy were alive, he would be on this platform speaking for the minority." (An abstract truth, perhaps, but not a practical one. If Kennedy had been alive and a viable candidate, he would have been most unlikely to break convention custom by appearing in the hall before the nominating procedures were complete.) Much mention of "principle" and "morality" was made, but the fundamental thesis was a hard-nosed argument that the war had to be wrapped up because of the damage it was doing to America's social fabric and its distortion of economic priorities. Wayne Morse questioned the premises of the whole operation and paid the penalty for doing so in such a circumscribed debate: he sounded cantankerous.

The speakers for the majority plank were, predictably, less distinguished. Theirs was the tougher case to argue. Edmund M. Muskie, the Senator from Maine, did not try very hard. He emphasized the similarities between the two planks, and apparently impressed many regulars with the wisdom of the deduction that the differences were over ends, not means. Governor Warren E. Hearnes of Missouri, however, expressed alarm at those differences. He was impressed by the perils to American servicemen implicit in the minority plank, and urged delegates, "Don't play God with their lives." Wayne L. Hays, a crusty Congressman from Ohio, lifted the emotional content of the debate while cutting its intellectual quotient very nearly in half. He was affronted by the demonstrators, who, he apparently thought, had dictated the minority position to the convention. He had cunningly crafted some reflections on the nature of demonstrators and gave the delegates the benefit of his alliterative analysis: "They would substitute beards for brains, license for liberty. They want pot instead of patriotism, sideburns instead of solutions. They would substitute riots for reason." It was not clear, since Congressman Hays did not have a beard, what he had substituted for a brain. Mayor Daley was observed clapping enthusiastically. Hale Boggs concluded the proceedings by divulging the contents of his confidential White House briefing: enemy strength in the DMZ, according to General Abrams, would increase five hundred per cent if the bombing stopped. The President had given Boggs permission to use it. Thus were the opinions of the military, whose insensitivity to the problems of Vietnam had done so much to render America's role there futile, lobbed into the endorsement of a discredited policy.

At four-thirty, the vote was taken: 1567 for the majority, 1041 for the minority plank. It was an impressive vote for the peace position—200 more than all the peace candidates together garnered that night. And the final effort to whip the Humphrey men in line had failed to corral figures like Representative Don Fraser of Minnesota, Grant Sawyer, the former Governor of Nevada, and Harold Gibbons, the Teamsters' Union vice-president. But they were operating against the declared sentiments of their candidate and, thus, against the authority of the machine. Their perception that Humphrey could not reasonably hope to win in November, tied to the majority plank, was entirely accurate. But that afternoon they were party heretics.

To the McCarthy people, the defeat seemed to mean that *all* their efforts had been in vain. The system had beaten them. And the end of the roll call produced an outpouring of emotion. Mrs. Anne Wexler from Connecticut sobbed on the shoulder of one of our reporters, "They got us in a corner and did this to us." Delegates from New York, California, Wisconsin, Colorado, Oregon, and New Hampshire, the core of the McCarthy-McGovern coalition, tied black bands around their arms and pinned black crepe on their badges. Hundreds of them began to sway together to the slow rhythm of "We Shall Overcome," led by the folk singer Theodore Bikel, a New York delegate. Another crowd of delegates stood in one of the aisles, shouting, "Stop the war, stop the war!" A priest knelt down in the midst of the New York delegation and others knelt with him as he prayed: "God's greatest gift is peace, make us aware of our potential for creating peace." When he finished there were cries of "Shalom" and "Amen."

That evening, when the convention reconvened for its climactic nominating session, the masters of the proceedings, confident of the outcome, dispensed with subtlety. The partisanship of the security guards and policemen was now unconcealed. Uniformed policemen tacked up signs saying WE LOVE MAYOR DALEY. On earlier nights, members of officially recognized challenging delegations could not get into the hall; now the galleries suddenly filled with Daley's henchmen. One hulking fellow appeared in the press gallery with "news credentials." When asked what paper he was from, he kept repeating, "Fifteenth ward, fifteenth ward." Security men grabbed a young girl who was handing out peace leaflets and made her drop them. When she bent to pick them up, a security man kicked her hand. One of our reporters shouted at him to stop. An American reporter beside him turned and said, "If you don't like this country you shouldn't be here."

At eight o'clock, the convention hall was a mass of Humphrey banners; hardly a McCarthy poster was to be seen. The reason, learned later, was that police had "accidentally" tear-gassed the supply of posters at McCarthy's storefront headquarters near the Hilton that afternoon and rendered them unusable. For if Mayor Daley's methods inside the Amphitheater were ruthless, in the streets around the Conrad Hilton they were almost completely unbridled. As the delegates assembled to the strains of brass bands blaring "Chicago, Chicago, you wonderful town," the police downtown were preparing for their most flagrantly brutal action of the week.

Police violence is always sickening. But what distinguished the

police action in Chicago from anything previously seen by members of
our reporting team—whose collective experience covered riots in Paris,
Belfast, Berlin, Calcutta, New York, Cleveland, and Detroit—was not
simply its ferocity; it was the fact that the police went, quite literally,
berserk. It happened twice on Wednesday. The first occasion was in the
afternoon when ten thousand people assembled in Grant Park for the
only open-air demonstration of the week to be given a city permit, a rally
under the auspices of David Dellinger's Mobilization Committee. A dangerously explosive situation arose after a demonstrator was arrested for
hauling down the Stars and Stripes near the bandshell. It was, however,
in the process of being brought under control by the rally marshals when
forty policemen in flying-wedge formation moved briskly through the
crowd, rhythmically swinging their billyclubs and chanting "Back-back-
back." Demonstrators hit by the wedge were randomly trampled and
clubbed. It was a pointless operation. After the policemen had gone
through, the crowd simply merged again to tend its wounded and listen
to the speeches. A few minutes later, this police detail was removed. One
of the policemen said to his replacement, "Go in, fella, and have some
fun."

That was the matinee. The real ugliness was reserved for the evening
performance, the scene that, televised, shocked much of the world. Only
the camera can fully recapture the horror of the occasion. But here, for
the benefit of those who did not see or cannot recall the television coverage, is an abstract from a memorandum of one of our reporters outside
the Conrad Hilton:

> At 7:50 p.m. the crowd was mounting outside the hotel. It was
> clear, however, that the demonstrators would not be allowed to march
> on the convention. Only the Poor People's mule train was allowed
> through the police lines to proceed up Michigan Avenue. There was a
> lot of confusion as nobody seemed to know what to do. Most of the
> demonstrators were obviously still suffering from the tear-gas attack
> that had broken up the attempt to form a march an hour earlier. There
> was no effective leadership, though there was a ragged attempt to stage
> a sit-down demonstration. I'd say most of them were pacifically inclined
> middle-class kids. There were some hippies, but probably just as many
> Chicago citizens rubbernecking. Then at 8 p.m. it happened. Cohorts
> of police began to charge into the crowd from a street north of the
> Hilton, Balbo. The kids screamed and were beaten to the ground by
> cops who had completely lost their cool. Some tried to surrender by
> putting their hands on their heads. As they were marched to vans to
> be arrested, they were rapped in the genitals by the cops' swinging
> billies. I saw one girl, surrounded by cops, screaming, "Please God,

help me. Help me." A young man who tried to help got his head blood-
ied by a flailing club. Some of the demonstrators were thrown against a
window of the hotel and pushed through it. The cops were using Mace
indiscriminately. But then there was no discrimination about any of it.
One policeman I overheard said with a delighted smile, "They're really
getting scared now." It was a sadistic romp. One of the more unforgettable vignettes was of an Illinois politician, he must have been a state
senator, sauntering out of the front door of the hotel to observe the
carnage. A police sergeant turned from the beating that was going on
at his feet and inquired politely, "How are you this evening, Senator?"
"Fine," said the senator, puffing on his cigar, "just fine."

Senator McCarthy and his campaign staff watched, horrified, from
the window of his twenty-third-floor suite. "It's incredible," said the
Senator, "like a Breughel." The bird's-eye view did lend a certain artistic
quality to the scene: the television lights gave it a frame in which the
sky-blue helmets of the police focused sharply against the indeterminate
mass of color that was the crowd. It was perhaps more like a Bosch.
Humphrey, two floors above McCarthy, saw less of the action. The tear
gas seeping through the hotel had irritated the Vice-President's skin and
eyes. He had to take a shower.

Over at the Amphitheater, things were steaming up independently.
The action outside the Hilton was not televised "live." Because of the
telephone technicians' strike, the media had been unable to install power
lines from the main convention hotels. So it was not until nine-thirty that
the first films of the affray flashed up on the screens placed in the corridors around the convention floor. By eight-thirty, however, when the
nominating roll call had already started, the delegates were involved in
a fracas of their own. The *casus belli* was a refusal by New York delegate
Alex Rosenberg to show his credentials to a security guard on the floor.
The guard "did his job," called on two of his comrades, and began to
remove Rosenberg forcibly. Paul O'Dwyer, the New York Senatorial
candidate, tried to intervene and started a melee that brought a posse
of Chicago policemen onto the convention floor. State Chairman John
Burns fought his way through the crowd to identify Rosenberg, only
to find himself ignored. The CBS newsman Mike Wallace was socked in
the jaw. Eventually, O'Dwyer and Rosenberg were hauled into a police
room, where they were interrogated by security guards for half an hour.

While this lively incident was being resolved, McCarthy's name was
placed in nomination by Harold Hughes. Meanwhile, word pictures of
the scenes outside the Hilton were being telephoned in by McCarthy and
McGovern staffers to their delegation leaders at the convention. Projects,

and rumors of projects, that would display their abject disgust for the occasion circulated around the hall. One of the more imaginative had been shot down earlier that day: William vanden Heuvel had suggested that Johnson's name be placed in nomination on the grounds that only he could run honorably on the Vietnam plank. It tickled the black humorist in Dick Goodwin: "Why take the dummy when you can have the ventriloquist himself?" The idea had been rejected because it was thought that it might hold the office of the Presidency up to ridicule. Now it was going the rounds again, with a host of other schemes—adjournment to another city, a walkout, withdrawal of McCarthy's candidacy.

At ten o'clock, Humphrey held an eve-of-triumph press conference in his Hilton suite. Yes, he was upset by the demonstrations. (But the reason for his upset seemed to be that they had spoiled his day.) Of the dissenters, he remarked, "They don't represent the people of Chicago. They've been brought in from all over the country. We knew this was going to happen. It was all programed." (It is worth mentioning that of the ten thousand demonstrators in Chicago, probably little more than half were from outside the city. They did not represent the people of Chicago, of course. But then this was a *national* convention. The demonstrators were focusing on a sentiment expressed by eighty per cent of the primary voters and by forty per cent of the convention delegates that afternoon.)

Back in the convention hall, the peace forces had made a tactical decision to move for an adjournment. A few minutes after ten, Bob Maytag, a lanky rancher from Colorado, requested the chair to compel Mayor Daley to suspend his "police-state tactics." It was designed as a lever for an adjournment motion. Carl Albert ruled the question out of order.

The roll call went on. "Connecticut." The slight figure of Senator Abraham Ribicoff came to the podium. Ribicoff had had a tough year in Connecticut. He had been a Kennedy man. He is a liberal but a cautious liberal, in a state split between John Bailey's machine and the McCarthyite insurgents. He was up for re-election and could not afford to alienate either faction. So he compromised. He was about to go through the futile but unexceptionable motion of nominating George McGovern for the office of President. In the middle of his address, he said, "With George McGovern we wouldn't have Gestapo tactics on the streets of Chicago."

Stunned silence. Then pandemonium. The television cameras focused on Daley, purple with rage and mouthing an expletive that looked to millions of lip-reading television viewers like an expression he was said never to use. The semantic riddle has never been satisfactorily solved, but the sentiment was unmistakable. Ribicoff stuck to his guns. Staring down at the Mayor, less than twenty feet away, he repeated, "How hard it is to accept the truth. How hard it is." There was dignity in it, but perhaps, too, an element of calculation. The McCarthy forces had been wary of Ribicoff all year, but on the bus home from the convention that night, Anne Wexler said, "I'm going to get everyone to work their guts out for Abe for what he said tonight." Ribicoff won big in November.

Around eleven o'clock, McCarthy went down to his fifteenth-floor volunteer-staff headquarters, which had been turned into an emergency first-aid post. Bruised and bleeding demonstrators from the street below had been brought up for treatment. Conrad Hilton bed sheets were torn up to be used as bandages. The Senator moved from bed to bed asking after the welfare of the injured. He did not say much, but his voice shook a little when he remarked, "This is typical of the way my staff has had to operate all this year." Afterward he rang an aide at the Amphitheater, asking that his name be removed from the ballot. It was too late.

At eleven-twenty, Carl Albert, having just overruled an adjournment motion introduced by Don Peterson of Wisconsin, announced the start of the balloting. There were no real surprises: Humphrey 1760¼, McCarthy 601, McGovern 146½ (rather more than predicted, but they included votes expected to go to McCarthy), the Reverend Channing Phillips (favorite son of the District of Columbia and the first Negro ever to have his name placed in nomination for the Presidency, opposed to the Administration's policies in Vietnam) 67½, Governor Dan Moore (favorite son of North Carolina, the only Southern delegation to withhold its votes from Humphrey) 17½, Edward Kennedy 12¾ (the never-say-die vote), abstentions and others 16½.

Humphrey gave his victory whoop at eleven-forty-seven, with the announcement of Pennsylvania's vote—103¾ for Humphrey—carrying him past the magic 1312 figure. He had spent an earlier part of the evening in his bedroom quietly surrendering to the lachrymose side of his nature. But it was a dry-eyed Humphrey who sat, expertly totting up his delegate count, surrounded by aides, newsmen, and the ganglia of TV equipment incestuously recording the moment of triumph brought to Humphrey by the same medium. But a still shot which graced the next morning's front pages captured the moment best: Humphrey leaping from his seat and clapping his hands as Pennsylvania came through, his face suffused with the radiance of a man who knows it's all been worth it. Moments later, the image of Humphrey's wife, sitting in the VIP seats at the convention, flashed on the screen. Humphrey rushed over to the set and imprinted a kiss upon the cold glass—"Mom, I wish you were here." Then the routine calls of congratulation. One from Florida— Richard Nixon; another from Texas—Lyndon Johnson. Humphrey was ecstatic. To the President: "Bless your heart, thank you."

At midnight, an Illinois delegate moved, a traditional gesture at these gatherings, that the nomination be made unanimous. No vote was taken. Albert declared the motion carried while hundreds of delegates yelled hoarsely, "No, no, no." Lowenstein and Goodwin, prescient to, and beyond, the bitter end, had a supply of a thousand candles borrowed from a Chicago synagogue that afternoon. Now they were distributed to disconsolate McCarthy delegates to carry on a "funeral march" through downtown Chicago.

A few of the less ceremonial spirits hurried straight over to a caucus in the Drake Hotel, where Marcus Raskin was outlining plans for the formation of a fourth party. Raskin—earlier in the year one of five de- fendants, the most famous being Dr. Benjamin Spock, charged with in- citing avoidance of the draft in a widely reported trial in Boston, and the only one acquitted—was plotting the peace movement's fall-back posi- tion. It was no competition for the candlelight procession. Paul Newman was there, and so was Jules Feiffer, but of the more powerful figures in the McCarthy campaign there was no sign. Most of the hundred or so people gathered in the Drake were students. There was little but out- rage to go on. Raskin reckoned that if McCarthy could be persuaded to lead a fourth-party drive, then it would be possible to get on the ballot in twenty-five states, including New York and California. If not, the whole deal became problematical. Someone asked whether Paul Newman should be requested to accept the burden of leadership. The proposal was rapidly nipped in the bud by the actor himself. "My immediate program," he said, realistically, "is to get drunk, and stay drunk for the next two weeks."

Over in the Hilton, on the staircase curving down into the foyer, another group of students was chanting "The Democratic Party is dead," alternating with "Fourth party, fourth party." But McCarthy, holding a loser's press conference in the Grand Ballroom, showed no great inclina- tion to take up that particular torch. He made some characteristically mild observations about the convention's being "rather badly handled." His defeat he attributed to a failure of the procedures to respond to the judgment of the people. He had rung Humphrey and congratulated him but was not inclined at that stage to endorse him. The fourth party? McCarthy's position was unchanged. If it mobilized a large following, he "might" support it, but it was not his intention to lead it. (This was a hopeless situation: a new party could not generate support without McCarthy's endorsement, and yet that endorsement was contingent on its ability to generate support.)

On Thursday afternoon, however, McCarthy came closer to his constituency than he had at any time through the year. He perceived better than any of his supporters that the protest they had mobilized could not be ignored; that Johnson and Humphrey must now realize how fundamentally out of touch with the national mood they had become; and that, if they had an ounce of political instinct left (which they had), they would ultimately feel obliged to come close to adopting positions they had been resisting all year. Most movements end by having their policies taken over and put into effect by their political enemies. It was hard for those who had been in the movement, but it did not render their efforts nugatory. It was this kind of perspective that McCarthy tried to give to his supporters and staff on Thursday afternoon, more comforting in its way than any amount of railing against police brutality. He did it wryly, and with a hint of self-mockery, and implicitly showed why he could never lead a radical fourth-party movement. He is perhaps one of the few real believers in the system. The failure, in his view, had been the people's unwillingness to operate within it. Now he was more hopeful. "If you people keep on this way, I may—as we say—'lose my cool,' " he told them. But he never did. And his epilogue on what had been the most important political phenomenon of the year was informed by the same humane conservatism that had inspired his candidacy.

> So what we do is to go on, to continue to present to the people as best we can for judgment between now and November the issues we have been raising for nine months in this country. We will continue to demand explanations from the candidates. But more important than that, we will proceed as best we can to support those candidates, particularly for the United States Senate, who have stood with us, and to identify those issues with our candidates. I hesitate to say that the fate of the Republic may rest upon the United States Senate; it might cause great grief in the land, and despondency. But the fact is that this may well be, with reference to issues that face us—particularly in foreign policy. I have, in the course of this campaign, spoken not only about the need to have every person in this country be a fully responsible citizen. I have said that every institution we have developed, whether it be the House of Representatives or the Supreme Court or the Senate itself—that we had to get from each of these the fullest measure of

strength and of power that it was possible to get; that I disapproved of what had happened in this country in the last four years, in which there has been a kind of transfer of power to the Executive Branch of the government. . . .

We have had a great victory to this point, one which should reassure us about the system itself. But more important than that, if we had any doubts—and I think most of us really were without doubt early —about the people of this country, I think we are on the way in 1968 to preparing the way for the judgments that need to be made, perhaps somewhat less clearly, perhaps with our getting less credit than we might have liked if we had the White House. But we are willing to share that, and to forgo it, if we can accomplish these things for the country. I think that the outlook is one that must be reassuring: one of confidence and one of optimism—not really of our own making, but by virtue of our having discovered it to exist in the minds and in the hearts of the people of this country. Your credit is not altogether in putting it there—excepting insofar as you yourselves had it—nor is my credit. But I think that we can say that we were willing to open the box and to see what America was. We had that kind of trust and that kind of confidence. And when we opened it, we found that the people of this nation were not wanting. Thank you very much.

Then, through the police lines and over to Grant Park, where McCarthy addressed the now sadly bedraggled ranks of the demonstrators, calling them "the government in exile." The message there went to a deeper level, perhaps because of the intellectual competition: Robert Lowell and Norman Mailer were also on the bill. McCarthy recalled how he quoted a poem of Lowell's at the beginning of his campaign:

And I want to end this before he comes on, because I think that the change from the America he describes and the world he describes is what my purpose is and what yours is. He made reference to our condition in these words:

Only man thinning out his kind
sounds through the Sabbath noon, the blind
swipe of the pruner and his knife
busy about the tree of life. . . .

We can turn back from that and make our nation one in which—I don't say the traditional—but the proper outlook is one of confidence and one of hope and one of trust in our fellow men and in other people around the world. If we proceed in this spirit, I do not think many of us will remain afraid of those billion Chinese with whom we have been threatened by Dean Rusk. It is in the year two thousand, anyway; you can wait until then. We do not have to worry about it—not to be afraid, not to be threatened, not to live in a Kafka-like burrow in which we can always hear, if we listen closely, some kind of scratching sound. The

idea of defense and of more defense, missiles and then antiballistic missiles and then antiantiballistic missiles, to infinity—this has never been
the attitude or spirit of this country, when we were doing what we
should do.

Enmity to the mechanistic forces in American life—the common ground
of true conservatives and true radicals: it was, ultimately, what the
McCarthy campaign had been all about.

But Chicago still had a few more blind swipes of the pruner's knife
to deliver. On Thursday evening, Dick Gregory made an attempt to lead
a march on the Amphitheater, under the guise of a "walk" to his home,
which happened to be in the stockyards area. At the intersection of
Eighteenth Street and Michigan Avenue, still a full three miles from the
objective, the march/walk came to an abrupt halt. Three canisters of
tear gas exploded outside the Michigan Avenue motel where we were
staying. And within seconds the street was a boiling mass of fleeing
Gregory "walkers," trundling National Guard armor, and masked policemen. The last attempt to mount a "peace march" had gone the way of
all the others. Two of our reporters in the crowd invited some of the
more distressed demonstrators into the motel. Five policemen roamed
through, pounding on doors and ordering demonstrators back into the
now-suffocating street. One quietly dressed, middle-aged man wearing a
McCarthy button kept saying over and over, "I can't believe it. I can't
believe it. This is America."

At the convention hall the machine ground on. David Hoeh, chairman of the New Hampshire delegation, found he could operate the electronic credentials verifier with a Dartmouth College ID card. He gathered
together a posse of newsmen to watch him work the trick again, a token
of his derision at "the nineteen-eighty-four phenomena manifested at this
convention." But it failed to work a second time, and a struggling Hoeh
was roughed up by the guards and borne away for interrogation.

A short film of Robert Kennedy's life brought on another cascade of
emotion, with the peace forces singing again, this time the "Battle Hymn
of the Republic." It seemed that they would never stop. Albert looked
flustered and angry. Lou Breese and his fifty-piece orchestra, the usual
device for throttling such manifestations, were no match for this. But
Daley was equal to the occasion with a move that showed that the Mayor,
when he puts his mind to it, is a master of finesse. One of his Negro
delegates, Ralph Metcalfe, mounted the platform to deliver an unscheduled tribute to Martin Luther King, Jr. The singing had to stop.

Humphrey made his acceptance speech. It was clearly calculated to be a testament of love—"Each and every one of us should reaffirm to ourselves and our posterity that we love this nation, we love America"; and hope—"We stand at the end of an era and at the beginning of a new day"; and gratitude—"And tonight, to you, Mr. President, I say thank you. Thank you, Mr. President." He saw the vision of peace in Vietnam. And how all could press forward to that vision: "Let those who believe our cause in Vietnam has been right—and those who believe it has been wrong—agree here and now: neither vindication nor repudiation will bring peace or be worthy of our country." He abhorred disorder: "Neither mob violence nor police brutality has any place in America." And the events of the preceding night prompted the reflection: "May America tonight resolve that never, never again shall we see what we have seen." After the speech, McGovern joined Humphrey on the platform—a symbolic endorsement. McCarthy was a conspicuous absentee. The applause was warm, but it was therapy for the team rather than adulation for the candidate.

Earlier that week, one of the demonstrators in Grant Park had held aloft a placard: THERE ARE TWO SIDES TO EVERY QUESTION—HUMPHREY ENDORSES BOTH OF THEM. It was close to the mark, but not quite central. Humphrey was a more worrying phenomenon: a man who could say, "Let there be light," and apparently believe the act of utterance alone is enough to dispel the Stygian gloom. It was impossible to resist the thought that an optimism so detached from reality might be a dangerous quality to carry into the Presidency. In such a mental climate even a mushroom cloud might have a silver lining.

The convention formally endorsed Humphrey's selection of Edmund Muskie as his running mate. There had been some mild unpleasantness. The McCarthy supporters had attempted to nominate their "boy wonder," Julian Bond, for the office—not out of any special desire to upset Muskie, but as a device for securing the privilege of making nominating speeches from the platform. These could then be used as a vehicle for unloading a few pertinent reflections on Daley's Chicago. The project collapsed with the revelation that Bond was still seven years below the qualifying age for the office. So Muskie it was—aged fifty-four, the son of a Polish immigrant tailor, a large, comfortable man with a good vote-getting record. In 1954 he had become the first Democratic Governor of Maine in twenty years. His Senate record was diligent and liberal. He displayed some of his chief's disquieting ability to see both sides of the question and leave it at that. Of the Chicago riots, Muskie was to say, "There were excesses on both sides." (A remark with a long, but not especially distinguished, pedigree. It was, for instance, used by a British newspaper proprietor in 1937 when asked, on returning from a visit to Nazi Germany, what he thought of the Jewish problem in that country.) Still, he had a way about him, the useful kind of *gravitas* that seems to transmute political banalities into profound insights. He was an asset to the ticket. Richard Goodwin did less than justice to the Maine Senator's talents when he remarked, "In the land of the blind, Muskie looks good."

The epilogue to Chicago belonged, inevitably, to the police. At four o'clock Friday morning, a posse of policemen raided the fifteenth floor of the Conrad Hilton on a tip from the National Guard that objects were being thrown from the window of room 1506A. But the brief to investigate this room was rapidly expanded by the mood of the force. Brian Harrison, a McCarthy staffer from Massachusetts, happened to overhear four officers talking in the lobby just before the raid was made. One said something had been thrown at the National Guardsmen and it might have come from the fifteenth floor. "O.K.," said another, "give the order to drag them all in and give them a beating. Teach them a lesson."

Most of the McCarthy staff people were in bed, physically and emotionally exhausted. Some were playing bridge, others singing softly. The more practical were very drunk or asleep. The police lined those who were awake against a wall and, using pass keys obtained from the management, entered rooms where others were sleeping. Some of the invaded rooms did not face the avenue; others were so situated that missiles could not have been thrown from them into the street. But the police were not deterred by the laws of physics. George Yumick, an advance man from Boston, challenged the right of the police to act in this way. He was beaten by three policemen. Another officer threw whisky at him, grinned, and said, "Sorry about that." Yumick, subsequently, considered himself "radicalized" by the experience and told a reporter, "I don't like people pissing on my head and calling it rain." After the raid, four people were taken to the hospital with head injuries.

McCarthy, roused from his bed by his staff people, came down when the worst was over. "You can't just come up here and knock heads," he complained to the police. But they could; and they had.

7

The Big Lie

"The great masses of the people will more easily fall victims to a big lie than to a small one."

—Adolf Hitler, *Mein Kampf*

"I think you newsmen missed the point. No one was killed."

—Richard J. Daley, Mayor of Chicago

At a meeting of the American Socialist Party in Washington in 1963, the veteran black activist Bayard Rustin described what he saw as the dilemma of dissent in the United States. Most middle-class white Americans believe in freedom and justice, he said. But they believe even more strongly in law and order. The strategy of dissent must be to awaken the first belief without running foul of the second, because—in Rustin's judgment—if it came to a choice between the two sets of values, law and order would always win.

The sequence of reactions to Daley's iron hand at the convention hall and to his policemen's rampagings in the streets and in the Hilton Hotel tended to confirm this gloomy analysis. During the convention itself and immediately afterward, neither press nor television stopped short at reporting what happened. They took sides editorially, and the great majority took sides against the Mayor. "The truth was," wrote Tom Wicker of the *New York Times,* "these were our children in the streets, and the Chicago police beat them up." And with Olympian solemnity, the *Times* editorialized on August 30 that "one Richard J. Daley" was guilty of "rigidity," "insensitivity," and "repression."

As late as September 7, the *Washington Post* went a good deal further. It printed on that date a column by Leroy Aarons which compared Daley's real Chicago to the mythical gangland Chicago of Berthold Brecht's play *The Resistible Rise of Arturo Ui*. The column ended with the play's last line, in which the actor who plays the gangster-dictator takes off his Hitler mustache and warns the audience that, though Hitler is dead, "the bitch that bore him is in heat again."

That mood did not last long. (The mood of the editors, that is: it is not suggested that Aarons or most of the on-the-spot correspondents changed their view.) Less than three weeks later, the *Washington Post* was half-apologizing for police brutality against student demonstrators with the argument that "of course" policemen must be expected to be annoyed by the sight of people wearing beards. (Which drew an epigrammatic protest from a lady reader: "Dear Sir, What about Lincoln? What about Moses? What about God?") The editor of the *Chicago Daily News* publicly criticized one of his reporters who had shouted, "For God's sake stop that!" to policemen who were clubbing three young girls and who had spent two days in the hospital as a result of the beating it got him. "He acted as a human being," lamented the editor, "but less than professionally. He was there as a reporter and not to involve himself." The mandarins of the press were genuinely horrified to find themselves in a situation where their vaunted code of objectivity, based on a Talmudic separation between "fact" and "comment," did not help them. They were also alarmed to find how far they had gotten out of touch with the reading, viewing, and advertisement-buying public.

On September 3, for example, even the fashionable columnist Joseph Kraft, who had never previously shown much concern for readers in union halls and Veterans of Foreign Wars posts, suddenly discovered an urgent need for "those of us in communications [who] are well-educated and comfortably off" to get back in touch with the "low-income whites" in something he had discovered called "Middle America," and to sympathize more with them when they felt threatened by Negroes or young people.

Few went through more convolutions than Jack Mabley, a columnist and assistant managing editor of *Chicago's American*. Mabley started the convention week as a profound admirer of the city's police work, writing warmly about their disciplined patrol techniques. As the week progressed, doubts began to filter in. And on Thursday morning, August 29, his column contained this passage:

> Scores of people under the Palmer House canopy watched in horror as a policeman went animal when a crippled man couldn't get away fast enough. The man hopped with his stick as fast as he could, but the

policeman shoved him in the back, then hit him with a night stick, hit him again, and finally crashed him into a lamppost. Clergymen, medics, and this cripple were the special pigeons last night.

Then came the reader reactions, stronger than anything Mabley had experienced in thirty years in the newspaper business. It was apparently a humbling experience for Mabley—"80 to 85 per cent of the callers and letter writers cheering for Daley and the cops. You can't help that gnawing feeling—can all these people be right and I be wrong?"

Mabley, presumably, would not take much cognizance of a mailbag informing him that popular sentiment held that two plus two equals five. Yet here he was displaying a pious willingness to accept judgments which ran counter to his own eyewitness impressions.

It is a curious syndrome. The only area where arrogance in a reporter is justified, indeed essential, is in a preparedness to stand by the evidence of his own eyes. Without such an attitude, the press becomes a mere tool for the confirmation of prejudice.

Within a month, in fact, the convention had become a symbol not, as might have been predicted at the time, of the dangers of "piety and iron," but of the opposite. With honorable exceptions, most notably *Newsweek* and *Time,* many of whose reporters had been personally roughed up and were not inclined to forget it, the press and the public came to accept Daley's version of events more or less uncritically. Cars in Chicago blossomed with bumper stickers saying WE SUPPORT MAYOR DALEY AND HIS CHICAGO POLICE, and this reaction was by no means limited to Chicago. More than nine out of ten of the seventy-four thousand letters the Mayor received in the first couple of weeks took the same line, or so he claimed.

Partly, this was a spontaneous reaction. Millions of Americans had become sick and tired of marches and protests and demonstrations. The belief in law and order, as Rustin had guessed, was proving stronger than other, more permissive, beliefs for them. Others were genuinely troubled by the question where the line should be drawn. In part, no doubt, Daley —like George Wallace and Richard Nixon—was the passive beneficiary of a real public mood.

But Daley was not the man to sit back and wait for public opinion to come round to his way of seeing things. He mounted a massive public-relations campaign to polish up his image and that of his beloved city. He cynically set about fanning the flames of reaction against the left. The record of his statements after the convention, and the report prepared for him by his chief counsel, Raymond F. Simon, read like a primer of the propagandist's art, in which he deployed every trick known to Dr. Goebbels and his imitators: the smear, the imputation of guilt by association, *suppressio veri, suggestio falsi,* and the Big Lie itself. Liberal connoisseurs of the Freudian slip might treasure Daley's remark at one press conference: "Get the thing straight once and for all. The policeman isn't there to create disorder; the policeman is there to preserve disorder [*sic*]." But there was no gainsaying the over-all effectiveness of the campaign.

It is worth taking a close look at the details of this operation, not only because it is a pleasure and a duty to nail a lie, but because it gives a good idea of the importance, for even the most old-fashioned of American politicians, of playing the press like a violin.

The Big Lie on which Daley's whole campaign was founded was the wholly false idea that police brutality was the only alternative to allowing "a lawless violent group of terrorists to menace the lives of millions of our people, destroy the purpose of this national political convention, and take over the streets of Chicago." That remarkable statement comes from a television interview which Daley gave to Walter Cronkite on the last night of the convention.

The fatherly Cronkite had been genuinely shocked by what he had seen at the convention and outraged that a CBS cameraman had been among the injured. He had allowed his feelings to show. Perhaps he had been called to heel by the management. Whatever the reason, his manner with Daley was anything but aggressive. He repeatedly addressed him as "sir." He introduced him with the ingratiating remark that "maybe this is a kiss-and-make-up session, but it's not intended that way. . . . I think we've always been friends." From that point on, as a senior CBS executive conceded privately with an unbelieving shake of the head, "Daley took Cronkite like Grant took Richmond."

Even for Cronkite, however, the smear which Daley attempted on his opponents at one point during the interview was a bit steep. The exchange went like this: Cronkite was asking Daley about a statement by one of his lieutenants which described some of the leaders of the demonstration as Communists.

> DALEY: Well there isn't any doubt about it. You know who they are.
> CRONKITE: No, I don't actually.
> DALEY: Well, you know Hayden, don't you, and what he stands for?
> CRONKITE: I don't know he's a Communist.

DALEY: You know the head of the Mo— well, you know the head
of the Mobilization. You sure know Dellinger, who went to Hanoi.
Why don't, why isn't anything said about those people? They're the
people who— Go over now, see if your cameras will pick them up in
Grant Park. Rennie Davis. What's Rennie Davis?
CRONKITE: Well, I don't know that they're Communists.
DALEY: Well, neither do I, but . . .

Dave Dellinger, the head of the National Mobilization Committee is, as
we have seen, a radical Quaker pacifist. Tom Hayden, the former leader
of Students for a Democratic Society, was a co-organizer of the Mobilization. Needless to say, neither he nor Davis nor Dellinger is a Communist.

The most startling justification which the Mayor produced for the
behavior of his police is that he had secret intelligence of plots to assassinate Hubert Humphrey, Eugene McCarthy, and his own good self.
He produced these allegations with a master propagandist's sense of
melodrama, spliced with a strain of Auld Irish sentimentality, in the
interview with Cronkite:

> It's unfortunate that the television industry didn't have the informa-
> tion I had . . . on my desk, that certain people planned to assassinate
> two contenders to the Presidency. Certain people planned to assassinate
> myself. But I've had that constantly. My family, God love them, has
> lived through all of that . . . so I took the necessary precautions. No
> mayor wants to call the National Guard, 'cause some people think it's
> a reflection. But the day I went in office I took an oath of office. . . .

In his official report "The Strategy of Confrontation," published on September 6, the Mayor repeated the story with a new twist. Police intelligence, the report said, knew of plans "to assassinate Senator Eugene
McCarthy, Vice-President Hubert Humphrey, Mayor Richard J. Daley,
and other political leaders. Perhaps the most unnerving rumor was one
of a plan to murder a young female supporter of Senator Eugene Mc-
Carthy and 'blame it on the police.' "

Did the Mayor and his men really believe these plot stories? As the
Mayor himself implied, rumors of assassination attempts are a dime a
dozen ("I've had that constantly"). It is perfectly true that on August 23,
apparently as a result of a police intelligence report of August 20, sixteen
witnesses, including leaders of a black street gang, the Blackstone
Rangers, and of white peace groups, were subpoenaed to appear before
a grand jury investigating the assassination stories. But the timing is
curious. On August 20, the District Attorney said that an assassination-
plot story produced by a prisoner in the county jail was "completely

unverified." On August 22, he met several Chicago police officers and ordered the grand-jury investigation, saying he had "new information." Yet Daley's report mentions only information received on August 20. Was there any new information on August 22, or was the whole investigation cranked up for political reasons? Certainly nothing of concrete value came out of the highly publicized inquiries.

But the gravamen of the case against the Mayor for using assassination stories to divert attention from the real issue of police brutality in Chicago is that it was in no way relevant. The grossest instances of police excess occurred in the back streets around Lincoln Park, when the candidates' personal safety was in no conceivable danger. Moreover, had there been a cold-eyed candidate-killer in town, he would almost certainly have been delighted to find himself in a situation where the local law-enforcement agencies had so completely lost their cool.

Such "plot" stories, however, come as no surprise after scrutiny of the shrewd workmanship displayed in "The Strategy for Confrontation." The whole "objective" report is peppered with the breath-taking statements and omissions that are the hallmarks of propaganda. Some examples merit discussion in detail.

Guilt by association. Throughout the report demonstrators are indiscriminately referred to as "hippies" or "yippies" or, in some of the more trenchant sections, as "terrorists" and "revolutionaries." The "overwhelming majority" of those arrested, says the report, were "adult trouble-makers who came to Chicago for the avowed purpose of a hostile confrontation with law enforcement."

In fact, there were many other breeds of demonstrators. On the later evenings in particular, the crowds included many ordinary citizens and not a few convention delegates. It is true that many of those obliged to spend a few hours in the lock-up were adults, but many of them could hardly be considered advanced in the art of trouble-making. They included, for instance, men from such staid organs as the *Saturday Evening Post,* the *New York Times,* and the *Los Angeles Times.* Others on the roster were men like Harris Wofford, head of the Old Westbury campus of the State University of New York and formerly associate director of the Peace Corps; and, most remarkably of all, Thomas Frazier, an Oklahoma delegate who had come to Chicago to vote for Humphrey. Frazier, a World War Two veteran now confined to, but extremely mobile in, a wheelchair, is hardly anybody's idea of a peacenik. "My idea of peace in Vietnam," he told a reporter, "is a small-sized atom bomb right in the middle of Hanoi." But, like so many other delegates, he was sick and tired of being pushed around both inside and outside the convention hall. Out of frustration, he joined Dick Gregory's "walk" to his own home on Thursday night and so became another digit in Daley's statistics of "adult trouble-makers."

Suggestio falsi. Citing a "police intelligence report," presumably from one of those conspicuous undercover agents, Daley's report quotes Rennie Davis as saying at a Chicago Peace Council meeting before the convention, "If trouble starts at the Democratic National Convention, among other things the Loop will fall." Read quickly, this passage is frought with dire overtones, seeming to suggest that Davis was advocating the physical destruction of Chicago's much-admired city center. Of course, he was advocating no such thing. Still less was he in a position to bring it about. He was merely predicting, in an excited and rhetorical way, that if the police were tied up at demonstrations near the convention hall, they could not simultaneously prevent demonstrations downtown.

An even finer example of this technique of misrepresentation is contained in a tenderly written section of the report entitled "Mule Train Rescued by Police." The mule train involved in this saga was the demonstration group led by Dr. Ralph Abernathy, Martin Luther King's successor as chairman of the Southern Christian Leadership Conference. He had brought this living symbol of Southern black poverty to both conventions to plead the cause of his people. When, on Wednesday night, Dr. Abernathy and his followers appeared in the downtown area, he was surrounded by demonstrators who cheered him and escorted him on his march. The train paused for some time and one of its members actually addressed the crowd, congratulating them on their stand.

The Daley report puts a diametrically different gloss on this sequence, conjuring up visions of dignified black dissenters suddenly engulfed by a tide of hostility. The black poor probably never realized how warmly, and protectively, Daley viewed their cause. In the report, Dr. Abernathy's train was surrounded by "a mob" who were screaming and spitting at the police. The members of the train were so alarmed that "a tall, well-built black man" approached officials, said he was in charge of the train, and asserted that he and Dr. Abernathy wanted to be rescued from the mob. After the train was separated from the mob, the same young man returned and asked for help for another six of his people "trapped" in the crowd.

The identity of this impressively built emissary between the "rescuers" and the "rescued" is not disclosed in the report. Nor, as it happens, was his existence apparent to the organizers of Dr. Abernathy's cavalcade. There is an element of truth in the assertion that they desired rescue—but from the police, not the demonstrators.

Our inquiries about this incident produced the following statement from the SCLC:

> We pulled out of the crowd because we had seen how the police had treated the demonstrators, beating and gassing them, and we wanted to avoid this.
> In fact, the SCLC was sympathetic to the demonstrators and Dr. Abernathy later told them Daley and his police were trying to run some kind of Fascist state. At no stage did we ask, or need, to be rescued from demonstrators, who had our support.

Suppressio veri. In this context, the most amazing passage in the report is its account of the famous police raid on the McCarthy head-quarters in the small hours of Friday morning. As we have seen, the police did have cause to investigate the activities in Room 1506 A, from which empty beer cans and other missiles had been projected onto the street below. But in describing this incident, the report narrows its focus to this particular room, never hinting at the alarming readiness of the police to raid many of the other rooms on the same floor.

"The police spoke softly and dealt gently," says the report. "Nobody was shoved or prodded. The only real instance of force was when one of the men from the group lifted the fifteenth-floor message table above his head and struck a uniformed patrolman on his chest. Then, as he raised the table above his head again, the patrolman struck him with his baton. . . ." The table wielder's injury is described as "a small lacera-tion (2 mm. in length)."

The passionate care for detail exemplified by the measurement of this wound fails to inform the rest of the analysis. As far as "soft speech" is concerned, the police rudely woke up two young women asleep in a neighboring bedroom. One of them, a Negro, had the clothes stripped off her bed by a policeman, who said, "Get the hell out of here." The other was called a bitch by another officer.

There are numerous eyewitness accounts of the police's "gentle dealing." Richard Goodwin put it more accurately in two sentences than Daley's report could manage in three pages: "The thing is simple. The police came up and cleared out the entire McCarthy floor with clubs." One of Hubert Humphrey's aides, nine floors higher up, was called and told what the police were doing. "I know," he said in horror, "I can hear the screams up here."

"Afterward," the report goes on, "some of the persons removed from Room 1506 A threatened a sit-in in the main lobby of the hotel, but after a few minutes dispersed." Another exquisitely trimmed description. Neal Gillen, a lawyer who worked for Humphrey, who happened to be passing, told how this dispersal took place: "I saw an officer with no provocation at all take his club and proceed to beat these people on the floor randomly." Eventually, this policeman had to be dragged away by his colleagues.

Daley's talent for insinuating that on his Animal Farm the chickens are a danger to the fox is perhaps best exemplified by two appendices of his slim volume: Appendix C, "Weapons used by dissidents," and Appendix E, "Police officers injured." In the first, the Mayor finally crosses the line from the dishonest to the absurd. Remember, we are dealing with "terrorists" bringing "menace to the lives of millions of people." Here is how the report lists the armaments used by the revolutionary army:

> Some were merely disgusting such as: Cellophane bags of human excrement, cans of urine, paint hurled at officers.
> Others were lethal weapons such as: Rocks, bricks, two-by-fours, dart guns, glass ash trays, golf balls with nails impaled therein, potatoes with razors hidden inside, live black widow spiders, Molotov cocktails, knives and stilettos, cherry bombs, cans of noxious chemicals, a piece of metal with tenpenny nails attached to it, aerosol can with contents which acts as a stink-bomb (scissors to puncture same), a piece of wood with a razor attached (has the word "peace" written on the wood), golf ball with nail forced through it, one-half of a wooden rolling pin filled with lead, bottle top with a wick for use with inflammable liquid, empty beer cans, baseball bat inscribed "Cops are pigs," stape nails taped together to be used as a weapon (sometimes called guerrilla mine).

An array of these sophisticated weapons was solemnly displayed at Chicago police headquarters. It was hard to believe that possession of the entire arsenal would have been much use against two determined Chicago policemen, let alone twelve thousand. Yet even this list was highly suspect. For instance, none of the sixty-three hundred reporters present in Chicago reported that a Molotov cocktail was thrown, nor have subsequent independent investigations managed to establish that one was ever used.

The curious case of the "live black widow spiders" is even more instructive. This spider was dealt with at some length in the Walker Report. One such spider did, as it happens, make the Chicago scene. It was, safely incarcerated in a bottle, thrown into the car of a private citizen by someone who may or may not have been a demonstrator. The occupant of the car, a special agent for a railroad company, was told by the individual that he had just gotten rid of a score or more of these "pets" in police cars, and those ones "weren't in bottles." The captive spider was turned over to the police. Subsequent investigation by the Chicago police failed to locate any black widows—alive, dead, or bottled—in any of the squad cars. In fact, nothing was found to budge the initial conclusions of the police captain put on the case that he was dealing with an apolitical action by a "nut."

There is one highly significant, and easily available, piece of weaponry that finds no place in Daley's list: guns. It did not apparently strike the authors of Daley's report as remarkable that, in a country where there are more small arms than adults, not one of the alleged terrorists brandished a firearm.

The most grotesque suppressed truth in the report concerns injuries. One would have thought that, on the absurd evidence of this part of the report alone, every newspaperman would have dismissed the whole document. In many instances, quite the reverse happened. For Daley's injury "statistics" persuaded many to revise their opinions on what had taken place: incredibly to anyone who saw what happened, the report conveyed the impression that more injuries were sustained by the police than by the demonstrators.

First, the police. Appendix E listed 198 policemen who had suffered some casualty during the week. The list includes 24 gassed—with their own gas, of course—and 70 suffering from "injuries" which would draw a reprimand for cowardice if complained of to the matron of an English boarding school: "abrasion to thumb," "laceration to tip of left finger," "split fingernail," "bruised left ankle." A large proportion of the injuries were to hands: a circumstance that led one unrepentant Chicago columnist, Mike Royko, to suggest that a lot of dastardly citizens must have been going round smashing policemen's knuckles with their faces.

On civilian casualties, Daley's report had this to say: "The partial survey of the Chicago Hospitals indicates that approximately 60 persons were treated at hospitals for injuries sustained during the course of the disorders." Thus, the casual reader would have the impression that for every one demonstrator injured at least three policemen were similarly incommoded.

Of course, the mind that could so imaginatively expand the demonstrators' arsenal was perfectly adjusted to contracting the number of demonstrator casualties. A less "partial" survey of the hospitals in the area would have revealed that the number of civilian casualties, arising out of the disorders, treated therein was in the region of a hundred. More astonishing was the omission of even a mention of the treatment carried out by the Medical Committee for Human Rights. This voluntary group of doctors and medical workers, originally set up to provide care for civil-rights victims of police brutality in the South, had no less than seven units in the vicinity of the demonstrations. As many policemen saw, these units occasionally did a land-office business in head-mending and rudimentary first aid. Dr. Quentin Young, a former national chairman of the organization, has notes of 425 patients treated at these facilities. Of this number, about one-third had neck or head injuries, and one-fifth had injuries in the lower abdomen and groin area. He further estimated that more than 200 more persons were treated on the spot by mobile medical teams, and that over 400 more were given first aid for tear gas or Mace.

Thus, if one includes gas victims (as the Daley report does on the police side), one comes out with a radically different police-civilian injury ratio than that suggested by the report. Taking Dr. Young's injury figures, which total over a thousand, into the equation, the new ratio works out at more than five demonstrators injured for every one policeman—which is very much the way it looked at the time.

Before composing the report, Daley's scribes did not even trouble to ask the Medical Committee whether it had any treatment figures. Presumably, since they could not have been ignorant of its activities, this was because they realized how damaging these figures would be to the case they were trying to present. Or perhaps they were reluctant to hear the Medical Committee's verdict on the police. "In general," said Dr. Young after the disturbances, "the police action in the South was more restrained than in Chicago."

The final trick of the Daley report, inevitably, was to turn the media into a scapegoat. "The news media," the report concluded, "responded with surprising naïveté and were incredibly misused." The technique is much older than Goebbels, but it still has its uses. Some of the press did allow themselves to be "incredibly misused," but the manipulation was done by Mayor Daley, not by the demonstrators.

The story ought to have a happy, if limp, ending. After Daley's propaganda counterthrust, the subject died a natural death in the newspapers. It seemed then that the mayor of America's second most important city could not only get away with what he wanted politically and brutally crush dissent, but could also rewrite history with his own crude brand of Newspeak. Then, long after Daley's version had time to take hold, came the exhaustive and excellently documented *Rights in Conflict*.

Compiled by a Chicago lawyer, Daniel Walker, this report drew on the work of 212 investigators and nearly 3500 eyewitness accounts. Walker was careful to bring out as much evidence as possible about abuse and provocation of the police by the demonstrators. But his summary found much evidence of "unrestrained and indiscriminate police violence." Accounts of the incidents in the Lincoln Park area convinced Walker "of the presence of what can only be called a police riot."

Surely, even at this late stage, this would put the Mayor's nose ever so slightly out of joint. Not at all. With masterly aplomb, Daley called yet another press conference and announced his admiration for "an excellent study." He was pleased to see that the report noted "the majority of policemen did act responsibly under extremely provocative circumstances." An undeniable reflection. But did this mean that one had to worry only if over six thousand of the twelve thousand police on duty that week stepped out of line? The theory of majority rule in law enforcement is a novel contribution to democratic thought. Daley did have one reservation about Walker's work, however. "My only basic criticism," he said, "is the summary, which, if used alone, would mislead the public."

The Mayor was on sound propagandist ground here. Most newspapers were for reasons of space unable to print much more than extracts from the report's summary. And Daley must have been well aware that the market for a 362-page report would be extremely limited, particularly among his loyal constituents.

Most of his loyal constituents, however, and many people in other states, did read an editorial on the subject in the *Chicago Tribune* after the Walker Report was issued. The editorial also appeared in the form of a full-page advertisement in the *New York Times* under the imprimatur of a group called Interested Citizens of Chicago. With loving fidelity to the Mayor's line it criticizes the report's summary and then moves into an impassioned defense of the policemen's conduct. The advertisement eloquently pleads: "Please read the *whole* Walker Report." It would have been more convincing had the editorial writer and those Interested Citizens not shown such conspicuous evidence of not having read the whole report themselves. The editorial contains the apparently imperishable canard: "If this was a 'police riot,' how did it happen that more police than members of the mob suffered injury?" Yet the Walker report had contained (and it did not question) the treatment figures supplied by the Medical Committee for Human Rights, which knocked the whole Daley thesis lopsided. There could hardly have been a more fitting demonstration of the indestructible quality of the Big Lie.

ACT XI

See How They Run

1

The Ghost of 1960

"During the 1936 campaign Stuart Chase wrote a book called *Rich Land, Poor Land,* in which he dramatized with brilliant persuasiveness the appalling waste of irreplaceable fertile soil. No one seemed to doubt that the statements were true or that the situation was serious. Did the political candidates make a major issue of what they were going to do to remedy this evil? They did not. The proposal of a practical plan might have been ruinous to either party."

—Thurman Arnold in 1937

Consecrated at last by their parties, equipped with running mates and with suitably flexible but inspirational platforms, Richard Nixon and Hubert Humphrey were now free to launch themselves upon the electorate. George Wallace had been free to do so all along, since his present strength, and eventual weakness, derived from his lack of a party bureaucracy. (Wallace's "nomination" did not occur until the convention of the American Independent Party in Dallas on September 16. It was a formality of formalities, and no running mate was produced.)

Few campaigns have been more energetic than Hubert Humphrey's and none so meticulous, or expensive, as Richard Nixon's. Yet the overall effect of both was not regarded with pleasure by political enthusiasts, except those who were actively backing one of the runners. For many people the elimination process had disposed of the candidates they found really attractive, and a spectatorial interest in the furious progress of George Wallace could not make up for their loss—although Wallace was undoubtedly the finest working demagogue seen for years in the top-class company. The desperate closeness of the contest, at the end, did a good deal to rekindle passion—but to judge by the poorness of the turnout on November 5, the public tended to share the coolness of the *aficionados.*

607

This was a pity, because the campaign was an interesting exercise. For one thing, certain close-in exchanges between the candidates affected the fascinating balance of nuclear peace. And it was a campaign in which some important—though by no means irreversible—political trends showed up more clearly than before. Indeed, from a technical viewpoint, 1968, with its dramatic fluctuations in party loyalty and sharp contrasts in political method, was a most remarkable campaign.

The charge most frequently made was that the campaign lacked content; that not many important things seemed to happen. Still, as one epigraph to this chapter attests, the observation that Presidential campaigns lack apparent content is not a new one. The complaint goes back before Thurman Arnold, who was not really complaining but trying to explain to the liberal community the difficulties faced by practicing politicians.

Although the 1968 campaign was probably little better or worse than most others, in terms of content, it occupied a narrative position calculated to emphasize its deficiencies. The preceding events of the year—even, on occasion, the political contest itself—had dramatized questions that were unarguably important. People were inclined to judge the campaign according to whether or not it resolved those questions. And by that standard it did not rate high.

Yet this is a misleading, even dangerous, standard to judge a campaign on, for it is only in the necessary mythology of democracy that a final campaign resolves questions. In practice, the main thrust of the enterprise must be to rally support, working within a framework of definitions made earlier—more or less hazily. Resolution of questions must take second place to the consolidation of coalitions. The mythological version of an election campaign helps, however, to secure general allegiance to the process. It should therefore be understood, and deferred to with care, by people with a particular interest in politics. Indeed, it is necessary that the campaign include some actual debate, since a myth with no element of truth loses its power to convince.

Frequently, Presidential campaigns seem unspectacular because the wrong kind of spectacle is expected. If someone accustomed only to the customs of horse racing goes to an auto race, it appears to him at first that the cars are not even racing against each other. It seems very dull. In fact, the action of the race is extremely complex but needs to be looked at in a different way. The political contest is often described figuratively as a race: in modern politics, the metaphor of a Grand Prix auto race is more useful than that of a horse race.

In an auto race, the spectator should be aware of the great complex of decisions—about what kind of cars, engines, tires, and fuel to have—which have already been made when the racers reach the starting grid. Certain kinds of surprises, such as the real outsider bursting through to victory, have been prepared against with as much scientific care as possible. Similarly in politics, it has been plain since parties were first organized that more and more of what matters takes place before the nomination of candidates. Horses, being simpler in construction than politicians and less easy to modify than machinery, are thus harder to understand than either. Essentially, this is why an account of the contest for the Presidency has to deal at greater length with the nomination of the candidates than with the subsequent competition between them. The auto race itself is important—also interesting and fraught with the possibility of miscalculation and disaster. But the building and selection of the cars takes more time and more varieties of effort.

The nature of the phenomena dealt with is quite different once the campaign has begun. Instead of being concerned with relatively small, observable bodies of party officials, the protagonists are maneuvering for margins of potential loyalty among unwieldy and "invisible" bodies of voters. The single most important factor in the game is the inertial force of voting habit: with that discounted, the candidates are fishing for a few per cent of one hundred thirty million potential voters. It is a game in which there is very little room for maneuver: the subtle paradox is that he who fails to maneuver at all runs the risk of throwing the game away. The theme of the 1968 campaign is that the Republican candidate, with everything in his favor, resolutely failed to react to circumstance and very nearly contrived to turn imminent victory into defeat.

Some politicians argue that "you can't second-guess a winning campaign." But that is like the generals who argue that because the British "won"—or anyway, did not lose—the Battle of the Somme in the First World War, it is not permissible to argue that there was anything wrong with the bloody and wasteful methods by which it was fought.

The beginning of the campaign was startling. It was difficult not to believe that the Democratic candidate was heading for a defeat comparable to Goldwater's in 1964—a defeat so comprehensive as almost to threaten the two-party system. On September 3, the day after Labor Day—when the campaign traditionally begins—the Gallup poll began sampling opinion for its first trial heat since the Democratic Convention. The result indicated that 43 per cent of the voters favored Nixon, 31 per cent favored Humphrey, and 19 per cent Wallace, with 7 per cent undecided. Within a few days, the difference was even more dramatic. In a sample taken between September 20 and 22, Nixon still had 43, but Humphrey had slipped to 28, only 7 points ahead of Wallace, with 21. Republican euphoria was the natural consequence: These were the days in which the Nixon high command talked of taking New York. But this talk did not extend to all members of the Nixon team. For instance, ex-Congressman Robert Ellsworth—the man who maintained liaison between the campaign caravan and state organizations—said in retrospect, "I honestly never thought it would be that easy. You had to say that the Democrats had a lot of guys like Larry O'Brien and Ted Kennedy, who are very professional, and you had to say those men would get together and do something. And you had to say the unions would get behind the ticket and pull a lot of those Wallace voters back to the Democrats. Not that I didn't think we would win. (I used to bet people by saying I would pay them so much for every Electoral College vote we had under three hundred, if they would pay me the same amount for every one over three hundred.) I just didn't think we'd win that easy."

In other words, it was believed that the huge gap between the Republican and Democratic nominees was bound to narrow sharply as voting day approached. The difference between Goldwater and Humphrey was that whatever Humphrey's immediate troubles his political persona was essentially part of the American mainstream. Therefore, it was always possible for him to spring back.

The issue on which that possibility turned was Vietnam, despite all arguments to the contrary. It is perfectly true that Vietnam was an issue on which only a minority of American voters had strong and clear feelings, and for the majority, even those who felt deeply unhappy about the war, it was too confused an issue to shift a Presidential vote. Numerous studies have shown that *no* single issue, in a passably normal year, is perceived with enough clarity or felt with enough strength to perform that trick. Most of the evidence from academic studies, opinion polls, and the like indicates that the ordinary voter, whose involvement in politics is marginal, has only the haziest image of the candidates and their programs. But to leave it at that is grossly to oversimplify the dynamics of party organization and the mobilization of opinion among the electorate.

The most convincing way to consider the issue of the war in Vietnam as the campaign got under way, was as an issue which could move a considerable number of votes at second hand—by leverage, as it were.

This worked in several ways, the most obvious being among the liberal section of the Democratic elite, whose cooperation—as organizers, fund-raisers, publicists—is crucial to the presentation of an active campaign. Most voters may have hazy perceptions of the issues, but on the whole the party elites do not, especially not liberal Democrats. Vietnam, and the complex of ideas about American foreign policy which it represented, was a symbol that controlled their partisanship.

Less obvious, and harder to define, was the role of the informal "opinion leaders," who permeate the electorate at large: the people who attempt, with varying degrees of intensity, to proselytize among their fellow citizens. According to a classic study of the electorate, *The American Voter* by Angus Campbell et al., Institute for Social Research, University of Michigan, "in the somewhat unique setting of a presidential election campaign, about one out of every four persons reports engaging in informal attempts to convince someone else to support a given party or candidate." According to one sensible account of the structure of public opinion, these people form one tier of the "two-step flow of communications"—passing on information and interest they receive from the mass media and party propaganda to their less engaged fellow citizens. Clearly, it is difficult to say just what the potentialities of this diffuse and variable mechanism were at the beginning of the 1968 campaign—but it is known that personal influence on this level *can* be extremely powerful. According to *The American Voter,* "the casual nature of this behavior should not conceal its importance . . . as a means by which the final distribution of partisan preference in the electorate is achieved." Indeed, personal influence is probably the most effective means of persuading people who are uncertain about voting at all that they *should* vote. And voters of low motivation, once brought to the polls, are more likely than not to be Democrats. Similarly, the more people vote, the better for the Democrats, since there are more of them.

Naturally, Vietnam was not the only issue which would affect the final vote. There were many, and some could not be seriously affected by campaign maneuvers. There was, for instance, virtually nothing to be done about the reasons why Midwestern farm states go Republican. Also, variable pressures came into action almost regardless of how the campaign developed: for example, powerful labor-union pressure was bound to be exerted against Wallace in the North (much of its effectiveness coming from personal contact of varying kinds), simply out of the unions' desire to preserve their own power structure.

But Vietnam was a variable that was affected by tactical maneuvers during the campaign. It was an issue over which it was unusually possible to make people believe they had perceived real movement. Obviously, the Administration, because it was conducting the war, could make the most convincing movement—but it was also possible, at least in theory, that Nixon could stake out a position to which people would respond. In sum, the development of the Vietnam issue would determine directly the fate of a small but useful number of committed peace votes, would govern the morale and partisanship of the Democratic Party elite; and, by its effect on the activity of "opinion leaders" throughout the country, would play a large part in deciding how much the electorate might be energized by the campaign. On Labor Day, the Vietnam issue was still "frozen." There had been no serious progress in the Paris peace talks. Pham Van Dong, Premier of North Vietnam, reiterated that day the familiar demand that the United States "unconditionally stop its bombing raids" and promised to fight to "complete victory." Hubert Humphrey had still made no move that even psychologically distinguished his position from that of the Administration. And Richard Nixon had still said nothing to indicate that he would reduce the U.S. commitment to the war. So all the movement was yet to come. It was a situation made for an astute politician. But there was, and is, a question whether such a description applies to Richard Nixon.

It is hard to believe that a political campaign was ever run with such crisp, mechanical efficiency as Nixon's drive on the Presidency in 1968. Far from projecting the usual sense of emergency and improvisation, it seemed as cool and distinguished an organization as any of the solid American corporations represented by Nixon, Mudge. Like them, it drew liberally upon almost every usable device produced by the communications and data-processing industries, and not infrequently a certain institutional enthusiasm about all this hardware slopped right over into self-parody, as when campaign manager John Mitchell declared that it was his job to "program the candidate."

Perhaps the most remarkable subdivision of the Republican campaign was the Nixon version of "participation politics," organized around a computer which held in its memory bank sixty-seven Nixon positions on various issues. In Nixon offices around the country, voters were encouraged to speak into tape recorders brief questions, addressed to the candidate, on issues that concerned them. Each person who did so received a reply, a four-paragraph letter written by a computer-directed electric typewriter and signed by a signature machine. (The computer was programed to give a slightly different, "individual" answer each time.) Such personal-letter factories had been used by candidates before (including the "spontaneous" Robert Kennedy); but it was quintessentially Nixonian to organize one much more completely than anyone had ever done before (at a cost of two hundred and fifty thousand dollars) and then blandly to apply a label to it—"participation"—which had been one of the rallying cries for insurgent candidates, to whom it had meant something altogether different.

Thus, the outside world was always able to discover where Richard Nixon stood, or at least where a machine which faithfully reproduced his attitudes stood. At the same time, the candidate was matchlessly informed about the state of the outside world and what it thought of his campaign. As his personal turbojet caravan crossed and recrossed the country, constant touch was maintained with Nixon's New York and Washington headquarters. (Nixon found the radiophone extremely useful for calling Republican officials in states he was flying over and exchanging encouraging remarks about the progress of the campaign.) Contact with the headquarters was broken only for a few minutes a day, when the Nixon jet sank down to make its approach to each airport, briefly blanking out the radiophone equipment. But as soon as it rolled to a stop, technicians would run out with long leads to reconstitute the umbilical connection via the telephone network. Telexes on the plane could exchange long memos with New York, and speech drafts and regular bulletins on the details of the Republican and Democratic campaigns. At one stage they used to receive twice-daily reports from New York on the sexual progress, or nonprogress, of Chi-Chi and An-An, the two giant pandas who were being brought together in the London Zoo. At every stopover, there were at least two telexes in the hotel, arranged in advance, and specially secure telephones for the campaign staff and traveling researchers. Again, other campaigns had put together some of the same hardware—but never so much, so well.

On the sixth floor of the Nixon headquarters in New York, at 450 Park Avenue, there was a twenty-four-hour watch kept, and there was a special red phone—known as the "hot line"—equipped with a specialized and instantly recognizable ring. It was the link the communications room, on the floor above, tried to keep open to the candidate no matter what time it was or where he was. The staff had standing orders to drop whatever they were doing and spring to answer when the hot line rang.

A telecopier in the communications room was linked up each evening to the hotel Nixon was staying at. At about ten p.m. the first edition of the *New York Times* would be transmitted, almost entire, to the travelers. Even in the White House, Nixon could hardly be better served. "I don't think the boss ever had an operation quite like that before," said one of his staff. "I think he rather enjoyed it."

Others found it a nerve-racking vision of the future. The precision was frightening: this appeared to be the politics of manipulation, the promise of a computerized 1984—four terms ahead of schedule. This reaction seemed to be shared by both liberals and conservatives. Nixon, editorialized *The Progressive,* was "the fully automated candidate, programed to give on each public occasion the performance calculated to win friends and influence people." Garry Wills, *National Review* contributor and conservative theorist, described with distaste "the minute calibration that marks Nixon, the great calculator."

Yet appearances are often misleading, especially where great quantities of expensive and complicated machinery are involved. At the heart of all the computers, all the electronic equipment and opinion research, there was an old-fashioned, passably honest, and not particularly effective political campaign, which suffered from several internal contradictions and was so chronically inflexible that, in spite of every possible advantage, it almost managed to lose. In a sense, the boyish enthusiasm with which the Nixon men celebrated their own glittering mechanical mastery demonstrated the point. Few things in politics are more subtly damaging than a reputation—deserved or not—for chilly efficiency, and so this was deplorable public relations. The Nixon campaign put one in mind of Ettore Bugatti's remark about a particularly elaborate and cumbersome Rolls-Royce of the twenties: the "triumph of workmanship over design."

Nixon's campaign revolved around John Newton Mitchell, Nixon's newest law partner—almost exactly the same age as the candidate (born in 1913) but a very long way his junior in national political experience. This was the first campaign of any kind that he had run. Mitchell succeeded two other campaign managers: first, Dr. Gordon Parkinson, a man who had done much to revive the Republican Party in California but who had to withdraw because of his wife's health; second, Henry Bellmon, who withdrew to run (successfully) for a Senate seat in Oklahoma. When Bellmon withdrew in May, it might have seemed logical for Robert Ellsworth to succeed to over-all command, and indeed Ellsworth appears to have been one of those to whom it seemed logical. Instead, Ellsworth was put in charge of the Washington office and did a great deal of traveling with Nixon. Mitchell took over in New York, very much the center of the operation, on May 18.

Mitchell's approach to a political campaign was not exactly orthodox, if only because he made plain from the first his distaste for those creatures normally considered indispensable to a campaign—politicians. "We don't have any of them around here," he remarked. "That's why it seems so professional. Politicians are always after self-status. I don't want people who spend most of their time worrying over their own position or image. We're interested in the candidate." It is true that politicians, even Republican politicians, are difficult and argumentative fellows, but all the same, there are some sharp fellows among them, and their specialty, in so far as they can be said to have one, is knowing what voters want. Possibly, Mitchell might have been able to learn something from them: for instance, he was much impressed by Spiro Agnew and was inclined to take a good deal of the credit for bringing Agnew aboard the campaign. In view of Agnew's performance, that was perhaps a dubious achievement. A politician might have been able to warn Mitchell against the deceptive charms of the Governor of Maryland; he was one of those political figures who don't stand exposure. The usually urbane Senator Thruston B. Morton of Kentucky, for instance, after seeing Agnew in action a couple of times, described him bluntly as an "asshole."

Yet Mitchell himself has something of a reputation as a politician within his own circle. To most of his staff, he radiated unquestionable authority: a long, unsmiling face topped off by a high, bald forehead. But the same face can be mobile on occasion. "In a meeting," complained one Republican pollster, "Mitchell would always be the one who was nodding and winking at you, so that it looked like he agreed with you. But in the end you never knew what he was thinking." A member of Nixon's law firm described him, with more admiration: "Very shortly after we got to know him, we could see that here was a very stylish political operator."

Above all, Mitchell appears to pride himself on being bluntly practical, a "pragmatist" in the Nixonian sense of the word. (Among his first remarks on becoming Attorney General were some "pragmatic" words about the usefulness of wire-tapping.) He has always been a lawyer, but the expertise he developed during his career is more financial and organizational than legal: that is, he specialized for twenty-five years in matters of municipal and state financing, becoming, among other things, an adviser to Nixon's great enemy Rockefeller, and chief of the New York

State bond program. This quarter-century's work equipped Mitchell with a useful political network across the country, not reaching out into the Republican grass roots in the Nixon manner, but still useful for finding a finance chairman here and there. At the beginning of 1967, when Mitchell's small but successful firm of Caldwell, Marshall, Trimble and Mitchell was merged with Nixon, Mudge, it was dealing almost exclusively in public finance.

Nixon's friendship with Mitchell ripened into something like complete reliance with a speed which surprised some people and which is perhaps best explained by the assessment of one man who worked for him without entirely enjoying the experience. "Mitchell is a fantastically capable engineer, once you've decided which way you want the train to go. He'll do everything at the right time, in the right way, and he won't try to drive the train off in his own direction." This makes it clear why Nixon could leave Mitchell to run the campaign with what Mitchell described as "complete autonomy." (The relationship was summed up in an exchange—just before Nixon arrived at the Republican Convention—which became fairly famous. Nixon was working on his acceptance speech on Long Island and rang Mitchell in Miami Beach. "Is there anything I should know?" Nixon asked. "No, not really," said Mitchell.)

The *apparat* which Mitchell directed was formidable. Its center was an unlabeled suite at 445 Park Avenue (known to the more conspiratorial-minded members of the staff as secret headquarters, although it was not especially secret). Here Mitchell had his own office, along with his chief aide, Kevin Phillips, a young lawyer who regarded himself as the theorist of the "emerging Republican majority." Here was where the advertising schedules and the campaign journeys were mapped out. Leonard Garment, the other major figure from the law firm, also worked at 445 Park, and—among others—one face from the past, Murray Chotiner, who had managed Nixon's first campaign and his notorious Senate campaign of 1950 and who now practices law in Newport Beach, California. (In the intervening years, Chotiner had run into rather hefty criticism concerning some dealings in Washington, so he was not the most freely exhibited member of the operation.)

Across the road was 450 Park—the center for button dispensing, literature distribution, citizen groups, Nixonettes, and Nixon's rather stiff little group of microboppers, known as Future Citizens for Nixon-Agnew. More important, it contained the sixth-floor policy-research operation. This organization had a pedigree going back at least two years, to October 1966, when Nixon's lone speech-writer, Pat Buchanan, began to set up meetings. It reached its final form with a meeting on June 10, after Mitchell became manager, when three essential subdivisions were organized: domestic and economic policy, under Alan Greenspan; foreign policy, under Richard Allen; and "the Presidency," under Raymond Price. (Whereas, in the earlier days of the campaign, there had been some talk of a new liberalism in Nixon's staff, this setup was frankly conservative in orientation. Apart from the fact that Allen and Greenspan, on the right, outnumbered Price as the mild liberal, they were the only ones who had staffs and panels of outside consultants. Price produced his noble thoughts on the Presidency entirely off his own bat.) Shortly after this meeting, the research department lost perhaps the most talented of all its members, the journalist Richard J. Whalen, author of that brilliant study of Joseph P. Kennedy, *The Founding Father*. Whalen is a conservative—he was not out of tune with the slant of the campaign, but he felt that in its determination merely to go after the Johnson Administration, it was not dealing seriously with the issues.

Mainly, the setting up of the policy-research department indicated John Mitchell's massive confidence. The department was told not to bother with any material aimed at the convention but to go straight for the campaign proper. The same instruction applied to Fuller & Smith & Ross, the advertising agency hired to promote the campaign. The brief given to John J. Poister, vice-president of FSR, who ran the operation, was simply to work out a plan for reaching every voter in the United States who owned a television or radio set. The cost—which eventually ran over eleven million dollars—was not going to be a problem. (The contrast between Republican and Democratic finances has rarely been sharper: at the beginning, the Democrats were not certain that they would be able to spend more than two million.)

Also in June, Mitchell put together his opinion-research operation, headed by Professor David R. Derge of the Department of Government at Indiana University. Derge is no doubt a sound and competent analyst; he was introduced to the organization by the New York banker Peter Flanigin, who acted as Mitchell's deputy. But he was not exactly the best known of the numerous political consultants available to the Republican Party—such as the young men of Campaign Consultants or Market Opinion Research, who spent the autumn chiefly occupied with Congressional and Senatorial races. The difficulty, of course, was that such people tended to be infected with Rockefellerism or Romneyism, where Mitchell and Nixon, it was clear, valued reliability above all else.

Under Derge, the Opinion Research Corporation of Princeton was hired to undertake perhaps the most elaborate polling operation yet attempted in a Presidential election, at the substantial cost of a quarter of a million dollars. Opinion Research spends most of its time doing market research for groups like General Motors, Campbell Soup, Standard Oil, and the National Association of Manufacturers, but it also has a long-standing connection with the Republican Party. (In the 1964 elections, ORC conducted polls for Republican candidates in thirty-eight states.) The most important project in the ORC "package" was a set of panel polls, derivations of a market-research technique which is one of ORC's specialties. Panel polling was originally developed by political scientists to study changes in voting intention and the effect of political propaganda: the essential idea is that, instead of interviewing an entirely fresh sample of the electorate each time (as in an ordinary opinion poll), the same people are interviewed on successive occasions. Naturally, the technically difficult aspect of the work is preventing the successive interviewing from inducing bias in the respondents—for instance, by making them better informed than the population at large. Certain learned disputes continue in political-science journals over the alleged reinterview effect and the scholarly validity of the concept. In the meantime, panel polling has become an important commercial tool and is used for such things as measuring the effectiveness of one television commercial against another —scholarly minuteness not being required here.

For the Nixon campaign, ORC set up panels of 500 voters each in California, Illinois, Michigan, Missouri, New Jersey, New York, Ohio, Pennsylvania, and Wisconsin. Other panels of 500 were made up from each of the Carolinas, Virginia, and Florida. These patient folk, selected as reliably representative of their fellow electors after some 12,000 interviews had been conducted in July, were to be subjected to questioning in three "waves"—in early September, early October, and late October. Naturally, they were not informed that their questioners were working for the Nixon campaign—in some cases that information could have made the reinterview effect quite sharp. Additionally, ORC arranged for "instant" telephone polls which could be conducted to test reactions to campaign events as they occurred, "issue polls" designed to elicit what problems were uppermost in the voters' minds, and yet more polls designed to discover how Nixon's image differed from Humphrey's. It was an enormous amount of information-gathering machinery, but there seems to be some question how much it meant to the people paying for it. "I really doubt," said one of the men involved, "that it led to any serious policy movement in the campaign."

Early in 1968, Nixon used to remark that "this campaign is haunted by the ghost of 1960." Based on his conviction that 1960 had been "the classic campaign of our time," it was a remark which had numerous applications to the circumstances in which he turned the tables. If in 1968 Nixon's use of opinion research was unoriginal, in 1960 it appears to have been downright eccentric. (For instance, the private polls, and every other indication available, convinced Nixon's manager in that campaign, Leonard Hall—correctly as it turned out—that almost everything depended on Illinois. Hall tried to persuade Nixon that he must drop all peripheral commitments and concentrate on Illinois. During this time, Nixon took off to Alaska, in a hopeless attempt to redeem his ill-advised promise to campaign in every state of the Union.) He appears to share in full measure the attitude of many veteran politicians toward opinion research and its attendant subtechnologies—that is, a mixture of fascination and mistrust. For instance, one of the projects organized by his research *apparat* was a series of "semantic differential" tests designed to examine the public's perceptions of Nixon and Humphrey. These are the tests in which a respondent is asked to look at sets of opposed words (passive/active, for instance, or bad/good) and to place candidates on a scale between each set of opposites. In the Nixon tests, people were asked to place on a 7-point scale first their ideal President, then Hubert Humphrey, then Richard Nixon. The tests were ready to go, when some additional tests were requested by Nixon himself. They included shifty/direct, insincere/sincere, and politician/statesman. No doubt to Nixon's great relief, he usually came out a bit nearer the statesman end of the scale (7) than the politician end (0). Nixon's score tended to average around 3.5, with Humphrey a little under 3.

Yet while he was eager, even anxious, to find out what his "image" was, Nixon was vigorously determined not to be remodeled on the basis of the findings. "I'm not going to have any damn image experts coming telling me how to part my hair," he said at one point. And his staff members were always eager to explain that, although the polls were *useful,* they were also very *confusing* and so could never be used as the major factor in decision-making. Everybody was anxious to make clear that Nixon would not tailor his politics to fit what the research said people wanted—and, indeed, there is evidence that he did not do so. Yet Nixon, like most other politicians, has been content to modify his attitudes according to pressures less scientifically and more intuitively assessed. It is not the idea of finding out what people want and giving it to them which politicians are uneasy about—that, despite pieties to the contrary, has always been the business of politics, and it would be curious if it were otherwise. What does worry them is the idea of doing it precisely and rationally. It is an interesting instinct about the place of the irrational and unpredictable in human affairs. Would it become impossible for the politicians to justify it to themselves without the element of hit or miss? (Another worry, perhaps, is an instinctive reluctance to let rival experts muscle in on the politicians' preserve of saying what the people want.)

The most important indication that the campaign of 1968 was haunted by the ghost of 1960 was the guiding principle that Nixon's energy was a finite resource. Not that Nixon was physically weak or indolent. On the contrary, his industry and endurance were so great as to tempt him into excess of activity. Like Scott Fitzgerald's Last Tycoon, he was apt to become addicted to fatigue, as to a drug. Therefore, in place of the absurd overextension of 1960, 1968 was built around a self-denying ordinance: to campaign in as few states as possible. It was not quite an overcompensation—indeed, it was a proposition which was strategically most defensible—but if applied too rigidly it could be dangerous.

Nixon started with one enormous advantage in the matter of campaign planning. Whereas the Democrats had scarcely a single state they could ignore as safe, Nixon had a huge block of them. There were twenty-one states, with 117 votes in the Electoral College, which the Republican planners were able to forget about, for all intents and purposes, where the campaign could be left in the hands of state committees, with perhaps swift "prop-stop" meetings here and there to back up local candidates. There were several kinds of states in this group—Midwestern, such as North Dakota, Iowa, and Indiana; mountain, such as Colorado and Utah; the rocky ribs of New England, such as Maine and Vermont. A good example was Kansas, with its seven votes, which Nixon did not visit and in which the Nixon-Agnew national organization spent virtually no money. As Ellsworth said comfortably of his home state, "If you have to worry about Kansas, you don't have a campaign anyway." Of all the "safe Republican" states, only Washington, with nine electoral votes, went Democratic, and that by a fairly narrow margin.

The Democrats had no such bank: almost every state that Humphrey could win he would have to fight for. It had not always been so, of course, because the Democrats had once had the solid South—which, only narrowly held by Lyndon Johnson for Kennedy in 1960 and captured by Goldwater in 1964, now seemed the almost undisputed property of George Wallace.

That, so to speak, was the defensive sector of Nixon's plan. The offensive sector revolved around a list of fourteen states, selected by Nixon himself, as targets for personal campaigning and major advertising expenditure. The list was "not open to question," according to the Nixon staff: it was the boss's own production, and from its configuration everything else in the campaign followed. The states were California (40 votes); Florida (14); Illinois (26); Michigan (21); Missouri (12); New Jersey (17); New York (43); North Carolina (13); Ohio (26); Pennsylvania (29); South Carolina (8); Texas (25); Virginia (12); and Wisconsin (12)—for a total of 298 Electoral College votes, thus sufficient to win the Presidency on their own.

But Nixon did not have to win them all, by any means. If he could put together 152 votes from this list to add to his "safe" block, he would be past the target of 270 needed to win. And this was a necessary proviso, since there was one state on the list which was not seriously winnable, at least in the opinion of the candidate and most of his staff. This was New York. Kevin Phillips was apparently sanguine to the last about the chances of taking New York, and at the time the Democrats were at their nadir, the polls made it look conceivable. But Nixon was never convinced. "He just used to say, 'I don't believe it,' when people said he would win New York," according to one of his research staff. (The reason for campaigning in New York was simply that it was impossible not to: it was the natural headquarters of the campaign and is the main communications center of the nation. Even so, Nixon carefully limited his appearances in New York. In 1960 he had tried to win the state.)

What the second list amounted to, in fact, was a reconsideration of Nixon's old battlegrounds against Kennedy. Illinois, Michigan, Missouri, New Jersey, North Carolina, Pennsylvania, South Carolina, and Texas had all gone to Kennedy by slender, or at least reversible, margins. At the same time, California, Florida, Ohio, Virginia, and Wisconsin had gone to Nixon by similarly small margins. This was the bond that the fourteen had in common, but they were still very diverse slices of America.

The Southern and Border states represented the flanks of George Wallace's fortress—Texas, Florida, and North Carolina—and one section of the fortress proper—South Carolina. With only eight votes, South Carolina was the most inconsiderable state Nixon pursued and one of the victories which caused most surprise when it was declared. Yet Nixon planned, shrewdly, from the first, to take the state: even its eight votes were worth chipping away from Wallace. And South Carolina, although it appeared to be undisputed Wallace territory, was a place where Nixon had a special weapon: Strom Thurmond. Wisely, Nixon decided to make no challenge to Wallace in Alabama, Mississippi, Louisiana, Georgia— or even Arkansas, which at first glance might have seemed like promising country for a raid.

Florida would be the site of a three-way contest: a Southern state, a part of which was losing its Southern character, filling up with middle-class *émigrés*—like Nixon himself—from other parts of the country, and with an experience of politics outside the one-party tradition. Further, within the state, that tradition was decaying rapidly, as conservative Democrats like Governor Kirk switched to the Republican Party. Admittedly, some of the migrants to Florida were liberal Democrats from the Northeast, and together with the remains of the native reflex in the northern part of the state for the Democratic ticket and the poorly organized Negro vote, would help Humphrey. But essentially all the social trends in Florida which had given Nixon victory in 1960 had grown stronger since, and the more important threat was Wallace. Therefore, the Nixon people projected a heavy television campaign for Florida—an excellent weapon, anyway, in the more geriatric and idiot-box-bound sections of the state. Wallace, although not short of money, would find it difficult to match the relentlessly rational deployment of Nixon's wealth.

Texas was similarly New South, increasingly rich in middle-class businessmen and employees. Nixon and most other Republicans were convinced that the 1960 margin had been contrived by the mighty Texas Democratic Party largely out of thin air and graveyards. In 1968, the Texas Democrats seemed to be in hopeless disarray as the result of open warfare between Governor John Connally's conservative wing of the party and Senator Ralph Yarborough's liberal wing. It seemed—wrongly —to the Republicans that these warring factions might not be reunited in time to perform feats of magic at the polls. It is a large and exhausting state to campaign in, but here special emphasis was laid on "surrogate candidates": notably Congressman George Bush, a fine-looking fellow of excellent birth who represented the space-town suburbs of Houston and was not opposed in his district—an indication of the strength of the Republican technocracy in Texas. ("I don't know what went wrong," Bush muttered when interviewed in December. "There was a hell of a lot of money spent.")

The most important states of the fourteen were the big Northern industrial ones: Michigan, Ohio, Pennsylvania, and New Jersey, adding up to 83 votes, with the "hybrid" state of Missouri—part industrial, part farm; part Midwest, part South—added on to make 95. In 1960, Nixon had taken only one of this group—Ohio—and if that was the best he could do in 1968 the election would be lost.

The vital state, to the Nixon strategists, was Pennsylvania, and in the end it was to be their most shattering disappointment. (Only one Pennsylvanian was appointed to a high post in Nixon's Administration.) Despite Kennedy's showing in 1960, Republicans regard Pennsylvania as theirs by right—and with some historical justification. In one hundred years, it has gone for the Democratic candidate for President only five or six times, and in the same period there have been only four Democratic governors out of twenty-five. In 1960 Governor David Lawrence was one of these rare birds. The Democrats were in charge of the state's patronage apparatus, one of the most impressive in the country, which automatically provided them with large quantities of money and campaign workers. Further, Pennsylvania's heavy proportion of Catholics was reckoned to favor Kennedy. But even with so much going for him, Kennedy carried the state by only a modest one hundred thousand votes. Since then, Republicans reconquered the state machinery, and Wallace arrived on the scene to menace the Democratic vote in the blue-collar suburbs. In August, private polls for the state Republican party showed Nixon leading Humphrey—and although by mid-September this had slipped to an even 41–41, with Wallace at 18 per cent, the belief in revenge, come November, did not lose ground.

The dynamics of taking Pennsylvania traditionally revolve around Philadelphia, and this was where Nixon and his minions somewhat miscalculated. It has always been believed that if a Republican can get 40 per cent or more of the vote in Philadelphia, the Republican vote in the rest of the state will carry him to victory. If this is to be done, it means some really tough "street-fighting," for in few cities of the country are the Democrats better at getting their vote out and at making sure that the vote appears in the finest possible light. (To anticipate slightly: on Election Day it was found that in the Sixty-fifth Ward *seven out of ten* voting machines had been tampered with in one way or another.) The only way to combat this is with a Republican army of poll-watchers and canvassers comparable at least to the ten thousand people the Democrats turn out to cover the city on Election Day. The task of raising such a force was entrusted to William Meehan, chairman of the Pennsylvania

Turnpike Commission, who satisfied Robert Ellsworth that he would be able to hold the Democrats on their own ground. It was not unreasonable to believe he would. Meehan was the son of the famous Austin "Boss" Meehan and the man who had reassembled the Pennsylvania Republican Party after the disaster of 1960. From his post on the Turnpike Commission, he was the unofficial dispenser of state patronage under Governor Raymond Shafer, and thus a man of no little standing in the community. But the armies he promised to Nixon never appeared on the streets. (It is only fair to add that Meehan was up against a Democratic boss, Mayor Tate, who was fighting with special passion. Tate was said to be most anxious to see a Democratic administration in Washington, because of certain inquiries which the Department of Labor had been conducting into Philadelphia labor-union affairs. Tate apparently felt that these inquiries should not be directed by any partisan spirit in Washington.)

The other miscalculation in Nixon's plans for Pennsylvania was over the matter of the Negro vote. In 1960, Nixon had taken nearly 20 per cent of the Negro vote in Pennsylvania. During the intervening years, the percentage of Negroes in Philadelphia rose from 28 to over 34, and so not surprisingly the Pennsylvania Republican leaders now believed they needed at least 15 per cent of the black vote to win the state. But Goldwater's candidacy in 1964 had comprehensively shattered relations between the Negroes and the Republican Party, and although people tried to comfort themselves with the reflection that Nixon's civil-rights record could be made to look reasonably good, it soon became apparent that some positive gesture would be required to repair the situation in Pennsylvania. And Nixon, far from making any such gesture, had been rather manifestly bowing in the direction of the Republican Party's new segregationist wing.

The Pennsylvania Republicans implored Nixon to make some move to reconcile the Negroes in their state. Early in September, W. Thatcher Longstreth, head of the Philadelphia Chamber of Commerce and an old admirer of Nixon's, urged him, "When you come to Philadelphia, drive through the streets, make your speeches, and then have a private meeting in your hotel with some Negro leaders who are Republicans." (This would have been easy to arrange, because hundreds of Negroes hold patronage jobs in Pennsylvania.) There was no need, Longstreth claimed, to make any specific commitment—but Nixon would not take up the idea. His reasons were somewhat obscure, but it was plain that he would not defer in private to Negro sensibilities as he would to Southern ones. "What's the use?" Nixon asked Longstreth. "I'm not going to say any-

thing. I am not going to campaign for the black vote at the risk of
alienating the suburban vote. . . . All we can do is not say anything or
do anything which will cause the Negroes to lose confidence in me, because I am going to be President of the United States, and no President
can do anything without having the confidence of the black community."
He added, "If I am President, I am not going to owe anything to the
black community." The idea appeared to be that the Negroes' confidence
would be preserved by promising them nothing—and then delivering it.
It is hard to know whether the attitude derived from political clumsiness,
honest consistency, callousness—or a mixture of all three.

Of the big targets, Ohio was the safest for Nixon. Putting it another
way, if he could not take Ohio (the only big state to break with Roosevelt in 1944), he could not take any of the others. Michigan and New
Jersey were much more problematical, and their fate depended on the
Wallace vote. This was the subject of much inquiry by ORC and Professor Derge, and on September 26 Derge presented Nixon and Mitchell
with the collated results of a series of inquiries, wrapped up into a set of
findings and inquiries. The tempting point was that more than half the
Wallace supporters said they would favor Nixon in a two-way race with
Humphrey. (Three days earlier, the Harris poll reported that with Wallace at 21 per cent, half of the Wallace supporters favored Nixon.) But
according to ORC's research, the majority of Wallace's supporters said
they might change their allegiance before Election Day. The question
was: What would they do then? It was not an easy matter to predict,
because Wallace's strength was drawn from dissidents in both major
parties, with a sprinkling of independents and people who had previously
been too alienated to vote.

One solution was right out of court. Nixon could not attract the
Wallace voters by moving further to the right and outbidding Wallace
with even sterner talk of law'n'order. The research showed that the
people who liked Wallace simply were not going to believe that anyone
else could rival their first choice in the iron-fist department. In the weeks
after the Chicago convention, it was easy to overestimate the degree to
which the electorate had moved to the right—and although Nixon was
praised on occasion for his "statesmanlike" refusal to plunge into a
flaming reactionary campaign and sweep the nation, it would in fact
have been electoral suicide for him to do so. Intelligent self-preservation
suggested that Nixon not rush onto the same reef as Goldwater.

Another error would have been an attack upon Wallace himself.
His supporters were already sufficiently resentful of orthodox politicians,

and direct attacks would confer much-needed status. The course which Derge recommended and Nixon adopted was the plainest and most obvious one, which was simply to hammer away at the argument that as Wallace could not win the Presidency, a vote for him would be a wasted vote. Once this argument was accepted, the only remaining rationale for a Wallace voter was to try to deadlock the election—too radical a strategy for most.

Nixon had an extremely effective weapon to deploy in the battle against Wallace's credibility—Barry Goldwater, the hero of the right, who was ready to repay in kind Nixon's loyalty of 1964. In a number of speeches, and in a specially written leaflet, Goldwater told his old followers that although Wallace said a lot of important things, and said them well, and although he was a man for whom Goldwater had a good deal of respect, there was no chance that Wallace could advance the cause of the right. The "can't win" strategy was entirely sound so far as it went, but like much else about the campaign it was not especially subtle. In certain respects, it was liable to help Humphrey.

It was clear that a good number of the Wallace voters would go to Nixon when they broke away. But merely because a majority *said* they favored Nixon, it could not be guaranteed that they would actually *vote* for Nixon (any more than that they *said* they would vote for Wallace guaranteed they would do so). The likeliest prospect was that Wallace voters, when they lost confidence in their own man's chances, would take the simplest way out and return to their previous voting allegiance. In the Northern states, this meant they would vote Democratic; in Michigan, for instance, Wallace voters were almost five-to-one former Democrats, according to the opinion polls. In that state, therefore, the best chance of Nixon's winning lay in the Wallace vote's holding together, rather than breaking up.

This was more than just a difficult technical point: it had to do with a real strategic difficulty in Nixon's campaign and in his list of target states. In the industrial North, there was no question of Wallace's winning a state. All that he could do was be a nuisance, and, in the nature of things, he was doing vastly more harm to Humphrey. But in the South and the Border, it was different. If Nixon allowed the feeling to grow that Wallace was worth voting for, Wallace might well win several states outside his Deep South fortress—he would win them from Nixon, not Humphrey, and it would increase his chance of deadlocking the election. There were five states at risk in this way, with a total of 71 votes: Texas, Florida, North Carolina, South Carolina, and Tennessee (not on Nixon's list because it was a state which, it was thought, would come into line because of Agnew. In the end, Nixon campaigned fairly hard in Tennessee). The most Machiavellian plan Nixon could have pursued was to find a way to attack Wallace's credibility in the Border and South without attacking it in the North. It would not have been easy, because nationwide communications have made such "differential" campaigns hard to contrive. In fact, Nixon chose to do the opposite. He preached as fervently against Wallace's credibility in the North as in the South. Indeed, he made one of his most cogent speeches on the subject in Flint, Michigan, something of a center of Wallace sentiment. He therefore probably contributed a good deal to the disintegration of the Wallace vote in Michigan, which was the immediate reason for Humphrey's winning the state.

One cannot be certain whether Nixon's strategic miscalculation sprang from a genuine distaste for Wallaceism or a mistake about the role of habit in the behavior of voters who are uncertain about what to do—probably both elements were present. Also, it is important that the basic philosophy of the Nixon campaign derived from a belief that the Republicans were riding what Leonard Garment called "a major historical trend in the Border States and the South." This thesis was most clearly articulated by Kevin Phillips, with the claim that the Republican Party should be "the new Populist Party," basing its support on the newly emergent middle and lower-middle classes of the South and West and fanning out into such parts of the country as southern Pennsylvania which he maintained was rich in migrants from the South. "This is a new American revolution," according to Phillips, "coming out of the South and West, like other American revolutions, such as FDR's." (Bringing with it, he would admit, values strikingly at variance with FDR's.) There has been evidence for some time of changes in the pattern of Republican support—but this seemed rather visionary stuff on which to base a campaign, especially when extended to New York. It is a corollary of Phillips's theory that "all you've got to do with American politics is work out who doesn't like whom and you've got it." The story of America, he claims, in a kind of mirror version of Democratic ethnic politics, is "the melting pot that never melted"; therefore the Irish of New York will turn Republican because "they don't like the Jews and Negroes who control the New York Democratic Party now." (It must be said that the New York party of John Burns, Frank O'Connor, and Paul O'Dwyer contrived to hold Nixon below his 1960 level in most of the suburbs where the Irish live.)

The obsession with white suburban votes, especially south of Maryland, was largely responsible for the liability of Spiro Agnew's candidacy. Strategically, his function was to bring home two states in which Nixon did not plan to campaign heavily: Tennessee, which was won, and Maryland, which was not. Tactically, Agnew was thought to be a bright and promising politician but sufficiently inexperienced to be gratefully docile —after his experiences with Henry Cabot Lodge, who kept making policy off his own bat, Nixon was feeling rather gun-shy about Vice-Presidential aspirants. The chief objection to Governor Howard Baker of Tennessee, another contender who had many of the same colorations as Agnew, was that he had too much of a mind of his own.

It was thought at first that Agnew had more of a mind than he turned out to have. There is every reason to believe that Nixon and Mitchell, after a fairly cursory inspection, felt they had found the ideal package for the Republican revolution, and reliable too. But one shrewd Republican operative who spent a lot of time with Agnew thought that they were simply taken in. "He fooled me for a few weeks," this man said. "Seems to take in data very quickly and has a couple of ideas that seem to suggest he might have an original mind. Nixon has a vacuum-cleaner mind, and so far as I know he only had a couple of talks with Agnew. He probably extracted those few ideas of Agnew's and thought there might be more in the pipeline. He couldn't have been more mistaken."

The Republicans comforted themselves with the thought that their QRC polls showed that most of the public didn't think the Vice-President made much difference and that very few of them were aware of the remarkable bloopers that Agnew floated with monotonous regularity. But that was not the point: what Agnew was doing was giving the Democratic elite—who knew exactly who he was—someone to hate and someone to organize against. And the more energetic they became, the more people they would bring to the polls who might vote Democratic without knowing who Humphrey was. There was, indeed, one occasion when Agnew almost lost the election for Nixon.

Shortly after Agnew remarked that Humphrey was "squishy-soft on Communism," Stephen Hess, a Republican intellectual of some practical experience, was dispatched to join his staff. (Hess ran into a tide of resentment there, because the columnists Evans and Novak wrote a story saying that he was being sent to look after Agnew. The trouble was that Evans and Novak were right.) When he caught up with Agnew's caravan, Hess found to his horror that the candidate and most of his staff were delighted with the effect the "soft on Communism" speech had had.

Apparently, they were infected by the Billy Rose approach to publicity: don't read it, measure it. Hess arrived just in time to stall more
diatribes on the same subject. Such crowd-pleasing gambits as "Communists in our midst" and "lists of names" were under consideration. At
this point, it emerged that Agnew genuinely did not know that these
phrases were the slogans of McCarthyism. Indeed, he may not have
known what McCarthyism was. He was vaguely aware that Joe McCarthy
had been a bad guy of some kind, but he had no idea why. In 1953,
Agnew had been an apolitical manager of a supermarket, and in the
years since he hadn't bothered to find out about McCarthy.

As it happened, the Democrats nearly came together in time to
deprive the Republicans of victory. The spectacle of Agnew giving a
road-show revival of *The Senator from Wisconsin* would have brought
them together six weeks earlier, and in one galvanic jerk.

Apart from the "geographical" difficulties of the Nixon campaign
and its lack of subtlety in assessing voter behavior and the role of minority groups ("Are they really part of the political process?" Leonard
Garment once asked), there was another general difficulty. It was, as
John Sears, a delegate-hunter in the days before Miami, said cheerfully,
"a negative campaign." That is, it was aimed quite frankly at criticizing
the shortcomings of the Johnson Administration, while making few
positive—i.e., controversial—propositions of its own. The aim was to
conserve the huge but deceptive lead Nixon had acquired since Johnson
had begun the decline of the Democrats—to preserve the coalition of
dissent by not saying anything that might cause sections of it to break
away. Nixon's rather grander way of putting it resembled his negative
formula for inducing Negro confidence: he would not make "empty
promises." From this proposition developed his glossy but curiously
inactive campaign.

Yet it would not have done to have the campaign be too obviously
negative—and in fact many speeches had been compiled even before
the campaign began, with more to follow, the massive texts of which
could be used to persuade skeptics like Richard Whalen. But committed
Republicans, perhaps naturally, were rather more impressed by these
than other people were, despite the ingenuity of such proposals as the National Computer Job Bank. ("If computers can match boys and girls
for college dates, they can match job-seeking men with man-seeking
jobs." It was not explained how the Computer Bank would project the
ghetto dweller into the suburban area, where the jobs were apt to. be
located.)

This strategy was entirely sound so long as the opposition was in bad shape, but it started to become dangerous the moment any recovery began on the other side. When the campaign was a few weeks old, not all Republicans were as sanguine as the Nixon high command. On September 26, Walter De Vries, a consultant for Republican Congressional and Senatorial campaigns, wrote to John Mitchell one of the more prescient political letters of the year. After explaining that he wrote purely in a personal capacity, De Vries said:

> . . . What is really starting to bug me, the Nixon vote, indeed for five or six months now, is staying the same—about forty per cent. This is not only true for Gallup and Harris, but is also the case in all of the private polls (marginal states and congressional districts). *I believe this forty per cent represents the "hard core" Nixon vote, and even if he picked up a few Wallace voters and Undecideds his percentage would not go much above the range it has been in all of these months* (two conventions and the campaigns notwithstanding).
>
> If this is true, and the trend continues, *the volatility is in the sixty per cent of the vote divided between Humphrey, Wallace, and the undecided—and, point number two: this race is by no means in the bag for Nixon.*
>
> One thing we think we know about political behavior is that when people are severely cross-pressured (e.g., McCarthy, Rockefeller supporters, and straight Democrats now splitting for Wallace), they often resolve their dilemma by reverting back (in the voting booth) to their traditional party behavior. And it is highly unlikely they will resolve their dilemma by non-voting—*they will* go to the polls.
>
> Parenthetically, the issue structure on racial problems still shows that most Americans still favor socio-economic aid, educational programs, the expansion of rights, and the elimination of discrimination; only a small minority go the real hard-line approach. . . .
>
> This lack of movement in Nixon's support and the volatility of the other sixty per cent suggest to me that a lot of action could occur in the last few weeks (unlike 1964). Thus far, as I read it, your strategy has been one of caution and playing it down the middle-of-the-road. If the Wallace vote starts to break off for Humphrey and the undecideds start moving the same way, a change in strategy or in emphasis might be in order.
>
> One of the strongest themes in appealing to independents and frustrated/alienated Democrats is that Nixon, at least, offers the opportunity for change—the chance to make things different. Humphrey doesn't even offer the *opportunity* to do things differently. I think you have got to hit this theme harder, and add the programmatic specifics to back it up (reduce our commitment in Vietnam; more and better trained police to get at crime; better educational programs; joint private-governmental efforts on urban problems; etc.).

Perhaps I have overstated the case; but, I think there should be a strategy and a plan in the tank in case events or voter movement start to overtake you during the last few weeks.

Mitchell, who was busy managing the large and intricate machinery of the Nixon campaign, did not even answer the letter. And when the voters did begin to move, there was nothing else in the tank.

2

You Taught Me How to Love You, Now Teach Me to Forget

"Thank God I'm normal,
I'm just like the rest of you chaps,
Decent and full of good sense,
I'm not one of these extremist saps,
For I'm sure that you'll agree,
That a fellow like me
Is the salt of our dear old country
—Of our dear old country."

—Archie Rice's song, in John Osborne's *The Entertainer*

"Here was our situation right after Chicago," one of Hubert Humphrey's managers remembered with a shiver after it was all over.

> We had no money. We had no organization. We were fifteen points behind in the polls. We did have a media plan, but we didn't have the money to go with it. And we were going to have to change our ad agency anyway. The worst thing was that we didn't have enough time. The candidate approved the campaign plan in Chicago on August 30. That was the Friday before Labor Day, which is the day the campaign begins, traditionally. Instead of having three or four weeks to mount a campaign, we had three days. And so the candidate went on the road, and he was a disaster.

As we shall see, that was no exaggeration. It was about this time that Larry O'Brien had breakfast with the candidate and is reputed to have said, "Look, I'm going to work my tail off for you, but as your manager I have to say to you—right now, you're dead." Certainly, Humphrey was short of everything a well-organized campaign needs, including the time and money to make up for other deficiencies. But that was not the heart of the trouble. The plain truth was that he had come out of the convention in Chicago literally hated by one large and active fraction of the party—the wing of it, what was more, to which he had always appealed in the past. And he was suspected, if not despised, by plenty of people in less liberal sections of the party. And yet this campaign, which began as a disaster, or a "nightmare," as Walter Mondale recalls it, ended in one of the most dramatic finishes in the history of Presidential elections, losing the popular vote by only one quarter of one per cent and coming within a whisker of achieving an upset that would have made Truman's win in 1948 look like a foregone conclusion.

On Monday, September 9, Humphrey began his formal campaign with two appearances, one in Philadelphia and one in Denver. In Philadelphia, the police commissioner, Frank Rizzo, a zealous satrap of Democratic Mayor Tate, insisted with absurd loyalty that a hundred thousand people were there to hear Humphrey speak. There were, probably, anything between seven and ten thousand. There were chants and jeers and slogans, and sometimes they almost drowned out the feeble cheers of the city employees and their families who had been dragooned out as a claque.

In Denver, it was worse. Because of bad advance work, the candidate's motorcade coincided with suppertime and drove through depressingly empty streets. Hecklers with peace banners made up half the crowd of three thousand that met Humphrey outside the Union Convention Hall where he was due to speak. They greeted him with shouts of *"Sieg heil!"* and "Dump the Hump."

The luckless Hump was caught between a nether and an upper millstone. In Philadelphia, still pursuing the phantom of the "politics of joy," he made a cheery reference to troop withdrawals from Vietnam. Grimly, at an afternoon news conference, Secretary of State Rusk put him down. That night, Humphrey called Clark Clifford, the Defense Secretary. "That's right, isn't it—what I said?" he asked, and was told no, it wasn't quite right. The troops he had mentioned, a regiment of Marines, would be leaving Vietnam, but they had only been on temporary assignment there and their withdrawal would not affect force levels.

Poor Humphrey, apparently confused, repeated the statement next day in Houston, and this time the President slapped him down brutally. "No man can predict" the homecoming of the troops, the Commander in

Chief said to an audience of cheering superpatriots at an American Legion convention in New Orleans. And he dismissed the idea of a bombing halt—that same bombing halt that Humphrey's advisers had urged him to advocate—as "the suggestion made by some of our enemies abroad and some of our friends at home. . . ." George Christian still insists that nothing was further from the President's mind than to cuff his Vice-President into line. He says that the New Orleans speech had been written a week before Humphrey's statement, that the President went over the text on the plane to New Orleans with two speech-writers, and that at no time was Humphrey's statement mentioned. He grins ingenuously. "We goofed," he says. "Of course, those reporters were going to interpret it as a roundhouse swing at *our* candidate." But when you put this explanation to Humphrey's manager, Larry O'Brien—a man whose knowledge of Democratic politics at any given moment is usually something like total—he smiles hugely. "That isn't how I remember it," he says.

It was not only on Vietnam that Humphrey was trapped between demonstrators and Administration. He was still equivocating on law and order. In his acceptance speech, he had seemed to throw out the faintest hint of future reconciliation to the hurt and angry liberals by suggesting that Daley was not, perhaps, above all reproach. Then, even before his campaign began, in a telephone interview from his home in Waverley, he said, "It's time to quit pretending that Daley has done anything wrong."

Jogging on the beach with his trousers rolled up like a middle-aged paterfamilias, or having his picture taken howling out a barbershop version of the "Whiffenpoof Song" with Governor Hughes of New Jersey, Humphrey sometimes seemed to be going out of his way to live up to his reputation as a corny political glad-hander. Watching him at this stage of the campaign, as he bounced around the country with one hand always outstretched and his mouth usually open, it was hard not to think of Archie Rice, the plucky but pathetic Entertainer in John Osborne's play. "Somebody else was supposed to have played to three-thousand-odd a week at Brighton with one of those shows," Archie's wife says wistfully at one point. "But by the time Archie got started with it, it had all petered out. People didn't want it any more."

Yet eight weeks and one day after that gelid start in Philadelphia, Humphrey was to arrive home to vote in Minnesota with only one affliction: that he was tired from celebrating the night before. For, according to the pollsters, the election which had originally been scheduled as a massacre had become "too close to call."

Many explanations can be given for that recovery. Some, like the political scientist Richard Scammon, brush aside the campaign and argue that the Humphrey revival was produced merely by an inertial return to party loyalty. Others give the credit to Larry O'Brien and his two lieutenants in the Democratic National Committee, Ira Kapenstein and Joe Napolitan.

The labor unions must take some share of the credit. It was their intensive propaganda that brought the blue-collar workers back from their flirtation with Wallace in crucial states like Michigan and Pennsylvania. All these points can be argued, just as veterans of the Desert War argue over what it was that turned the tide at El Alamein, Auchinleck's organization of the defense of Cairo, Montgomery's disposition of his tank forces, or the naval blockade that strangled Rommel's supply lines.

But nobody who fought alongside Humphrey has any doubt about when his El Alamein was. It came on September 30 in Salt Lake City. That was when he went before the national-network television cameras for the first time since his nomination, and—for the first time in an even longer period—said what he thought about Vietnam. But before he reached that breakthrough, Humphrey had to pass through many deep and dreadful troubles. In the middle of September, he was in the trough.

The man who said there was no money was looking on the bright side. The Democrats actually had minus money: a debt of roughly one million dollars run up by United Democrats for Humphrey during the preconvention period and another four-hundred-thousand-dollar debt in the Democratic National Committee. What was particularly galling was that seven hundred thousand dollars of Democratic party funds were sitting in a bank in New York—which the Humphrey people could not get their hands on.

It appears that, in the autumn of 1965, when Lyndon Johnson still ruled the land in the golden glow of consensus (at least, so far as the business world was concerned), he began to take thought for the morrow and provide for the campaign of 1968. Richard Maguire, then treasurer of the Democratic National Committee, had raised a million and a half dollars for the 1964 campaign by selling tax-deductible advertisements in the official program for the Democratic Convention. A year later, Maguire repeated the trick in different form, and sold six hundred thousand dollars' worth of advertisements, at fifteen thousand dollars a page, in a book imaginatively called *Towards an Age of Greatness*. There were, however, a couple of problems with this happy device. One was that the corporations who had turned out willing to unbelt to a so-called Committee on Voter Education and Registration (a tenuous disguise for the Democratic National Committee) included a rather disturbing proportion of defense contractors. Many others, not actually defense contractors, were railway and airline corporations—people whose business is closely regulated by the government. The second problem was that the whole operation sounded to many lawyers as though it could be prosecuted under the Federal Corrupt Practices Act. The President himself is said to have been infected by panic. The money, six hundred dollars plus three years' interest, was placed in trust. And in trust it stayed throughout the autumn battles of 1968, anguished cries from Humphrey's treasurer, Bob Short, notwithstanding.

There were several reasons why money was so desperately tight. The usual Democratic Party contributors are often wealthy liberals. Not only had they been thoroughly fished by the McCarthy, Kennedy, and Rockefeller campaigns before Short's men could get to them, but also many of them, especially the wealthy Jewish business people of New York and Los Angeles, were unresponsive on principle. "They were far more policy-oriented this year," said one DNC fundraiser. "They wanted a piece of the action on positions." He did not seem to think it quite proper that the fat cats should turn ideological.

Not only did Humphrey's position—or rather his lack of a position —on Vietnam shut off liberal contributions. His fund-raisers found they couldn't get the other kind of money, which normally flows to a candidate in the hope of favors to come. Humphrey was so low in the polls that many rich men who had contributed to Lyndon Johnson's campaign in 1964 had decided that poor Hubert was never going to be in a position to do favors.

Inevitably, the problems became self-reinforcing. On September 15, he was 12 points behind Nixon in the Gallup poll (31 to 43, with Wallace 19). How could those figures be improved? The press could have helped, but the reporters kept writing about those small and chilly crowds. How could the crowds be improved? By money. By advertising—on television above all, but also by drumming home the candidate's name, face, record, personality, and even policies by radio, newspaper ads, billboards, lapel buttons, and bumper stickers. But advertising requires cash on the barrelhead: the networks implacably refuse credit.

And many of the other suppliers of democratic goods and services—the button-makers, for example—were still owed from before the convention. The regional offices were crying out for Humphrey-Muskie buttons and bumper stickers to show the flag against the rash of Wallace buttons and stickers (which the Wallace people were *selling*). But it was not until September 23 that O'Brien could find a hundred thousand dollars to buy a first order of designs that had been ready and waiting for weeks. And, at a grander level than buttons, there was the whole case of the agency and the media plan.

> Hail to B.B.D. & O.
> It told the nation how to go!
> It managed by advertisement
> To sell us a new President . . .
> Philip Morris, Lucky Strike,
> Alka-Seltzer, I like Ike.

When Marya Mannes wrote that sour little verse about the packaging of General Eisenhower by the advertising agency of Batten, Barton, Durstine & Osborn, there still seemed to be something vaguely shocking to most Americans about bringing in an advertising agency to sell a Presidential candidate like a hangover cure. But that was in 1952. By 1968, people had become used to the idea. Back in May, one of the first things the Humphrey people had done was retain an advertising agency— just as Nixon had engaged Fuller & Smith & Ross; Rockefeller had engaged the Jack Tinker agency; Kennedy had Papert, Koening, Lois; and even Gene McCarthy was very professionally sold by Carl Ally, whose talents are also devoted to Hertz Rent A Car, I.B.M., and a product called Sleep-Eze. Humphrey had hired the highly regarded agency Doyle, Dane, Bernbach, which, in view of his position and their most famous advertisement theme, could hardly have been more apt. Doyle, Dane, Bernbach invented for Avis Rent A Car the slogan "We're only Number Two. We have to try harder." Perhaps less suitable was the fact that D.D.B. also handle Winchester rifles; Humphrey, after all, is a gun-control advocate.

The Humphrey account was entrusted by Bill Bernbach to his youngest vice-president, Arie Kopelman, then not quite thirty. Kopelman had worked, in a previous career, for Procter & Gamble, one of whose products is called Joy. (Others: Bold, Cinch, Dreft, Zest, and—yes—a detergent called Mr. Clean.) His specialty was packaging, a branch of the business which involves relatively unsubtle, broad-brush creative work, directed by extremely refined statistical analysis, at which Kopel-

man was universally acknowledged to be brilliant. His major work at
D.D.B. had been on the Heinz soup account, and he does not shy away
from the layman's possible inhibitions about the idea of packaging
candidates like products. On the contrary, he embraces the concept with
a frankness bordering on self-parody. "When I wrote the media plan,"
he says, "we looked at it as if we were marketing a product for Heinz
or Procter & Gamble."

Kopelman and D.D.B. were extremely enthusiastic about the work.
By the time of the Chicago convention, he had fifty-seven people working on the account, including twenty space-salesmen standing by to grab
time for commercials and half-hour documentaries as soon as they got
the word. He had already begun trial runs with an elegant little computer
operation, which would work out refinements like "rotation patterns."
The computer would be able to tell you, for example, what the marginal
value of repeating a commercial on, say, civil rights would be in a given
city x days after first time of showing. And he had an elaborate timetable showing just what jobs ought to be done each day, right up to
November 5.

But in Chicago, Kopelman began to discover how different a campaign for the Presidency of the United States can be from a Procter &
Gamble marketing operation. Kopelman went to Chicago with a team of
fifteen copy-writers, film directors, visualizers, ready and waiting for the
word to go. According to his timetable, production of commercials ought
to start on August 30. In Chicago, he was introduced to Joe Napolitan.

The Humphrey campaign, rather than proceeding like a well-
planned marketing operation, was fighting for its life. And the chain of
command was not so unambiguous as those in the organization charts
recommended by the best management schools. Larry O'Brien, as we
have seen, had come in purely to run the campaign up to the convention. After that, he intended to retire to one of several very well-paid
jobs. He had actually signed contracts for one of them, and Humphrey
had planned to hand the management of the post-convention effort to
another ex-Kennedy hand, Kenneth O'Donnell. In the end, the desperate
Humphrey persuaded O'Brien to stay on. But before he managed to do
so, there was a period of power vacuum, in which half a dozen contenders
competed for authority.

There being no one else to do it, O'Brien, with his two helpers,
Kapenstein and Napolitan, prepared the campaign's own media plan.
This was done in the time left after nursing delegates, and all they had
to go on was a brief prepared in a large black notebook by Secretary

Orville Freeman, another aspiring campaign manager. The Freeman black book amounted to little more than a summary of what everyone—including the energetic Kopelman at D.D.B.—wanted to do. Knowing what he did of the financial crisis, Freeman should have been perfectly well aware that large sections of what he had written down were extravagant to the point of fantasy. O'Brien whittled it down, and on August 29, while the candidate was waiting to give his acceptance speech, O'Brien showed him a rough plan. Humphrey approved it.

But it was not until September 5 that Kopelman felt he had received the go-ahead he wanted. His creative people started work on three commercials which were shown to Napolitan in the form of storyboards. Then, on September 13, the blow fell. Bill Bernbach, in Mexico, got a cable telling him that the campaign was being taken away from his agency and given to Campaign Planning Associates, an outfit set up for the purpose by Napolitan with another New York advertising agency, Lennen & Newell. The exact reasons for the row are hard to unravel; and not all the details are relevant. But three or four fascinating issues were involved.

The first was money. The kind of operation D.D.B. was proposing involved an expenditure on the order of six or seven million dollars. This was modest by Nixon standards but simply out of the question for O'Brien and Napolitan. Nor was it any good suggesting, as D.D.B. did, sensibly enough from their point of view, that the Democrats accept their plan and decide later how many weeks of it they could afford. The Democrats had no idea when, or even whether, they could afford half-hours on national television. In the event, they did virtually no advertising until late September. There were no half hours, there were very few television spots, no radio and no newspaper advertisements—at a time when Nixon was saturating the air waves. That D.D.B. were quite normally demanding a ten-per-cent commission had its effect. Lennen & Newell were prepared to do it for a flat fee.

But when Allan Gardner, Lennen & Newell's man, moved in, he too was aghast at the shortage of cash. He went in to see Robert Short, the campaign treasurer, and mapped out some ideas for a "very conservative" campaign costing six and a half million. Short told him, "I *may* be able to give you two and a half million." Gardner and his assistant "nearly dropped our briefcases." Actually, at that Short was whistling in the dark. He had to get on the phone that week to raise the money to meet the payroll.

The second problem was a clash between two concepts of professionalism. The young men from D.D.B. considered themselves experts in what they call "communications." Joe Napolitan is a professional in the deployment of certain political techniques. Brought up in the same small city—Springfield, Massachusetts—as Larry O'Brien, he made his name by managing the campaign of an eccentric radio manufacturer named Milton Shapp, who spent two and a half million dollars of his own money running for Governor of Pennsylvania in 1966. Largely because of Napolitan's shrewd use of rather rough-and-ready polls, and a crafty documentary made for him by a free-lance director named Shelby Storck, Shapp won the primary. He was smashed in the general election by the Republican, Ray Shafer, and has not been heard of since. But Napolitan—and Storck, who made the "personal" film of Humphrey that went out on election eve—made their names. Napolitan is a gruff, abrupt fellow with no patience for what he considers irrelevant. The D.D.B. men were horrified when he watched one presentation and barked, "That's not an effective use of television, and I think it's terrible." "You just don't talk to Mr. *Bernbach* that way," complained one acolyte.

But the third issue was ideological, and it was the advertising men who felt that they stood on the side of principle. Several of the creative people at D.D.B. had worked for McCarthy as volunteers early in the year. This had caused considerable suspicion in the Democratic National Committee. And the suspicion was not allayed when several of the committeemen began grilling the Humphrey people on issues of principle. "Why didn't Humphrey come out against Daley?" the advertising people asked, causing the Democrats to suspect incipient sabotage. This went further when they produced a mock-up of a commercial on law and order. "We had some rather liberal ideas," one of them remembers ruefully. "Stressing the dimension of social justice. Well, Joe Napolitan actually said, 'I don't want to see any black faces in this stuff. I don't want to argue about it. No black faces!' "

There were other, more positive things that Joe Napolitan was doing in those first hectic weeks after Chicago. His job was to get the ordnance factories producing the ammunition for counterattack. Bringing in Shelby Storck to make a documentary was an act of faith, because no one knew where the money was coming from to show it. Napolitan—as will emerge later—also commissioned certain private polls designed to make Humphrey's image look less tattered than the national polls did. And there were plenty of things Larry O'Brien could do to drag the wagons of the campaign out of the mud.

But there was only one person who could lead the sortie, and escape from the ring of iron, which led from low polls by way of a hostile press through poor crowds, poor morale, a shortage of money and therefore advertising, back to low polls again. Hubert Humphrey had to do the leading himself. And the only way he could do that was by separating himself at last, clearly and unequivocally, from Lyndon Johnson. And the only issue that counted in the context was the one of which Johnson was most spectacularly resentful of challenges.

John Reilly's White Paper advocating a bombing halt in Vietnam, which had come so close to being made into a speech before the convention, was still there. As a matter of fact, one copy of it had crisscrossed the country for six weeks in Ted Van Dyk's briefcase. But the arguments were still there—on both sides. Zbigniew Brzezinski and his professors, John Reilly, and John Stewart in the Executive Office Building in Washington, were more in favor of a Vietnam peace than ever. Bill Connell and Jim Rowe were still against.

But the argument in September was by no means a replay of the argument that had gone on in August. For one thing, the political situation had changed radically. In August, it was possible to look at the delegate count and not be convinced that Humphrey had to dissociate himself from the President's policy to get the nomination. By mid-September, his situation was so desperate that most people thought it was the only thing he could do to save his campaign from annihilation. "We badly miscalculated," one of Humphrey's shrewdest staff men admitted afterward. "We hadn't really focused in and realized how very aggressive the press corps was going to be over every dotted *i* and crossed *t* and every answer the candidate might give in that freewheeling style of his." One might think it more surprising if the press corps had *not* watched for *i*'s and *t*'s when dealing with a matter of war and peace; that such clever men should get this wrong is yet another proof of how isolated people in Washington can be from the mood of the country. This was the attitude that lay behind Humphrey's startled remark to Fred Dutton in June.

But if, by the middle of September, the candidate hadn't quite "focused in," some of his staff had. They understood that what they had to do, as one of them said to us, was "formulate a policy, thrash it out with him, have him understand the issues, get a policy stated, and then hang on to it." And so one of those cumbrous, grinding processes by which American foreign policy slowly moves—by which the consensus is painfully shifted—got under way at last. In September, three powerful political figures threw their weight onto the side of the doves. One was

Senator Fred Harris, cochairman of the campaign. He had been a dove
of sorts all along. Now, swallowing perhaps some disappointment over
the Vice-Presidency, he was traveling with the candidate. Larry O'Brien
was the second. His private views on Vietnam, he now says, were "close
to Hubert Humphrey's." If so, they were divided and confused. But his
sense of practical politics made the actual needs clear to him in September. And the third was George Ball. In theory, as Ambassador to the
United Nations he had no part to play in the Humphrey campaign and
no business playing one. In fact, he was the decisive figure.

Before the middle of September, the whole elaborate speech
machine was creaking into action again. It seemed to have more working
parts than ever. In the Executive Office Building, the White Paper was
dusted off again: the same "Draft No. 10" we have met before. Barry
Zorthian, back from a spell as a U.S. spokesman in Saigon, worked on a
new draft in the State Department. Norman Cousins, editor of the
Saturday Review, wrote a draft of his own. Arthur Goldberg, Ball's
predecessor as Ambassador to the UN, worked on yet another with one
of his law partners in New York.

This time, the White House was not the problem. Whether even
Johnson had felt his "roundhouse swing" in New Orleans to have been
a bit over the odds, or whether he never became aware what was happening—the Humphrey doves had certainly learned a lesson in discretion
—there was no serious pressure from the White House to keep foreign-
policy speeches tightly controlled. Nothing was heard now of the famous
"third offensive." A brief upsurge of fighting in Vietnam a month before
had served as a justification for those in the press, like Joseph Alsop, who
made dire prophecies of what would happen if Humphrey proposed a
bombing halt. But it was not to Vietnam, but rather to Paris, that Humphrey and his advisers now had to look.

It was not that there was any startling development in the talks,
which still dragged stubbornly through the ritual of accusation and
counteraccusation. On September 11, Ambassador Averell Harriman, the
chief American negotiator, admitted frankly in a radio interview that no
progress had been made; none was to be made for a full month. But the
Paris negotiations had taken on the role, in the tortured debate within
the Humphrey camp, that the warnings of the "third offensive" had taken
in August. Humphrey now was worried about Harriman. If the Vice-
President was to make any meaningful statement at all on Vietnam, one
that would genuinely differentiate his position from that of the President,
then he must call for a bombing halt as an act of faith and gesture of good

will designed to unfreeze the negotiations. But, Humphrey worried: *suppose Harriman repudiated the speech next day?* It would then be worse than useless; it would be the *coup de grâce* for his campaign.

Therefore, it was vital to know in detail where Harriman stood. Humphrey's sense of responsibility, his obsession with loyalty to the President and the Administration, meant that there was not the slightest hope of his making the necessary speech unless he was sure that Harriman would back him up. Also, Harriman, if it could be shown that he was not hostile to the initiative, would be a face card for the doves in a showdown with Connell and Rowe. Neither of these two gentlemen could claim any credentials as a foreign-policy expert—or, indeed, any credentials as a hawk—to lay against those of the man who had warned Roosevelt against Stalin before Yalta.

Harriman and Humphrey had actually talked together when the former Governor was in Washington in August. But they did not discuss Humphrey's speech on that occasion, since he had not then decided to make one. There was another difficulty: the inner secrets of Vietnam policy were being kept very close indeed inside the Administration. The President had learned that lesson. When the breakthrough in the Paris talks did come on October 12, even the Secretary of Defense was not told for a week. Only two people in the State Department, apart from cable clerks, were told immediately: Dean Rusk himself and his assistant, Ben Read. Read, however, was an old Washington grapevine friend of Bill Welsh, on Humphrey's staff. (They had been Senate staff assistants together.) Gingerly, Welsh began discreet inquiries concerning the state of play.

At about the same time, in early September, an emissary from Paris saw Larry O'Brien and reassured him that Harriman would be sympathetic. That was still not enough, if only because O'Brien, not being a foreign-policy expert, was not the man to define the areas of freedom with the minuteness required. And so George Ball, still formally in the Administration, entered the play.

Ball is a big, burly fellow with a large nose, rather unruly gray hair, and surprisingly often a look of suppressed frivolity on his face, as though he had just thought of an improper joke. He is not, despite a chain of diplomatic appointments that go back to 1961, a diplomat by training or experience. Before he went to the State Department, he was a lawyer and a keen amateur politician: the livery he wore was that of Adlai Stevenson. Ball's particular usefulness, his "commodity," as it were, was that without for a moment sacrificing official respectability he had established a reputation for controlled heterodoxy when the situation called for it. Ball is a good man to have around when your are reassessing.

On September 17, Ball was due in Brussels for a NATO meeting. Taking advantage of this announced trip, Ball made an unannounced trip to Paris on the way, where he arrived on September 15 and had two long, private chats with his friend and colleague Governor Harriman. The master negotiator was more than reassuring. He explained to Ball that, since August 19, he had been moving closer and closer in negotiation (with the President's permission) toward the San Antonio formula of September 1967. That proposition, since heavily thicketed around with reservations, stood as the most unguarded offer of a bombing halt that the United States had made. Ball told Harriman about the contents of Humphrey's White Paper, and Harriman said that it sounded well on the safe side of what he and Cyrus Vance were saying to the Vietnamese in Paris.

By the time Ball returned to the United States, Humphrey's speech had been readied in yet another draft, and things were fast approaching a crisis. The breaking point was reached a few days later. On September 25, Humphrey flew to Los Angeles—or rather, he slid into the third city of the country like a thief in the night. He did not speak at a public rally or in the Civic Center, or in Griffith Park, where Robert Kennedy had denounced the "darker impulses of the American spirit." He did not speak on the campus of either of the city's two great universities, U.C.L.A. or U.S.C. His schedulers did not dare let him go near any such fixture.

His organization in southern California was a ghost army. Nominally, it was being run by Mrs. Carmen Warschaw, but Charmin' Carmen had taken herself off to Europe and did not plan to come back for weeks. An obscure second-rank figure in the local party, Kenneth Hahn, succeeded in persuading the Humphrey people to book their candidate into his alma mater, an extraordinarily obscure institution named Pepperdine College. Pepperdine, if it was known for anything at all, was known for being "anti-Negro," as Humphrey's advance man, Martin O'Donnell, warned his headquarters in anguish. Moving like a jolly zombie, still shaking hands and chattering compulsively, the candidate on that day in Los Angeles carried a stench of disaster with him. After Pepperdine, he spoke to a lily-white, largely Republican audience of old folks at a depressing place called Leisure World in Orange County. He then taped an appeal to go out over KHJ, one of the lowest-ranking TV stations in Los Angeles (no one knew why he chose it), and fled to Sacramento.

There, because of another muddle, no microphones were on hand at the airport.

Now the urgency of the situation was getting through to Humphrey. Although few people were listening, in Los Angeles, he mentioned a bombing halt and blurted out, "The President has not made me his slave, and I am not his humble servant. The President is not trying to force me. He is not screening my speeches." At last, it was true. This time no thunderbolt arrived from the White House.

On Thursday, Eugene McCarthy got back from the south of France, where he had been vacationing since the convention, looking fit and re-laxed, and told reporters in New York that he had no intention of sup-porting Humphrey. That was not a surprise, nor was it fatal in itself. What mattered was that none of his *followers* were supporting Humphrey. "The people who were most disenchanted with Humphrey," as one staff man recalled it, "were desperately needed. Not because of their votes—there weren't many of them—but because they are the people who work and write and get active in campaigns: graduate students, young profes-sors, lawyers, upper-middle-class housewives, the elite of a Negro com-munity. They are also the journalists and the people the journalists talk to." It is, of course, this edge which the Democrats have among the educated bourgeoisie that normally countervails the Republicans' advan-tage in financial muscle. And Humphrey didn't have it.

Also on Thursday, the President announced that George Ball was resigning as Ambassador to the United Nations to work for the Hum-phrey campaign. But there was not much time for his efforts to make an effect. Three days earlier, Nixon's man Bob Ellsworth had said with con-tempt, but perfect accuracy, that Humphrey was in "desperate straits." That had been confirmed on Tuesday by the Harris poll, which published a reckoning of the voters' first-choice preferences. Nixon was on top with 22 per cent, and Humphrey was in *fifth* place, behind Ted Kennedy, George Wallace, and Nelson Rockefeller. Only 8 per cent of Harris's sample, it seemed, wanted Humphrey as President. And on Thursday night, Humphrey got the worst news of all. In the Gallup poll, due to be published on the weekend, Humphrey would be seen to have slipped 3 points and Nixon to have gone up 4, putting Humphrey 15 points behind Nixon's 43 per cent. George Wallace, showing strong support in the blue-collar states, was at 21 per cent. And if the voters followed *those* preferences on election night, the Democratic candidate might run a poor third in the Electoral College.

So that night, Larry O'Brien decided on a gambler's throw. It had been only on Monday that he had managed to procure the hundred thousand dollars he needed for buttons and stickers. Now, he and the candidate made up their minds to spend another hundred thousand on a half-hour national television broadcast. The most convenient moment available was next Monday, September 30, when the candidate would be in Salt Lake City at the end of his Western swing. Next morning, Friday, George Ball got to work on his new job: he flew to Portland, Oregon, to meet Humphrey. Shortly after midnight, Ball and Fred Harris were closeted with their man in his suite. The serious work of persuasion had begun.

Humphrey was in a plastic mood, for that day in Oregon, McCarthy country, had been perhaps the worst yet. He had stood in silence, white in the face, as several hundred boys and girls from Reed College and Portland State University rose at a signal and walked out shouting, "End the War!" Humphrey gave the signal for work to start on the definitive version of the speech. The proof that he needed it was rammed home the next night in Seattle. A big, shaggy-haired fellow with a bullhorn stood up in the crowd and shouted that Humphrey ought to be tried in a United Nations court for "crimes against humanity." Humphrey lost his temper and shouted back. The man with the bullhorn bellowed, "We've come to arrest you, not to talk to you," and the demonstrators swarmed up onto the platform. "Knock it off!" the Vice-President of the United States was shouting. "Now you've had your equal time, now shut up!"—until at last the police had shoved the demonstrators out of the auditorium. "I shall not be driven from this platform by a handful who believe in nothing," Humphrey said. "Now we face the danger of tyranny by an organized minority."

The question now was what the speech on Monday would actually say. On Saturday afternoon, Larry O'Brien was sitting in his corner office on the sixth floor of the Watergate Building in Washington, gloomily discussing the state of the finances with some of his minions, when he first saw a draft of the speech. He did not like what he saw. He liked it so little that he dictated what an awed subordinate remembers as the hottest memo he has ever handled. It said, in effect, that the speech was a weak, vacillating abomination; that it was the kind of thing that an Assistant Secretary of State might say in a bad year but that it would not do for a candidate for the Presidency; and that it was not worth spending the campaign's last hundred thousand dollars on. This remarkable explosion was all the more devastating because O'Brien is a man who rarely raises his voice, who has trained himself to think long and hard before he growls. The steaming memo was placed in a machine called a telecopier. A telephone receiver was cradled in the machine, the number of the hotel in Seattle was dialed, and through the grace of certain processes patented by the Xerox Corporation, the candidate was made aware of his manager's feelings.

As soon as he received this incandescent message, Humphrey called O'Brien. He was not upset, but rather apologetic. "Your comments are valid," he said. He explained that he had only just had a chance to read the speech himself, and it sure wouldn't do in its present form. O'Brien had better get out to Seattle and talk about it.

O'Brien arrived on Sunday afternoon and went straight to Humphrey's suite. They talked quietly, and mainly alone, until it was time to catch the plane for Salt Lake City. Humphrey had canceled an intended salmon-fishing jaunt, and for the first time in ten days he had an opportunity to sit down and think his situation through. There was a speech in Salt Lake City on Sunday evening, and, when he got back to the hotel there, he was still surrounded by some of the local spear-carriers. Gradually they drifted away, and gradually his staff gathered in the suite, sensing that a crucial debate of policy and strategy was in the making.

The debate centered, in the end, on a single short paragraph in the forthcoming speech. The nub was: what would Humphrey say about a bombing halt, and what qualifications and reservations would he put around it? In the draft which lay in front of everyone, dictated that morning in Seattle by Van Dyk on the basis of the earlier drafts that had outraged O'Brien, there were three short but essential paragraphs. In the first, Humphrey said that he would be willing, as President, to take the risk of stopping the bombing in the hope of ending the war. In the third, he said he would start the bombing again if the Vietnamese did not respond in good faith. The sticker was the second paragraph, which made the willingness of Hanoi to abstain from military action in the Demilitarized Zone the test of whether Humphrey should stop the bombing.

The debate ranged far and wide. There were about a dozen people in the suite, sitting around with copies of the speech, yellow legal pads, and pencils. Most of the staff men kept quiet, except for technical suggestions. George Ball had had to go back to New York to be interviewed on "Face the Nation," so O'Brien and Harris led for the doves, arguing that to give the speech the political impact that was essential, it must be seen as a clear and unequivocal offer. And because they believed that the position must not look as though it had been weaseled, they wanted to cut out the second clause—the qualification over the DMZ. Rowe and Connell, the hawks, not only argued that he shouldn't do that; they argued, with scarcely diminished vehemence, that Humphrey shouldn't make the speech at all.

The argument centered on the rival two-man teams, with elaboration from others. Some argued that Humphrey must make the plain commitment, and others said it would produce a denunciation from Lyndon Johnson. Some warned of the counterattack that Nixon could mount. And, of course, Connell and Rowe relied on the argument that, if Humphrey said on September 30 that he would order a bombing halt as soon as he was inaugurated in January, then he would be wrecking the negotiations. Why should Hanoi concede anything—such as Saigon's participation in the talks—in exchange for a bombing halt, if it could get one for free in January? Ball was contacted on the telephone, and once again he contacted Harriman in Paris, this time via the State Department. Once again, Ball was able to put down the argument that Harriman might repudiate the speech. This time, the put-down was fairly definitive.

At one point, the candidate had had enough. "My God!" he cried. "Some of you are worrying about what Harriman's going to say, and some of you are worrying about what Johnson's going to say, and some of you are worrying about what Nixon's going to say. Let's worry about what I'm going to say, for a change!" And he took a pad of paper and wrote a draft himself in longhand, which became the basis of the speech that was finally agreed on.

At five-fifteen in the morning, the session broke up. O'Brien was back in the candidate's suite at seven-forty-five; he was tired, but he had what he wanted, and so had Harris. They had made concessions on the DMZ, but they had got the speech, and still in strong form. What was more, they felt that at last they had a candidate of some strength—a man who knew what he wanted to say and would say it.

Humphrey went off to give the traditional morning speech at the Mormon Tabernacle, and the pens crawled over the draft yet again. George Ball, back again, applied a few final strokes of polish. But at last the moment arrived when the NBC producer would no longer be denied. Just before they left the hotel, O'Brien asked Humphrey how long he thought it was. Humphrey had made a few telerecordings in his time, and he thought for a moment and said, "Twenty-six and a half minutes." O'Brien just had time to rush to a phone and call Ira Kapenstein in Washington. Just before he flew out, he had suggested that if there was to be any spare time in the half hour, they should use it for an appeal for funds. Kapenstein had taken the precaution of arranging a box number, and when he got the news from O'Brien that there should be half-a-minute's leeway, he got moving. There was just time to call the network and arrange for a card to be made with the box number on it. It would be fed into the network from Chicago with, voice-over, an appeal for funds.

"Tonight," Humphrey began, "I want to share with you my thoughts as a citizen and as a candidate for President of the United States. I want to tell you what I think about the great issues which face this nation. I want to talk to you about Vietnam. . . . I have paid for this television time this evening to tell you my story uninterrupted by noise, by protest, or by secondhand interpretation." And then he came to those three short paragraphs:

> As President, I would be willing to stop the bombing of North Viet-nam as an acceptable risk for peace, because I believe that it could lead to success in the negotiations and a shorter war. This would be the best protection for our troops.
> In weighing that risk—and before taking action—I would place key importance on evidence, direct or indirect, by deed or word, of Communist willingness to restore the Demilitarized Zone between North and South Vietnam.
> If the Government of North Vietnam were to show bad faith, I would reserve the right to resume the bombing.

A camel, they say, is a horse designed by a committee. And there is certainly a camelious awkwardness about those sentences, especially the middle paragraph, where much comparative anatomy had been done. From a literary point of view, the most noticeable feature of the whole passage, over which so many highly educated men labored so long, is the dying fall. It slides inexorably down from the high hope of the promise in the beginning—"I would be willing to stop the bombing"—to the caution at the end.

Nor was the speech a great breakthrough diplomatically. Governor Harriman's spokesman, checking with him before going on to brief the press in Paris, found the Governor unfazed by the speech. He duly recorded the bland comment for relay: Averell Harriman, as chief nego-tiator, found nothing in the speech which could upset the negotiations, whatever Nixon might say. Substancewise, as they are horribly apt to say in the Executive Office Building, the labor had brought forth not a horse, or even a camel, but a mouse.

Still, it was a frisky mouse. "The strange part," said one of the men who sat in on the Salt Lake City session, "is that, when all was said and done, there was very little in the way of actual policy difference from earlier drafts." (This was a man who had worked on the White Paper six weeks before.) "But that wasn't the point. The greater effect was the therapeutic one on the people involved, the fact that the candidate was willing to sit down at last and face these issues, that he had the ability to to take part in these discussions at a high intellectual level. And the speech itself was strong enough to get us some of the peace people—not Gene McCarthy, but some of the others." There is no doubt: from that long night onward, Hubert Humphrey himself felt like a different candidate. And so he began to look like one.

It was just as well that Ira Kapenstein managed to get the box-number card fixed with the network. Humphrey did get through with half a minute to spare. The appeal went out, and straight away the phones began to ring. Altogether, the broadcast brought in a hundred and fifty thousand dollars, in contributions averaging fourteen dollars. The enterprise made a profit. And subsequent telecasts brought in a million more. In August, O'Brien had said privately, "Hubert paid a high price for being a good boy." In September, it seemed that virtue was its own reward.

3

The Rednecks Are Coming

"He stands up for law and order,
  The policeman on the beat.
He will make it safe to once again
Walk safely on the street.
He'll uproot the seeds of treason,
He'll restore the courts of law,
So justice can prevail.

Won't you stand up with George Wallace!
Won't you stand up with George Wallace!
Won't you stand up with George Wallace!
So all men can be free!"

> —Wallace campaign song in 1968, sung to the tune of "The Battle Hymn of the Republic"

"My God! The galoots are loose!"

> —Charles Morgan, Jr., of Alabama, southern regional director of the American Civil Liberties Union

On Monday, September 30, the day that Hubert Humphrey made his speech in Salt Lake City, George Wallace flew to Chicago from Montgomery. Nobody was laughing at him now. The polls were giving him twenty-one per cent of the vote, and there was every reason to believe that his support was still rising. That week, the golden shower of letters falling on P.O. Box 1968, his campaign address in Montgomery, was richer than ever: between seventeen and twenty thousand letters a *day,* with—pinned to them in small checks, money orders, and dollar bills—almost half a million dollars in campaign contributions.

Douglas Kiker, himself a Southerner and a seasoned political reporter, wrote that at this point in the campaign

> It is as if somewhere, sometime a while back, George Wallace had
> been awakened by a white, blinding vision: they all hate black people,
> all of them. They're all afraid, all of them. Great God! That's it! They're
> all Southern! The whole United States is *Southern!*
>
> Anybody who travels with Wallace these days on his presidential
> campaign finds it hard to resist arriving at the same conclusion.

The day before, Wallace received a letter from Rensselaer, New
York. "Governor Wallace," it said, "is the only one, outside of God, who
can get us out of this mess and bring our Glorious Country back where it
was before the Roosevelt inauguration."

That day in Chicago, the Wallace cavalcade arrived in Lockheed
Electras instead of the DC-6 that had carried them thus far. The faces
of the Negro freight handlers as they took the Wallace signs out of the
baggage hold were a study in careful disdain. The atmosphere between
reporters and police as they waited for Wallace was tense. And the first
sight of the candidate on the steps of the plane was a shock. His eyes
were black-ringed—not with mascara, one's first thought—deep-set with
exhaustion and strain. He wore a shiny blue suit, its breast pocket
jammed with cigars, spectacles, and the handkerchief he occasionally
removed and carefully spat into. A red-stone fraternity ring glowed on
his left hand. "Governor, do we need all these people here?" asked a CBS
man, pure hatred in his voice, gesturing at the Secret Service men and
police. Wallace ignored him and cordially shook hands with the policemen, as usual. A fair-sized crowd along the fence cheered, and Wallace
thanked them with a sort of parody of a salute, at once cocky and ingratiating. Then he set off to meet the people of Chicago.

Wallace is not known for a delicate sense of irony, but he is a man
with a certain sense of black humor. More than almost anything in his
1968 adventure, he must have enjoyed the moment at which his enemies,
the "pointyheads" who had resolutely ignored or underestimated him all
the earlier part of the year, suddenly flopped over and did the opposite.
The August 2 issue of *Life* magazine, for example, consecrated to him
an excited feature called "The Wallace Clout" about what it called "The
Surge Nobody Foresaw." The *Life* editors, caught as usual between the
desire to be up to the minute and the early closing dates imposed by the
economics of advertising, were a month late. In the course of July the
danger from Wallace had already been so clearly recognized that two

serious efforts had been hastily mounted to stop him from using his strength and the eccentricities of the Constitution to hold the country to ransom.

The Electoral College system, like much else in the American Constitution, was designed for circumstances that no longer exist and was not designed for the circumstances that do exist. This is now hardly an original or even an unorthodox thought. The American Bar Association has recommended abolishing the college; and the Johnson Administration proposed to reform it drastically. It is worth pointing out here that there are two separate weaknesses in the system, both of which Wallace found himself in a position to exploit. The first is that while in general the Electoral College discourages third-party candidates, and indeed almost guarantees that they will be unsuccessful, it does not so discriminate against third-party candidates who start with a block of states in their pocket. The point has been neatly summarized by Professor Alexander Bickel in his book *The New Age of Political Reform:*

> In 1912, William H. Taft, the real third-party candidate in the extraordinary circumstances of that year, had 23.2% of the popular vote, and 8 electoral votes, and in 1924 Robert M. LaFollette had 16.6%, and 13 electoral votes. Only from a regional base can a third party penetrate the electoral college. Thus in 1948 Strom Thurmond had such a base, and Henry Wallace did not. Each got 2.4% of the popular vote, but Thurmond had 39 electoral votes (31 more than Taft in 1912, with his 23.2%) to Wallace's none.

One might quarrel with this analysis in one respect. It is possible to imagine a formidable third-party candidate without a regional base but running on an issue which united the votes of certain states—for example, a right-wing candidate attracting votes in the Far West as well as in the Deep South. But it was plain in 1968 that George Wallace, whether or not he succeeded in raiding electoral votes in the North or along the Border, would in any case start with a useful bloc of votes from the Deep South.

The second weakness of the system is the procedure it specifies for dealing with a deadlock. The eventuality of no candidate's winning an absolute majority in the Electoral College is covered by the Twelfth Amendment, ratified in 1803 as a result of the disputed election of 1800. When the electoral votes have been taken to Washington (as fast as post horses can gallop over muddy roads) and counted by the President of the Senate, then

if no person have such majority, then from the persons having the
highest numbers not exceeding three, on the list of those voted for as
President, the House of Representatives shall choose immediately, by
ballot, the President. But in choosing the President, the votes shall be
taken by States, the representation from each State having one vote . . .
And if the House of Representatives shall not choose a President, whenever the right of choice shall devolve upon them, before the fourth day of
March next following, then the Vice-President shall act as President . . .

Once it was allowed to get this far, plainly the system was a pre-
scription for chaos. Who was to decide how a state delegation would cast
its single vote? What if the delegation was evenly split? What would
happen if the country were left in doubt for almost three months who
would be the next President? Those were only the most obvious of a
dozen questions that crowded into the minds of lawyers, politicians, and
journalists as soon as they began to contemplate the possibility of the
election's "going into the House." They were new questions for almost
everyone, because that possibility arises only if two exceptional conditions are both satisfied in the same year: a third-party candidate in the
field with a firm grip on a bloc of states and the two major-party candidates running close enough for a third bloc of votes in the college to
prevent either of them from getting a majority. By the beginning of July,
that was exactly what seemed to be happening.

In July, Wallace's standing in the polls, which had held steady at
around thirteen per cent for several months, began to climb. In the first
part of the month, we asked a number of political analysts in Washington whether they thought there was any chance that the election might
go into the House, and we were astonished to find how many of them
thought it was truly possible. Gerald Ford, for one, predicted flatly that
it would happen, and he was calculating that Wallace would get no more
than 50 to 70 electoral votes, a lot less than many others were beginning
to fear privately that he might get. As early as June 19, Gallup published
the results of a survey of three thousand Democratic county chairmen,
which suggested strongly that Wallace would at least carry Alabama,
Mississippi, Louisiana, Georgia, and South Carolina: 47 electoral votes,
for a start. Careful inquiries we made at the time suggested that Wallace
might in the end get roughly twice that number. And before the conventions, the race between the two major candidates looked as if it was going
to be close. Three or four Senators, half a dozen Congressmen, two of
Humphrey's closest advisers, and a White House aide were among those
who told us at the time that there was a strong possibility that the election would be decided in the House. And if it was, they pointed out, that

meant that George Wallace would be in a position to bargain for his help as a kingmaker.

On July 7, the *Washington Post* published what it called "A Proposal for Outfoxing Wallace" by a young assistant professor of government at the University of Virginia, Gary Orfield:

> Having found a way to translate the raw racism of Alabama politics into a potent expression of the uncertainties, discontents and hates of millions of Americans, Wallace may find himself in a position to dictate the racial policies of the next Administration. GOP and Democratic leaders must act before November to eliminate this possibility. . . .
>
> The basic need is for an agreement from both parties against dealing with Wallace and providing a way to elect a President without his assistance in the case that neither party has a majority either in the electoral college or in the House. . . .
>
> Both parties should agree before the election that if the normal procedures fail, they will provide the necessary votes in the House to elect the candidate with the largest popular vote. This would guarantee the most democratic result. . . . The first step would be clear commitments from the leading party candidates and in each party platform promising that there would be no bargain with Wallace in any circumstances.

A few days later a similar plan got more powerful support. Two Congressmen, Charles Goodell (Republican of New York) and Morris K. Udall (Democrat of Arizona) started drumming up signatures to a bipartisan compact to stop Wallace. "This would be done," Goodell said, "through a previous agreement among candidates—seated and non-seated—for the House of Representatives that they would vote for the Presidential candidate who received a plurality of the popular vote." By July 23, the *Washington Post* was able to report that the idea of "erecting a bipartisan barrier" against a deal with Wallace "had the informal endorsement of Richard Nixon and Hubert Humphrey, the two front-running candidates of the major parties, of several members of the Senate, and of at least fifty members of the House."

Understandably, perhaps, Congressman Goodell smiled wryly when he read out to a roomful of colleagues and reporters George Wallace's reaction to this plan. "These national Republicans and Democrats," Wallace wired, "now publicly display their willingness to enter into a conspiracy to circumvent the Constitution." But was Wallace altogether wrong? To circumvent the working of the Constitution is exactly what was proposed. No doubt the plan was conceived out of the highest and most public-spirited motives. No doubt it would have been a terrible thing from the point of view of the *Washington Post* and the two candidates—even, perhaps, from the point of view of the majority of the voters —if Wallace had held the balance of power in the Electoral College. One can well agree—one can hardly deny—that this was a weakness in the Constitution. But the proper method of remedying such weaknesses, surely, would have been to amend it, not to circumvent it. These improvised stop-Wallace schemes were based on two premises: first, that Wallace was a uniquely wicked fellow and his racial doctrines so intolerable that he deserved to be singled out for a unique exclusion from the constitutional/political process; and, second, that the fundamental law of the Constitution is that the will of a majority, even of a plurality, must triumph—so that where, through an oversight, a conflict might appear between the letter of the Constitution and this fundamental law, the Constitution must give way. Neither proposition will stand much examination.

At the best times, it is not a very good idea to suggest changing the rules in the middle of the game. To try to change the rules in the middle of an election is to invite your opponents to have recourse to any nonconstitutional methods at hand with a good conscience, since this is exactly what he will think you have done. But in this instance it would have been particularly foolish and dangerous. For it would have played into Wallace's hands. One of the main sources of his strength was precisely the suspicion of a large number of Southerners and of a fair number of people outside the South that the institutions of the country —the Supreme Court, above all, but also the Presidency, and the Federal government as a whole—had fallen into the hands of an unscrupulous elite who could be counted on to rig the game against the ordinary folks, even at the expense of strict construction of the Constitution. It would be hard to imagine an issue that Wallace could have done more with.

What, in fact, was Wallace's strategy? Did he in fact plan to let the election get into the House and there exact his pound of flesh? The balance of evidence is that he did not. When he first announced his candidacy in February, he said, "I am in the race irrevocably. I will run to win." Three days later, the *New York Times,* citing no particular evidence, glossed this to mean that Wallace planned to force the election into the House and there exact a deal—"Wallace electors for a blackball on the Supreme Court." Was it as simple as that? It was not.

The seeds of Wallace's campaign plans were sown in 1964. Much attention has been paid to his role in the first half of that year, to his three primary campaigns, which showed that he could win a heavy vote in at least certain parts of the North. But what happened to him in the second half of the year has received very little attention. It is not at all well known that after his primary successes he had what one of his close friends described to us as "very attractive offers" to turn Republican. Another intimate of his told us that Wallace was actually within days of announcing his conversion in September 1964, when Strom Thurmond beat him to it. (Negotiations were conducted partly through the auspices of the wealthy South Carolina textile magnate Roger Milliken, who is the state Republican finance chairman and Thurmond's backer. Wallace may well have felt that in that setup Thurmond would always have the inside track. "Wallace thought that one was enough," one of his friends hinted to us.)

Wallace certainly got some financial help from Milliken and from other Republican sources in 1964. But the main lesson he learned from his brief flirtation with the party of Lincoln was that he could command a high political price. Rightly or wrongly, Wallace believes that he persuaded Goldwater's people to give him a veto over appointments of an Attorney General and of Supreme Court justices if Goldwater won. If a successful run in three Northern primaries could be parlayed into that kind of national power, then what might not be achieved by a full-blown Presidential campaign?

But 1968 was not necessarily the year Wallace was planning for. In point of fact, at the time he was preparing for 1968, Wallace and his advisers naturally assumed that Johnson would win the Democratic nomination. They were thinking of 1972. One should never forget Wallace's Southern background when trying to understand his thinking; and one of the most hallowed precepts in Alabama politics is that you run twice, once to be known, and the second time to be elected. Until the President withdrew, Wallace reckoned he was running in 1968 to be known in 1972, when he confidently expected to be running against Robert Kennedy. That was the real reason why the news of the President's withdrawal came as such a blow, until he and his friends realized that the riots after Dr. King's death transformed the situation in his favor again.

The truth was that Wallace's strategy was flexible. It evolved with his growing success. The one thing that can be said with some certainty is that he never intended to let the election get as far as the House before he started whatever bargaining he might be able to do. Between Election Day and the meeting of the new House of Representatives, between November 6 and January 22, there was a long interval in which the situation in the Electoral College would be known; the actual meeting of the electors on December 16 would be as meaningless as the formal counting of their votes at a joint session of Congress on January 6. It would be during that interval that Wallace would have to exact his price.

Wallace always insisted that he was running to win. He may even have believed at times that he could. "Just think," he said, looking out the window of the plane on the way back from one of his trips in California late in 1967, "one day I may be President of all this." When he did hint at compromise, he always insisted he was not talking about letting the crisis drag on until the House met. On June 17, he announced on the ABC-TV program "Issues and Answers" that he was working for "a coalition government," and two weeks later, on another television program, NBC's "Today," he claimed that he would win because one of the other candidates would "throw his votes to me *in the electoral college.*" Much later, at the height of his success, he hinted broadly that he would negotiate to get his price for breaking a deadlock, if there was one, after the election but before the Electoral College met on December 16. At the height of the boom, he really did seem to think he could win. This confidence spread to his retinue. "It's going to be mighty funny next January 20," said Sam Smith of the American Independent Party Band with a dreamy smile, "when we have a country music band a-pickin' in the East Room of the White House!"

The best guess is that Wallace was running to win if he could. But if not, then he was still running—to prove something to himself, to get as high a price as he could for conservatives and for the South, and to see how far he could go. "Can a former truck driver . . . be elected President of the United States?" "He'll keep trying," predicted a doughty Alabama opponent, Judge Roy Mayhall, with something like grudging admiration. "The day after the election, the other candidates, winners and losers, will go fishing, or do something else to relax. Not George. He'll be out on the street in Montgomery shaking hands, right back campaigning. He doesn't know anything else."

For the candidate, the campaign was an obsession. For the rank and file, it was a crusade. But for many of the inner circle of Wallace's buddies from Alabama, it was a cross between an adventure and a racket.

Any Presidential candidate tends to surround himself with men from his own state: he knows he can trust them not to look for a better deal from one of his rivals, because he can destroy them politically at home if they try. But Wallace's campaign was run by Alabamians even more exclusively than Johnson's was by Texans, or Goldwater's by Arizonans, or Humphrey's by his "Minnesota Mafia." With the unimportant exception of lawyer Tom Turnipseed from South Carolina, one of the four in charge of the ballot drive, *all* the people who ran the Wallace campaign were from Alabama. This annoyed the Northern enthusiasts, and later in the campaign that tension was an important source of dissension and probably hindered the effectiveness of the operation.

The four top men, known jealously as the "Palace Guard," were Seymore Trammel, national campaign chairman; Cecil Jackson, national campaign director; and the two national campaign coordinators, Ed Ewing and Bill Jones, both ex-press-secretaries of Wallace's. Trammell, as we have seen, had his hands on the finances and might also, since Wallace was supremely bored by administration, be said to have been *de facto* governor under Wallace. He wears glasses and has crinkly hair and carefully manicured hands, and an equally careful manner of bland evasiveness. Behind this mask, he struck everyone who met him as being a toughie. Robert Kennedy was particularly unfavorably impressed. "I suppose I can understand the Governor's position," he muttered to a newsman after meeting the two of them during the crisis at the University of Alabama, "but that Trammell is a son of a bitch. He wants someone killed."

Jackson is Wallace's legal adviser. Thin, dark, intense, and crippled, he was resented by other members of Wallace's entourage for his haughty manner. One of Wallace's best friends got so fed up with trying to get an appointment with Jackson that he called the Governor direct. "Say, Governor," he began, "can you kindly fix me up an appointment with your legal adviser?" "What's the trouble?" Wallace asked sympathetically. "Hell, no, it ain't that. I can get hold of *you* whenever I want to. It's just your goddamned legal adviser who's too high and mighty to see me these days."

Bill Jones was the intellectual of the group—a status he earned not by any particularly coherent insights into society, nor even by especially vehement right-wing views, but simply by virtue of having written the authorized Wallace biography, a work of uncritical hagiography. He is a lugubrious man, bald and bespectacled, and a worrier. He has a penchant for curious shiny coffee-colored suits, which he was proud of lending occasionally to Wallace. He hero-worshipped Wallace and used to make a point of being seen whispering in the candidate's ear on the platform. But in fact he really does have a good deal of influence with Wallace, and occasionally overrules him.

Bill Ewing, the one large man in the inner circle—Wallace is sensitive about being a bantam in a society that respects physical bulk—acted as a general factotum and was also in charge of the dozen or so regional coordinators.

The regional coordinators were, almost to a man, lawyers from Alabama, most of them drinking companions and political allies of Wallace's for many years. (Politics is the recreation of most gentlemen and the occupation of most lawyers in Alabama.) It would be entirely wrong to suggest that they are, as a group, sinister or unpleasant. On the contrary, to spend an evening with, they are friendly and amusing company . . . on any subject but one. One of us spent such an evening with one of them, a successful lawyer in Montgomery, a contemporary and close friend of Wallace's, and one of his earliest advisers. Like most Southerners, he is accustomed to concealing his feelings on certain matters from strangers, and it took several hours of drinking excellent bourbon and sparring warily even to approach sensitive ground. When it was reached, he talked intelligently and with an open, judicious mind. "We have tended to blame the breakdown of law and order on the courts," he said, for example. "That assumption may be false. I don't know." He went on to discuss the problems of racial integration in the South calmly and rationally. Then, quite suddenly, he wandered into the next room, bourbon in hand, to join his law partners. They were guffawing over a gross "joke" about roasting and eating the hindquarters of a "fine nigra." He told no jokes himself. But he listened with amusement to a detailed analysis of the merits of a blue film of Negro women.

He insisted, as a good host, on driving us home—but circuitously, to show us the Negro section of Montgomery, in which it dawned on us we had more contacts than he had. It was nine-thirty at night, and there was not a soul in the streets. "That's law and order in Alabama for you," he said proudly. "They know better than to be on the streets after dark." We drove on, out of the Negro section; but with a strange passion our host suggested another detour, this time to "a real, and I mean *real,* nigra area." It looked much the same as anywhere else, a parody of a *Saturday Evening Post* small town, with the autumn leaves swept into neat piles by the roadside, and each white wooden porch lit by a bulb over the front door. On the front lawns there were swings and tricycles, and the only sign of poverty was that the cars in the garages were five or six years old. Yet for Wallace's friend this was obviously tiger country. "Yessir!" he said with some bravado as we rattled on along unpaved, empty streets, "this is a real nigra section!" He maintained that he knew the people in these neat houses and that they liked him. "Let's pull up at any house," he kept proposing. "We'll knock on the door, and I'll say, 'It's lawyer C——,' and we can go inside, and they'll give us coffee. Any house." We declined this gracious offer of someone else's hospitality, and he seemed hurt. "The nigras down here would be glad to see us," he repeated, "not like them up North."

The nearest thing to a black ghetto in Monroe, Michigan, is the district on the wrong side of the tracks where the town's six hundred Negro families live in modest comfort. Monroe is a small industrial town on the shores of Lake Erie—bang in the middle of the Midwestern industrial heartland. Almost everyone in town works either for the Ford Motor Company, which has a components plant there, or for the local paper mill. Assembly workers at Ford get three dollars and forty-three cents an hour, exactly a dollar an hour more than ten years ago, and the average family income in Monroe, at around seventy-seven hundred dollars a year, is close to the national average. It is, in short, on the surface at least, a modestly comfortable, egalitarian, cozy sort of place.

Yet in the last week in September a poll found that twenty-seven per cent of the voters there said they would vote for George Wallace. "I'm not for him myself," a young Ford worker told us. "You can't ship twenty million blacks out. You just can't kill them all. But up at Ford's, oh, I'd guess a third or more [of the workers] are for Wallace." This conjures up a rather graphic idea of the sort of policies Wallace's admirers understood him to be proposing.

The Wallace movement in Monroe was self-starting. Some Wallace organizers came down from the Michigan state headquarters in Battle Creek and got nowhere. Then, in August, a young Monroe man called Ray Smith went to the Wallace state convention and came back fired with enthusiasm to convert Monroe.

Smith is in his late twenties, a pleasant, slightly introverted young man who is popular enough with his workmates at Ford, where he is a die-maker, to have been elected to a union office. He says he is not a racist, and since to be elected he must have gotten the votes of a large number of Negroes who had been working alongside him for five years or so, there is no reason to disbelieve him. He was for Kennedy in 1960 and was particularly stirred by Kennedy's inaugural—"Ask not what your country can do for you . . ." But he says he was disillusioned when he discovered that Kennedy was a "true liberal." Smith calls himself a conservative, and he is particularly upset by what he sees as the trend to remove control of local affairs to Washington. He voted for Goldwater in 1964 and preached Goldwater to his mates, but he was not active in the campaign.

After the state convention, Ray Smith and his friends held a meeting in the community room at the bank and wrote to Montgomery for campaign materials. They had to buy them, and Smith advanced the money out of his own pocket. Next he rented a storefront headquarters on East Front Street. He suspects the rent was cheap because the man who owned it was sympathetic. He and his wife spent three days cleaning it up, and then two of his buddies from Ford came over and helped to fix up the big red-white-and-blue sign: WALLACE FOR PRESIDENT.

It is hard to be sure where the support for Wallace in Monroe came from. Some of it, perhaps, came from transplanted Southerners, of whom there are a good many in industrial Michigan. But if so, it would be hard to prove. People born in the South were a minority among the Wallace supporters we talked to, and those who admitted to being from the South seemed ashamed of it and kept emphasizing how much they felt themselves to be Michiganders now. There is no obvious tradition of conservatism in Monroe, and there had been no racial trouble to speak of there for as long as anyone could remember. But after the Detroit rioting in 1967 (Detroit is only forty miles away), eighty Monroe ex-servicemen formed a "riot squad" to be ready. "We don't lock doors in Monroe," we were told, "but when you see all this stuff on television it looks so real." Not all the members of the riot squad turned out to be for Wallace. Still, it is hard to isolate any reason for the Wallace boom in Monroe other than racial anxiety, focused and distorted by the mass media.

Wallace may have learned to talk in a code which could be understood in the North ("I don't talk about race or segregation any more," he admitted candidly during a plane ride from Montgomery to Knoxville one day in September. "We're talking about law and order, and local control of schools, not those other things."), but his Alabama operatives still found it difficult to talk the same language as the Northern enthusiasts like Ray Smith. This conflict between the Northern and Southern wings of the Wallace staff cropped up almost everywhere outside the South. It can be seen very clearly in the case of Chicago, where Wallace began his crucial offensive aimed at the rich deposits of electoral votes in the industrial Middle West.

The man Wallace first sent to Chicago from Alabama was a lawyer and Alabama State Senator named William G. McCarley. Like most

Wallace missionaries, he arrived in town flat broke and had to borrow three hundred fifty dollars from a lady lawyer named Mrs. Joan Nelson to open a headquarters. It was Mrs. Nelson who had descended on Montgomery earlier and by the sheer force of personality—she is a big, handsome thirty-three-year-old redhead—persuaded Wallace that it was worth making a big effort in Illinois. She ran things in Chicago with the help of a tough ex-cop called Art Kelly, who had put in eight years on the homicide squad and now ran a saloon on the north side. McCarley kept getting under their feet. (At one point, he tried to turn the operation over to another lady, who had given him a sizable campaign contribution and wanted a career in politics for her son.)

There was also a real difference of political strategy between them. McCarley's one idea was to harp on the racial string. (Many of Wallace's Alabama people seemed to have the same highly oversimplified idea of Northern racial attitudes, no doubt largely derived from the media—where else could they get it? In upstate New York, for example, one day in early October, one of us spent the morning with some young Wallace workers who were spending their first day outside the South. A police cruiser drove by with a wire grid attachment at the rear window. "Look at that!" said one of the Alabamians excitedly. "They must have had some riots here!" In fact there had been no riots: the grid was a routine precaution.) The Northerners, on the contrary, were anxious to play down the racial element. They preferred to see the Wallace movement as a Populist rebellion of the people against their masters. "This thing is coming out of the sidewalks in the three-dollar wards!" said Mrs. Nelson.

Both ideas may well have been based on a misapprehension encouraged by the media. On August 2, *Life* magazine reported that *"rather surprisingly,* Wallace raids into the alien north have found a welcome among many people of substantial place and means [our italics]." We have already pointed out that the political scientist Michael Rogin had found that in Wisconsin in 1964 "the center of racist strength was not in working-class areas but in the wealthy upper-middle-class suburbs of Milwaukee." And the University of Michigan's Institute for Social Research report on racial attitudes in fifteen cities also found that "suburban white people . . . differ very little from whites within the city limits in their attitudes on most aspects of racial integration." Such evidence notwithstanding, *Life* repeated the familiar oversimplification on September 20 under a symbolic picture of the Gary steel mills: "Wallace's folks for the most part are hard-working members of the lower middle class—steelworkers, waitresses, mechanics, clerks"—in other words, what anyone not under the thrall of the Luce illusion that there is no working class in America would call the working class.

The point is not that Wallace support came more from the middle class than from the working class. It did not. "The greatest number of Wallace supporters come from the working class and particularly from the upper-income segment of the blue-collar class," according to a careful study in Michigan by the pollster Fred Currier. But many factors other than social and economic class are likely to affect something so emotional and volatile as racial attitudes. (Rogin has shown that physical proximity to the ghetto is an important factor here, and there are many, many others.) The point we would make is that by repeating the rather comforting doctrine that racial hostility was to be found among the working class and particularly among that part of it not so politely called "the ethnics," rather than among "people of substantial place and means," the media were spreading an unproven simplification and one that was in danger of being self-verifying.

Rightly or wrongly, Mrs. Nelson and the native Wallaceites in Chicago wanted the candidate to appeal to generalized Populist discontent. They wanted a major registration drive among poor white people in the city, whether or not there was any evidence of racial tension. They even wanted Wallace to speak to Negro audiences. McCarley and the people at headquarters brushed all this aside. They wanted Wallace to speak to the converted. They therefore scheduled only one stop for the candidate on his visit to Chicago, apart from a motorcade through the Loop: in Cicero, a white community threatened by the expansion of the overflowing west-side ghetto, where there had been serious racial trouble before.

There was another cause of dissension between the Alabamians and the Northerners: money. Most of the Northerners were putting money into the campaign because, for one reason or another, they believed in it. Many of the Alabamians took it for granted that there was money to be made out of it. And there was—a great deal of money.

The most shamelessly corrupt aspect of the campaign arose out of the system for selling campaign materials. The theory was that anyone who wanted to set up a Wallace for President storefront ordered a two-hundred-fifty-dollar kit—hats, buttons, ties, bumper stickers, and so on —from Central Supplies at headquarters in Montgomery. These supplies were then supposed to be sold for three hundred and fifty dollars retail, leaving a hundred toward campaign running costs. However, many, perhaps most, of the enthusiasts who wanted to help simply didn't have two hundred and fifty dollars to spend. Smaller quantities were needed. Several of the regional coordinators saw their chance. They set themselves up as middlemen, breaking bulk and taking a handsome rake-off. The profits were enormous. Hats, six dollars a dozen from Montgomery, supposedly to be sold for a total of nine dollars, were reaching the storefronts priced at a dollar each. The same with buttons: four cents out of Montgomery, eight cents from the middleman, ten cents for the Wallace supporter. Bumper stickers, which should have been priced at ten cents, were selling for fifty cents in Cicero on September 30. And at about this time, when the campaign was really taking off, supplies were sometimes taking two weeks to arrive from Montgomery. Several big Wallace groups simply ordered their own supplies direct from the manufacturers. Other coordinators took kickbacks from the manufacturers: five per cent on hats, in one instance. Most of the local coordinators were honest; one was sent into a large Northern state with a hundred dollars and the simple order, "We want to take the state." He failed, of course, and he stayed as broke as he began. But others didn't. One man's secretary told us that her boss made more than ten thousand dollars out of the campaign.

It was no more than a little cream skimmed off the top of money which began to bubble into Wallace's churns after—though not necessarily because of—the Democratic Convention.

"We're not overrun with money, that's true," said Wallace as he set out on a fund-raising trip on June 11. He was not poor-mouthing. His wife's illness had prevented him from campaigning, and her death, establishing Albert Brewer in the Governor's mansion, threatened the flow of such funds as the government of Alabama might have yielded. Wallace aides, who had been talking expansively about a fifteen-million-dollar campaign, lowered their sights and began to speak of ten million.

The ballot drive was a leapfrog operation. "We raised money for California in the first place," Dick Smith, the hound-faced little weekly-newspaper editor who was campaign finance chairman, told us. "Then we raised enough in California for the next place, and so on." The ballot drive as a whole cost not less than two and a half million dollars— "Round a dollar a name," Cecil Jackson said after it was mostly over, and a check with other sources suggests that he was not far off.

How much did the campaign itself cost? Seven million dollars, not counting the ballot drive, Dick Smith told us on two occasions. There is reason to believe that this estimate is a bit low. Smith told a dinner audience in August that it was costing "two hundred dollars a minute,

eight hours a day, six days a week, just to keep this campaign rolling."
That works out to ten and a half million dollars—and the rate of expenditure was certainly higher in October than in August. At least one
and a half million was spent on television advertising, and perhaps substantially more.

Where did the money come from? Not from the legendary fatcats
of liberal conspiracy theory. H. L. Hunt, for example, according to Bill
Jones, contributed "around five hundred dollars, two cases of liquor,
and a whole stack of pamphlets." A relative of Hunt's, no friend of his
political beliefs, confirms that this is quite likely. There were a few rich
men who contributed to the Wallace campaign on a generous scale, but
far less than was often supposed. Among the names we heard mentioned
again and again as major contributors were those of Leander Perez, boss
of Plaquemines Parish, Louisiana; Colonel Sanders, the "finger-lickin'
good" fried-chicken king; Edward Ball, the Florida lawyer whose sister
married a DuPont, and who is one of the arch-conservatives behind the
Southern States Industrial Council; and the potato and oil magnate Paul
Pewitt. Perhaps the most surprising name is that of John Wayne, who
gave such an impassioned address to the Republican Convention. According to one of the women in the department that handled contributions
in Montgomery, "The Duke" sent three weekly checks for ten thousand
dollars each—the last one inscribed on the back, "Sock it to 'em, George!"

Smaller sums were collected from the moderately rich at luncheons
and dinners. In Dallas on September 16, for example, a thousand-dollar-
a-plate lunch brought in at least fifty thousand dollars and perhaps
twice that; a twenty-five-dollar-a-plate supper the same day brought in
at least thirty thousand dollars more; and the careful Robert Novak and
Rowland Evans reported that subscription forms passed out at the rally
the same night were expected to bring in another hundred thousand
dollars.

The sale of campaign materials, in spite of all the racketeering that
cut into the profits, was another major source of income. The head of
Central Supplies told us that between January and August his operation
sold three million bumper stickers, four million buttons, and about a
hundred fifty thousand straw hats. "We managed to make a small
profit," he conceded. Actually, there is reason to believe that the profit
margin, on a turnover of around seventy-five hundred dollars a day, was
between a hundred and two hundred per cent, which comes to about two
and a half million dollars.

Last but by no means least of the teats at which the Wallace campaign sucked the milk of unkindness from the angry, the alienated, and the curious in 1968 was the sudsbucket, a device the candidate learned from his first master, Big Jim Folsom.

If the Wallace campaign was a strange, wholly Southern blend of crusade and racket, the Wallace meeting was in the direct line of descent from the revival and the camp meeting. The Lord was praised—but the ammunition was expected to be passed. It was not a question, as it had been for Humphrey at Salt Lake, of tacking on a cautious plea for funds as an afterthought. Fundraising was built into the very structure of a Wallace rally. The warm-up speaker was almost always Dick Smith, the finance chairman. "Welcome to the fastest-growing political movement in the history of our nation," he would begin. Then he would drop some oblique hints about the cost of bringing the word to the people, like any professional evangelist on the Southern back-country sin-and-soda circuit. Occasionally, he would essay an ideological thought about freedom or anarchy. It would usually fall flat. But invariably he would promise that "the Wallace girls will come among you." The sudsbuckets were made of yellow plastic. The girls made no great effort to comb the audience. They merely wandered around looking fetching, in white blouses and black skirts, red-white-and-blue Wallace boaters perched on their heads, and Wallace sashes taut across their bosoms. Roughly, one person in every three put something in the little yellow buckets, and the cash went into a big trunk known affectionately as "the woman"—because, as Dick Smith explained, "we never let our hands off her, not even at night."

Sex and salvation have always been intimately mingled in Southern old-time religion, which would not have lasted so well if it had not been grounded in the unchanging facts of human nature. The last of the planter-aristocrats to be Governor of Mississippi at the beginning of this century, Leroy Percy, had a scathing phrase for the demagogues who had ousted his class from its political birthright: "the kind of people," he called them, "who attend revival meetings and fornicate in the bushes afterward." The Wallace girls were infinitely too respectable, too daintily nurtured and ladylike, even to be imagined in so gross a context. But there was an unmistakable perfume of erotic adventure blended with the revivalist excitement of the Wallace caravan just the same. The girls—they were mostly related in one way or another to various members of Wallace's circle—were almost all both pretty and friendly and smartly turned out in the lamentably unfashionable style of Southern sorority queens. Their bleached-blond hair was swept into fantastic, obsolete coiffures—ringlets and beehives—and lacquered into place with heroic regularity, considering the irregular hours they kept. One of the great mysteries of the campaign was how such elaborate structures could have been restored to the consistency of crispy noodles between the hour when the hotel night club closed and the baggage call at, say, six o'clock in the morning.

The great *frisson* of the campaign was provided by Miss Ja-Neen Welch, who declared her love for the candidate at a press conference. Miss Welch left her job as the lady who urged a presumably panting TV audience of consumers to join "the Dodge rebellion" because of a vision —so she said—that told her George Wallace was going to be President. She was so moved that she got herself, the day of Wallace's first visit to Chicago, in the reception committee at the foot of the airplane steps. "Look what we've got here," her hero muttered to a friend as he spied her. They met, that evening: imagine the candidate's surprise when he got up to his room and found Miss Welch there! In some alarm, he summoned a friend, and Miss Welch was persuaded to withdraw. "She's nuts," the candidate was heard to observe unkindly. But Miss Welch didn't mind. She gave up her job and joined the caravan, and loyally tramped around gymnasia and union halls, offering to kiss any fellow who would give up twenty dollars out of his paycheck to help her hero.

It is not possible to say for certain what was the total income from all these sources—from the lunches and the dinners, the buttons and the bumper stickers, the checks from the fatcats and the money orders in the mail, and from the sale of poor Ja-Neen's kisses. But, computing all that we have been able to discover, and making all due allowance for some leakage and seepage over and above an expenditure of somewhere between twelve and thirteen million dollars, it seems likely that there is still something left over for 1972.

But that is to jump ahead. On October 1, when he left Chicago and flew to Grand Rapids, Michigan, Wallace looked as dangerous as Lee on his march to Gettysburg. He claimed the whole South and the Border as his, with 170 votes in the Electoral College. Even Nixon's staff was reported to concede him between 90 and 100 votes. Sober and unsympathetic observers, including the *New York Times,* thought he was running ahead of Humphrey. And now he was storming the citadel where the decisive votes in an American Presidential election are stored—Illinois, Michigan, Ohio, Pennsylvania. As he gleefully pointed out at every stop, in a three-way race you only need one more than a third of the votes to win a plurality. And, right in the very states he was now entering, the very block of voters who had kept the Democrats in power in seven out of the last nine Presidential elections seemed to be veering toward him. The white inhabitants of the great industrial cities now seemed so alienated that they might abandon their traditional allegiance. He had the money. In "law'n'order," after the Democratic convention, he had the issue. He had the impetus.

It was, of course—everyone hastened to say—unthinkable that he could win. The polls gave him no more than twenty-one per cent as yet. Everything turned on whether that was an under- or an overestimate. Was the Wallace vote, as so shrewd a judge as Larry O'Brien suggested to one of us earlier, "the vote a guy doesn't tell the pollsters about—the mean vote a guy keeps in his gut, until he goes in that booth, and sees red, and pulls that lever"? Or was the Wallace talk a new way of griping, a protest against everything that seemed wrong with the country, against the war and the riots and all the rest of the mess—but a protest that Americans had too much sense to take to the length of throwing away a vote? At the beginning of October, nobody could answer that question for certain.

ACT XII

Some of the People, Part of the Time

1

The Old Quarterback

"Seldom, if ever, has a candidate for office spoken out as fully on as wide a range of issues as Richard M. Nixon has during the Presidential campaign of 1968."

—Nixon-Agnew Campaign Committee

"Mr. Nixon has published a collection of positions he has taken on 167 issues. It seems a pity he could not have made it a round 170 by adding Vietnam, the cities, and civil rights."

—The *New York Post*

"Richard Nixon avoided bringing the war into his campaign."

—Max Ascoli, giving his reasons for endorsing Nixon

F ew items of American political folklore have been better established than the notion that a Presidential campaign is a warm, spontaneous adventure. Accompanied by a band of reporters, who become his friends, the candidate barnstorms through the infinite variety of the heartland, taking his case to the people. He faces their questions and senses their mood. It is expected that on occasions serious political intercourse will take place. In the age of the jetliner and the computerized opinion poll, this picture no longer corresponds precisely with reality, if it ever did. But something of the tradition remains, and most of the campaigns of 1968, in their different ways and to different degrees—even George Wallace's—tried to do something to keep it alive.

The campaign of the winner, Richard Nixon, was not like that. The relationship between Nixon and the reporters who were supposed to be conveying his propositions to the electorate was of such frigidity as to make any act of communication difficult. After a few weeks of campaigning, the newsmen scarcely bothered to maintain even the mask of professional camaraderie which is usually the last barrier between their feelings and their subject—something which emerged rather clearly, for instance, when the caravan reached Opa Locka airport, Miami, around one-thirty a.m. on October 13.

The reporters were in a particularly bleak mood. For some time, they had been pressing Nixon's staff for an opportunity to put questions to the candidate in some context more serious than a scrambled press conference on an airport apron. So far, they had been unsuccessful, and their tempers were not improved by the fact that Nixon did not appear pressed for time: a few hours earlier on television in Dallas, he had rambled through a good part of the program talking football. The Nixon staff had apparently noticed the tension, and chose the worst possible way to relieve it. As people began to move toward their buses and cars, Nixon's aide Charlie McWhorter handed him a suspiciously mint football. Nixon promptly hefted it in the best Bart Starr fashion, and called to the dozens of reporters around him, "Who's going to run for my pass?" These somewhat stylized occasions are normally seized upon as a means of breaking down the natural tension between candidate and reporters: witness Robert Kennedy's numerous touch-football games, Hubert Humphrey racing the press along the beach, and even the reserved Gene McCarthy swinging a friendly baseball bat.

This time, no one moved. After a short, chilly silence, Nixon said, a couple of times, "I *can* throw it, you know." People shuffled a little and turned away to the transport. Nixon, looking rather stricken, slumped into his car.

Nixon's campaign has been generally regarded as "efficient." It was efficient in the sense that it was superbly organized on the mechanical and logistical level. The appearances and disappearances of the candidate were managed with precision: airplanes took off and landed on time; halls were nearly always filled; and the schedule usually worked. Yet Nixon only barely won his election, just as it was quickly forgotten how narrowly he was beaten by Kennedy in 1960. A situation in late October where Gallup poll figures pointed toward a five-million-vote plurality was turned by election day into one of the smallest popular-vote margins on record. That is not prima-facie evidence of efficiency, however smoothly oiled the wheels seemed to him.

If Nixon's approach represents the best way of fighting a modern

Presidential campaign, there are some dismaying consequences for the future of politics. Certainly it means that the traditional picture of the Presidential hustings with which we opened this chapter has finally become irrelevant. The elements in that picture of more than sentimental value—elements of spontaneity and development, the hope that some new thoughts will be born in the give-and-take of debate—were the qualities farthest from the Nixon campaign; and it is doubtful whether its chief architect, the candidate himself, or his right-hand man John Mitchell would object to such a description. Their intention from the start had been a meticulously planned assault upon Democratic Washington, and only at the very end, when the sheer closeness of the thing began to oppress their nerves, is there any evidence that they departed at all from their intentions.

It was always vividly apparent that the campaign existed on two levels. There was the relaxed, almost soporific national campaign intended to preserve the unassailable lead that Nixon was thought to hold in the nation at large. (The temptation—or opportunity—to make new converts was steadily resisted.) This, naturally, was the level which occupied, and bored, most of the newsmen who traveled regularly with Nixon. Beneath this bland superstructure, altogether grittier localized campaigning went on, aimed at ensuring that certain key states fell into line to fulfill the Nixon strategy in the Electoral College. Sometimes, the hard-nosed propositions employed in the second level of the campaign clashed with the abstract principles enunciated at the higher level, but at the time there were no objections.

The physical circumstances of the campaign were leisured and comfortable. Occasionally, before his nomination, Nixon's campaign had looked as rickety as any other: he was still not the leader of the party, so that he had to live on less respect, and even his formidable logistical operation was not quite perfectly run. Three weeks before Miami Beach, for example, there was a dismal journey into Romney's Michigan, which started badly with Nixon's usual jet being unavailable. An elderly chartered turboprop lugged the candidate and his party to their destination well over an hour late. At an airport press conference, the microphones didn't work properly—which may have been just as well, since Nixon was producing rather vulnerable simplifications like "This is a two-party system, and those who want a change, or those who want things as they are, should vote for one of the nominees of the two major parties." At the fund-raising dinner in the evening, Nixon was introduced by Governor Romney and had to smile creakily through a set of "jokes" (Nixon had brought his daughter Julie along with her fiancé, David Eisenhower, against Romney in New Hampshire, "and you can't beat a Nixon-Ike combination"), coupled with helpful remarks about how courageously Nixon had overcome his "mistakes" in California, and the disadvantages of his five-o'clock shadow.

After Miami, the three tri-jet Boeing 727s (Nixon's own *Tricia,* named for one daughter, and two supplementary press planes, *Julie* and *David*) were on duty every campaigning day. The acoustics worked flawlessly, as far as anyone could see, and as he swept into each state, former mortal enemies within the party cast respectful palms before the anointed leader. Nelson Rockefeller himself, as late as October 18, when signs were turning in altogether other directions, committed a little of his political capital to a flat prediction that Dick Nixon was going to take New York.

The most obviously leisured aspect of Nixon's campaign was the amount of time spent in the sun at Key Biscayne: two days at the end of September, another three-day break in mid-October when only three weeks' campaigning remained. (True, Key Biscayne was handy for Florida, itself a swing state, and for the crucial border states. But mostly Nixon simply vanished from public view there.) Even on the road, the tempo was less than demanding. Correspondents hardened to the perpetual motion of a Kennedy campaign found it difficult to believe that baggage call was usually no earlier than ten thirty a.m. and that after only one or two stops the day would be over by eight thirty p.m. It was a pace to make even Eugene McCarthy look frenetic.

Partly, of course, this was simple reaction from Nixon's famous over-enthusiasm of 1960, when his rash promise to campaign in fifty states resulted in something like physical self-immolation—and the haggard look which was thought to have contributed to his poor appearance on television against the eupeptic Kennedy. It was, however, more scientific than a simple urge to protect the candidate from strain: Nixon and Mitchell had decided that a good deal of what goes on in the usual political campaign was wasted effort. For instance, they had worked out that the big night-time rally, although useful occasionally, should not have too much nervous energy expended on it, because it was usually too late to get onto television news programs.

Television, rather than actual contact, was plainly the way to reach most of the voters: the personal event, therefore, existed chiefly as something for television to report. So the ideal day contained, relatively early, a suitable event. It did not matter if this was something largely irrelevant in itself, such as an afternoon rally packed with school children too young to vote. Sometimes the school-children device—the boys and girls, having been given a holiday in order to attend, were usually very enthusiastic—became a little overloaded, and the hungry cameras demanded fresh sustenance. This was not always easily managed with Nixon, on whom, to his credit, hokum sits ill.

Some rather desperate contrivances came up from time to time, like the hydrofoil ride in Seattle on October 25. Visiting the harbor, Nixon was installed in the prow of the hydrofoil, where he assumed a curious attitude apparently modeled upon that of stout Cortes. The boat then rushed purposefully around the harbor while jets of water were sent up. Nixon apparently got carried away: three-quarters of an hour later, a glance down any of the numerous vistas of the Seattle dockside was apt to reveal in the middle distance the hydrofoil buzzing past, with the tiny figure of the Presidential candidate gesticulating in the bow. The effect, in the end, of the numerous passings and repassings was oddly like some slapstick movie of the twenties, and parties of people in boats were in danger of falling overboard in sheer hilarity.

Apart from televisable events for the national and local news programs, Nixon gave a great deal of time to special appearances, both interviews and paid spots, on local television. But two features common to most campaigns were almost entirely absent: the "background" interview with the national press, and the confrontation with national television cameras. Nixon's evenings, after as little as two daytime meetings, were frequently given over to private taping sessions. A typical schedule (although with an earlier start than usual) was Friday, September 20:

9:15 a.m.   Baggage should be at 450 Park Avenue for transporting to Airport.
10:55 a.m. Depart New York City en route Philadelphia, Pa. Flying time 35 minutes.

HOTEL HEADQUARTERS: Marriott Motor Hotel, City Line and Monument Ave.

11:30 a.m. Arrive Philadelphia International Airport.
11:50 a.m. Depart airport en route downtown Philadelphia.
12:10 p.m. Motorcade in downtown Philadelphia.
12:50 p.m. Arrive Marriott Motor Hotel.
7:00 p.m.   Depart hotel en route WCAU-TV (across the street from hotel).
7:05 p.m.   Arrive WCAU-TV studio, City Line & Monument. Viewing Room will be provided for the press.

7:30 p.m.	MR. NIXON will appear on live Pennsylvania Television.
8:30 p.m.	Conclusion of television program.
8:40 p.m.	Return to Marriott Motor Hotel for overnight.

In questions of physical comfort the service given was extraordinary. This also appears to have been in part a reaction from 1960, when Nixon and his people felt that the press took out on Nixon their discontent at poor working conditions. There is a characteristically virtuous denial in Nixon's *Six Crises* of the idea that "I might have received better treatment from the press had I courted them more, or had Herb [Klein] provided the more elaborate facilities for entertainment that Salinger, with greater funds at his disposal, was able to provide." Perhaps in 1968 Nixon was trying to prove how much money could be spent without gaining press friendship, for, especially at Key Biscayne, facilities for enjoyment far outstripped anything the jovial Salinger ever dreamed of. One thing Klein did that Salinger never thought of was to go round to the newsmen, safely installed in the Royal Biscayne Hotel, and assure them that as *no one* was going to get anything out of Mr. Nixon during the Biscayne stay, *everyone* could relax happily around the pool and forget about the competition.

Free cars—Lincolns, Cadillacs, Chrysler Imperials—were provided by devoted supporters and put at the disposal of the press. There were trips in a large yacht, and water skiing, also free of charge. Entertainments, with ample free food and booze, were laid on at night, during which Congressman Melvin Laird—now Secretary of Defense—acquired the name of "Snakehips" because of the elegant, olde-world manner of his rotations on the dance floor with Nixon's private secretary, Rose Mary Woods. These pleasures culminated with a lavish party on October 14 at the Key Biscayne Yacht Club. There were oyster and clam bars, vast piles of lobsters, gallons of free drinks, and two bands for dancing under the palms. It beat anything the Kennedys ever turned on in similar circumstances. Ostensibly, the purpose of the party was to introduce John Mitchell, Leonard Garment, and other Nixon lieutenants to the press, but they turned out to have very little to say of a political nature, and the ratio of information to ingestion must have set a new low for affairs of this nature. Reporters, who are great ones for complaining, spend much of their time wishing for an assignment which combines luxury and idleness in the largest possible quantities; having found it, they did not like it. This may have been due entirely to their own professional thirst for news, but in any case it was reinforced by their editors, who were not getting any shipments of booze and lobsters and merely noticed the lack of interesting stories.

The problem, from a news viewpoint, was that there were really only three kinds of Nixon meeting. There was, first, the airport stop outside such small cities as Sioux Falls, South Dakota, or Bismarck, North Dakota. Three or four hundred people attended upon the candidate, who was seated on the back of a flat-bed truck with local congressional candidates, prospective senators, and perhaps the governor, where he was a Republican. Often there would be a high-school band, and always balloons. (The Nixon organization either thought balloons very important or had the support of a balloon manufacturer.) These meetings were held almost exclusively in states like the Dakotas, which there was no chance Nixon could lose, and their aim, of course, was to help local candidates. In South Dakota, Nixon spoke fervently about Archie Gubbrud, the conservative Republican running against George McGovern for the Senate. Standing up in the sharp wind with the red-faced and inarticulate Gubbrud, Nixon described the urgent need he felt to have "Archie" in Congress when he got to the White House—a wish which was disappointed, in the event. McGovern related later that the chief difficulty in opposing Gubbrud was his naïveté. "To attack Archie Gubbrud on an intellectual level," he said, "was like kicking a dog."

Such occasions rarely lasted more than a half hour, so the candidate offered no more than a skeletal version of his standard speech, sometimes clipped to little more than an assembly of proven "applause lines." Nixon traveled the country with a small but serviceable bouquet of axioms and witticisms, selected apparently for the fact that they remained comprehensible amost irrespective of the order in which they were put together. Some of those he found most useful were:

> We had a head wind today as we came out here. Well, that was a wind that's going to blow the old Administration out of Washington. . . .

> We had a tail wind today as we came out here. Well, I hope that's a tail wind that's going to blow us into the White House. . . .

> I have traveled, as I have indicated, to most of the nations of the world. And I have studied the history of Man—and, my friends, from the whole beginning of time if I were to pick a time in which to live, and of all the nations in the world, if I were to pick a place to live—I'd pick the United States of America, nineteen sixty-eight. This is the time. This is the place. . . .

> Poor Hubert. When he said "All the way with LBJ," he didn't mean it meant all the way back to the ranch. . . .

Our objective in the next four years should not be to get more people on welfare rolls—we want to get more people on payrolls. . . .

We're going to build up this country so that no one will dare use the U.S. flag for a doormat again. . . .

Hubert says he's captain of the team now. Well, he may be captain, but that old man on the bench—and I mean President Johnson—is still giving the signals. . . .

My friends, I was Vice-President for eight years. I am proud of the fact that in those eight years I served in an administration that ended one war and kept the country out of another war for eight years. . . .

[In farm states:] I know Mr. Freeman [then Secretary of Agriculture] . . . and I think he's a very good lawyer. But we need a new Secretary of Agriculture—one who will recognize that it is his duty to speak *for* the farmers *to* the White House rather than *to* the farmers *for* the White House. . . .

I've just seen a sign waved by someone in the crowd. It says: "Trade Hubert for the Pueblo." Well, I don't think North Korea would take him. . . .

They say the Democrats are going to try to win this year like they did in 1948. Well, I say it's one thing to give 'em hell, but it's another thing to give 'em Humphrey.

These well-tried lines became so familiar that the waiting reporters tended to mouth them in a chorus, finishing slightly ahead of the candidate. The outspokenly nationalistic ones which dealt with the massive superiority of the American Way were frequently met with ostentatious groans from Swedes, Finns, Frenchmen, Englishmen, and other lesser breeds.

Nobody, of course, expects anything very profound from such "prop-stop" meetings, but, where some candidates take them as an opportunity to relax a little, on the Nixon campaign they were as stylized as a Noh drama. The same was true in the second kind of Nixon meeting—the major daytime rallies, which were usually held in states where Nixon needed to consolidate support. These big rallies differed only according to whether they were indoors or outdoors. In each case, Nixon usually delivered his standard speech. There was, for instance, his rally at five p.m. on September 25 in the big open space on Welton Street in Denver, Colorado (an important center for the mountain states, none of which he expected to lose, but some of which, like Nevada and New Mexico, could use a little work).

Some two thousand people were warmed up by Peanuts Hucko's

jazz band and by the girlish cheers of the Nixonaires and Nixonettes. Nixonaires were the smaller, elite group, composed of off-duty air hostesses, who assumed the additional task of ushering. Nixonettes, chiefly the daughters of local Republican stalwarts, just cheered. The standard speech, naturally, was preceded by some half-humorous local references:

> I am proud that the man that introduced me, Senator Peter Dominick, not only has one of the great records in the United States Senate, but he is one of the men I am counting on in the new Senate to give that new Administration the support that it needs. How about sending him back with a big majority? . . .
>
> Could I be permitted a word about a very good friend . . . Governor Love of this state? Now, Governor Love is one of the leading members of our Truth Squad, and believe me they have a double task this year. They have the responsibility of following Hubert Humphrey around the country and of answering what he says. Now the trouble is we have had to two-platoon him. One squad has to answer what he says in the morning, and the other squad has to answer what he says in the afternoon, which is just the opposite. . . .
>
> Then as I stand here before this audience, I, of course, recall the many other occasions that I have come to Denver. I recall the occasion in nineteen sixty. I didn't think then the crowd could be bigger, but you have done it. This is the biggest crowd we have ever had.

Then to the main matter, the assertion that "something's happening across this land, and I want to tell you about it." Nixon informed the people of Denver that they were part of a great movement for change which he had detected in Charlotte, North Carolina; Indianapolis; Des Moines; and Seattle (to whose citizens, of course, he had just imparted a similar message). The young people, said Nixon, were out—which was hardly surprising, seeing that Nixon's advance men had been going to their school principals and soliciting half-holidays for them to come out.

> I see it also in signs along the road. Oh, they are very interesting. I have seen some interesting ones today, both for and against. I will talk about the ones that are for. My friends, the other day in Philadelphia, Pennsylvania, I saw an old lady—later I learned she was eighty-five years of age—sitting on the side of the street in a wheel chair. She had a great big sign, "Sock it to 'em, Dick." . . . And then another one that we saw yesterday when we were in Idaho, up at Boise, and this one said, "Smile, you are on the way to the White House."

Americans were out, Nixon said, who had never been out before— the people who had not been shouting and demonstrating and violating the law, but had been paying their taxes, sending their children to school, and supporting their churches. These were the "forgotten Americans." This suggestion that they were hard done by seemed to touch a chord in the audience, although the people so addressed in Denver, as elsewhere, looked prosperous and well clad, rather than forgotten.

Then to a trusty line, slightly improvised:

> My friends, I was Vice-President for eight years, and I am proud of the fact that I served in an Administration that ended one war and kept the nation out of other wars for eight years. . . . And, my friends, I am proud that I served in an Administration in which we had peace in the United States, in which we did not have this problem of violence and fear which pervades this nation and its cities today. . . . I am proud that I served in an Administration in which crime in the nation's capital went down by seventeen per cent instead of up by a hundred and seventy-five per cent, as it has in the last eight years.

The need for a new respect for law and order blended, naturally, into the need for a new respect for the United States in foreign parts. Civil rights, also, were dealt with in this section of the speech, with the reflection that the civil right in which "every American, whether he is a black American or a white American," was most interested was the right to be secure from domestic violence—not a proposition with which many would quarrel.

Then came the need for a sound dollar and an end to inflation, especially on behalf of the twenty million retired people in America (who, not infrequently, at daytime meetings, made up a segment of the rally audiences second in importance to the college and high-school students). The inflation that was eroding the dollar and the inability of the Federal government to maintain suitable farm prices—another matter of which the speech complained—were attributed to reckless spending on social-reform programs.

> And here we have the clearest choice of this campaign. . . . On the one side a man who says and honestly believes that the answer to problems is a knee-jerk reaction of government program, a Federal government program, that is. . . . Over the past four years and the past eight years we have government jobs, government housing, government welfare, billions and billions of dollars poured into those programs. And the result? Failure and frustration and riot across the land. . . .
>
> And so rather than continuing down that road and pouring more billions into programs that have failed, I say to you today, why not a new road?

The new road, it must be said, sounded fairly familiar. It was introduced with the thought that "the war on poverty in America didn't

begin five years ago. It began when America began a hundred and
ninety years ago." It had been, said Nixon, the most successful ever
waged (which, if nothing else, was a testimonial to the staying power of
poverty). The objective in the next four years, must be to get millions
onto payrolls rather than millions onto welfare rolls. The powers of
government would be used to enlist private enterprise in the struggle with
poverty. In accordance with Nixon's express determination not to make
unkeepable promises, he offered no rough date for victory over the
enemy afflicting thirty million Americans, but the *envoi* of the speech
was calculated to inspire everyone for the struggle:

> I say to you, my friends, today, we in this state of Colorado make
> history this year. Let's make great history. Great history for this state,
> great history for America, but, more than that, great history which will
> mean that peace and freedom will survive in the world for the next third
> of a century. We can do it. Now let's go out and win it big in November.

The enthusiasm which greeted Nixon on this occasion was impressive, as it was at nearly all his outdoor rallies. But they were dwarfed by
Nixon's third type of meeting—the great indoor rallies, which were the
setpieces of the campaign. The audiences here were bigger; not un-
typically, at Southern Methodist University in Dallas on October 11,
Nixon had ten thousand people. But their make-up was even more reliably friendly, since, in addition to the effect of the time of day, which
filtered out manual workers, admission to the event could be controlled.
The most spectacular effect of this policy occurred in St. Louis the day
after the Denver open-air rally. Although St. Louis is forty-per-cent
black, the Nixon advance men managed to assemble in a central auditorium a crowd of three thousand which contained just six black faces.
In a remarkable application of the principle which Nixon had so sternly
opposed at the Republican Convention, white high-school children had
been bussed in from the suburbs to make up the crowd.

But even when such mechanical devices were not employed, the
biggest crowds remained largely lily-white—as at Knoxville, in the traditionally Republican area of East Tennessee on October 15. Although
there were fifteen thousand people outside the hall and five thousand
inside, the journalists could still play their wager of "five dollars for
each black face" with no serious chance of loss. Apart from high-school
and college students, rally tickets were dispensed only to citizens thought
to be suitably solid, a proposition which rarely went wrong. (One occasion when it did was when a ticket for Madison Square Garden on

November 1 was sent to Hubert Humphrey's chief New York fundraiser, the textile boss Marvin Rosenberg. "I guess they thought that all
businessmen are Republicans," he said in some amusement. "In the
textile business in this city, it is not so.") But even for those who
obtained tickets, there sometimes remained further obstacles: at Madison Square Garden, for example, scores of ticket-holders were barred as
"undesirables." Fred Carlin, a member of the state Republican Committee, said "Anyone who doesn't look right is pulled from the line." It
was, he said, "just an eye test"; those who failed to pass it included
Negroes in African garb, bearded youths, tieless people, and three
bearded Hassidic Jews. It was an interesting commentary on Nixon's
remark (in a radio address on September 19) that "the lamps of en-
lightenment are lit by the spark of controversy; their flame can be
snuffed out by the blanket of consensus."

Those who were chosen and got in usually had their spirits raised
by a huge brass band and, at several rallies, by a thousand-voice choir.
This would sing the "Battle Hymn of the Republic" in a very slow tempo
and using all the words, the middle bit being taken solo by the ripest local
baritone. At the musical crescendo, the biggest of all balloon showers
would descend on the audience. The extra size of the audience, however,
did not entitle it to any further elaboration of political thought. These
excerpts from Knoxville on October 15 may be compared with Denver
on September 25:

> The question of whether we have peace at home, that's on the line
> in this campaign. Whether we are going to be able to restore respect for
> law and respect for order. . . .
> Let's look at what we have. Over the past four years listen to the
> figures. Crime has been going up nine times as fast as population. We
> find that all over this nation we have had problems, problems with
> regard to riots, problems that have caused death and destruction in our
> cities. . . .
> We have a basic difference between the two candidates. On the one
> side one who says, "We shall go forward with the programs of the past,"
> and look what they are. Over the past four years we have poured billions
> of dollars into programs for Federal jobs and Federal welfare and Fed-
> eral housing, and what's happened?
> Well, my friends, I say this, that when you are on the wrong road
> and you reach a dead end, the thing you do is to get off that road and
> onto a new road. . . . Let me show you the exciting new direction.
> Rather than more millions on welfare rolls, let's have more millions on
> payrolls in the United States of America. . . . And so I say to you
> tonight, we stand at a great moment of history.

It appeared at times that these carefully selected, carefully prepared audiences were there almost as much for the benefit of the candidate's self-assurance as his actual electoral fortunes. They represented, very strictly, the section of white and prosperous America which needed no converting. Day after day they roared their approval, even their love, at him—and he seemed almost to bathe in it from the stage, smiling and smiling again, with his arms upraised in his favorite gesture, straight from the shoulder, with the fingers of each hand extended in a Victory sign. One could hardly begrudge Nixon his acclaim. He had been, in the past, unfairly rejected and unfairly abused. Nor in a democracy, can one fairly complain at the spectacle of a major section of the population demonstrating their approval of the man who, they believe, will look after their interests. But there was a frightening air of self-intoxication about it: the constant repetition that *this* is the real America, *you* are the real Americans seemed to lead to the assumption that there were no other Americans.

When, occasionally, the voice of another America did break in, briefly, as at Akron, Ohio, on October 10, it was greeted with glassy incomprehension. There, at the university, some student radicals who had slipped into the crowd began to shout some rather well-worn slogans: "Hell, no, we won't go," "Stop the war," and even "Chicago, Chicago." Did they have their candidates mixed up? Nixon's face set in a rigid smile, and he raised his voice to drown them with the aid of the public-address system. If he ever knew the technique for dealing with hecklers, he had forgotten it. (Kennedy and McCarthy were particularly competent at this. Witness McCarthy with similar protestors in California— "They say I'm a stalking horse for Kennedy." *"Yeah!"* "And they say I'm a Judas goat for Johnson!" *"Yeah!"* "Awful hard to be both.") His technique being so inflexible, he ground on with his text, saying "This great crowd here today, of people who want new leadership, whose enthusiasm will carry me on . . ." while he was being shouted down. Yet the hecklers failed, in that there was not even the level of communication required for their kind of act: every now and then they would stop, and the hall re-echoed to Nixon, shouting at the top of his voice to drown the now silent protest.

It was, however, only a momentary eddy in a placid progress. The speeches, variations on the standard, so rapturously received, dealt largely with the abstract and the unexceptionable, save for the special matter of the Crusade against Crime. However, that was not to say that Nixon could not make a good, hard, nitty-gritty sort of appeal in the places where a state's vote was crucial and its interests recognizably special. On these occasions, it was noticeable, the notion of Federal largesse was by no means so poisonous to self-respect and the American virtues as Nixon had proclaimed it to be in the abstract. In Texas, for example, a swing state, Nixon made a blunt commitment on a matter some Texans regard as vital:

> As Senator, Richard Nixon supported the oil-depletion allowance at its current level; I supported it as Vice-President. I will maintain it.

In Austin, he made equally clear that there was one project which would not suffer through the pressures on the Federal treasury:

> The present Administration's passion for parity has caused America to fail to gain the lead in space. . . . I consider the space program a national imperative. . . . Although the resources of America are now under severe strain because of four years of bankrupt economic policies, we must gain the lead in space. I pledge an Administration in which the space program will not be looked upon as a luxury but as an integral part of America's march forward. . . . Leadership in space will thrust America forward in scientific research, and in the military superiority needed to negotiate a lasting peace in this generation.

In East Tennessee, even the standard speech was less than usually stern about Federalism—but then Ronald Reagan himself has been known to moderate his conservative transports in the land of the Tennessee Valley Authority. And lest the message should be lost, Nixon drummed it home with a special statement coupling the TVA rhapsodically with the great Oak Ridge National Laboratory:

> Right now, the Oak Ridge National Laboratory is engaged in a project which can illustrate how our scientists and the awesome power of the atom, together with our American talent for huge regional development programs such as the TVA, can be a tremendous force for peace. . . . I refer to the Oak Ridge Laboratory's investigation of the Eisenhower plan for building nuclear desalting plants to bring rivers of clear fresh water to the Middle East.

Equally forthright language could be heard on the question of the protection of industries:

> While I am here in North Carolina [October 15], the locale of such an important part of this country's great textile industry, I want to reiterate the position I have taken previously on crucial factors affecting that industry. . . . One such consideration involves the impact of dramatically increasing imports on the 2.4 million people directly employed in the nation's textile and apparel industries. . . . The present Admin-

istration . . . has permitted much of the rest of the world to establish or maintain barriers to the products of our industry while we have provided foreign textile-producing nations virtually unlimited access to our markets. As President, my policy will be to rectify this unfair development. . . .

In Johnstown, Pennsylvania, Nixon equally promised vigorous action to deal with rising imports of foreign steel. There was, of course, no reason at all to object to a campaigner addressing himself to the regional interests of his nation—but it was noticeable that the proposals Nixon put forward in these cases seemed more detailed and firm than his remarks about the process of bringing private enterprise to deal with the problem of domestic poverty. Sometimes one yearned for an equivalent to the famous put-down that transfixed British Prime Minister Harold Wilson during a 1964 visit to the naval base of Chatham (which also constitutes a standing warning to all politicians on the dangers of the rhetorical question). "Why do I emphasize the role of the Royal Navy?" asked Wilson. "Because you're in Chatham," came a clear voice from the back of the hall.

More than in any stump speech or written statement, the spirit of Nixon's campaign flourished in the calm of regional television studios. He was lavish with interviews to local stations, and it was inevitable that the suggestion should be made that he preferred their questions to those he might face from the network men. Certainly, when one puts together some of the questions Nixon was asked on these occasions, they do not look formidable. For instance, on WAVE-TV in Louisville, Kentucky, September 26:

> Mr. Nixon, at this point in the campaign, what do you find as the greatest concerns of the people? . . .
>
> Have you encountered any surprises at all? I suppose not? . . .
>
> The polls that we have seen show you ahead nationally. Is there any hazard at all to being a leader?

The answers to these questions scarcely need recording. Perhaps the only tricky question Nixon was asked on this program was whether the national unease over crime was based on fact or was a product of rhetoric. Nixon said it was based on fact.

Again, the questions asked on WFAA-TV in Dallas, Texas, on October 13 were hardly brain-teasers:

Mr. Nixon, in your acceptance speech in Miami Beach, you said that the Republican Party has the leadership, the platform, and the purpose that America needs. What is there about your leadership that America needs? . . .

Mr. Nixon, do you believe, sir, that under your leadership the Republican Party today has more to offer the black Americans than at any time in its past history?

It was not often than Nixon ran into a questioner like Don McGaffin of KOMO-TV, Seattle (September 24):

Mr. Nixon, today you said that Mr. Humphrey is stuck with the record of the past four years and that he must defend that record. . . . Well, you too were part of an Administration for eight years, and you are stuck in a sense with that record. One of the most persistent criticisms of American foreign policy is that the United States finds itself propping up military dictatorships. . . . Why does it seem that way?

To this Nixon had to reply:

It is true that when you look at either the Eisenhower Administration or the Truman Administration before it, or the Kennedy Administration or the Johnson Administration, that inevitably it seems that the United States does end up supporting governments abroad that do not fit our ideals of what a representative democracy ought to be.

These interviews, however, were maelstroms of controversy compared to the device, used on a number of occasions, of the "Nixon Format." This was simply a period of bought time on which Nixon appeared with a panel and moderator appointed by his own people. The panelists, held to represent the ordinary citizens, naturally did not tend toward hostile questions. A fairly typical example went out to Texas, Arkansas, New Mexico, and Oklahoma from KLRD-TV in Dallas on October 11. This was the occasion on which Nixon indulged in a lengthy discussion of football with Bud Wilkinson:

. . . And I always remember that Oklahoma was a great third-quarter team under Bud, and that third quarter, whatever happened in the first half, they zinged ahead, and then held on in the fourth quarter, usually to win. That meant they had to have an offense in the third quarter and a defense in the fourth quarter. And yet I look—for example, if you are going to talk about football, I look at the Dallas Cowboys. Now, you take Tom Landry, he was a great defensive coach with the Giants. He comes down here to Dallas and he produces a great offensive team. After all, with Meredith throwing and Hayes catching, it's going to be a great offensive team. You can be sure of that. But unless he had a great defense, he wouldn't be able to be in there, as he was right up to the Super Bowl or at least almost to the Super Bowl last year.

I am digressing in football again, but that's my favorite subject. But to go on with the other question. What I'm going to say is this. We are going to have an offense and a defense. We are going to sock it to them on the offense and defend on the defense. How's that?

[Panelist Field Scovell, a businessman:] I think you've got a pretty good hand in Bud, and I think old Bud's got a pretty good hand in you.

Other questions were equally chummy:

[Scovell:] You took a little of the starch out of my questions when you carved up our alleged Attorney General and then you handled the bussing situation that I was going to ask about. Now Mr. Nixon, in our problems in Vietnam we continue to hear . . . from quite a few sides the fact that this is going to be handled and brought to an honorable end. Can you elaborate on that any and tell us just kind of what that means, what is covered in that statement?

[Nixon:] What an honorable end to the war means to me is ending it on a basis that will discourage future wars. . . .

Reporters and columnists who had covered Presidential campaigns for many years began to be assaulted by a sense of unreality. Eventually, they realized, even accepted, that it was not going to be possible to put questions to the candidate. They fell into a state of what one can only call astounded torpor. As a mark of the state that intelligent men and women could be reduced to by this organized tedium, there was the controversy which broke out in South Dakota over whether or not Nixon shaved his nose. There were two schools of thought on this: some said that bristles on the nose are unheard of, others that Nixon did have them. After much craning and peering, the matter was settled by a distinguished columnist who declared that at a certain angle he could see the cut hairs glinting in the sunlight.

There was, after all, nothing else to talk about.

Bombs Away
with Curt LeMay

"When the military man approaches, the world locks up its
spoons. . . ."

—George Bernard Shaw, *Man and Superman*

In Cicero, Illinois, on the afternoon of his Chicago visit, a month after
the Democratic Convention, George Wallace was preaching to the converted. It was an alarming spectacle.

Cicero is a shabby industrial suburb of Chicago, immediately across
the city line from the city and its bursting southwest-side ghetto. Its main
thoroughfares are punctuated with an extraordinary number of bars,
from which rough-looking men emerge blinking and staggering at most
hours of the day and night. It has a tradition of toughness going back to
the days of Al Capone and his fellow heroes, who used it as a kind of
privileged sanctuary when the heat was on in the city. It has a population
of seventy thousand—and none of them are black. The first and only
Negro family brave enough to move in, about ten years ago, was driven
away by a fire bomb thrown through a front window. In May 1966, a
seventeen-year-old Negro boy was beaten to death by four white toughs
merely for having come into town to look for a summer job. On September 4 of the same year, the National Guard had to open fire to rescue a
civil-rights march of Chicago Negroes from a mob of several thousand
local whites who, after pelting the nonviolent demonstrators with eggs,
firecrackers, stones, and bottles, then tried to rush them.

Wallace spoke from an improvised platform under some trees outside the sports field of the Western Electric Company and across the
street from a shopping center with a policeman watchfully posted on the

roof. The crowd was clearly out for blood and thunder, if not for blood alone, from the start. Wallace began by introducing the folks on the platform with him, and mentioned that a Negro friend of his, Jim Collins, had just brought in some money from Negro supporters in Indiana. Wallace mentioned these Negro supporters several times. (We never saw any evidence of their existence. Jim Collins, who also never materialized in our presence, was mentioned by so many people that whether he existed or not he had clearly achieved the status of a myth in the Wallace campaign—his function being to "prove" that it was not a racist campaign, just as the figures showing that the Negroes in Selma had voted for Lurleen Wallace performed the ritual function in the South.) Wallace apologized for Jim Collins' absence in Cicero. The Ciceronians were unimpressed. "How the hell would you expect him to get through this crowd!" asked a rough voice from the back.

As Wallace swung into his usual speech, thickets of placards waved overhead. THE DEMOCRATS WON'T, THE REPUBLICANS CAN'T—significant distinction—WALLACE WILL SAVE AMERICA!, SUPPORT YOUR LOCAL POLICE, and THE TRUTH IS NOT RADICAL. There were only five open dissenters in the whole crowd, and they happened to be jammed against the car one of us was standing on. The oldest was twenty, the youngest seventeen: four girls, all very neatly dressed, and a boy in a blue windbreaker. In shaky ballpoint, their signs read, DON'T LET WALLACE TURN AMERICA INTO A POLICE STATE, and LOVE. The crowd didn't just heckle them. It surged against them, obscenely full of hate, overtly sexual. "Hey!" said a middle-aged woman with a daughter much the same age as the five dissenters, "look at those four Lesbians and a homo!" "Take your whores and go home," shouted a spotty youth in a dirty tee-shirt, adding, "Those kooks hate us!"

On the platform, Wallace could be heard orating, ". . . I have never in my life made a speech reflecting on the race, color, creed of any citizen of this country . . ."

"Hey!" shouted a swarthy man, pointing at one of the girls with a dissenting sign, "I bet she shacks with niggers!" The crowd laughed. A girl in a peppermint-striped jersey, rhythmically chewing gum, suddenly turned around and hit the boy in the face—casually, but hard. Without pause in her chewing, she turned back to concentrate on what Wallace was saying.

This emboldened a big burly middle-aged fellow, all of two hundred and fifty pounds, to push the girls aside, grab their placards, and tear them up. The girls began to cry, eyeshadow smudging their cheeks.

Asked what their parents thought about their demonstrating, one of them jerked a thumb toward Wallace and said between sobs, "My mother's for him!" But they didn't give up. All five raised their arms, with fingers extended in the V-for-victory sign. Strangely, this gesture acted as a focus for other dissenters as the placards had not. Soon seven, and finally eight, other arms went up. Their owners were all young and white-faced with fear. But, even more strangely, there was no more violence. Having torn down the offending placards, the crowd seemed bored with its easy victory. One youth looked for a new world to conquer. "Hey, Moishe," he shouted to a reporter from New York, whose name happens to be Marty. "Go ahead, Moishe, are you writing this all down backwards?" He added, superfluously, "I hate Jews too."

Later, we asked Wallace about what had happened. "I'm sorry it happened," he said. "If I had my way, no one would get hit. I acknowledge the right to picket peacefully." And he told a story about a time he and his wife had been trapped in a car by demonstrators, and he had been afraid that the car would be turned over. He remembered that Lurleen had been frightened. He seemed genuinely shocked at the memory of that kind of violence—yet it was the inevitable consequence of the kind of speech he was making, night after night.

That was Monday, September 30. Wallace spent a long day Tuesday stumping Michigan—Grand Rapids, Kalamazoo, Lansing, Flint. On Wednesday, he flew to Pittsburgh by way of Akron, Ohio. And Thursday, October 3, at a little after ten-thirty in the morning, in the number-three ballroom of the Pittsburgh Hilton Hotel, he dropped the big one. The setting was dramatic, even Wagnerian, in an absurd, incongruous way. The ballroom was brilliantly lit for television. The big windows looked out over the wide, swirling waters where the Allegheny meets the Monongahela to form the Ohio, and on to the sheer bluffs beyond. The reporters sat on little gilt chairs, like ladies at a fashion show, facing a dais. Next door a meeting of something called the Galvanizers was in session. But Thor, the God of Thunder, was also in town.

"I am extremely pleased," said George Wallace, looking pleased with himself, "to present to you and commend to the people of the United States the very capable gentleman whom I have selected as my Vice-Presidential running mate, General Curtis Emerson LeMay." Seven minutes later, after one of the most remarkable press conferences since Moses brought down the tables of the law from Mount Sinai, George Wallace had fallen from the peak of his power and menace.

It was a last-minute choice, and three weeks overdue at that. After breakfast that morning, General LeMay had still not finally made up his mind to serve. And it was a reluctant choice on Wallace's side as well. He had not wanted to have a running mate on his ticket at all. He took the view that no one could add to his magic for his constituency, and in that he may have been right. "Whaddya mean, a balanced ticket?" he snarled at one of the interminable staff discussions to thrash the question out. "Goddamn it, who wants one of those?" But state law in several states demanded that there be another name beside Wallace's on the ticket, and most urgently in Pennsylvania, where nomination papers with the name of both Presidential and Vice-Presidential candidates had had to be filed by March 6, and petitions began circulating February 14.

Roy Harris had proposed the name of his old friend Marvin Griffin to fill the space. Talking to Griffin in the cluttered office of the neat little photo-offset weekly newspaper he owns and edits in Bainbridge, Georgia, one cannot possibly dislike him. His hospitality is too natural and his stories too funny. It is hard to imagine him being mean to an individual human soul. Nevertheless, the record makes it lamentably plain that when he was Governor of Georgia he was an unashamed racial dema-gogue and an administrative disaster. An Atlanta columnist, Charlie Pou, summed up his administration with the phrase "If you ain't for stealing, you ain't for segregation." A grand jury found "perfidious con-duct of state officials" in his administration "hitherto inconceivable in the minds of citizens." And his successor, Ernest Vandiver, conceded drily that in Griffin's term, 1954 to 1958, "the state of Georgia was buying rowboats that would not float. Some were wisely sent to parks without lakes."

In the first week of February, Seymore Trammell and Cecil Jackson had traveled over from Montgomery to summon the Cincinnatus of Bain-bridge from his ten years of retirement to a higher duty. Griffin was unenthusiastic. He thought his name on the ballot would make the Wal-lace cause too sectional. "He lives on one side of the Chattahoochee River, and I live on the other." But a couple of days later, Wallace called up and asked him to come over to Montgomery the next day for a talk. Griffin flew to Montgomery and agreed to let his name go forward, "on one condition, that you let me do it on an interim basis." So they flew to Atlanta together and announced this unusual arrangement. Griffin slightly marred the effect by one unfortunate regional slip of the tongue: he said he was happy to lend his name to Wallace's ticket "till we've treed the coon."

For the next eight months Griffin enjoyed his provisional eminence in a spirit of high good humor and even levity. He began to be annoyed by "all these damn-fool Yankee reporters" who kept calling him up and asking him whether he had heard one name or another mentioned as the choice to replace him. One day he decided to float a name of his own. "I never lie to the press," he told us piously. "I told this feller one friend of mine thought John Wayne would be a great choice, and one friend of mine did—a feller I meet in the barbershop." Within hours there were reports all over the country that John Wayne would be Wallace's running mate.

Wallace's first choice, according to more than one source within his palace guard, was a daring flight of fancy: he is said to have sent at least two emissaries to approach Governor John Connally of Texas. In general, the Wallace camp considered two categories of names: Southern and Border politicians, on the one hand, and national figures with an appeal to the conservative and particularly the conservative working-man's vote, on the other. Virtually all the Border governors were seriously considered; and so was Ezra Taft Benson, the ultraconservative Secretary of Agriculture in the Eisenhower Administration. Among the nonpoliticians whom Wallace more or less seriously considered at various times during the summer were Colonel Sanders, the "finger-lickin' good" chicken baron who was suspected by dyspeptic reporters of having supplied the interminable fried chicken on Wallace campaign planes; Paul Harvey, the superpatriotic ABC radio commentator; Louise Day Hicks, who ran as a conservative for mayor of Boston in 1967; and—most appetizing of all, from Wallace's point of view—J. Edgar Hoover himself, the high priest of law'n'order. But the silence that was the only response to a few tentative feelers from Hoover was deafening, and most of the others, politicians or laymen, who were approached demurred, saying, as Dick Smith put it, "nothin' political, just plain scared."

Apparently, it was a wealthy Indiana trucker and landowner named Wilfred Gray who first suggested the name of General LeMay. Seymore Trammell seized on the idea. His shrewd mind saw that LeMay was the ideal man for binding on to Wallace's Southern and working-class law'n'-order vote the middle-class conservative Goldwater voters. In the middle of August, LeMay went to Montgomery for a talk.

LeMay is a bomber. That sums him up. He has grown up with the most destructive weapons in the history of the world, but unlike everyone else, he has always been the man *behind* the weapon. He transferred from fighters to bombers as a young Army Air Corps officer in the thirties "because I could see the future for them," and he was right. At thirty-seven, in 1943, he was a major general, having acquired a reputation as a brave and technically competent officer. He also acquired the nickname Old Ironpants for insisting that his bombers fly through defenses without evasive action, to improve their accuracy. He led several such raids himself, but for all that, LeMay is one of a generation of fighting-men air-force commanders for whom war is neither a chivalrous nor even a necessarily risky affair, but simply the pitiless exertion of overwhelmingly superior force. It is a set of circumstances that breeds bullies. LeMay played a minor part in the decision to bomb Hiroshima and Nagasaki in 1945. He commanded the United States Air Force in Europe in the years of the Cold War and of maximum U.S. superiority. He then returned to run the Strategic Air Command in the heyday of the doctrine of massive retaliation. He rose to be Air Force Chief of Staff under President Kennedy, who, however, refused to extend his term of command for more than a token year. Kennedy mistrusted his loud support for Big Bombs, Big Bombers, and Big Stickism generally, and particularly resented his opposition to the nuclear-test-ban treaty. He resigned in 1965 and in 1968 published an able and extremely outspoken attack on the defense policies of the administration he had served, in a book called *America in Danger*. Short of immediate pre-emptive nuclear war, no doctrine seems too aggressive for LeMay. He has looked longingly back to the days when "we might have destroyed Russia completely and not even have skinned our elbows doing it." In his book LeMay brushed aside such new-fangled "no-win" ideas as graduated and flexible response or limited war—which in themselves, as we have seen, could lead to some pretty frightening consequences. Even deterrence was too passive a strategy, to his way of thinking. "Deterrence cannot be assured in a vacuum. It must rest, not upon the ability to withstand a first strike and retaliate effectively, but on the ability to launch a first strike and win if necessary." He called for a "comprehensive defense system including an effective ABM [antiballistic missile]." He denounced the idea that mere nuclear parity with Russia was enough and he specifically welcomed nuclear proliferation. As for Vietnam, he called not for less bombing but for more. "We must be willing to continue our bombing," he concluded grimly, "until we have destroyed every work of man in North Vietnam if that is what it takes to win this war." He actually spoke happily about bombing North Vietnam "back to the Stone Age."

On the other hand, if LeMay's military thinking was as hard and hawkish as you could find, even among retired officers of the Air Force, in other respects his political views were no more than the conventional conservative growls of his class. He had, to be sure, no sympathy with civil-rights militants: "The trouble is being caused by a bunch of professional no-goods, Communists," he said. "I think the Communists are up to their eyes in the civil-rights movement. As a matter of fact, I know it. I've seen some of the reports. These reports are never made public." Yet he was certainly no racist. He was proud of his part in integrating the Air Force and, particularly, SAC. "What we finally did," he explained, "was to pick out a few people, good solid-citizen-type colored people who wanted to make things work. . . . But in addition to that, if they were radar mechanics, they had to be top-notch radar mechanics. . . . And we sent a few of them out. And when they appeared at the mess hall the night before, a few eyebrows were raised, but the people were inherently courteous and polite."

This is hardly the credo of a committed racial liberal, but Wallace discovered to his surprise that it was honest pride and that it meant something to the general. Wallace had not been overkeen on LeMay; he didn't particularly care for the idea of a running mate with a national reputation that outshone his own, and there may also have been traces of shyness at the idea of a former sergeant in the 20th Air Force giving orders to his former commanding general. What is more, Wallace was shrewd enough to fear the memory of what a reputation for being quick on the nuclear trigger had done to Goldwater in 1964. But in August, as Bill Jones said in a dazed way, "we kind of took off." It was now becoming urgent to find a serious national figure to put on the ticket. And Trammell was arguing hard that LeMay was the man. But, to Wallace's amazement, LeMay turned him down flat in August. LeMay was not sure that Wallace was sound on the bomb; he *was* sure that he didn't like Wallace's racial stand. He didn't disagree about what to do with rioters, but he was for firm, orderly integration, military-style, and no argument would budge him.

That gave the other group in Wallace's circle its chance. Bill Jones, Dick Smith, and the others who had been on the road were very impressed with the evidence of working-class support in the Border States and in parts of the North. What was wanted, they felt, was a popular, Populist figure who would frighten nobody and solidify that vote. Their choice was A. B. (Happy) Chandler, twice Governor of Kentucky and twice Senator, but better known as a former baseball commissioner. An amiable, mild-mannered man of seventy who plays a round of golf every day in the middle to upper 70s, still takes an occasional law client, and raises an acre of Burley tobacco as a Kentucky gentleman should,

Chandler is also a moderate conservative, and he, too, was proud of his achievements on behalf of the Negro. He had integrated the schools in Kentucky in 1947 without fuss, and he was baseball commissioner when Jackie Robinson became the first Negro in the major leagues.

On August 30, Chandler spent several hours with Wallace in a motel in downtown Louisville, and the thing seemed to have been decided. Chandler was to leave Kentucky on Monday night, September 9, for Washington, where Wallace would announce his choice at a press conference the next morning. Wallace retired for a brief rest in Miami. Then something went wrong. A certain Pete Brown, claiming to be the chairman of Wallace's Kentucky executive committee and a Wallace elector, announced that he was resigning in disgust and taking eight other Wallace electors with him. He asserted that he had met with "dissension, disrespect, and disloyalty" from Wallace aides in Montgomery, and, less publicly, he denounced Chandler as an integrationist. On September 9, three Wallace aides, one of them Trammell, paid a call on Chandler. Exactly what was said is not clear. But it seems that Chandler was asked to denounce his own record as a racial liberal, which he indignantly refused to do. "A retreat on that?" he said later. "What do you think would happen? Chaos in this country." Apparently, Trammell also left Chandler with the impression that his selection had been vetoed by a mysterious "Mr. Big." "I don't know who Mr. Big is," Chandler said. "My own opinion? I don't think this fellow makes his own decisions. As I have the thing figured out, he's got some fellows behind him with some money and they are pretty tough." Asked whether these "fellows" were Southwestern oil men, Chandler said, "Deep down in my heart, I have a feeling maybe they are." It was a suspicion ideally tailored to the liberals' conspiracy theory about Wallace. But it is more likely that Mr. Big was none other than Seymore Trammell himself. No doubt there were conservatives in Texas, in Kentucky, and, for that matter, elsewhere who wanted more segregationist red meat than they would have gotten from Chandler. But it suited Trammell's book to have Chandler vetoed and to lay the blame further afield.

In any case, it was LeMay's turn again now. He was still reluctant. But Trammell went to California to see him and appealed to his vanity. He succeeded in persuading LeMay that only he and Wallace stood between America and the fate of the Cities of the Plain. There was another motive, less recognized perhaps, which popped out later when LeMay was explaining his decision. "I certainly didn't want to do it," he told a press conference. "My wife and I were living comfortably out in

California, in a house we could call home for the first time in our lives. I dread going back to the eighteen-hour day. I dread the responsibility I have finally been able to relieve myself of." This was orthodox let-this-cup-pass-from-me stuff in the best tradition. But then he lifted a veil. "For twenty-one years I have been right at the end of a telephone, and it might ring any time. For a long time I listened for that telephone. And then it occurred to me that nobody cared where I was going any more. Nobody wanted to know." He steadied himself on the brink of self-pity and self-revelation and swerved away. "I didn't want to do this. I didn't need to do this. I think it's necessary, for the benefit of my country."

Still he hesitated. He paid a final visit to Montgomery, the last weekend in September, and there managed to extort two conditions. One was a financial guarantee: he was afraid, rightly as it turned out, that he might lose his sixty-thousand-dollar-a-year job with a California electronics firm if he joined Wallace. The second was that Wallace would come out against nuclear parity between the United States and Russia.

As we have seen, LeMay didn't finally make up his mind until Thursday morning, October 3, and George Wallace had a substitute standing by: none other than the indestructible Jimmie H. Davis, former yodeling instructor and twice Governor of Louisiana, elected in 1944 and again in 1960. Davis is best known as the composer of "You Are My Sunshine," though friends claim for him that he has also composed finer and less printable ballads, such as "I'm a Bear Cat Momma from Horner's Corners." It seems odd that such a sunny fellow is also a relentless segregationist and was the author of the heartless legislation that took Negro women with illegitimate children off the relief rolls and left them to hustle or starve. No doubt the Wallace campaign would have been enlivened if the singing governor had answered the call for the last yodel. But as it was, Old Ironpants played his big scene as high comedy in a style all his own.

The two of them stood on the dais in the middle of the line, LeMay's suburban family from California on the left and the ferrety faces of Wallace's palace guard on the right. LeMay is a gray and ponderous figure. His hair is iron-gray, and so are his suits, which seem to have been tailored to fit an oil drum. The meaty, cigar-chomping all-American vigor of his postwar face has been deadened by a stroke into mere fleshy heaviness, with a permanently testy expression. Wallace was smaller, and never more physically vulgar with his slicked-back cowlick than when he was striking the statesman's pose. And yet he was the one with vitality, the master on his own ground.

It was all over in seven minutes flat. One reporter was so stunned that he forgot to switch on his tape recorder. A CBS reporter, broadcasting live, had to take a grip on himself not to shake his head with sheer astonishment as he listened. A veteran British reporter who had slipped out for some refreshment at the bar came back in as LeMay finished. "Did I miss anything, old boy?" he asked. He sure did.

"We seem to have a phobia about nuclear weapons," the candidate for Vice-President began. "The smart thing to do when you're in a war—hopefully you prevent it. Stay out of it if you can—but when you get in it get in it with both feet and get it over with as soon as you can. Use the force that's necessary. Maybe use a little more to make sure it's enough to stop the fighting as soon as possible. So this means efficiency in the operation of the military establishment. I think there are many times when it would be most efficient to use nuclear weapons. However, the public opinion in this country and throughout the world throw up their hands in horror when you mention nuclear weapons, just because of the propaganda that's been fed to them.

"I don't believe the world would end if we exploded a nuclear weapon," he went on, warming to the work of reassurance. Why, he said, he had seen a film of Bikini atoll after a series of twenty nuclear tests, and he painted a picture of paradise regained. "The fish are all back in the lagoons; the coconut trees are growing coconuts; the guava bushes have fruit on them; the birds are back. As a matter of fact, everything is about the same except the land crabs. They get minerals from the soil, I guess, through their shells, and the land crabs were a little bit 'hot,' and there's a little question about whether you should eat a land crab or not." The rats, on the other hand, he concluded fair-mindedly, "are bigger, fatter, and healthier than they ever were before." Thus life imitates satire.

By this time, Wallace was in anguish. "General LeMay hasn't advocated the use of nuclear weapons, not at all," he said desperately. "He discussed nuclear weapons with you. He's against the use of nuclear weapons, and I am too."

But LeMay would not leave well enough alone. "I gave you a discussion on the phobia that we have in this country about the use of nuclear weapons. I prefer not to use them. I prefer not to use any weapons at all."

"If you found it necessary to end the war," someone insisted, "you would use them, wouldn't you?"

"If I found it necessary, I would use anything we could dream up —anything that we could dream up—including nuclear weapons, if it was necessary."

Wallace decided the time had come for a pre-emptive strike of his own. "All General LeMay has said—and I know you fellows better than he does because I've had to deal with you—he said that if the security of the country depended on the use of any weapon in the future he would use it. But he has said he prefers not to use any weapon. He prefers to negotiate. I believe we must defend our country, but I've always said we can win and defend in Vietnam without the use of nuclear weapons. And General LeMay hasn't said anything about the use of nuclear weapons."

Still LeMay wouldn't let it alone. "Let me make one more statement. Wait a minute now. Let me make sure you've got this straight. I know I'm going to come out with a lot of misquotes from this campaign. I have in the past. And I'll be damned lucky if I don't appear as a drooling idiot whose only solution to any problem is to drop atomic bombs all over the world. I assure you I'm not."

It would, perhaps, have been better if he had before the press conference been given the advice that experienced Vice-Presidential hand Marvin Griffin gave him a few minutes later: "Keep yo' bowels open, and yo' mouth shut!"

One of the Wallace organizers in New York is a man who worked for Goldwater in 1964. Well before the announcement that Wallace had picked LeMay we asked him what lessons he had learned from 1964. "Keep off the bomb!" he said simply.

Perhaps the General was right about one thing after all. Perhaps the American people, like other peoples around the world, do have something of a "phobia" about nuclear weapons. Perhaps they feel they should scrutinize with special care any man who might come even close to decisions over their use—and reject him if they detect even the slightest sign of lightheartedness where such terrible responsibilities are concerned.

But even the hawks' tame columnist, William S. White, who has represented the views of the Air Force generals and their friends on Capitol Hill for years, saw the danger. In a column unctuous with sympathy for "an authentic hero of air combat" who had never shown "the smallest white feather to any enemy in combat," White conceded that LeMay represented Wallace's "first capital mistake." White discerned that the ignorant rabble who made up "a critical mass" (an interesting

lapse into the jargon of nuclear technology) among the Wallace supporters was "Populist at heart and is not actually interested in any kind
of war."

Wallace himself seemed to realize his mistake as soon as he had
made it. The very night of the press conference, in Toledo, Ohio, a
reporter went up to the speakers' platform to ask LeMay to expand his
statements of the morning. LeMay was quite willing to do so, but Wallace
was not willing to let him. His aide Joe Fine snapped that the General,
whose mouth was just opening to answer, was not available. And the
reporter was hustled away by the Secret Service.

(Incidentally, the Secret Service's involvement in the Wallace
campaign appeared to go far beyond what was required to insure the
candidate's safety, though that must have seemed a pretty tough assignment at certain times and in certain places. It was not that the young
Secret Service men seemed particularly sympathetic to Wallace; though
they occasionally gave some sign to demonstrators and even to the press
of sharing Wallace's attitude, their deportment was on the whole scrupu-
lously apolitical. It was simply that, being tidy-minded young men with
a proper military sense of duty and initiative, they moved into a vacuum
and took over a considerable share of the administration of the campaign
because nobody else was doing it—or rather, because so many other
people were doing it that it was in a chronic state of chaos. So many
people were dabbling in the simplest arrangements—what time should
the baggage call be in the morning, how long was a stop, where should
the buses park—that the press and the candidate were both in a frenzy.
Wallace raved, but his staff was so small and so adept at juggling the
blame that he couldn't fire anyone. At one point, a deputation from the
press approached Wallace and said that if he would appoint a press
liaison man, the press would club together and pay his salary. It was a
joke, but it had a serious intent. Eventually, press problems tended to be
handled by the top Secret Service man on the trip, David Frarex. He is
a tall, tough, Nordic, crew-cut fellow, friendly and extremely bright.
From that point on, he was not only a kind of press liaison man: he
seemed just about to run the campaign. He was far too cool and professional to let anyone guess what he actually thought of Wallace until the
end. If pressed, he kidded his way out. We asked him if he didn't worry,
sometimes, about the power he had. "No," he said cheerfully, "I'm just
getting ready to kick the can out from under him!" On the last day of
all, when Wallace went to vote in Clayton, there was a milling mob of
ecstatic supporters in the square. As Wallace disappeared into their

midst, Frarex suddenly saw that his security control had disappeared with him for the moment. He turned to one of his colleagues and snapped urgently, "Who's running this thing politically, anyway?" The other Secret Service agent deliberately misunderstood. "You?" he suggested, deadpan. They both grinned from ear to ear.)

The LeMay press conference coincided with the zenith of Wallace's fortunes. From that day on, they began to decline. This is not to say that LeMay was the only, or even the main, reason for the decline. At about the same time Wallace began to feel the force of the unions' counterpunch.

The Wallace movement, like any other national political movement in America—or, for that matter, in any country—was a coalition. At the risk of oversimplification, it can be said that after the Democratic Convention Wallace could count on two elements: the Deep South and the right-wing lunatic fringe. He could hope to get at least a good share of the vote of a third element: the traditional conservatives. The absolutely critical question, now squarely posed, was how many votes he could draw from a fourth and much larger group: the white working class and lower-middle class in the urban and industrial areas of the North and Middle West.

On September 15, the Gallup poll, which gave Wallace 19 per cent nationally, showed him clearly in the lead in a three-cornered race in the South. It is often forgotten that the South has a quarter of the population of the United States. In a thirteen-state region, including Oklahoma and Kentucky as well as the eleven former Confederate states, Wallace had 38 per cent to Nixon's 31 and Humphrey's 25. In the hard-core states of the Deep, or "inner," South, his lead was even more marked. In the end, he polled 40 per cent in Arkansas, 43 in Georgia, 48 in Louisiana, 63 in Mississippi, and 65 in Alabama. One of the editors of the *Atlanta Constitution,* Reese Cleghorn, in a pamphlet analyzing the Wallace phenomenon (*Radicalism: Southern Style*), has pointed out that "if Wallace was not a sectional candidate, at least he was a particular kind of peculiarly southern candidate running nationally."

But the Southern political tradition which bred the Wallace movement was not the ancient history of slavery and reconstruction, defeat and differentness. Wallace and his friends had very little to say about John C. Calhoun or Robert E. Lee, nor did they "take their stand" on any distinctively Southern tradition of chivalry or agrarianism. They talked about the things that have seemed to threaten or outrage the average white Southerner in the last fifteen years—court decisions and Fed-

eral guidelines, the threat of Communism and the prospect of desegregation. And while those older traditions were ones which by definition
Northerners could not share, the new Southern politics was based on
grievances which were only more prevalent in the South as a matter of
degree.

Cleghorn cites a study by a political scientist at the University of
Wisconsin, Ira S. Rohter, which suggests that most right-wing extremists
are to be found among the "decliners, the new arrivals, and the value-
keepers"—those, in other words, who fear that as a result of social
change they "do not have the prestige and power they would have if the
world were just—and their enemies have too much." One might well ask
who in the world is not to some extent in one or another of those categories. Yet Cleghorn is surely right in saying that the South is peculiarly
prone to such fears and to their expression as right-wing extremism
because it has experienced not, as many Americans in other parts of the
country would probably still assume, *less* social change but more. The
growth of the urban population, the decline in the farming population,
the movement into the cities and the consequent breakup of traditional
habits of work and living have been far sharper in the South than in the
North, as a glance through the national census will show. Moreover,
other less concrete but far more disturbing changes, such as the assault
on traditional beliefs about God, country, and family, the sexual revolution, and above all the black rebellion, have all had a far more traumatic
impact on the conservative society of the South than elsewhere. They
have conspired to produce in an unusually large proportion of Southerners that insecure and threatened social psychology, that political paranoia, which is the soil in which the demagogues and fanatics of the
Radical Right thrive.

But the same tensions, changes, and influences that have produced
so much political paranoia in the South have bred it also, in greater or
lesser degree, everywhere else in the country. Almost without exception,
the Radical Right was for Wallace. What is more, in many states his
campaign was either run or at least heavily influenced by members of
extreme right-wing groups like the John Birch Society, the various Klans,
the White Citizens' Councils, anti-Semitic groups, and even paramilitary
organizations like the Minutemen. The list of Wallace backers, managers,
and electors in many states reads like a national directory of extremists,
a political bestiary.

In Alabama, we have seen, the Klansmen Robert Shelton and "Ace"
Carter were active in the beginnings of the Wallace drive.

In California, there were two rival Wallace committees. William K. Shearer, who has been listed as secretary-treasurer of the California Citizens Council, headed one of them; Opal Tanner White, long-time associate of the arch-anti-Semite Gerald L. K. Smith, was secretary of the other. The chairman of the American Independent Party's central committee in Los Angeles County, Kenneth S. Waite, has attended a secret training session of the armed Minutemen.

In Connecticut, at least two of the eight Wallace electors were well-known Birchers, Harold Richard Greene of Westport and Monroe Sherrow of Hartford. On August 24, four armed Minutemen attacked a pacifist camp near Voluntown and four of them were wounded in a gun battle with the police: one of the four wounded, Louis J. Rogers, was chairman of the Wallace-for-President committee in Lisbon, and another, Frank D. Barber, was cochairman in Norwich.

And so one might go on down through a list of all the states. Roy Harris was state chairman for Wallace in Georgia, and Leander Perez was state chairman in Louisiana. In their different manners—Harris is a far more diplomatic and less hard-fisted operator than Perez—these two are perhaps the most important architects of the last ditch of Southern resistance. In Texas, the state chairman, Bard Logan, and at least twenty-seven of the thirty-one members of the Wallace committee were Birch Society members. In New Jersey, in addition to Birchites, the Wallace committee included a certain Ernest T. Bradow, who claimed to have organized a white vigilante group called PRE-ARM—People's Rights Enforced Against Riots and Murder. Robert de Pugh, founder of the Minutemen and a fugitive from justice wanted for conspiracy to rob a bank, issued a pro-Wallace appeal from his underground headquarters. At no stage did Wallace do or say anything effective to dissociate himself from such supporters; he seemed to have no intention of alienating the formidable help they brought him in terms of both enthusiasm and cash. Thus, for example, when the Dallas oil millionaire Henry L. Seale, on whose planes, loaned or leased, Wallace flew more than forty thousand miles during the campaign, was asked why he supported Wallace, he replied, "He's like us on the nigger situation." Wallace's comment was, "Mr. Seale is a good friend of ours."

The strategy, as Wallace saw it at the height of his popularity in late September and early October, took account of all these separate elements, if in a characteristically vague and airy way. The extremists had already done their part, in fundraising, in the ballot drives, and in getting the state and local organizations off the ground. The regional politics of the South would provide an irreducible base. "We'll carry every state from the Potomac to the Rio Grande," said Roy Harris grandly when we talked to him in early October. The eleven Confederate states would in fact have provided 128 electoral votes, if Wallace could have won them all: and even the *New York Times,* in mid-September, conceded him 77. To get to the White House, in theory, in a three-cornered race, he needed only 180 votes. Most political statisticians reckon that the "Goldwater vote," the stanch but not radical conservatives, make up one of the stablest elements in the country's political chemistry, perhaps some fifteen to sixteen per cent of the electorate. Depending on this sector proved perhaps the most illusory of Wallace's calculations: virtually all the "Goldwater vote" outside the South seems to have gone to Nixon. But in September, Wallace saw it as a foundation to build on in states like Indiana, Michigan, Missouri, and Illinois. After that, everything depended on whether Wallace could achieve a breakthrough with the supposedly alienated working-class voters in the industrial Midwest.

It was not as if there were no evidence to encourage Wallace when he set out on his crucial foray through the industrial states. He was drawing capacity crowds in all the industrial cities. There were reports of enthusiasm for Wallace from plant after plant, high votes for Wallace in straw polls, even Wallace endorsements from union locals. Steelworkers, automobile workers, all the aristocracy of the industrial working class, seemed infected with the Wallace virus. "This is wild Wallace country," wrote a *New York Times* reporter from Homestead, Pennsylvania, of all places, hallowed ground in the traditions of American labor militancy as the site of one of the great strikes of the nineteenth century. "Over in the boiler shop," a low-level union official at the United States Steel plant told him, "I bet you they're ninety-two per cent Wallace." At a Ford plant in New Jersey, sixty-two per cent said they were for Wallace, and nobody took much notice of the union official who pointed out that, since the poll was based on only a hundred interviews, it was "haphazard, unscientific, and misleading." At the Ternstedt plant of General Motors in Flint, Michigan, United Auto Workers Local 326, with more than four thousand members, endorsed Wallace. And, more ominous still, Local 659, at the huge Chevrolet plant near by, with twenty thousand members, refused to endorse any candidate for President. "Listen," said a high UAW official in mid-September, "the men in the plants want to zap the Negroes by voting for Wallace. It's as simple as that."

It wasn't quite so simple as that. Scenting a major shift in the struc-

ture of American political allegiance, the journalists poured into Flint
and Gary. Nationally syndicated columnists whose Washington by-lines
were only occasionally varied by a jaunt to Paris or London or a conducted tour of Saigon began to file from Toledo, Warren, and Kalamazoo. They found plenty of copy. Everywhere, foundry and assembly-line
workers were only too ready to growl about law and order and grumble
about how the union hierarchies took them for granted. Here was a major
story: a counteralienation to offset the militancy of the blacks and the
intellectuals. Evans and Novak's column in the *Washington Post* on the
day Wallace spoke in Chicago at the outset of his Northern tour appeared
under the headline "Auto Workers' Support for Wallace May Foretell a
Political Revolution." The Washington columnist Joseph Kraft, fresh
from his discovery of "Middle America," also reported that "a great
many workers in Flint resent the union leadership. In particular, they
resent union stands being taken on behalf of political candidates and
social issues without what they feel is adequate consultation of the rank
and file." But, Kraft added shrewdly, "the Wallace noises are probably
being exaggerated by internal union considerations. A large number of
those now talking Wallace to spit in the eye of the union will probably
not vote for him on Election Day."

The truth was that the Wallace drive caught the unions at a time
when they were deeply divided in several directions. The AFL-CIO was
at loggerheads with the UAW, on the issue of the war but also because
of a gulf of personality and temperament between George Meany and
Walter Reuther, a gulf that was reflected at lower levels in the union
hierarchies. Years of relative affluence and bureaucratization had inevitably divided the politicians, the intellectuals, and the administrators in
the head offices from the elected officials at the grass roots. And the
lower echelons had been badly shaken by the surge of Wallace sentiment.
Some of them, elderly men particularly, to some extent shared the insurgents' attitudes. They were neither racists nor Fascists, but they were
troubled by Negro advancement, shocked by the rhetoric of Negro militancy, and appalled by what they had seen on television in the way of
riots and demonstrations. And even those who had no such sympathies
were understandably wary of standing in the way of a stampede if that
was what the Wallace movement turned out to be. "We've got to stir
these local union leaders to get a confrontation with their members,"
said Michael Johnson, executive vice-president of the Pennsylvania
AFL-CIO. "They are reluctant to have a confrontation. They need these
white guys for election support within the union."

The unions were divided and perplexed. But they were not ready to give up. The journalists were far too quick to underestimate both their political resources and their determination. "Sure we're hurting, and Wallace is obviously making things worse," said Thomas Kean, of the New Jersey AFL-CIO. "But we plan to do something about it."

Within the union hierarchy, even down to the plant level, the Wallace penetration was negligible. At a regional and area meeting of UAW delegates early in September, on a secret ballot, 87.8 per cent went for Humphrey, 1 per cent for Nixon, and 10 per cent for Wallace. A few days later, elected delegates from local lodges of the International Association of Machinists at their Chicago convention were 90 per cent for Humphrey, 2 per cent for Nixon, and 8 per cent for Wallace.

At the height of the Wallace surge, in mid-September, Louis Harris found only 16 per cent of union members outside the South were for Wallace: far more than anyone would have expected a year earlier, no doubt, but still far less than the straw polls and the newspaper stories were suggesting. The Wallace people in the industrial areas, as opposed to the candidate and his friends from Alabama, had few illusions about their own power if they were pitted frontally against the power of the unions and the loyalty of their leaders. "I could have my local endorse Wallace," one Michigan Wallace organizer said, "but I won't, because that would be slapping Walter Reuther in the face." "I reckon when the time comes," said Ray Smith, the Wallace man in Monroe, Michigan, "they're going to flood us with propaganda."

And that is exactly what they did.

"Don't let anyone fool you into voting against your best interests!" said the Machinists' election guide, published on September 26. "Wallace's Alabama is a low-wage, right-to-work state. . . . How sympathetic could you expect him to be to demands for higher wages?" "A top aide of George C. Wallace is . . . trying to break a strike by the United Steelworkers of America in Selma, Alabama," said the Steelworkers' newsletter the next day.

The UAW was stung to action by the straw polls in August, which produced what one official called "alarming results." A lot of the polls were known to have been rigged by Wallace supporters, but there was plenty of evidence of a heavy potential Wallace vote even so. Summer schools turned up more evidence of dissatisfaction that could turn into Wallace support. So the decision was taken to go after Wallace on all fronts. A "Wallace desk" was set up in Solidarity House in Detroit, and the whole operation was lavishly funded as a matter of top priority.

UAW officials will not say how much money was spent, but there is no doubt it was a massive sum. In three Eastern states alone, more than a hundred thousand copies of one pamphlet were distributed. And the literature was supplemented by word of mouth, both at meetings and informally. The decision was made to attack Wallace on political and ideological grounds, not merely from the standpoint of the workers' self-interest. Wallace's labor record was attacked. Heavy stress was laid on the fact that for all Wallace's talk about law and order and how his no-nonsense Southern methods would put a stop to crime, Alabama had the highest murder rate in the country. At UAW meetings in the East, local officials told their members about the "Fascist" implications of what Wallace was saying.

One of the most effective weapons in this paper barrage was a memorandum from COPE (the AFL-CIO's Committee on Political Education) in Washington. The front page, boldly laid out in blue, black, and white with a black outline map of Alabama, read as follows:

> *George Wallace's Alabama*
>
> * WALLACE'S ALABAMA ranks 48th among states in per-capita annual income and is $900 below the national average.
>
> * WALLACE'S ALABAMA meets only one of eight key standards for state child labor laws.
>
> * WALLACE'S ALABAMA ranks 48th among states in per-pupil expenditures in public schools.
>
> * WALLACE'S ALABAMA ranks 49th in welfare payments for dependent children.
>
> * WALLACE'S ALABAMA ranks higher only than Mississippi among south-eastern states in increase in manufacturing jobs in recent years.
>
> * WALLACE'S ALABAMA has one of the highest illiteracy rates in the nation.
>
> THESE CONDITIONS PREVAILED BEFORE HE BECAME GOVERNOR. THEY REMAIN BASICALLY UNCHANGED DESPITE HIS FOUR YEARS AS OFFICIAL GOVERNOR AND 1½ YEARS AS UNOFFICIAL GOVERNOR. TODAY, HE SEEKS YOUR VOTE AS A CANDIDATE FOR PRESIDENT OF THE UNITED STATES.

But the counterattack on Wallace was not only launched from the top. Local union men pitched in as well. Max Brydenthal, for example, the AFL-CIO man in Indianapolis, didn't wait for the glossy leaflets to arrive from Washington. He went out and spent a few hundred dollars on copying equipment and produced his own handbills right in the office. They made much the same points as the nationally distributed pamphlets —in one of them, for example, Brydenthal drew attention to Wallace's having said, "I'm not going to be outnigguhed again." And indeed sometimes the most effective ammunition, he found, were Wallace's own speeches, reproduced from local papers at minimal cost. Brydenthal found he could produce his own handbills for two cents each or less, where printed leaflets from the head office cost fifty cents or more. What was even more to the point, he could get his stuff out quicker. At first, some of the local union officials were rather nervous about giving out the handbills. But when they found that Brydenthal's people got very little adverse reaction, they joined in and ordered handbills and distributed them themselves. In the end, the Indianapolis AFL-CIO produced and distributed three hundred thousand handbills in little more than a month.

The experts had all been assuming—it had become an axiom in Washington—that the white American worker was so affluent that he could no longer be reached by appeals to his pocket and that he no longer felt he needed a union to protect his interests. "Party leaders doubt," wrote Evans and Novak, "that labor's emphasis on bread-and-butter issues has much impact on today's affluent workers." More cynically, it was also being assumed that these same affluent industrial workers had lost the political ideals they had held in the hard days of the Depression. The only social forces, it had become fashionable to say, which could move the blue-collar vote now were appeals to racial prejudice, jealousy, and frustration. At every level, from Walter Reuther in Solidarity House down to elected plant officials, the leadership of labor decided to test these pessimistic and indeed insulting assumptions.

It should be noticed that they took Wallace on frontally, on his own ground. The union propaganda—and it was propaganda—made the economic case against Wallace, and made it at times pretty roughly. Wallace and his backers might be antilabor. But it was not perhaps strictly fair to blame them for the wage differential between North and South. But what matters more than that is that they also attacked Wallace for being a racist and an enemy of democracy. "The Wallace formula of divide-and-rule," said the lengthy resolution in which the UAW endorsed Humphrey after an unprecedentedly long hesitation (not because of any Wallace sentiment but because of the scars of the Kennedy and McCarthy campaigns) "is a formula for national disaster. The hatreds and fears he is trying to exploit would be worsened, not cured.

America should turn again, as it always has, to the fundamental wisdom of the Constitution which links domestic tranquillity with the promotion of the general welfare. . . . We must work together to make America whole, to build one nation united in the belief in the worth and the dignity of every person." One could find the rhetoric a trifle fustian. But one could hardly accuse those who endorsed it of running away from the issue of principle between themselves and George Wallace.

The issue was squarely joined, in spite of all the doubting prophecies. The glove Wallace had thrown down had been fairly taken up. It remained to be seen who had most accurately judged where the working class's ultimate political loyalty lay.

On September 15, a reporter showed Wallace one of the first of the AFL-CIO leaflets. In blue on white on the cover it said, "George Wallace could cost you one thousand dollars a year." The reporter asked him how he would answer that. "I don't have to answer that," he said. "It falls flat on its face. Nearly all the rank and file support me."

But if he was to prove that a Southerner could be elected President of the United States, he did have to answer it.

3

"A Damned
Close-Run Thing"

"You might get better, but you'll never get well!"

—Luis Russell, blues lyric

Two days after Humphrey's Salt Lake City speech, which marked
the rejection of his advice on foreign policy, William Connell, Humphrey's faithful executive assistant, sat down to write a memorandum
on something he knew a lot more about. An assessment of Humphrey's
state-by-state position in the wake of what Connell himself called the
"disastrous" Gallup poll of September 22 that showed Humphrey lagging
15 points behind Nixon, it was headed, significantly, "Preparation for
the Harris poll of October 7." And it was the beginning of an operation
which is a classic illustration of the way polls, press, and politicians
interact in a Presidential campaign.

The danger was that the Gallup poll would influence the press to
write Humphrey off, and their coverage and comments would then
be reflected not only in still more low poll figures but also in dwindling
financial contributions, which would mean less advertising, and start
the downward spiral all over again. Connell boldly proposed a campaign
not merely to counteract Gallup but to discredit him.

His memorandum listed twenty-seven states to which Humphrey
should confine his activities. Fourteen of them were listed as "probable":
these included New York, Michigan, New Jersey, Missouri, and
Pennsylvania and came to 194 electoral votes. A further nine states were
listed as "real possibilities": rather optimistically, they included not only
Ohio and Washington but also such apparently safe Nixon states in

711

the West as New Mexico and even Nevada on the grounds that they were "Democratic states," which Joe Napolitan, for one, regarded as doubtful. If Humphrey could carry all twenty-three, he would be home, with 276 votes. Four states, with another 64 votes—California, Alaska, and the Carolinas—were listed as outside chances for Humphrey, and Illinois was simply described as "too big to ignore."

Connell commented that the polls which Joe Napolitan had commissioned for Humphrey at the time of the Gallup blow gave him a "fighting chance" to be over the top in the Electoral College. If the Harris poll on October 7 showed any improvement, he argued, "not only can we point to a turnup by Harris, but we can point to the Gallup poll and stress a *remarkable* [Connell's emphasis] change from Gallup." The sort of thing he had in mind is clear from a later memo he wrote on October 22, headed "Gallup's Credibility Gap." "What is Dr. Gallup's track record?" he asked, and he mentioned the Dewey/Truman election of 1948 and the disagreement—or apparent disagreement—between Gallup and Harris on Republican contenders on the eve of the Miami Convention.

Connell had grasped one idea very firmly. The polls should not be meekly awaited as Acts of God. "We should prepare a full-scale orchestration," he proposed, "on the theme: 'The swing is on to Humphrey.' We should hit key columnists, writers, and financial people with the news that we were already in the ballgame at the time the bad Gallup poll was taken, and with this new national upsurge, we have strengthened ourselves . . . in enough states to win the election in the electoral college." "Larry," scrawled Joe Napolitan, passing these thoughts on to O'Brien, "not a bad memo. You should read."

The difference between two stories in the *New York Times* illustrates how willing the orchestra was to respond to the conductor's baton. On October 6, the *Times* led with an article that sounded like a sentence of death on the Humphrey campaign. Warren Weaver, Jr., basing his story "on interviews with several hundred political leaders," announced that in the all-important commodity—Electoral College votes—Humphrey was running third, well behind Wallace as well as Nixon. He gave Humphrey a mere 28 electoral votes, against 66 for Wallace and 380 for Nixon! The story did point out that most of the interviews it was based on predated the Salt Lake City speech. But that was buried at the bottom of the column; the headline said "Humphrey Leading in 4 [states] as He Drops Further Behind."

Three days later, the *Times* ran another story, by Max Frankel, under an eight-column headline saying "Democratic Leaders, Calling Polls Misleading, Say Humphrey Can Win." Without making any reference to the dramatic predictions of only three days earlier, this second story said, "After an extensive state-by-state survey, including many polls, that cost $250,000," the Humphrey camp was convinced that their candidate "retains a fair chance to win the presidency."

What had happened in the intervening three days was that the *Times,* along with other newspapers, had been fed the results of the polls Napolitan had commissioned, with O'Brien's agreement, at the time of Gallup shock. The same day that the *Times* published them, October 9, Connell put these figures into a memorandum to be shown to selected reporters for less favored newspapers. The memorandum was by no means composed in a spirit of disinterested scientific research, to judge from its heading, "Humphrey on the Upswing, Gallup or Not!" It was a selling document. It adduced two categories of evidence. The first was the results of telephone polls carried out for the Democratic National Committee by Sindlinger and Company. (Telephone polling is much used in commercial market research, and Sindlinger is very highly regarded in that field. But most political pollsters treat the results of telephone polls with some suspicion.) Connell drew attention to the "sharp rise in the undecided vote following the Democratic Convention, and the gradual swing back to Humphrey of that undecided vote since mid-September." The other evidence came from the private polls commissioned by the Democrats. Connell did not mention that the five cited in the memo had been carried out by none other than Joe Napolitan himself, or that other polls, by Oliver Quayle and others, had not been released. "The central point," Connell summed up, "is this. . . . Somebody is wrong—either Gallup is wrong or *all* of the five state polls [the Napolitan ones] are radically wrong and Sindlinger is wrong as well." A note from Connell to O'Brien the next day, enclosing more of the same kind of ammunition, was frank enough. "Larry," it said, "the attached memorandum prepared by our polling people should be used with selected columnists, etc. I think it is highly significant and persuasive."

Unfortunately for O'Brien, Napolitan, and Connell, not all the journalists accepted their figures as obligingly as the *New York Times* had done. Rowland Evans and Robert Novak, for example, launched a broadside against "dubious" surveys "not taken seriously by the polling fraternity or the Democratic National Committee's own research division," and against "releasing questionable data to bolster sagging morale." Humphrey's people denied the charges indignantly, of course. But it was perfectly true. The Napolitan-Connell trick was a desperate attempt to bolster morale.

What Evans and Novak missed about the whole operation was that it was highly successful. Most newspapers swallowed it hook, line, and sinker. And it was aimed not only at the press. Connell's original plan had been to "hit key columnists, writers, *and financial people*," and that was just what was done. That same week, telegrams were sent off to all state chairmen and to state coordinators of Citizens for Humphrey. "The public polls," they said, in effect, "show us trailing Nixon, but they may be wrong. We have private polls which tell a different story. We have great television commercials prepared, but we can't afford to pay for them. All we need is money. Go and tell the good news about our polls to potential contributors in your state, and we'll send you the material."

Such appeals began to have their effect. For various reasons, in fact, money was at last becoming easier. "The President helped here," one of Humphrey's top aides confided to us. "He turned loose some of his top fundraisers from 1964 in New York." And Robert Short, chief of the Vice-President's campaign fundraising operation, had managed to persuade some very rich men to come to Humphrey's help with loans, if not straight contributions.

There is little relation between the realities of how money flows into campaign chests and the Federal statutes that are supposed to police the process. One obvious example is the statutory limit of five thousand dollars for an individual's contribution, which is evaded by an infinity of fictions, many of them variations on the idea of a "committee" set up as a conduit for contributions.

At the beginning of the campaign, right after the convention, Humphrey's situation was desperate. Short's only hope was to borrow money. After the election, sixty-six Democratic money committees filed records of a total of 9.7 million dollars in contributions. Short admitted that another 3 million was contributed but not recorded, because it went directly to pay campaign bills instead of being funneled through a finance committee. And he estimated that about half of what he raised was in the form of loans.

The first group of loans came in just at the time of the Connell-Napolitan wizardry with the polls, and there can be little doubt that some of the wealthy men who loaned Humphrey money were shown the data in Connell's memos, as had been suggested, in the effort to persuade them that the Vice-President's cause was not lost. Humphrey himself had to spend far more of his time soliciting for these loans than he should have. On one of his visits to New York he is known to have spent several hours, which might have been used in campaigning, on the telephone pleading with businessmen to help him.

A very large proportion of the money he did receive came from a very small number of individuals, and from their friends, business partners, or codirectors. Much of this money came in the form of bank loans, a technique that offers tax advantages to wealthy contributors. The lender borrows money from his bank on his own name and lends it to the campaign. He pays the bank the interest on the loan, and when the campaign repays him—out of the proceeds of fundraising dinners after the election—he repays the bank. What he has contributed to the campaign out of his own pocket is only the interest on the loan for a few months. But, unlike a straight campaign contribution, this interest is tax deductible. Federal law forbids "national banks" from making such loans; but not all banks are national.

Short managed to borrow a million dollars in September, and on October 21 he reported a further two million dollars. A third batch came in during the closing days and hours of the campaign. In all, less than thirty people contributed a third of the twelve to thirteen million dollars spent on the Humphrey campaign, and perhaps substantially more. Moreover, many of the contributors can be grouped in clusters, as it were, around a very small number of major fundraisers. Thus, for example, of eighteen contributors listed as having lent more than 100,000 dollars each in reports filed in late October, three—Arnold M. Picker, Robert S. Benjamin, and Robert Dowling, all of New York— are fellow members of the board of the United Artists motion-picture corporation with Arthur Krim. Krim was one of the Johnson fundraisers of 1964 whom, we were told, the President had "turned loose." Another three—H. E. Gould, Francis M. Levien, and Edwin L. Weisl—are all members of the board of Gulf & Western Corporation, the fast-growing conglomerate which is one of the star growth stocks on Wall Street, or of its subsidiary, Universal American Corporation, which manufactures aircraft and missile components. Weisl has been known for years as Johnson's principal political lieutenant in New York. A third group centers around Hubert Humphrey's Minnesota friend Dwayne Andreas, who lent 5000 dollars in his own name and at least another 95,000 in the name of various committees with his address. Another interesting contributor was Bernard Cornfeld, the head of Investors

Overseas Services of Geneva, whose international mutual-fund stocks were barred from sale within the United States by the Securities and Exchange Commission.

Short seems to have shown some virtuosity in developing variations on the time-honored committee system. He artfully established a network of about twenty little committees as conduits to receive money from the wealthy givers and lenders and channel it to the big-spending committees: Pharmacists for Humphrey, Retailers for Humphrey, and so on. Each had a list of contributors, a list of lenders (always a variation on the basic group of twenty-one big lenders), and a list of transfers out. Entertainers for Humphrey, for example, and Lawyers for Humphrey turned out to be the same people. They filed virtually identical reports. Each of them listed 8500 dollars in contributions from Mrs. Doris Lanier of Bal Harbor, Florida, John J. Hooker of Nashville, Tennessee, and Henry Ford II, and identical lists of 5000-dollar loans each from Arthur Krim's friends Benjamin, Dowling, and Picker; Weisl, Levien, and Gould; Short; and Jeno Paulucci; Arthur Houghton of Corning Glass; John Loeb of Loeb, Rhoades; and other citizens, twenty in all. On each list there was also a twenty-first loan from a committee in Minnesota. In each case, the name of the committee had been typed over the erased name "Dwayne Andreas." And both in their capacity as "lawyers" and in their capacity as "entertainers," Humphrey's friends spent their money in almost identical ways. Both contributed exactly 74,000 dollars to the Humphrey-Muskie Media Committee, for example. Later, as the pressure of the campaign increased, Short's imagination seems to have failed him. Three separate groups of Educators for Humphrey appeared, and Citizens for Humphrey-Muskie groups almost beyond numbering.

It is far harder to generalize about the men who contributed heavily to Humphrey than about the Nixon backers. Nixon was supported by a broad cross section of the business class; Humphrey by a strange mixture. Many of the connections seem to be largely personal: like those of Andreas, Paulucci, and Short himself to Humphrey, and those of Krim, Weisl, and their friends handed on from Johnson to Humphrey. Some of the heavy Humphrey backers—Ford, Houghton, and Loeb spring to mind—are men of established, "old money" wealth whose contributions were presumably motivated by feelings about the issues. We have the word of one of Humphrey's closest advisers that one of those three was passionately interested in the issue of peace. But, in general, there is a flavor of new and venturesome money about the list, and several of the lenders are in businesses which either have experienced or might experience at any time Federal regulation or investigation. Jack I. Wolgin, for example, who lent 45,000 dollars, is chairman of the board of Sunasco, whose subsidiary, Atlas Corporation, holds second-mortgage notes from mortgage firms that have come under Federal investigation.

Hubert Humphrey was getting help from both some of the most established and some of the most entrepreneurial figures in American capitalism at the same time as he was getting even more critical help, perhaps, from labor.

On October 25, Bill Connell sent off one of the shrewdest and, in the over-all perspective of the whole campaign, perhaps the most significant of his memos. "With 10 days to go," he minuted on it, "there are still 8 to 10 million votes either undecided or not firmly committed to any candidate. The attached memorandum measures and identifies the blocs of voters where you should concentrate your maximum efforts."

One group was identified as "basically Rockefeller-oriented Republicans and Independents" who were said to be uneasy about Nixon's economic policies. And the second was the "soft" Wallace blue-collar vote. "With much talk about strong Wallace sentiment in many labor unions," Connell wrote, "it is refreshing to get reports this week of statistically significant switches from Wallace to Humphrey—*and no measurable switches from Wallace to Nixon*—among labor-union members." The labor counterattack was beginning to work.

Confronted with the very serious crisis of the Wallace challenge on their own ground, the unions entirely outperformed the middle-class liberals who had been criticizing them so severely for their lack of sensitivity to the moral issues raised by the war in Vietnam. Of course, Wallace could not be fought by the middle-class liberals. They did not have the nexus of past commitment to the working class that the unions had. It was not *what* was said about Wallace that was crucial—there were plenty of people who could have made a case against him. What mattered was *who* said Wallace was no good, and it came best from the unions. Perhaps the operation did not match up to the ideal of Periclean debate, but there was not a lot of time for Periclean methods. The unions had been much criticized for their attitude earlier in the year. They deserve some credit for redeeming themselves.

By the mid-point in the campaign the Democrats had found themselves with an unlooked-for asset: the contrast between the Vice-Presidential nominees of the two parties. And this was more telling than in normal years because of the low popular standing of the two Presidential candidates themselves. The press, eager to find something new to write about, lovingly fell upon the tidbit of comparing and contrasting the characters of the two newcomers to the national electoral scene: Ed Muskie and Spiro Agnew. And Muskie rapidly emerged as the journalists' favorite, almost their pet.

It was not so much what he said as the way he said it. While Humphrey, for instance, was showing an ineptitude with hecklers (at the Seattle Center Arena, the Vice-President called on the police to clear demonstrators out of the hall), Muskie was evolving novel techniques for dealing with this particular campaign hazard. His most frequently used device was to call on the noisiest of the heckling group with the invitation, "You want the microphone? You can have it!" And he'd let him have it. Nothing much of substance ensued. On the war, Muskie stuck doggedly to his line that the Democrats were more capable of ending it than the Republicans. But his meetings, undoubtedly, had a more cordial atmosphere than those of the other major candidates.

Like Agnew, Muskie had been selected partly for his "ethnic appeal." Unlike Agnew, however, the ethnicity seemed to mean something in Muskie's case. The Democrat's staple speech would dwell long and fondly on how his family had fled from Poland to escape Czarist oppression and how America had provided a refuge and a hopeful outlet for the family's talent. Agnew could have said very much the same thing about his own odyssey but never did. He was not very close to his Greek roots in any case. ("The only thing Agnew ever did for the Greek community in Baltimore," said a Greek-American legislator in that city, "was leave it as soon as possible.")

The point was, of course, that Muskie had no opposition. He was a cautious, competent politician with a good presence, and these attributes, useful though not uncommon, were magically transformed to great virtues when set beside the lean talents of Agnew. While the Republican went on his unmerry way dropping ethnic bloopers—calling Polish-Americans "Polacks" and a Japanese-American reporter "a fat Jap"—all an opponent had to do was to watch his own manners. It was hard in one sense on Agnew, for his ethnic *gaffes* invariably proceeded not from malice but from insensitivity. And he was ever-ready to apologize for offending people's feelings. But the self-abasement of the apologies seemed to suggest that Agnew just was not equipped to be "a heartbeat away from the Presidency." Nobody could make that deduction about Muskie.

By the end of the campaign Humphrey's campaign staff was playing on this contrast for all it was worth (several polls suggested that if Muskie had been the Democratic nominee, then his party would have emerged victorious). One of the most potent TV campaign ads simply read: "Spiro Agnew for Vice-President"; the sound-track was a long burst of near-hysterical laughter. Finally, the words flashed up on the screen: "This would be serious if it wasn't so funny."

It was in a rather different area that the campaign produced its meed of actual debate. This was the exchange between Nixon and Humphrey about the degree to which it was necessary for American nuclear power to surpass that of the Soviet Union. The number of voters on whom this had an effect may not have been large; but the debate was important as an example of how exposure during the Presidential campaign may contribute toward the redefinition of an issue as important as the balance of nuclear terror. The unusual vivacity with which this exchange was conducted derived largely from the role played in its origins by political espionage.

John Reilly, Hubert Humphrey's foreign-policy adviser, realized from the first that there was a possibility that Nixon would attack the Democratic Administration for failing to make America stronger vis-à-vis Russia. Such a step would be entirely consistent with Nixon's record as an advocate of the proposition that the Russians must always be confronted with overwhelming nuclear superiority. It would also be consistent with the views of Richard Allen, Reilly's opposite number on Nixon's staff.

The Nixon camp had given a hint of its intentions at the end of May, when the Senate discussed the proposal that work be started on a system of missiles designed to intercept and destroy enemy missiles on their way to American soil. The system proposed was the Sentinel "thin" ABM (antiballistic missile) system. The argument about the validity of this system was deeply embedded in the complex logic of deterrence. Originally, Sentinel had been proposed as a defense against the somewhat remote danger of missile attack by China. Secretary McNamara had been strongly opposed to the idea of constructing even this "thin" system of antimissile missiles, although by the standards used in such matters the cost was small—some seven billion dollars. McNamara claimed that the system was simply not required for defense against the Chinese and would be entirely inadequate for defense against the Russians. If the goal was protection against Russia, the Sentinel could be no more than a first step toward a system so complex and costly that it might do major damage to the economy. Certainly, it would comprehensively distort all domestic priorities—a "thick" ABM system, it was estimated, would cost over fifty billion dollars. Even then, McNamara was doubtful that it would be of any practical use—although, of course, it would be the largest bonanza in the history of the defense industries.

Nevertheless, the Sentinel had many friends in Congress—such as Senator and Reserve Major General Strom Thurmond. Senator Richard Russell of Georgia, chairman of the Senate Armed Services Committee, made a powerful speech saying that the purpose of an ABM system *should* be anti-Russian, and the sooner it was started the better. (It is Senator Russell's view that if there has to be another Adam and Eve to start things up after a nuclear holocaust, they should be an American Adam and Eve.) Although nearly every member of the Administration supported McNamara in his initial stand against the Congressional pressure and against the Pentagon officials who supported the ABM, his successor, Clark Clifford, was less intransigent.

By the time the matter reached the floor of the Senate in May, the Sentinel ABM program was fairly thoroughly identified as part of the nuclear contest with the Soviet Union. It had come to separate the sheep, who believed that American nuclear power was broadly sufficient, from the goats, who felt it was dangerously inadequate. To the first group, the ABM program was a wasteful and dangerous initiative which would start another crippling lap of the arms race and might well make it impossible to negotiate any arms-control treaty with the Russians. To the second group, such dangers were less alarming than their own nightmare of the Russians' steadily eroding the margin of American superiority. To them, the antimissile system was necessary because it would, by canceling some part of Russia's power, improve the balance in America's favor. In May, Nixon and Allen were firmly at one on the need for the ABM and the danger from the Russians. Nixon issued a crisp statement vigorously supporting the Senate's decision to go ahead with the ABM system—and saying that he was especially glad to see that America's growing weakness compared to Russia was being appreciated. In Allen's view, the statement cleared the way for a major attack during the campaign upon the sad impoverishment of America's strategic armory. "The funny thing," he reflected privately, "is that we're going to win this election on a missile gap, just like Jack Kennedy in nineteen-sixty. Only our gap is real, and his was phony." On the other side of Capitol Hill, John Reilly and his boss Humphrey were equally firmly committed to a set of attitudes in which United States power was quite adequately superior to Soviet power; in which the ABM concept was dangerous boondoggling; and in which the great prize in foreign relations would be to achieve a treaty with the Russians on arms control.

The "winning" of arguments on an issue like this depends more upon tactics and timing than content, the subject being so complex and abstract that the other side can always make some kind of counterclaim given time. For Reilly, it was therefore an important break when he received information about where the attack was likely to fall.

Reilly had working for him a "task force" of academics to study arms control and disarmament. Around September 20 it met, and one of the professors let it be known that he had a student who was working on a big speech with Richard Allen. So far as could be gathered from the student's careless talk, this was likely to be Nixon's major initiative in the area of foreign and nuclear policy. It seemed that the speech was not likely to go into the ABM question or into disarmament as such. It would simply warn that Russia was catching up. Reilly naturally had plenty of materials on hand for such an argument, and he started two of his assistants working them up into a speech for the Vice-President. Reilly then worked the drafts into a unified speech and sat back to wait for Nixon's punch. It was a long time coming—and for a rather curious reason.

Reilly's information about Nixon's plans was right, but for the wrong reasons. At the time the Democrats received their tip about a missile speech, no such speech existed. The decision to prepare it had not even been made.

When Nixon retired to Key Biscayne for his three-day pause in the middle of October, however, he decided to launch a new series of major speeches for the last phase of the campaign. (It was as near as he got to a concession that the campaign had not been sufficiently active.) The policy researchers, Greenspan, Price, and Allen, were summoned from New York for a conclave with Nixon, Leonard Garment, Bryce Harlow, and Thomas Keogh (who had taken leave from his job as executive editor of *Time* to organize publicity for Nixon). The enterprise was entitled "Operation Extra Effort," and Garment was authorized to purchase ten additional radio-network slots to display its products.

One subject proposed was a missile-, or "security"-, gap speech. That afternoon at Key Biscayne, Allen and Harlow began to rough it out together. But before the speech got very far it was interrupted by a diversion which illustrates the remarkable confidence in the Nixon camp at this time. Monday morning, October 14, before moving off again on his campaign, Nixon said, "I want a book made up of all my positions so far, and I think we ought to put it out." For most of the rest of the week, the staff at 450 Park Avenue worked around the clock—not on developing new policy statements for "Extra Effort" but on editing existing ones into a fat book. *Nixon on the Issues* went to bed Wednesday, October 16, and was issued the next day. It was no small feat of editing, for the book contained 194 pages and was claimed to include positions on 227 issues. On October 17, one of the research girls from 450 Park flew to Boston to intercept the candidate and present him with the first, specially bound copy, inscribed *"Nixon socks it to 'em—presented by the staff."* He is said to have been much delighted. "We certainly did sock it to 'em," he said. This done, the staff returned to Extra Effort. By the middle of the following week, Allen and Harlow had the security-gap speech ready for delivery.

It was only later, after Humphrey's swift and vehement response to it, that the Republicans realized there had been a leak. The odd thing was that the real speech had *not* been leaked. Back in early September, a RAND Corporation staff member sent an unsolicited draft of a security-gap speech to Nixon's research office. It was not looked on as a serious policy document but was thought interesting enough to be circulated fairly widely within the office. This was the document the Democrats had learned about—and, as it happened, it resembled the final product closely enough that the Democrats were not misinformed.

Nixon gave his speech over a national radio hookup on October 24. Reading the final draft through beforehand, he said, "This is a hardhitting speech, but it needs to be said." Hard-hitting it certainly was. "The present state of our defenses," Nixon began, "is too close to peril point, and our future prospects are in some respects downright alarming. We have a gravely serious security gap." He then ran through a series of disasters which had overtaken the nation under the Democrats—including the Bay of Pigs, a venture planned under Eisenhower and supported by Nixon himself!

> Now let's measure where we are today. . . . First, let's check our weapons. Eight years ago, our numerical advantage over the Soviets in bombers was thirty per cent. Now it's more than the other way around. Today the Soviets are fifty per cent ahead of us.
>
> Eight years ago, in nuclear submarines, we had a five-hundred-percent advantage. Already it is down four-fifths and each year shrinks still more. Eight years ago we had a decisive lead in tactical aircraft. Now the Soviets are ahead not only in numbers but also in quality. We

have produced only one new aircraft of this type since nineteen-sixty, while the Soviets have put out seven.

Nixon deplored the fact that the Vietnam war had led to the expenditure of a large part of the strategic stockpile of weapons. There was, he said, far more at stake than military hardware: America's defense apparatus was the guardian of peace.

> Soon after the Eisenhower team left office, the new administration reached a grave misjudgment. The idea was, if America kept up her numerical superiority, if we also stayed ahead in new weapons, we would provoke Communist leaders, and this would dash our hopes for friendly relations and peace.
>
> Apparently, these planners had persuaded themselves they could quickly reconcile our differences with the Communist world. . . . It was concluded that by marking time in our own defense program, we could induce the Communists to follow our example, slacken their own effort, and then we would have peace in our time.
>
> Such were the dreams that crimped our national defense program. Out of it all evolved a peculiar, unprecedented doctrine called "parity." This meant America would no longer try to be first. We would only stay even.

The argument, then, was that "parity" actually meant relative *superiority* for the Soviet Union, since the Soviet economy was smaller than the American, and Soviet technology less advanced than the American. If the Russians once got even, therefore, they would be ahead in terms of "commitment and will." This would encourage them to go the rest of the way and become superior.

> So the Soviets have vigorously advanced their military effort as we put ours in second gear. They have raised the quantity and quality of their ballistic missiles. They have greatly increased their submarine-launching ballistic missile capacity. They have developed a land-mobile version of an intercontinental missile. . . . They have tested and developed an orbital bombardment system. . . . Recently, we learned that they are perfecting ballistic-missile multiple warheads far more powerful than our own. This is a grave menace to the United States.

By 1970 or 1971, Nixon declared, the United States could have a "survival gap"—that is, be "irretrievably" behind in the "most crucial areas." It was hard-hitting, all right.

Normally, a detailed counterspeech on such a subject might involve a good day's hard work for a speech-writing team. By the time policy decisions have been made, advisers contacted, and drafts cleared, it can be two or three days before the counterattack reaches the public. In the meantime, the attack is making mileage. But in this case, Humphrey's counter was already prepared. The necessary policy discussions had already been held. It was simply a matter of striking back as soon as Nixon made the move.

Humphrey was in California the night of October 24. First thing Friday morning, in Los Angeles, Humphrey read out to the reporters and the cameras a long and detailed critique of what Nixon had said. Reports were circulated about the great help provided overnight by Defense Department specialists in Washington, giving the impression that speed of response had been achieved by desperate burning of the midnight oil. In fact, Reilly and his chief aide, Robert Hunter, had needed only two or three hours to edit the reply.

In most parts of the country, people who had seen Nixon's speech in their morning papers were able to read Humphrey's reply in the evening. Humphrey alleged, as one might expect, that Nixon was being "irresponsible" and threatening "the whole frail architecture of peace" so carefully constructed by Johnson, Kennedy, and Eisenhower. Nixon had described an America so enfeebled as to make war possible; Humphrey described an America so mighty that peace was probable:

> Charge: Mr. Nixon has charged that eight years ago, our numerical advantage over the Soviets in bombers was thirty per cent; now, the Soviets are fifty per cent ahead of us.
> Fact: Today we have over five hundred heavy strategic bombers and over six hundred tankers; the U.S.S.R. has only about one hundred fifty heavy bombers and fifty heavy dual tanker-bomber aircraft. . . .

> Charge: Eight years ago in nuclear submarines we had a five-hundred-per-cent advantage. Already it is down four-fifths.
> Fact: Today we have seventy-five nuclear submarines, compared with only eighteen in 1961. The U.S.S.R. has only fifty-seven nuclear submarines, compared with twelve in 1961. . . .

> Charge: Eight years ago we had a decisive lead in tactical aircraft. Now the Soviets are ahead. . . .
> Fact: The U.S. today has over seven thousand tactical aircraft, the U.S.S.R. has only about fifty-four hundred. Our aircraft have over two hundred sixty-five per cent as much payload capacity as the Soviet force today. . . .

> Charge: Recently we learned they [the Soviets] are perfecting ballistic-missile multiple warheads far more powerful than our own.
> Fact: The Soviets are at least two years behind us in simple multiple warheads, and these have already been made obsolete by our technology.

For Humphrey, Nixon's most outrageous allegation was the general one that the Democrats had allowed America's military effort to slip into "second gear," while the Russians had been making spectacular progress. No one, Humphrey felt, could have pursued Peace through Strength with more vigor than the Democrats. The United States, he declared, possessed and would possess for the foreseeable future, enough nuclear destructive power to "obliterate any aggressor nation or nations." He continued:

> Today, we have three times as many strategic nuclear weapons in our strategic alert force as we had at the end of the last Republican administration, including a fifteen-hundred per cent increase in numbers of ballistic missiles—a thousand Minutemen ICBMs, as opposed to twenty-eight then; forty-one Polaris submarines with six hundred twenty-five missiles, as opposed to three submarines with forty-eight less-powerful missiles then. . . .

This was massive retaliation, and it seemed to wipe out Nixon's second-strike capacity. Theoretically, there were always more arguments for the Republicans to deploy: for instance, the argument that Russian bomber strength was really bigger than the Democrats admitted, because the Russians might not care whether their crews came back or not—therefore Russian bombers with sufficient range for only a one-way trip to the U.S. ought to be included. And who, after all, could be sure just how good or bad Russian warheads might be? But there would have been little point in going through such arguments. Nearly all newspapers favored Humphrey's position: in the view of the "judges"—commentators and editorial writers—Humphrey had "won."

(On election night, when the election seemed for a while to be sliding into deadlock, Thomas Keogh told people that it was the security-gap exchange that had made the difference in Humphrey's catching up with Nixon, and it probably did help to restore the Humphrey campaign's confidence and to reconcile the dissident elements of the Democratic elite. But those processes had begun with Humphrey's Salt Lake City speech and received a more considerable boost from Johnson's imminent announcement of a bombing halt. The more important effect of the exchange was, perhaps, to make Nixon think again about the automatic salability of the "hard line." In May, Nixon had been keenly in favor of the ABM. But after the election, he hired Henry Kissinger, formerly a Rockefeller adviser, to become his chief foreign-affairs assistant in the White House. Kissinger is hostile to the ABM, and he wants to achieve an arms-control agreement with the Soviet Union. It seems certain that

there will be increases of defense spending under the Republican Administration, but perhaps, because of John Reilly's spy, they will be smaller
increases than they would otherwise have been.)

Five days after the security-gap exchange, the log jam broke on
an issue which still had far more potential explosive power in sheer
political terms: Vietnam. On October 31, the President announced that
all bombardment of North Vietnam would cease from eight a.m. the
next day. There were four campaigning days left to drive home the advantage for the Democrats. And it was going to give the Democrats an
advantage, despite the fact that the South Vietnamese government was
being energetically obstreperous about taking part in the Paris peace
negotiations.

Johnson's announcement was the result of a passage of diplomacy
sufficiently intricate to give nightmares to Metternich, during which the
North Vietnamese played the Americans against the South Vietnamese,
the South Vietnamese tried to play the Democrats against the Republicans, and the Johnson Administration, with no one to play against anyone else, tried to get the North, the South, and the National Liberation
Front to sit down around a table with them. Their worst problem was
trying to get South Vietnamese agreement to the formula for a bombing
halt. At least since the beginning of the year, the regime in Saigon had
nurtured a suspicion that the Americans might find it dispensable. These
suspicions were inflamed by Humphrey's speech in Salt Lake City and
were almost confirmed a few days later when Humphrey told a questioner that he was for a bombing pause, with "no periods, no commas, or
semicolons." The South Vietnamese, according to one State Department
man, believed that they would not be given a veto over a decision to stop
the bombing. Their suspicions were correct.

As the American negotiators saw it, the deadlock in Paris began to
move on October 9, in the secret meetings the diplomats had set up to
provide themselves with a more relaxed *ambiance* than that of the
Majestic Hotel, where the official talks were supposed to be going on.
Until then, there had been about as much contact between the delegations, even in secret session, as between boxers fighting in different
rings. However, on the 9th, the American negotiators came away with
the impression that the North Vietnamese were prepared to talk about
the subjects on which the U.S. wanted to get some concessions. Essentially, the Americans wanted to get assurances that fighting in the Demilitarized Zone would cease; that attacks on the "population centers"

of South Vietnam would cease; and that "meaningful" peace talks could begin quickly after the bombing stopped. Without giving anything away, the North Vietnamese seemed willing to talk. On October 11, Johnson and Rusk agreed that this ought to be encouraged.

The critical exchange is said to have occurred the next day between Averell Harriman, head of the American delegation, and Colonel Le Duc Tho. Although the Colonel was not the official head of the North Vietnamese delegation, he was known to be an important North Vietnamese Politburo member. He and Harriman were drawn to each other as one scarred veteran to another. Colonel Tho asked whether the United States would stop bombing, unconditionally, if the South Vietnamese government were admitted to the talks. Harriman replied that he could not readily talk about "unconditional" cessation of bombing but would pass the question on to Washington—where, naturally, its mere arrival created euphoria. The next day was Sunday, October 13, and an account of the developments in Paris was sent to Ambassador Ellsworth Bunker in Saigon with instructions to bring President Thieu up to date. Bunker saw Thieu the same day, and here, it seems, one of a series of "misunderstandings" between the Americans and the South Vietnamese arose. Bunker told Thieu that agreement now seemed possible with Hanoi. The "package," as it was called, would consist, approximately, of assurances on the DMZ, assurances on the population centers, swift commencement of talks, and participation of Thieu's government in the talks. As Bunker saw it, there were no difficulties at the meeting: Thieu "concurred." In the light of later developments, the word "concurred" assumes a somewhat uncertain meaning. It may have been that Thieu was amenable simply in extension of the known earlier attitude of his government that Hanoi would never seriously negotiate. He did not understand that the Americans considered that perhaps agreement with Hanoi was now so likely that it would be worth putting the formula to the North Vietnamese formally. (Or perhaps he did not realize that Harriman and Colonel Tho had achieved a measure of rapport with each other.)

Meanwhile, Johnson was sounding out his generals and his other allies on the tactical advisability of a bombing halt—and getting positive answers. On October 14, after a meeting with the Joint Chiefs of Staff, Walt Rostow, and other advisers, he instructed Harriman to go to the North Vietnamese on October 16. He was to ask that the enlarged talks begin one day after the end of the bombing. A message was sent to Saigon telling Ambassador Bunker to make contact with Thieu and get his assent to a joint communiqué which could be issued by Washington and Saigon if the North Vietnamese said yes to Harriman.

To judge by Thieu's conduct, he was unpleasantly surprised to find that an agreement was imminent. Bunker went to see him at six a.m.— it had to be that early because Paris is seven hours behind Saigon and Harriman was to go to Tho the next morning, Paris time—and took with him a draft communiqué which said that serious and direct peace talks were about to get under way in Paris. This communiqué to be issued in the event that a bombing halt was agreed upon was apparently flexible enough in its wording to allow for Thieu's most hated enemies, the National Liberation Front, to be invited to the table in Paris. In fact, Bunker gave Thieu to understand that the NLF *would* be there but, he hoped, integrated into the North Vietnamese delegation. Then, if the South Vietnamese were integrated with the United States delegation, both could save face. . . .

Not surprisingly, Thieu was enormously agitated and called his National Security Council to talk the matter over. As the Americans remember it, Thieu again "concurred." Thieu, however, later insisted that it was only a draft communiqué and that he had laid it before the Council as such. The Council did not like the document at all, and within a few hours rumors were flying all over Saigon—and from there all over the world. In Washington, the White House issued formal denials that any "breakthrough" had taken place in Paris, and the President had to telephone each of the candidates and tell them, in general terms, what was happening. For at least one, Richard Nixon, the terms were all too general, and he still suspected that Johnson was getting ready to drop a political bomb on him. The same night, October 16, offered a conspicuously suitable occasion: the Al Smith memorial dinner in New York, one of the great Democratic political junkets of the year. Nixon himself was attending the dinner, as a rare Republican, and it probably occurred to him that few things would have given a Democratic President more pleasure than to announce a triumph of his statesmanship in such circumstances. Nixon had Bryce Harlow and Richard Allen sitting in a room at the Waldorf-Astoria, poised over a typewriter in case a reply was required.

But there was not a chance of its happening then. Hanoi, having apparently been on the brink of agreement, was balking. It was clearly the sensible thing for them to do, since it was not hard to discern that some considerable differences existed between Washington and Saigon.

If Hanoi stalled, those differences might widen and make the Americans lose patience. So the North Vietnamese began to ask for such concessions as two- or three-week gaps between the bombing halt and the peace talks. They knew the Americans would not risk so long a gap—for domestic political reasons, if nothing else.

A few days of acute tension now began for the handful of officials in Washington who knew what was really happening under the shifting clouds of rumor. As so few people could be told what was going on, Dean Rusk's two most important Vietnam advisers—William P. Bundy, Assistant Secretary of State for Far Eastern Affairs, and Benjamin H. Read, director of the State Department's executive secretariat—had to take turns sleeping in the office to man the green Securiphone. In Paris, Harriman and Cyrus Vance worked to get the North Vietnamese back to where they had been before. Meanwhile, they were having considerable difficulties with Pham Dang Lam, South Vietnam's observer at the talks, over the interpretation of what they were saying to Colonel Tho and his friends. In Saigon, Bunker and his staff were trying to bring the South Vietnamese back into line. They noticed, rather sourly, one fringe benefit: the rivalry between Thieu and Marshal Ky, which they had been trying to damp down for months, had been entirely subsumed in anti-American solidarity. On October 21, Pham Dang Lam cabled to Saigon an account of what appears to have been a fairly impressive dressing-down from Harriman about what he could and could not expect. It may have helped to produce Thieu's rather grudging agreement the next day to send a small delegation to Paris—and to concur in a bombing halt if he liked the look of Hanoi's guarantees. What the South Vietnamese really wanted, though, was for Hanoi to recognize their government, which at that stage was something of a pipe dream.

Domestic political tension built up in Washington as Election Day loomed nearer and nearer—and as it became more and more apparent that with one good break the Democrats might just scrape home. Probably, from around October 20, there would have been little problem with the North Vietnamese, who had carefully withdrawn their troops from contact with the Americans as far as possible. (On October 21, the Americans released fourteen North Vietnamese prisoners who, presumably, had been kept on hand for such a good-will gesture, since prisoners as a rule were turned over to the South Vietnamese.)

But the President was moving with almost agonizing deliberation, taking careful—and, some of his advisers thought, almost repetitious—

military soundings. On October 23, for instance, he consulted General Momyer of the Tactical Air Command, who said that he did not think a bombing pause would be militarily dangerous—although it was not clear what Momyer could add to General Abrams' cables from Saigon. Essentially, Johnson seemed to be holding off in the hope that Ambassador Bunker could persuade the South Vietnamese to "sign up," as Secretary Clifford put it. Johnson's problem of timing was an intricate one: It would be worth waiting for an agreement that Saigon would go along with, for, in terms of domestic political impact, it would make the announcement of a bombing pause enormously more effective. But, as he knew, there was every chance that the "agreement" would fly apart, and very likely at the most awkward possible moment.

By October 27, time was running out. That evening, the President got word that Hanoi was again prepared to agree to a halt, military disengagement, and swiftly mounted talks. But the question of the status of South Vietnamese and NLF delegations in Paris remained vague. The question was whether Bunker could get Saigon to agree to a joint communiqué. Meanwhile, General Abrams was to fly to Washington to give the President personal, final military assurances. For a brief while, it seemed that Bunker had succeeded and that Johnson's waiting had been worth while. President Thieu had been raising numerous procedural points about the prospective talks in Paris. Would the delegations display their flags? Would the South Vietnamese delegation have a name plate? In retrospect, it is clear that Thieu was fencing around the old question of whether the NLF was to be given any serious role in the talks and whether Hanoi would recognize Saigon. Bunker's method of dealing with this was to say that there should be no flags, plates, or other symbols, and that each side should arrange its own seating.

On this basis, there was apparent agreement on Monday, October 28, on the form of a joint communiqué. The communiqué would say that North Vietnam was about to start direct and serious talks with South Vietnam and with the United States; that neither of these powers would "recognize the National Liberation Front as an entity separate from North Vietnam." The communiqué carefully would not say that the NLF could not be at the talks or that it could not, if present, regard itself as a separate entity. It was the old diplomatic device of the studiously blind eye, and, in the opinion of Bunker and his staff, the South Vietnamese knew perfectly well that it was. Certainly, the tenor of Thieu's questions indicated that he was aware the NLF would be involved.

There was another burst of euphoria in Washington on Monday evening. In the early hours of Tuesday, General Abrams gave the President a last military reassurance. As dawn broke, Johnson went through a set of final checks with Rostow and Richard Helms of the CIA, and again with Abrams. Arrangements were started for the President to broadcast the news next day, October 30. The first indication that there was anything wrong came in a message from Bunker about seven a.m.: Thieu could not get a delegation together for Paris by the date to be specified in the joint communiqué, November 2. At first, the mood in Washington did not break, but as the day lengthened, so did Thieu's objections. It became clear that he was objecting to the presence of the NLF in Paris: exactly what the Americans had been convinced he had agreed to a few hours before. Angrily, the officials in Washington postponed the President's broadcast for another day, in an attempt to sort out the dispute.

What had gone wrong? In Saigon, Thieu and Ky were making much of a message from Phan Dang Lam in Paris, who reported that he had been told by Harriman that the North Vietnamese had agreed to nothing beyond Saigon's representation at the talks. Theatrically, the two South Vietnamese leaders claimed they had been tricked, even insinuating that Bunker and Harriman were somehow in league with the North Vietnamese.

The American negotiators were puzzled. They had no reason to think that Thieu and Ky had learned anything new about the negotiations that would account for their change of heart. The Americans were quite clear in their own minds that Saigon had understood the joint communiqué for what it was: a piece of window dressing intended to make it possible for Saigon to swallow the participation of the NLF in the talks.

Suddenly the suspicion exploded behind the scenes in Washington that the South Vietnamese were trying to play with American politics; that their aim was to sabotage the talks, thereby helping the Republicans to win the election—and then get a better deal from them afterward. There is also reason to believe that the Administration was in possession of information from tapped telephones and other intelligence sources, which made them suspect that the South Vietnamese had been encouraged by someone to believe that the Republicans would help them to play this game. What the Administration did not know was whether this game of finesse had the approval of Richard Nixon or his staff.

Understandably there was deep suspicion among the handful of officials who knew just how delicately balanced the fate of the negotiations was, and who had been working and hoping for their success for months. The South Vietnamese "had come to a series of expectations about Nixon," said one of this inner circle of officials darkly at the time. "And they had been encouraged in those expectations. It was very dirty work." He was, as it happens, quite right in believing that the South Vietnamese had been encouraged to look to the Republicans for a better deal. But he was wrong if he guessed that the encouragement had the approval of the Republican candidate or of his staff.

What is true is that because of the unchartered activities of a Republican campaign worker both the White House and the Republican campaign high command were on tenterhooks, each fearing that the other could precipitate one of the ugliest election-eve rows in the history of American politics. It took a secret personal telephone call from President Johnson to Mr. Nixon to take the electricity out of the atmosphere.

One of the co-chairmen of the Women for Nixon-Agnew National Advisory Committee was Mrs. Dwight D. Eisenhower. The other was a beautiful forty-five-year-old Washington lady of Chinese descent called Anna Chennault. Mrs. Chennault was born in Peking and married the World War II war hero General Claire L. Chennault, commander of the Flying Tigers, in 1947. General Chennault died in 1958, but Mrs. Chennault, who had become an American citizen in 1950, continued to make her home in Washington. There she was a well-known hostess in political circles and a welcome guest at many embassies, including that of South Vietnam, whose ambassador, Bui Diem, she counts among her many friends. As her presence on a level with Mrs. Eisenhower suggests, she is very prominent in Republican fundraising. She contributed over a thousand dollars herself to the Nixon campaign and claims to have raised a quarter of a million.

As early as June, Mrs. Chennault wrote a letter to one of Mr. Nixon's foreign-policy advisers, pointing out that President Thieu would be in Washington shortly, and offering to arrange for Nixon to meet the South Vietnamese president if he wished to do so. The adviser who received this letter was immediately aware of the interpretations that could be put on such a meeting—so much so that he scrawled in capital letters in the margin of Mrs. Chennault's letter "NO! NO!" And he minuted to "R.N." that "this not be done for *any* reason and under *no* circumstances. Proposal dangerous in the extreme and injurious to our Vietnam position—that is to U.S. national interests."

Mrs. Chennault subsequently called several people on Nixon's staff. She was given no encouragement. "The boss was absolutely adamant that he should not get mixed up in the Vietnam peace talks," one of his staff told us.

On Wednesday, October 30, John Mitchell made telephone calls to certain members of his staff, asking with a certain menace in his voice, "Have you been in touch with any embassies?" If the answer was yes—which it quite legitimately could be—Mitchell followed up by asking, "Which embassy?" As a result of his calls, Mitchell was able to reassure the White House that no member of Nixon's staff had been in touch with the South Vietnamese.

But the situation was still obviously potentially lethal. That same night, in Paris, American negotiators met the North Vietnamese secretly and assured them that President Johnson would announce the bombing halt the next day, and that the bombing would actually stop on November 1, whatever happened. The South Vietnamese had not given their agreement. From the White House's point of view it was still desperately desirable to get Saigon to agree to join the talks if at all possible, but in any case not to jeopardize either the talks or the Democrats' chances. From the Republican point of view, a charge of intriguing with the South Vietnamese to delay the peace negotiations would be a catastrophe—even though there was the possibility that it might backfire. From both sides' points of view, the idea of charges and countercharges of playing politics with the peace negotiations on the very eve of the election was a nightmare. "I thought that if this thing hit the fan," one man who knew what was going on said, "it would be on Monday, and that would make for an unprecedented mess on the eve of voting."

On Thursday Mrs. Chennault made a lot of phone calls. In one of them, to one of Mr. Nixon's oldest and most trusted advisers, she complained that she could no longer get through to John Mitchell. She said she was attempting to reach Mr. Nixon through other channels. And she indicated that she had played a role in the recent endorsement of Nixon by eleven South Vietnamese Senators. She called some of her contacts in the Nixon campaign as often as four and five times a day, but still got absolutely no encouragement.

It was on Thursday evening, October 31, that the President went on the air and announced the cessation of bombing, as he had promised the Vietnamese to do. He said that talks would begin the following Wednesday in Paris—the day after the election—and South Vietnam would be "free to participate." The principle of self-determination, he said, required that the government of South Vietnam "play a leading role in accordance with our agreement with President Thieu at Honolulu." Simultaneously, Defense Secretary Clark Clifford held a press conference, announcing that the bombing halt had his full support and that of the Joint Chiefs and General Wheeler. Adequate assurances had been received from Hanoi, he said.

It was the best that could be done. But on November 1, local time, President Thieu issued a communiqué saying that the American decision was "unilateral." His government did not support it, he said, and the cessation of bombing was not justified by concessions from North Vietnam. Next day, the South Vietnamese National Assembly adopted by acclamation a communiqué condemning President Johnson for "betrayal of an ally."

It was Saturday, allowing for the time difference, when the news that Thieu was balking came over the wire in the United States. Nixon was campaigning in Texas and southern California. In New York, his staff were sufficiently alarmed at the prospect of a major row breaking out that at least one man stayed at his post specially until three o'clock on Sunday morning.

Finally, on Sunday afternoon, President Johnson placed a call to the Nixon entourage. He spoke to one of Nixon's aides, who handed the phone to Nixon. The President himself now brought up Mrs. Chennault's name, and appeared to be well informed about her activities. Mr. Nixon was able to satisfy him that these activities had been in no way chartered or encouraged by anyone with authority from him, and the President changed the subject. When the South Vietnamese opposition to the talks had become known, Nixon's friend Robert Finch had made a remark to the press about his having thought that the President had "all his ducks in a row." This had apparently incensed Mr. Johnson. "Who is this man *Fink?*" he demanded scornfully. When he hung up, Mr. Nixon and his friends collapsed with laughter. It was partly out of sheer relief.

Hubert Humphrey had his bombing halt at last, and no doubt it helped him. Presumably it would have helped even more if the South Vietnamese had not refused to go along with it. Whether their refusal made the critical margin of difference; whether, without the intransigence of Thieu and Ky, the Democratic candidate might just have scraped through, no one can say with certainty. The margin of defeat was so slight that it could have been the case. But if that is what lost Hubert Humphrey the election, it was not Richard Nixon's fault. One of the few times when he became really angry in the campaign was when, earlier and on quite another issue, it was suggested that he might make political capital out of the war. "I'm not going to make the war a political issue even if it costs me the election," he said indignantly. One way and another, it was the Democrats it cost an election.

4

The End of an Affair

"I am one, my liege,
Whom the vile blows and buffets of the world
Have so incensed that I am reckless what
I do to spite the world."

—William Shakespeare, *Macbeth*

The morning of Saturday, November 2, a busload of forty student volunteers from Boston University pulled up outside the Rockville Centre, Long Island, headquarters of the Democratic Congressional candidate in the Fifth District of New York. There was nothing new in that. Busloads of students had been arriving every weekend for six weeks, to the point where the good suburban citizens of that part of Nassau County were bewildered at the attention they were getting from the educated young. This particular consignment of volunteers, however, was unusual. For after the briefest visit to campaign headquarters, a fashionably disorganized suite of shabby fourth-floor offices, these students stumped downstairs, clambered back into their bus, and indignantly requested their driver to head straight back to Boston.

The reason for their gesture of high displeasure was ideological. They had just learned that the candidate they had come to help had done the unforgivable. Allard K. Lowenstein, the President-slayer, architect of the McCarthy campaign, inspiration of the student crusade, had gone over to the enemy. Or, at least, he had just endorsed Hubert Humphrey —and must therefore be adjudged to have rejoined the system. From the viewpoint of the students, this amounted to treason. They were not moved by the fact that Lowenstein's Congressional opponent, a lawyer named Mason Hampton, was one of the most hair-raising Republicans in the state. (He had advocated an air strike against North Korea in retalia-

736

tion for the seizure of the *Pueblo*. When asked about the possible consequences for the *Pueblo* crew, he had replied, "You can't worry about
eighty-three men in a situation like that.")

The incident was not entirely typical. Other busloads of students
arrived the same day, received the same daunting intelligence, and concluded that on balance their distaste for Hampton outweighed their
aversion to Lowenstein's eleventh-hour support of the Vice-President.
They stayed in Nassau and worked for the candidate. But it was one of
the more graphic illustrations of the anguish among the erstwhile supporters of Eugene McCarthy that lasted down to, and beyond, polling
day.

Ultimately, Humphrey managed to get all the professional politicians
in line. Lowenstein and Paul O'Dwyer were the last to be ushered into
the fold. Their endorsements had been prompted by the bombing halt
and by the new, if tangled, phase of the Paris negotiations. McCarthy
himself had rendered his endorsement, a lukewarm one, two days before the announcement of a bombing halt. But his constituency did not
automatically follow suit. This was no Talmudic detail, no irrelevant
question of whose political hands were empty but clean. If McCarthy's
hard-core supporters had endorsed him Humphrey would almost certainly have succeeded in deadlocking the election and might even have
emerged a clear victor. California, Wisconsin, and Oregon, states in
which McCarthy had shown great strength in the primaries, all ultimately
went to Nixon, by the narrowest of margins. Had California stayed in
the Democratic column, the election would have been deadlocked. Had
all three gone to Humphrey, plus Illinois (another state narrowly won
by Nixon, and one with a strong antiwar vote, though its expression had
been partly muffled through the year by Daley's iron grip on the party
apparatus), then Humphrey would have been home free. Over three
and a half million Democrats voted for McCarthy in the primaries. What
happened to them? Nobody can be quite sure, but there are some clues.
Shortly before the election, Nixon's private polling outfit, the Opinion
Research Corporation, sampled opinion among former supporters of
McCarthy's candidacy and found that only four out of ten were prepared
to vote for Humphrey. A similar pool of adherents of Robert Kennedy
revealed that little over half of them would pull a lever for the Vice-
President. Many of those not reconciled to the Vice-President fell into
the category of "opinion leaders." And while they may—as a result of
the bombing halt—have, ultimately, voted for the Democratic nominee,
few were eager proselytizers on his behalf.

The evidence, in fact, suggests that while most of the political generals in the dissident movement came over to Humphrey, a substantial proportion of the foot soldiers in the New Politics of participation decisively rejected him at the ballot box, in most cases by simply not voting. One general who did not conform to the pattern was Tom Mechling, who had run McCarthy's delegate-intelligence bureau before the convention. (He had quit a very comfortable job with the Xerox Corporation to work for McCarthy.) Mechling ended the year as the communications chief of New York Citizens for Nixon. Mechling had a freedom of choice not vouchsafed to Lowenstein or O'Dwyer: he was not running for office. But for this very reason his view probably came closer to rank-and-file sentiment in the peace movement. "My reasoning was very simple," said Mechling after the election. "I thought the United States could only get out of the war if we cleared out everybody who had been locked in to Johnson's policies. And that meant getting rid of Humphrey."

The endorsements of McCarthy and Lowenstein—the two personalities with most influence on the antiwar constituency, though to the extent that its votes were ideological, they were not in anybody's gift— came too late to make much difference. By that time, attitudes had hardened, at least among those capable of seeing through the careful semantics of Humphrey's Salt Lake City speech. Last-minute endorsements by quondam leaders were just as likely to be seen as betrayal—the view of the busload of Boston students—as they were to be seen as evidence of the new-found acceptability of Hubert Humphrey.

To understand why these endorsements came so late, and so ineffectually, it is necessary to look back at the situation of the peace forces immediately after Humphrey's nomination. McCarthy had once described himself as not so much a leader as the "accidental instrument" of a popular movement. After the chaos of Chicago, there were many in that movement who felt that the "instrument" could still be used to good effect. The first to attempt to wield it was Marcus Raskin's fourth-party organization, and there were many outside Raskin's immediate operation who hoped to keep McCarthy's candidacy buoyant. Defeated McCarthy organizations in various states met, recriminated, and determined to remain intact to spearhead petitions, independent-elector slates, or write-ins for McCarthy on the November ballot. The Senator was under strong pressure from some of his advisers to support these efforts. Convinced that McCarthy had impressive electoral strength in the two largest states—New York and California—their argument was that the candidate (like Wallace) should work for a deadlocked election that would force the final decision into the House of Representatives. Write-ins or elector slates put forward in key states, creating a four-way Nixon-Humphrey-Wallace-McCarthy split, could conceivably result in McCarthy's capturing New York's 43 electoral votes and California's 40, and possibly others. The argument, in brief, was that a small plurality in such a confused electoral situation might give the peace constituency decisive leverage. Louis Harris's first post-convention poll seemed to some to buttress the case: Nixon 39 points, Humphrey 31, Wallace 21, Undecided 9. It suggested the inevitability of deadlock. Surely the McCarthy people ought to have some stake in the bargaining process that would follow such a result.

However, to have any hope at all, such a policy needed McCarthy's strategic support and a national base which he alone could give. None of the existing radical parties offered much prospect of channeling the dissent mobilized by McCarthy. The liveliest of these, the Peace and Freedom Party, had adopted as its Presidential candidate Eldridge Cleaver, Minister of Information of the California-based Black Panther group. Cleaver was a man of considerable talent; his book *Soul on Ice,* one of the year's best sellers, displayed a better appreciation of America's structural problems than anything said by any of the other candidates. As a vote-getter, however, he had severe limitations. The very name of the Panthers—who had first achieved prominence by affecting military-style dress and exercising their "right to bear arms" in public—struck terror into most suburban neighborhoods. Cleaver himself was on parole awaiting trial on an attempted murder charge (he subsequently went into hiding when the parole expired). He was also too young to be President. Clearly, the antiwar protest had to steer clear of the wilder fringes of dissent. It needed a new party; and it needed McCarthy. A clear green light from McCarthy would accelerate the drive to put his name on the ballot in the crucial states. Initially, it seemed that he was beguiled by the idea. Despite his coolness toward fourth-party initiatives in Chicago, it was not until some weeks after the convention that McCarthy finally closed this door. In fact, early in September, he came close to being convinced. The occasion was a highly secret meeting on fourth-party election tactics at the Sheraton Hotel in Washington.

It was in no sense a radical-fringe operation. Convened by Seymour Hersh, McCarthy's press officer in New Hampshire and Wisconsin, the meeting was attended by professionals of the caliber of Dick Goodwin, Adam Walinsky, and Pat Lucey. Marcus Raskin came armed with feasibility studies. Goodwin argued forcefully that the project could easily be financed—at that stage, of course, Humphrey as a no-hope candidate was getting few funds from the liberal establishment. At one point in the discussions, McCarthy generated tremendous excitement. "I guess," he observed laconically, "we could win New York, California, Oregon, Minnesota, and maybe even Wisconsin." That was the nearest Raskin ever came to luring the Senator into the race. As the practicalities of his remark were discussed, McCarthy's interest seemed to evaporate. The formula he eventually adopted was the result of what one of his aides described sarcastically as "one of his typical Solomon-like decisions."

He would withdraw his name from the ballot in all states—if necessary, by overt action—except California. There, he would allow his name to go forward if by the deadline, which was midnight, September 20, his supporters could collect the 330,000 signatures legally required. The consequences of this decision, though not immediately obvious, were important. The decision had a built-in delayed reaction. It was likely to have the effect of delaying any Humphrey-McCarthy *rapprochement* until the end of September, whatever their respective supporters might wish. For, once his name was on the ballot in competition with Humphrey's in the nation's most populous state, McCarthy was hardly in a position to endorse Humphrey nationally. Possibly that thought had not escaped his mind.

Why did McCarthy make California the exception? There may have been sentimental reasons: His candidacy had been born there. He may have felt that he could not have turned off the movement in California even if he had wanted to. What he said was that his name on the ballot in California in November would bring out thousands of voters who might otherwise have stayed at home in disgust. Once in the polling booths, they might stay on to vote for more or less like-minded Congressional and local candidates like Alan Cranston, Democratic candidate for the Senate. But if that rationale was good for California, why was it not sound for New York (to help Paul O'Dwyer), in Pennsylvania (to help Joe Clark), in Ohio (to help Jack Gilligan), or in any other states where liberals who had supported him were running against the war? Clearly it was not a rationale, but a rationalization.

Before leaving in mid-September for two weeks of rest on the French Riviera—there were plenty who found the symbolism of that gesture unattractive—McCarthy made it plain that he would have nothing further to say about supporting Humphrey, at least until mid-October. And he asked Jerry Eller to start scheduling speaking dates for him on his return, but only on behalf of like-minded candidates. Not all of those candidates were grateful for his support. Harold Hughes in Iowa and Wayne Morse in Oregon let Eller know that McCarthy would not be welcome in their states until he had come out for Humphrey! (Jack Gilligan, who accepted the offer, was less than thrilled with the service, feeling that McCarthy was too parsimonious with his time. "If you believe in a cause," growled Gilligan after McCarthy left Ohio, "you don't dole yourself out in teaspoons."

With McCarthy out of the country, the attitude of his key supporters toward the Presidential race lost cohesion. There was a split in the ranks. Those who held office or thought they might seek it needed to identify themselves with the party. The rest felt little disposition to support Humphrey. For them, the prospect of Humphrey's defeat was not particularly daunting. If there was one thing on which the supporters of Robert Kennedy, George McGovern, and Eugene McCarthy found themselves able to agree, it was that the party needed remaking. It would be easier to rebuild the party if Nixon won. A Democratic victory might have the effect of sanctifying the methods used by Humphrey, Daley, and Connally. An electoral setback, it was thought, would "cleanse" the party.

Still, the war was the main issue. If Humphrey made real concessions on this, much of the feeling against him would melt away. After September 20, there were no organizational obstacles to a reconciliation between Humphrey and McCarthy. As McCarthy may well have foreseen, his followers in California failed to meet that deadline by over 50,000 votes. Still the California liberals did not give up. Against the express wishes of Gerald Hill, on Sunday, September 22, the directors of the California Democratic Council voted in favor of a write-in drive for McCarthy. This did not help the prospects of reconciliation with Humphrey and his supporters, even though McCarthy himself was noncommittal and did nothing to encourage the write-in. Its timing, too, could not have been more awkward. For it came just as the Humphrey camp was pulling out all the public-relations stops for the candidate's Salt Lake City speech.

All day Sunday, September 29, phone calls went out from Humphrey's Washington headquarters to McCarthy and Kennedy leaders. Senior Humphrey men called McCarthy state chairmen to describe the advance text of the speech and to argue that it represented "a major new independent position" for Humphrey. The speech was warmly described as "a major concession" to the McCarthy point of view, and McCarthy state chairmen, among others, were urged to make appeals for party unity immediately after it. Some, without hearing or even seeing the speech, did just that. David Hoeh, for example, now busy with his own campaign for Congress, had his staff issue a favorable reaction for immediate release.

McCarthy received an advance text from Tom Finney, who had been acting ever since Chicago as an unofficial liaison man between McCarthy and the doves on Humphrey's staff. But McCarthy made no public comment on it, favorable or otherwise. In private, he told his friends that he considered Humphrey's new position no move at all, and saw no reason to change his oft-repeated stance that Humphrey could not expect his endorsement unless he made a "significant" move away from the President's position. He was strengthened in this attitude by a letter from Gerald Hill in California saying that his supporters there would be terribly let down if he did not hold out for a radical change in Vietnam policy.

The day after the Salt Lake City speech, McCarthy tried to reach Hill in his San Francisco law office to answer this letter by phone. Before he could get through, it was time for him to leave Washington for St. Louis, where, as part of his personal program for unwinding, he was due to report the World Series, with many folksy reminiscences of the Great Soo League of his youth, for *Life* magazine. He had jotted down on the back of the envelope Hill's letter had arrived in, the points he wanted to make to Hill, including the conditions he felt Humphrey would have to agree to before he could earn his endorsement. McCarthy asked Eller to telephone these points to Hill, and, later that day, reading from the notes, Eller did so. McCarthy considered the conversation a private exchange of viewpoints and thought no more about it.

It happened that the next weekend, October 5 and 6, the New Democratic Coalition, uniting the leaders of the Kennedy, McGovern, and McCarthy movements, held its first organizing meeting at the Dyckman Hotel in Minneapolis. Among the two hundred leaders from forty states who attended were three of the most important of those who had set out to look for a champion so many months before: Gerald Hill, Don Peterson of Wisconsin, and Allard Lowenstein. The dream of the NDC, which had sprung from the trauma of Chicago, was to forge a new Democratic Party which would not be dominated by Richard Daleys and John Connallys. It was a powerful and representative gathering of the effective left. Paul Schrade was there, and

so was Adam Walinsky. Don Green and Curtis Gans, of McCarthy's
national staff; Jim Bogle, Dave Martin, and Arthur Herzog, who had
run the McCarthy campaigns in the Indiana, Nebraska, and Oregon
primaries, respectively; Jack Gore, from Colorado, and David Hoeh;
Sarah Kovner, cochairman of the New York Committee for a Democratic Alternative; Sanford Gottlieb of SANE; Michael Harrington . . .
and Jerry Eller.

Eller's presence was a surprise. The Coalition's organizers were
trying hard to play down the personalities of the three liberal Presidential candidates. They had decided in advance that there was to be
no discussion of the endorsement or nonendorsement of a Presidential
candidate. They were already thinking further ahead than November 5.
It was a lively, optimistic meeting on that basis. Harrington put it
best: "After all, we picketed outside the Democratic Convention in
Los Angeles eight years ago. This year we picketed inside." A St.
Louis psychiatrist, taken aback at the left's propensity for controversy,
suggested the inclusion of a group-dynamics specialist to curtail the
stridency of future meetings. But much of the controversy, to be fair,
did not come from the prophets of the NDC, but was inspired by
Eller.

Before the Saturday afternoon meeting, Eller ran into Gerald Hill
and told him without preliminaries that "the Senator has no objection
to your revealing the exchange if any interested newspaper should ask
about it." Hill promptly and happily leaked what he understood to have
been McCarthy's conditions to two newspaper reporters—Robert Walters
of the *Washington Star* and Bernie Shellum of the *Minneapolis Tribune*.
Hubert Humphrey learned for the first time in their stories the four
conditions he would have to meet to warrant McCarthy's endorsement.
Walters' story, checked with Eller, was run under the headline: "Mc-
Carthy Sets Terms for Aid to Humphrey." McCarthy's demands, it said,
were that Humphrey

> 1. Publicly call for an immediate halt to all U.S. bombing of North
> Vietnam.
> 2. Endorse the concept of full elections in Vietnam, involving all
> elements engaged in the conflict there including the National Libera-
> tion Front, the political arm of the Vietcong.
> 3. Advocate broad reform of the country's selective-service laws,
> including provision for conscientious objection to specific wars, such as
> that being waged in Vietnam.
> 4. Support the efforts of those seeking to bring about full-scale
> structural and institutional reform of the Democratic Party . . .

Was this authorized? If so, it suggested that the gap between
the two Minnesotans would be almost impossible to close. It might
please McCarthy's followers in California, but for people like Tom
Finney it was disquieting. Was it just a leak to test the public reaction?
If so, it was a clumsy one. Its timing seriously embarrassed many of
McCarthy's friends at the NDC meeting. Hill, for instance, had to rebut
allegations that he made disclosure as part of a plan to further Mc-
Carthy's long-range political aims. Earl Craig, a Minneapolis Negro, and
one of the organizers of the event, stalked out of a press conference,
angrily railing against attempts to force the NDC "into a box" over personalities. McCarthy himself, pressed by reporters to confirm or deny his
conditions, characteristically did both. Asked about the story the *New
York Post* reported on Tuesday, October 8, McCarthy said, "I never
drew up a list, and if I had, the demands would not be four but probably
two and a half." But that same night, at a fundraising dinner for Paul
O'Dwyer, he came out with the very four conditions which Eller and Hill
had mentioned. He would withhold his endorsement, he said—he did not
mention Humphrey's name—unless the party promised to halt the bombing of North Vietnam, declared a willingness to accept a new government
in South Vietnam, charged the draft laws, and set about restructuring the
party. (Presumably, Eller had reminded McCarthy in the course of the
day of those pregnant jottings on the back of Hill's letter.)

It was still not clear which was the real Eugene McCarthy talking.
But, then, that had not been entirely clear all year. What was perhaps
understandable was that Hubert Humphrey, from that point on, never
budged an inch toward McCarthy's position. He was "not prone to
meeting conditions," he said.

The clumsy and amateurish way in which McCarthy allowed Eller
to leak his "conditions" to Hill placed him publicly in a more intransigent
position than he had perhaps intended. Before the month was out, he
had convinced himself that Humphrey would, after all, make a better
President than Nixon. The question seemed to him a finely balanced
one at the margin; it was Nixon's abrupt discovery of a "security gap,"
more than any positive virtue on Humphrey's part, that seems to have
convinced him. The pity was that when he did finally endorse Humphrey
on October 29, it was not only terribly late; to many of those who might
have been influenced by his judgment, his decision seemed in direct
contradiction to his famous "four conditions." It was neither a fulsome
nor a flattering endorsement at that. "The position of the Democratic
candidate," McCarthy said, "falls far short of what I think it should be."

But, he went on to say, confronted with the choice between Humphrey and Nixon, he felt that Humphrey had shown "a better understanding of our domestic needs" and seemed more likely to start "scaling down the arms race and reducing military tensions in the war." Unnecessarily, since whatever else he might be criticized for, he was not to be suspected of sycophancy, McCarthy felt he had to add that his statement was "in no way intended to reinstate me in the good graces of the Democratic Party leaders." And as if to prove it, he said he would not run for the Senate in 1970 and would not "seek" the Democratic nomination in 1972. The next day, in Los Angeles, he made his submission, or as close as he would come to one. "I'm voting for Humphrey," he said, "and I think you should suffer with me." The liberals had been suffering with him one way or another ever since the convention. It had been a tough period for McCarthy, but his own conduct had made it tougher for his supporters. The contempt for the conventional rules of political maneuver that had originally made his candidacy so refreshing now spoiled his every initiative. In mid-September, when asked by a reporter what he and his supporters could now do to further their cause, McCarthy had replied, "Perhaps we can set an example." Yet he had not been able to do even that effectively. He might have stood aloof on the issue of principle. Or he might have decided that in the end he would rather see Humphrey than Nixon in the White House. He could not bring himself to do either. He endorsed Humphrey, but he could not concentrate his attention long enough to exact the conditions to which he was entitled for his endorsement. And when he did bring himself to bestow a grudging accolade, he did not do it effectively enough to make a difference.

5

And Then There Was the One

"You know, Dick, a shift of only fourteen thousand votes, and we would have been the heroes, and they would have been the bums."

> —Leonard Hall, Richard Nixon's campaign manager in 1960, after the election of that year.

When Nixon came down to the ballroom of the Waldorf-Astoria hotel in New York, just after eleven-thirty a.m. on November 6 to make his victory statement, it was natural that he should choose the language of national unity. He produced the famous Presidential seal which his daughter had made for him in crewelwork. He said that the object of his Administration would be to build bridges. And he took as his motto the sign which he had seen held up to him during the campaign in Deshler, Ohio, imploring him to "Bring Us Together."

It sounded rather moving at the time, but the symbolism was treacherous, as it is apt to be. Thirteen-year-old Vicki Cole, the Methodist minister's daughter who had waved the sign, had not made it herself. Her own original thought, written on a banner that had been lost in the crush, had been more partisan. "LBJ Taught Us," she had written, "Vote Republican!" Worse, it also turned out that young Vicki had not been for Nixon at all. She thought both Nixon and Humphrey were "good men," but subsequently confessed shyly that her first favorite had been Robert Kennedy. Nixon had chosen to make Vicki Cole a symbol of the American people's aspirations for unity. In so far as one thirteen-year-old girl could fairly be taken as a symbol of anything, she was a far better symbol of something less anodyne: the fact that for a large majority of the American people, the result of the election was a foregone disappointment, because none of the nominated candidates was their first choice. Between them an assassin's bullets and the nominating convention system had seen to that.

The language of Nixon's speech was restrained, and he showed himself graceful toward his defeated opponent. "A great philosophy," he said,

> is never won without defeat. It is always won without fear. What is important is that a man or a woman engage in battle, be in the arena, participate, and I hope that all of those who supported Mr. Humphrey will continue their interest in politics. They will perhaps be in the other party; we may be contesting again. Who knows?

He gave no such invitation to the Wallace supporters. But he pledged that

> this will be an open Administration, open to new ideas, open to men and women of both parties, open to critics as well as to those who support us.

Proper obeisance was naturally made in the direction of various national figures: to Hubert Humphrey, for example, to ex-President Eisenhower, and to President Johnson. One figure, however, was conspicuously not mentioned: Nixon's own running mate.

That was understandable, too. For this was the moment for high thoughts and talk of national unity; and Governor Agnew had not only shown himself the specialist in below-the-belt politics: he had been specifically chosen to exploit national division, and his choice had been an integral part of Nixon's essential strategy. The election had not been won on promises of unity or reconciliation. It had been won by making a mathematical calculation that, as George Wallace had said, "there's more of us than there is of them." Early in the year, Richard Scammon had reminded Americans in danger of being bemused by the Kennedy and McCarthy campaigns that the majority of the electorate was made up of "the unyoung, the unblack, and the unpoor." Nixon had grasped that point. He had calculated that he could be elected without significant help from the poor, the foreign, the black, the angry, or the troubled, and he had been right. But it had been a desperately close thing.

In the end he had been elected by a smaller proportion of the voters—43.4 per cent—than any President since Woodrow Wilson in 1912. And this was not only because of the unavoidable competition of

George Wallace. It was also true that a shockingly high proportion of the electorate remained indifferent to all the issues and all the candidates' attempts to engage their interest, and just plain didn't bother to vote. Voter participation has historically been far less keen in the United States than in Europe, where 75-to-80-per-cent turnouts are normal. Since 1948, however, the percentage of Americans voting had been creeping up, and the average for the five elections between 1948 and 1964 had edged above 60 per cent. Nineteen sixty-eight, in spite of all the excitement and the earnest importance of the issues, marked a pause in that improvement, and the final figure for participation was almost exactly the running post–World War II average: a fraction over 60 per cent. That meant that out of one hundred and twenty million Americans of voting age, roughly forty-eight million did not vote.

What happened to the missing forty-eight million? About four million could not vote because they were technically aliens, or were in prisons or mental hospitals. Another seven million were either sick or disabled. Three million were away from home, and another three million claimed they could not leave their jobs to vote. (These figures are projected from a Gallup survey carried out after the election.) No less than five million were prevented from voting in a *national* election by *state or local* residence requirements—a little-noticed anomaly of American Federalism. That left at least twenty-six million who did not vote essentially because they didn't want to or didn't bother to. ("At least," because there is no way of knowing how many of those who claimed they were unable to vote because they were away from home or at work might have managed to vote in other circumstances or in another country.) Of the twenty-six million, fifteen million were registered voters, but either didn't like any of the candidates or were totally uninterested. Ten million could have registered but didn't. And another one million failed to obtain absentee ballots. In other words, those who either didn't bother or didn't choose to vote amounted to at least 36 per cent of those who did, and perhaps more. For all the tumult and the shouting, the campaigns had failed to get through at all to more than a quarter of those who were not prevented from voting.

Nixon's campaign strategy had been low-key from the start. He knew that a high vote favors the Democrats, and he had aimed at keeping the excitement low. In terms of the proportion who voted, he had been successful. Even so, he came closer to losing than would have seemed possible a month before the election. Up to the eve of polling, John Mitchell continued to make blandly confident noises about a five-million plurality. But he knew better than that. His own polls, by Opinion Research Corporation, were telling him by then that Nixon would be lucky to scrape together enough popular votes to carry the Electoral College, and everything depended on where they were.

Exactly as Walter de Vries had foretold in September, the voters made their minds up later than ever in 1968. Blocks of voters were still swinging turbulently from one candidate to another in the last few days and hours. The big gap between Nixon and Humphrey disappeared startlingly fast. On the Friday before the election, Louis Harris reported Nixon leading 40–37. On the Sunday, Gallup reported 42–40. On election day, Harris reported the election "too close to call," but with Humphrey a nose ahead. Cautiously, after a traumatic year, all the pollsters agreed that opinion was so fluid that prediction was unsafe, and perhaps meaningless.

There is more detailed evidence that an unusually large number of voters were making up their minds at the last minute. A post-election survey in the vital swing state of Illinois, for example, showed that although well over half the voters had made up their minds how they were going to go by the time the conventions were over, as usual, nearly 17 per cent of them said they were still undecided on November 1. It may have been coincidence that the news of the bombing halt finally came on October 31. In any case, the last few days of the campaign, always a climax, were a photo finish in 1968.

Half instinctively, the politicians responded to their sense that the national mood was moving and shifting under their feet. Struggling to keep their feet, they let loose with wild haymaker swings. In Cleveland, Humphrey declared that all the workers had got from the Republicans was "small doses of political and economic arsenic." In Beaumont, Texas, Wallace responded ferociously to his sinking poll figures. The funniest thing he had read in his paper, he said, was not "my long-term favorites Dick Tracy and Steve Canyon—but a new comic strip entitled the Gallup Poll." And in Fort Worth, Texas, Nixon told workers at the General Dynamics plant where the F-111 is made, "I am the one that stands for a stronger U.S., and Mr. Humphrey for a weaker U.S."

There was probably little any of them could have done in terms of rationally conceived action with calculable results to affect the vote at this stage. All they could do was lash themselves into final, frenetic paroxysms of exhortation, and hope for the best. But at least Humphrey stood to gain from this last-minute excitement. Nixon's position was more difficult in this respect. From a coldly rational standpoint, the best thing he could do was nothing. His best chance of winning the election now lay in keeping the poll down; the more people grew interested enough to go out and vote, the more likely it was that the Democratic total would rise. Theory and calculation urged that he should do nothing. Yet psychologically inaction was impossible for a man who had waited so long only to see the prize hovering tantalizingly close to his reach. So Nixon, like Humphrey, crammed on more sail, put out more flags, and sailed into a last blind attack with all his guns firing.

It was fitting that the last act was played out in California, the last destination of America, the place where Nixon's long climb off the canvas had begun, and where, too, the revolt against the war which had given the politics of 1968 their disastrous aspect for the Democrats had broken out. Proverbially most volatile of the states, California was now also one of the most finely balanced. Both candidates arrived there by way of Texas. Nixon made an unscheduled trip through Texas, starting on October 31, because it looked as though the Democrats' chances there had been saved at the last minute by a startling pair of eleventh-hour reconciliations. Two Sundays before the election, Humphrey had appeared at the giant Astrodome in Houston with Johnson. They were introduced by a yet more masterly showman, Frank Sinatra, but although there were some who maintained that a good deal of the ear-splitting enthusiasm was for Sinatra, the Republicans knew that the public anointing of Humphrey by the President at long last was a spectacular they could scarcely hope to match. One Republican who only watched the coronation from afar said afterward, "You could feel the emotion on that TV screen. I knew we'd lost Texas when I saw that."

Even more amazing to connoisseurs of Texas politics was the reconciliation of the two savagely opposed wings of the Texas Democratic party. Humphrey had actually shared a platform at the same time with Governor John Connally and Senator Ralph Yarborough, champions respectively of the conservative and liberal factions, and two men who had missed no opportunity for cutting lumps off one another for years. The danger that Texas might go Republican had, unbelievably, united them: it was a bit like a public reconciliation between the Kremlin and the Vatican. True, the conversation was stilted. Those who craned close enough heard the two warriors say no more than "Hi, Ralph!" "Hi, John!" Still, they had spoken, and the roof had not fallen in. United for the first time for many years, the Texas Democrats threw their titanic energies for once into fighting the Republicans, and not each other.

Nixon was not giving up so easily, though. The issue now seemed to turn on the Mexican-Americans of Texas, a community of some six hundred thousand, roughly half of them in the San Antonio area, and about four hundred thousand of whom could be expected to vote. In state and local elections, the Texas Republicans had been capturing a respectable proportion of the Mexican-American vote. But that was against conservative Democratic candidates. In a national election, they could be expected to go pretty solid for Humphrey, but it was worth a special effort for Nixon to cut that proportion down as much as he could.

He pulled out a very special effort indeed. It was hard for him to point to any solid record of achievement on behalf of Mexican-Americans; his campaign so far had done little more to attract brown than black Americans. But Nixon did his best. In San Antonio, before an audience of sixty-five hundred, he produced the Cuban couple who have been his and his wife's personal servants for some years: Mexican, Cuban, it's all the same thing. He claimed that both his daughters had studied Spanish. And he even eagerly pointed out that he and Pat had spent their honeymoon in New Mexico. In Lubbock, he promised to retain the oil depletion allowance, in Fort Worth he promised to keep building the F-111 there, and for space-industry workers in Houston and all over the state he said he would "keep America first in space." His pitch for the Mexican-Americans was particularly cunning in the manner in which it avoided antagonizing the white suburban vote. "They have not been rioting," Nixon said of the Mexican-Americans. "They have not been breaking the law." The black ghettos might be getting all the attention, but everyone knew it was "the wheel that squeaks that gets the grease." The silent Mexican-Americans were getting their squirt of grease now. But it was a little late. The degree of their interest in his campaign is suggested by the fact that not a brown face was to be seen in the San Antonio audience.

Nixon's refrain, as he stumped his way through Fort Worth, Lubbock, Austin, and El Paso on his way to the West Coast, was this: "If we take Texas, we've won. If the Democrats take Texas, they can't win, and they might cause a constitutional crisis." But in point of fact Texas was already gone, and Nixon could—just—afford to lose it. But he could not afford to lose California, where he arrived late on Saturday, November 2.

The Golden State was showing all its legendary volatility. According to the state poll, Nixon's lead had melted from fourteen points to a single point. That meant that California, like the nation, was too close to call. The Democrats there, who had scarcely dared to hope for survival, were in transports of optimism. Pat Brown was moved to call up Larry O'Brien over the weekend with an excited psychological prognosis. "I know that guy Nixon," he said. "I beat him in 1962, and he's going to blow it again."

Not if he could help it, he wasn't. Tight as the finish might be, Nixon did not mean to let the tension show. The nearest he came to it, very briefly, was on Monday, when he made an unscheduled stop at the campaign headquarters in Los Angeles. The very fact of an unscheduled stop in the well-ordered progress of Richard Nixon indicated a nuance of concern in itself. The aim in this case, sensibly enough, was to warm up the morale of those who would be helping to get out the vote the next day. The visit might not be a great headline maker, but it was obviously an improvement from the reporter's point of view on the scheduled plan of yet another period of "conferring in his hotel with aides."

In his headquarters, surrounded by an orderly and well-barbered posse of fifty or so campaign workers, Nixon stood on a chair and declared, "As we come down to the wire, I think the major issue in your final telephone calls that you should emphasize is the issue of peace." Descending from his perch, the candidate seemed a little preoccupied. He fell back on his usual small-talk resource for such occasions, but this time it went slightly astray. At one point, he could be seen imparting a good deal of football lore to a young man whom he apparently took for a local party worker. He was actually one of his traveling party, whom Nixon had momentarily failed to recognize, and who already felt he knew as much about pro football as he needed to know.

It may well be that this preoccupation owed something to the ordeal by television which was to round out the evening, and the campaign. Both the Republicans and the Democrats had booked time for four-hour telethons, to be put out from Los Angeles on the eve of the poll. Since the two shows all but overlapped—Humphrey's started half an hour earlier—serious or masochistic viewers, by switching from channel to channel, could get the closest thing to a direct confrontation between the two candidates that had been available all year. It was almost unanimously agreed that Humphrey came off the winner in that test, however he would do in the more important test the next day.

Nixon was not at his best. He seemed hampered by the format, which had him sitting formally and talking straight to camera for a large proportion of the time. He was introduced by the fat and lugubrious comedian Jackie Gleason, but the general tone was anything but spontaneous and was only lightened once, and that involuntarily, when Nixon angrily dismissed criticisms of Agnew as "political nut-cutting." The very first question put to him was whether he would pick Agnew if he had it to do over again. He said naturally he would choose him again, but he didn't look any too happy about it.

It was noticed that he took every opportunity to denigrate the bombing pause. On several occasions, both in the studio and talking to volunteers beforehand, he first praised Johnson faintly, then damned him by talking about the "tragic breakdown" of the talks. He spoke of "cities still being shelled by the enemy, hundreds of Americans still being killed, and thousands of tons of supplies coming down the Ho Chi Minh trail." It was obvious that he felt that the announcement of the bombing halt had hurt him, and that he was doing all he could to play it down.

Humphrey, on the other hand, was in top form. The motorcade he took with Senator Muskie through downtown Los Angeles that afternoon covered much the same ground as Robert Kennedy had covered in the summer, and evoked something like a repetition of the same electric excitement. In striking contrast to the Nixon crowds, the people who pressed in on the car in which Humphrey and Muskie stood waving through a hail of confetti and ticker tape were largely black- and brown-skinned. Their enthusiasm was such that the Secret Service men had to hang on to Humphrey's legs to stop him being hauled overboard in sheer enthusiasm. "I wish," one old lady shouted, "that I could vote for you a thousand times." It was an extravagant wish, but one which Democratic organizers in other cities would soon be doing their best to satisfy.

The Humphrey telethon had something of the same ebullience. The difference between Democrats and Republicans, when all else is said, often comes down to the fact that the Democrats have more fun. Humphrey had the advantage of appearing with the attractive Ed Muskie, and the two of them were soon swatting questions with the practiced coordination of a long-established tennis doubles team at the net.

They were backed up by a large turnout of the Hollywood aristocracy. Paul Newman, Joanne Woodward, Burt Lancaster, and Kirk Douglas were among those who manned the banks of telephones, and also occasionally asked questions. Edward G. Robinson read a patriotic recitation in his inimitable growl, and to cap it all Senator Ted Kennedy came up on film to eulogize Humphrey. It was a three-keyboard performance, with all the stops out. Strolling through the family compound in Hyannis Port, Kennedy recalled stopping outside his brother Bobby's house on election night in 1960 and playing with the children as they waited for the results to come through that would show that their big brother had beaten Nixon.

Some of the calls were answered by the stars, while others came straight through to the Vice-President, who was as usual not at a loss for words. On the Nixon telethon, questions were intercepted first by a hundred telephone girls, and then fed to the mighty football coach, Bud Wilkinson, who decided which ones should be lateraled to Nixon.

Nixon could not produce a genuine political happening, like the call Humphrey received from Senator McCarthy, who encouraged his supporters to vote for Humphrey far more warmly than he had done in his grudging official endorsement. An act of grace had been performed. It was perhaps too late to be what the theologians call efficacious grace.

Neither side passed up any expedient for tugging at the voters' heartstrings. After the telethon, the Democrats showed the attractive, rambling documentary Joe Napolitan had commissioned about the life of Humphrey. It included a fairly breathtaking section in which Humphrey played with one of his grandchildren, an adorably pretty child who happens to be mentally retarded, and reflected tearfully that through this affliction he had learned the power of human love.

Nixon struck back at the viewers' emotions by producing Ike's grandson David at the end of his telethon. "I think," said Bud Wilkinson archly, "that you have a message for us?" And indeed David had, from the grand old general, who to nobody's surprise sent his good wishes to his former Vice-President, and implored the voters to save the country by voting Republican.

After his telethon, Nixon climbed aboard his Boeing 727 and sped for New York, spending most of the flight asleep. The Humphrey entourage, however, decided to relax rather more boisterously before taking the traditional road to the candidate's home town. Politicians, journalists, Hollywood figures, photographers, and a remarkable cross section of hangers-on such as only Los Angeles could have produced repaired to the rambling home of Mr. Lloyd Hand in an expensive-looking section hard by the Sunset Strip. Mr. Hand, who had been a Humphrey fundraiser, had provided a marquee, a band, and a generous flow of refreshments. Exhilarated by the feeling that they might have captured California—a feeling which grew more boisterous as the night wore on—the Democrats began to celebrate with great abandon, and the accompanying press, apparently Democrats to a man, joined in. It was by any standards a very good party indeed, good enough for the candidate to feel moved to perform a very creditable Charleston. But when the plane took off for Minnesota in the small hours, the reaction started to set in. As the plane flew over the Rocky Mountains, very few people found themselves able to sleep. Everyone was in a rather odd mood compounded about equally of exhaustion, liquor, and—since they were mostly Democrats—a feeling that some kind of disaster was about to overtake them.

One of the women reporters on board became suddenly overcome with conscience because she had made no arrangements to cast her vote. She began to wonder, desperately, whether she could possibly get home to New York in time to do so. It appears, from the recollections of those on board, that a large number of people became emotionally involved in this crisis, and it was decided that the best thing to do would be to approach Fritz Mondale when they got to Minneapolis. Senator Mondale, as a campaign manager, was often known to have a spare airplane, and might be able to find one for this deserving cause.

When the party arrived at the Minneapolis–St. Paul airport at seven-thirty on a chilly winter morning, several people conducted the lady through the sleet over to Senator Mondale, who was deep in conversation with a local political veteran. The problem was explained to him, and of course he sympathized. But he simply did not have a spare airplane. In this crisis, the Minneapolis veteran stepped forward. "Why," he asked, "does the lady have to go to New York? We'll be happy to vote her in the Sixth Ward." It was not, however, quite as easy as that. The veteran conducted the party to the Sixth Ward, and explained the problem to the people in charge. But the ward, as it happened, was one of those which had been taken over by the upright McCarthyite liberals in the springtime revolution. Clean-cut to the last, they would not hear of even so minor a voting irregularity. After some negotiating, a compromise was struck: the lady and a professional colleague who had accompanied her could strike their blow by doing an hour's telephone canvassing. They sat down, and were given careful instructions by the young McCarthyites. . . .

But the saga of She Who Must Vote, though perhaps a portent of the possibilities of creative fusion between the old pros and the new politicians, was hardly enough to stop the defeatist mood now galloping through the Humphrey retinue. "It's just as well," growled Orville Freeman, "that we had the celebration party last night!"

The machinery was in motion, and there was, as far as the principals were concerned, only one more thing to be done. Each of the candidates could cast one pebble into the ocean on his own behalf, and Humphrey drove out of Minneapolis, even past his own home at Waverly, to Maryville, a tiny hamlet on the edge of the prairie, to cast his. Efficiently and unsentimentally, Nixon had already arranged for an absentee ballot. Wallace was fighting his way through the crowd outside the shiny glass courthouse he had himself been instrumental in bringing to Clayton. In the three corners of the country, the three seconds were doing the same: Agnew from his exquisite eighteenth-century mansion in Annapolis, LeMay in California, and Muskie in Maine.

Anyone could see that the bird of fortune had flown from Wallace's side by now. For the last four weeks of the campaign there was an unmistakable smell of failure about him, and if there is one thing Americans are frightened by, it is failure. It wasn't only the polls. He found it oddly hard to cope with a new style in heckling he was meeting. He had known how to use the old, frontal heckling. He used to drive it along to build up the tension, until violence became all but inevitable, knowing that on television it would come over as confirmation of his thesis that it was the students who were threatening the peace of America. But instead of trying to shout him down with cries of *Sieg heil!* the kids, especially in California, began to do what they should have done all along: to laugh at him. They shouted, *"Sieg heil,* y'all!" and laughed. What got on his nerves most of all was the boys and girls with long hair pretending to be on his side.

At Madison Square Garden, on his last visit to New York, two weeks before polling day, he managed to get something of the old atmosphere. Beefy industrial workers could be seen spitting in the eyes of anyone who looked hostile or neutral. One small, quite young man with an Eastern European accent, perhaps a postwar refugee from Hungary or Poland, walked up to a neatly dressed young girl wearing a Humphrey button, pulled out his wallet, waved it insanely in front of her face, and shouted, "I can buy tresh like you for twen'y dollars!" But the sheer frenzy of Wallace's meetings in the North was beginning to tell against him. Here and there busloads of decent-looking industrial workers and off-duty policemen could be seen sitting stolidly through his rallies in New York and other Northern cities. It was getting increasingly hard to ignore the proportion of his adherents, at least in the Northeast, who were drawn from groups who are without honor in their own country: the embittered, the obsessive racists, the failed, the frustrated, and the tough kids looking for a safe fight.

Back home, it was different. Yet even in Montgomery, the hall that

had been hired for the victory celebration was half empty by the time
Wallace got there. He made one attempt, just before midnight on election night, to claim, "The electoral process is not over, I think everyone
understands that," a broad hint that the real period of negotiation was
about to begin. But from the very earliest results it began to be clear
that, however well he had done in the Deep South, Wallace had been
disappointed in the border states, and substantially rejected by his clients
in the North. He still might be right. The election might yet be deadlocked. But if so, it was clear by eight o'clock, even, on election night,
that it would be because the two major candidates were exceptionally
close, not because Wallace had done particularly well.

And by that time, there was nothing either of them could do about
it either. The jury of seventy million plus had retired to consider its
verdict, and there was nothing left but to wait. Humphrey and Nixon
settled themselves for the ordeal according to their different natures.
Humphrey chose to suffer gregariously among his family and friends;
Nixon alone, in the fatuous surroundings appropriate to one who—even
if he were to stumble once again on the threshold of the White House—
had nevertheless Made It. He had caused two suites to be rented, one for
himself and one for his wife and family, in the towers of the Waldorf-
Astoria, a somewhat characterless but extremely expensive type of accommodation commended perhaps by the fact that two famous Republicans before him had actually chosen to live there: Douglas MacArthur
and Herbert Hoover. Their omens might be considered mixed.

Hubert Humphrey got some badly needed sleep in the afternoon at
his own house on the lake at Waverly, and then drove into town to have
dinner with Dwayne Andreas at his house on the banks of the more
fashionable Lake Minnetonka. (In Minneapolis a man's standing is
judged by how far the lake he fishes on is from the center of town.) One
detail seemed perfectly to exemplify the effort of Humphrey's world to
reconcile homeliness with sudden prosperity. The menu of the Andreases'
dinner party—it was carefully relayed to the waiting reporters at Robert
Short's Leamington Hotel—was full of folksy touches, such as "home-
made apple pie." But it was not made by Mom; it was delivered by Town
and Country Caterers, Inc.

While Humphrey was enjoying a cautious highball with the Andreases and his three grown-up children, Nixon was soaking in the
luxurious bathtub of his suite at the Waldorf, and Mrs. Nixon, Tricia,
and Julie were down the hall in another suite. He was not to see
them until the night was almost over. Humphrey went in, after dinner, to

the Leamington, to watch his fate on three television sets tuned to each of the three networks. Nixon ordered his staff to switch off the television and got his information—reports would be the better word— over the telephone from carefully chosen subordinates in key cities and even precincts.

Nixon was probably wise not to subject his nerves to the last unnecessary strain of the brilliantly staged drama which the networks serve up on election night. There is, of course, an element of hokum in these performances. There is the hot breath of commercial competition to be the first with a prediction, even if it turns out to be premature. There is some doubt about the reportorial value of those early figures, fragmentary and sometimes inconsistent. What, for example, does it mean to say that a computer's "national estimate" with 2 per cent of the vote in is that Nixon will get 43 per cent of the vote, Humphrey 35, and Wallace 22? Either it means that this is too small a sample for the computer to make a valid prediction from, or it means that the computer is badly programed. The commentators, too, add their characteristic touch as entertainers: there is the coyness of David Brinkley, saying that "if it went into the Electoral College, no one would understand it, not even me." And there is the lump in Theodore H. White's throat as he says how "prideful" he feels to be able to walk across Park and Fifth Avenues without hearing gunfire on election morning. But one should not be unreasonable; a man cannot be expected to talk sense on camera for fifteen hours. There is another, more important sense in which the tele-drama of election night is spurious: it is the voters who have buried the evidence of their decision during the day, and the order in which the computers exhume the fragments of it may be deceptive.

But having said all that, there was real suspense on the night of November 5, 1968. It was at about ten past eleven, Minneapolis time— ten past midnight in New York—when CBS reported that Humphrey had carried New York, and not just carried it, but swept it by a margin that turned out to be half a million votes. An hour earlier, when CBS predicted that he would take the state, Humphrey had said "By golly, we might do it!" and for the next five hours the result was in real doubt.

Just before midnight, Senator Mondale agreed to come down to the press room in the basement of the Leamington, and he looked happy. "We still have strong hopes that the Vice-President will receive a majority of the Electoral College votes," he said, "but it's too early to predict that in the light of the fact that the returns from the West Coast are just beginning to come in." The first returns from California would be from the San Francisco Bay area, habitually more liberal than the South, and a lead there meant little. Still, Mondale could fairly say, "We are encouraged by the fact that at least at this point the Vice-President is ahead in California, he's ahead in Texas, and we've carried Pennsylvania, and we carried the state of New York by a remarkable margin, and wherever we look we are doing at least as well—in many places far better—than many have predicted."

That was fair comment. Larry O'Brien appeared about the same time, beaming like a large and happy ginger cat, and Humphrey was seen briefly by the watchers in the Leamington, flecked with snow and trying hard to hide the hope not even he had expected to feel so solidly at this stage.

Richard Nixon was completely the master of his feelings in his suite at the Waldorf. They were not untinged with doubt. He ordered his staff —John Mitchell, Bob Haldeman, the faithful valet Dwight Chapin, his old friends Bob Finch and Murray Chotiner moved in and out—to make calls, checking every development with their own sources, bypassing the ups and downs of the networks. At eleven thirty-five, New York time, it was decided to bluff the press—why, it is hard to say, since the matter was out of the press's hands now. Herb Klein, poker-faced, went down and walked into the vast press room. "We still think we can win by three to five million," he shouted, "but it looks closer to three million at this point." It looked nothing of the kind. At midnight, New York time, Humphrey went ahead of Nixon for the first time, with 36 per cent of the vote counted: Humphrey 42 per cent, Nixon 41 per cent, Wallace 17 per cent. Half an hour later, with half the votes counted, according to NBC, Humphrey was 600,000 ahead in the popular vote and closing up in electoral votes, so far as could be calculated. About that time, in the front row of the crowded Leamington press room, a group of reporters crowded round John Reilly to ask him about possible appointments as Secretary of State and Secretary of Defense. Brutally, someone called from in front of the television set, "It's slipping!" and the conversation was never finished. A few minutes later Nixon walked along the hall to his wife and daughters' suite and reassured them that "it all depends on California, but California's all right."

The calculation had become a little more complicated than that. Nixon's original equations had not been solved. Of his fourteen states, three of the richest in electoral votes—New York, Pennsylvania, and Michigan, with 93 votes among them—were gone already, and Texas, with another 25, was to go in the end. Bill Connell's list of estimates, compiled almost at Humphrey's darkest hour, was to prove more durable: of the thirteen states Connell listed as "probable for Humphrey," he was to lose only New Jersey, and he also picked up three off Connell's list of "real possibilities": Washington, Maryland, and West Virginia.

But in the small hours the arithmetic of victory narrowed down to a handful of states: to seven, in particular: California (with 40 electoral votes), Illinois (29), Ohio (26), Texas (25), New Jersey (17), Missouri (12), and Agnew's Maryland (10). If Nixon could win the three biggest of those seven states—California, Illinois, and Ohio—then he was impregnable. If he lost California, he might be vulnerable to certain combinations of other states; and even if he won California, he could be beaten if he lost the next two in size, Illinois and Ohio.

In Ohio, the Republicans were doing a lot less well than they had hoped all night. Partly this was because Cleveland delivered an enormous vote to Humphrey, much of it black. And Jack Gilligan was locked in a desperately close race with William Saxbe, the Republican State Attorney-General, for the Senate. Gilligan lost in the end, but the attractiveness of his personality and the enthusiasm of his workers had much to do with slicing back Nixon's lead to 106,000—in a state where Wallace won 460,000 votes.

Gradually it became plain that California was indeed safe, as Nixon had told Pat. Illinois, meanwhile, offered what would have been comic relief if the whole fate of the election had not turned on it. Settling into his chair for the night at the Waldorf, Nixon had specially instructed his people to watch Illinois like hawks. It was not simply that he had lived for eight years with the bitter question whether he had been robbed of the Presidency by Richard Daley's manipulation of the Illinois vote. There was specific reason to watch Illinois carefully again this time.

The Republicans had organized a special poll-watching drive in Chicago, called Operation Eagle Eye, to cut voting fraud in Daley's Cook County to a minimum. Even so, they were not able to do more than reduce the scale of the shenanigans. In the Twenty-Fourth Ward in the West Side ghetto, columnist Robert Novak, disguised as a poll-watcher, reported that Democratic election judges were actually telling voters to pull the Democratic lever under the eyes of silent "Republican" judges. For days before the election, the Chicago papers were full of tales of heavy crops of bums and derelicts being registered in West Side flophouses to provide the names for a fine Democratic turnover. And suspicion became certainty in the press rooms at the Leamington and the

Waldorf when it was learned that "computer breakdowns" and "disputed vote counts" were holding the Illinois decision back. Veteran reporters could be heard explaining to the green, the trusting, or the foreign how the game was played in Illinois: how both the iron Mayor and his Republican enemies downstate would "hold back" hundreds of precincts in an effort to finesse each other to give a hint of the size of the total they had to beat; how they would release a few precincts as bait to lure the other man into giving away some of his; and how the Mayor's "river wards," on the twilight perimeter of the Loop, could usually win the day if Daley was in earnest.

For hours in the middle of the night, Illinois hung in doubt. There came a moment, indeed, when Humphrey had only to win Illinois to deny Nixon 270 votes in the electoral college, the margin of victory. But the Mayor was not trying as hard in 1968 as he had tried in 1960. That, at least, was what knowledgeable people in the Humphrey organization said afterward. They pointed to his failure to appoint the strongest possible candidates to help the ticket, and to his apparently much greater efforts on behalf of local candidates than for the national Democratic ticket. Who can search the heart of Richard Joseph Daley? But there were those who thought that, ironically, the Mayor's efforts on election night might have been inhibited by his irritation on the previous Saturday, when Humphrey came to his city, kept his contact with the Mayor to a minimum, and then had the audacity to say, "Chicago last August was filled with pain."

However that may be, it all turned in the end on Illinois again, and Illinois went for Nixon by 140,000 votes. By three o'clock in the morning, New York time, Richard Nixon was able to savor a little private ritual. It was precisely the eighth anniversary of his defeat. He called his closest helpers into his room—Mitchell, Chotiner, Finch—and allowed himself to voice the unspoken hope, now established fact. Ohio was safe. California was safe. Illinois was safe too. *Quod erat demonstrandum.* The equation had turned out to contain more variables than when first drawn up on those yellow legal pads; but it had worked out just the same. The White House was safe. Nixon allowed himself to play with the thought of an immediate announcement, then prudently allowed himself to be talked out of it. He would wait for Humphrey's concession, which came in a telephone call the next morning a quarter of an hour before it was given publicly. But a few minutes after three o'clock, Nixon allowed himself to savor the luxury of belief. This time, he had won.

That is what happened on election night. But what really happened on election day? The Democratic candidate was beaten for the Presidency. But the Democratic Party as such did not fall apart, was not routed, was not even badly scathed by comparison with most of the forecasts that had been made. The Republicans gained five state governorships. (Taking into account the fact that Governor Agnew would be replaced by a Democrat, since the Maryland legislature, which would choose his successor, was Democrat-controlled, the net Republican gain would be four governors.) They would also gain five seats in the Senate, taking their strength there to the highest point since 1956. But in the House, where they had seriously hoped to win control, they gained only 4 seats out of 435, which left them 26 seats short of control.

The Democratic coalition—the South, the big-city bosses, the Negroes, the unions, and the intellectuals—was widely supposed to be on the verge of falling apart. Leaving aside the question whether one big city boss did or did not cost him the election, Humphrey in the end lost only one of these five elements of the party in a total and catastrophic sense: the South. He carried only one Southern state—Texas—and that by a hair's breadth. This was far the worst showing in terms of states that a Democratic candidate had made in the South since Reconstruction: not even Alfred E. Smith in 1928, "wet" as he was, did so poorly. Even so, Humphrey's showing in the South was not quite so catastrophic as it might seem, if one looked toward the future. In both the Carolinas, for example, he ran only two percentage points behind Wallace, in each case mainly thanks to the newly registered Negro vote in those states.

We have seen how the total vote in 1968 was lower than had been generally expected. It would have been lower still but for the fact that about one million voters, new since 1964, took part in Texas, Alabama, Mississippi, and Louisiana. This was the first fruit of the 1965 Voting Rights Act, and of the elimination of the poll tax in Texas, and of the vigorous registration drives that Negroes and Mexican-Americans organized to persuade their people to take advantage of their new practical freedom to vote. Negro registration in the South, increasing dramatically, produced a certain offsetting degree of backlash registration among whites. But the over-all effect was clear-cut.

In Texas, relieved at last of the poll tax, just over three million people cast their votes for President—*437,422 more than in 1964!* The increase, concentrated among Mexican-Americans and Negroes, was more than enough to give Hubert Humphrey the state.

More Negroes came out to vote than in any previous year. Their turnout, nationally, was up by about 7 per cent. They had been activated by the threat of Wallace, and also caught up in the registration efforts of the unions. And they were pretty thoroughly of one mind: a black vote for Nixon was almost as rare as a black face at a Nixon meeting. Nationally, 88 per cent of Negroes voted for Humphrey and 12 per cent for Nixon. True, it was more than Goldwater had received; but then Goldwater could be considered something of a freak. Nixon in 1960 had won 32 per cent of the Negro vote.

The tendency was even more dramatically clear in certain cities. In Houston, for example, there were about 58,000 Negro votes for Humphrey, and about 800 for Nixon. In the 109th Precinct there, Humphrey got 1061 votes; Nixon and Wallace got 4 each. In the 169th, Humphrey got 1286, Nixon 11, and Wallace none. "You'd think," said Republican Congressman George Bush sadly, "that there would have been more people just come in there and make a mistake!" But making all allowance for block voting habits and local black bosses, it seems that the black voters were just not in a mood for mistakes.

The Mexican-American vote went the same way. In eighteen Mexican-American precincts of San Antonio, the Humphrey vote was over 95 per cent.

All over the country, the minority groups Nixon had planned to do without struck back at him. They were very largely responsible by themselves for the fact that the Republican ticket carried no big cities —a fact pregnant with meaning for a future in which the cities must be any President's most urgent domestic problem. Nowhere was the pattern plainer than in Philadelphia, where Nixon's hopes of winning Pennsylvania, one of his fourteen states, must turn. His refusal to campaign for Negro votes wrecked his hopes of winning the state.

A Democratic candidate for the Presidency needs to come out of Philadelphia with a margin of a quarter of a million votes to win the state. Humphrey got 271,000. Something like 150,000 of those came from the black wards. One aide of Congressman Bill Green admitted later that they had been worried. "We didn't know whether the Democratic organization had the muscle to get out the Negro vote. But they came out in droves."

Muscle, it must be said, was vigorously wielded in Philadelphia.

Apart from any other reasons for not wanting a Republican in the White House, that fine Irishman Mayor Tate is said to have cherished the hope of serving his country as Ambassador to Dublin. Tate's friends in the labor unions got busy: some ten thousand union men, some paid, some volunteers, took the day off to work as poll-watchers and the like. In Philadelphia, the "watching" is sometimes a little partisan, which may account for the fact that twenty-four voting machines were found to have counted votes before polling day. A clean-ballot organization had fifty attorneys out with walkie-talkies touring the city, but they could hardly have kept an eye on all Tate's soldiers. By the end of the day, a bundle of complaints had been filed about electioneering "too near the polling booth" (within ten feet!) and seven out of ten voting machines in the 65th Ward were found to have been "adjusted." Nobody saw much sign of Billy Meehan's Republicans.

The black voters served the old Democratic coalition more loyally than ever. White working-class voters did not stay quite so well in line. Humphrey's recovery was due to the return of the errant workers who had flirted with Wallace, no doubt; but not all the footloose ones came home. Wallace received nationally some 15 to 18 per cent of the union members' votes. Perhaps a third of those were habitual Republican voters. If so, the leak to Wallace was substantial, though not catastrophic, as the Democrats and the union leaders had feared in September. Wallace's vote collapsed fast, as voters came closer to the realities of election day. In Michigan, Wallace had stood at 16 per cent of the statewide vote early in October. By the day before polling, the *Detroit News* poll reported that his strength had slipped to 11 per cent, and on the day he got 10 per cent. Gus Scholle, head of the Michigan AFL-CIO, did not even bother to wait for the votes to be fully counted before boasting, "We pulled the state for the Democrats!" and no one saw any reason to disagree.

As for Richard J. Daley, Mayor, he kept his own counsel. And in the meantime "the unyoung, the unblack, and the unpoor" had been enough—just enough—to elect an un-Democrat.

6

A Great Day
for Key Biscayne

"Mr. Nixon lacked the self-awareness which intellect produces. . . . His reason for running . . . was the hope of his own success, and he believed success was enough because nobody had ever told him otherwise."

—Mark Harris, *Mark the Glove Boy, or The Last Days of Richard Nixon* (an account of the 1962 California gubernatorial race)

Key Biscayne is a narrow island about two miles long, lying about a mile and a half off the tip of Miami Beach. It was once a coconut plantation, and it used to belong to a wealthy family who thought they might turn it into a nature reserve. However, showing good business sense, they compromised and made half the island into a nature reserve, selling off the rest very profitably to developers, who are busily erecting hotels, little shops, and concrete blocks of holiday apartments. It has been for some time Mr. Nixon's favorite part of America—or at least the part that he finds most relaxing and congenial—and once his victory had become clear, he wasted as little time as possible getting there. On the evening of November 6, he flew down to Key Biscayne from New York, pausing briefly in Washington to pay his respects to Dwight Eisenhower in the hospital. On arriving, he drove straight to the six-room house on Biscayne Bay which he had rented from Senator George Smathers and went to sleep for nine hours.

For seventeen years, since he went there to recuperate from his bitter struggle with Helen Gahagan Douglas, visits to Key Biscayne have punctuated the stages of Nixon's career. (As the new Administration got under way, Key Biscayne found itself designated as the location of the "winter White House." It was on the way to becoming a kind of lackluster Hyannis Port.) It is quite a pleasant place: its being under development, rather than developed, means that the palms have been smashed down only in the commercial area, and although the foundations of hundreds of buildings have been laid, not many have been built. It is still possible to walk along the long white beaches and pass only two or three people on the journey from one end of the island to the other. But it is well on the way to its natural fulfillment as a Miami resort of the expensive but rather staid variety: a place for retired soft-drink executives to buy apartments, a place to fish and swim and go to bed early. There will not be vast white hotels like those that crowd Miami Beach's sandless shore. There won't be forty-piece orchestras and Sammy Davis, Jr., in ornate ballrooms. There won't be call girls, and Jewish delicatessens, and cut-rate retirement homes at the cheap end of town. There won't be a cheap end of town.

A night out in Key Biscayne is naturally a somewhat limited affair: dinner at the Jamaica Inn, followed, perhaps, by a few drinks at the Royal Biscayne Hotel. Nixon used the Jamaica a good deal when he was a private citizen, and he was dining there after the 1960 election when he got the call saying that Jack Kennedy would like to arrange a meeting with him. The Jamaica has elderly waitresses in "authentic" Elizabethan serving-wench gear, and there is a bar done in the Olde Englysshe style —which is to say, heavily laden with pewter mugs. The Royal Biscayne is liberally decorated with the British coat of arms, and in the dimly lit bar a cocktail pianist raises unfailing laughter with mildly risqué jokes. (Sample: the one about the priest who tried to jump on a donkey but missed and fell down a well—because he didn't know his ass from a hole in the ground.) It is not very exciting, but it is a good place to go to escape from the sophisticates of New York and the right-wing supermoralists of the West. It is full of sober sensible Americans, who, like Nixon himself, have made a bit of money.

Nixon's purpose in departing for Florida was not, as campaign manager John Mitchell put it, to escape from anything—but simply to "soak up the sun and clear from his mind the campaign cobwebs." The craving for sunlight was understandable, since there seemed to be very little brightness about New York or Washington in the aftermath of so indecisive an election. The air was full of heavily conciliatory remarks by Democrats, as maniacally determined to be "good losers" as the English after a cricket match. It was a rather unreal atmosphere, in which one of the few genuine responses was the elegant sourness of Eugene McCarthy in Washington: "It is a day for visiting the sick and burying the dead. It's gray everywhere—all over the land."

But Nixon in Florida had no need to worry about McCarthy's cracks. On the morning of November 7, he awoke, much refreshed, and put in a call to Hubert Humphrey in Washington. Its purpose, which was successful, was to invite Humphrey to a meeting, a symbolic reconciliation, of the kind Jack Kennedy had extended to him. That done, Nixon spent most of the day lounging around in the spacious yard of the house next to Smathers', which is owned by Nixon's—and Smathers'— good friend Charles Gregory ("Bebe") Rebozo. What sort of men are these that the President-elect chooses to celebrate with? What is this Florida milieu that means so much to him?

George Smathers, the man who introduced Nixon to Florida, could hardly be described at this stage as an attractive political figure, having for some time combined savagely McCarthyite anti-Communism with opposition to civil rights and stanch friendship for such Latin American dictators as the bloodthirsty Rafael Trujillo. He started his career as a liberal Democrat under the aegis of Florida's Senator Claude Pepper, then betrayed Pepper by running against him as the candidate of conservative Florida business interests, notably the duPont group. Despite their nominal party difference, Nixon and Smathers clearly decided, as freshmen Senators, that they found each other congenial. The connection prospered during the fifties and did not weaken noticeably during the sixties, when Smathers' reputation began to grow somewhat odorous. (Gorgeous George, as he is sometimes called, was rather frequently discovered pulling lucrative chestnuts out of the fire for Floridian business interests. A notable coup was his part in writing special legislation in 1962 which enabled the duPont family to escape income tax when antitrust laws compelled them to sell their three-and-a-half-billion-dollar holding in General Motors. Mrs. Jessie duPont of Florida and her brother Ed Ball, a long-time Smathers backer, owned stock in E. I. duPont de Nemours and in G.M. worth together about two hundred and fifty million dollars. And he also managed to get involved in the Bobby Baker affair. During the inquiry, it emerged that Smathers and his legislative assistant, Scott I. Peek, had been in a land deal at Cape Canaveral with Baker. After some confusing discussion of the amounts involved, Smathers simply declared that his memory of the affair had collapsed.) Smathers' continued closeness to Nixon sorted ill with Nixon's own tight standards of conduct and frequent demands for the greatest of purity in Washington

—just as Smathers' intimacy with President Kennedy sorted ill with his virulent opposition to most of Kennedy's liberal programs. It is curious that a man like Smathers, a conservative demagogue and wheeler-dealer, can be the intimate of a liberal Democrat and of a Republican puritan —both Presidents of the United States.

It was Smathers who introduced Nixon to Bebe Rebozo. In detail, he arranged for Rebozo, his friend since schooldays, to act as host for Nixon on the vacation after his campaign against Helen Gahagan Douglas. Rebozo, who appears to be a withdrawn but kind and considerate man, looked after the weary Nixon like a mother hen. "I guess we just hit it off," Rebozo says now. The friendship that resulted made Nixon a full member of the Rebozo-Smathers Florida set—and a limited participant in their business deals. Leaving aside some of the activities of the flamboyant Smathers, there is nothing sinister about this group—it is just that their *ambiance* is one of Florida real-estate dealing, not perhaps the most engaging aspect of American life.

Rebozo, who traveled a good deal with Nixon during the 1968 campaign, is almost certainly Nixon's closest friend outside his strictly political world—and maybe that qualification is unnecessary. (He sat with the Nixon family in Los Angeles in 1960, watching the returns come in.) He was born in the same year as Nixon, also to a poor family, and had the same experience of hard and early work: he started on a paper route at ten and had a period as one of Pan American's first stewards. He is now reckoned a millionaire, having come up via eighty hours' work a week and a series of deals in service stations, finance companies, and land speculation on the sandy keys south of Miami Beach. He is not one of the old rich or even the super-rich; he is neither a great buccaneer nor a great creator. He is simply a diligent, fortunate man whose success is part of the Florida boom and the superlatively comfortable environment that Florida provides for the business operator, if not for other social types, among its citizens. Rebozo, indeed, is Nixonian Man almost to the last detail. (In loyalty to his old friend Smathers, he remained a registered Democrat until 1968. However, as Smathers has now retired from the Senate—and presumably does not need Bebe's vote in the primary—Rebozo says he will re-register as a Republican.) He is president of the bank in Key Biscayne and is building a shopping center there with finance provided largely by the Federal Small Business Administration, which is a use of corrupting Federal money with which his friend Richard Nixon presumably finds no ideological fault.

Nixon's interest in the commercial future of Key Biscayne and its environs extends over some years. He has owned several pieces of the action, the most important one being in Fisher Island, an undeveloped triangle of 220 acres, north of Key Biscayne and just 300 yards south of Miami Beach. Gar Wood, the speedboat racer, sold 195 acres of the island to a Rebozo syndicate for $1,950,000 in 1958, and it was a little later that Nixon was brought into the syndicate—shortly after his 1960 defeat, almost certainly. The holding was scarcely known of until October 10, 1968, when all three Presidential candidates published their net worth, and $401,382 of Nixon's $515,830 (Hubert Humphrey recorded $281,423 net worth and George Wallace $77,000) was put down as "undeveloped land in Florida," which was almost entirely his share in Fisher Island. Rebozo said he had urged Nixon to buy into the syndicate in 1958 but that Nixon refused at the time, only beginning to do so when he was a private citizen. Oddly, Rebozo could not remember whether he had sold Nixon some of his own shares in Fisher Island, Inc., or whether a new issue had been made. In any case, it seemed clear that a special effort had been made to bring Nixon in. Along with Rebozo, Nixon's companions in the enterprise included Sloan McCrea, a lifelong friend of Smathers'; Hoke T. Maroon, a banker and treasurer of Smathers' first Senatorial campaign; R. B. (Bun) Gautier, a former state senator; Rebozo's lawyer; and Rebozo's sister. No matter how you examine them, they do not look like a team of public benefactors.

Rebozo said that Nixon had not invested "anything like" $400,000 but that his shares might have risen to that value. Indeed, the speed at which such land can gain in value was shown by the fact that the syndicate nearly managed to sell Fisher Island to the city of Miami for $5,750,000—but, although Mayor Elliott Roosevelt was in favor of the deal, it fell through.

In the end, the value of Fisher Island will depend on the building of a causeway to link it to the mainland and thus allow hotel and apartment development to go forward. So far, the Dade County authorities have refused permission, although Rebozo says confidently that the apotheosis of Fisher Island is only "a matter of time." The danger for Nixon, clearly, will be if permission should be granted during his term in the White House: it would be difficult to prevent cynical people, and Democrats, from saying that "the county doesn't want to offend the President." Reflected glory, even some business fallout for the Miami islands, is one thing. But a new causeway would be too much of a Great Day for Key Biscayne. (Indeed, the business fallout was soon to become certain: shortly after the election Nixon bought the Smathers house, which he had previously leased, and one next to it on Bay Lane. He paid $127,000 to a rich Cuban named Manuel Arca for the second house, and about the same to Smathers for the first. On January 1, 1969, Key Biscayne real-estate dealer Don Berg raised the price of his lots by twenty per cent.)

It will be surprising if the handsome, discreet Rebozo does not remain close to Nixon throughout the new President's reign. Certainly that was how it started off, with the President-elect giving his very first press conferences under the palms in Rebozo's ample back yard. It was here that rather grisly ritual was announced: the meeting with the defeated candidate. It was to occur next day, and Humphrey was to come to Florida to meet Nixon. (In 1960, it had been the other way around: the victorious Kennedy journeyed to Key Biscayne to meet Nixon. But the arrangement apparently suited Humphrey, who was on his way to vacation in the Virgin Islands.)

On November 8, Nixon set off in a motorcade from Key Biscayne to Opa Locka Coast Guard station, just north of Miami, where an Air Force Convair disgorged a surprisingly large party: Hubert Humphrey, Mrs. Muriel Humphrey, their daughter and her husband, and the Humphrey sons, Hubert III and Robert, with their wives. Then there were Senator Edmund Muskie and his wife, with four young Muskies. They all looked fairly unhappy about it except the imperturbable Muskie, and Humphrey himself, who put on his usual show of impenetrable ebullience. Among the rather contrived exchanges at the Coast Guard station, however, there was at least one which did ring true, and that was Nixon's greeting to Humphrey. "I know exactly how you feel," said the President-elect.

The two men went through an elaborate show of conferring, after which Nixon said that during the next four years he would "call upon Vice-President Humphrey for his advice and for his counsel . . . particularly in matters of foreign policy." This must have been one of the most unbelievable remarks made during the entire year, but as the occasion was a ritual affirmation of national unity, rather than a serious political transaction, nobody was so rude as to say so. Humphrey, characteristically, seemed to get a little carried away by the spirit of the moment and went perhaps a little further than respectable for a partisan politician:

> He's going to be our next President, and I'm going to be one of his fellow citizens. And I'm going to want his Presidency to be an effective Presidency. Because as he succeeds, we all succeed.

Senator Muskie returned a little balance to the scene. He wasn't going to say anything himself, he said, because Nixon and Humphrey had already said it all. And "in Maine, we have a saying that you don't say anything that doesn't improve on silence." The proceedings were wound up with an appalling set of bantering interchanges between Nixon and Humphrey.

> HUMPHREY: I'll have it a little easier over the next few weeks.
> NIXON: That's right. You can take a vacation. I have to go to work.
> HUMPHREY: You bet. Take care. Good-by.

The same day, the other major political visitor to Key Biscayne arrived. This was Vice-President-elect Agnew. Nixon had not directed many signs of affection at Agnew during the closing days of the campaign, and he had not bothered to mention him in his victory speech. The pattern did not change now: Nixon did not go to the airport to meet Agnew or talk to him when he arrived at Key Biscayne. Instead, Agnew had dinner with Robert Finch and was led into Nixon's presence only at breakfast the next day. An hour and a half later, the two of them came out to talk to the press under Rebozo's palm trees, and Nixon produced a collector's item of double talk.

Agnew, he said, would have special new responsibilities of a type which would be made clear later. These would be so special and so responsible that Agnew would not have his own executive or press staff.

Instead, he would have an office just down the corridor from the President's in the west wing of the White House, and would share the services of the President's executive and press staff. This was a state of serfdom that even LBJ had not imposed on Hubert Humphrey—but Agnew, who is nothing if not a trouper, managed to keep smiling. Indeed, he said that he was "terribly heartened" by the boss's generosity and that as a result, he felt he would be "interjected into the mainstream to a degree beyond my expectations." Nixon, who was rather chilly about it all, did not even make anything of the fact that it was Agnew's fiftieth birthday. He was said to be much more interested in another visitor: his 1960 running mate, Henry Cabot Lodge, who was in process of being hired to replace Averell Harriman at the Paris peace talks. (A few months earlier, in nearby Miami Beach, Nixon had shuddered at the recollection of Lodge's performance eight years ago, and had hoped—vainly, it turned out—to avoid another trauma of that kind by anointing Agnew.)

By now, the time was approaching to leave the pleasures of Key Biscayne and get back to the power centers. Nixon had drawn from the island the refreshment he required. As one of his staff put it, the purpose of the stay had been "largely one of decompression," and Mr. Nixon had now "completed the decompression, shifted gears, and begun to lock into the enormity of the problems ahead of him." Sobered by his own mechanical eloquence, the staff man added that it was "not a happy prospect for any man."

Nixon, however, was clearly untroubled. He had succeeded in his enterprise, and that, for the moment at least, was certainly enough. Success, measured by direct and uncomplicated criteria, was the pattern behind his friendships and the keystone of such philosophy as he seemed to possess. Key Biscayne is not the place for a man who has any real questions to ask about the condition of America and the world. It is a place for the satisfied, a place in which it is possible to be solemn, but hardly serious, about the problems confronting the nation. Men like Rebozo and Smathers—whatever other qualities they may possess—do not provide the kind of intellectual climate that a man would seek who wanted to think with any care about the condition of the Presidential office. Would the Presidency mean any more to them than a higher point on the same continuum that includes speculative transactions in sand and palm trees? Neither of them has given a sign that it might.

The period of decompression concluded, as might have been expected, on a pious note. On Sunday, Nixon attended Key Biscayne Presbyterian Church, where the service was conducted by the Reverend John A. Huffman, a close friend and admirer of Billy Graham's. Outside the church, there was a crowd of some three or four hundred people, and a ten-year-old boy pushed forward and presented the President-elect with a Bible. The next day, Richard Nixon flew to Washington to discuss with Lyndon Johnson the transfer of power.

CODA

CODA

And He Shall
Judge among the Nations

"Great praise the Duke of Marlbro' won,
  And our good Prince Eugene."

"But what good came of it at last?"
  Quoth little Peterkin.
"Why that I cannot tell," said he;
  "But 'twas a famous victory."

—Robert Southey, "The Battle of Blenheim"

Americans have lived since 1961 in the glow of a potent political symbol. John Kennedy in the White House was not able to fulfill all the expectations he aroused. And the time he was allowed was too short to judge whether he would have been able to fulfill them. But the great majority of his countrymen—not only those who had voted for him, but many of those who had voted against or had not voted at all—felt that he offered them a seductive vision of how they ought to be led, and of what they might hope to become. Neither disillusionment nor tragedy have been able to wipe from the national consciousness the image of the young victor of 1960, dedicating himself and his countrymen in the elegant rhetoric of his inaugural to a new ambition for excellence under a new conception of the Presidency.

So appealing was the vision which President Kennedy showed to his countrymen, so perfectly did he himself fit the ideal which they had come to have of the Presidency, that it became almost blasphemy to recall how close another man had been to that office in his place. By the beginning of 1963, if some satirist had been audacious enough to imagine that five years later Richard Nixon would stand where Kennedy had stood and take the inaugural oath, after a prayer offered by the Reverend Billy Graham, the fantasy would have been dismissed as in the poorest of taste. And if he had gone so far as to suggest that by that time Nixon's daughter would have been married to President Eisenhower's grandson by the Reverend Norman Vincent Peale, that would have been set down to mere evil-minded scurrility.

Yet the 1969 inaugural was neither a grotesquely undignified nor even a specially unhappy occasion. It was noticed that while President Johnson suffered the proceedings with stoical attentiveness and Hubert Humphrey could hardly hide his disappointment, Mrs. Johnson was unfeignedly happy that it was all over, and not dishonorably. There was something about the way she looked at her husband that brought to mind Kent's lines at the end of *King Lear*: "He hates him much/ That would upon the rack of this tough world/Stretch him out longer." They were all tired. As they packed for a quick vacation in Florida or the Virgin Islands before going back to their classrooms or their law firms, most of the rump of those who had gathered in Washington with such high hopes eight years before would have been happy to pronounce the same *finis* over the Administration they had served.

The symbolism of the inaugural ceremony was confused. Reporters, who examine the auspices on such occasions with the sharp-eyed superstitiousness of priests poring over the sacrificial entrails, came up with no clear line. The weather, for example, was neither good nor bad. It was a cold overcast day that turned to rain only after the last bands had tootled past and the last float had rumbled mercifully away. It was observed that security precautions were almost oppressively heavy. The crowd around the Capitol and along Pennsylvania Avenue, estimated at a quarter of a million people, which was less than a quarter of the crowd in 1965, was watched by a total security force of some fifteen thousand armed men—soldiers, National Guard, police, Secret Service, and other Federal agents. Behind triple cordons of police, paratroopers, and guardsmen, Nixon was virtually invisible to the crowd in a car specially equipped with bulletproof windows and a bombproof floor. His car drove to the White House preceded by a flying wedge of thirty motorcycle policemen, and flanked by others. Two carloads of Secret Service men followed close behind, and twelve hand-picked agents dogtrotted alongside, their hands in their pockets and their eyes warily circling the crowds. Two Marine helicopters circled noisily low overhead. When the new President made an uncharacteristically impetuous break to cross the road outside the White House and shake hands with the crowd, the Secret Service dragged him back.

Yet it could hardly be maintained that these precautions were unnecessary. Large numbers of demonstrators had come to Washington to express their distaste for Nixon, and though the great majority of them were resolved to make their point quietly, about a thousand militants, some fitted out with helmets and gas masks, were waiting for the Presidential limousine between three blocks and one block of its journey to the White House. As the big black car drew level with them, they screamed their slogans. "Four more years of war!" "Peace now!" and *"Sieg heil!"* and chanted "Ho, Ho, Ho Chi Minh, the NLF Is Going to Win!" More in impotent rage and frustration than with any real intent to do damage, they pelted the car with pennies, sticks, empty tin cans, small stones, even with a spoon and fork. As one youth tossed what turned out to be nothing more dangerous than a large ball of aluminum foil, the Secret Service panicked. The big car shot forward, and the agents trotting alongside crouched and broke into a run.

Next it was the Vice-President's turn. As the *New York Times* put it with charming prudishness, "there was a chanted obscenity that included his name." Then the first of the military bands arrived to save the day by drowning the shrill small voice of protest with its massively reassuring oompah-oompah. Only those immediately on the spot would have noticed the big man with fair hair who plowed into a group of demonstrators shouting, "Filthy Communist swine!"; or the black man and the white man who were exchanging bitter racial insults; or the crowd of demonstrators who surrounded a policeman later that evening, shouting, "Kill the pig!"

It is very much to be hoped that Vicki Cole was unaware of such scenes. She was the dear little thirteen-year-old daughter of a Methodist minister in Deshler, Ohio (population two thousand), who had been spotted by the candidate holding up a banner which said "Bring Us Together." Naturally, Vicki and her big sister Brenda had been given an expenses-paid trip to Washington to hold up their sign on one of the floats in the inaugural parade. It was the spotlight of public attention that prompted Vicki to confess that it had not, originally, been her placard and that she had preferred Bobby Kennedy to all the other candidates.

Whether because of the appalling revelations of Vicki Cole, or for some other reason, Nixon soon dropped "Bring Us Together" as the slogan of his new Administration. When he announced his Cabinet and other principal appointments in a curiously stilted and tedious television spectacular on December 12, there was little that the omen-watchers could seize on as solid evidence of an intention to put the healing of national disunity at the top of the President-elect's list of priorities. The two most striking appointments he announced were not to the Cabinet at all but to the White House staff. Dr. Henry Kissinger, once a self-righteous Cold War pedant but young and intelligent enough to question his original assumptions, was to come over from Rockefeller's retinue to be the top White House adviser on foreign policy and military affairs. And the chief adviser on racial and domestic questions was a recruit from the Democrats, the intensely controversial Daniel Patrick Moynihan. Moynihan is a specialist in the problems of the ghettos, a man of high intellectual caliber and a deep knowledge of the issues involved. But he had managed to make himself profoundly suspect to many Negro leaders, first—and unfairly—because the implications of his work on the Negro family were resented; and then, compounding his difficulties as a conciliator, because of a certain brusque insensitivity in his method of giving the blacks and their white allies the benefit of his analysis. It seemed either exceptionally brave or rather unwise of Nixon to have appointed him.

As for the Cabinet, Nixon insisted that "these are strong men, these are compassionate men, they're good men." He anointed them lavishly with the adjective "great." They were "great" bankers, "great" educators, members even of "great" law firms. They had, he said, great records, great distinction, great leadership to offer. Like the ring announcer at a world title fight, introducing so many "great little battlers," he actually used the phrase "extra dimensions" eight times about his twelve men. So far as anyone could judge, he had in fact chosen a highly competent Cabinet. Three out of the four key jobs—State, Justice, and Health, Education, and Welfare—went to close and trusted personal associates: William P. Rogers, John Mitchell, and Robert Finch. The fourth, Defense, was given to the supple right-wing politician Melvin Laird. The other portfolios were distributed to more or less worthy nonentities and the two political also-rans, Governor George Romney of Michigan and Governor John Volpe of Massachusetts. Nelson Rockefeller had been adroitly maneuvered out of the running. It was, Max Frankel enthused somewhat faintly in the *New York Times,* "a team of moderates." Of rather moderate moderates, one might have said. It contained, moreover, no Negro, no woman, and no Jew, and no one who could be considered an intellectual. It was a steering committee of the conformist middle class triumphant: not a gesture in the direction of unity so much as a demonstration of the defeat of dissent.

When the President-elect abandoned "Bring Us Together," he made his Administration the first to take office for thirty-six years without the blazon of a slogan. If there was a principal policy theme in the inaugural speech, it was peace. "The greatest honor history can bestow," Nixon said, "is the title of peacemaker. This honor now beckons America—the chance to help lead the world at last out of the valley of turmoil and on to that high ground of peace that man has dreamed of since the dawn of civilization. . . . This is our summons to greatness."

The speech enunciated another and more original theme, a suggestion that Americans "lower their voices." Nixon said,

> In these difficult years, America has suffered from a fever of words; from inflated rhetoric that promises more than it can deliver; from angry rhetoric that fans discontents into hatred; from bombastic rhetoric that postures instead of persuading.
>
> We cannot learn from one another until we stop shouting at each other—until we speak quietly enough so that our words can be heard as well as our voices.

There were millions of Americans who could say amen to that. Some might feel that the most noticeable sound in the American ether was not the noise of protest but the insistent drone of the advertising Muzak and the portentous vibrato of the news media, until the whole country seemed in danger of self-dramatizing itself into a frenzy. Still, it seemed a sensible self-denial for the President to propose. Was there, too, perhaps even on the winners' stand, a half-conscious memory of 1961, a cautious unwillingness to challenge comparison with the eloquent ghost of John Kennedy? Only a few days before his election, Richard Nixon had said on national television, "I know I do not possess that quality people call charisma." If it was so, it was a prudent modesty for which many people could feel grateful.

Yet even here the theme was not clear. For in almost the same breath the President went on to make the highly rhetorical suggestion that "we can build a great cathedral of the spirit." And before the end, his inaugural had scaled heights of bombast rarely attempted since the days of Colonel Robert Ingersoll. "We have endured a long night of the American spirit," Nixon concluded in a tearing burst:

> But as our eyes catch the dimness of the first rays of dawn, let us not curse the remaining dark. Let us gather the light. Our destiny offers not the cup of despair but the chalice of opportunity. So let us seize it, not

in fear, but in gladness—and "riders on the earth together," let us go forward, firm in our purpose, cautious of the dangers; but sustained by our confidence in the will of God and the promise of man.

After which solemnities, it was time for what J. Willard Marriott, chairman of the organizing committee, described in the official handout as "the usual inaugural balls." There were six of them. The one the President himself attended was slightly spoiled by the fact that guests at a reception for Vice-President Agnew the previous night had stripped the place of its flowers, worth twenty-five thousand dollars. The reign of the solid citizens might have begun; but there were still Republicans ready to grab a gulp from the chalice of opportunity.

We have suggested that the election campaign, which had its moments of high tragedy, of low comedy, and even of farce, resembled most of all a melodrama. Certainly it was "characterized by sensational incident and violent appeals to the emotions." It had the proper blend of rhetorical bombast and unscrupulous intrigue. Whether the ending is thought to be a happy one depends on a partisan political judgment which we, as foreigners and as reporters, are doubly disqualified to make. But, in any case, this is the point where all resemblance to melodrama ceases. For when the writer of a melodrama feels the imminence of his final curtain, he can clear the stage. Some of the characters will be foully done to death. Some will be hauled off to durance vile. Others will live happily ever after. And the audience can chatter out into the night, happily aware that the doings at the old red barn were quite unreal. Political drama is not so neat. Some of our actors have left the stage, but most of them haven't. The audience doesn't get up and go out. And as one play is ending, the next is beginning to unfold.

At about a quarter past noon on Inauguration Day, the man with the little black bag known as "the football," which holds the electronic keys of nuclear war, left Johnson's side and attached himself to Nixon. The king is dead; long live the king! They had always said how much Lyndon Johnson savored power, how ruthlessly he would want to cling to it. But now that it was gone, he managed a very passable imitation of a man who was glad to be relieved of the cares of office. He rationalized, of course. "It was our decision," he said. And so it was, in the sense that the towel had flopped into the ring a few seconds before the referee could begin the count. On his first day back at the ranch, he amused himself by chasing some of his deer in a Lincoln Continental, and the next morning he went for a horseback ride with his wife around his acres. Wearing a yellow shirt and a Stetson hat, he looked tired but pleased with himself. He admitted that "anyone who's been as active in public office as I have will notice when they call the roll and he doesn't answer. But I want to miss it." He looked out at the Pedernales River, shaded with live oaks, and the private airport, and the ranchlands planted with wildflowers by Air Force personnel on fatigue, and he added happily, "It hurts good." Only the twelve Secret Service agents who were expected to shadow him for the rest of his life were left as a reminder that this had once been the most powerful and one of the most hated men in the world.

It hurt Hubert Humphrey bad, and he didn't try to conceal it. His departure from the political stage was something less than final. He planned to go and do a little teaching at Macalester College in St. Paul, make a few lecture tours, and supervise the writing of a book (the drudgery was going to be done by the faithful Norman Sherman). But he kept his apartment in Washington, and it was said that he planned to spend about half of his time there. At a lunch in New York, a week before the inauguration, he was already passing out broad hints that he still lived in hope. "I want you to know that I'm not done yet," he chirped. "I feel very healthy, oh so healthy, and you and the *New York Times* can make your own interpretations of what that means!"

For some of the major actors, the inauguration made no outward difference in their lives at all. Nelson Rockefeller was still Governor of New York and still giving little lunches in the house on Fifty-fourth Street. Ronald Reagan was still Governor of California and threatening to keep open the embattled campuses of the university if he had to do it "at the point of the bayonet."

"Sure I voted," said the elderly Negro, the morning after the election, fumbling to put a dime in a parking meter on Dexter Avenue in Montgomery. "But I don't reckon the election settled anything."

He was wrong, of course. The election of Richard Nixon as President of the United States cannot be called nothing. But in a larger sense, it was perfectly true that most of the soldiers in the political armies continued to disagree. The McCarthy volunteers had gone back to their campuses and their suburbs, but most of them were obviously more determined than ever to "work for a Democratic alternative in 1972." And George Wallace's people also felt that the battle wasn't over yet. Wallace himself had not stayed long in Buck's Pocket to lick his wounds. In Montgomery, the Wallace for President headquarters was still running full blast on Inauguration Day. And in Augusta, Roy

Harris was still making cheerful predictions. "I think Wallace will run again in seventy-two," he said. "I think he'll have more money and a better organization and he'll make a much better showing, because by that time people will be as sick of Nixon as they were sick of Johnson."

Allard Lowenstein was finding it rather harder to attune himself to the style of Congress than it had been to overthrow a President. He was chagrined to find that the liberals in the Democratic Study Group, among whom he had expected to feel at home, were in no hurry to fight for a change in the Speakership or in the House rules, and he was furious that the Democrats couldn't even muster enough votes to censure a Congressman who had worked openly for Wallace. And finally, to put him in his place, he had been given the last committee assignment he wanted: Agriculture. "So, after a week," he said bravely, "my mind is much clearer." And he set himself to work to stir up support in the country. That was one thing he did know how to do.

Eugene McCarthy was as unhappy and as enigmatic in his Senate office as ever he had been on the day Lowenstein first came to see him. He had announced that he wouldn't be running for the Senate in 1970, but he had been careful not to say that he couldn't be available to run for the Presidency. On the other hand, it didn't seem likely that he would be a knight in shining armor a second time. He had done two things, in his sudden, unexplained way, that his followers found unpalatable. He had given up his seat on the Foreign Relations Committee, to make room for Senator Gale McGee, a war hawk. And he had voted for the incumbent Russell Long for Senate Whip—against Edward Kennedy.

It was not until the day after Christmas that Kennedy finally decided to see if he could round up enough votes to be elected Whip—the number-two job in the Senate Democratic hierarchy, under Senate Majority Leader Mike Mansfield. The groundwork was laid, with typical Kennedy magnificence, in a series of long-distance phone calls from a luxury ski lodge in Idaho. But there was nothing casual or dilettante about it. Long before that, the Kennedy retainers knew that for one candidate the campaign for 1972 had already begun. "Here we are," said one of them, a month earlier, "sitting talking about 1968, when Ted's already thinking about next time." Being elected Whip would be a firm stride in that direction. The job itself is not particularly important, though with a Republican President in the White House the Democratic Congressional leadership would be sure to get a good place in the limelight; and both Lyndon Johnson and Hubert Humphrey had made it a step on the way up. But Senator Russell Long, while not particularly loved by the Senate establishment, was strongly entrenched behind a wall of favors from the oil and natural-gas companies and other industries whose interests he had tenderly cared for as chairman of the Senate Finance Committee. To beat him would be an impressive proof of strength. And what was more, though Kennedy did not know it until later, his nearest rival for the 1972 nomination, Edmund Muskie, had quietly canvassed his colleagues a few days before Kennedy picked up the phone in Idaho and found that Long was too strong for him. Twenty-nine votes would be needed to secure the job. Muskie might be the heir presumptive, and everyone liked him, but he could get no more than twenty-four promises of support. He dropped out. Kennedy—hurling promises, charm, phone calls from backers of every description, tactful deference, and the silkiest of political muscle into the fray like so many battalions—got thirty-one votes.

Senator McCarthy's was not one of them. He bluntly refused when Kennedy asked him for his support, face to face. What was more, he stubbornly insisted that the whole affair was of no conceivable importance. "I went against Lyndon Johnson last year because I thought there was a great issue at stake. I would have voted against Russell Long, too, if I had thought there was some cause or principle involved. But what was it? You come back in two years' time and show me how the Senate is changed or improved by having Teddy as Whip instead of Russell Long." What else was McCarthy doing, he was asked, besides writing his memoirs? "What else is anyone doing right now?" he replied. "The ball is in the other fellow's court. This is a time for waiting and watching."

It is a lot easier to describe the battle than to answer little Peterkin's question. Much fame was deservedly won by "our good prince Eugene" and others. There were brave charges, and heroic stands, and one or two subtle stratagems, and many a noble speech to the troops. But what good came of it at last? What did it all mean, beyond the replacement of Johnson by Nixon as the man with the football?

The first thing that can be said is that the worst did not happen. None of the more apocalyptic disasters came to pass. After the terrible explosion in April, the year was relatively free from really destructive rioting—though too much comfort should not be drawn from this phenomenon. Passivity in the ghetto is not an indication of the restoration of calm; for most it is an index of resignation, and for a few it is pause to reassess strategy. The development of Black Panther–style cadres in many ghettos proceeded apace. And if the conditions that breed this new style of black militance are not alleviated, then future eruptions in the ghettos could reach unprecedented levels of ugliness. The negotiations in Paris did begin, they did not break down, and at the time of writing they are still creaking steadily along. The dangers of the war in Vietnam have been reduced though by no means eliminated. Most important of all, the election was a severe setback for the radical right and offered comforting evidence to support the optimistic view that, short of a major economic or political crisis, there is a high watermark beyond which the extreme right wing cannot hope to advance in elections. Whether or not that general proposition is true, Ronald Reagan's candidacy was a failure, and Max Rafferty was easily beaten in the California Senate race.

George Wallace, above all, failed to prove his contention that "there's more of us than there is of them." His vote in the North melted away once the unions turned their political blowtorch onto it. He failed to deadlock the election. He even failed to do well enough to force the two major parties to pay Danegeld.

Nineteen sixty-eight was not, after all, a year of decision. The election itself was as close to a tie as you are likely to get. In the early part of the year, there were many who thought that America was moving to the left. There was much talk of a new radical politics. And the outstanding phenomenon of the year seemed to be the New Hampshire primary—the radicalization of the young and a large section of the middle class and the rebellion on the left of the Democratic Party against the President and the war. In the second half of the year, on the other hand, many other persons pronounced with equal confidence that the center of gravity had shifted to the right.

There was suddenly much talk of the "forgotten man," a political animal now happily forgotten again, whose principal distinguishing characteristic was held to be that he could be reached only by appeals, whether covert or strident, to his fear of racial violence and crime. That was the time when there was talk of a great new permanent Republican majority, replacing the New Deal coalition and destined to reign for a generation.

It was hard to see at the time that both these theories could be true, though contradictory assumptions about novel phenomena are common enough in American politics. ("They say I'm a stalking horse for Bobby," Senator McCarthy had said. "They say I'm a Judas goat for

LBJ. Awful hard to be both!") In the event, the voters proved at the polls that neither was true.

Nineteen sixty-eight was not the year of the New Politics. Indeed, one of the most striking features of the political process in the first half of the year was the residual strength of the regular politicians. In each of the two major parties, they were able to hold off exceptionally dangerous insurgencies. The fact that the candidates nominated by the Republicans and the Democrats in 1968, in spite of all the swirling turbulence of the year, were Richard Nixon and Hubert Humphrey, was remarkable testimony of the grip which the men of the center, who are also the professionals, have on the political system and to the resources which bureaucratic politics can deploy against the politics of charisma.

Nixon's edge came from the fact that the insurgency on the right, divided as it was between the conservative faction within the party and the Wallace movement, did less damage to the Republicans than the insurgencies on the left did to the Democrats. And the relative failure of the Wallace movement in the end was still more evidence of the grip the regular parties still have on the minds of the voters.

Indeed, one way of looking at the political process in the first, preconvention, phase of 1968 is as a series of filters, systematically eliminating all the strongest political personalities, until only the safest and blandest were left. Even if one sets the death of Robert Kennedy aside as an accident—and we have tried to suggest that there are important ways in which neither his murder nor Dr. King's can be entirely so regarded—it is still true that the men who were filtered out all had stronger political personalities than the men who survived. In American Presidential politics, the race may be to the swift, but the battle certainly isn't to the strong. In their very different ways, Johnson, Rockefeller, McCarthy, and Wallace all addressed themselves to what were generally regarded as the main issues far more specifically and unambiguously than Humphrey and Nixon, for all their floods of position papers, policy papers, and the rest. It was the men who were eliminated, not the men who were nominated, who told the American people frankly where they stood on the war, on race, poverty, and crime. It can be said with only a trace of epigrammatic exaggeration that Humphrey managed to be nominated because he talked about every issue except the one that mattered to his party; and Nixon was elected because he talked about every issue except the ones that mattered to the country. If one had to sum up the whole electoral process in terms of decisions between personalities, one would have to say that, after the preliminary stages had filtered out all the more positive candidates, in the end enough Americans were unhappy about the state of the country after eight years of Democratic Administrations that they marginally preferred a safe Republican to a safe Democrat. There are surely no great ideological shifts to be made out of that.

There is one historic trend, which did not begin in 1968 but became more apparent in the course of the year, which may have the effect of shifting the center of gravity of American politics to the right for a few years at least. It is not an ideological shift so much as a geographical one. The Electoral College system means that winning a Presidential election is a matter of winning states as well as winning popular votes. But, half-buried under the constitutionally recognized Federal system uniting the states, there is rough but crucial equilibrium of the great geographical sections. We have seen that the relations between one of those sections, the South, and the others had been unbalanced by the great migration, the Federal attack on segregation, and the civil-rights revolution. In Presidential politics, the Solid South has been breaking up since 1948. But in 1968, the fragmentation became total. The Democrats carried only one Southern state, Texas. Wallace and Nixon shared the rest between them. But it would be a mistake to jump to the simple conclusion that the conservative South has now left the Democratic column forever. For in the industrialized states of the South—in North Carolina, Texas, even Georgia, for example—heavy Negro registration may lead to the emergence of a new, integrated, and moderately liberal Democratic Party capable of carrying states in a three-way race and even one day perhaps in a two-way one.

The implications of the disappearance of the old Democratic South are of the first magnitude. As long as Republican states in the West and the Farm Belt balanced off Democratic states in the South, the balance of power in Presidential elections was held by the large industrialized states, and especially by the members of minority groups— including Negroes—concentrated in the key cities of those states. This had the effect of giving Presidential politics a more liberal bias than Congressional politics. But if a new band of states that could go either way appears around the perimeter of the Deep South, then in Presidential campaigns both parties may be expected to compete for the small-town and suburban white Anglo-Saxon Protestant votes there with the same solicitude with which for a generation they have wooed ethnic voters in, say, Illinois and Pennsylvania. Since, in an age of national mass media, it is hard to aim one type of appeal to voters in one part of the country and another to others somewhere else, this change—only one of the multiple effects of the breakup of the traditional South—is bound to shift the center of debate to the right for at least a time. The choice of Spiro Agnew as the Republican Vice-Presidential candidate in 1968 may be considered a recognition of these new developments.

If 1968 was a year in which the traditional politicians could congratulate themselves, that does not mean it was a wholly reassuring year for them by any means. The McCarthy, Kennedy, and Wallace insurrections were all failures in the obvious sense. But it remains to be seen whether George Wallace will be able to do any better in 1972 than he did in 1968. It seems clear enough that he will try and that his success will depend on how much progress the Nixon Administration makes in improving the objective conditions in the areas of greatest racial tensions.

As attempts to install their men in the White House, both the Kennedy and McCarthy campaigns also failed. It seems likely that Robert Kennedy hesitated too long and that, had he lived, he would not have been nominated, but that is mere hypothesis. What is not in doubt is that he looked more capable than anyone else of beginning the great task of reconciliation between black and white.

McCarthy did much of what he set out to do. He never supposed that he could be President—never, that is, before New Hampshire, whatever wild dreams he may have allowed himself during the spring. His achievement—and the achievement of the remarkable collection of people who worked in his campaign—was to put a President out of office and to push the Administration into a more conciliatory approach to Vietnam. (The poison, however, is still in the system. And at the time of writing a new and dangerous confusion between rhetoric and reality over the war is developing. The spectacle of the Paris negotiations seems a beguiling pointer to the imminence of peace. The reality in Vietnam is that since the Nixon Administration took over, American military action has been intensified. The purpose, undoubtedly, is to underpin the negotiating position of the unpalatable Ky-Thieu regime with territorial acquisitions. The end product could be a pacification of fear under a military dictatorship.) But we would like to stress that McCarthy's effort is likely to have a permanent effect on the Democratic Party. There are, for a start, more than half a dozen states in which a liberal faction took control in the course of the 1968 battles. There are young people who have been attracted into politics by the McCarthy campaign —the Reverend Joseph Duffey in Connecticut, to take a single example. And at every level in the party in many states these people are likely to have more and more influence. They have already exerted a startling influence on some of the most important of the old politicians: two such leaders as Jesse Unruh in California and Stanley Steingut in New York are apparently numbered among the converts, and even old-style politicians like John Bailey and Neil Staebler, who were breathing forth fire and slaughter against the New Politics a year ago, have shown signs that they too may have seen the light on the road to Damascus. Paradoxically, the Democratic Party may have been strengthened by its year of upheaval. The unions showed both more courage and more political strength than expected when Wallace tested them. So of the traditional Democratic coalition, the only permanent loss may turn out to have been in the Southern conservative wing; and that could be a good wing to lose. One consequence of the nightmare in Chicago is likely to be that the South will never have such influence over the choice of a Presidential candidate again: the abolition of the unit rule will work in that direction, and so will the failure of the Southern Democrats to carry their own states.

Conversely, in 1968 the South acquired more power in the Republican Party than it has ever had before. We have tried to show not only that Nixon in fact owed his nomination to the South but that he knew very well in advance that this would be so and specifically bargained for Southern support. It is likely that if the Southern Republicans hoped they could exact their pound of red meat in exchange, they will be disappointed. Nevertheless, the Republicans' position in the hour of their triumph cannot be said to be enviable. With the Democrats in the wildest array which even such a turbulent party is likely to fall into in a generation, the Republicans still almost lost the election. They failed to win control of the House of Representatives or even substantially to improve their position there. In the Senate, they may be bailed out on some issues by the Southern conservatives, but, inevitably, there are going to be times when Nixon pulls levers and finds there is nothing at the end of the wires. Nixon is a minority President in several senses. He was elected by roughly a quarter of all Americans of voting age. He was the *first* choice of an even smaller proportion of the American people, if the preference polls are anything to go by. And, *pace* Miss Vicki Cole, his campaign did not aim to unite. It set out, on the contrary, to divide.

It may be argued that there was nothing Nixon could have done about this; that if the party had wanted to have taken the other route, of that moderate urban Republicanism of which Governor Rockefeller, Mayor Lindsay, Senator Hatfield, and Senator Percy are the symbols, it would have chosen one of them, and not Nixon. That may be so. The fact remains that Nixon made no substantial gesture during the campaign to those groups who are the natural antagonists of his own supporters. In particular, he made no gesture to the blacks. (His talk about "black capitalism" may be considered as designed to appeal more to capitalists than to blacks.) He actually said in so-many words that he owed the blacks nothing, and it was perfectly true. His choice of Governor Agnew as his running mate was a clear indication that this was his strategy, and his appointments as President have confirmed it. Whether he had any choice in the matter or not, Nixon owes his election to the votes of the middle class, old stock, Protestants of the West, the Middle West, and the Southern Border, and in general to the business class and its allies. He won those votes because he bade for them. And he is more exclusively the choice of those classes than any President since Herbert Hoover.

We have suggested that for us the most disturbing problem in American politics is not this issue or that, not the war, nor even the failure to solve the problems of race and poverty, but something deeper that seems partly to explain both of those things: namely, the gap between rhetoric and reality. For in an American Presidential election, rhetoric overwhelms reality.

The President is an elected politician. He gets elected, in reality, as best he can. Like any other politician in a democracy, he is supported by people who think he will uphold their interests. And there is nothing shocking about this. But the President is not only an elected politician. He is also magic. He is the monarch, emblem, and protector of national unity, defender of the American faith. And so the gap opens again between the rhetoric and the reality. It is not enough that he should be a decent, honorable, sensible man who has succeeded, as Disraeli said when he became Prime Minister, "in climbing to the top of the greasy pole." He must be the divinely ordained leader. But the ordination of Richard M. Nixon was not divine. It was, as we have tried to show, extremely human.

Index

Index

Aarons, Leroy, 592–93
Abbott, George, 494, 495
Abel, I. W., 144, 153, 548
Abernathy, Ralph D., 11, 598–599
ABM system, 447, 695, 719–21
Abrahams, Al, 220
Abrams, Creighton, Jr., 535, 580, 730
Acheson, Dean G., 248, 419
Adams, Earl C., 224
advertising and politics, 46–47, 92, 204–205, 207–208, 299, 342, 383–393, 617, 632, 636–41, 719
AFL-CIO, 144, 503, 542, 706, 707, 708, 709, 710
Agnelli, Gianni, 360
Agnew, Spiro T., 17, 220–23, 423, 467, 474, 491–93, 499, 615, 616, 627–29, 673, 718–19, 747, 753, 756, 762, 771, 777, 780, 787, 789; background, 490–91; election campaign, 615, 627–29, 673; named as Vice-Presidential candidate, 482, 484–90, 494–95
Ahmanson, Howard F., 318, 319
Aiken, George D., 122
Alabama primary, 284–85
Alanson, Anne, 139, 324
Albert, Carl, 535, 540, 541, 562–63, 584, 585, 586, 589
Alexander, Howard, 274

Allen, Richard V., 257, 617, 719, 720, 721, 722, 728
Alsop, Joseph, 305, 360, 642
Alsop, Stewart, 360
American Independent Party, 284, 285, 288
American Medical Association, 193
American Party, 284
Americans for Democratic Action (ADA) 52, 60–62, 64, 83, 395
Anagnostopoulos, Spiro Theodore. See Agnew, Spiro T.
An-An, 613
Andreas, Dwayne O., 143, 152, 715, 716, 757
Arnold, Thurman W., 538, 607, 608
Ascoli, Max, 673
Ashbrook, John M., 470
Ashton, Frederick, 360
Asplin, Leslie, 137
assassination, 3, 349–50, 352, 354–362 passim, 367–68; of Robert F. Kennedy, 311, 349–50, 352, 354–355, 356–62, 371, 402–403, 526, 564, 785; of Martin Luther King, 11–12, 15–18, 144, 207, 262, 289, 312, 362–63, 367, 491, 512, 517, 525, 785; of Presidents, 367–71

Bailey, John M., 183, 394–95, 397, 398–400, 550, 584, 788

Baker, Bobby, 152, 767

Baker, Howard, Jr., 188, 487, 488, 628

Baker, Russell, 359, 434

Ball, Edward, 666, 767

Ball, George W., 152, 419, 421, 641, 643–48

Barber, Frank D., 704

Barbieri, Arthur, 397

Barkan, Al, 152

Barnet, Richard J., 25, 27

Barnett, Arthur D., 422

Barnett, Ross, 271

Barr, Joseph, 153, 548, 558

"bastard feudalism," 210–14, 565 *ff.*

Batten, Barton, Durstine, & Osborn, 637

Bay of Pigs, 110, 250–51, 341, 348, 722

Bayh, Birch E., Jr., 157

Bell, Charles, 407

Bellmon, Henry, 614

Benjamin, Robert S., 715, 716

Benson, Ezra Taft, 694

Berg, Don, 770

Berlin, Isaiah, 109, 360

Berman, Edgar, 152

Bernbach, William, 637, 639, 640

Bernstein, Alfred, 274

Bernstein, Leonard, 360

Bickel, Alexander M., 230, 368, 653

Bikel, Theodore, 549, 581

Bilbo, Theodore, 270, 283

Birdsong, Cindy, 417

Birkenhead, Lord, 543

Birkhead, Kenneth M., 137

Black, Shirley Temple, 325

Black Panther Party, 578–79, 739

blacks, 3, 11–16, 32–36, 38, 39, 57, 106, 135–36, 147, 162–65, 173–174, 187–88, 200, 256, 277–79, 321, 323, 330–34, 342, 344–45, 389–90, 417–18, 440, 441, 499, 510–12, 516, 517, 553, 624–25, 660–61, 662–64, 683, 688, 690–693, 696–98, 763–64, 778, 786. *See also* racism

Bliss, Ray C., 186, 455, 488

Blondheim, Charles, 286

Bobst, Elmer H., 252, 255

Boddy, Manchester, 247

Boe, Nils A., 221

Boggs, T. Hale, 531–36, 540–41, 580

Bogle, Jim, 743

Bond, Julian, 360, 555, 556, 558, 578, 590

Bootin, Bernard L., 94, 95, 99

Bottum, Joseph, 67

Botway, Clifford, 383

Boyarsky, Bill, 190

Bradley, Bruce, 440–42, 474

Bradley, Omar N., 419

Bradley, Thomas W., 321

Bradow, Ernest T., 704

Brandeis, Louis D., 237

Branigin, Roger D., 157–60, 163, 167–70, 171, 172, 176, 177, 360, 558

Braun, Theodore W., 222

Brecht, Berthold, 593

Breese, Lou, 589

Breslin, Jimmy, 360

Brewer, Albert, 290, 665

Brewster, Kingman, Jr., 122

Brinkley, David, 360, 451, 758

Brock, Jack, 274

Brock, William E. III, 486

Broder, David S., 198, 490

Brody, Marvin, 318, 338

Brooke, Edward W., 185, 458

Brooks, Preston S., 479

Broslawski, Farrel, 320, 325

Brown, Edmund G. ("Pat") 139, 194, 206, 323, 752

Brown, Edmund G. ("Pat"), Jr., 325, 327

Brown, H. Rap, 33

Brown, Pete, 697

Brown, Sam, 63, 64, 133, 411, 412, 531, 552, 555

Brownell, Herbert, 486, 487

Bryan, William Jennings, 212

Brydenthal, Max, 708–709

Brzezinski, Zbigniew, 152, 422, 641

Bubb, Henry A., 205

Buchanan, Patrick J., 256, 257, 616

Buchwald, Art, 78

Buckley, William F., Jr., 256

Bugatti, Ettore, 614

Bundy, McGeorge, 53, 55, 56, 57, 303, 419

Bundy, William P., 303, 729

Bunker, Ellsworth, 727, 728, 730, 731

Burden, Carter, 108

Burke, David, 566

Burkhardt, Robert J., 137

Burnham, James, 256

Burns, John, 114, 408, 409, 410, 540, 543, 549, 550, 583, 627

Bush, George H. W., 622, 763

Butler, Andrew P., 479

Butler, J. R. ("Butch"), 201, 208, 443

Calhoun, John C., 702

Califano, Joseph A., Jr., 151, 542

California Democratic Council, 60, 62–63, 327

California primary, 207–208, 285–287, 300–301, 311–55, 737

Callaway, Howard H. ("Bo"), 188, 485

campaign financing, 86, 91, 101, 158, 228–30, 272–75, 285, 317–19, 525; of Humphrey, 404, 632–33, 635–640, 714–17; of Kennedy, 317–19; of Nixon, 101, 228–29, 716; of Rockefeller, 391; of Wallace, 273–275, 287, 664–69

Campbell, Angus, 33–34, 36, 611

Capone, Al, 508, 690

Capote, Truman, 360

Cargo, David, 437, 466

Carl Ally agency, 637

Carlin, Fred, 684

Carlson, Frank, 472, 475

Carmichael, Stokely, 33, 282, 491, 492

Carpenter, Renée, 123

Carpenter, Scott, 123

Carter, "Ace," 269, 703

Carter, Hodding, 555

Carver, George, 419, 420

Case, Clifford P., 283, 471–72, 475

Casey, Gene, 383

Cecil, David, 360

Central Intelligence Agency (CIA), 29, 59, 152, 302, 303, 419–20, 731

Cermak, Anton, 368

Chachiris, George, 173

Chafee, John H., 186, 221, 291, 494

Chambers, Whittaker, 236, 242, 244–246

Chandler, A. B. ("Happy"), 696–97

Chapin, Dwight, 759

Chaplin, Sylvia, 99

charisma, 127, 307–10, 312, 323, 337, 369, 484

Chase, Stuart, 607

Chavez, Cesar, 118, 313–17, 320, 321, 360

Checkers, 229

Chennault, Anna, 732–33, 734

Chennault, Claire L., 732

Chi-Chi, 613

China, 303

China policy, 22, 23–24, 167, 303

Chinoy, Ely, 45

Chotiner, Murray, 248, 616, 759, 761

Christian, George, 11, 12, 80, 122, 634

Church, Frank, 60, 65, 67, 107, 363

Churchill, Winston S., 496

CIA. *See* Central Intelligence Agency

cities, 3, 10, 31–33, 39–40, 364–67, 440, 505; migration to, 277–79, 703. *See also* ethnic politics; urban crisis

civil-rights legislation, 35, 188, 438, 459–60, 478–79; Civil Rights Act of 1964, 35, 278, 280, 453, 462–463

Clark, Blair, 85, 86–87, 90, 91, 95, 132, 135, 136, 150, 403, 410, 411, 527, 528

Clark, Bob, 339, 340, 343

Clark, Jimmy, 286

Clark, Joseph S., 60, 67, 140, 406, 740

Clark, William, 532

classes, social, 45, 162–65, 246, 322, 592–93, 663–64, 704–710 *passim,* 717, 789

Cleaver, Eldridge, 739

Cleghorn, Reese, 702, 703

Clement, "Foots," 266–67

Clifford, Clark, 60, 107, 121, 122, 123, 419, 420, 633, 720, 730, 734

Coalition for an Open Convention, 411, 517–23 *passim*

Cole, Brenda, 777

Cole, Vicki, 746, 777, 788

Collins, Jim, 691

Communism and Communists, 55, 192–93, 281–82, 290, 293, 314, 447, 460, 595–96, 696; Nixon on, 242–53

Communist Control Act (1954), 148

Concerned Democrats, 63

Condon, Edward U., 230

Congress, 41, 185, 192; Senate, 68–70, 71, 314–15, 465, 587; Senate Foreign Relations Committee, 69, 118

Conlisk, James B., Jr., 517, 518

Connally John B., 412, 541, 542, 543, 557, 558, 559, 622, 694, 741, 742, 750

Connecticut primary, 396–98

Connell, William, 151, 153, 408, 423, 557, 641, 643, 648, 711, 712, 713, 714, 717, 759

Connor, "Bull," 270

Conservative Party (Wallace in Kansas), 284

Consiglio, Thomas, 317

Conway, James, 529

Cooke, Jesse, 441

Cooper, John Sherman, 122

Coover, Robert, 433

Corman, James, 322

Cornfeld, Bernard, 715

Costello, William, 229

counterinsurgency, 24, 25–26, 27, 55

Courage Party, 284

Cousins, Norman, 642

Cowan, Geoffrey, 396

Cowles, Gardner, 143, 380

Craig, Earl, 744

Cranston, Alan, 740

crime, 38, 46, 200, 282, 366–71, 453, 682, 685, 704. *See also* violence; mental health; "law'n'order"

Crisswell, John B., 541

Cronkite, Walter, 124, 435, 595–96

Crossley, Archibald, 392–93

Crowley, Patrick, 413

Crowther, Bosley, 191

Cuban missile crisis, 308

Cudahy, Richard, 134

Cuneo, Henry, 350

Curia, John, 361

Currier, Fred, 377, 546, 664

Czechoslovakia, 128; Soviet invasion of, 532, 535, 560

Daley, Richard J., 16, 89, 108, 116, 120, 121, 122–23, 127, 173, 321, 412, 413, 414, 432, 503–505, 506–507, 508–512, 514, 515, 517, 518–519, 520, 521, 522, 523, 539, 541, 543, 544, 547, 558, 562, 566–67, 568, 569–70, 571, 575, 578, 580, 581, 584–85, 589, 592–604, 634, 640, 737, 741, 742, 760–61, 764
Daniel, Margaret Truman, 142
Daniell, Eugene, 93
Darin, Bobby, 305
Davis, Jefferson, 267
Davis, Jimmie H., 698
Davis, Rennie, 516, 596, 598
Davis, Sammy, Jr., 766
Dawson, William L., 512
Dean, Arthur, 419
DeCourcy, Ed, 82
defense contracts, 79, 325, 749, 751
De Gaulle, Charles, 238, 368
Dellinger, David, 516, 582, 596
Democratic Convention, 423, 427, 503–604; credentials, 543–44, 551–559 *passim;* demonstrations, 517–523 *passim,* 539, 581–83, 584, 585, 589, 592–604 *passim;* floor debate and vote on peace plank, 579–81; Johnson's role in, 515, 518–19, 531–32, 535–37, 538–44, 561, 562–63, 578; (1964) at Atlantic City, 320; peace plank, 61, 524–37 *passim,* 541–43, 579; Platform Committee, 529–37 *passim,* 540, 551, 557; unit rule, 556–59 *passim;* vote on Presidential candidate, 581–86
Democratic National Committee, 505, 539, 541, 713

Democratic Party, 62, 98, 112, 120, 127–28, 147, 228, 376, 434–36, 438, 478, 507, 524, 525, 526, 545–547, 548, 552, 553–54, 564, 572, 574, 578, 586, 612, 627, 743, 745, 762, 786–88; finance of, 632–33, 635–41; organization of, 632–33; in South, 128, 277, 762; in Texas, 622, 750–51
demonstrations, 416–17, 633–34, 646. *See also* Democratic Convention; heckling
Dempsey, John, 399–400
Dent, Harry, 437, 439, 445, 448, 455, 459, 461, 468, 474, 481, 486
de Pugh, Robert, 704
De Puy, William, 419, 420
Derge, David R., 617–18, 625, 626
Devise, Pierre, 511
DeVries, Walter D., 377, 378, 630, 749
Dewey, Thomas E., 183, 226, 393, 434, 712
Di Carlo, Joseph, 284, 291
Diem, Bui, 732
Diem, Ngo Dinh, 25
Dillon, Douglas, 360, 419
Dirksen, Everett M., 452–53, 455, 467, 474, 488
DiSalle, Michael V., 566, 570, 571
Disraeli, Benjamin, 789
Doherty, William, 352
Dolan, Joseph, 111, 117
Dominick, Peter, 681
Dougherty, Gerald, 160, 161–62, 172
Douglas, Helen Gahagan, 247, 248, 765, 768
Douglas, Kirk, 360, 753
Douglass, Bobby, 392
Dowling, Robert, 715, 716
Doyle, Dane, Bernbach, 637, 638, 639, 640
draft, 39, 58, 131, 139

Draper, Theodore, 28
Duffey, Joseph, 395–96, 397, 398, 399–401, 788
Dulles, John Foster, 23, 237, 302, 304
Dunfey, William L., 93, 94, 118, 119
DuPont, Jessie, 767
Dutton, Frederick G., 108, 110, 114, 115, 118, 129, 138, 376, 528, 529, 533, 566, 641
Dymally, Mervyn, 321
Dzu, Truong Dinh, 561

Eastland, James O., 360
Edelman, Peter, 111, 112, 115, 125, 138, 307, 314, 332, 338, 566
Edwards, Don, 65, 375
Eisenhower, David, 241, 676, 754, 776
Eisenhower, Dwight D., 45, 187, 196, 216, 217, 226, 236, 237, 278, 282, 307, 360, 369, 370, 378, 393, 464, 471, 483, 495, 496, 637, 676, 688, 694, 723, 724, 765
Eisenhower, Julie Nixon, 241, 676, 751, 757, 776
Eisenhower, Mamie, 732
Eldridge, Ronnie, 89, 107
election results (1968), 747–48, 758–764
elections (1960), 162, 250–51, 619, 620, 674, 676, 678, 753–54; (1964), 184–85, 193–94, 271, 451, 620–21; (1966), 185, 186, 197, 254
Electoral College, 620, 621, 645, 653, 656, 658, 668, 675, 712, 749, 758, 786
Eller, Jerome, 67, 77, 85, 91, 550–552, 740–44
Elliott, Carl, 269

Ellsworth, Robert, 253, 489, 610, 614, 620, 624, 645
English, Jack, 114, 407, 408, 409
Epstein, Mary, 549
Ernst, Harry, 148
Erwin, Frank C., Jr., 557
establishment, Eastern Republican, 226–27; liberal intellectual, 51–58
ethnic politics, 173, 508–509, 664, 705–710 *passim*, 718
Evans, Daniel J., 454
Evans, Elizabeth, 357
Evans, Randall, 287
Evans, Rowland, 360, 473, 560, 628, 666, 706, 709, 713, 714
Evers, Medgar, 367
Ewing, Ed, 285, 659, 660

Fabrizi, John, 407
Fannin, Paul, 486
Farley, Frank, 471–72
Farley, James A., 409
Fasig, Dan, 166
Feiffer, Jules, 116, 125, 549, 586
Feldman, Martin, 189, 441
Finch, Robert, 197, 225, 254, 486, 489, 734, 759, 761, 771, 778
Fine, Joseph, 284, 701
Finney, Thomas, 301, 410, 411, 412, 413, 551, 742, 744
Fisher, Carl G., 428
Fitzgerald, F. Scott, 216–17, 223, 620
Flanigin, Peter, 617
Foley, Eugene, 404, 408
Folsom, Big Jim, 266–67, 272, 477, 667
Fong, Hiram L., 222, 434–35, 472, 475
Ford, Gerald, 455, 463, 488, 654
Ford, Henry, II, 143, 281, 380, 716
Forsythe, Dall, 6

Fortas, Abe, 465, 480–81, 487
Fortson, Ben, 288
fourth-party movement, 412, 586, 738–40, 742–45
Fowler, Henry H., 230
Frady, Marshall, 265, 267
Frankel, Max, 712, 778
Frankenheimer, John M., 350
Fraser, Donald M., 580
Frazier, Thomas, 597
Freckles, 302
Free, Lloyd, 221, 385, 386, 387, 388, 389, 390, 393
Freeman, Orville L., 151, 152, 422, 639, 680, 755
French, Eleanor Clark, 406, 408, 409
Freundlich, Larry, 91
Friedman, Milton, 360
Fulbright, J. William, 38, 66, 67, 107, 124, 531
Fuller & Smith & Ross, 617, 637

Galbraith, John Kenneth, 51, 52, 53, 56, 58, 65, 83, 96, 109, 113, 132, 136, 320, 484, 531, 532, 560
Gallup poll, 166, 186, 198, 293, 386, 387, 392, 393, 454, 544, 604, 609, 630, 636, 645, 654, 674, 702, 711, 712, 713, 748, 749
Galyen, Roy, 315
Gans, Curtis, 62, 63, 76, 77, 90, 132–133, 135, 136, 137, 139, 167, 396, 410, 411, 412, 552, 555, 743
Gardner, Allan, 639
Gardner, James C., 458
Garfield, James A., 367, 368
Garment, Leonard, 253, 254, 256, 616, 627, 629, 678, 721
Garson, Barbara, 352
Garson, Marvin, 352
Gary, Elbert, 172
Gavin, James M., 23, 66, 89

Gautier, R. B., 769
Geer, Peter Zack, 287
General Electric, 193–94, 202
General Motors, 221, 767
Geoghegan, William, 534
George C. Wallace Party, 284
Georgia primary, 287–88, 555–56
Gess, Nelson, 407
Gibbons, Harold, 580
Gifford, Dun, 566
Gilbert, Bil, 281–82
Gillen, Neal, 600
Gillespie, Chester, 499
Gilligan, Ellen, 525
Gilligan, John J., 525–26, 527–29, 532–37, 542, 551, 579, 740–41, 760
Gilpatric, Roswell L., 122
Ginsberg, Allen, 522
Ginsburg, David, 151, 422, 423, 529, 531, 532, 534–35, 536, 579
Glass, Carter, 264
Gleason, Jackie, 752
Glenn, John H., Jr., 109
Goebbels, Josef, 595, 602
Goldberg, Arthur J., 642
Goldman, Eric F., 214
Goldstein, Ira, 357
Goldthwaite, Alfred, 469
Goldwater, Barry M., 27, 78, 157, 164, 170, 184, 185, 186, 187, 188, 190, 194, 198, 201, 217, 226, 232, 253, 254, 256, 271, 322, 360, 382, 436–38, 444, 451, 455, 459, 465, 478, 479, 480, 486, 487, 556, 609, 610, 621, 624, 625, 626, 657, 659, 662, 694, 696, 700, 705, 763
Goldwater, Monroe, 409
Goodell, Charles E., 493, 494, 655
Goodwin, Richard N., 7–8, 51, 52, 55, 57, 58, 64, 65, 78, 93, 96, 100, 109, 110, 111, 114, 115, 119, 132–133, 139, 352, 358, 410, 411, 530,

531, 533, 557–58, 563, 570, 571–575, 584, 586, 591, 599, 739
Gordon, Kermit, 53
Gore, Jack, 743
Gorman, Paul, 301, 338, 358, 412
Gottlieb, Sanford, 743
Gould, H. E., 715, 716
Graham, Billy, 360, 482, 486, 772, 776
Graham, Katharine, 145
Graves, Hampton, 262, 265
Gray, Henry, 286
Gray, James, 556
Green, Don, 743
Green, Edith, 300, 324
Green, Wilbur ("Young Bill"), 153
Green, William, 140, 763
Greene, Harold R., 704
Greenfield, Jeff, 111, 125, 138, 212–213
Greenspan, Alan, 256–57, 617, 721
Greenville Group, 439, 440, 449
Gregory, Dick, 516, 578, 589, 598
Grier, Roosevelt, 213, 360
Griffin, Marvin, 287, 693–94, 700
Griffin, Robert P., 487
Gronouski, John A., 151
Groppi, James, 136
Gross, Nelson, 471–72
Gubbrud, Archie, 679
Gulf & Western, 715
Guthman, Edwin O., 110, 309, 375
Gwirtzman, Milton, 213

Habib, Philip C., 419, 420
Hagerty, James C., 360
Hahn, Kenneth, 644
Halberstam, David, 85
Haldeman, Robert, 389, 759
Hall, Gus, 126
Hall, Leonard W., 381, 389, 454, 494, 619, 746

Halleck, Charles A., 27
Hamill, Pete, 112, 115, 116, 138, 324
Hamilton, George, 131
Hampton, Mason, 736–37
Hand, Fred, 287–88
Hand, Lloyd, 754
Hanna, Mark, 210
Harding, Warren G., 574
Harlow, Bryce N., 721, 722, 728
Harper & Row, 213, 230
Harriman, W. Averell, 87, 360, 642–643, 644, 648, 649, 727, 728, 729, 731, 771
Harrington, Michael, 45, 360, 743
Harris, Fred R., 118, 124, 146, 151, 153, 178, 404, 557, 641, 646, 648
Harris, Roy, 271, 280, 282, 287, 288, 693, 704, 705, 781–82
Harris poll, 176, 198, 218, 289, 293, 377–78, 386, 391, 392, 393, 414, 454, 566, 625, 630, 645, 707, 711, 712, 739, 749
Harrison, Brian, 591
Harrison, Noel, 327
Hart, Philip A., 566
Hartke, Vance, 65, 157
Harvey, Paul, 694,
Harwood, Richard, 360
Hatcher, Richard, 174
Hatfield, Mark, 185, 298, 299, 455, 457–58, 473–74, 486, 488, 789
Hayden, Tom, 109, 360, 516, 595, 596
Hayes, Bob, 688
Hayes, Brad, 18
Hayes, Wayne L., 580
Hazen, Robert, 207
Hearns, Warren E., 580
heckling, 139, 292–93, 633–34, 646, 685, 718
Heinz, H. J., II, 380
Helms, Richard M., 419, 731

Hemingway, Ernest, 216
Hersey, John, 366
Hersh, Seymour, 90, 93, 95, 135, 136, 739
Herzog, Arthur, 743
Herzog, Herta M., 383
Hess, Karl, 257
Hess, Stephen, 234, 492–93, 628–29
Hickel, Walter J., 472
Hill, Gerald, 63, 67, 301, 325, 327, 741–44
Hill, Robert C., 255
Hilsman, Roger C., 23, 24, 531
Hinman, George L., 216, 218, 220, 221, 222, 380, 381, 383, 393, 454
Hiss, Alger, 229, 236, 242, 244–46, 248, 249
Hitch, Charles, 53
Hitler, Adolf, 268, 592, 593
Ho Chi Minh, 9, 95
Hoeh, David, 83, 84, 85, 87, 88, 90, 94, 99, 589, 743
Hoeh, Sandy, 83
Hoff, Philip, 530–31
Hoffa, James R., 315
Hoffer, Eric, 256
Hoffman, Abbie, 513–15, 517, 519, 522, 523
Hofstadter, Richard, 44, 248, 281
Hogg, Quintin, 264
Hooker, John J., 716
Hoover, Herbert C., 245, 246, 484–485, 757, 789
Hoover, J. Edgar, 167, 307, 328, 346, 365, 694
Houghton, Arthur, 716
Houston, William, 286
Hovard, Jack, 321
Hruska, Roman L., 360, 485
Hubbard, George, 493
Hucko, "Peanuts," 680
Huffman, John A., 772

Hughes, Emmett John, 216, 218, 220, 221, 250, 380, 381, 384, 385–86, 390, 393
Hughes, H. Stuart, 57
Hughes, Harold, 108, 413, 415, 559, 583, 741
Hughes, Richard J., 554, 556, 566, 634
Huie, William Bradford, 15, 268–69
Humphrey, Hubert H., 6–7, 17, 60, 61, 69, 73–75, 111, 136, 139, 140, 142–55, 157, 159–60, 165, 166, 176, 178, 198, 201, 228, 261, 262, 282, 300–302, 309, 310, 317–19, 330, 334, 336, 351, 379, 380, 391, 392, 402–11, 413–18, 420–24, 478, 483, 504, 525, 526, 528–30, 531, 533–37, 566, 568–71, 575, 580, 581, 583–87, 589–90, 596, 599, 600, 607, 610, 612, 618–20, 622, 623, 625–28, 630, 651, 654–55, 659, 667–68, 674, 679–81, 684, 688, 702, 707, 709, 726, 736–45, 746, 749–64, 767, 769–71, 776, 781–83, 785; campaign financing, 143–45, 404, 632–33, 635–40, 714–17; campaign organization, 151–52, 422–23; concedes, 761; declares candidacy, 145–46; election campaign, 632–50, 711–25, 734, 736–45; pre-Convention campaign, 156–79
Humphrey, Hubert, III, 770
Humphrey, Muriel, 7, 143, 770
Humphrey, Robert, 770
Hunt, H. L., 666
Hunter, Robert, 724
Huntington, Samuel P., 152, 422
Huntley, Chet, 451, 513
Hyett, Arnold, 91

Ickes, Harold, Jr., 406

Indiana primary, 156–79, 288, 299, 743

Ingersoll, Robert, 779

Inouye, Daniel K., 541, 547

Jack Tinker & Partners, 383–87, 389–90, 637

Jackson, Cecil, 659, 665, 693

Jackson, Jesse, 11, 12

Janeway, Eliot, 214

Javits, Jacob K., 283, 452, 494

Jenkins, Roy, 213–14

John Birch Society, 703, 704

Johnson, Hiram, 322

Johnson, Lady Bird, 4, 10, 94, 538, 776

Johnson, Lyndon B., 16–17, 26, 28–31, 35, 37–38, 41–42, 52–58, 60–65, 74, 76–83, 94, 96–99, 106–107, 109, 111–14, 117–18, 120–123, 132, 134, 137–44, 146–48, 150, 153–54, 159, 165, 168, 177, 184–85, 188, 200, 214, 218, 231–232, 253, 262, 278, 282, 289, 291, 293, 298, 300, 303, 305, 317, 319, 320, 322, 327, 330, 339, 341, 370, 376, 378, 380, 395, 403, 410, 416, 418, 420–24, 465, 480, 487, 504, 510, 515–16, 519, 524–25, 531–532, 535–43, 548, 553–54, 560, 562, 570, 578, 584, 586–87, 590, 620, 629, 635, 636, 641–42, 648, 653, 657, 659, 679, 680, 685, 688, 715–16, 724, 726–28, 730–34 738, 742, 747, 750, 753, 771–772, 776, 780, 782–85; on Vietnam, 9, 99, 418–24, 535, 641–50, 726–735 passim; withdrawal, 4–11, 403

Johnson, Michael, 706

Johnson, Rafer, 335, 349

Jones, Eric, 450

Jones, William, 659, 666, 696

Jorgensen, Frank E., 251

Joseph, Geri, 70

Kampelman, Max, 151, 152

Kapenstein, Ira, 635, 638, 648–49, 650

Kastenmeier, Robert, 134

Katzenbach, Nicholas deB., 75, 342

Kaysen, Carl, 53, 54, 122, 360

Kean, Thomas, 707

Keating, Kenneth B., 316, 360

Kelly, Art, 663

Kempton, Murray, 549

Kendall, Donald M., 252

Kennedy, David, 350

Kennedy, Edward M., 110, 112, 114, 115, 118, 119, 121, 124, 127, 128, 129, 133, 134, 138, 160, 161, 162, 213, 318, 358, 404, 414, 529, 544, 563, 564–76, 578, 585, 610, 645, 753, 782–83

Kennedy, Ethel, 6, 108, 110, 112, 117, 336, 354, 358, 361

Kennedy, Jacqueline, 358

Kennedy, John F., 3, 5, 24–26, 27, 42, 52, 55, 56, 65, 74, 75, 85, 86, 88, 108, 112, 120, 122, 124, 125, 127, 162, 171, 173, 228, 236, 242, 250, 251, 253, 255, 300, 301, 303, 304, 326, 335, 337, 338, 348, 368, 370, 380, 394, 411, 416, 436, 459, 504–509, 510, 620, 621, 623, 661, 674, 688, 695, 720, 724, 766–67, 768, 770, 775, 776, 779

Kennedy, Joseph P., 214, 215, 569, 617

Kennedy, Joseph P., II, 358, 361, 565

Kennedy, Kathleen, 358

Kennedy, Robert F., 6–9, 18, 35, 52, 57, 60–67, 75, 78, 83, 89, 91, 93–

94, 96, 98, 100, 105, 136–37, 144–
145, 151, 153–54, 157–60, 168,
170–71, 188, 200, 212, 216, 228,
236, 261–62, 282, 289, 291, 297–
298, 372, 375–79, 384, 398, 402–
408, 414–15, 420, 423, 504, 524,
526, 529–30, 534–35, 545, 548,
551, 564, 566–68, 579, 584, 589,
612, 636–38, 644, 657, 659, 674,
685, 709, 737, 741–42, 746–47,
753, 777, 785; assassination, 349–
350, 354–55, 356–62, 371; in California before campaign, 129–32,
138; campaign financing, 317–19;
campaign organization, 300–301,
317–24; debate with Eugene Mc-
Carthy, 337–49; decision to run,
65, 89, 105–126, 129, 132; funeral, 359–62; primary campaign,
127–32, 138–41, (California) 300–
301, 311–24, 327, 329–54, 357,
(Indiana) 162–67, 172–79, (Oregon) 297–310, (South Dakota)
352

Kennedy, Robert F., Jr., 358
Kennedy, Rose, 576
Kenworthy, E. W. (Ned), 301, 304
Keogh, Thomas, 721, 725
Keppel, Francis, 54
Kerner Report, 39, 118, 492, 536
Kerr, Chester, 397
Kerr, Clark, 529
Kerr, Robert, 70
Khrushchev, Nikita S., 250, 252
Kiker, Douglas, 652
Killian, Robert K., 399
Kimball, Penn T., II, 377, 378
King, John W., 94, 97, 98
King, Martin Luther, Jr., 11–12, 14–
16, 17, 33, 39, 62, 144, 207, 261,
262, 289, 312, 346, 362, 363, 367,
380, 384, 491, 492, 498, 511–12,
517, 528, 589, 598, 657, 785

Kirk, Claude R., Jr., 188, 432, 460,
468, 622
Kirkpatrick, Lyman B., 29
Kissinger, Henry A., 53, 214, 216,
725, 778
Klein, Doris, 194
Klein, Herbert, 457–58, 678, 759
Kline, Richard, 319, 323–24
Knott, Walter, 194
Knowland, William F., 206
Koenig, Julian, 91, 92
Kopelman, Arie, 637–38, 639
Kosygin, Alexei N., 578
Kovner, Sarah, 406, 743
Kraft, John, 108, 117, 118
Kraft, Joseph, 360, 593, 706
Krassner, Paul, 514, 521–22
Krim, Arthur, 715, 716
Krupa, John, 174
Ku Klux Klan, 156, 292, 367, 703
Kuchel, Thomas H., 350
Kurwitz, John, 205
Ky, Nguyen Cao, 340, 729, 734

labor unions, 144–45, 316, 317, 338,
611, 635, 661, 705–710, 717, 784
La Follette, Robert M., 212, 653
Laird, Melvin R., 678, 778
Lancaster, Burt, 753
Landry, Thomas, 688
Lanier, Doris, 716
Lanz, Rupert, 555
Larner, Jeremy, 301, 330, 338, 358,
412
LaRue, Fred C., 485
Lausche, Frank J., 525
Lawford, Patricia Kennedy, 110, 130,
177, 358
"law'n'order" as political issue, 164,
207, 294, 363–64, 371, 497, 519,
625, 634, 669, 682, 704, 706
Lawrence, David, 623

Lawrence, William H., 339, 346, 347
Lawson, James, 13–15
Lazarus, Ralph, 380
Le Duc Tho, 727, 729
Lee, Robert E., 285, 668, 702
Lehrer, Tom, 278
LeMay, Curtis E., 690, 692–93, 694–696, 697–702, 756
Lennen & Newell, 639
Le Vander, Harold, 221, 222
Levien, Francis M., 715, 716
Lewis, Ben W., 508
Lewis, Claude, 523
Lewis, Sinclair, 282
Liberator, Americus, 178
Lincoln, Abraham, 367, 384, 480, 496, 505–506, 568, 593, 657
Lindsay, John V., 184, 185, 189, 213, 221, 451–52, 457, 460, 475, 486, 487, 488, 493–95, 789
Lingo, Al, 268
Lippmann, Walter, 42, 214, 215, 365
Liuzzo, Viola, 367
Lodge, Henry Cabot, 255, 446, 628, 771
Lodge, John D., 255
Loeb, Henry, 13–14
Loeb, James, 65
Loeb, John, 153, 716
Logan, Bard, 704
Long, Huey, 262, 264, 270, 368
Long, Russell B., 360, 782–83
Longstreth, W. Thatcher, 624
Losee, Tom, 383, 384, 387, 390, 391
Louis, Joe, 418
Love, John A., 221, 681
Low, Robert, 408
Lowell, Robert, 70, 86, 338–39, 360, 411, 413, 505, 588
Lowenstein, Allard K., 58–60, 61, 62–64, 65–66, 76–77, 87, 88, 89, 100, 109, 112, 113, 124, 129, 137, 166, 351, 352, 360, 395, 396, 405,

407, 410, 411, 412, 517, 519, 547, 571, 586, 736–38, 742
Luce, Henry R., 244
Lucey, Patrick J., 114, 117, 118, 304, 305, 739
Lum, Henry, 428
Lynch, Thomas, 319, 357

Maas, Peter, 574, 575
Mabley, Jack, 593–94
MacArthur, Douglas, 757
MacLaine, Shirley, 360
Maddox, Lester G., 149, 556, 578
Magnuson, Walter, 479
Maguire, Richard, 151, 635
Mahoney, George, 220
Maier, Henry, 136
Mailer, Norman, 430, 496, 588
Malcolm X, 367
Mallory, Stephen R., 480
Manchester, William, 55, 360
Mankiewicz, Frank F., 62, 107, 111, 117, 124, 138, 356, 357, 358, 527, 530
Mannes, Marya, 146, 637
Mansfield, Mike, 122
Marriott, J. Willard, 780
Marshall, Alton, 381, 384
Marshall, Burke, 118, 565
Marshall, Thomas R., 483
Marshall, Thurgood, 59
Martin, David, 743
Martin, James, 458, 469–70, 474
Marx, Karl, 515
Massachusetts primary, 83
Mathias, Bob, 254
Mathias, Charles McC. (Mac), 494–495
May, Stephanie, 396, 398
Mayer, George H., 184
Mayhall, Ron, 658
Maytag, Robert, 584

Mazo, Earl, 229–30, 234
McAdoo, William, 156
McCall, Tom R., 221
McCarley, William G., 662–63, 664
McCarthy, Abigail Q., 73, 132
McCarthy, Eugene J., 5–6, 8–9, 17,
  42, 68–77 *passim,* 106, 115, 117–
  119, 124–28, 137–41, 145, 150,
  153–54, 157, 159, 162–66, 183,
  201, 212, 228, 293, 313–14, 319–
  320, 351, 357–58, 364, 379, 381,
  384, 392, 394–417, 505, 506, 519,
  524, 527–30, 532–34, 536, 566,
  568, 570–71, 574, 576, 579, 581,
  583–91, 596, 599, 629–30, 636–
  637, 640, 645–46, 650, 674, 685,
  709, 736–45, 747, 754, 767, 781–
  785, 787; background, 69–77;
  campaign organization, 324–30,
  394–401; at Convention, 541, 543–
  562; debate with Robert Kennedy,
  337–49; decision to run, 67, 76–
  100, 113–14; in New York, 405–
  414; primary campaign, (California) 300–305, 324–34, 336–49,
  357, (Indiana) 166–67, 176–78,
  306, (Nebraska) 306, (New
  Hampshire) 79, 81–101, (Oregon)
  297–307, 309–10, (South Dakota)
  352, (Wisconsin) 133–41
McCarthy, Joseph, 247, 248, 486,
  527
McCarthy, Margaret, 407
McCarthy, Mary (daughter), 76,
  78, 133, 328
McCloskey, Herbert, 546
McCone, John A., 29–30
McCoy, Thomas, 410
McCrea, Sloan, 769
McDonald, Myron, 383
McFarlane, K. B., 210–11
McGaffin, Donald, 688
McGee, Gale, 533, 782

McGovern, George S., 60, 61, 66–
  67, 107, 414, 415, 527, 528, 531,
  533, 560, 561, 562, 566, 570, 581,
  583, 584, 585, 590, 679, 741, 742
McGregor, Clark, 485
McGrory, Mary, 70, 78, 195, 413
McHale, Frank, 170–71, 175
McIntyre, Thomas J., 85, 94, 98,
  99
McKeithen, John, 144, 557
McKenna, John H., 175
McKinley, William, 368
McKinnis, Carlton, 263
McKissick, Floyd, 360
McLuhan, Marshall, 375, 515
McNamara, Robert S., 26, 27, 29,
  84, 107, 118, 122, 347, 447, 565,
  719, 720
McWhorter, Charles, 494, 674
Meany, George, 144, 317, 526, 542,
  706
Mearns, Hughes, 538
Mechling, Thomas, 414, 415, 551–
  552, 738
Meehan, Austin ("Boss"), 624
Meehan, William, 623–24, 764
Memphis garbage strike, 11–15
Mencken, H. L., 428
mental health, 267, 370–71. *See also*
  crime; violence
Mercer, John, 204, 205, 208
Mercouri, Melina, 108, 110
Meredith, Don, 688
Meredith, James, 360
Merk, Frederick, 43
Metcalf, Lee, 67
Metcalfe, Ralph, 589
Mexican-Americans, 313–17, 323,
  335, 336, 342, 344, 750–51, 762,
  763
Miller, Arthur, 394–95, 397, 545,
  546, 550
Miller, Bill, 381, 494

Miller, J. Irwin, 380, 381
Miller, Jack R., 486, 487, 494
Milliken, Roger, 657
Minutemen, 703, 704
Mitchell, John N., 189, 257, 458,
    459, 489, 612, 614–16, 617, 628,
    630, 631, 675, 676, 678, 733, 749,
    759, 761, 766, 778
Mitchell, Stephen, 410
Mixner, David, 552, 555
Moley, Raymond, 225–26, 240
Momyer, William W., 730
Mondale, Walter F. ("Fritz"), 146,
    151, 153, 154–55, 178, 404, 633,
    755, 758–59
Montgomery, Bernard L., 635
Montgomery, Robert, 170, 176
Moore, Dan K., 557, 585
More, Thomas, 75–76
Morgan, Charles, Jr., 651
Morgan, Howard, 298, 299
Morse, Wayne L., 67, 264, 298, 299,
    300, 527, 580, 741
Morton, Rogers C. B., 223, 467, 488,
    489, 490
Morton, Thruston B., 221, 223, 381,
    615
Mott, Stewart, 221
Movetti, Robert, 321
Moyers, Bill D., 4, 28, 154–55
Moynihan, Daniel P., 53, 214, 778
Muchmore, Donald, 201, 346
Mundt, Karl E., 486–87
Murfin, William, 439, 467–69, 486
Murillo, Joseph, 335
Murphy, Charles, 536
Murphy, George, 488, 489
Murray, Willard, 321
Musil, Robert, 564
Muskie, Edmund S., 580, 590–91,
    637, 716, 718–19, 753, 756, 770–
    771, 783
Myrdal, Gunnar, 277

Namier, Lewis, 211
Napolitan, Joseph, 201, 377, 378,
    635, 638–39, 640, 712, 713, 714,
    754
Nathan, Robert, 151
National Association for the Ad-
    vancement of Colored People
    (NAACP), 14
National Farm Workers' Association,
    314
National Mobilization Committee to
    End the War in Vietnam, 515–23
    passim, 582, 596
Navasky, Victor S., 227
Nebraska primary, 133, 178–79, 204,
    207, 220–21, 299, 743
Negroes. See blacks
Nelson, Gaylord, 134, 531
Nelson, Joan, 663, 664
Nestigan, Ivan, 114
Neustadt, Richard, 53
New Hampshire primary, 8, 78–102,
    157, 204, 206, 223, 313, 676,
    787
New Left, 38, 395–96, 515–23 passim
New York primary, 403, 405–10
New Politics, 375–400 and passim
Newfield, Jack, 65, 107, 109, 112,
    117, 333, 376
Newman, Paul, 97, 397, 586, 753
Nickerson, Eugene, 405
Nimoy, Leonard, 327
Nixon, Donald, 234
Nixon, Frank, 232–34
Nixon, Patricia R., 229, 751, 757,
    760
Nixon, Patricia (Tricia), 243, 676,
    751, 757
Nixon, Richard M., 5–6, 18, 23, 44,
    114–15, 137, 144, 158, 178, 184–
    185, 188–89, 197, 199, 201–202,
    205–206, 208, 218–19, 221–58
    passim, 281–83, 289, 291, 293, 325,

329, 334–35, 337, 369, 379–82, 384–87, 390–93, 414, 421, 423–24, 427, 432, 437, 453, 476, 481–82, 492–93, 544, 553, 577, 586, 594, 631, 636–37, 639, 645, 648–49, 655, 668, 702, 705, 707, 711–12, 714, 716–17, 719–25, 728, 731–34, 737, 741, 744, 746–54, 756–61, 763, 776–80, 783, 785–89; acceptance speech, 495–99; background, 224–40; campaign financing, 101, 228–29, 716; campaign organization, 253–58, 485–90, 612–31; at Convention, 433–35, 439–40, 455–575, 483–90, 494–99; election campaign, 607–630, 673–89, 734–735; Inauguration, 776, 779–80; pre-Convention campaign, 254–58, 446–48; primary campaign, (Indiana) 156–79, (New Hampshire) 82, 96, 101–102; wins election, 761

Nofziger, Lyn, 205
Norstad, Lauris, 122
Novak, Kim, 360
Novak, Robert, 473, 560, 628, 666, 706, 709, 713, 714, 760
nuclear-weapons treaties, 57, 695–96, 698, 699–701, 719–26
Nugent, Luci Johnson, 538
Nugent, Patrick Lyndon, 538
Nunn, Louie, 454, 457, 486

Oates, Mary Lou, 135, 136
Oberdorfer, Don, 474
O'Brien, Lawrence F., 8, 137, 304, 305, 306, 329, 423, 568, 610, 632–633, 634, 635, 637, 638–39, 640, 642, 643, 645–50, 669, 712, 713, 752, 759
O'Connor, Frank, 408, 627
O'Donnell, Kenneth, 114, 115, 118, 527, 528, 531, 532, 535–36, 537, 579, 638
O'Donnell, Martin, 644
O'Donnell, Peter, 442–44, 488, 489
Odum, Howard, 276
O'Dwyer, Paul, 405, 407, 583, 627, 736–37, 740, 744
oil-depletion allowance, 70, 686
Olsen, Jerry, 381
Opinion Research Corporation, 617–618, 737, 749
Oregon primary, 133, 204, 207–208, 220–21, 288, 297–307, 313, 743, 737
Orfield, Gary, 655
O'Rourke, Terry, 173
Osborne, John, 632, 634
Oswald, Lee Harvey, 368, 370

Paini, Arthur, 413
Palevsky, Max, 327
Papert, Koenig, Lois, 637
Paris peace talks. *See* Vietnam
Parkinson, Gordon, 614
Patterson, John, 267
Paulucci, Jeno, 152
Peace and Freedom Party, 320, 325, 739
Peace Commission, Robert Kennedy's proposal for, 119–24, 316
peace movement, 52–53, 57–58, 60–67, 298, 515–18, 524–37 *passim*, 546 *ff.*, 738–45 *passim*. *See also* fourth-party movement
peace planks. *See* Democratic Convention; Republican Convention
Peale, Norman Vincent, 240–41, 247, 482
Pearson, Drew, 346
Peck, Abe, 513
Peek, Scott I., 767
Pell, Claiborne, 527

Penn, Lemuel, 367
Pennsylvania primary, 153–54, 548
Pepper, Claude, 767
Percy, Charles H., 184, 186, 189, 254, 256, 457, 474, 789
Percy, Leroy, 667
Peretz, Martin, 91
Perez, Leander, 271, 666, 704
Perry, Herman L., 252
Perry, James M., 377, 378
Peterson, Donald O., 64, 562, 585, 742
Pettis, Jerry, 254
Pewitt, Paul, 666
Pham Dang Lam, 729, 731
Pham Van Dong, 612
Phillips, Channing, 585
Phillips, Kevin, 616, 621, 627
Picker, Arnold M., 715, 716
Pierson, DeVier, 121
Pigasus, 522
Placencia, Arthur, 349
Poister, John J., 617
police in Chicago, 517–23 *passim,* 581–83, 584, 585, 591, 592–604 *passim*
polls and pollsters, 8–9, 79, 84, 98, 99, 100, 117, 118, 202–204, 165–166, 176–77, 198, 218, 293, 300, 304, 391–93, 414, 609–10, 617–619, 625, 635, 636, 645, 651, 654, 673, 702, 711–14, 749, 751–52
Pomerance, Rocky, 431
Pool, Ithiel de Sola, 43
Pou, Charles, 693
poverty in the United States, 38, 41, 42, 45, 200, 277, 326, 330–34, 342–43. *See also* war on poverty
Presidency, 10, 29–30, 241, 369–71, 789
Price, Raymond K., 231–32, 256, 257, 617, 721
primary system and primaries, 9, 10, 80–81, 203. *See also* under individual states
Proxmire, William, 134
Pueblo, 109, 207, 498, 680, 737
Pulliam, Eugene S., 170
Pye, Lucien, 422

Quayle, Oliver, 713. *See also* Quayle Associates poll
Quayle Associates poll, 98–99, 176
Quigley, Stephen, 404
Quinn, Katherine, 398–99

racism, 33, 35–36, 39, 45, 177, 187–188, 194, 220, 226–73, 276–81, 497, 553 *ff.,* 660–61, 662–64, 690–693, 705–710, 756, 771
Radford, Arthur W., 23
Rafferty, Max, 257, 325, 350, 468, 784
Rainwater, Lee, 32
Randolph, Jennings, 535
Randolph, John, 264
Raskin, Marcus, 586, 738–40
Rauh, Joseph L., Jr., 60–61, 62, 64, 65, 66, 83, 113, 148, 152, 414, 415, 527, 528, 552, 553, 554, 556, 558, 559
Ray, James Earl, 15
Rayburn, Sam, 279
Read, Benjamin H., 643, 729
Reagan, Nancy D., 193, 206
Reagan, Ronald, 17, 163, 178–79, 186, 189–208 *passim,* 226, 314, 322, 326, 363, 378, 435, 453, 481, 486, 487, 489, 494, 549, 686, 781, 784; background, 189–97; at convention, 437–50, 454–59, 461, 465–70, 472–75; declares candidacy, 450; pre-convention campaign, 197–208

Rebozo, Charles ("Bebe"), 767–72

Reddin, Thomas, 349

Reed, Clarke, 439, 440, 445, 447, 456, 466, 474

Reed, Thomas, 203, 204, 205, 208, 326–27, 442

Reilly, John, 151, 422, 423, 641, 719, 720, 721, 724, 726, 759

Reischauer, Edwin O., 54, 122, 422

Republican Convention, 189, 196, 427–75 *passim;* choice of Miami for, 427–32; choice of Vice-Presidential candidate, 460, 461–62, 465, 473, 476, 482–95; peace plank, 452–53; platform, 452–53; vote on Presidential candidate, 457, 467, 473–75

Republican Party, 183–89; in California, 186, 189, 190, 197, 201–202, 207; finances of, 193–94, 196, 199–200; in Indiana, 178, 258; in Nebraska, 178–79; organization of, 186–87, 210, 218–20; in Pennsylvania, 623–25; in South, 184, 186–89, 432, 437, 438–50, 479–80, 482, 683–84, 788; in Texas, 442–44, 750–51

Resnick, Joseph Y., 405

Reston, James, 146, 362–63

Reuss, Henry, 134

Reuther, Walter, 317, 413, 529, 706, 707, 709

Reynolds, Frank, 339, 346

Rhodes, George, 34

Rhodes, James A., 195, 449–50, 470, 472, 475, 486, 487, 494

Rhodes, John J., 486

Ribicoff, Abraham S., 400, 584–85

Ridgway, Matthew B., 23, 29, 122, 419

Rights in Conflict. See Walker Report

Riis, Jacob A., 365

Riley, Michael, 161

riots: in Baltimore, 16–17, 491; in Chicago, 16–17, 256, 363, 364–67, 371, 491, 517, 706, 783–84; in Detroit, 16–17, 34, 39, 365, 366, 662; in New York, 16–17; in Newark, 16–17, 365; in Washington, 4, 16–17, 34; in Watts, 34, 39, 365. *See also* Democratic Convention

Ripon Society, 436

Rizzo, Frank, 633

Robards, Jason, 360

Roberts, Juanita, 16

Robinson, Edward G., 753

Robinson, Jack R. (Jackie), 697

Robson, Robert, 435

Rockefeller, David, 215

Rockefeller, John D., 214, 215

Rockefeller, John D., III, 215

Rockefeller, John D., IV, 360

Rockefeller, Margaretta Murphy ("Happy"), 217, 220

Rockefeller, Nelson A., 17–18, 38, 102, 144, 186, 188–89, 202, 206, 208–223 *passim,* 226–27, 240, 253, 258, 261, 283, 293, 377–93, 437–38, 440–42, 453, 483, 485, 491, 494, 615, 617, 630, 636–37, 645, 676, 717, 778, 781, 785, 789; background, 214–17; campaign financing, 391; campaign organization, 379–93; at Convention, 454–457, 459–61, 466–75; first decision to run, 218–23; first withdrawal, 221–23; primary campaign, 156–79, 382–94; re-entry, 379–82

Rockefeller, Winthrop, 17, 188, 215, 221, 472, 474, 475

Rogers, Louis J., 704

Rogers, Will, 274

Rogers, William P., 778

Rogin, Michael, 663, 664

Rohter, Ira S., 702

Rommel, Erwin, 635

Romney, George, 184–86, 189, 198, 210, 223, 258, 283, 378, 449, 470, 472, 475, 487, 495, 617, 675–76, 778; primary (New Hampshire), 82, 87, 100–102, 134

Ronan, William, 377, 383

Roosevelt, Eleanor, 59

Roosevelt, Elliott, 769

Roosevelt, Franklin D., 277, 368, 369, 406, 525, 625, 627, 643, 652

Roosevelt, Theodore, 310, 496, 506

Roper, Elmo, 79, 98

Rose, Billy, 629

Rosenberg, Alex, 541, 583

Rosenberg, Marvin, 152, 684

Ross, Diana, 417

Rossetti, Frank G., 410

Rostow, Eugene V., 57, 216

Rostow, Walt W., 9, 24, 25, 26, 54, 56, 57, 303, 419, 420, 727, 731

Rowe, James H., 8, 60, 137, 151, 423, 533, 641, 643, 648

Rowen, Henry, 53

Royko, Michael, 601

Rubel, A. C., 194

Rubin, Jerry, 514

Rumsfeld, Donald, 486

Rusk, Dean, 26, 42, 55, 75, 167, 216, 278, 303, 307, 328, 347, 419, 422, 532, 533, 588, 633, 643, 727, 729

Russell, Richard B., 150, 479, 720

Rustin, Bayard, 14, 592, 594

Ruth, G. H. ("Babe"), 384

Saarinen, Eero, 396

Saint, Eva Marie, 327

St. Angelo, Gordon, 159, 160, 166

Salinger, Pierre, 111, 114, 129, 138, 178, 304, 323, 329, 356, 358, 551, 565, 579, 678

Salvatori, Henry, 194, 197, 198, 323

Sanders, Colonel, 666, 694

SANE (Committee for a Sane Nuclear Policy), 57, 743

Sanford, Terry, 557

Sawyer, Grant, 531, 580

Saxbe, William, 760

Scalapino, Robert, 28

Scammon, Richard, 21, 635, 747

Schapp, Milton, 548

Schauinger, Herman, 6, 75

Scheer, Robert, 57

Schlesinger, Arthur M., Jr., 25–26, 51, 52–53, 55, 56, 57, 58, 64, 65, 111, 112, 113, 114, 115, 116, 117, 119, 125, 132, 186, 530

Scholle, Gus, 764

Schoumacher, David, 133, 574–75

Schrade, Paul, 313, 314, 315, 316, 317, 318, 320, 338, 355, 357, 542, 742

Schuman, Howard, 33–34, 36

Scott, Hugh, 221

Scovell, Field, 688

Scranton, William W., 283, 487, 494

SDS. *See* Students for a Democratic Society

Seale, Bobby, 578

Seale, Henry L., 704

Sears, John, 257, 485, 629

Seaton, Frederick A., 255

Sedida, Jo, 328

Senate. *See* Congress

Sevareid, Eric, 42, 145

Severini, Antoinette, 361

Shafer, Raymond P., 221, 470, 624, 640

Shapiro, Samuel H., 557, 566

Shapp, Milton, 640

Shearer, William K., 704

Shellum, Bernie, 743

Shelton, Robert, 269, 273, 703

Sheppard, Martin, 342

Sherman, Norman, 149, 151, 781

Sherman, William T., 444
Sherrill, Robert, 148, 267, 477
Short, Robert, 151, 636, 639, 714–15, 716, 757
Shoup, David N., 360
Shriver, Eunice Kennedy, 576
Siegenthaler, John, 110, 118, 565, 566
Sikes, Stan, 284
Simon, Raymond F., 594
Sims, Hugo, 557
Sinatra, Frank, 431, 750
Sinclair, Upton, 508
Sirhan, Sirhan, 311, 349, 350, 357, 368, 371, 403
Slote, Leslie, 382, 391
Smaby, Alpha, 64
Smathers, George A., 247–48, 557, 765, 767–70, 772
Smith, Alfred E., 762
Smith, Dick, 665, 667, 694, 696
Smith, Gerald L. K., 704
Smith, Jean Kennedy, 110, 130, 358
Smith, Ray, 661–62, 707
Smith, Sam, 658
Smith, Stephen, 108, 109, 110, 112, 114, 117, 119, 128, 129, 138, 162, 304, 324, 358, 569–76
Smothers, Tommy, 360
Snazelle, Greg, 204, 205, 207, 208
social mobility, 45, 187, 321–22, 703. *See also* classes, social
Song, Alfred, 321
Sorensen, Theodore C., 93, 108, 111, 114, 115, 118, 121, 122, 123, 125, 138, 162, 351, 408, 415, 527, 529, 533, 551, 565, 566, 567–68, 579
South Dakota primary, 352
Sparling, Edward J., 518
Spencer, Stu, 318
Sperling, Godfrey, 106, 109
Spock, Benjamin, 586
Staebler, Neil, 8, 137, 788

Stagg, Tom, 465, 482
Stalin, Joseph, 643
Stans, Maurice H., 254–55
Starr, Bart, 235
Stassen, Harold E., 178, 472, 475
Stassen, Robert J., 472
Steel, Ronald, 56
Stein, Harold, 91
Stein, Howard, 136
Steingut, Stanley, 408, 409, 410, 788
Stempler, Randall, 407, 408
Stennis, John, 150
Stevenson, Adlai E., 248, 249, 250, 326, 410, 436, 643
Stewart, John, 151, 422, 641
Stokely, Hilda, 556
Stokes, Carl, 144
Stoll, Irwin, 357
Stone, Martin, 325–27
Storck, Shelby, 640
Studds, Gerry, 83, 87, 88, 93, 99
students, 79–80, 96–98, 128, 136, 139–40, 298, 299, 328–29, 330, 363, 371, 372, 683, 685, 736–739
Students for a Democratic Society (SDS), 62, 516, 596
Styron, William, 360, 394, 397
suburbs, 194, 324, 344–45, 663, 683
Sumner, Charles, 479
Supreme Court, 230–31, 342, 462, 465; 1954 desegregation decision of, 35, 278
Susskind, David, 514
Sweet, Robert, 493, 494
Swett, Leonard, 506
Symington, Stuart, 74

Taft, Robert A., 226
Taft, William Howard, 506, 653
Taggart, Tom, 156
Talmadge, Eugene, 270

Tate, James H. J., 140, 153, 416, 548, 558, 624, 633, 764
Taylor, Maxwell D., 419
Teamsters' Union, 580
Ted offensive, 564–76. *See also* Kennedy, Edward M.; Democratic Convention
Tennessee Valley Authority, 193, 686
Tet offensive, 9, 30, 92–93, 94, 109, 397, 402–403
Thayer, Walter N., 380
Thieu, Nguyen Van, 340, 727, 728, 729, 730, 731, 732, 734, 787
Thomas, Norman, 59, 62
Thomson, James C., Jr., 22, 24
Thompson, Llewellyn, 16
Thurmond, Strom, 188, 271, 434, 435, 437–38, 447–48, 451, 455, 458–61, 465, 467, 468–70, 472, 473, 475, 476–81, 483, 486, 487, 488, 490, 526, 622, 653, 655, 720
Till, Emmett, 367
Tillman, Benjamin R. ("Pitchfork Ben"), 270
Tinker, Jack, 377. *See also* Jack Tinker & Partners
Tocqueville, Alexis de, 364–65, 367
Tonkin Gulf, 27, 30
Tower, John G., 442–44, 487, 488–489, 490
Trammell, Seymore, 273–74, 286, 659, 694, 696, 697
Tree, Marietta, 408
Trevor-Roper, Hugh, 245
Trujillo, Rafael, 767
Truman, Harry S., 183, 248, 249, 370, 393, 526, 633, 688, 712
Tuck, Richard, 129, 130, 307
Turnipseed, Tom, 284, 659
Tuttle, Holmes, 194
Twining, Nathan F., 23

Udall, Morris K., 655
unit rule, 438, 471, 556–57, 562
United Auto Workers (UAW), 317, 413, 542, 705, 706, 707, 708, 709
Unruh, Jesse, 62, 107–108, 112, 118, 119, 127, 129, 195, 278, 316, 317, 318, 319, 320, 321, 323, 324, 325, 349, 415, 539–40, 543–44, 549, 550, 568, 569–70, 575, 578, 788
urban crisis, 34–36, 38–41, 330–34, 343–45, 371, 453, 496–97
USSR, 719, 720–21, 722–25

Valenti, Jack, 542
Vance, Cyrus R., 419, 644, 729
Vance, Robert, 128
Vance, Rupert, 276
vanden Heuvel, William, 6, 110, 114, 119, 125, 300, 584
Vandiver, Ernest, 693
Van Dyk, Ted, 151, 402, 422, 529, 641, 647
Vanocur, Sander, 360
Vardaman, John K., 270
Victoria, Queen, 368
Vietnam, 3, 10, 21–31, 38–39, 41, 74–75, 114, 118, 184, 200, 219, 325, 326, 418–24, 454, 610–12, 787; Branigin on, 168, 169; Humphrey on, 147–48, 154–55, 418, 421–24, 612, 633–35, 641–650, 726–35 *passim*, 741–45; Johnson Administration and, 26–31, 418–24, 641–50; Johnson on, 9, 99, 418–24, 535, 641–50, 726–735 *passim*; Kennedy Administration and, 24–26, 56–57, 340–41; R. F. Kennedy on, 108–109, 116–117, 119–24, 130–31, 166, 339–341; LeMay on, 695; McCarthy on, 71, 75–77, 93, 96, 301–303, 339–41, 404, 741–45; negotiations,

9, 16, 40, 179, 420, 339–40, 612, 642, 649, 726–35 *passim,* 771, 787; Nixon on, 23, 101, 184, 423–424, 463–64, 496–97, 723, 726–35 *passim;* Romney on, 101. *See also* Democratic Convention: peace plank

Vietnam Peace Commission. *See* Peace Commission, Robert Kennedy's proposal for

violence, 311, 362–71. *See also* crime; "law'n'order" as political issue; mental health

Volpe, John A., 443, 487–88, 490, 778

Voorhis, Jerry, 236, 244

Vorspen, Albert, 407

Waite, Kenneth S., 704

Walinsky, Adam, 111, 112, 114, 125, 138, 166, 305, 307, 338, 375, 376, 530, 566, 567–68, 739, 743

Walker, Daniel, 603–604

Walker Report, 514, 603

Wallace, DeWitt, 255

Wallace, George C., 5, 17, 32, 45, 129, 145, 159, 162–63, 188, 200, 261–62, 276, 312, 360, 371, 391–392, 444, 446–47, 449, 461, 477, 481, 488–89, 517, 553–54, 594, 607, 610–11, 621–23, 625–27, 630, 635–37, 645, 651–69 *passim,* 673, 712, 717, 738–39, 747–48, 756–57, 759–60, 762–64, 769, 781–82, 784–88; background, 263–75; campaign financing, 273–75, 287, 664–669; campaign organization, 284–289, 658–64, 701–702; election campaign, 651–69, 690–710; pre-convention campaign, 278–94

Wallace, Gerald, 263

Wallace, Henry A., 653

Wallace, Jack, 263, 264

Wallace, Lurleen Burns, 262, 264, 272, 285–86, 289–90, 691, 692

Wallace, Mike, 583

Walters, Robert, 743

war on poverty, 32, 38, 682–83

Warner-Lambert Pharmaceutical, 252

Warren, Earl, 282

Warschaw, Carmen, 318, 320, 644

Warschaw, Louis, 318

Wasserman, Lou, 319

Watson, Billy, 267

Watson, Marvin, 7, 137, 541–42, 562

Wayne, John, 666, 694

Weaver, Warren, Jr., 712

Weber, Max, 307–310, 323

Wechsler, James A., 76

Weinberg, Sidney, 143

Weisel, William, 355, 357

Weisl, Edwin L., 715, 716

Welch, Ja-Neen, 668

Welsh, Matt, 159

Welsh, William, 422, 534, 536, 643

Wentworth, John, 505

Westmoreland, William C., 419

Wexler, Anne, 398, 399, 401, 581, 585

Wheeler, Earl G., 419, 734

Whelan, Richard J., 617, 629

Whipple, Blaine, 298–99

White, F. Clifton, 198, 200, 201, 202, 205, 435, 441, 448, 455, 457, 459, 469, 470, 472–73

White, Howard, 274

White, Opal Tanner, 704

White, Theodore H., 53, 758

White, William S., 214, 700

White Citizens Councils, 703, 704

Whitney, John Hay, 380

Whittaker, James, 360

Wicker, Tom, 56, 592

Wiesner, Jerome, 54, 447

Wilkins, Roger, 518–19

Wilkins, Roy, 14
Wilkinson, Charles B. ("Bud"), 688–689, 754
Williams, Andy, 109
Williams, John Bell, 439
Williams, Walter W., 255
Wills, Garry, 614
Willkie, Wendell, 226
Wilson, Bob, 488
Wilson, Harold, 687
Wilson, Malcolm, 389, 390
Wilson, Mary, 417
Wilson, Woodrow, 747
Wilvers, Robert, 383
wire-taps, 346–47, 615
Wirtz, W. Willard, 152
Wisconsin primary, 8, 79–80, 132, 133–38, 204, 206–207, 737
Wofford, Harris L., Jr., 597
Wolgin, Jack I., 717
Wood, Gar, 769
Woodcock, Leonard, 413

Woods, Rose Mary, 678
Woodward, Joanne, 753
Wordsworth, William, 376
Wriggins, Howard, 422
Wyatt, Wilson W., 531
Wyman, Eugene, 144, 214, 319, 320
Wyman, Jane, 193

Yarborough, Ralph W., 479, 558, 622, 750
Yarmolinsky, Adam, 54
Yippies, 514–16, 517–23 passim, 597
Yorty, Samuel W., 321, 335, 360
Young, Andrew, 11
Young, Quentin, 602
Yumick, George, 591

Zablocki, Clement, 579
Zorthian, Barry, 642